Inclusive Wealth Report 2012
Measuring progress toward sustainability

The *Inclusive Wealth Report 2012* is a joint initiative of the United Nations University International Human Dimensions Programme on Global Enivronmental Change (UNU-IHDP) and the United Nations Environment Programme (UNEP) in collaboration with the UN Water Decade Programme on Capacity Development (UNW-DPC) and the Natural Capital Project.

This volume may be cited as: UNU-IHDP and UNEP (2012). *Inclusive Wealth Report 2012. Measuring progress toward sustainability*. Cambridge: Cambridge University Press.

Inclusive Wealth
Report 2012

Measuring progress toward sustainability

CAMBRIDGE UNIVERSITY PRESS

Cambridge, New York, Melbourne, Madrid, Cape Town, Singapore, São Paulo, Delhi, Dubai, Mexico City

Cambridge University Press
The Edinburgh Building, Cambridge CB2 8RU, UK

Published in the United States of America by Cambridge University Press, New York

www.cambridge.org
Information on this title: www.cambridge.org/9781107683396

First published 2012

Printed in the United Kingdom at the University Press, Cambridge

A catalogue record for this publication is available from the British Library

ISBN   978-1-107-03231-6 Hardback
ISBN   978-1-107-68339-6 Paperback

Editorial Consultant: Stu Slayen Consulting
Cover illustration: Louise Smith © UNU–IHDP
Design and layout: Louise Smith
Project assistant: Pablo Fuentenebro

Contents

Figures

Boxes

Tables

Contributors

Science Advisor

Partha Dasgupta – University of Cambridge

Report Director

Anantha Duraiappah – IHDP Executive Director

Science Director

Pablo Muñoz – IHDP Academic Officer

Authors

Matthew Agarwala – London School of Economics and Political Science

Giles Atkinson – London School of Economics and Political Science / Centre for Climate Change Economics and Policy

Edward B. Barbier – University of Wyoming

Elorm Darkey – University of Bonn

Partha Dasgupta – University of Cambridge

Anantha Duraiappah – IHDP Secretariat

Paul Ekins – University College London

Pablo Fuentenebro – IHDP Secretariat

Juan Sebastian Lozano – The Nature Conservancy (Colombia)

Kevin Mumford – Purdue University

Pablo Muñoz – IHDP Secretariat

Kirsten Oleson – University of Hawaii

Leonie Pearson – University of Melbourne

Charles Perrings – Arizona State University

Chris Perry – UN-Water Decade Programme on Capacity Development (UNW-DPC)

Steve Polasky – University of Minnesota

Heather Tallis – Stanford University

Stacie Wolny – Stanford University

Foreword

The preliminary findings of the *Inclusive Wealth Report* (IWR) initiative are presented in this publication: they provide for policymakers an initial analysis towards a broader and comprehensive way of measuring inclusive progress within their economies.

There has for some time been a shared recognition that conventional indicators such as gross domestic product (GDP) or the Human Development Index (HDI) are failing to capture the full wealth of a country. These limitations may be in part fueling environmental decline and degradation because changes in natural or "nature-based" assets are not factored into national accounts, rendering those accounts less useful as an indicator of changes in human well-being.

This report, produced by the UN University International Human Dimensions Programme on Global Environmental Change and UNEP, builds on the findings of the Millennium Ecosystem Assessment of 2005. It echoes, too, the conclusions of the Stiglitz-Sen-Fitoussi Commission of 2009 which argued that measuring well-being requires a shift from conventional production indicators to metrics that incorporate non-economic markets-based aspects of well-being, including sustainability issues.

The preliminary IWR gives an overview on the evolution of some relevant categories of natural capital, such as forests, for a range of countries over a 19-year period, comparing their decline or increase against two other areas: produced capital, such as roads and factories; and human capital, including levels of education, knowledge, and creativity. The preliminary findings indicate that it is possible to trace the changes of the components of wealth by country and link these to economic growth, including highlighting the impact of declines or increases in natural capital as an economic productive base.

While many economies do appear to be getting wealthier, it is happening often at the expense of the natural capital base which, in the future and over generations, may move the Inclusive Wealth Index (IWI) from the black into the red.

Achim Steiner

UN Under–Secretary–General and UNEP Executive Director

Preface

Although there have been a number of successes in creating a more sustainable global economy, a new report by the United Nations Secretary-General's High-Level Panel on Global Sustainability — *Resilient People, Resilient Planet: A future worth choosing* — recognizes the current global political-economic order's failures, even inability, to implement the drastic changes necessary to bring about true "sustainability."

The Panel's report presents a vision for a "sustainable planet, just society, and growing economy," as well as 56 policy recommendations for realizing that goal. It is arguably the most prominent international call for a radical redesign of the global economy ever issued.

Despite significant advances in the past 25 years, humanity has failed to conserve resources, safeguard natural ecosystems, or otherwise ensure its own long-term viability.

But, for all its rich content, *Resilient People, Resilient Planet* is short on concrete, practical solutions. Its most valuable short-term recommendation — the replacement of current development indicators (gross domestic product or variants thereof) with more comprehensive, inclusive metrics for wealth — seems tacked on almost as an afterthought. Without quick, decisive international action to prioritize sustainability over the *status quo*, the report risks suffering the fate of its 1987 predecessor, the pioneering "Brundtland Report", which introduced the concept of sustainable development, called for a paradigm shift, and was then largely ignored. *Resilient People, Resilient Planet* opens by paraphrasing Charles Dickens: the world today is "experiencing the best of times, and the worst of times." As a whole, humanity has achieved unparalleled prosperity; great strides are being made to reduce global poverty; and technological advances are revolutionizing our lives, stamping out diseases, and transforming communication.

That said, inequality remains stubbornly high, and is increasing in many countries. Short-term political and economic strategies are driving consumerism and debt, which, together with a growing global population — set to reach nearly nine billion by 2040 — is subjecting the natural environment to growing stress. By 2030, notes the Panel, "the world will need at least 50 percent more food, 45 percent more energy, and 30 percent more water — all at a time when environmental limits are threatening supply."

Despite significant advances in the past 25 years, humanity has failed to conserve resources, safeguard natural ecosystems, or otherwise ensure its own long-term viability.

Can a report — however powerful — create change? Will the world now rally, unlike in 1987, to the Panel's call to "transform the global economy"? Perhaps, in fact, real action is born of crisis itself. As the Panel points out, it has never been more clear that we need a paradigm shift to achieve truly sustainable global development.

But who will coordinate an international process to study how to encourage such a shift, and who will ensure that scientific findings lead to meaningful public-policy processes?

We need new indicators that tell us if we are destroying the productive base that supports our well-being.

The 2010 Report by the Commission on the Measurement of Economic Performance and Social Progress, commissioned by French President Nicolas Sarkozy, echoed the current consensus among social scientists that we are mis-measuring our lives by using per capita GDP as a yardstick for progress.

The United Nations University's International Human Dimensions Programme (UNU-IHDP) and the United Nations Environment Programme (UNEP), together with other partners, have been working to find these indicators for this *Inclusive Wealth Report* (IWR), which proposes an approach to sustainability based on measuring natural, manufactured, human, and social forms of capital. The IWR aims to provide a comprehensive analysis of the different components of wealth by country; their links to economic development and human well-being; and policies that are based on social management of these assets.

The IWR represents a crucial first step in transforming the global economic paradigm, by ensuring that we have the correct information with which to assess our economic development and well-being — and to reassess our needs and goals. While it is not intended as a universal indicator for sustainability, it does offer a framework for dialogue with multiple constituencies from the environmental, social, and economic fields.

The report might suffer from incompleteness in data but it presents a valuable framework for tracking sustainability. This report also highlights where more work is needed in plugging the data gaps and adding more information incrementally as it becomes available. But rather than wait for complete accuracy, the report makes a bold attempt to illustrate with the available data whether countries are sustainable and, if not, where they are under-performing and where interventions are needed to rectify the situation. The framework also offers a useful tool for macroeconomic planning agencies as it pays equal attention to all three pillars of sustainable development (social, environmental, and economic). It also talks the language of economic and social institutions and not just the language of the environmental community.

Our situation is critical. As *Resilient People, Resilient Planet* aptly puts it, "tinkering around the margins" will no longer suffice—a warning to those counting on renewable-energy technologies and a green economy to solve our problems. The Panel has revived the call for far-reaching change in the global economic system. Our challenge is to follow words with action this time.

Partha Dasgupta
Science Advisor to the *Inclusive Wealth Report 2012*, and Frank Ramsey Professor Emeritus of Economics at the University of Cambridge

Anantha Duraiappah
Report Director to the *Inclusive Wealth Report 2012*, and Executive Director of the International Human Dimensions Programme on Global Environmental Change

Acknowledgements

The *Inclusive Wealth Report* (IWR) is an outcome of a cooperative effort. Many individuals and organizations participated in various capacities. The IWR would not have been possible without the numerous contributions from authors, reviewers, UNU-IHDP staff members, funding agencies, and many others who at one point or another contributed to the project. We are extremely grateful to all of them and would like to thank and acknowledge them here for their dedication and long hours.

Science Advisor

We would like to begin by extending special thanks to Professor Sir Partha Dasgupta, Chair of the International Human Dimensions Programme Scientific Committee, who served as the report's Science Advisor. His untiring efforts as an author and advisor were instrumental in the production of this report.

Authors

We would like to thank all authors who contributed to this report: Matthew Agarwala, Giles Atkinson, Edward B. Barbier, Elorm Darkey, Partha Dasgupta, Anantha Duraiappah, Paul Ekins, Pablo Fuentenebro, Juan Sebastian Lozano, Kevin Mumford, Pablo Muñoz, Kirsten Oleson, Leonie Pearson, Charles Perrings, Chris Perry, Steve Polasky, Heather Tallis, and Stacie Wolny.

Reviewers

The IWR benefited greatly from all of the feedback and comments provided by our reviewers, including John Agnew, Peter Bartelmus, Patrick ten Brink, Julia Bucknall, Dabo Guan, Michael Harris, Rashid Hassan, Nicolas Kosoy, Jens Liebe, Hal Mooney, Edwin Muchapondwa, Eric Neumayer, Timothée Ollivier, Unai Pascual, Alan Randall, Bart Schultz, Stanislav Shmelev, R. Kerry Turner, Marcelo Villena, Jeff Vincent, and Aart de Zeeuw.

UNU-IHDP

As a core project of the UNU-IHDP Secretariat, the IWR project has involved many people from its early stages. Anantha Duraiappah, Executive Director of IHDP, who conceived of the idea for an IWR as early as 2008, took the lead as the IWR Director. Pablo Muñoz, Academic Officer at IHDP, who coordinated and oversaw the scientific inputs to the report served as Science Director of the report. Elorm Darkey provided analytical support in the production of the database and numerical computations. Special thanks to Anne-Kathrin Raab, Communications Manager; Lou Smith, art and layout designer; and Carmen Scherkenbach, our editor. We would like to thank Pablo Fuentenebro, Benjamin Zhu, and Sabrina Zwick for their technical and logistical support.

We are equally grateful to our interns who devoted their time to this project, including Workineh Asmare, Ara Beittoei, Mert Cetinkaya, Elorm Darkey, Pablo Fuentenebro, Michelle Lowe, Umberto Muratori, Carlos Torres, Ekaterine Rogava, and Sijia Yi.

Finally, the report benefited significantly from the editorial expertise of Stu Slayen.

UNEP

This is a joint project with the United Nations Environment Programme, and many people from UNEP played a role in developing this report. We would like to specifically acknowledge the support of Ibrahim Thiaw, Director of the Division of Environmental Policy Implementation, for providing the institutional support for this initiative. Special thanks also go to Pushpam Kumar, Chief of the Ecosystem Services; Neville Ash, Coordinator, Biodiversity and Ecosystem Services Branch, and Chief, Biodiversity Unit and chief of the Biodiversity Branch; and Makiko Yashiro Programme officer, the Ecosystem Services Unit.

Funding bodies

The IWR was made possible by a grant from the United Nations Environment Programme (UNEP). The National Science Foundation and the German Federal Ministry of Education and Research (BMBF) provided additional funding through their core support to the UNU-IHDP. The Chinese National Committee for the International Human Dimensions Programme (CNC-IHDP) provided additional funds to facilitate outreach and dissemination of the IWR. The project also received in-kind support from the UN Water Decade Programme on Capacity Development (UNW-DPC) and the Natural Capital Project.

Finally, we would like to thank our publisher, Cambridge University Press, for the time and flexibility given to us throughout the production and printing of the report. Special thanks to Chris Harrison, Publishing Director for Social Sciences at Cambridge University Press.

Abbreviations

6EAP . . . . . . Sixth Environmental Action
Programme
ANDP . . . . . . adjusted net domestic product
ANS . . . . adjusted net savings
BEA . . . . Bureau of Economic Analysis
C . . . . carbon
CBP . . . . consumption-based principle
CES . . . . constant elasticity of substitution
CGSDI . . . . . Consultative Group on
Sustainable Development
Indicators
CIA . . . . United States Central Intelligence
Agency
CO2 . . . . carbon dioxide
CNC . . . . critical natural capital
CPR . . . . common property resources
CVM . . . . contingent valuation method
DMC . . . . . . domestic material consumption
DMI . . . . direct material input
EA1 . . . . SEEA Environmental Asset:
Natural resources
EA2 . . . . SEEA Environmental Asset: Land
and surface water
EA3 . . . . SEEA Environmental Asset:
Ecosystems
EF . . . . ecological footprint
EFTA . . . . . . European Free Trade Association
EPA . . . . United States Environmental
Protection Agency
ESI . . . . Ecological Sustainability Index
ESP . . . . ecosystem services product
EU . . . . European Union
GBC . . . . Goulburn-Broken Catchment
FAO . . . . Food and Agriculture
Organization
GDI . . . . gross domestic income
GDP . . . . gross domestic product
GF . . . . UKNEA scenario: Go with the
Flow

GHG . . . . greenhouse gas
GNS . . . . gross national savings
GPI . . . . Genuine Progress Indicator
GPL . . . . UKNEA scenario: Green and
Pleasant Land
GS . . . . genuine savings
GTAP . . . . . . Global Trade Analysis Project
HC . . . . human capital
HDI . . . . Human Development Index
HIPC . . . . . . heavily indebted poor country
ICID . . . . International Commission on
Irrigation & Drainage
IGBP . . . . . . International Geosphere–
Biosphere Programme
IMF . . . . International Monetary Fund
IO . . . . input-output
IOT . . . . input-output tables
IPCC . . . . Intergovernmental Panel on
Climate Change
ISEW . . . . . . Index of Sustainable Economic
Welfare
IWI . . . . Inclusive Wealth Index
IWIadj . . . . . Adjusted Inclusive Wealth Index
IWR . . . . Inclusive Wealth Report
LS . . . . UKNEA scenario: Local
stewardship
MA . . . . Millennium Ecosystem
Assessment
MAG . . . . Ministerio de Agricultura y
Ganadería del Ecuador
MRIO . . . . . . multi-regional input-output
NC . . . . natural capital
NCI . . . . Natural Capital Index
NDP . . . . net domestic product
NIPA . . . . national income and product
accounts
NNI . . . . net national income
NNP . . . . net national product
NOx . . . . nitrous oxides
NPV . . . . net present value
NS . . . . UKNEA scenario: National
security
NSGAP . . . . normalized sustainability gap
NTFB . . . . . . non-timber forest benefits
NW . . . . UKNEA scenario: Nature at work
OECD . . . . . Organisation for Economic
Co-operation and Development

PBP . . . . production-based principle
PES . . . . payment for ecosystem services
PF. . . . . production function
PIM. . . . . . . Perpetual Inventory Method
PM–10 . . . . . particulate matter
PPP. . . . . . . purchasing power parity
PPP. . . . . . . polluter-pays-principle (Chapter 6)
PSR . . . . pressure-state-response
R&D . . . . . . research and development
Rio+20 . . . . 2012 Earth Summit
SC. . . . . social capital
SCC . . . . social cost of carbon
SDI . . . . sustainable development
          indicators
SEEA . . . . . . System of Environmental and
          Economic Accounts
SEEAW . . . . System of Environmental-
          Economic Accounting for Water
SGAP. . . . . . sustainability gap
SNA . . . . System of National Accounts
SOx . . . . sulfur oxides
SW . . . . soil water
TEEB . . . . . . The Economics of Ecosystems
          and Biodiversity
TFP. . . . . total factor productivity
TMC . . . . . . total material consumption
TMDL. . . . . . total maximum daily loads
TMI. . . . . total material input
TMO . . . . . . total material output
TMR . . . . total material requirement
TN. . . . . total nitrogen
UKNEA . . . . U.K. National Ecosystem
          Assessment
UN . . . . United Nations
UNCSD . . . . United Nations Conference on
          Sustainable Development
UNDP . . . . . United Nations Development
          Programme
UNEP. . . . . . United Nations Environment
          Programme
UNFCCC . . United Nations Framework
          Convention on Climate Change
USGS. . . . . . United States Geological Survey
UNU. . . . . . . United Nations University

UNU–IHDP. United Nations University
          International Human
          Dimensions Programme on
          Global Environmental Change
USDA. . . . . . United States Department of
          Agriculture
USGS. . . . . . United States Geological Survey
USLE . . . . . . universal soil loss equation
VSL. . . . . value of a statistical life
WAVES . . . . Wealth Accounting and Valuation
          of Ecosystem Services
WC. . . . . water closet
WM . . . . UKNEA scenario: World markets
WWF . . . . . . World Wildlife Fund
YS . . . . years-to-sustainability

Executive summary

This Inclusive Wealth Report (IWR) is the first of a biennial series of reports on the sustainability of countries. The report looks at the productive base of economies, based on capital assets – produced or manufactured capital; human capital; and natural capital. This first report of the series is focused on natural capital and will be released at the Earth Summit 2012 (Rio+20) to be held in Rio de Janeiro, Brazil, in June 2012. The two main themes of Rio+20 will be the green economy and international environmental governance. The United Nations Secretary-General's high level panel report on global sustainability – *Resilient People, Resilient Planet: A Future Worth Choosing* – was released in April of 2012 to inform the discussions and negotiations at the summit. The report highlights the potential of a green economy and also calls for new ways of measuring progress in a green economy. The IWR provides such a measure.

The IWR is a joint collaboration between the United Nations University International Human Dimensions Programme (UNU-IHDP) and the United Nations Environment Programme (UNEP). The group of authors for the report was selected based on their expertise in inclusive wealth and environmental economics, and an extensive publication record in the area of natural capital, human well-being, social welfare, and valuation, among others. A review process was also established and each chapter was reviewed by a minimum of two external referees using standard academic criteria. The reviewers were chosen again based on their expertise in the field, strong academic credentials, and a good publishing record in the relevant fields covered by this report.

The goals of the Inclusive Wealth Report

The primary objective of the Inclusive Wealth Report is to provide quantitative information and analysis that present a long-term perspective on human well-being and measures of sustainability. In addition, the main objectives of the IWR are:

- to undertake a preliminary analysis of whether countries were on a sustainable path, and provide national governments with a metric to assess transitions towards the so-called "Green Economy";
- to carry out a comprehensive analysis of the various components of wealth by country and their link to economic development, highlighting in particular the importance of natural capital;
- to become an indicator of progress towards sustainable development with the production of biennial reports monitoring the well-being of countries. In the long-term, we expect inclusive wealth to become an important criterion in assessments of societal progress;
- to help countries formulate and stimulate policies based on the notion of asset portfolio management, wherein nations follow plans to comprehensively manage diverse assets – natural, manufactured, and human – to create productive and sustainable economic bases for the future, and emphasize how an inclusive wealth report can be used by nations to guide their investment strategies for sustainability; and
- to highlight where extra research is needed to make the Inclusive Wealth Index and the report a useful tool for economic, environmental and social planning.

Structure and content of the report

The primary audience of the Inclusive Wealth Report will be governments. More broadly, the report will be of use to development practitioners as well as researchers and the wider development community. The inclusion of environmental damage in the accounts – as well as damages from global environmental change such as climate change – can be useful in determining cross-country compensations and a guide for international negotiations on the consideration of transboundary assets. The report will also be useful for national economic planning agencies when considering macroeconomic fiscal policies. Changes in the various capital assets and their contribution towards the inclusive wealth of a country can provide information on where to target future investments in order to get the best returns for increasing the productive base of the country.

The report is presented in two parts. Part i (Chapters 1–5) introduces the concept of inclusive wealth and provides the first results for a set of 20 countries used as a pilot in the 2012 report.

In Part ii of this report (Chapters 6–11), we present some key insights on developing ecosystem services accounts and the challenges faced when attempting to value the changes in the capital stocks over time.

Each chapter presents a number of "key messages," as presented in the next pages.

Key Messages

CHAPTER 1

Well–being and wealth

- The true achievement of sustainable development must focus on human well-being. When we talk about human well-being, we cannot only talk about today. The definition of human well-being – and, indeed, our efforts to achieve it – must entail the well-being of future generations.
- Studies on sustainable development performance evaluate societal change over time. To be complete, these studies must effectively evaluate a society's productive base.
- Wealth is the social worth of an economy's assets: reproducible capital; human capital; knowledge; natural capital; population; institutions; and time.
- Shadow prices are key to understanding inclusive wealth. The shadow price for many market-traded goods is the market price, but these should be used with caution as many prices do not take account of externalities.

CHAPTER 2

Accounting for the inclusive wealth of nations

- This chapter analyzes changes in the inclusive wealth index (IWI) and its components for 20 countries for the period from 1990 to 2008. Wealth is primarily assessed here as the value of manufactured, human, and natural capital stocks. The Index is additionally adjusted for population changes by presenting per capita measures.

- 6 out of the 20 countries analyzed decreased their IWI per capita in the last 19 years. In 5 out of 20 countries, population increased at a faster rate than inclusive wealth, resulting in negative changes in the IWI per capita.
- The majority of the countries in our sample have had an increase in their stocks of manufactured capital per capita. In China, India and Chile, the positive changes in IWI has been mainly driven by manufactured capital. Russia, Nigeria, and Venezuela saw a decrease in their manufactured capital base.
- When the three capital forms measured are adjusted for total factor productivity – oil capital gains and carbon damages the performance of some countries increases considerably, particularly for Nigeria, Saudi Arabia and Venezuela.
- Human capital, being the prime capital form that offsets the decline in natural capital in most of the economies, has increased in every country.
- This chapter demonstrates that the IWI provides a different perspective for assessing the performance of an economy - this by switching the focus of attention from flows (income) to stock metrics (wealth). This stresses the importance of preserving a portfolio of capital assets to ensure that the productive base can ultimately be maintained to sustain the well-being of future generations.

CHAPTER 3

The significance of the natural wealth of nations

- This first IWR focuses on quantifying components of natural capital that are largely driven by those resources for which markets exist. It is easier to obtain physical inventories and data on these stocks.
- Shadow prices would be an effective tool for measuring an asset's contribution to well-being because they also reflect the relative importance of the different capital forms

within the wealth accounting framework. The lack of such shadow prices presents a significant shortcoming. So instead, this analysis relies on rental prices, meaning market prices minus production costs of the resources.

- We see that in almost all countries, potential gains in renewable resources were not enough to compensate for the depletion of exhaustible stocks, like fossil fuels. The fishery is a specific illustration where, although a renewable resource, fish are being "mined" at a rate that challenges renewal of the stock.
- The general trend is that population has been growing in most of the countries, exacerbating thereby the decline in natural capital growth rates, as resources are accounted for among a larger number of people.

Readers are encouraged to review the Methodological Annex and the Data Annex at the end of the publication. These annexes shed light on the processes used to arrive at the information in Chapters 2 and 3.

CHAPTER 4

Measuring inclusive wealth at a sub-national level: lessons from the United States

- This chapter is the first attempt to construct an accounting of the capital assets of each of the 48 contiguous u.s. states.
- The study looks at four types of capital: exhaustible natural capital (mainly coal, oil, and natural gas); land; physical capital (like buildings, homes, and equipment); and human capital (based on education, wages, and number of working years remaining). Despite the limitations in data availability, using housing and stock market data to value physical capital is an important contribution to the literature on sustainability.
- The results show a very low level of wealth inequality across states. The Gini coeffi-

cient is 0.09, which represents a fairly equal distribution of wealth.

- The study demonstrates that the rate of economic growth as measured by inclusive wealth can be quite different than the rate of economic growth suggested by GDP figures. Data show that those states with high GDP growth rates tend to have much lower rates of inclusive wealth growth.
- It is essential that governments collect capital stock data so that inclusive wealth accounting can become increasingly accurate, comprehensive, and useful. More complete data would enable states to measure their rate of inclusive investment. Such data would also make it clear to policy-makers whether current GDP growth rates are sustainable in the long-run.
- An important conclusion drawn here is that if states with an inclusive wealth per capita annual growth rate that is less than their GDP per capita annual growth rate want to sustain higher GDP growth rates for the long term, increased inclusive investment will be required. This means that state governments would have to encourage education, reduce the extraction of natural resources, and increase the construction of public infrastructure.

CHAPTER 5

Are national economies (virtually) sustainable?: an empirical analysis of natural assets in international trade

- This chapter explores the impact of international trade on sustainable development and the measurement of genuine (or adjusted net) savings at both the global and domestic levels.
- The chapter draws crucial distinctions between production- and consumption-based approaches to measuring changes in inclusive wealth, as well as between the notions of domestic and global sustainability,

where the latter is defined in terms of the global genuine savings rate.

- By looking only at per-country inclusive wealth accounting, we potentially weaken our understanding of global performance. The chapter addresses this by examining how changes in resource wealth are embodied in internationally traded goods and services.
- Specifically, the chapter uses a disaggregated multi-regional input-output model (MRIO) to measure the value of resource depletion and the social costs of carbon emissions in the context of international trade.
- The term "virtual sustainability" is introduced here as a way to consider the implications of trade and the role of consumption in understanding a country's contribution to global sustainability.
- Our empirical findings indicate that the magnitudes of the (change in) natural assets embodied in trade can be substantial, both in dollar value terms and in relation to national economies. This could challenge both the conventional thinking on sustainability and the claims of progress made on this front by individual countries.

PART II

CHAPTER 6

Natural capital as economic assets: a review

- In calculating total wealth, depleting a type of natural capital and substituting it with another form of natural capital or with manufactured capital is frequently uneconomical in most countries. The assumption of absolute substitutability is not a realistic one.
- Externalities are the effects of activities on the well-being of people who have not been parties to the negotiations that led to those activities. An example is the impact of upstream deforestation on downstream farmers. Without correction, the use of natural capital is implicitly subsidized by people who suffer from the externalities.
- A large part of what nature offers is a necessity and not a luxury. There are options for some level of substitutability, but in consideration, caution must be taken for irreversible processes that might cause a decrease in well-being.
- The social worth of natural resources can be divided into three parts: use value, intrinsic value, and option value – in varying proportions.
- Property rights are currently focused on individual ownership. However, many of nature's services are public and therefore it is difficult to assign property rights to them. Moreover, if those rights are assigned, they are typically assigned without due accord to social justice. Ill-specified or unprotected property rights typically prevent markets from forming or make markets function wrongly when they do.

CHAPTER 7

The road to wealth accounting

- It is clear that human activity has had a profound effect on our environment, and that these effects, in turn, have had an impact on human well-being. While the importance of this relationship is appreciated, there are still few reliable indicators of the value to people of biosphere change.
- The Millennium Ecosystem Assessment was able to quantify the physical changes in ecosystem services that had occurred in the previous half century, but it was unable to assign a value to the loss of non-marketed ecosystem services.
- This chapter considers the issues involved in developing metrics of the social importance of biosphere change. What is needed is a measure of the impact of biosphere change on wealth and wealth distribution.

The chapter discusses the welfare-theoretic foundations of wealth accounting, and the steps taken so far to build wealth accounts. It then considers what is required to evolve wealth accounts from the current system of national accounts (SNA).

- The SNA provides an incomplete picture of wealth because it includes only property that generates private claims to future benefits. It therefore excludes parts of natural capital that is essential to human well-being but cannot be privately held (e.g., the atmosphere or the open oceans).

- Two major efforts to advance our understanding of wealth are discussed here: the World Bank's idea of adjusted net savings, and the System of Environmental and Economic Accounts (SEEA). Both are important steps on the road to wealth accounting, but neither fully address the issues of what environmental stocks should be included, and how they should be measured and valued (the double counting caused by the SEEA's inclusion of ecosystems is particularly problematic).

- Ultimately, country wealth measurements should include all natural assets that are under a country's jurisdiction and that contribute to human well-being, whether those assets are privately owned or not.

- More work is still required on understanding and measuring the relationship among assets, environmental externalities, and poverty in an effort to advance human well-being.

CHAPTER 8

Ecosystem services and wealth accounting

- Ecosystems should be treated as an important asset in an economy and, in principle, ecosystem services should be valued in a similar manner as any other form of wealth. Quantifying these services is very challenging.

- The purpose of this chapter is to review progress in economics and ecology in assessing ecosystem services and their values, and to discuss the resulting implications for including such services in a wealth accounting framework.

- Understanding the relationship between ecosystems, their structure and functions, and the ecological services they generate is essential to determining how the structure and functions of an ecosystem provide valuable goods and services to humans.

- Since the purpose of new investment is to increase the quantity and quality of the economy's total capital stock, or wealth, adjusting gross domestic product (GDP) for depreciation in this stock would measure more accurately whether net additions to capital are occurring.

- If net domestic product (NDP) is to serve as a true measure of the changes in an economy's wealth, it must include any appreciation or depreciation to human and natural capital as well.

- The approach developed here requires, first, recognizing ecosystems as a component of natural capital, or ecological capital; and second, measuring these important assets in terms of the land area, or ecological landscape, which defines their boundaries.

CHAPTER 9

Inclusive wealth accounting for regulating ecosystem services

- Studies that have sought to value natural capital have typically focused on "provisioning" services or natural resource stocks such as oil and natural gas, minerals, timber, and fisheries. Other than the cost of CO_2 emissions *vis-à-vis* climate regulation, regulating services have not been considered in any great depth.

- An important first step for including regulating services in an inclusive wealth framework is to have well-defined individual services.

The present typology of regulating services does not lend itself well to wealth accounts because multiple services are embedded within common regulating service category. Identifying individual services also simplifies the valuation process.

- It is important to identify servicesheds in order to estimate the value of ecosystem services. A serviceshed is the area that provides a specific benefit to a specific individual or group of people. It is further characterized by three factors: (1) ecosystem supply; (2) institutions; and (3) physical access.
- Due to the high degree of uncertainty in estimating the value of regulating services, it will be useful for policy-makers to see a range of values with lower and upper bound estimates. We provide such uncertainty analyses for climate regulation through carbon sequestration.
- The marginal net benefit of regulating services is large enough to justify undertaking future research in identifying servicesheds, unbundling regulatory services into explicit benefits, and producing value estimates for inclusion in wealth accounts.

CHAPTER 10

Accounting for water: stocks, flows, and values

- As water becomes increasingly scarce, as sectoral competition for water intensifies, and as humanity increasingly interferes with nature's hydrological cycle, the need to measure and value water flows and stocks has increased.
- Such evaluation must proceed in two discrete steps: first, the construction of physical water accounts, designed to figure out how much water there is, where it is, when it is available, how accessible it is, and with what reliability; and second, when the accounts are in place, the analysis can proceed towards placing a value on these resources.

- The UN's System of Environmental-Economic Accounting for Water (SEEAW) is an important step forward in understanding the flows and stocks of water. The flows comprise abstraction, consumption, and return flows; the stocks, which are harder to assess, look at groundwater resources, lakes, snowpack, and the like.
- SEEAW has important strengths. It is multi-sectoral; it clearly distinguishes between consumptive and non-consumptive uses of water; it is hydrologically consistent with the law of conservation of mass; and it can be applied at various scales (project, sector, region, country, and basin).
- While SEEAW has been promoted for a few years, Australia is the only country for which detailed implementation plans and progress seem to be available. The process has been lengthy and detailed and has resulted in many reports, reviews, and studies.
- SEEAW accounts should be expanded to include the "unmanaged" natural landscape; "managed" areas; and rainfed agriculture.

CHAPTER 11

Safeguarding the future of the wealth of nature: sustainability, substitutability, measurement, thresholds, and aggregation issues in natural capital accounting for human well-being

- Nature is very different from human, social, and manufactured capital stocks in that it predates humanity and it operates through its own complex laws and systems.
- Most accounting for natural capital involves assigning monetary values to the flows of benefits from that capital. A monetary measure suggests that one capital stock can be substituted for another when trying to measure a country's total wealth in a multi-capital model. For natural capital, there is an emerging body of opinion that such substitutability is not complete, therefore

accounting for it in this way could be seriously misleading.

- The assumption of more or less complete substitutability between natural capital and other capital stocks is sometimes referred to as the "weak sustainability" assumption; while an assumption of limited substitutability is termed the "strong sustainability" assumption.

- The assumption of strong sustainability in respect of certain important aspects of natural capital would seem more consistent with the scientific evidence. Starting with this assumption when trying to understand the interactions between different forms of capital allows substitutability to be considered to the extent appropriate. Starting with an assumption of complete substitutability (the weak sustainability perspective), and proceeding directly to monetary valuation, tends to obscure those situations where this assumption is not valid.

- While consumption is important to well-being, it is also affected by a number of other crucial factors. The contribution of natural capital to well-being has not been widely recognized in the literature, but that has started to change in recent years as diverse contributions have been revealed through ecosystem assessments.

Overall lessons, findings, and recommendations

Lessons learned

A number of key lessons emerge from this first report, including: 1. substitutions among the different capital assets vary and in many cases become uneconomical; 2. the importance of not just one capital but the emphasis on a basket of inter-dependent capital assets; 3. population changes and their impact on the returns to a nation's productive base; 4. interconnected externalities that accrue, particularly from the degradation and decline of the natural capital base; and 5. estimation of shadow prices, which are so critical in computing the inclusive wealth of a country. These are elaborated upon in the Conclusion.

Key findings

KEY FINDING 1

70 percent of countries assessed in the 2012 Inclusive Wealth Report present a positive Inclusive Wealth Index (IWI) per capita growth, indicating sustainability.

KEY FINDING 2

High population growth with respect to IWI growth rates caused 25 percent of countries assessed to become unsustainable.

KEY FINDING 3

While 19 out of the 20 countries experienced a decline in natural capital, six of them also saw a decline in their inclusive wealth, thus following an unsustainable track.

KEY FINDING 4

Human capital has increased in every country, being the prime capital form that offsets the decline in natural capital in most economies.

KEY FINDING 5

There are clear signs of trade-off effects among different forms of capital (manufactured, human, and natural capital) as witnessed by increases and declines of capital stocks for 20 countries over 19 years.

KEY FINDING 6

Technological innovation and/or oil capital gains outweigh declines in natural capital and damages from climate change, moving a number of countries from an unsustainable to a sustainable trajectory.

KEY FINDING 7

25 percent of assessed countries, which showed a positive trend when measured by GDP per capita and the HDI, were found to have a negative IWI.

KEY FINDING 8

The primary driver of the difference in performance was the decline in natural capital.

KEY FINDING 9

Estimates of inclusive wealth can be improved significantly with better data on the stocks of natural, human, and social capital and their values for human well-being.

Recommendations

Inclusive wealth offers policy-makers a comprehensive accounting tool for measuring the assets available in the economy. The understanding of such asset portfolios and their changes over time has important implications for sustaining the consumption needs of present and future generations.

RECOMMENDATION 1

Countries witnessing diminishing returns in their natural capital should build up their investments in renewable natural capital to increase their inclusive wealth and the well-being of their citizens.

RECOMMENDATION 2

Countries should mainstream the Inclusive Wealth Index within their planning and development ministries so that projects and activities are evaluated based on a balanced portfolio approach that includes natural, human, and manufactured capital.

RECOMMENDATION 3

Countries should support/speed up the process of moving from an income-based accounting framework to a wealth accounting framework.

RECOMMENDATION 4

Governments should move away from GDP per capita and instead evaluate their macroeconomic policies – such as fiscal and monetary policies – based on their contribution to the IWI of the country.

RECOMMENDATION 5

Governments and international organizations should establish research programs for valuing key components of natural capital, particularly ecosystem services.

The conclusion to the IWR elaborates upon the findings and recommendations identified here, and discusses the prospects for future for future work on inclusive wealth.

Inclusive wealth:
an overview

This is the first of a series of biennial reports on the sustainability of countries. The report looks at the productive base of economies, based on capital assets – produced or manufactured capital; human capital; social capital; and natural capital. This first report of the series is focused on natural capital and will be released at the 2012 Earth Summit (Rio+20) to be held in Rio de Janeiro, Brazil, in June 2012. The two main themes of the Rio+20 summit will be the green economy and international environmental governance. The report of the United Nations Secretary-General's High-level Panel report on Global Sustainability – *Resilient People, Resilient Planet: A future worth choosing* – was released in April of 2012 to inform the discussions and negotiations at the Rio+20 summit. The report highlights the potential of a green economy and also calls for new ways of measuring progress in a green economy. This report provides such a measure.

The IWR is a joint collaboration of the United Nations University International Human Dimensions Programme (UNU-IHDP) and the United Nations Environment Programme (UNEP). The group of authors for the report was selected based on their expertise in inclusive wealth and environmental economics, and an extensive publication record in the area of natural capital, human well-being, social welfare, and valuation, among others. A review process was also established and each chapter was reviewed by a minimum of two external referees using standard academic criteria. The reviewers were chosen again based on their expertise in the field, strong academic credentials, and a good publishing record in the relevant fields covered by this report.

Context

The primary objective of the *Inclusive Wealth Report* is to provide quantitative information and analysis that present a long-term perspective on human well-being and measures of sustainability.

The congruence of economic, social, and environmental crises over the past decade has forced political, business, and civil society leaders – as well as the general public – to question whether our present model of fostering human well-being is sustainable or even ideologically correct. The focus on material wealth as the key constituent of well-being and economic growth – and the only way to understand prosperity – is being increasingly questioned. We have forced ourselves to believe that we can grow ourselves out of the multiple crises we face today. There is no doubt economic growth is an important determinant of well-being. But it is not the *only* determinant and not should not be seen as an end in and of itself, but simply as one of many means to improving human well-being. Social and ecological factors are also important determinants of well-being, and in some cases, are direct *constituents* of well-being (MA 2005; DASGUPTA 2001; STIGLITZ ET AL. 2010). Examples are education, health, clean air and water, and spiritually significant ecological landscapes, among others. These things not only help us achieve well-being, they are elements of well-being in and of themselves.

In addition to broadening the measurement of well-being, there is also the issue of addressing the well-being of future generations. Some would say that focusing only on the present generation's pursuit of well-being – however defined – is unethical. The exact composition of the well-being of future generations is hard to determine as we have little idea of what the aspirations and desires of future generations will look like. But that does not exempt us from leaving a productive base from which these future generations can determine the type of lives they would value and pursue.

This report begins the unpacking of the various constituents and determinants of well-being and explores the productive base a country needs to ensure well-being is maintained and/ or improved for future generations. The report provides such an analysis for a group of 20 countries selected for their variety of geographical, social, economic, and ecological characteristics. The results reported should be seen as an exploratory exercise into the empirical estimations of many capital assets that do not have market prices – and in fact exist outside of the market – but are still critical for the maintenance and improvement of well-being.

What we measure and what we manage

Traditional indicators such as gross domestic product (GDP) per capita and the Human Development Index (HDI) have been the main determinants used to measure the progress of nations. GDP per capita was developed just after World War II by economist Simon Kuznets. It was constructed by Kuznets to measure the level of economic production and to provide guidance to policy-makers on which sectors of the economy are growing and which are slowing, and the throughput that is used by the economy. It was, therefore, always meant to be used strictly as an indicator for economic production. But somewhere along the line, GDP came to be used by policy-makers to measure the overall progress and performance of a nation, and that implied the well-being of its citizens. This caused some fundamental problems, not with the indicator itself, but with the way it has been used. Increases in total economic production do not translate into improvements in well-being. They might increase employment and might increase the income of individuals, but all these are just possible outcomes and not automatic consequences of economic growth.

In an attempt to broaden the perspective of well-being beyond economic growth and income, the Human Development Index (HDI) was developed. The HDI added literacy and mortality to the equation of income. Although an improvement over just using income to measure well-being, it has a number of internal inconsistencies that make it problematic to use to determine whether the well-being of a country's citizens has really improved or not. We shall not go into details of these inconsistencies, as that is not the main purpose of this report. Readers can refer to Sagar and Najam (1998) and others for a detailed discussion of the shortcomings of the HDI.

Putting aside the breadth of coverage of well-being and methodological issues, neither GDP nor the HDI reflect the state of the natural environment and both focus on the short-term, with no indication of whether current well-being can be sustained. The flagship development reports of the international institutions (the *Human Development Report* of UNDP; the *World Economic*

The flagship development reports of the international institutions share a common weakness when it comes to measuring social progress: they are all focused on current, short-run measures with little or no consideration of the natural capital base of an economy.

Outlook of the IMF; and the *World Development Report* of the World Bank) share a common weakness when it comes to measuring social progress: they are all focused on current, short-run measures with little or no consideration of the natural capital base of an economy.

There have been recent advances in addressing the weaknesses in contemporary measures of welfare that are used to judge the progress of nations. The World Bank's *Where is the Wealth of Nations?* (2006) and the more recent, *The Changing Wealth of Nations* (2010) are two such initiatives. Using a welfare framework as the basis of computing the comprehensive wealth of an economy, these reports provide for the first time an accounting of the use of the natural capital base. However, there are some strong assumptions behind the underlying model that might weaken its usefulness as a measure of sustainability. Some of these are discussed further in Chapter 1.

The main message is that important elements of a wealth report do already exist, but there are significant gaps where research and analysis will be required to increase the depth and breadth of the wealth estimates. This report draws on the World Bank measures of comprehensive wealth but goes beyond them by revising the theoretical framework and the methodology of computing the various capital asset bases. These are clearly elaborated in the data and methodological annexes presented at the end of this report.

What we need to manage and what we need to measure

The call for going beyond material wealth to gauge our well-being and make sure that well-being is achievable and sustainable for future generations has long appeared in much of the sustainable development, environmental, and ecological economics literature, significantly less in economics and development literature. The present pre-occupation with the Green Economy, we fear, will not provide the change we seek if we do not address the fundamental problem of what precisely we are measuring and the indicators we need to develop.

The concept of, if not the actual term, "sustainable development" has been around for centuries, but the most recent modern-day expression can be traced back to 1983 (DURAIAPPAH 2003). In 1983, then Secretary-General of the United Nations, Javier Pérez de Cuellar, appointed Gro Harlem Brundtland from Norway to head a special commission to address the rapid deterioration of the human and ecological environments. The resolution establishing the commission by the General Assembly in A/RES/38/161 in 1983 stipulates the following terms of reference:

(a) To propose long-term environmental strategies for achieving sustainable development to the year 2000 and beyond;

(b) To recommend ways in which concern for the environment may be translated into greater co-operation among developing countries and between countries at different stages of economic and social development and lead to the achievement of common and mutually supportive objectives which take account of the interrelationships between people, resources, environment and development;

(c) To consider ways and means by which the international community can deal more effectively with environmental concerns, in the light of the other recommendations in its report;

(d) To help define shared perceptions of long-term environmental issues and of the appropriate efforts needed to deal successfully with the problems of protecting and enhancing the environment, a long-term agenda for action during the coming decades, and aspirational goals for the world community.

In 1987, the commission published *Our Common Future*. The report emphasized the notion of sustainable development and defined it as "development that meets the needs of the present without compromising the needs of future generations to meet their own needs" (WORLD COMMISSION ON ENVIRONMENT AND DEVELOPMENT 1987). Although the terms of reference given to the Commission might, at first sight, seem to have been narrowly confined to the environment, the Commission's members had the foresight to understand the importance of addressing these issues within an integrated framework bringing together the social, economic, and environmental spheres to address the notion of sustainability. At the end of the day, it is the welfare of humans about which we are concerned, not just the present generation but future generations as well.

The Commission called for a new era of economic growth that was socially and environmentally sustainable. The report did an excellent job of informing us of the state of the planet, emphasizing the need for urgent action, and advising on what needed to be done and where action was required both across regions as well as in key focus areas. But the report fell short on providing guidance on how to quantify progress in a way that could provide support to policy-makers in considering interventions and responses. The call for a new era of economic growth without any suggestion for new metrics for evaluating progress left countries with little choice but to continue using GDP to track progress.

The situation has changed in the follow-up to Rio+20. The report of the High-Level Panel Global Sustainability of the UN Secretary-General, *Resilient People, Resilient Planet: A future worth choosing*, as emphasized earlier, calls for not just a new form of economic growth that works within ecological boundaries while pursuing social equity, but also for new measures to track progress. And it calls explicitly for going beyond our present generation of indicators, such as GDP and the HDI. This report provides such a metric and presents the strengths of the inclusive wealth measure but also its weaknesses and ways to improve the measure over time.

The inclusive wealth framework

The inclusive wealth framework proposed in this report is a theoretical framework based on social welfare theory to consider the multiple issues that sustainable development attempts to address. First, the inclusive wealth framework moves away from the arbitrary notion of needs and redefines the objective of sustainable development as a discounted flow of utility which, in this case, is consumption. The framework is flexible enough to allow consumption to include not just material goods, but also elements such as leisure, spiritual aspirations, social relations, and environmental security, among others.

The elegance of the inclusive wealth framework comes from the equivalence theorem whereby the framework allows the move from the constituents of well-being to their determinants. In this case, we refer to the various capital assets a country is able to accumulate. This asset base is called the productive base of the nation. The productive base forms the basis for sustainable development and provides a tangible measure for governments to use and track over time. But, more importantly, the framework provides information for policy-makers – particularly planning authorities – on which forms of capital investment should be made for ensuring the sustainability of the productive base of an economy.

The IWR 2012: natural capital

The report will be produced every two years. Each edition will focus on a specific thematic area. In the case of this first report, the focus is on natural capital and, in particular, "ecosystem services." The concept of ecosystem services is relatively new and there is a significant gap between using the term ecosystem services and accounting for these services within wealth accounts. It was therefore felt that a first report focusing on natural capital and ecosystem services would serve to highlight the importance of natural capital, but also illustrate the work required to ensure a near complete accounting of this critical capital for the productive base of an economy – a task that has been ignored by most planning strategies and tools. The IWR series will progressively increase the coverage of asset values over time, particularly with respect to ecosystem assets (and their associated services) as well as the impacts of climate change and other environmental impacts on these assets. Underpinning this progressive increase in coverage will be a research program on these and wider topics in asset accounting.

Audience and structure of report

The primary audience of the *Inclusive Wealth Report* will be governments. More broadly, the report will be of use to development practitioners as well as researchers and the wider development community. The inclusion of environmental damage in the accounts – as well as damages from global environmental change such as climate change – can be useful in determining cross-country compensations and a guide for international negotiations on the consideration of transboundary assets. The report will also be useful for national economic planning agencies when considering macroeconomic fiscal policies. Changes in the various capital assets and their contribution towards the inclusive wealth of a country can provide information on where future investments should be targeted to get the best returns for increasing the productive base of the country.

The report is presented in two parts. Part I introduces the concept of inclusive wealth and provides the first results for a set of 20 countries used as a pilot in the 2012 report. This section of the report has a total of five chapters. In Chapter 1, the concept of sustainable development is revisited and the redefinition of sustainable development and sustainability from needs to well-being is presented. This chapter also provides the theoretical framework wherein the link with well-being and wealth is made through a welfare theoretic conceptual framework. In this chapter, the notion of the productive base of an economy, the foundation for this productive base, and the maintenance of well-being are developed and introduced. The chapter also lays down the necessary definitions and equations to make the link with well-being and the different forms of capital that constitute the productive base of the economy and the role of shadow prices. Some of the key differences between the wealth accounts presented in this report and the wealth accounts developed by the World Bank are also discussed in Chapter 1. The final section of the chapter presents the key assumptions and caveats underlying the inclusive wealth framework.

> The framework emphasizes not only the importance of maintaining any one particular asset base, but also of maintaining the total capital asset base.

Chapter 2 presents the empirical computations of wealth across 20 countries for the period of 1990–2008. The countries were chosen in a manner to distinguish differences in stages of development, natural resource bases, population dynamics, and geographical locations. It is hoped that this list will be expanded in future reports. Particular attention is paid to the changes in inclusive wealth and the respective changes across human, natural, and produced capita. Comparisons to GDP are made for all countries to provide a comparative analysis between the inclusive wealth and GDP accounts. A key component of this chapter is the differences between absolute changes in inclusive wealth and the respective capital asset bases with changes on a per capita basis to demonstrate the role population growth plays in sustainability. This chapter also provides some key policy guidance on where to focus investments in order to improve the inclusive wealth of a country. Chapter 3 follows with a more detailed analysis of the natural capital accounts. The drawdown or build-up of the various assets within natural capital are analyzed, paying particular attention to forests and their role in the decline or increase of natural capital. Chapter 4 provides a more detailed analysis of the wealth accounts of the United States of America and provides some key insights on how inclusive wealth accounts can be used at a sub-national level. Chapter 5 follows with an overview of how trade influences wealth accounts and provides some preliminary findings on the dynamic role trade plays in determining the inclusive wealth of nations.

In Part II of this report, we present some of the key lessons learned on developing ecosystem services accounts and the challenges faced when attempting to value the changes in the capital stocks over time. Chapter 6 provides an overview of the role natural capital plays within wealth accounts and sets the foundations of computing the value of natural capital. The chapter discusses ecosystem services and the various ways shadow prices can be computed for the various components of natural capital. Chapter 7 makes the distinction between flows and stocks and their relevance to wealth accounts. In this chapter, the relevance of the system of environmental accounts and the way ecosystem services can be reflected in these accounts are discussed. The primary objective of this chapter is to lay the groundwork for future work in national accounts in order to capture the value of ecosystem services. In Chapter 8, a more detailed description of valuing non-market ecosystem services is discussed. The use of ecological production functions is expanded and the complexities of these functions are explored.

The next two chapters focus on regulating ecosystem services. Chapter 9 provides an overview of the three regulating services of soil erosion control, water purification, and carbon sequestration. Tools used to value these services such as INVEST are described and some examples of valuation of these services using these tools is provided. Chapter 10 provides an overview of water services and describes the complexities of accounting changes in water-related ecosystem services. The focus in this chapter is on the physical accounts and leaves the valuation of these stocks as a research question for future studies.

Chapter 11 completes part two of the report by highlighting some of the issues relating to substitutability among the various categories of capital and discusses the notion of strong and weak substitutability. The chapter goes on to provide some information on ecological thresholds and the complexities of deriving tipping points in both the social and ecological spheres expanding on issues discussed in Box 1 in Chapter 1. The chapter provides a discussion on the unique characteristics of natural capital and the complexities of using the inclusive wealth accounting framework from an empirical perspective.

The reader is encouraged to review the data and methodological annexed at the end of the report to get a more detailed discussion of the methods used to get the results presented in Chapters 2 and 3 of Part I.

The report ends with a concluding chapter, in which key lessons, findings, and recommendations are offered. In addition, a brief description of the next report is presented.

REFERENCES

DASGUPTA, P. (2001). *Human well-being and the natural environment*. Oxford: Oxford University Press.

DURAIAPPAH, A.K. (2003). *Computational models in the economics of environment and development*. Dordrecht, Holland: Kluwer Academic Publishers.

MILLENNIUM ECOSYSTEM ASSESSMENT (MA). (2005). *Ecosystems and human well-being: Synthesis*. Washington, DC: Island Press.

SAGAR, A. & NAJAM, A. 1998. The human development index: A critical review. *Ecological Economics, 25*(3), 249-264.

STIGLITZ, J.E., SEN, A. & FITOUSSI, J.P. (2010). *Mismeasuring our lives: Why GDP doesn't add up*. New York: The New Press.

UNITED NATIONS GENERAL ASSEMBLY. (1983). *Resolutions adopted by the general assembly at its 38th session*. Retrieved from http://www.un.org/depts/dhl/resguide/r38.htm

WORLD BANK. (2006). *Where is the wealth of nations?* Washington, DC: World Bank.

WORLD BANK. (2011). *The changing wealth of nations: Measuring sustainable development in the new millennium*. Washington, DC: World Bank.

WORLD COMMISSION ON ENVIRONMENT AND DEVELOPMENT. (1987). *Our common future*. New York: Oxford University Press.

CHAPTER 1

Well–being and wealth

Partha Dasgupta and Anantha Duraiappah

KEY MESSAGES

The true achievement of sustainable development must focus on human well-being. When we talk about human well-being, we cannot only talk about today. The definition of human well-being – and, indeed, our efforts to achieve it – must entail the well-being of future generations.

Studies on sustainable development performance evaluate societal change over time. To be complete, these studies must effectively evaluate a society's productive base.

Wealth is the social worth of an economy's assets: reproducible capital; human capital; knowledge; natural capital; population; institutions; and time.

Shadow prices are key to understanding inclusive wealth. The shadow price for many market-traded goods is the market price, but these should be used with caution as many prices do not take account of externalities.

1. Introduction

Economic development is customarily evaluated in terms of its contribution to human well-being. Well-being should not just be considered for people living today, but for future populations as well. This inter-generational perspective on well-being is essential and is intended in this chapter with the use of the term "well-being." The term refers to today and tomorrow.

Economic development is evaluated for two purposes: prescribing and assessing. The purpose of policy evaluation, including project evaluation, is to arrive at policy prescriptions – for example, when a government project evaluator carries out a study to determine whether a wetland should be drained to build a housing estate. The idea is to evaluate a society at a point in time before and after a hypothetical change (the policy change) has been made. In principle, policy evaluation, including project evaluation, can be used to identify optimum development, which is a development path a society would ideally wish to follow.

In contrast, the literature on sustainable development studies ways to assess an economy's performance. That literature has grown in response to the realization that the development process of nations and regions has been accompanied by deterioration of a number of key environmental characteristics. Sustainability analysis is about evaluating societal change over time.

We will call the person doing the evaluation the social evaluator. The social evaluator could be a citizen (thinking about things before casting his or her vote on political candidates); he or she could be an ethicist hired to offer guidance to the government; she or he could be a government decision-maker, and so on. In what follows, modern convention is adopted by replacing the "social evaluator" with "society."

Although the idea of optimum development dominated development economics from the 1950s through the 1970s (CHAKRAVATERY 1969; LITTLE AND MIRRLEES 1968, 1974), interest has shifted in recent years to the notion of sustainable development. The literature on the latter subject is now vast. The theory underlying the concept was presented by Hamilton and Clemens (1999) and Dasgupta and Mäler (2000), and reviewed with extensions by Dasgupta (2001 [2004], 2009). Empirical studies on whether in recent decades economic development has been sustainable in various countries have been conducted by Hamilton and Clemens (1999), Dasgupta (2001 [2004]), Arrow et al. (2004), World Bank (2006, 2010), and Arrow et al. (2010).

The literature on sustainable development grew in response to the concern that humanity's use of environmental natural resources is not taken adequately into account in economic decisions. But writings on what one may call "natural capital" are scattered in journals and books. This chapter offers an organized view of how environmental natural resources can be introduced seamlessly into sustainability analysis and contains an account of the way natural capital should be included in the calculations that are necessary for studies of sustainable development.

2. The idea of sustainable development

In their pioneering work, World Commission on Environment and Development (1987: 70) defined sustainable development as "... development that meets the needs of the present without compromising the ability of future generations to meet their own needs."

What should we make of it?

Notice that the definition makes no specific reference to human well-being. Similarly, it makes relatively weak demands about justice among the generations. In the Commission's view, sustainable development requires that future generations have no less of the means to meet their needs than we do ourselves; it requires nothing more. As needs are the austere component of well-being, societal development could be sustainable in the Commission's sense without having much to show for it.

Notice also that the Commission's definition is directed at sustaining the factors that satisfy

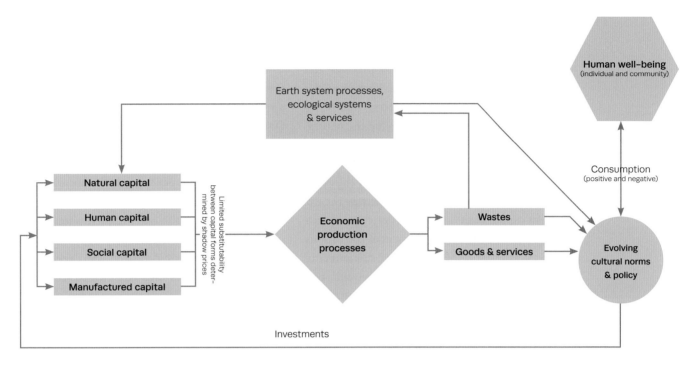

FIGURE 1

The productive base and human well–being

needs (food, clothing, shelter, personal relationships, leisure activities). But those factors would be available only if the society in question had an adequate productive base to produce them. So, in the Commission's view, sustainable development requires that relative to their populations, each generation should bequeath to its successor at least as large a quantity of what may be called a society's productive base as it had itself inherited from its predecessor. That raises another problem with the Commission's reasoning: it doesn't explain how the productive base should be measured.

The requirement that an object should be sustained over a period of time means that it shouldn't diminish over the period. In accordance with the recent literature on sustainable development, we have

> Definition 1. By sustainable development we mean a pattern of societal development along which (inter-generational) well-being does not decline.

A comparison of Definition 1 with that of the Brundtland Commission suggests therefore that we should seek an aggregate measure of a society's productive base with the property that it moves through time in the same manner as does well-being. In other words, we should seek a measure of a society's productive base that increases during any specified period of time if and only if well-being in that society increases during that same period of time.

3. Capital assets

It is intuitive that the elements comprising a society's productive base are not only the capital assets to which people there have access, but also the social infrastructure that influences the way those assets are put to work for human use, now and in the future as illustrated in Figure 1. The conceptual framework we use for the report begins with human well-being as the end. Well-being is to a large extent governed by the evolving cultural norms and policy which in turn influence the way societies use the different forms of capital assets. The capital asset base is, according to the conceptual framework, the foundation for the economic production process which then goes on to produce the goods and services which feed back into the norms and policy before influencing well-being. Ecosystems are critical in supplying the natural capital asset base. The drawdown of natural capital, subsequently impacting the way ecosystems are used, is heavily influenced by the evolving cultural norms and policy. The way the different capital assets are used is determined, to a large extent, by the shadow prices of the various capital assets and their respective components. The foundational base for the economic production system is therefore the different form of capitals and their respective shadow prices governing their use. It therefore makes sense then to invoke a broad notion of assets. We do that here and discover that the list includes at least two categories of assets whose appearance could seem quixotic. Several categories, however, are familiar.

3.1 Familiar assets

They include:

(1) *Reproducible or also called manufactured capital or produced capital in this report (roads, buildings, ports, machinery, equipment).* In common parlance, including national accounts, this category pretty much exhausts the list of capital assets. When national income accountants and international organizations speak of investment, they usually mean the accumulation of reproducible capital.[1] Reproducible capital is frequently called "manufactured capital."

(2) *Human capital (education, skills, tacit knowledge, health).* This category is embodied in people. As teachers are painfully aware, human capital is not transferable without cost from one person to another. Education, skills, and health are ends as well as means. They have intrinsic

worth, but are also of indirect value (investment in human capital raises a person's productivity).

(3) *Knowledge (science and technology).* This category includes such items as nature's laws, abstract theorems, formulae, and algorithms. Once discovered, they are in principle there for all to use. But for someone to be able to apply knowledge, three conditions must be met: (i) a recognition by that person that the knowledge exists; (ii) the person should have the relevant skills (human capital!); and (iii) there should be no legal or social barrier to applying the knowledge. What one should broadly call "research and development," or R&D, are the investments required to advance codified knowledge, unless of course that knowledge can be obtained freely from external sources.

(4) *Natural capital (local ecosystems, biomes, sub-soil resources).* Today it has become commonplace that nature should enter explicitly in economic calculations. But because nature has been neglected for so long in the literature on social and economic development, natural capital is the focus of this report.

(5) *Population (size and demographic profile).* Conceptually, this category raises the deepest problems; in as much as people are both the reason well-being should occupy the core of sustainability analysis and the means to the realization of well-being.

3.2 Institutional capital

Categories (1)–(5) are not exhaustive. Today it is not uncommon for people to refer to "religious capital," "social capital," "cultural capital," and, more broadly, "institutional capital" when trying to understand the progress or regress of societies. So, we have a further category of assets to consider:

(6) *Institutions.* By "institutions" we mean the myriad of formal and informal arrangements among people (the rule of law, social norms of behavior, habitual social practices) that influence the allocation of resources both at a moment in time and over time. Institutions are

---

1   See, for example, the Tables on National Investment at the end of the World Bank's annual *World Development Report.*

"enabling" assets. Access to institutions should be (i) non-rivalrous in character and should be (ii) freely open to all. Institutions are often seen as public goods.

How do institutions enter sustainability analysis? They do so by influencing the value of other capital assets. Suppose the state apparatus in a country is corrupt, implying that the judicial system is unreliable. Because people find it difficult to protect their property rights, the value of their capital assets is small, other things being equal. Corruption reduces the social worth of assets.[2]

Institutions influence the composition of consumption and saving and the character of future institutions. There are institutions that foster progress by having in place a structure of incentives that encourage people to allocate goods and services in their most productive uses. But institutions aren't enough. If they are to progress, people must trust one another and have confidence in their institutions. Well-developed competitive markets, tight social norms and codes of conduct, and good governance together can help create and maintain trust and confidence. But mutual trust and the cooperation that can result from it cannot be guaranteed even, under sound institutions. Opportunistic behavior can beget opportunistic behavior. Institutions can break down under a cascade of opportunism unless there are checks and balances in place.[3]

In contrast, there are institutions that are a hindrance from the start. Under weak, misguided, or corrupt governance, goods and services end up in unproductive (even wrong) places. When vested interests govern social decisions, neither efficiency nor more generally justice gets much of a look-in. A society's capacity to flourish shrinks when its institutions deteriorate (owing to civil wars, ethnic strife, increased corruption) and its other assets don't accumulate sufficiently to compensate for that deterioration. Likewise, a society's capacity to flourish shrinks when its material assets (e.g., natural capital) depreciate and its institutions aren't able to improve sufficiently to compensate for that depreciation or turn behavior so that the assets begin to accumulate.

3.3 Time as an asset

We haven't quite yet covered the myriad of assets that comprise a society's productive base. Consider a small oil-exporting country. Being small, the country has no control over international oil prices. Meanwhile, or so let us imagine, an oil cartel, of which our country is not a member, raises the price of oil on a continual basis. Our country therefore enjoys capital gains on its reserves without having to engage in any form of capital accumulation. Its productive base expands.[4] Similarly, it could be that the country enjoys an expansion of its knowledge base by deploying scientific advances elsewhere without having to pay for that privilege. In both circumstances our country enjoys an expansion of its productive base simply by waiting. That tells us we should include time in a society's productive base.

The suggestion could seem perverse. We usually regard a commodity to be an asset only if it is durable, whereas time is fleeting. Moreover, unlike assets in categories (1)-(6), which can be accumulated or decumulated at will, time moves at a constant pace, namely, the pace it has set itself. But classifications are meant to serve a purpose, they are not cast in iron in some Platonic universe. A chief aim of sustainability analysis is to construct a measure of a society's productive base that can be used to judge whether it is pursuing a sustainable

---

2   No doubt the purpose of corrupt practice could be to enhance the market worth of assets owned by the practitioner. In the text we are referring to the social worth of assets.

3   On the role of trust in sustainable development, see Dasgupta (2011).

4   The same logic says that, other things being equal, an oil–importing country would find its productive base to shrink as the international price of oil rose over time.

development path. If that aim can only be achieved if we include time in the society's productive base, we should regard it as an asset. So we now have one further capital asset on our list, namely,

(7) *Time!*

4. The social value of capital assets: shadow prices

Goods and services are of value because they contribute to human well-being. What are the contents of a person's well-being? Here we note that they include the engagements that are open to a person; and that those in turn centre on the person's relationships with others, the consumption of goods and services involving herself and those to whom she relates, and her ability to meet her obligations to others, and to pursue her projects, purposes, and the many mundane things that define her life.[5] Many of those engagements we care about directly, others are of indirect value to us. That said, every engagement requires goods and services if they are to be carried out. It follows that in its reduced form, individual well-being, and therefore human well-being, is a function of the consumption and use of goods and services.

Capital assets in categories (1)–(6) are the means by which consumption goods and services are produced. Several are ends as well (health, education). At any given date, (intergenerational) well-being is determined by (a) the assets a society has inherited from the past, (b) the society's subsequent development (which in turn will be shaped by that inheritance), and (c) chance.

We consider the role of chance in sustainability analysis in Box 1. Here we focus on (a) and (b).

Excepting for time, assets are durable goods. Some are tangible (roads, wetlands), while others are not (knowledge, institutions, time). No doubt capital assets depreciate (machines and

equipment undergo wear and tear even when left unused, fisheries are destroyed when over-harvested, and societies have been known to forget their traditional knowledge), but they offer a flow of services over time. A desk offers the scholar an object on which she is able to read, write, and type. The value of the desk is the worth of the contribution it is expected to make to scholarly activity. In order to assess that worth, we need to estimate the value of the scholarly activity itself. The latter's value will include the enjoyment the scholar experiences from the activity and the benefits others enjoy from the fruits of that activity. Of course, it could be that she is fully compensated for the benefits others enjoy from her work, the compensation being, say, higher earnings and increased adulation. But it may be that the higher earnings and increased adulation, when taken together, are less than the totality of benefits others enjoy from the fruits of her scholarly activity. In the latter case we should estimate not only the value of the desk to the scholar – that would be the desk's private value to the scholar – but also that part of the value to others that does not get reflected in her increased emoluments and social esteem. In short, we should be interested in the desk's social worth. But the desk in question is one among (hopefully!) many writing desks. That particular desk can therefore be viewed as a marginal unit of the totality of all writing desks. The social worth of a marginal unit of an asset is called its shadow price. So we have

> Definition 2. The shadow price of a capital asset is the contribution a marginal unit of it is forecast to make to human well-being. For example, watersheds are known to provide water purification ecosystem services for human health. The shadow price of these watersheds is then the net benefit an additional unit area of a watershed conserved will contribute towards well-being which, in this case, will be the constituent of health.

An asset's shadow price depends on its future use, which is to say that it is a function of the forecast of the asset's use. That is an inevitable feature of the worth of anything. A writing desk

---

5   Williams (1985) is a classic study of the content of human well-being.

that is forecast to rest unused and unrecognized is value-less. In contrast, if it is forecast that the desk will be used to good effect, its shadow price would be positive. Social evaluators who agree on everything but their forecasts would impute different shadow prices to the desk.

Forecasts are not mere guesses. If they are to carry conviction, forecasts must be based on a defendable theory of the social and natural processes that shape a society's future. That means shadow prices are based on counter-factuals: they are determined not only by the forecast of the shape of things to come, but also by the forecasts of future development had the current stocks of capital assets been otherwise. To put it another way, if they are to carry conviction, forecasts have to be based on a defendable theory of the evolving political economy shaping the society under study. Estimating shadow prices involves counter-factuals. Shadow prices contain an enormous quantity of information.

The inclusion of population change in sustainability analysis raises technical problems that are best excluded here.[6] The account of institutions as a category of "enabling" assets suggests that it will prove useful to keep them separate from the other categories of assets. Presently we will see why it proves useful to keep time separate as well. That leaves us with reproducible capital, human capital, natural capital, and knowledge (categories (1)–(4)). But each of those four is itself a broad category of goods, requiring disaggregation. In theory, the disaggregation can be as fine as we care to make it, but in empirical work it is inevitably coarse. For example, it is common in government and international publications to present estimates of investment in "industry," the sector being one that includes any number of capital assets (factories, machines, automobiles, and so on). A similar form of aggregation is involved in "mining" and "agriculture." Of course, if you are studying the automobile industry in an advanced industrial country, you will want to disaggregate some more and distinguish various brands of automobiles and the ancillary assets (repair and maintenance shops, gas pumps) that go to provide for the industry. Here we do not need to specify the extent to which the assets have been disaggregated to form our list. So we take it that capital assets in categories (1)–(4) are indexed by i and number N; that is, i ranges from 1 to N. The lack of specification of the category to which any particular i belongs means we can arrive at a measure of a society's productive base without prior presumptions about the relative importance of various capital assets that comprise that base.

Let t denote time. For convenience, we suppose t is a continuous variable such that $t \geq 0$. Suppose t is the date at which sustainability analysis is being conducted. We denote the evolving political economy by $\mathbf{M}$ and by $V(t)$ inter-generational well-being at t. Let $K_i(t)$ be the stock of asset i at time t and $\mathbf{K}(t)$ the N-vector of the stocks of capital assets (that is, $\mathbf{K}(t) = \{K_1(t),\ldots, K_i(t),\ldots, K_N(t)\}$. An economic forecast at t is a prediction of the future development path, based on $\mathbf{K}(t)$, M, and possibly t itself. Thus we have:

EQUATION 1

$$V(t) = V(\mathbf{K}(t),\mathbf{M},t)$$

Let $\Delta K_i(t)$ be a small increase in asset i at time t. We may interpret ΔK_i as a gift some external source makes to the economy. The gift "perturbs" the economy. *Other things remaining the same*, let $\Delta V(t)$ be the small change in $V(t)$ consequent upon that gift. Let $P_i(t)$ be the shadow price of asset i at time t. From Definition 2 and EQUATION (1) it follows that

EQUATION 2

$$P_i(t) = \Delta V(t) \big/ \Delta K_i(t) \qquad i = 1,2,\ldots,N$$

In very exceptional (i.e., idealized) circumstances, an asset's shadow price would equal its market price. Thus market prices of natural capital are rarely equal to their shadow prices. Those reasons have to do with the presence of "externalities," an ubiquitous phenomenon that is linked to the weak property rights that

---

6 See Dasgupta (2001, [2004]) and Arrow, Dasgupta, and Mäler (2003) for a detailed analysis.

BOX 1
Chance, thresholds, bifurcations, and potential catastrophes

Accommodating chance in sustainability analysis is to invite the language of probabilities (be they subjective probabilities or empirical probabilities, or a combination of the two). Unless we need to consider chance explicitly in our discussion, we will embed it in our analysis without mention. For example, readers could, should they wish, read "expected well-being" when we write "well-being," and the expectation could be thought of as being constructed out of an implicit set of probabilities. Here, we study the way to introduce uncertainty explicitly into sustainability analysis.

In defining shadow prices (Definition 2), it was assumed that a small increase or decrease in the stock of asset $i(\Delta K_i)$ leads only to a small change in human well-being (ΔV). That amounts to supposing that human well-being (V) is a smooth function of the stocks of capital assets (K_i). The requirement would appear to go against a general finding, that the dynamics of natural systems (e.g., ecosystems, climate systems) are non-linear, harboring *thresholds* that have the property that if a system would undergo discontinuous changes if it were to cross one. Formally, thresholds are known as *separatrices*.[1]

Thresholds are loci of points on the space of capital stocks that divide a dynamical system into distinct regions. Dynamical systems are confined to the region they happen to be in unless and until external forces "tip" them into another region. Classic examples of such tipping phenomena include the destruction of previously thriving fisheries. Over-harvesting can reduce fish populations to below their thresholds, tipping them into sizes that spell doom.

Bifurcations are different from thresholds. Earth systems operate at spatial scales ranging from the "miniscular" to the entire globe and running at speeds that range from the "near-instantaneous" to the "glacial." Suppose the social evaluator is studying the ecology of a grassland. Although it is embedded in the climate system, the speed with which the grassland's cover responds to changes in the (local) climate is at least an order of magnitude faster than the speed with which the local climate (as an expression of, say, global climate change) shifts. So, for all intents and purposes the social evaluator can regard climate as one of the parameters defining the grassland system. But it is a parameter that changes slowly and inexorably.

Bifurcations in a dynamical system are critical loci of points on the space of the system's parameters. They are "critical," in the sense that the loci divide the system's space of parameter values into separate regions, with the property that its dynamics differ from region to region. So it can be that a long-established grassland "tips" into a shrubland when the climate crosses a bifurcation. The existence of both thresholds and bifurcations call into question the assumption that V is a smooth function of (i) asset stocks and (ii) those relatively constant parameters that characterize the society under study. Let us see how we should respond to the doubt.

Of the pair, (i) is of particular interest because shadow prices have been defined on its basis (Equation [1]). In Equation (1) we assumed that V is a smooth function of K. How do we justify that in the presence of thresholds? Note first that the location of a threshold is never known with certainty. The social evaluator may know there is a threshold for, say, a population, but she or he would never know what it is. There are far too many particularities of the system the social evaluator will never understand, which is why the location of thresholds

---

1   Scheffer (2009) and Steffen et al. (2004) offer excellent accounts of the abrupt changes that nature and society are prone to in the face of non-linearities in the dynamics that drive them.

remains uncertain. Interestingly, that uncertainty smoothes V.

As illustration, consider a fishery. Its stock is denoted by K. We suppose the social evaluator has studied fisheries well enough to know that there is a threshold population size, call it K_c, such that the fishery would be doomed if the population were to drop below it, but would survive indefinitely if the population remained above it. To formalize the loss that would be suffered if the fishery were to cross the threshold, imagine that $V(K_c)$ is the value of the fishery if K is marginally in excess of K_c, but would be a small fraction, α, of $V(K_c)$ if K were marginally less than K_c. Crossing the threshold would result in a discrete loss in well-being, amounting to $(1-\alpha) V(K_c)$. That means $V(K)$ is discontinuous at K_c. Obviously, Equation (1) is meaningless at K_c. What could the fishery's shadow price mean in such a situation?

Suppose that, even though the social evaluator does not know the true value of K_c, she knows that it is not above K^{**} and not below K^*. So she knows that K_c lies somewhere in the range $[K^*, K^{**}]$. To have an interesting problem, imagine that the stock is currently above K^{**} but that there are signs of over-fishing, which is why the social evaluator has been called upon to study the fishery.

Let us imagine that the social evaluator constructs a discrete analogue of the fishery by dividing the interval $[K^*, K^{**}]$ into N equal sub-intervals of length Δ. So, $\Delta = (K^{**}-K^*)/N$. For simplicity of exposition we imagine that the social evaluator believes that K_c lies in one of those N sub-intervals with equal probability. Currently the fishery's size is just above K^{**}. Suppose under business-as-usual the fish population at time t would drop to $(K^{**}-\Delta)$. The expected loss in well-being would be $(1-\alpha)$ $V(K_c)/N$. If N is large, the expected loss is small, meaning that the expected value of V is a smooth function of K at K_c. But that means the shadow price of a marginal unit of fish, $P(K_c)$, is well-defined.

Imagine that a policy analysis persuades the social evaluator that the risk to the fishery under business as usual is worth it. She or he recommends business to remain as usual and the fishery enters the interval $[K^{**}\Delta),K^{**}]$. There are now two possibilities:

(a) It is discovered that the threshold did in fact lie in the interval $[K^{**}-\Delta,K^{**}]$. As the fishery is now known to be doomed, society will have entered a new accounting regime. All shadow prices will have to be recomputed. But Proposition 1 (on page 55) would continue to hold from that moment.

(b) The fishery is discovered to be safe. The social evaluator realizes that the threshold lies in the interval $[K^*,K^{**}-\Delta]$. But now there are $(N-1)$ sub-intervals left. So, the social evaluator, being a good Bayesian probabilist, concludes that the probability that K_c lies in any of them is $1/(N-1)$. That's still a small number, so the previous argument continues to hold. And it will continue to hold so long as the probability that K_c lies in the next sub-interval remains small. But once that probability becomes appreciable, the fishery's "shadow price" becomes a meaningless term. Both policy analysis and sustainability analysis would require the social evaluator to estimate the discrete loss in human well-being that would result from the fishery crossing its threshold.

prevail over environmental resources. Both sustainability analysis and policy analysis require the use of shadow prices. Shadow prices are the link between capital assets and the human well-being they are forecast to protect and promote.

It is customary to regard an asset as a "good" if its shadow price is positive, and as a "bad" if its shadow price is negative. The estimation of shadow prices involves "values" (the particular conception of human well-being that is deployed); "theories" (the character of the social and natural processes on the basis of which forecasts are made); and "facts" (the size distribution of various capital assets, the extent of their substitutability among one another, the determinants of the demand and supply of goods and services, and so forth). So it should be no surprise that even reasonable people could disagree over the magnitude of shadow prices. In recent years, those disagreements have been sharpest over the social worth of natural resources such as carbon and nitrogen concentrations (which at current levels are "bads") and the oceans (which taken together are a "good" in a multitude of ways).

Shadow prices are not Platonic objects, nor can they be plucked from air on mere whim and prejudice. We will never get shadow prices "right," but we can try to narrow the range in which they are taken by reasonable people to lie. The social evaluator estimates shadow prices, but recognizes that others may question her estimates. In democratic societies those differences are resolved through the ballot box. Chapters presented in Part II of this report provide an overview of many of methods that can be used to estimate shadow prices and the challenges we face when estimating the shadow prices of the many components within natural capital.

5. Wealth and the productive base

How is a society's productive base to be measured? We are interested, remember, in an index that tracks human well-being over time. Below we show that the required index is the society's wealth. Let us see how wealth should be measured if it is to have the property we want it to have.

In empirical work, it has proved impossible to disaggregate assets to the extent we have done in Equation (2). For example, when environmental economists have recommended that the shadow price of a ton of carbon in the atmosphere is of the order of 150 international dollars today, they haven't distinguished rich people from poor people, nor people in the tropics from people in temperate zones. The figure has been taken to be the shadow price of a ton of carbon in the atmosphere, period. In empirical work (ARROW ET AL. 2004; DASGUPTA 2001 [2004]; HAMILTON AND CLEMENS 1999; WORLD BANK 2006), distributional issues were ignored as a first cut into what is a new and very difficult exercise. The shadow prices the authors estimated were of capital assets, not person-specific capital assets.

Definition 3. Wealth is the social worth of an economy's capital assets.

Let Δt denote a small passage of time following t and let $Q(t)$ be the shadow price of asset time; that is,

EQUATION 3

$$Q(t) = \Delta V(t) \big/ \Delta t$$

If $W(t)$ denotes wealth at t, Definition 3 says that

EQUATION 4

$$W(t) = Q(t)t + {}_i\Sigma P_i(t)K_i(t)$$

Wealth is a weighted sum of a society's assets. Because the Index aggregates the society's *entire* productive base (institutions are reflected in the P_is via **M**, remember), W is referred to as *inclusive wealth* by some (DASGUPTA 2001 [2004]; WORLD BANK 2006) and *comprehensive wealth* by others (ARROW ET AL. 2010). In what follows, we continue to refer to W simply as "wealth."

Equation (4) is an expression for wealth, not well-being. However, the two are synchronous in time. Formally, we have:

Proposition 1: Inter-generational well-being increases over a short period of time if and only if wealth at constant shadow prices increases over that same period of time.

To prove Proposition 1, we return to Equation (1). Differentiating both sides of the equation with respect to t and using Equations 2 and 3 yields

EQUATION 5

$$dV(t)\big/dt = {_i}\Sigma P_i(t)dK_i(t)\big/dt + Q(t)$$

From Equation (5) it follows that

EQUATION 6

$$dV(t)\big/dt \geq 0$$

if and only if $_i\Sigma P_i(t)dK_i(t)\big/dt + Q(t) \geq 0$

The condition expressed in Equation (6) is Proposition 1.

Proposition 1 has become the basis for sustainability analysis. As it identifies wealth as the appropriate index of an economy's productive base, it is as well to illustrate its significance with the help of a numerical example.

Imagine a closed economy. In a given year it invests US$5 billion in reproducible capital, human capital, and research and development. Assume too that time does not enter V exogenously, implying that $Q = 0$. *GDP* would be recorded as increasing, as would the United Nations' Human Development Index; but suppose that natural capital is depleted and degraded that year by US$6 billion. Equation (6) would record that the country was becoming poorer in wealth by US$1 billion, implying that development was unsustainable that year.

But for such exceptions as carbon in the atmosphere, forest as sources of timber, and sub-soil resources, natural capital is usually ignored in national statistics. In Chapter 6, we look closely at the content of natural capital and review the methods that are available for estimating shadow prices for its various constituents.

6. Inclusive wealth and comprehensive wealth

Many researchers working on wealth accounts have used the terms inclusive wealth, comprehensive wealth, and just wealth interchangeably. In this report, we use the terms inclusive and comprehensive wealth to describe the wealth accounts produced for this report. However, for the purpose of this section only we refer to the wealth accounts developed by the World Bank as comprehensive wealth accounts. In this section, we highlight some of the key differences between the inclusive wealth accounts we present in this report and the comprehensive wealth accounts developed by the World Bank. The comprehensive wealth accounts and the genuine savings indicator, also called adjusted net savings, were developed by World Bank researchers in the late 1990s in an attempt to track the sustainability of economies. The World Bank acknowledging the limitations of GDP began developing comprehensive wealth accounts together with genuine savings and have published estimates of these for countries in a series of publications beginning with the 1997 publication, *Expanding the Measure of Wealth* (WORLD BANK 1997). There are similarities between the comprehensive wealth accounts and the inclusive wealth accounts. They both come from an economic welfare model. However, there are some key differences between the two worth highlighting here to give the reader a clear understanding of the information each of the wealth accounts provide for policy-making and their underlying assumptions.

6.1 Comprehensive wealth accounts and the genuine savings (GS)

There are a number of significant differences between comprehensive wealth and inclusive wealth accounts on two fronts. The first is at the theoretical level while the second is at the empirical computation of some of the assets components within the wealth accounts. Let us begin with the theoretical framework.

First, the World Bank computes comprehensive wealth in the following manner. It begins by making the assumption that wealth is the discounted flow of consumption. The formulation inadvertently assumes that consumption is always on a sustainable path. This then implies that savings will be sufficient to offset the depreciation of capital that might occur. In years where the adjusted net savings – gross national savings minus depreciation of produced capital plus expenditures on education minus natural resource depletion minus damage from pollutants and carbon emissions – is negative, then the negative adjusted net savings is subtracted from consumption to get a level of consumption which would have kept the capital stock intact (WORLD BANK 2006). This adjusted level of consumption is called the sustainable consumption level. In the comprehensive wealth accounts framework, the three main capitals computed were primarily natural, human, and produced capitals. The remaining capital category was called intangible and was treated as a residual in the computation of the capital asset base.

In the case of the inclusive wealth accounts, no assumption of sustainability of consumption is assumed. In the inclusive wealth framework Proposition 1 in the previous section makes it clear that inter-generational well-being increases over a short period of time if and only if wealth at constant shadow prices increases over that same time period of time. And following definition three which explicitly states that wealth is the social worth of an economy's capital asset base. Therefore, in the inclusive wealth accounts, changes in wealth are measured directly from the changes in the asset base. It therefore can and will reflect unsustainable trajectories and highlight which capital assets are in decline and where investments might be needed to improve the overall well-being of a country.

There are a number of important points to highlight between the theoretical frameworks used for comprehensive wealth and inclusive wealth. In the case of comprehensive wealth, wealth is defined as the present value of an exogenously defined flow of consumption. In the case of inclusive wealth, wealth is defined as the shadow value of all capital assets a country owns. This implies that in the case of comprehensive wealth, sustainability is assumed while in the case of inclusive wealth, sustainability is analyzed. Arrow et al. (2012) highlight some of the key problems policy-makers might face if using comprehensive wealth as a measure of sustainability. Summarizing their main points: (i) if per capita consumption is taken to be known to be growing at a positive rate, the sustainability of economic development in their list of countries is assumed, not studied; (ii) there is, and really can be, no empirical basis for estimating future consumption without measuring the present basis for it, namely, comprehensive wealth; and (iii) the identification of comprehensive wealth with the present value of consumption is valid only under the (stringent) assumptions that the economy under study is following an optimal path and the production structure there exhibits constant returns to scale.

At the empirical level, the inclusive wealth accounts presented in this report follows the methods used by Arrow et al. (2012) to compute the shadow values of four categories of capital. These are the human, natural, produced, and health. Unlike comprehensive wealth accounting, where a major part of the wealth values are embedded in the intangible capital category, the inclusive wealth accounts try to capture as much as possible of the wealth within distinct capital categories. This was done for two reasons. First, as illustrated above, the inclusive wealth accounts do not assume a sustainable flow of consumption. Second, to provide as much information for policy-makers on changes in actual identifiable capital assets and therefore provide guidance on future investments.

One of the critical advantages of using the wealth accounts is the direct accounting of environmental damages. The comprehensive wealth and inclusive wealth accounts account for these damages. However, the computation of carbon emissions damage was fundamentally different. In the case of comprehensive wealth, carbon emissions damage was computed using a damage estimate from climate change studies and then multiplied by the carbon emission for each country. In the case of the inclusive wealth accounts, the damage accruing from carbon emissions was computed based on the global emission damages and then using a formula developed by Nordhaus and Boyer (2000) who appropriate proportionately the damage for each country. The basic difference between the two is that in the case of inclusive wealth, the assumption is that damages to a country are not dependent on the actual emission of that country but is based on global emissions. We acknowledge that there is much room for improving the methodology and estimates for carbon emission damages across countries. The Nordhaus and Boyer estimates are now quite outdated and new study figures will need to be incorporated.

The inclusive wealth report has taken a first step to untangle the ecosystem services typology and to provide a basis for including regulating and cultural ecosystem services in addition to the present provisioning services. In this first report, an attempt was made to include fisheries in the actual estimates presented in Chapter 3 while Chapters 9 and 11 reflect on the challenges in including water-related ecosystems services in future reports.

Last but not least, population has to be acknowledged as a critical factor in sustainability. Although the comprehensive wealth accounts do provide per capita figures, the underlying assumption is that population is kept constant. In the case of the inclusive wealth estimates, population growth is intrinsically captured in the framework and the growth rate has been factored in the analysis. Not surprisingly, results show significant differences between estimates with and without population growth.

7. Key assumptions and caveats

We complete this chapter with an explanation of some of the key assumptions adopted in the inclusive wealth accounts presented in this report and also some caveats underlying the framework that the reader should be aware.

First, shadow prices are key to inclusive wealth. The shadow price for many market-traded goods is the market price. However, even these have to be cautiously used as market prices of many traded goods do not take into account of the externalities they might have caused in the production process. Examples would include prices of agricultural products that might have caused pollution of water bodies and degradation of soil. This however is not to say that the methodology and framework underlying the inclusive wealth accounts is flawed. What it highlights to us is the need to start doing better at internalizing these externalities within the production process.

Second, valuing of non-market goods and services poses a more serious problem. These will include in particular the regulating and cultural services provided by ecosystems. Ecologists and ecological economists consider many of these regulating services as services or goods that cannot be substituted with other forms of capital. In the case of inclusive wealth, much of this criticism is deflected, in a theoretical sense by the use of shadow prices. The shadow prices capture the substitutability of the capital assets not just in the present period but also in the future. Therefore, as some of the regulating services reach thresholds, the shadow prices of these services becomes exceedingly high making it uneconomical to further draw down these assets. These high shadow prices will in fact point to the need for reinvestment in these capital assets. The key challenge however is to get the shadow prices of these ecosystem services. For example, the shadow price of the climate regulation service is extremely difficult to compute, but a first order approximation based on the damages occurring from a change in that specific service might suffice for our needs.

Third, the issue of non-linear process and in particular ecosystem processes where incremental changes might not result in any substantial changes in welfare till a threshold is reached whereby sudden shifts are observed.

Can the inclusive wealth framework accommodate these non-linear properties of natural systems and provide the warnings early on in the process to avert such thresholds from being reached? The quick response to this factor is in the shadow prices used in the computation. If shadow prices are estimated using the production function approach whereby shadow prices of many life-supporting systems are captured through a production function, then a shadow price function dependent on the level of natural capital can be estimated and used in the computation of changes in natural capital and inadvertently changes in inclusive wealth. But we are far from having these prices schedules and it is an area where much research is required. But until those shadow price schedules are computed, the next best solution is to use the willingness to pay shadow prices. Then based on a dual observation of the quantity and value of assets available, expert opinions can be used to evaluate if thresholds are being reached in each asset base and prudent measures can be taken to re-invest in these asset categories.

Fourth, is the dichotomy between the scales at which natural systems occur and at which the inclusive wealth is computed. The unit of analysis at the moment is the national level. However, many ecosystem services a country enjoys are dependent on the use of natural capital in neighboring countries but in some cases, in countries across the world. Therefore, the shadow price of a ton of carbon is now computed as the damage that a country occurs because of the global pollution. But the onus of responsibility is left wanting. For example, the countries emitting the most carbon will have a larger part of their inclusive wealth reduced because of the role they have on the inclusive wealth of other countries. This is an important extension of the framework that can be carried out as a future feature of the framework. The information released could be useful in computing the compensation countries might have to pay for destroying a global natural capital, the global common inclusive wealth, which is also part of country national accounts.

REFERENCES

ARROW, K.J., DASGUPTA, P. & MÄLER, K.G. (2003). The genuine savings criterion and the value of population. *Economic Theory, 21*(2), 217-225.

ARROW, K., DASGUPTA, P., GOULDER, L., DAILY, G., EHRLICH, P., HEAL, G.,...WALKER, B. (2004). Are we consuming too much? *The Journal of Economic Perspectives, 18* (3), 147-172.

ARROW, K.J., DASGUPTA, P., GOULDER, L.H., MUMFORD, K.J. & OLESON, K. (2010). Sustainability and the measurement of wealth. *NBER Working Paper No 16599.*

CHAKRAVARTY, S. (1969). *Capital and development planning.* Cambridge, MA: MIT Press.

DASGUPTA, P. & MÄLER, K.G. (2000). Net national product, wealth, and social well being. *Environment and Development Economics, 5*(1), 69-93.

DASGUPTA, P. (2004). *Human well-being and the natural environment (2nd Ed).* Oxford: Oxford University Press.

DASGUPTA, P. (2009). The welfare economic theory of green national accounts. *Environmental and Resource Economics, 42*(1), 3-38.

DASGUPTA, P. (2011). A matter of trust: Social capital and economic development. In J. Lin and B. Plescovik (Eds.) *Annual World Bank conference on development economics, 2009: Lessons from East Asia and the global financial crisis.* New York: World Bank and Oxford University Press.

LITTLE, I.M.D. & MIRRLEES, J.A. (1968). *Manual of industrial project analysis in developing countries: Social cost benefit analysis.* Paris: OECD.

LITTLE, I.M.D. & MIRRLEES, J.A. (1974). *Project appraisal and planning for developing countries.* London: Heinemann.

NORDHAUS, W.D. & BOYER, J. (2000). *Warming the world: economic models of global warming.* Cambridge, MA: MIT Press.

WILLIAMS, B. (1985). *Ethics and the limits of philosophy.* London: Fontana/Collins.

WORLD BANK. (2006). *Where is the wealth of nations?* Washington, DC: World Bank.

WORLD BANK. (2011). *The changing wealth of nations.* Washington, DC: World Bank.

WORLD COMMISSION ON ENVIRONMENT AND DEVELOPMENT. (1987). *Our common future.* New York: Oxford University Press.

CHAPTER 2

Accounting for the inclusive wealth of nations: empirical evidence

Pablo Muñoz, Elorm Darkey, Kirsten Oleson, and Leonie Pearson

KEY MESSAGES

This chapter analyzes changes in the inclusive wealth index (IWI) and its components for 20 countries for the period from 1990 to 2008. Wealth is primarily assessed here as the value of manufactured, human, and natural capital stocks. The Index is additionally adjusted for population changes by presenting per capita measures.

6 out of the 20 countries analyzed decreased their IWI per capita in the last 19 years. In 5 out of 20 countries, population increased at a faster rate than inclusive wealth, resulting in negative changes in the IWI per capita.

The majority of the countries in our sample have had an increase in their stocks of manufactured capital per capita. In China, India and Chile, the positive changes in IWI has been mainly driven by manufactured capital. Russia, Nigeria, and Venezuela saw a decrease in their manufactured capital base.

When the three capital forms measured are adjusted for total factor productivity – oil capital gains and carbon damages the performance of some countries increases considerably, particularly for Nigeria, Saudi Arabia and Venezuela.

Human capital, being the prime capital form that offsets the decline in natural capital in most of the economies, has increased in every country.

This chapter demonstrates that the IWI provides a different perspective for assessing the performance of an economy - this by switching the focus of attention from flows (income) to stock metrics (wealth). This stresses the importance of preserving a portfolio of capital assets to ensure that the productive base can ultimately be maintained to sustain the well-being of future generations.

1. Introduction[1]

The aim of this chapter is to analyze changes in "inclusive wealth" and its components for 20 countries from 1990 to 2008. Wealth is primarily assessed here as the value of manufactured, human, and natural capital stocks[2] for each nation (as discussed earlier) with the next chapter focusing specifically on the role and significance of natural capital. In wealth accounting, these forms of capital are crucial pillars that are passed down from generation to generation to sustain future needs. Thus, the wealth-based measure at hand can be used to determine whether a nation is on a sustainable development path and whether its wealth is growing. If so, then it can be said that the nation is developing sustainably. This condition would reflect that we are passing on at least the same productive base that we use today to the next generation, in order to allow them to fulfill their own needs. Conversely, a decline in the productive base would compromise the ability of future generations to meet their needs.

This chapter draws to a large extent on the method outlined in Arrow et al. (2012), but also goes beyond it by carrying out a more comprehensive assessment of natural capital. The new assets included here are coal and fisheries. Moreover, one of the important contributions of the IWR wealth accounts refers to the elapsed time span. While most of the studies built up their accounts every five years (e.g., WORLD BANK [2011] or ARROW ET AL. [2012]), the IWR covers 19 years presenting annual wealth estimates from 1990 to 2008, thereby enriching substantially the empirical evidence available so far. The length of this period additionally corresponds to almost one generation, shedding light on the productive base down to the next generation. This also facilitates the comparison of inclusive wealth with other common income-based measures of national progress, for example, the gross domestic product (GDP) and the Human Development Index (HDI).

We investigate the change in wealth for 20 countries (see Figure 1), covering about 58 percent of the world's population and 72 percent of the world's GDP in 2010. As natural capital is the major focus in this first Inclusive Wealth Report, we selected countries where nature plays an important role for their economies, as with oil in Ecuador, Nigeria, Norway, Saudi Arabia, and Venezuela; minerals in Chile; and forests as in Brazil. We also sought to include major economies on all of the continents.

There are many challenges concerning an inter-country wealth-based analysis, not least the fact that no government currently collects capital stock data. The ultimate target is to provide empirical insights to policy-makers when determining whether a country is on a sustainable development path. As much of this chapter is based on incomplete data, it should not be read as a definitive assessment of wealth accounting, but as a major step in the right direction.

The rest of this chapter is organized as follows: Section 2 discusses the empirical construction of the wealth accounts for each capital form. On methodology, we largely follow Arrow et al. (2012). We refrain from presenting the computation of each capital category in detail. Instead, this section highlights the basic assumptions, the extensions to existing work in this field, and some of the challenges in the construction of wealth accounts. We then move to the analysis of the results in Section 3. In Section 4 we take the analysis further by including three determinants (namely carbon damages, oil capital gains and total factor productivity), which affect the size of the productive base of a nation. In Section 5 we compare the IWI to GDP and HDI, while Section 6 serves as our conclusion.

---

1   We are most grateful to Kevin Mumford for very valuable guidance and comments.

2   These capital forms are also adjusted by environmental externalities (particularly carbon damages) and oil capital gains (see Section 2).

2. Methodology

The Inclusive Wealth Index (IWI) offers a capital approach to sustainability. The Index seeks to measure the social value of capital assets of nations by going beyond the traditional economic concept of manufactured (or produced) capital. Indeed, the Index is inclusive in the sense that it also accounts for other key inputs as important components of the productive base of the economy, such as natural capital (NC), human capital (HC) and, ideally, social capital (SC) (excluded here due to the lack of empirical measures).[3] As it has been previously shown (see Chapter 1), the basket of assets (or productive base) is concretely measured by adding up the social worth, which acts as a weight in the Index, of each capital type of a country, resulting in the Inclusive Wealth Index, or wealth (see Equation 1).

---

3   See Chapter 1 for a comprehensive list of different capital forms.

FIGURE 1

Average IWI per capita growth rate

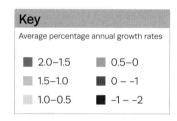

Key

Average percentage annual growth rates

■ 2.0–1.5		■ 0.5–0	
■ 1.5–1.0		■ 0 – –1	
■ 1.0–0.5		■ –1 – –2	

- Australia
- Brazil
- Canada
- Chile
- China
- Colombia
- Ecuador
- France
- Germany
- India
- Japan
- Kenya
- Nigeria
- Norway
- Russian Federation
- Saudi Arabia
- South Africa
- United Kingdom
- United States
- Venezuela

EQUATION 1

Wealth = P_{mc} x Manufactured Capital (MC) + P_{hc} x Human Capital (HC) + P_{nc} x Natural Capital (NC)

Moreover, the Index emphasizes changes in wealth (or per capita wealth) over the time period studied. Thus, changes in wealth – or *inclusive investment* – are directly measured by assessing the changes in the physical asset base of a nation over time, and subsequently adjusting by population:

EQUATION 2

ΔWealth = Inclusive Investment = P_{mc} x Δ MC + P_{hc} x Δ HC + P_{nc} x ΔNC

It is worth highlighting that changes in IWI are solely driven by changes in the physical side of the economy, since prices (or the weights in the Index) are assumed to be constant and represented by the average price of the time span under evaluation. In this way, changes in wealth are induced by real changes in the physical amount of the various capital forms, and not simply by price fluctuations that could be subject to contingent situations (e.g., market bubbles). From an environmental sustainability viewpoint, assessing the physical change in natural capital tends to provide a more meaningful indication of the ecological changes. Over the long run, however, price changes may be important, and could influence inclusive wealth estimates.

2.1 Capital assets in the IWR

We measure wealth in our accounts by studying various assets that can be grouped into the following four categories: human capital; manufactured capital; natural capital; and health capital. The later capital is treated separately from the other capital forms as modest changes in health capital would outweigh any changes in the other three assets. There are additionally three adjustments made to these accounts: (1) the potential damages that climate change may cause on the wealth of a nation; (2) the study of how increases in oil prices may benefit (harm)

some countries in building other capital forms; and (3) the role of technical progress as reflected by the change in total factor productivity. While the rest of this section aims at sketching the approach used to measure each of these capital forms and how they break down, Box 1 provides an overview of the key variables involved in the computation of the IWI.

2.1.1. Human capital[4]

To calculate human capital, we followed the work of Arrow et al. (2012), who based their method upon Klenow and Rodríguez-Clare (1997). In this former study, human capital is primarily captured by measuring the population's educational attainment and the additional compensation over time of this training, which is assumed to be equivalent to the interest rate (8.5 percent in this case). As the interest rate is constant over time, changes in human capital are basically caused by either the change in number of people educated or an increase (decrease) in the years of education. It is additionally assumed that the amount of human capital per person increases exponentially with the interest rate, and with the average educational attainment per person. The shadow price per unit of human capital is obtained by computing the present value of the labor compensation received by workers over an entire working life. Notice that these latter estimates are subject to various demographic parameters such as birth or mortality rates as well as other parameters related to the labor market, like the participation of the population in the labor force by age and gender. In our case, for each nation we computed these shadow prices for every year within the 1990–2008 time period, and then used the average of this rental price of one unit of human capital over time as the representative weight for entering

---

4   While both education and health can be considered as components of human capital, we refer here to human capital as the contribution of education to the productive base only, and we use the term health capital for the study of the progress made in the life expectancy of the population.

human capital into the wealth accounting framework.

2.1.2. Manufactured capital

With regard to manufactured capital, we follow the method developed in King and Levine (1994), who based their calculations on the Perpetual Inventory Method (PIM) by setting an initial capital estimate. Indeed, one of the big difficulties in the manufactured capital computation concerns the fixing of the initial amount of capital available at the beginning of the accounting period. Once this departure point is obtained, changes over time are captured by using the net capital formation reported every year in the system of national accounts. Regarding the initial estimate, steady-state estimates are used, thus assuming that the capital-output ratio of the economy is constant in the long-term (for details on this method, see KING AND LEVINE [1994]). Once this ratio is measured, it is subsequently multiplied by the final output (GDP in this case) of the economy under study, in order to obtain a first estimate of the manufactured capital stock. This approach can only give a rough estimation of the fixed capital assets available in a specific period. In order to minimize errors in the time period under study (1990–2008), we carried out our initial estimate in 1970; as capital depreciates over time (we assumed an annual depreciation rate of 7 percent) the initial capital estimate retained in 1990 would be of about 22 percent and only 5 percent in 2008. This means that any potential error in the departure point (year 1970) would be minimized during the relevant period under analysis. Subsequently, the perpetual inventory method allows capturing the dynamics in the manufactured capital accumulation by looking at the annual changes in investment. Finally, regarding the lifetimes of the assets, we

BOX 1

Key variables used in the measurement of wealth

Human capital
- Population by age and gender
- Mortality probability by age and gender
- Discount rate
- Employment
- Educational attainment
- Employment compensation
- Labour force by age and gender

Produced capital
- Investment
- Depreciation rate
- Assets lifetime
- Output growth
- Population
- Productivity

Natural capital
A. Fossil fuels
- Reserves
- Production
- Prices
- Rental rate
B. Minerals
- Reserves
- Production
- Prices
- Rental rate
C. Forest resources
- Forest stocks
- Forest stock commercially available
- Wood production
- Value of wood production
- Rental rate
- Forest area
- Value of non–timber forest benefits (NTFB)

- Percentage of forest area used for the extraction of NTFB
- Discount rate
D. Agricultural land
- Quantity of crops produced
- Price of crops produced
- Rental rate
- Harvested area in crops
- Discount rate
- Permanent cropland area
- Permanent pastureland area
E. Fisheries
- Fishery stocks
- Value of capture fishery
- Quantity of capture fishery
- Rental rate

Health capital
- Population by age
- Probability of dying by age
- Value of statistical life
- Discount rate

Adjustments in IWI
A. Total factor productivity
- Technological change
B. Carbon damages
- Carbon emission
- Carbon price
- Climate change impacts
- GDP
C. Oil capital gains
- Reserves
- Oil production
- Oil consumption
- Prices
- Rental rate

have assumed indefinite depreciation periods (see methodological annex for further details).

2.1.3. Natural capital

Natural capital assets are primarily measured in this report by the following five categories: (1) forests, represented by timber and non-timber forest benefits (NTFB); (2) fisheries (only for four countries); (3) fossil fuels (oil, natural gas, and coal); (4) minerals (bauxite, copper, gold, iron, lead, nickel, phosphate, silver, tin, and zinc); and (5) agricultural land. The way of valuing each capital asset shares a relatively common accounting method, where total wealth is estimated by multiplying the physical amount available of the asset under study by its corresponding resource rent. As previously mentioned, the resource rent is represented by the average market value of one unit of natural capital over the years 1990–2008. While the key variables used in each category are presented in Box 1, those readers specifically interested in natural capital should refer to Chapter 3 where these accounts are elaborated in further detail.

2.1.4. Health capital

Our health capital estimates also rely on the study of Arrow et al. (2012). In this work, positive (negative) changes in this capital form are essentially captured by extensions (reductions) in the individual's life expectancy. Such changes are basically analyzed by calculating the years of life remaining of a given population in different time periods, with the population age distribution and the people's probability of death being therefore the key inputs into the model. As far as the shadow price of health capital is concerned, it is measured by the multiplication of discounted years of remaining life of a person with the value of an extra year of life (ARROW ET AL. 2012). The shadow price is constant over time and taken from the Value of the Statistical Life estimated by United States Environmental Protection Agency (EPA). Therefore, it is primarily the changes in people's life expectancy that translate into changes in health capital.

2.2 Adjustments to the IWI

We shall refer to "Adjusted Inclusive Wealth Index" (IWI$_{adj}$ hereafter) when countries' capital assets are corrected for specific factors that further affect the size of the productive base of a nation. In the following, we briefly describe the three components that we will take into account: (1) carbon damages; (2) oil capital gains; and (3) total factor productivity.

2.2.1. Carbon damages

Some of the adjustments needed to be done to the countries' wealth relate to those stemming from environmental externalities. In particular, one of the issues that arises is how climate change can affect countries' inclusive wealth. In these wealth accounts, we introduce this correction of the indicator by following the method developed by Arrow et al. (2012), where in a first step, the total annual carbon emissions are estimated and subsequently multiplied by its social cost (US$50 per carbon tonne[5] - Ct). For calculating the distribution of these social damages that each region will suffer we refer to Nordhaus and Boyer (2000). This study presents the distribution of damages as a percentage of the regional and global GDP. By using information on each country's GDP, we recovered the total global damages in absolute level, and then derived the share of each nation in this total. We used this proportion to allocate the total social cost previously estimated, that is US$50 per Ct multiplied by the total global annual emissions (for additional details see ARROW ET AL. [2012]).

---

5   The damages per ton of carbon released to the atmosphere are estimated US$50 per tonne of carbon (Tol 2009).

2.2.2. Oil capital gains

Rental prices have been kept constant over time as we previously mentioned. However, in this section we explore potential wealth gains that may stem from continuous price increases in a particular natural resource type. Some countries with large endowments of some specific natural resources (e.g., oil in Nigeria or copper in Chile) may also want to compute this change in prices as one further category in their wealth accounts, as these wealth gains may be beneficial for building other capital forms, for example, human capital. In this report, we concretely explore gains stemming from a change in oil prices. In line with Arrow et al. (2012), we assume an annual increase in the rental price of 5 percent over the period 1990–2008.[6] These changes in the rental price are multiplied by the stock of oil available in each subsequent period. While some countries enjoy higher rental prices for their oil asset, other countries, which depend on oil imports, may be negatively affected, since their capacity to build other capital forms is diminished by these higher prices. We therefore redistribute those capital wealth gains obtained by oil extractive economies to those nations that consume this commodity. There are, of course, some countries that extract large amounts of oil at the world level (for example the United States, which is the second largest producer in the world), but at the same time are an important consumer of this material. This fact leads us to compute the "net" oil capital gains as the difference between oil capital wealth gains and losses. See methodological annex and Arrow et al. (2012) for additional details.

2.2.3. Total factor productivity

Total factor productivity (TFP) growth measures the change in aggregate output that cannot be explained by the growth rate of observable inputs (BARRO AND SALA-I-MARTIN 1995). This residual in growth accounting can be understood as a proxy variable of technological progress, which is hard to measure directly. Given the empirical evidence that TFP growth accounts for a substantial part of the overall growth rate in real GDP (see, for example, CHRISTENSEN ET AL. [1980]), it is important to consider this variable in wealth accounting as well. Adjusting for TFP in this context means that the same productive base can lead to an increase in aggregate output over time because technical change renders each capital asset more productive. For further details see Arrow et al. (2012).

2.2 Data limitations

We have measured four capital forms here, plus carbon damages, oil capital gains, and total factor productivity. There are, however, other capital stocks not accounted for yet; a clear example of this is social capital. Even more, within some natural resource categories, for example fisheries and minerals, we still lack data among the countries under study. This renders the comparison between countries quite difficult. Other caveats to bear in mind relate to the annual changes in wealth; with regard to several variables, the data points used to construct the accounts represent points at the end of a decade. For example, some parameters in our models are obtained from the Life Tables (WORLD HEALTH ORGANIZATION 2012), which report information only for the years 1990, 2000, and 2009. This implies that we needed to fill the years in between by carrying out linear interpolations. We therefore caution readers about these interpolations when taking conclusions from inter-annual variations (see methodological annex for more details).

3. The wealth of nations

This section gives an overview of the results for our country sample over the 1990–2008 period. All variables are measured at constant U.S. dollars for the year 2000. The analysis is

---

6 This 5 percent corresponds to the annual average oil price increase during the years 1990–2008 (BP 2011).

organized as follows: First, we will discuss the Inclusive Wealth Index based on three types of capital assets: human, manufactured, and natural capital. Since health capital dominates the total capital asset base, we have treated these computations separately from the other capital forms (see Box 2).

The key variables we shall address in this chapter are: (i) the average annual growth rates in Inclusive Wealth Index (IWI) over the time period 1990–2008 as shown in Table 1 and Figure 2 respectively; (ii) the percentage change in IWI and the three capital assets per capita as presented in data annex; and (iii) the composition of the productive base of the economy in relative and absolute terms shown in Figure 4 and Appendix 2 respectively. In addition, we provide estimates of the IWI but adjusted for oil capital gains, carbon damages, and total factor productivity. In Section 5 of this chapter, we shall also provide a comparative exercise of the IWI against GDP and the HDI to illustrate the differences across these three indices for the 20 countries.

Given the enormous amount of information available, we restrict ourselves to summarizing our main findings. The interested reader can also find the entire data set in data annex of this chapter.

3.1. How has each country been doing in the last two decades from an inclusive wealth perspective?

The desired output would be positive growth rates for the IWI. Countries with positive growth rates of IWI would ideally demonstrate that their productive base is not being eroded and they have maintained the asset base to produce the same level of output for consumption of future generations. Table 1 shows that all countries have positive IWI growth rates except for Russia. China, Kenya, India, and Chile exhibit the highest growth among all countries studied.

FIGURE 2

Average annual growth rates (per capita) disaggregated by capital form

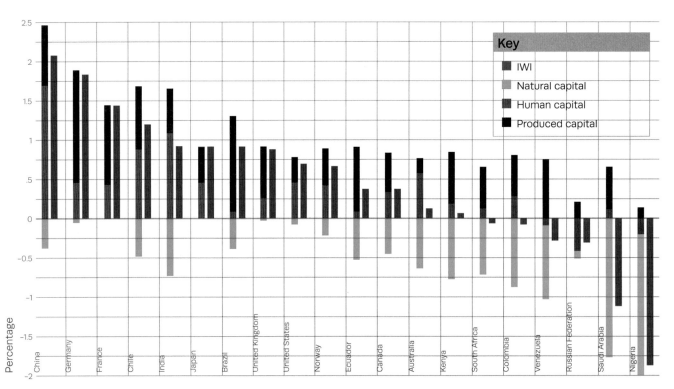

However, the figures presented in column (1) of Table 1 have only limited explanatory power in the scope of an inter-temporal analysis, simply due to the fact that population changes over time. This has to be borne in mind when we talk about sustainable consumption paths of a country. An increase in total wealth does not necessarily indicate that future generations may consume at the same level as the present one; as population grows, each form of capital is more thinly spread over the society, so that productivity growth based on capital accumulation alone might eventually cease. Therefore, we need to extend the analysis by considering per capita values of total wealth.

Column (2) in Table 1 shows the demographic development of the countries under study. In this regard, Kenya, Saudi Arabia, and Nigeria top the list with average annual growth rates of population of at least 2.4 percent. The status of some countries change drastically when population growth is taken into account. We see a major shift of countries with respect to their IWI growth rates when population is factored into the analysis, as shown in Figure 3.

Kenya for example which returned a relatively high IWI rate of 2.85 only managed to have a growth rate of 0.06 IWI per capita. This demonstrates that the rate of return of its capital asset base per person is very low and either it improves on its IWI or reduces its population growth rate. The picture is worse in the case of Saudi Arabia and Nigeria who move into a non-sustainable position, as they depict negative IWI per capita growth rates. But these are not the only countries switching from positive to negative IWI growth: Colombia, South Africa, and Venezuela also moved in the same direction because of higher population growth rates than their IWI growth rates. These countries have, at least, two options to reverse this trend. They either have to reduce their population growth rates or reinvest in the different capital asset bases to increase the rate of IWI growth. The question on which capital asset base to focus will be addressed in the following section.

BOX 2
Health Capital

Health capital of a nation's population reflects the expected discounted value of years of life remaining. This is, understandably, a large number; indeed, we find that health capital makes up more than 90% of the capital base for all countries in the study. In the nations under study, the amount of health capital that each person owns outweighs all other forms of capital combined. Given a population, slight changes in mortality rates result in more or less health capital each year. Most countries in the study experienced gains in per capita health capital over the period 1990–2010. The exceptions were South Africa, Russia, and Kenya, which lost health capital; and Japan, Australia, and Venezuela, which remained stable. Most nations saw a slight but persistent increase in per capita health over the entire period, but in some nations recent health improvements are accruing health capital after earlier stagnation (Nigeria) or recovering health capital losses suffered during the 1990s (Kenya). Differences between the countries' rates of change in per capita health reflect national policy choices as well as demographic differences. Improvements in mortality rates in an older population (e.g., Japan) will not affect per capita health capital as much as those same mortality gains in a younger population (e.g., Kenya).

Because health capital constitutes such a large portion of the capital base, its change renders insignificant any other capital changes. It is obviously a key point to consider that health capital is as important as it is, and to direct policy attention to reducing mortality to continue to increase that component of wealth. In theory, these gains in the productive base can substitute for declines elsewhere. However, policy-makers also need to know the relative rates of change in human, natural, and reproducible capital. It is to gain resolution fine enough to speak to these changes that our analysis in this chapter omits health capital.

The situation is slightly reversed in Russia: although the country's IWI growth rate per capita is still negative, the situation has been slightly alleviated, because population had decreased steadily since 1993. The impact of high population growth rate is again highlighted by comparing India and China. Both countries showed strong IWI of 2.66 and 2.92 respectively. However, after including population growth rate, the IWI per capital of India fell to 0.91 while that of China dropped to only 2.07 because of the slower population growth rate in China. In the case of Venezuela, South Africa, Saudi Arabia, Nigeria, and Colombia, the population growth rates were higher than the growth rate of the IWI thus pushing these countries on a unsustainable trajectory.

3.2 What is the contribution of the different capital forms to per capita wealth creation?

Figure 2, as mentioned before, illustrates the average contribution of the different capital types to the development of the average Inclusive Wealth Index per capita for each of the 20 countries. It is interesting to note that among the top five performing countries appear three middle-income economies – China, India, and Chile – where wealth changes are driven by high growth rates of manufactured capital. In the case of France and Germany, the other two of the five top countries, much of the growth in average IWI per capita came from the growth in human capital. Note also the low change in natural capital for Germany and France in comparison to the rest.

Turning to the bottom five countries in average annual IWI growth per capita, we see that it is in fact the decline in natural capital that explains the negative wealth trend.[7] The only exception is Russia, where the negative IWI growth is triggered by the steady decline of manufactured capital. For the bottom three countries (Venezuela, Saudi Arabia, and Nigeria), natural capital and in particular fossil fuels represent the main component of wealth as will be shown in Chapter 3. Since the natural capital accounts in these countries are based to a large extent upon exhaustible resources, these results come as no surprise. As the basis of renewable natural resources is too small to offset this decline, the advisable rule would be to invest and achieve higher returns in other types of assets, namely manufactured and/or human capital. In this context, Norway, despite being an important oil extracting country, depicts

TABLE 1

Measuring countries' progress. Average annual growth rates, period 1990–2008.

Countries/ Indicators	IWI	Population growth rate [2]	IWI per capita [3]
Australia	1.41	1.29	0.12
Brazil	2.30	1.38	0.91
Canada	1.41	1.03	0.37
Chile	2.56	1.35	1.19
China	2.92	0.83	2.07
Colombia	1.62	1.70	−0.08
Ecuador	2.14	1.76	0.37
France	1.95	0.51	1.44
Germany	2.06	0.23	1.83
India	2.66	1.74	0.91
Japan	1.10	0.19	0.91
Kenya	2.85	2.79	0.06
Nigeria	0.53	2.44	−1.87
Norway	1.33	0.67	0.66
Russia	−0.50	−0.19	−0.31
Saudi Arabia	1.57	2.72	−1.12
South Africa	1.57	1.64	−0.07
UK	1.26	0.38	0.88
United States	1.74	1.04	0.69
Venezuela	1.70	1.99	−0.29

---

7   Those readers interested in more information about natural capital are referred to Chapter 3.

FIGURE 3
Inclusive wealth index

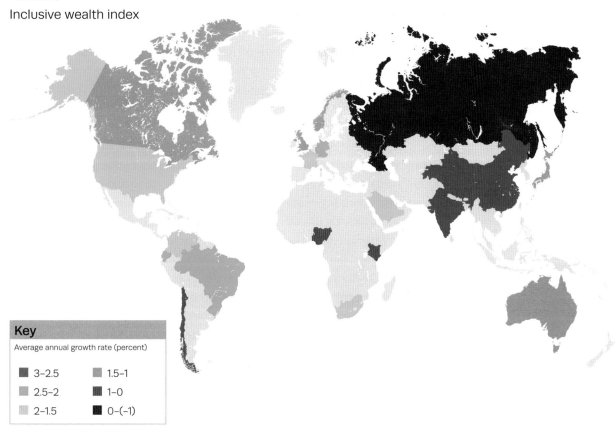

Key

Average annual growth rate (percent)

■ 3–2.5	■ 1.5–1
■ 2.5–2	■ 1–0
■ 2–1.5	■ 0–(–1)

Inclusive wealth index per capita

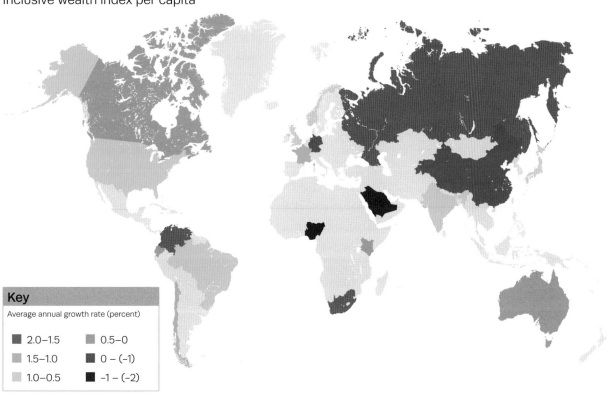

Key

Average annual growth rate (percent)

■ 2.0–1.5	■ 0.5–0
■ 1.5–1.0	■ 0 – (–1)
■ 1.0–0.5	■ –1 – (–2)

positive growth of the IWI and a relatively modest decline in natural capital (see Figure 3).

Health capital of a nation's population reflects the expected discounted value of years of life remaining. This is, understandably, a large number; indeed, we find that health capital makes up more than 90 percent of the capital base for all countries in the study. In the nations under study, the amount of health capital that each person owns outweighs all other forms of capital combined. Given a population, slight changes in mortality rates result in more or less health capital each year. Most countries in the study experienced gains in per capita health capital over the period 1990–2008. The exceptions were South Africa, Russia, and Kenya, which lost health capital; and Japan, Australia, and Venezuela, which remained stable. Most nations saw a slight but persistent increase in per capita health over the entire period, but in some nations recent health improvements are accruing health capital after earlier stagnation (e.g., Nigeria) or recovering health capital losses suffered during the 1990s (e.g., Kenya). Differences between the countries' rates of change in per capita health reflect national policy choices as well as demographic differences. Improvements in mortality rates in an older population (e.g., Japan) will not affect per capita health capital as much as those same mortality gains in a younger population (e.g., Kenya).

Because health capital constitutes such a large portion of the capital base, its change renders insignificant any other capital changes. It is obviously a key point to consider that health capital is as important as it is, and to direct policy attention to reducing mortality to continue to increase that component of wealth. In theory, these gains in the productive base can substitute for declines elsewhere. However, policy-makers also need to know the relative rates of change in human, natural, and reproducible capital. It is to gain resolution fine enough to speak to these changes that our analysis in this chapter omits health capital.

So far, we have looked at the *average* annual change of the Inclusive Wealth Index over the entire time span. This approach, however, excludes details about how per capita wealth has evolved *within* the reference period. The full trend line is presented in data annex. Note that the relative change of each capital form over time relates to one common base year, that is to say that per capita wealth of 1990 is indexed to 0 for all countries under study.[8]

In general, the various capital categories have contributed differently to the IWI growth per capita. The highest cross-country discrepancies can be observed with manufactured/produced capital. As expected, most of the countries in our sample have increased their stocks, in particular the more recently industrialized countries – China, Chile, and India – feature the highest rise in manufactured capital (China more or less quintupled its stock of manufactured capital while Chile and India show an increase by 183 percent and 168 percent, respectively). The human capital on the other hand in these three countries increased at a much lower rate while natural capital declined. The key question we need to ask ourselves is if this trend is sustainable? To answer this question we need to look at the composition of the asset base in these countries. In all three countries, the weight of produced capital was approximately 17 percent versus human and natural capital weights of 37 percent and 46 percent respectively on average. This implies that although these countries witnessed the largest increases in produced capital, its overall weight within the inclusive wealth index is the lowest. In other words, we might interpolate this as every single unit increase in produced capital contributes less towards the IWI than a single unit decline in natural and human capital.

However, not all countries have increased their produced capital. Russia, Nigeria, and Venezuela actually show negative growth in manufactured capital (with the stock decreasing

---

8 Notice that the IWI path cannot be simply computed as the sum of each of these trajectories as they are weighted differently within the wealth accounting framework.

by 37 percent, 42 percent, and 12 percent respectively). Russia was the only country in the sample of 20 countries had a decline in its IWI caused largely by a decline in produced capital. Most other countries witnessing decline in IWI were caused either by declines in natural capital or high population growth rates as in Venezuela. Three countries, Brazil, Ecuador, and Kenya, reported a more or less constant stock of manufactured capital until 2005.

The changes in inclusive wealth in Brazil, Germany, and Saudi Arabia were driven primarily by rapid growth in human capital of 48 percent, 46 percent, and 43 percent respectively. The increase in human capital was found to be the prime factor that offsets the decline in natural capital that occurred in almost all nations. In most cases, human capital is accumulated by between 20 and 36 percent over the years under study. The lowest growth in human capital since 1990 was experienced by highly industrialized countries such as Australia and the U.S. with 8 percent within 20 years, Japan with 12 percent, the United Kingdom with 14 percent, and Norway with 15 percent. All of these economies had already accumulated a high stock of human capital before 1990. This result was driven primarily by the variable we used in this report, which is the years of total schooling of the population. A key lesson to be learned from this result for the developing countries is the diminishing returns on human capital as the years of schooling reaches a maximum. The continued decline of natural capital in countries where the human capital has reached diminishing returns suggests a strategy to reinvest in natural capital.

Most countries with the exception of Japan saw a decline in their natural capital asset base at a per capita level. The biggest declines occurred in the United Kingdom and Saudi Arabia, where the decrease was caused by a decline in the fossil fuels asset base. The countries, which saw a fall in their IWI because of declines in natural capital were Colombia, Kenya, Nigeria, Saudi Arabia, and South Africa. The precise information of which components of the natural capital played a key role in the overall decline are presented in Chapter 3.

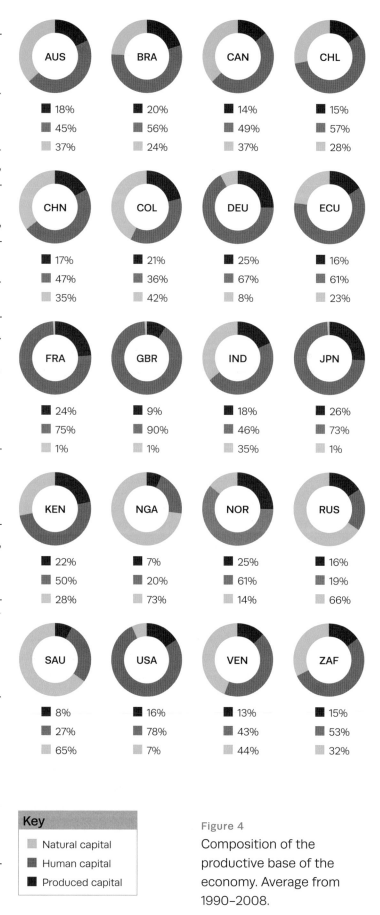

Key

	Natural capital
■	Human capital
■	Produced capital

Figure 4

Composition of the productive base of the economy. Average from 1990–2008.

FIGURE 5

Composition of productive base for France, Germany, Japan, Norway, United States, and United Kingdom,

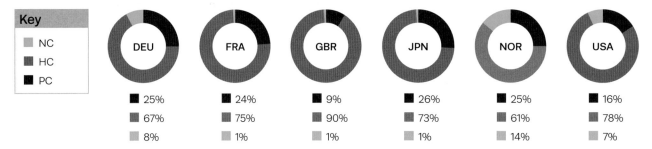

Key
- NC
- HC
- PC

DEU	FRA	GBR	JPN	NOR	USA
■ 25%	■ 24%	■ 9%	■ 26%	■ 25%	■ 16%
■ 67%	■ 75%	■ 90%	■ 73%	■ 61%	■ 78%
■ 8%	■ 1%	■ 1%	■ 1%	■ 14%	■ 7%

FIGURE 6

Change in productive base for China, Chile, India, and Kenya (US$, year 2000)

Key
- NC
- HC
- PC

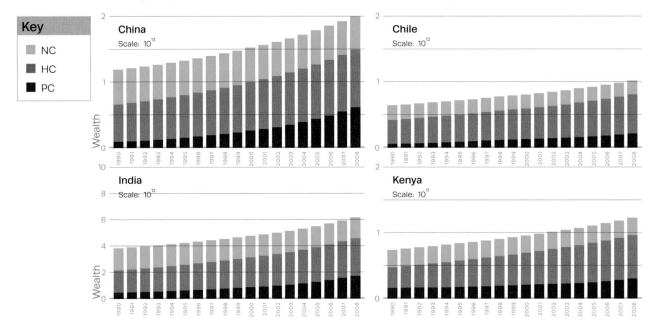

The configuration of the capital portfolio indicates which capital plays a predominant role in the respective countries. Figure 4 shows the capital composition of the 20 countries as an average between 1990 and 2008. Manufactured capital represents on the average only 17 percent of the wealth portfolio, with little variance among countries. While it is not surprising that manufactured capital is being overshadowed in every country by human capital, its share in the composition of wealth is also less than the share of natural capital; only in the highly-industrialized countries of this sample – France, Germany, Japan, Norway, United Kingdom, and United States – as shown in Figure 5 do fixed capital assets contribute more to the productive base than natural resources.

However, among the countries with relatively low shares of produced capital, Nigeria, Saudi Arabia, and the United Kingdom have even lower shares of produced capital. The United Kingdom has a particularly disproportional share structure with human capital dominating with a 90 percent share with the United States following closely with a share of 78 percent. Natural capital, on the other hand, tends to be more relevant in developing countries such as Venezuela and Colombia and is the prevailing factor in those economies whose GDP is largely driven by oil extraction, such as Nigeria, Russia,

Figure 7

Change in productive base
for Brazil, Kenya and Saudi
Arabia

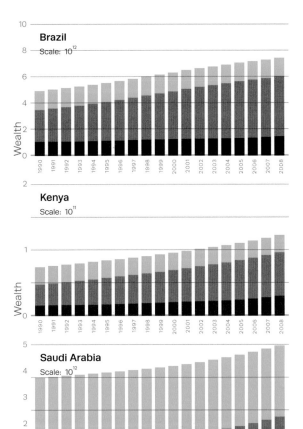

and Saudi Arabia. The countries with the lowest share of natural capital as a share of the total capital asset base were France, Japan, and the United Kingdom where natural resources constitute only 1 percent of total capital value.

3.4 What is the absolute wealth level of the country in terms of manufactured, human, and natural capital?

Again, the *average* capital composition over the entire time span does not give insights into the dynamics behind wealth accumulation; for this, we need to know in which way the stock of each

capital form has changed in absolute terms. Data annex depicts the evolution of the different capital forms within the reference period, this time without correcting scale effects due to population growth. Thus, we are dealing with the question of how rich a country has performed overall in terms of manufactured, human, and natural capital. In this regard, total wealth has been increasing for all countries except for Russia.

India, Chile, Kenya, and China shown in Figure 6 produce the highest rate of change in their productive base with China increasing its productive base by about 70 percent in the time span under analysis, with manufactured capital being the primary growth engine. As one can see from the comparison of the diagrams, human capital served as the main driver of capital accumulation. Conventionally defined, developing countries starting from a low level of human capital such as Kenya and Brazil shown in Figure 7, have been clearly catching up to the more industrialized economies in the sample. Manufactured capital remained relatively stable in Brazil, Venezuela, Saudi Arabia, and the U.K., while for Russia and Nigeria, manufactured capital has even declined in absolute terms. This trend, primarily caused by falling saving/investment rates, has led to an overall decrease in total wealth in the case of Russia. The diagrams in Appendix 2 also give a clear picture of the availability of natural resources in the countries under study: Nigeria, Russia, and Saudi Arabia thereby present the highest stock in natural capital (driven by oil reserves), in comparison to the other assets, whereas the productive base of the industrialized economies, as already mentioned, depends on relatively few natural resources. While this overall picture is unambiguous, we need to be careful with interpreting the exact numbers, since data availability concerning the different subcategories of natural capital varies highly among the countries. For example, we do not possess data about Japan's fishery stocks, which is an important natural resource for this economy. Improving on the value of the natural capital asset base will provide us with a more

FIGURE 8

Adjusted IWI

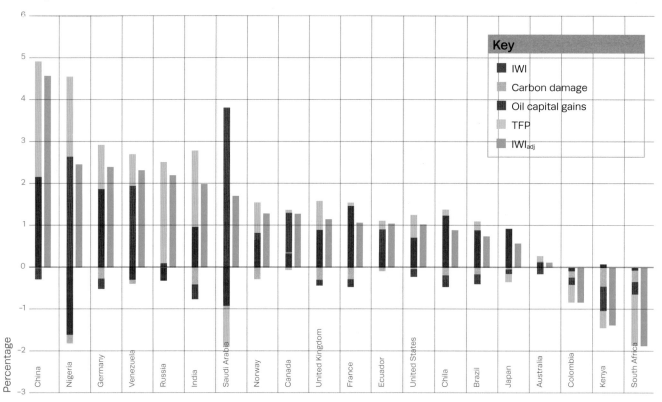

realistic understanding of the weight of natural capital within the productive base of a country. However, it should be noted that the relatively high weighting associated with natural capital already informs us of the relative importance natural capital plays in a country's sustainability tract.

4. Adjusted Inclusive Wealth Index

In this subsection we take the analysis one step further, by including three determinants that somewhat alter a country's productive base or its aggregate output. These are: carbon damages, accounting for the potential damages of climate change in the country's wealth; oil capital gains, capturing how changes in oil prices may benefit (frustrate) the construction of other capital forms; and total factor productivity (TFP), measuring the extent to which the capital

stock, *ceteris paribus*, became more (less) productive in the generation of goods and services. When these factors are taken into account the resulting indicator will be called the "Adjusted Inclusive Wealth Index" (IWI$_{adj}$).

We have added these adjustments to the average annual growth rates per capita presented in Figure 3. Results show that while China and Germany still remain in the top five countries in terms of growth rate, Nigeria, Venezuela, and Russia appear as new members in this group (see Figure 8). This huge jump in the ranking from the bottom to the top five economies is primarily attributed to TFP growth as well as oil capital gains, as Nigeria and Venezuela have large endowments of this natural resource. After adjusting the IWI, not only did Nigeria, Venezuela, and Russia moved away from unsustainable consumption paths, so did Saudi Arabia, another oil-based economy, due to the steady increase in the price of crude oil over the last decade. However, for other nations that depend on oil imports, the reported IWI growth was reduced by the adjustments, as in Kenya, for example, where oil price fluctuations severely hit the economy, reinforced by the decline of total factor productivity. In comparison to Figure 3, Colombia and South Africa still have negative growth rates, because oil prices and TFP mainly accentuate the negative wealth growth. The impact of climate change on the total value as measured here seems to be of considerable relevance in Kenya.

5. A comparison of IWI, GDP, and HDI

So far we have studied the composition and evolution in total wealth, taking into account demographic development. However, societal progress (regress) can be also assessed from other angles, most typically, by the relative change in the gross domestic product (GDP) and the Human Development Index (HDI) over time. The former measures the value of all final goods and services, manufactured in an economy within one year, while the latter entails a broader concept of societal development, extending gross national income per capita by other determinants of social well-being, as evidenced by life expectancy as well as expected years of schooling. These indicators generally lead to different empirical findings concerning the progress of a nation. Table 2 compares IWI, GDP, and HDI for our sample of 20 nations for 1990–2008.[9] The IWI column in this table summarizes results based on the average annual per capita change within the reference period. The numbers presented in column two depict the rate of change of the HDI while those in column three show the rate of change of GDP per capita. Let us begin evaluating countries by looking at their HDI and IWI rate of change.

---

9 We again revert to the unadjusted IWI, since we are interested in the role of the capital categories under study for socio–economic development, being aware that other factors (such as technical change) may offset deteriorations in the productive base.

If countries are purely evaluated on the HDI, then all countries except South Africa have seen an improvement in their HDI over the time period. South Africa returned an average growth rate of 1.3 percent of GDP over the same time period, but also saw a negative growth rate in the IWI. The three low ratings for South Africa suggest that urgent interventions should be made that might include improving all three types of capital, particularly human and natural capital.

There are five other countries that had positive growth rates in the HDI and GDP per capita but had negative growth rates for the IWI: Colombia, Nigeria, Russia, Saudi Arabia, and Venezuela. Most of these have large reserve of fossil fuels. They have basically been drawing down their oil reserves but yet not increasing their produced and human capital bases as fast as they should to ensure an overall positive growth in IWI. Although all five would have posted positive GDP per capita growth rates, the negative IWI growth rates suggest an unsustainable track and most of the GDP growth has come at the expense of the natural capital base.

India and China warrant special attention because of the size of their populations and economies. Although China demonstrated the highest IWI growth rate, earlier discussion had already highlighted the need for China to re-evaluate its development strategy and begin increasing its investment in natural capital and get higher returns on its produced and human capital. India faces a more dire situation as its inclusive wealth has only growth by 0.9 percent over the past 19 years compared to China's 2.1 percent. These results might suggest that India will need to improve its rate of build up of human capital as it decreases its natural capital even further to maintain a positive inclusive wealth growth rate. This again brings us back to the contribution to the IWI from a single unit increase or decrease of the respective capital assets. But the question of critical levels of natural capital comes into play and these results suggest a more detailed investigation of the natural capital categories in India and to the extent they have been destroyed and the level at which this decline can continue.

If we use the HDI, Colombia and Nigeria are in the top five, although they are among the bottom countries from an IWI perspective. The explanation may be largely based on the fact that HDI does not consider in its computation the depletion of natural capital, which acts as the main driver behind the negative growth rates in these countries.

Turning now to GDP, the traditional tool for judging the performance of economies, a different picture is drawn altogether. According

TABLE 2
Comparing average growth rates per annum in IWI per capita, GDP per capita and HDI.

Countries/ Indicators	IWI per capita	HDI	GDP per capita
Australia	0.1	0.3	2.2
Brazil	0.9	0.9	1.6
Canada	0.4	0.3	1.6
Chile	1.2	0.7	4.1
China	2.1	1.7	9.6
Colombia	−0.1	0.9	1.7
Ecuador	0.4	0.6	1.8
France	1.4	0.7	1.3
Germany	1.8	0.7	1.5
India	0.9	1.4	4.5
Japan	0.9	0.4	1.0
Kenya	0.1	0.4	0.1
Nigeria	−1.8	1.3	2.5
Norway	0.7	0.6	2.3
Russia	−0.3	0.8	1.2
Saudi Arabia	−1.1	0.5	0.4
South Africa	−0.1	−0.1	1.3
United Kingdom	0.9	0.6	2.2
United States	0.7	0.2	1.8
Venezuela	−0.3	0.8	1.3

to this approach, all economies have enjoyed at least some progress. Let us discuss the relationship between our Inclusive Wealth Index and the traditional income-based measure in greater detail. In this regard we look at Chapter 4, which undertakes a very similar analysis of inclusive wealth for 48 of 50 U.S. states from 1990 to 2000 and compares the capital accumulation rate to the GDP growth rate. The comparison gives information about whether the respective economy is over- or under-consuming. Accordingly, if the capital stock cannot keep pace with the growth in GDP, less and less capital will be available to feed the production system. We have a situation where we consume more than we could produce in the future (assuming no changes in technology). Reverting to our country sample, Table 2 displays large differences between GDP and IWI growth rates at a per capita level. In fact, in most of the cases GDP growth rates tend to be larger than those based on an inclusive capital approach (except for France and Germany), casting some doubts on the sustainability of such GDP records in the long run for the economies under analysis.

6. Conclusion

This chapter offers an analysis of the inclusive wealth of nations and its changes over time in terms of several relevant assets for 20 countries, over a time period of 19 years. We showed that the IWI provides a different perspective for assessing the performance of an economy, by switching the focus of attention from flows to stock metrics (contrary to GDP). The preservation of such stocks is essential for ensuring that aggregate output can be sustained in the long run, therefore enriching the measures by which economic development can be captured. On the empirical grounding, we found that the annual average growth rates in IWI per capita in six out of 20 nations report a decline in wealth. This result has, in fact, been exacerbated by rapid population change. Figures, however, improve for some countries, when considering adjustments to the three accounted-for capitals. For example, Saudi Arabia could move into a sustainable consumption path, not because of the building of the capital base, but due to the increase in oil prices which in fact triggered the move in that direction.

The global picture that can be drawn from the discussion makes evident that natural capital has been steadily declining in per capita terms. Even though this development could be offset by the accumulation of other assets, it is important to have in mind that whereas manufactured and human capital are reproducible factors, natural capital has limited substitutability with respect to the other capital forms (see Chapters 3 and 11).

On a methodological level, the inclusive wealth framework offers a comprehensive accounting tool covering various socio-ecological aspects, which allows policy-makers to track the changes in countries' physical assets portfolio. In this study, we additionally accounted for the effects of oil prices, an approach that can be extended to other relevant commodities depending on the country under study. Other adjustments considered within the tool regard the carbon damages on the economy. This analysis could also be expanded to the study of the impact of climate change on other capital assets, in particular natural capital. We do not yet have a way to apportion the damages across capital forms, but this should clearly be a point of discussion when measuring countries' wealth, in order to keep gaining accuracy over previous estimates.

Some of the aspects that still need to be addressed are: the accounting for social capital that has been excluded due to the lack of a methodological and empirical framework; the absence of shadow prices which have been here substituted by rental prices; and the limitation of our study to the analysis of some specific natural capital components. The wealth accounts that we have established in this study can be certainly extended to other categories such as regulating services (see Chapter 9) or water (see Chapter 10) as well.

Besides the sound theoretical foundations of the Inclusive Wealth Index, one should bear in mind the uncertainties and restrictive assumptions inherent in these empirical calculations, which are mainly subject to data availability. These results should therefore be understood as rough trends in wealth accumulation. However, even with this strong caveat, our findings warrant further investigation. Thus, the current analysis represents a relevant step towards illuminating the significance of the inclusive wealth approach for long-term economic development.

Percentage change in IWI per capita and the three capital forms: human, manufactured, and natural capital, 1990–2008.

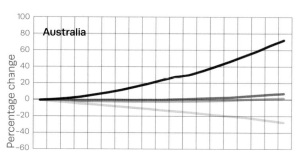

Key

- IWI
- NC
- HC
- PC

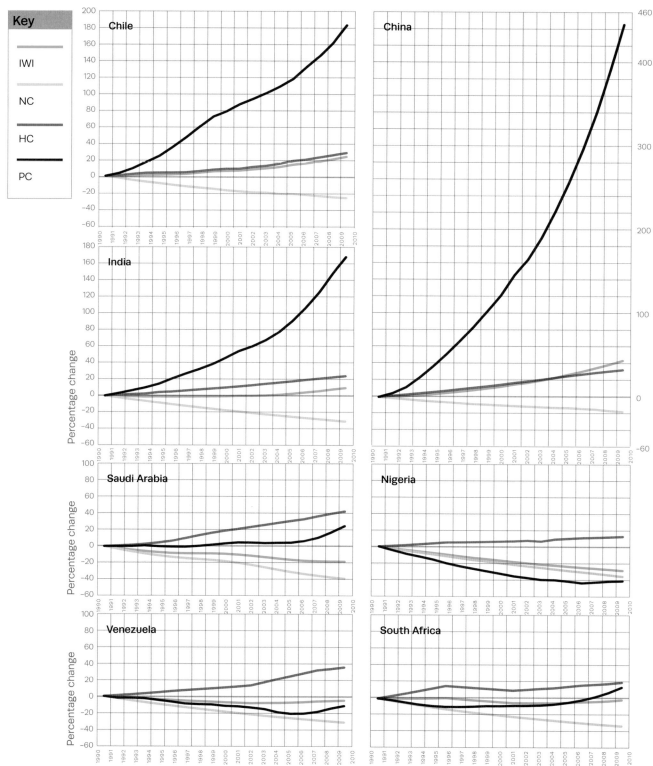

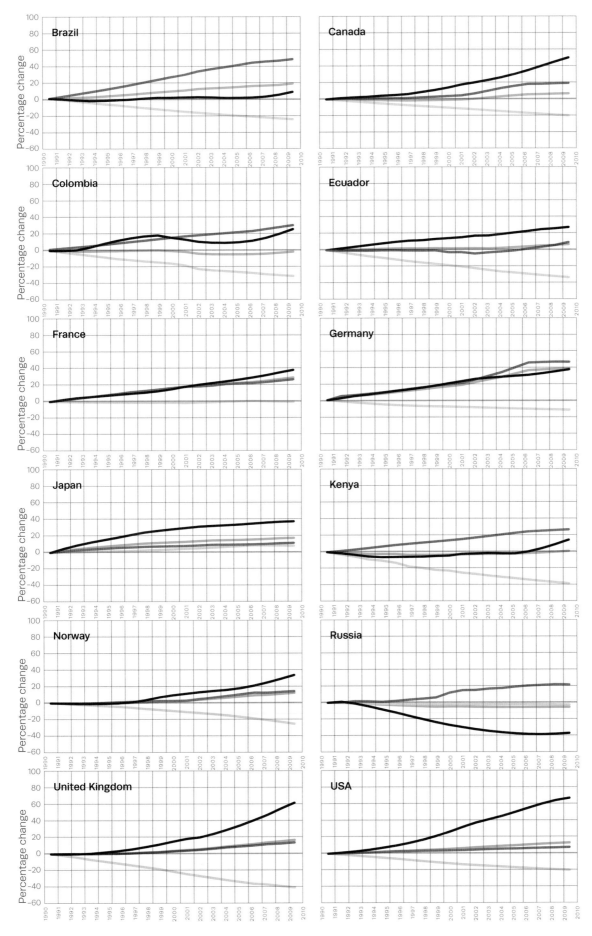

Composition of the productive base by form of capital, 1990–2008.

(US$, year 2000).

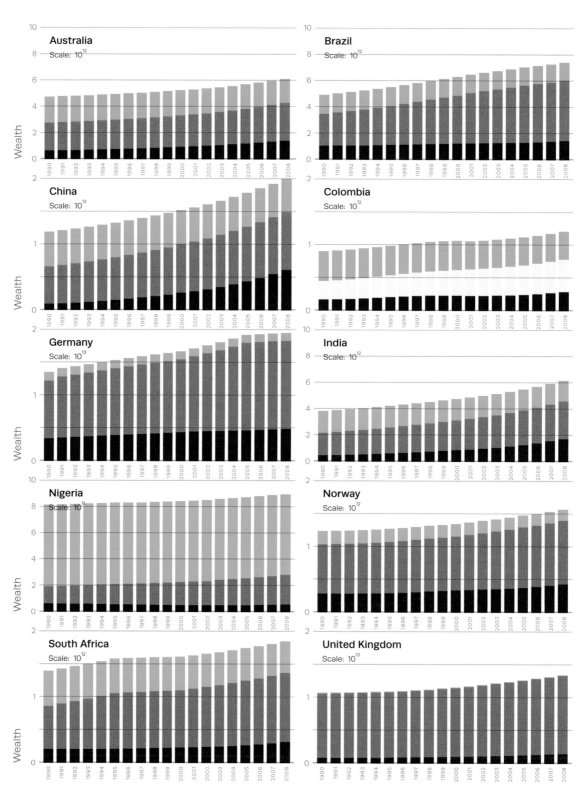

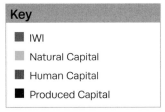

Key
- IWI
- Natural Capital
- Human Capital
- Produced Capital

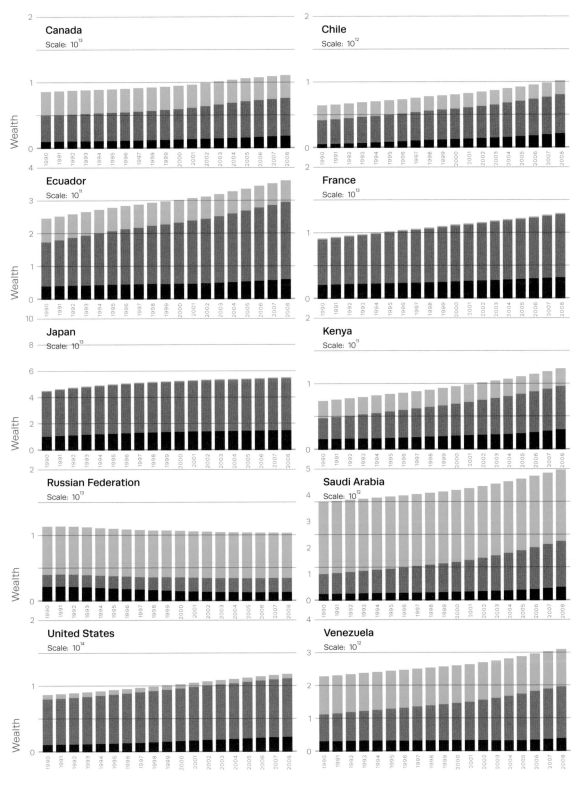

REFERENCES

ARROW, K., DASGUPTA, P., GOULDER, L., MUMFORD, K. & OLESON, K. (2012). Sustainability and the measurement of wealth. Forthcoming in *Environment and Development Economics.*

BARRO, R. & JONG-WHA, L. (2010). A new data set of educational attainment in the world, 1950-2010. *NBER Working Paper No. 15902.*

BARRO, R. & SALA-I-MARTIN, X. (2004). *Economic growth.* Cambridge, USA: MIT.

BP. (2011). *Statistical review of world energy 2011.* Retrieved May 2011, from http://www.bp.com/statisticalreview

BOLT, K., MATETE, M. & CLEMENS, M. (2002). *Manual for calculating adjusted net savings.* Washington, DC: Environment Department, World Bank.

CHRISTENSEN, L.R, CUMMINGS, D. & JORGENSON, D.W. (1980). Economic growth, 1947-1983: An international comparison. In J.W. Kendrick & B. Vaccara (Eds.) *New developments in productivity measurement and analysis, NBER conference report.* Chicago: University of Chicago Press.

FOOD AND AGRICULTURE ORGANIZATION OF THE UNITED NATIONS. (2011). *FAOSTAT.* Retrieved May 2011, from http://faostat.fao.org/site/291/default.aspx

FOOD AND AGRICULTURE ORGANIZATION OF THE UNITED NATIONS. (2011). *Fisheries and aquaculture department. Global production statistics.* Retrieved May 2011, from http://www.fao.org/fishery/statistics/global-production/en

FOOD AND AGRICULTURE ORGANIZATION OF THE UNITED NATIONS. (2011). *Global forest resources assessment.* Retrieved May 2011, from http://www.fao.org/forestry/fra/fra2010/en/

HESTON, A., SUMMERS, R. & ATEN, B. (2002). *Penn world table version 6.1.* Center for International Comparisons at the University of Pennsylvania (CICUP).

HERTEL, T., TSIGAS, M. & NARAYANAN, B. (2007). *Primary factor shares.* GTAP 7 Data Base Documentation. Center for Global Trade Analysis.

INTERNATIONAL MONETARY FUND. (2011). *International financial statistics.* Exchange Rate Archives. Retrieved May 2011, from http://www.imfstatistics.org/imf/

KING, R.G. & LEVINE, R. (1994). Capital fundamentalism, economic development, and economic growth. *Carnegie-Rochester Conference Series on Public Policy, 40*(1), 259-292.

KLENOW, P.J. & RODRÍGUEZ-CLARE, A. (1997). The neoclassical revival in growth economics: Has it gone too far?" In B. Bernake & J. Rotemberg (Eds.) *NBER macroeconomics annual 1997.* Cambridge, MA: MIT Press.

KLENOW, P.J. & RODRÍGUEZ-CLARE, A. (2005). Externalities and growth. In P. Aghion & S. Durlauf (Eds.) *Handbook of economic growth.* Amsterdam: North Holland.

LAMPIETTI, J. & DIXON, J. (1995). *To see the forest for the trees: A guide to non-timber forest benefits.* Washington, DC: World Bank.

NARAYANAN, B.G. & WALMSLEY, T.L. (EDS.) (2008). Global trade, assistance, and production: The GTAP 7 data base. Retrieved from www.gtap.agecon.purdue.edu/databases/v7/v7_doco.asp

OLLIVIER, T. & GIRAUD, P.N. (2011). Assessing sustainability: A comprehensive wealth accounting prospect: An application to Mozambique. *Ecological Economics, 70,* 503-512.

RICARD, D., MINTO, C., JENSEN, O. & BAUM, J.K. (IN PRESS). Evaluating the knowledge base and status of commercially exploited marine species with the RAM legacy stock assessment database. *Fish and Fisheries.*

SEA AROUND US. (2011). *Exclusive economic zones.* Retrieved May 2011, from http://www.seaaroundus.org/data/

SUMAILA, U., MARSDEN, A., WATSON, R. & PAULY, D. (2005). *Global ex-vessel fish price database: Construction, spatial and temporal applications.* The University of British Columbia: Fisheries Center.

THE CONFERENCE BOARD. (2012). *Total economy database.* Retrieved January 2012, from http://www.conference-board.org/data/economydatabase/

TOL, R.S.J. (2009). The economic effects of climate change. *Journal of Economic Perspectives, 23,* 29–51.

UNITED NATIONS DEVELOPMENT PROGRAMME. (2011). *Human development reports. HDI trends 1980-2010.* Retrieved May 2011, from http://hdr.undp.org/en/statistics/hdi/

UNITED NATIONS. (2011). *National accounts main aggregates database.* Retrieved May 2011, from http://unstats.un.org/unsd/snaama/Introduction.asp

UNITED NATIONS. (2009). *Gross domestic product by expenditures at constant prices. National accounts official country data.* Retrieved September 2009, from http://data.un.org/Browse.aspx?d=SNA.

UNITED NATIONS. (2011). *UN data.* Retrieved May 2011, from http://data.un.org/Default.aspx

UNITED STATES ENERGY INFORMATION ADMINISTRATION. (2011). *International energy statistics.* Retrieved May 2011, from http://www.eia.gov/countries/data.cfm

UNITED STATES GEOLOGICAL SURVEY. (2011). *Mineral commodity summaries.* Retrieved May 2011, from http://minerals.usgs.gov/minerals/pubs/mcs/

UNITED STATES GEOLOGICAL SURVEY. (2011). *Mineral yearbook: Volume I - Metals and minerals.* Retrieved May 2011, from http://minerals.usgs.gov/minerals/pubs/commodity/myb/

UNITED STATES GEOLOGICAL SURVEY. (2011). *Mineral yearbook: Volume III - Area reports: International.* Retrieved May 2011, from http://minerals.usgs.gov/minerals/pubs/country/index.html#pubs

WORLD BANK. (2006). *Where is the wealth of nations?* Washington, DC: World Bank.

WORLD BANK. (2011). *Gem commodity database.* Retrieved May 2011 from http://data.worldbank.org/data-catalog/commodity-price-data

WORLD BANK. (2011). *The changing wealth of nations.* Washington, DC: World Bank.

WORLD BANK. (2011B). *Nationally protected areas.* Retrieved May 2011, from http://data.worldbank.org/indicator/ER.LND.PTLD.ZS.

WORLD HEALTH ORGANIZATION OF THE UNITED NATIONS. (2012). *Health statistics and health information systems. Life tables for WHO member states.* Retrieved January 2012 from http://www.who.int/healthinfo/statistics/mortality_life_tables/en/

CHAPTER 3

The significance of the natural wealth of nations

Leonie Pearson, Pablo Muñoz, and Elorm Darkey

KEY MESSAGES

This first IWR focuses on quantifying components of natural capital that are largely driven by those resources for which markets exist. It is easier to obtain physical inventories and data on these stocks.

Shadow prices would be an effective tool for measuring an asset's contribution to well-being because they also reflect the relative importance of the different capital forms within the wealth accounting framework. The lack of such shadow prices presents a significant shortcoming. So instead, this analysis relies on rental prices, meaning market prices minus production costs of the resources.

Empirical findings show that almost all the selected countries (19 out of 20) experienced a decline in natural capital per capita over the period of study.

We see that in almost all countries, potential gains in renewable resources were not enough to compensate for the depletion of exhaustible stocks, like fossil fuels. The fishery is a specific illustration where, although a renewable resource, fish are being "mined" at a rate that challenges renewal of the stock.

The general trend is that population has been growing in most of the countries, exacerbating thereby the decline in natural capital growth rates, as resources are accounted for among a larger number of people.

The growth in population explains more than half of the changes in natural capital per capita in 13 out of 20 countries.

1. Introduction

The aim of this chapter is to investigate the role and significance of natural capital in the measure of inclusive wealth. The analysis builds on Chapter 2 using the same data set – a 20-country analysis of wealth from 1990 to 2008. Natural capital in this report can be classified into the following two main categories: (i) non-renewable resources; and (ii) renewable resources. Coal, oil, natural gas, and 10 minerals are included in the non-renewable resource group while agricultural land, forest resources, and fisheries are included as renewable resources. We were not able to use the ecosystem services typology developed by the Millennium Ecosystem Assessment (MA) in this study due to the lack of data and the inconsistency of the MA's typology with economic valuation and accounting.

The report adds to the broader understanding of national wealth accounting by focusing on natural capital within wealth estimates, and by expanding the scope of natural capital as used by Arrow et al. (2012). New stocks in this capital form are fisheries in the renewable resource category – although, data for these resources was available for only four countries - and coal in the non-renewable resource category. In the case of coal, the data were quite extensive and the key role coal plays for many of the countries in this pilot report were significant to warrant inclusion in the wealth accounts.[1] Thus, it is intended that figures in this chapter provide a better understanding of how capital assets contribute to the sustainability of a country and where investment might be needed if some capital asset is being depleted to levels that can cause the overall wealth portfolio to decrease.

---

1 The inclusion of coal in this report will allow computing the environmental and health damage caused by the use of coal in future reports.

2. Methodology

This section builds upon Chapter 2 and provides further insights into the measurement of natural capital. Natural capital is defined in Chapter 11 as "everything in nature (biotic and abiotic) capable of contributing to human well-being, either through the production process or directly." Indeed, nature supplies every year multiple benefits to human beings that, in one way or another, influence people's well-being. This continuous flow of natural resources and services stemming from them largely justify the mainstreaming of nature as a form of capital. Within the wealth accounting framework, natural capital is defined as the sum of the worth of all natural assets in a given country (ARROW ET AL. 2012).

This first Inclusive Wealth Report (IWR), focuses on quantifying components of natural capital that are primarily (although not only) driven by those resources for which markets exist, since it is easier to obtain physical inventories and data on these stocks. The natural assets considered in this work are shared in Chapter 2, Box 1, where we also explore the inclusion of fishery stocks and their changes over time. This is a new natural resource category considered when compared to previous studies in wealth accounting, including Arrow et al. (2012); and World Bank (2011);. Note also that Chapters 9 and 10 of this report explore methodologically and empirically wealth accounts for three regulating ecosystem services and water accounting, respectively. However, the high degree of incompleteness of the estimates which is required for the wealth accounts made the use of presently available data problematic.

Turning the focus onto the valuation side of the assets, a key element in this regard is shadow pricing where externalities play a particularly important role. Shadow prices not only measure the asset's marginal contribution to human well-being, but also reflect the relative importance of the different capital forms within the wealth account framework, acting therefore as a "weight" within the Inclusive Wealth Index

(ARROW ET AL. 2012). Constructing the Index in this way facilitates the conversion of different asset forms into a common measure. However, the limited availability of such shadow prices presents a significant shortcoming. While there seems to be a growing literature on the social prices of the carbon emissions (e.g., TOL 2009), applications to other assets are rather scarce. This points to a significant gap in our knowledge base and highlights an area where a systematic and comprehensive research effort should be taken to begin compiling these missing shadow prices for many of the non-market ecosystem services. Due to this important limitation, we confine our empirical work to the use of rental prices, meaning market prices minus production costs of the resources, assuming that they provide a first rough guidance on the relative contribution of the different assets to sustaining social well-being.

One important step in the computation of the Index relates to the changes in market prices over time. As mentioned in Chapter 2, this study takes a static approach to these prices, that is, keeping them constant over time and representing them by the average price over the period under study, being the only exception manufactured capital. This is similar to other works in wealth accounting, for example Arrow et al. (2012) and Chapter 2 in this report. From an environmental sustainability viewpoint, estimating the indicator in this way underpins the analysis of physical changes in natural capital over time, and in the overall productive base of the economy. However, this also excludes shadow prices being used as warning systems when critical capital assets are approaching thresholds and tipping points. If averages are used, this important element might be lost. This approach is taken in this study as a first approximation primarily because of the lack of shadow prices and the use of market prices. Fluctuations in the market prices of many components of natural capital can be caused by a variety of reasons and not purely by increasing scarcity and externalities.

Another important methodological issue is the ranking of countries based on the net wealth measures across countries. While one may tend to rank nations according to their net wealth, it is not in principle advisable. The reason is that we used market exchange rates in this study, and not international dollars based on countries' purchasing power parity (PPP). In principle, this point can be resolved by using international dollars. However, this would not affect the results of the changes in wealth estimates on an intra-country level, as it would move up or down the estimates of wealth, reflecting an identical proportional change in wealth over time.

There is another reason that one should bear in mind before doing a final conclusion on these findings, which is the lack of an accepted uniform approach for collecting natural capital data, resulting in "missing data points" for some countries. In the case of minerals for example, where data from the U.S. Geological Survey (2011A; 2011B; 2011C) were used, some nations report production (extraction) statistics for these accounts, but they do not supply information on the corresponding reserves, leading us to exclude the respective mineral item in the accounts. Countries where we found poor data on mineral reserves are: Ecuador, France, Germany, Kenya, Nigeria, Norway, Saudi Arabia, South Africa, and the United Kingdom. In contrast, information on mineral reserves is quite comprehensive for Australia and Canada. A similar situation exists for fisheries. For the 20 countries studied, we found data available in the RAM Legacy Stock Assessment Database (RICHARD ET AL., IN PRESS) on biomass stocks for four of them. Even among these four countries, the number of species assessed varies considerably. For the United States, for example, the RAM Legacy Stock Assessment Database reports information for 80 commercial species in the United States, but only about 10 species in the case of South Africa, Australia, and Canada.

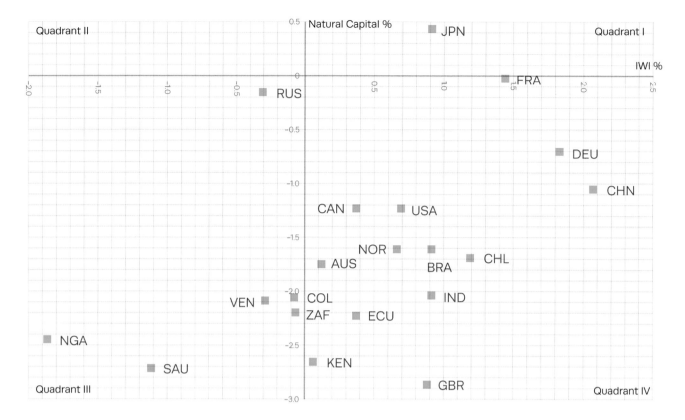

FIGURE 1

Measuring per capita
changes in natural capital
and IWI: average annual
growth rates

3. The natural wealth of nations

*What is the role of natural capital in inclusive
wealth?*

Natural capital represents an essential pool of
resources that can induce the building of other
capital assets, such as education, health, or manufactured capital. Trends in wealth accounting
indicate that natural capital constitutes, on
average, about 30 percent of national wealth
estimates for the country sample analyzed here
(see Chapter 2), but it ranges from 1 percent for
France, Japan, and the U.K. to 65 percent, 66
percent, and 73 percent in Saudi Arabia, Russia,
and Nigeria respectively. In this section we start
presenting the average annual growth rates in
wealth and natural capital at a per capita level.
To facilitate the understanding of these per

capita growth rates, we classify the countries
into four groups regarding the growth (decline)
in wealth and natural capital (see Figure 1):

- Increase in wealth and natural capital
  (quadrant I in Figure 1).
- Decline in wealth and increase in natural capital stocks (quadrant II in Figure 1).
- Decline in wealth and natural capital
  stocks (quadrant III in Figure 1).
- Increase in wealth and decline in natural
  capital stocks (quadrant IV in Figure 1).

In general, the empirical findings show
that most countries (13 of 20) experienced a
decline in natural capital stocks over the period
of study, while achieving a growth in wealth
(see quadrant IV in Figure 1). Another group of
countries composed of six nations (Colombia,
Nigeria, Russia, Saudi Arabia, South Africa, and
Venezuela) present the least desirable situation,
as they are experiencing a decline in wealth as
well as in natural capital. It is worth highlighting that all these countries have relatively large
resource pools of fossil fuels. Most of these countries even with a high growth rate of human and
produced capital were not able to have positive
IWI rates because of the huge drawdowns of

their natural capital base. However it must be noted that population growth plus the high drawdown of natural capital caused many countries to fall into unsustainable trajectories. These results highlight the need to improve the transformation process of their natural capital – oil, in this case – to human, produced and even renewable forms of natural capital to achieve sustainability.

Additionally, no country in this sample exhibits a decline in wealth while increasing its natural capital (i.e. quadrant II in Figure 1). An inference from this early result might suggest that increases in natural capital will not come at the expense of a decline in overall inclusive wealth. This result might therefore refute the "environment at the expense of development" argument seen commonly in the climate change debate.

China surprisingly experienced a somewhat lower decline in natural capital compared to India and Chile, countries whom, together with China, experienced some very high GDP growth rates over the time period reported. China also showed a strong Inclusive Wealth Index (IWI) suggesting a positive sustainable track. However, caution should be shown as the rate of increase in human capital and produced capital has shown signs of slowing down, highlighting again diminishing returns of transformation and that its continued drawdown of natural capital cannot be sustained at the current rate. Interestingly, Russia, which showed a decline of -0.34 in natural capital in absolute terms, showed that the natural capital per capita decline is alleviated to -0.19 because of its declining population.

Japan depicts the most favorable situation, as it is experiencing wealth accumulation while at the same time increasing its natural capital stocks. This has been achieved primarily through investment in the forest sector. This position is also explained by a slower population growth rate in relation to other nations. This is to a large extent supported by the recent assessment of Japan's ecosystem services (DURAIAPPAH ET AL. 2012). However, before any final conclusions can be made, it is worth mentioning that the role of trade related to this country may provide important insights into the understanding of Japan's nature's demands. Some key points on trade and natural resource depletion are explored in Chapter 5 (for further details on growth rates see Table 1).

The analysis changes a bit if population growth is taken out of the calculations. First,

TABLE 1

Measuring Changes in Natural Capital: Average Annual Growth Rates, 1990–2008

Countries/ Indicators	Natural Capital Growth (Decline) (%)	Population Growth (%)	Natural Capital Per Capita (%)	IWI Per Capita (%)
Australia	−0.49	1.29	−1.78	0.12
Brazil	−0.26	1.38	−1.64	0.91
Canada	−0.21	1.03	−1.24	0.37
Chile	−0.36	1.35	−1.71	1.19
China	−0.24	0.83	−1.07	2.07
Colombia	−0.39	1.70	−2.09	−0.08
Ecuador	−0.50	1.76	−2.26	0.37
France	0.48	0.51	−0.03	1.44
Germany	−0.47	0.23	−0.70	1.83
India	−0.34	1.74	−2.08	0.91
Japan	0.63	0.19	0.44	0.91
Kenya	0.05	2.79	−2.74	0.06
Nigeria	−0.07	2.44	−2.51	−1.87
Norway	−0.96	0.67	−1.63	0.66
Russia	−0.34	−0.19	−0.15	−0.31
Saudi Arabia	−0.08	2.72	−2.80	−1.12
South Africa	−0.60	1.64	−2.24	−0.07
United Kingdom	−2.50	0.38	−2.88	0.88
United States	−0.21	1.04	−1.25	0.69
Venezuela	−0.14	1.99	−2.13	−0.29

FIGURE 2 (left)

FIGURE 2 (left)

Average annual growth rates disaggregated by natural capital and population change

FIGURE 3 (right)

Average annual growth rates disaggregated by natural capital and population change in France and Kenya

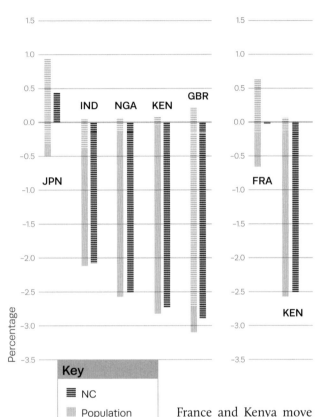

Key

≡ NC
▓ Population
≡ Other factors

capital to increase its overall inclusive wealth as the marginal contribution of a single unit increase in natural and human capital to IWI is greater than a single unit increase in produced capita.

Colombia, Nigeria, Saudi Arabia, South Africa, and Venezuela move from quadrant III to IV due to a positive turn in inclusive wealth. In these contexts, demographic development plays an important role in wealth change, an issue that will be addressed in answering the following questions.

Which components explain the decline (increase) in natural capital?

We can further explore the growth rates in natural capital by investigating what determinants are influencing the previous results. We start looking at the proportion that is attributed to the five aggregated categories of the natural capital accounts: agricultural and pasture land; forest resources; fisheries; fossil fuels (oil, natural gas, and coal); and minerals. By doing so, we also take into account changes in population over time. This is important insofar as a decrease in per capita natural wealth can be triggered either by depletion of the natural resources considered here, or because population grows faster than the change in natural capital, or both. Per capita measures are commonly used for comparing economies of different scale; in our analysis, however, the per capita index of natural capital is used to primarily show the pace at which the natural resource endowment of each member of the society is changing.

France and Kenya move from quadrant IV to quadrant I. While the latter country presents the highest population growth rate (2.79 percent), France, has one of the lowest rates (0.51 percent), only after Japan (0.19 percent), Germany (0.23 percent), and the United Kingdom (0.38 percent). Kenya moving into quadrant I is not surprising and it illustrates very clearly how its high population growth rate is unsustainable and highlights the need for population policies to address this driver of unsustainability. The situation for France is slightly different. The key message emerging from this analysis shows that France will need to increase its investment in natural and human

These results are illustrated in Appendix 1, which indeed identifies demographic development as the main driver behind the changes in natural capital. On the average for this country sample, population change explains 62 percent of the changes in natural capital. Moreover, the growth in population explains more than half of the changes in natural capital per capita in 13 out of 20 countries. The demographic pressure on natural capital is particularly evident for developing countries such as Kenya, Nigeria, and India, accounting for more than 90 percent of per capita wealth change. Saudi Arabia, on the other hand, even as a high-income country due to its high population growth rate falls into the same category as Kenya, Nigeria, and India. Conversely, in two high-income economies – the United Kingdom and Japan – population growth rates in the range of 12 percent showed minor effects in the changes in natural capital as illustrated in Figure 2. In the light of these figures, it is not surprising that if we account for inclusive wealth without population adjustments, Kenya and France move into a positive growth rate as shown clearly in Figure 3. There is, however, only one nation where demographic development contributed positively (about 33 percent) to the changes in natural capital per capita – Russia. Population growth in Russia has been decreasing over the past two decades; nevertheless, the relative decrease in population has not been enough to outweigh the overall decline in natural capital. Therefore, these findings empirically support the view that increasing population will place a higher burden on a decreasing natural capital asset base.

Turning to the contribution of the natural capital components, fossil fuels constitute the second main driver (21 percent) of changes in natural wealth. This can be attributed to the lack of data on many ecosystem services in this report. The proportion varies considerably depending on the natural resource composition of the countries. Fossil fuels explain, as shown in Figure 4, a large part of the negative growth rates in the United Kingdom (82 percent), which has been triggered by the depletion of natural gas. Similar are the cases of Germany, Russia, and Norway, where in the former country the decline is caused by the decrease in coal, whereas in the two latter economies it is mainly due to natural gas. Interestingly, as a third driver in this sample appears a renewable resource, forests, explaining on the average about 11 percent of the changes in natural capital on a per capita basis.

Discrepancies, however, are big among countries. In economies such as Japan and France, forest resources contribute positively to the changes in per capita natural capital rates (65 percent and 49 percent respectively). The initial results would point towards learning lessons from France and Japan who have been able to increase forest cover. Other countries where forest resources are relatively important are China and the United States with rates in the range of 15 percent as shown in Figure 5. The other components play in general a minor role, with the exception of minerals in Chile (21 percent), as well as agricultural and pasture land in Japan (18 percent). Fisheries, in comparison to the other components, are still at a very low level (less than 1 percent). In this context, it is important to bear in mind at least two aspects: (1) we account only for a few species due to data constraints, therefore, the figure could change once additional assessments of other species are added; and (2) despite the low contribution in

FIGURE 4

Average annual growth rates disaggregated by natural capital and population change, with focus on fossil fuels

FIGURE 5

Average annual growth rates disaggregated by natural capital and population change with a focus on forests

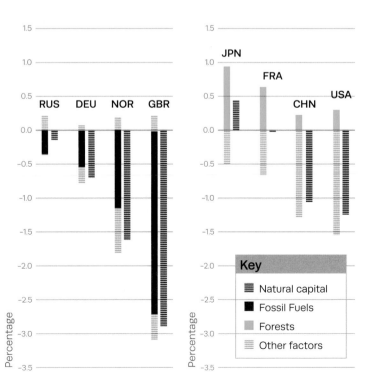

FIGURE 6

Percentage change in natural capital, 1990–2008

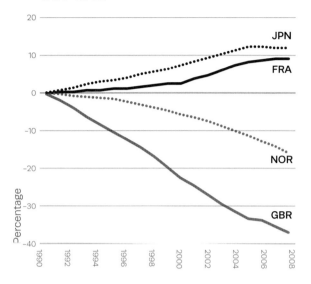

FIGURE 7

Percentage change in fish stocks, 1990–2008

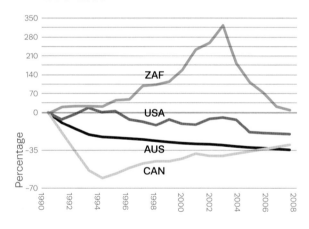

relative terms to natural wealth, it is of importance to have an understanding of this sort of wealth and how it has been changing (declining) over time. The evolution in the components of natural capital is presented in the next subsection.

How have different natural capital components been changing during the past two decades?

In this section we exclude population from our analysis and observe movements in the natural capital categories. We present an overview of how each natural capital component, as well as the aggregated (weighted) natural capital index has been changing with respect to 1990 levels. This analysis, when looked at a resource component level, provides us with information on the physical changes in the underlying assets under examination, as we used a constant rental price over time for weighting the Index (see methodological annex). A first over view indicates that the Natural Capital Index (NCI) has been mainly declining in the United Kingdom and Norway with a negative change of 36 percent, and 16 percent with respect to the 1990 levels respectively. On the other hand, positive changes were experienced by Japan and France as previously mentioned, with increases of 12 percent and 9 percent respectively (see Figure 6). In Annex 2, we additionally grouped the 18 natural resource types under study in the same categories previously presented: agricultural land, fisheries, forest resources, fossil fuels, and minerals. This analysis is presented in the following subsection.

Agricultural land

This category comprises two land types, cropland and pasture land, as defined by the FAO (2012). The major negative changes with respect to the base year (1990) can be observed in Japan (12 percent) and Australia (10 percent), although for different reasons. In Australia, the current trend is explained by pasture land, while for Japan it is cropland. Conversely, Brazil experienced positive changes in this asset, with agricultural land expanding by 10 percent, with a balanced increase in both cropland and pasture land. However, the way in which these changes affect the total NCI depends on how important these changes are with respect to the total change worth of the natural assets. Agricultural land changes in Australia, Brazil, and Japan tend to play a similar role in the natural capital index, contributing about 25 percent of the changes in the Index. In the case of Kenya, although cropland cover expanded by slightly over 2 percent which might seem small for the time span analyzed, these changes influence largely the Index as they explain about 70 percent of the changes in natural capital.

Fisheries

Fisheries in this report, for reasons stated earlier, are a small part of the overall natural capital of the four countries for which we have data. However, there are expectations that this resource will become more critical as we collect more data on stocks and shadow prices of this valuable asset. In the present computations, the scarcity of fish resources and their impacts on food security are not captured explicitly in the accounts. It is an area for future research both at the methodological and empirical level. The data available for analysis were complex and while extensive in many areas, were limited to only four countries and one common fishing zone. Within each country there was enormous variation in the type of fish stocks assessed and how prices were provided. The final analysis, using data from 1990 to 2006, consisted of varying fish stocks: 12 from Australia; 9 from Canada; 10 from South Africa; and 40 from the United States.

Fish stocks presented in Figure 7 show that all jurisdictions, except South Africa, have experienced declining fish stocks. South Africa's fishery stock is attributed primarily to the introduction of two new stocks – anchovy and sardine – which grew significantly, and then declined in 2003. While fish stocks can be managed as a renewable resource, the analysis shows that all countries use them as an exhaustible resource and fish stocks are "mined" over the period.

Forest resources

These accounts are built on the basis of two sub-categories: the stock of timber commercially available in the country, and non-timber forest services provided by the proportion of forest stocks accessed by the population. Moreover, these two forest accounts move in the same direction as they are linked to the forest surface available. Empirical measures in forest wealth accounts depict an interesting evolution of this natural capital category over the last two decades. The forest accounts explain on average[2] about a quarter (26 percent) of the changes in natural capital that occurred in this period, although with big fluctuations among countries. Interestingly, 10 out of 20 countries scored an increase in forest resources, of which six of them are high-income countries (see Annex 2). Forest accounts are of particular relevance in the case of Japan and France, as they lead an important part of the changes in natural capital accounts, explaining 75 percent and 81 percent of the changes, respectively. On the other hand, seven countries showed a decline in this account, five of them with the lowest performance in this regard are: Brazil (-7 percent), Ecuador (-26 percent), Kenya (-7 percent), Nigeria (-41 percent), and Venezuela (-10 percent). These changes have been of major relevance for understanding the changes in natural capital for Ecuador, Japan, and Brazil, where forest resources explain about 89 percent, 71 percent, and 66 percent respectively of the changes in the natural capital account when comparing with the 1990 levels. Forest stocks have remained constant to the forest resources assessments in Canada, South Africa, and Saudi Arabia.

Fossil fuels

Before moving to the analysis of the exhaustible resources categories – fossil fuels and minerals – it is important to bear in mind that based on the method employed for the study of these components, non-renewable resources are by definition depleted if used and therefore can be expected to decline in all countries. The results suggest fossil fuels on the average, contribute to more than half (53 percent) of the changes in the Natural Capital Index. However, in

---

2   This figure represents an average across countries, with all countries weighted equally.

the case of Saudi Arabia, Canada, the United Kingdom, and Russia, fossil fuels contributed 99 percent, 92 percent, 91 percent, and 90 percent of the changes in the NCI of these countries respectively.

The decline in fossil fuels is by itself only part of the story. For example, the decline in fossil fuels in the United Kingdom accounted for about 59 percent of the decline with respect to the base year, while in the case of Saudi Arabia, the decline was only 1.5 percent. Venezuela and Nigeria show a decline of 2 percent, and Ecuador a decline of 0.5 percent. These differences in magnitude across the countries indicate the size of reserves they have of the resource base. Canada and Russia, which have relatively large resource bases, suffered a decline of about 10 percent with respect to the 1990 level. On the other hand, there are other countries that showed large declines in fossil fuels such as France (69 percent) and Japan (40 percent) during this time span. However, these large declines were of minor relevance within the indicator, as fossil fuel explains less than 7 percent of the changes in natural capital in these countries.

Minerals

The impact of declines in minerals was greatest for Chile which experienced a decline of 30 percent over the time period causing a change of 79 percent to its NCI. This was caused primarily by the drawdown of its copper resources. Canada, South Africa, and Australia were also drawing down heavily their mineral resources by approximately 47 percent, 27 percent, and 21 percent respectively. These declines in the mineral base caused declines in the overall natural capital accounts by about 10 percent. Although the United States and Colombia saw relatively large declines in minerals by about 35 percent and 48 percent respectively, the overall changes in natural capital were substantially less at about 3 percent.

Lessons learned for policy

Inclusive wealth offers policy-makers with a comprehensive accounting tool for measuring the assets available in the economy and its changes over time. In this chapter as well as in Chapter 2, we have analyzed several changes in the productive base of the economy. In this regard, natural capital tends to mostly exhibit negative trends even if the productive base of the economy increases. This is somehow expected due to the trade-offs of, for example, across exhaustible resources and the other capital forms. Trend lines illustrating downward and upward movements in the various capital assets can be useful for providing an overview of how long can the drawdown of certain assets continue and how efficient the transformation has been in the past. In this realm, some of the challenges regard investigating ways of getting higher returns on its drawdown of natural capital by improving the total factor productivity (TFP), and the building up of higher levels of human capital through programs to increase literacy and employment rates in the country. The same goes for providing closer attention to achieving high returns to produced and human capital. This might indicate that thresholds are being approached, and that countries might be coming to a state where the transformation of natural capital is reaching diminishing returns to scale. This insight is useful to policy-makers in understanding the potential role and significance that natural capital has when countries might adopt a portfolio management approach to wealth, which is necessary for achieving sustainable development.

Let us take Kenya as an example. Although agricultural land expanded over the past 19 years, the amount of this expansion was insufficient to account for the population increase Kenya had also witnessed over that same period. This calls for larger investment in expansion of agricultural land but also an increase in forests, which actually declined in Kenya over the same time period. Policies focusing on management of population growth, expansion of cropland,

and increased forest cover can be seen as build-ing blocks for addressing the food security situ-ation in the country.

In the case of the United Kingdom, as another example, decline in its natural capital base, with an average negative rate of 2.5 per-cent per annum, reaching the largest depleting rate in 2000 with a magnitude of 3.5 percent, suggests the need for intervention strategies to reverse this decline, as shown in Figure 8

The decline was primarily driven by draw-down of its oil and natural gas resources. The negative Natural Capital Index illustrates that the rate of transformation of this drawdown of its natural capital assets, in this case its oil and gas, to human and produced capital were inefficient and below par. However, a promising sign is the upward trend seen in the build up of its natural capital base through an increase in forest stocks.

Lessons can be derived from having a closer look at Norway, (see Figure 9) which also saw a decline in its natural capital asset base, again driven by its drawdown of oil and gas resources. But in spite of a larger population growth rate, Norway exhibits a positive IWI. This can be traced back to a larger increase in its human and manufactured capital base illustrating a higher rate of return on its natural capital base.

What does a focus on natural capital tell us for wealth estimates?

This chapter has focused on the significance of natural capital in estimates of wealth using empirical insights. Understanding the constitu-ent parts of the wealth estimate is critical in determining the "best" portfolio management approach for each country to achieve sustain-able development (i.e., non-declining IWI). The analysis provides policy-makers guidance on which of the capital asset bases are declining and where investment is required. It does not necessarily always have to be investment in nat-ural capital, and there might be instances when the IWI might suggest investments in human and produced capital. It must be acknowledged

that countries must also have the critical levels for human and produced capital to improve the well-being of all its citizens.

Essentially, the IWI has to be acknowledged as a measure of weak sustainability (Neumayer 2010) and allows for the substi-tution between different capi-tals stocks, such as produced and natural capital. On the other hand, strong sustain-ability requires (broadly) that natural capital is non-substitutable with the other capital stocks (DALY 1995). As shown through our analysis, few nations achieve this very strict criterion (see). Additionally, this strict criterion does not allow investment from one capital into another, the essence of the portfolio line of attack to wealth management as currently practiced (see HAMILTON AND CLEMENS [1999], ARROW ET AL. [2012]; DASGUPTA [2008]). However, this might be a criterion that can be invoked once critical levels of each capital are reached beyond which un-sustainability becomes an endogenous prop-erty of country's development path.

United Kingdom

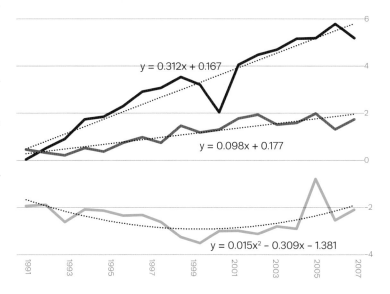

$y = 0.312x + 0.167$

$y = 0.098x + 0.177$

$y = 0.015x^2 - 0.309x - 1.381$

FIGURE 8

Transformation rate of capital assets in the United Kingdom

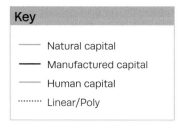

Key

—— Natural capital
—— Manufactured capital
—— Human capital
········ Linear/Poly

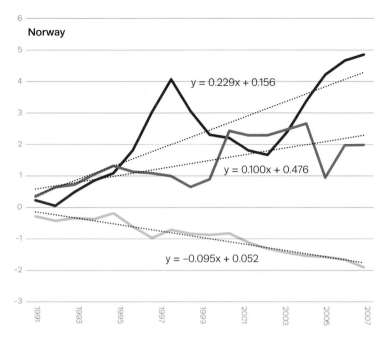

y = 0.229x + 0.156

y = 0.100x + 0.476

y = -0.095x + 0.052

FIGURE 9

Transformation rate of capital assets in Norway

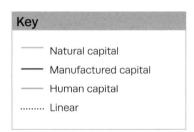

Key

——— Natural capital

——— Manufactured capital

——— Human capital

········· Linear

*What limitations and uncer-
tainties need to be resolved?*

There are two key areas of
limitation in the current
chapter. First are conceptual issues related to natural
capital in the IWI; second are
methodological issues.

A key limitation of the
IWI framework is its inability
to address two key concepts
in natural capital: first, how
critical is a type of natural capital; and, second,
the resilience of natural capital. As for "how
critical," there are some natural capital stocks
that are so important to human well-being that
they defy both measurement and substitution
(EKINS 2003). These capital stocks are considered critical because they either contribute
consequentially to human well-being and/or
there is a moral obligation for society to preserve them (PEARSON ET AL. 2011). These natural
capital stocks include: climate regulation, flood
regulation, fertile soil, biodiversity, drinking
water, etc. These have not been included in
this measure of wealth. However, Chapters 9
and 10 of the report address some of complexities related to their assessment. It is therefore
important for policy-makers to understand that

while the stocks of natural capital measured in
this analysis are important, the IWI presented in
this report does not account for fundamental
functioning of the earth's ecological systems
and therefore other assessments are necessary
to guide their management.

The second issue is the resilience of natural
capital, or the fact that natural capital and its
underpinning ecosystems do not always behave
in linear ways, exhibiting marginal change
responses to large shocks. Natural capital stocks
sometimes experience hysteric responses and,
as such, the consequences of declining a natural capital stock past a threshold of no return
is not a small change in value (ROKSTROM ET
AL. 2009). Conceptually, work by Walker et al.
(2010) tried to bridge this gap by including resilience of two critical capital stocks within the
inclusive wealth measure for a small catchment.
However the data and knowledge requirements
are so large, it has yet to be implemented yet at
the national level.

There are large methodological limitations
to the current analysis as discussed in the methodological annex. However this chapter has
highlighted that there is a porosity in the type of
data that are internationally comparable on natural capital stocks and ecosystem services. This
results in not only "value" being derived from
only tradeable goods, but also that the choice of
which stocks to measure is limited, ensuring a
bias or that a less-than-complete set of natural
capital stocks can be accounted. For example,
protected areas are assessed by the World Bank
as the value of pastureland and crop land. This
opportunity cost approach is at best a minimum
proxy of these significant land parcels that, in
some instances, house the last remaining habitat for endangered species. These types of proxy
measures and their associated capital stocks
have been excluded from the wealth accounts.
Although important, it was decided that they do
not contribute directly to the productive base of
the national economy, instead producing other
goods and services that are best measured and
managed by other means. This might be a matter
that falls outside the realm of simple economic

decision-making, but should exist in the domain of ethics and moral value theory.

4. Conclusion

This initial investigation of natural capital within a wealth assessment has provided some useful insights for policy-makers trying to achieve sustainable development and researchers trying to measure it.

Key findings are grouped into three areas. First, it was shown that most countries experienced decreasing natural capital over the assessment period, ensuring that potential gains in the renewable resources were not enough to compensate for the depletion trend of exhaustible resources (e.g., fossil fuels). Second, countries can be broadly grouped into three categories – 1 out of 20 countries is in this category: (i) those experiencing growth in wealth and natural capital; (ii) those experiencing growth in wealth while depleting natural capital – 13 out of 20 countries are in this category; and (iii) those experiencing a decline in both wealth and natural capital – 6 out of 20 countries are in this category. Third, population has been growing in most of the countries, exacerbating thereby the declining in the natural capital growth rates, as resources are accounted for among a larger number of people.

These findings assert that natural capital is central to the need to understand inclusive wealth. It is not enough for policy-makers to know that inclusive wealth is non-declining, as not all countries are satisfied with achieving a sustainable development path if it requires the depletion of natural capital stocks. However, for other countries, these natural capital stocks are exhaustible in any case, and their value may be invested into other forms of capital – for example, human capital (education) – to ensure a long-term sustainable future. This examination of natural capital has shown the strength of inclusive wealth as not only a leading indicator of national sustainability, but also for its ability to understand wealth at the level of each category of capital stocks.

TABLE 2

Understanding How Change in Wealth and Natural Capital is Different When Considered in Absolute and Per Capita Rates

	Changes in IWI and in natural capital	Per capita changes in IWI and natural capital.
Growth in wealth and natural capital	France	Japan
	Japan	
	Kenya	
Growth in wealth while 'mining' natural capital	Australia	Australia
	Brazil	Brazil
	Canada	Canada
	Colombia	Chile
	Chile	China
	China	Ecuador
	Ecuador	France
	Germany	Germany
	India	India
	Nigeria	Kenya
	Norway	Norway
	Saudi Arabia	U.K.
	South Africa	U.S.
	U.K.	
	U.S.	
	Venezuela	
Decline in wealth and natural capital	Russia	Colombia
		Nigeria
		Saudi Arabia
		South Africa
		Russia
		Venezuela

Average annual growth rates disaggregated by natural capital type

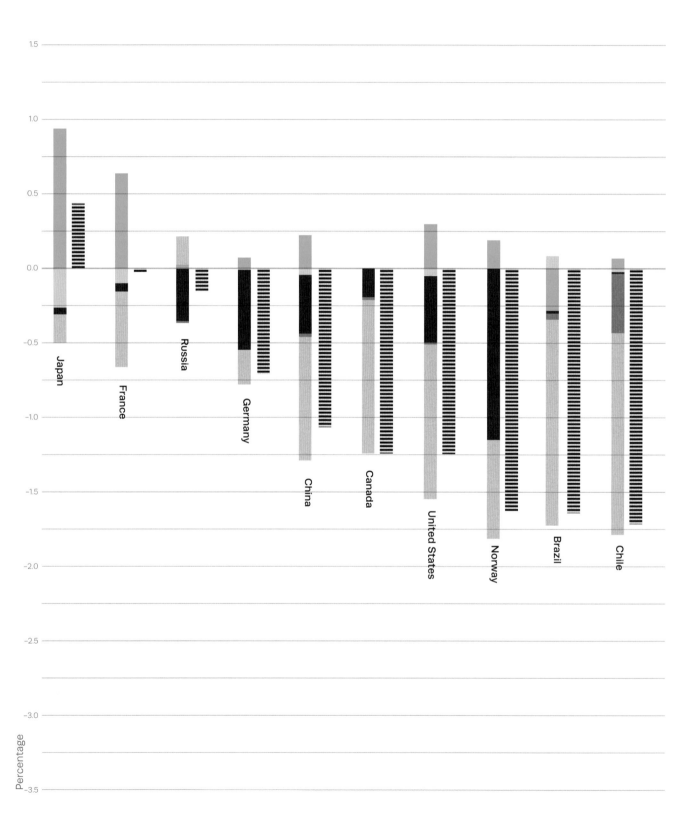

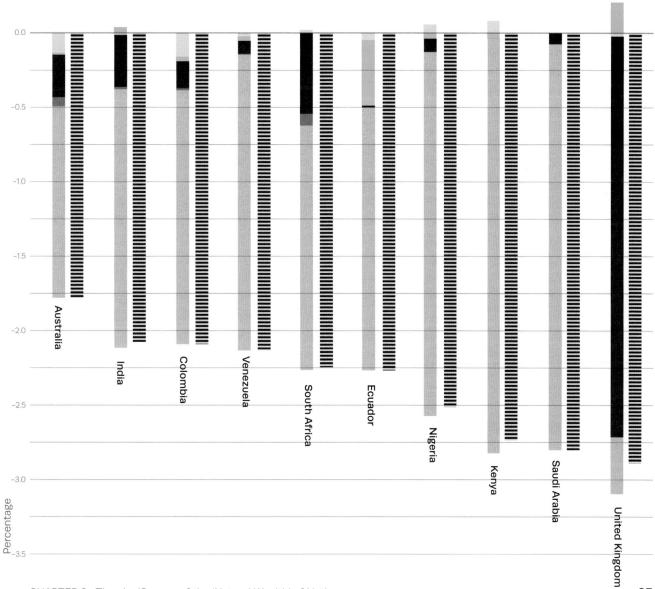

Annual growth rates disaggregated by natural capital type

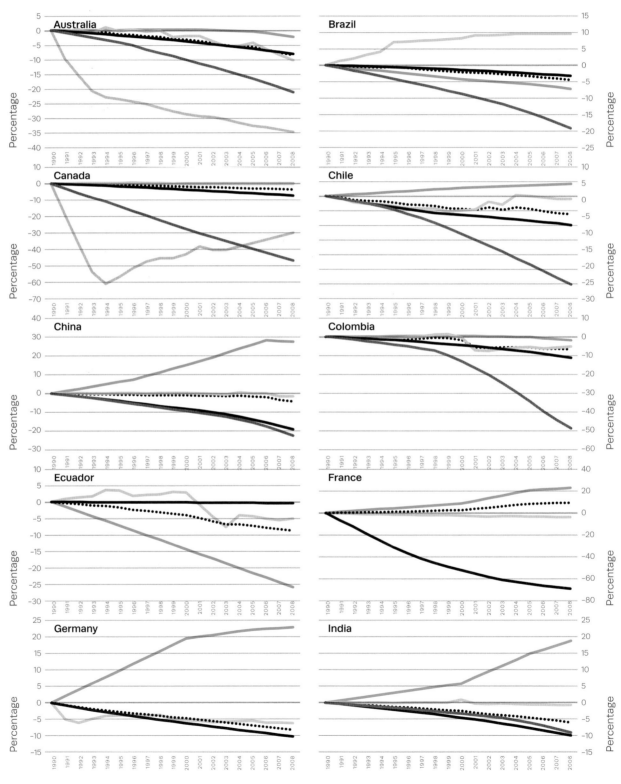

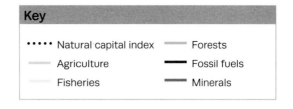

Key

···· Natural capital index   Forests

Agriculture   **Fossil fuels**

Fisheries   Minerals

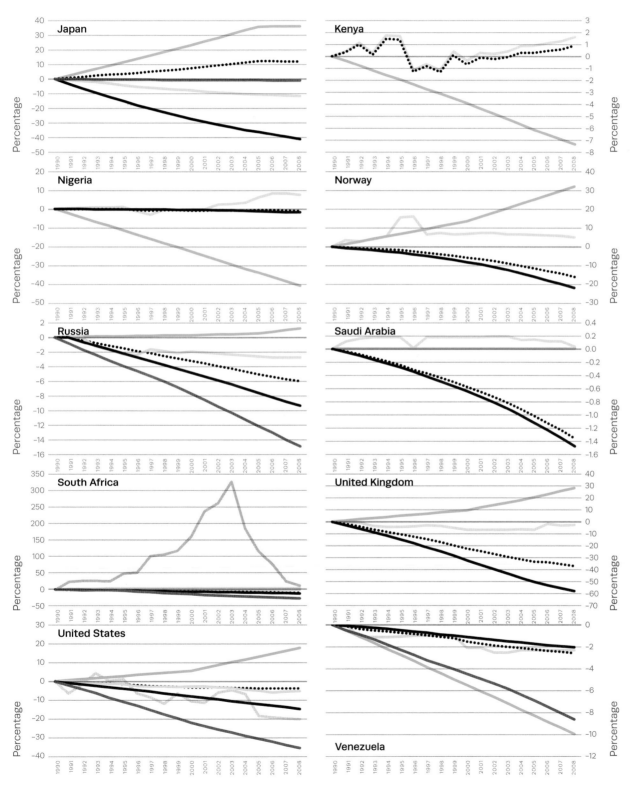

REFERENCES

ARROW, K., DASGUPTA, P., GOULDER, L., MUM-FORD, K. & OLESON, K. (2012). Sustainability and the measurement of wealth. Forthcoming in *Environment and Development Economics*.

DALY, H.E. (1996). *Beyond growth*. Boston: Beacon Press.

DASGUPTA, P. (2008). Nature in economics. *Environmental and Resource Economics, 39*(1), 1–54.

DURAIAPPAH, A.K, NAKAMURA, K., TAKEUCHI, K., WATANABE, M. & NISHI, M. (2012). *Satoyama and Satoumi: Socio ecological production landscapes of Japan*. Tokyo: United Nations University Press.

EKINS, P. (2003). Identifying critical natural capital: Conclusions about critical natural capital. *Ecological Economics, 44*, 277–292.

FOOD AND AGRICULTURE ORGANIZATION OF THE UNITED NATIONS. (2012). *FAOSTAT*. Retrieved May 2011, from http://faostat.fao.org/site/291/default.aspx

HAMILTON, K. & CLEMENS, M. (1999). Genuine savings in developing countries. *The World Bank Economic Review, 13* (2), 333-56.

NEUMAYER, E. (2010). *Weak versus strong sustainability: Exploring the limits of two opposing paradigms*. Cheltenham, UK: Edward Elgar.

OLLIVIER, T. & GIRAUD, P.N. (2011). Assessing sustainability, a comprehensive wealth accounting prospect: An application to Mozambique. *Ecological Economics, 70*, 503-512.

PEARSON, L., KASHIMA, Y. & PEARSON, C. (2012). Clarifying protected and utilitarian values of critical capital. *Ecological Economics, 73*, 206–210.

RICARD, D., MINTO, C., JENSEN, O. & BAUM, J.K. (IN PRESS). Evaluating the knowledge base and status of commercially exploited marine species with the RAM legacy stock assessment database. *Fish and Fisheries*.

ROCKSTRÖM, J., STEFFEN, W., NOONE, K., PERSSON, Å., CHAPIN III, F.S., LAMBIN, E.F.,... FOLEY, J.A. (2009). A safe operating space for humanity. *Nature, 461*, 472–475.

TOL, R.S.J. (2009). The economic effects of climate change. *Journal of Economic Perspectives, 23*, 29–51.

WALKER, B., PEARSON, L., HARRIS, M., MÄLER, K.G., LI, C.Z., BIGGS, R. & BAYNES, T. (2010). Incorporating resilience in the assessment of inclusive wealth: An example from South East Australia. *Environmental and Resource Economics, 45*, 183-202.

UNITED STATES GEOLOGICAL SURVEY. (2011). *Mineral commodity summaries*. Retrieved May 2011, from http://minerals.usgs.gov/minerals/pubs/mcs/

UNITED STATES GEOLOGICAL SURVEY. (2011). *Mineral yearbook: Volume I - Metals and minerals*. Retrieved May 2011, from http://minerals.usgs.gov/minerals/pubs/commodity/myb/

UNITED STATES GEOLOGICAL SURVEY. (2011). *Mineral yearbook: Volume III - Area reports: International*. Retrieved May 2011, from http://minerals.usgs.gov/minerals/pubs/country/index.html#pubs

WORLD BANK. (2011). *The changing wealth of nations*. Washington, DC: World Bank.

CHAPTER 4

Measuring inclusive wealth at the state level in the United States

Kevin J. Mumford

KEY MESSAGES

This chapter is the first attempt to construct an accounting of the capital assets of each of the 48 contiguous U.S. states.

The study looks at four types of capital: exhaustible natural capital (mainly coal, oil, and natural gas); land; physical capital (like buildings, homes, and equipment); and human capital (based on education, wages, and number of working years remaining).

The results show a very low level of wealth inequality across states. The Gini coefficient is 0.09, which represents a fairly equal distribution of wealth.

The study demonstrates that the rate of economic growth as measured by inclusive wealth can be quite different than the rate of economic growth suggested by GDP figures. Data show that those states with high GDP growth rates tend to have much lower rates of inclusive wealth growth.

It is essential that governments collect capital stock data so that inclusive wealth accounting can become increasingly accurate, comprehensive, and useful. More complete data would enable states to measure their rate of inclusive investment. Such data would also make it clear to policy-makers whether current GDP growth rates are sustainable in the long-run.

The study's use of housing and stock market data to value physical capital is an important contribution to the literature on sustainability.

An important conclusion drawn here is that if states with an inclusive wealth per capita annual growth rate that is less than their GDP per capita annual growth rate want to sustain higher GDP growth rates for the long term, increased inclusive investment will be required. This means that state governments would have to encourage education, reduce the extraction of natural resources, and increase construction of public infrastructure.

1. Introduction

Economic growth is usually defined as the increasing capacity to produce goods and services and is often measured by the growth in gross domestic product (GDP) per capita. While GDP measures the value of the goods and services produced, it is not a direct measure of the *capacity* to produce these goods and services. To directly measure a change in the capacity to produce goods and services would require a measure of the growth in a comprehensive accounting of all forms of capital (including human capital). GDP may still be useful as a measure of economic growth to the extent that it is similar to the growth in the capital stock. However, it turns out that these two measures are the same only if the economy is following an optimal growth path.[1] If the economy is not on an optimal growth path, then an income-based measure like GDP could lead to qualitatively different conclusions about economic growth than a direct measure of the growth of the capital stock.

Consider an economy that slows the rate of investment in capital and allows the capital stock to depreciate over time. This diminishes the economy's capacity to produce goods and services. However, the reduction in investment allows for higher levels of consumption and thus GDP growth is not immediately influenced. A direct measure of the change in the capital stock would reflect this reduction in the capacity to produce goods and services straight away. As a second example in which income-based measures and capital-based measures give different results, consider an economy in which an exhaustible resource is an input to production.[2]

If the economy increased the amount of this exhaustible resource used in production each period, this would increase GDP but decrease the capacity to produce goods and services in the future, all other variables remaining the same.

How different the GDP growth rate is from the capital stock growth rate is an empirical question. The purpose of this chapter is to construct an accounting of the capital assets of each of the 48 contiguous U.S. states. This capital-based measure is called "inclusive wealth" or "comprehensive wealth" and represents a complete accounting of all capital assets. The growth rate of the measure of inclusive wealth is computed for each U.S. state from 1990 to 2000 and compared to the GDP growth rate. This comparison is useful as an indicator of whether a given state is over- or under-consuming. If the rate of GDP growth exceeds the rate of capital stock growth, the state is consuming at a rate where it will not be able to sustain the rate of GDP growth in the long term.

Though appealing as a measure of economic growth, directly measuring the capital stock is more difficult than measuring GDP because there is no government collection of comprehensive capital stock data.[3] Even when capital stock data are available, many forms of capital are not traded in markets and thus there is no market price at which to value these assets. Some of these empirical difficulties have been addressed in work by Hamilton and Clemens (1999), Dasgupta (2001), Arrow et al. (2004), World Bank (2004), Arrow et al. (2010), World Bank (2011), and Arrow et al. (2012). This chapter is the first effort to apply the methodology developed in this literature to U.S. states.

As this is an initial effort to use state-level data to calculate inclusive wealth growth rates, the empirical work is not comprehensive. This chapter focuses only on a few of the most

---

1   For the capital stock growth rate to be the same as the GDP growth rate in a simple model with an optimal growth path, the production function must also exhibit constant returns to scale.

2   An exhaustible resource is a commodity whose available stock cannot be increased. See Dasgupta and Heal (1974) for the derivation of the optimal consumption path in a production economy with an exhaustible resource.

---

3   Wealth accounting initiatives at the OECD, the World Bank, and the United Nations University are working to make inclusive wealth data available to researchers. However, none of these efforts are focused on measuring inclusive wealth at the state-level within the United States.

important forms of capital: human capital, physical capital, land, and exhaustible resources. The U.S. state-level data allow the incorporation of housing valuation and stock market measures that the prior literature has been unable to use in comparisons across countries due to a lack of data.

The results from this empirical exercise indicate that there are large and meaningful differences between measuring economic growth through an income-based approach, like GDP, and measuring economic growth through an inclusive- or comprehensive- wealth-based approach. The wealth-based growth rates are similar in magnitude to the income-based rates, though the correlation between them is negative.

2. Measuring inclusive wealth

While this paper does not expand on wealth accounting theory, it offers a new application. A short description of the theory is helpful before explaining the methods employed. Following Arrow et al. (2012), inclusive wealth at time t is defined as the value of all capital assets:

EQUATION 1

$$W(t) = \sum_i p_i(t) \, K_i(t)$$

where $p_i(t)$ is the shadow price or marginal value of asset i at time t and $K_i(t)$ is the amount of asset i at time t. Non-decreasing wealth means that the economy has the capacity to produce at least as much as in the past and is consistent with the definition of sustainability that has been adopted in the wealth accounting literature (e.g. ARROW ET AL. 2012). Inclusive investment is defined as the change in the value of all capital assets holding prices constant:

EQUATION 2

$$I(t) = \sum_i p_i(t) \, \big(K_i(t+1) - K_i(t)\big)$$

Inclusive investment can be defined over any time period (month, quarter, year, or decade) as the data allow. A positive value for inclusive investment in period t implies that the productive capacity of the economy is greater in period

$t+1$ than it was in period t. However, this does not mean that the economy will enjoy higher consumption indefinitely as future declines in inclusive wealth are possible if inclusive investment is negative in the future.

Technological change can be regarded as yet another form of capital asset. As shown in Arrow et al. (2012), if the rate of saving is small, the shadow price for the usual measure of technological change, total factor productivity (TFP), will be approximately one. Thus, the TFP growth rate, $R(t)$, can be added directly to inclusive investment:

EQUATION 3

$$I(t) = R(t) + \sum_i p_i(t) \, \big(K_i(t+1) - K_i(t)\big)$$

To calculate inclusive wealth and inclusive investment, one would need estimates of the stock of each capital asset at the beginning and the end of the time period being considered as well as the shadow prices for each asset. For a non-renewable resource such as oil, the change in the stock is simply the negative of the amount extracted during the period. Ignoring externalities associated with the use, the shadow price corresponds to the rental value, which is the price less the marginal cost of extraction.[4] Data on physical capital (buildings, machines, equipment) and land are generally reported in dollars making the task of finding a shadow price unnecessary.

Human capital is more difficult to measure directly. Following Klenow and Rodríguez-Clare (1997), the amount of human capital per worker is defined as $exp(rT)$, where r is the appropriate rate of interest, assumed to be 8.5 percent per annum as in Arrow et al. (2012), and T is the average number of years of educational attainment. The stock of human capital is the human capital per worker multiplied by the number of workers. The shadow price of a unit of human capital is calculated as the total wage bill divided by the total stock of human capital.

Population growth is assumed to be exogenous, has no effect on prices, and enters the

4   The average cost of extraction is generally used due to data availability.

production function multiplicatively. Under these assumptions one can account for population growth simply by measuring all capital assets in per capita terms.[5] In this chapter, all forms of capital are ultimately valued in per capita terms by dividing by the state population for the appropriate year. The assumption of exogenous population growth implies an assumption that all migration is also exogenous.

3. Data and empirical results

In this chapter, data are used from the period 1990–2000 to analyze economic growth in the U.S. 48 contiguous states. Table 1 presents real GDP per capita by state in 1990 and 2000 and then calculates the annual growth rate. The state-level real GDP data were obtained from the Bureau of Economic Analysis, and the state-level population data were obtained from the U.S. Census Bureau. Both data series are publicly available. Over this 10-year period, the annual growth rates range from 4.5 percent in New Mexico to under 1 percent in Louisiana. Though not reported in Table 1, note that each state experienced some population growth over this 10-year period. North Dakota had the smallest population annual growth rate at less than 0.1 percent and Nevada had the largest at 5.2 percent.

The remainder of this section focuses on the calculation of inclusive wealth. The methods and data used for each general type of capital asset are presented separately.

3.1 Exhaustible natural capital

Exhaustible forms of natural capital include non-renewable energy and mineral resources. This chapter focuses on three energy resources

– oil, coal, and natural gas – as these are by far the most valuable forms of natural capital.[6] The state-level data for these resources are publicly available from the U.S. Energy Information Administration. For each resource, proven reserves and quantity extracted are reported for every year. Proven reserves are the known quantity that is economically recoverable given current technology. While the estimated proven reserve is available in every year, only the most recent year's data are needed. Proven reserves tend to increase over time as new resources are discovered and new methods of extraction are developed. This is true even after subtracting the amount extracted. However, the stock of energy resources is a non-renewable resource which means that it is non-increasing by definition.

Thus, the stock of the exhaustible resource, $K(t)$, in year t is defined according to:

EQUATION 4

$$K(t)=K(T)+\sum_{j=t}^{T-1} X(j)$$

where $X(j)$ is the total extraction for the state in year j and the most recent measure of proven reserves is given by $K(T)$. The most recent proven reserves data is for 2009, so extraction data for each state for years 1990–2008 are needed for the calculation. The extraction data for oil, coal, and natural gas is also obtained from the U.S. Energy Information Administration. The results are presented in Table 2.

The shadow price for each of these goods should be state-specific as the extraction cost for the resource differs by state. However, state-specific estimates of the extraction cost were unavailable and so a U.S. average extraction cost estimate from the World Bank (2006)

---

5   See Arrow, Dasgupta, and Mäler (2003) for a complete discussion of how population growth enters the theory and the conditions under which per capita values can be used.

6   Future work could investigate the availability of state–level reserves and extraction data for a large number of mineral types. Recent work by the World Bank (2011) and Arrow et al. (2012) has shown that minerals are not nearly as valuable as energy resources, so it is unlikely that the result would be very different, though this is just speculation that would need to be confirmed by a more comprehensive accounting of all forms of exhaustible natural capital.

data appendix is used. This is an important limitation as the cost of extracting oil, coal, and natural gas in some states is far greater than in others. The World Bank (2006) extraction cost estimates are an average over various types of U.S. extraction methods, not marginal costs. As a simplification, each resource is assumed to be homogeneous and an average price is used for the 1990–2000 period. This yielded shadow prices (average resource price less the average extraction cost) of US$2.48[7] per barrel for oil; $1.90 per short ton for coal; and $0.19 per thousand cubic feet for natural gas.

Another important limitation in this study is the disregard for capital gains. As explained in Arrow et al. (2012), as non-renewable resources are extracted the shadow price should increase for the stocks that are still underground. Thus, future consumers of non-renewable resources should expect to pay higher prices and future exporters of non-renewable resources should expect to make higher profits. However, data on the consumption and extraction behavior of not only every state, but also of the rest of the world would need to be obtained in order to calculate the capital gains. This pursuit is left for future research.

3.2 Land

Land is clearly an important capital asset and, fortunately, high-quality data are available for land use by state. The U.S. Department of Agriculture's Natural Resources Conservation Service conducts a survey of land use by state every five years. Developed urban land is ignored in this section as it should be captured in the value of housing and the value of physical business capital considered in Section 3.3. All federal land is excluded from the present analysis as it is not clear that this land should be counted as

part of the wealth of the state.[8] This leaves non-federal rural land. Table 3 reports the amount of non-federal rural land by state in thousands of acres for 1990 and 2000.[9]

Across the 48 states considered in this study, non-federal rural land declined by about 21 million acres from 1990 to 2000. Nearly 95 percent of this reduction in non-federal rural land was due to urbanization. The remaining 5 percent was due to expansion of federal land and the creation of new water areas. New water areas include ponds, lakes, reservoirs, and estuaries. These new water areas are excluded from the analysis because of the difficulty in valuation.

The average quality of rural land differs widely across states. The U.S. Department of Agriculture's National Agricultural Statistics Service provides estimates of the average price of an acre of rural land in each state. Not all years are available, so rather than take an average price over the 1990–2000 period, this chapter uses the 1995 values. Using the average price of an acre of rural land as the shadow price implies assuming that the land market is thick and that distortions from taxes and government subsidies are small.

The average value of an acre of rural land in each state, as well as the value of the change in the amount of rural land (primarily reductions due to development), are also reported in Table 3. The loss in rural land wealth for states that experienced a great deal of development would likely be offset by gains in housing wealth and physical capital, though this depends on the

---

8   The inclusive wealth of a state is the wealth owned by all inhabitants of that state. Land owned by the state government should obviously be included, but it is not clear how land owned by the federal government should be treated in the accounting. One option is that the value of federal land could be divided equally among all inhabitants of the country and thus assigned to the states in proportion to the population. However, this is an enormous task that would likely have little influence on the overall results.

9   The Natural Resources Conservation Service reports land use in 1987, 1992, 1997, and 2002. The 1990 and 2000 land use reported here are linear approximations using the two adjacent land use values.

---

7   All monetary values in this chapter are expressed in US$.

value of the rural land and housing market prices.

It would be interesting to disaggregate the rural land measure into its various component types such as pastureland, cultivated cropland, non-cultivated cropland, and forest. Over time, there is a great deal of conversion of one land type to another within the rural land category. However, average land values by sub-type and state were unavailable. Conducting the analysis with this finer level of detail would likely lead to smaller total land value losses as states convert less valuable rural land types into more valuable types. This gain is likely small compared to the loss from urbanization. Another limitation in this study is that the value of various renewable resources, such as groundwater and fisheries, is not included. Though these renewable resources are also likely small in value compared to the forms of capital that are included, these limitations point to the need for additional empirical work.

3.3 Physical capital

Physical capital is the stock of all buildings, homes, equipment, etc. Some of the stock of physical capital in a state is owned by investors outside of that state. This notion of inclusive wealth is the productive capital stock owned by a given state's residents.[10] So, where possible, this chapter allocates wealth based on ownership rather than location of the physical asset. This implies that migration from one state to another could have an important impact on wealth calculations.[11]

The Bureau of Economic Analysis (BEA) publishes an annual estimate of the stock of fixed reproducible tangible wealth. This includes estimates of the value of housing, consumer durable goods, and financial assets owned by households and non-profit organizations less home mortgages and other household debt. Assets owned by the government are included in the estimates. The value of assets owned by firms is not estimated directly as this should be captured by the value of corporate equities, equity in non-corporate business, and corporate bonds. The BEA constructs these estimates using the Federal Reserve Flow of Funds Accounts. Unfortunately, the BEA only publishes physical capital estimates for the nation as a whole; no data are available at the state level.

There is a great deal of state-level data on housing wealth. This chapter uses the state-level housing wealth series employed in Case, Quigley, and Shiller (2005). These estimates of housing wealth were constructed from repeat sales price indexes, state-level home ownership rates, and the number of households in each state. To simplify the analysis, all homes are assumed to be owner-occupied. This is an important limitation as about 30 percent of homes and apartments are rented rather than owned by the resident. The home value data also includes the value of the land.

To value the physical capital contained in businesses, this chapter uses the stock market holdings of all residents of the state. This allows for businesses in one state to be owned by residents of another state. The state-level stock market wealth series again comes from Case, Quigley, and Shiller (2005). These stock market estimates were constructed from the Federal Reserve Flow of Funds Accounts. For equities held by pension and mutual funds, the Survey of Consumer Finances is used to distribute the wealth to households geographically. Checking the state-level estimates against other data would have been preferred, but no alternative sources were known to the author.

Table 4 reports the housing and stock market wealth value by state in 1990 and 2000. Note that the stock market boom in the last half of the 1990s is likely responsible for an overvaluation of

---

10 This is similar to Arrow et al. (2012) where the physical capital wealth estimates depended on the ownership of physical capital, not the location of that capital.

11 Migration of people with higher than average wealth increases the wealth *per capita* of the destination state.

the true value of the physical capital owned by businesses. Using the book value rather than the market value of companies may be a better measure, though this would neglect real increases in the value of a business that are not captured by the purchase price of physical capital.

Housing and stock market wealth account for about 70 percent of the BEA estimate of the stock of physical capital. The remaining wealth is due to durable consumer goods, savings deposits, equity in non-corporate businesses, and government assets. Because there is no state-level source for these data, these types of physical capital in the analysis are ignored. This is similar to the treatment of non-energy forms of natural capital in Section 3.1 and the treatment of water areas in Section 3.2 and implies that the results here are underestimates.

The value of urban land used by businesses is included in the value of the business and thus it would be double counting to have included urban land data in the land calculations of Section 3.2. A potentially important limitation is the double counting of the value of some energy companies. To the extent that the state has transferred ownership of non-renewable resources to firms, there should be a reduction in the valuation of the non-renewable resource discussed in Section 3.1.

Despite the limitations, using housing and stock market data to value physical capital is an important contribution to the literature on sustainability. In particular, the stock market data allow for wealth accounting by ownership rather than by location. This is not a feature of the most widely-used OECD international capital stock data.

3.4 Human capital

The measure of human capital used here follows methods developed by Klenow and Rodríguez-Clare (1997) and Arrow et al. (2010). Using this method requires state-level data on the level of educational attainment and an assumed rate of return on human capital. The state-level of educational attainment data are obtained for

1990 and 2000 from the U.S. Census Bureau. Following Klenow and Rodríguez-Clare (1997) and Arrow et al. (2010), the rate of return of 0.085 is used for all states, though this could be made state-specific if there was empirical evidence suggesting that the rate of return differed by state.

The stock of human capital per capita in a state is defined as $exp(.085 \times T)$, where T is the average number of years of educational attainment in the state. The stock of human capital per capita is reported by state in Table 5 for years 1990 and 2000. The change in the stock of human capital over time comes only from the increase in the average level of education. Note that all states experienced an increase in the average level of education.

The shadow price of a unit of human capital is equal to the discounted sum of the wages it would receive (the rental price) over the expected number of working years remaining. To arrive at this shadow price, the first required step is to calculate the state-specific average annual wage as the total wage bill for the state divided by the number of workers. The total wage bill by state is obtained from the Bureau of Economic Analysis and the number of employees comes from the Bureau of Labor Statistics. The average annual wage reported in Table 5 is the average annual wage per worker (not per unit of human capital) in 1990. By dividing the average annual wage per worker by the average stock of human capital per worker, we arrive at the rental price for a unit of human capital.

This rental price for a unit of human capital is received each year over the number of working years remaining with the rental price for future years discounted at the same rate assumed to be the rate of return on education. The resulting shadow price of a unit of human capital ranges over states from about $120,000 to $200,000. The value of the change in the stock of human capital per capita is obtained by multiplying this shadow price of a unit of human capital by the difference in the stock of human capital per capita between 1990 and 2000. This value of the change in the stock of human capital is then

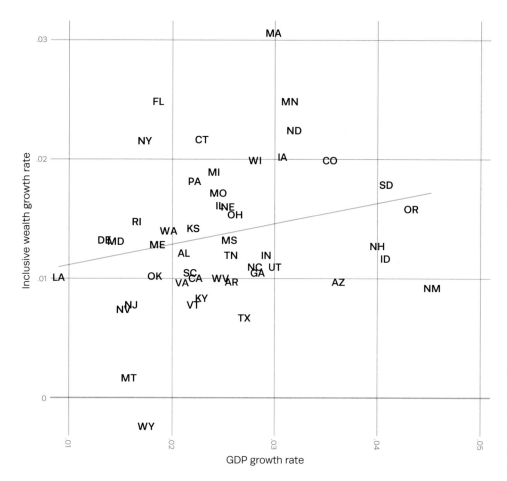

FIGURE 1

Per capita inclusive wealth
and GDP annual growth
rates

Notes: The per capita inclusive wealth
growth rate reported in Column (2) of
Table 8 is plotted against the per capita
GDP growth rate for each state along
with the linear regression line.

multiplied by the state population to arrive at the total change in the value of human capital for the state as a whole and is reported in the last column of Table 5.

3.5 Overall changes in capital: inclusive investment

Table 6 reports the value of aggregate changes in each of the forms of capital considered. Exhaustible natural capital is depleted in most states, but there is a great deal of heterogeneity with some states extracting trillions of dollars worth of energy resources over the 10-year period and other states extracting nothing. There is less heterogeneity in the decline in land capital as nearly all states experienced some loss of rural land due to development with the largest decline occurring in Florida. While there are large gains in human capital, the gains in physical capital are nearly an order of magnitude larger.

Table 7 reports the value changes in each form of capital per capita. This not only makes it easier to compare states of very different sizes, but also removes the effect of population growth. Again, physical capital gains dominate the other forms of capital. Somewhat surprisingly, the change in inclusive wealth per capita is found to be negative for Wyoming. This is because the gains in physical and human capital were not enough to overcome the US$54,000 per capita decline in natural resources over the 10-year period.

The final column of Table 7 reports that annual total factor productivity (TFP) growth rate over 1990-2000 from Sharma et al. (2007). As explained in Section 2, TFP can be thought of as another form of capital and because it has a shadow price of one, the TFP growth rate can be directly added to the growth rate of all other forms of capital in dollars.

The annual growth rate for inclusive wealth is reported in Table 8. The first column reports the inclusive wealth annual growth rate without accounting for population growth. The second column reports the inclusive wealth per capita annual growth rate. The third column adds the TFP growth rate to the inclusive wealth per capita annual growth rate reported in column (2). Finally, the fourth column reports the GDP per capita annual growth rate to serve as

FIGURE 2

Inclusive wealth + TFP growth rate

Notes: The sum of the per capita inclusive wealth growth rate and the TFP growth rate reported in Column (3) of Table 8 is plotted against the per capita GDP growth rate for each state along with the linear regression line.

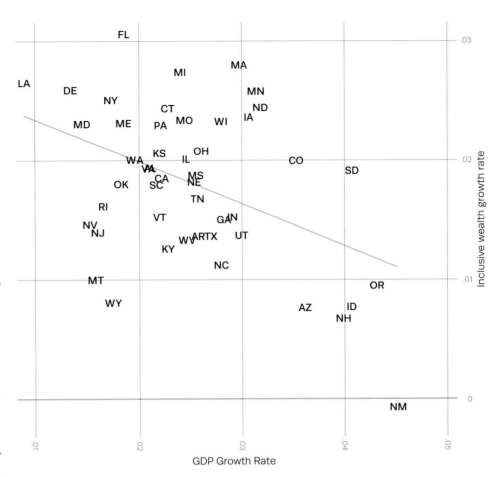

a comparison to the wealth growth rates reported in columns (2) and (3).

The relationship between the inclusive wealth per capita annual growth rate and the GDP per capita annual growth rate is illustrated in Figure 1. This figure shows that there is a slightly positive relationship but a great deal of heterogeneity. In general, GDP growth exceeds inclusive wealth growth for all but a handful of states. In New Mexico, for example, the annual growth rate for GDP per capita is 4.5 percent, the fastest growth rate in the U.S., while the annual growth rate for inclusive wealth per capita is less than 1 percent, one of the slowest growth rates. However, this does not necessarily imply that states are under-investing because Figure 1 does not include productivity growth.

Figure 2 illustrates the relationship of the sum of the TFP annual growth rate and the inclusive wealth per capita annual growth rate with the GDP per capita annual growth rate. The relationship is quite negative, implying that those states with the highest GDP growth rates tend to have lower inclusive wealth growth rates.

3.6 State–level inclusive wealth inequality

The results can also be used to investigate state-level wealth inequality. By ranking each state by its inclusive wealth per capita in 2000, a state-level inclusive wealth Lorenz Curve is created (see Figure 3). In this figure, all inhabitants of a state are assumed to have the average level of inclusive wealth of that state. The 45-degree line represents the percentage of total inclusive wealth in the 48 contiguous states owned by that percentage of the total population if all states had the same inclusive wealth per capita. The darker curved line represents the actual distribution of inclusive wealth over the population.

Figure 3 shows a very low level of wealth inequality across states. In fact, the Gini coefficient is 0.09 which represents a quite equal distribution of wealth. Financial wealth in the U.S. over households is estimated to have a Gini coefficient of 0.81, a very unequal distribution of wealth (BOVER 2010). It seems likely that the distribution of inclusive wealth would have a lower Gini coefficient than 0.81, though this is just speculation. Regardless, it seems that only a small amount of inclusive wealth inequality is due to state-level differences. It is likely that

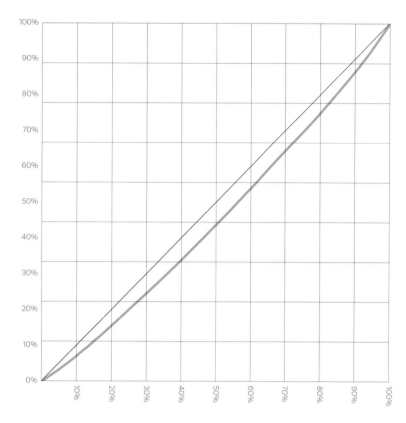

FIGURE 3

State–level inclusive wealth
Lorenz curve

Notes: This Lorenz curve shows the
distribution of inclusive wealth across
states but not within states. In this
figure all individuals within a state
are assumed to have the average
level of inclusive wealth in that state.
Calculations by the author.

inclusive wealth inequality across individuals within a state is much larger.

4. Conclusion

This chapter has applied the inclusive wealth framework to U.S. states from 1990 to 2000. The purpose is to apply this new approach of growth accounting to an environment with good data availability and reliability. One important lesson is that the rate of economic growth as measured by inclusive wealth can be quite different than the rate of economic growth implied by GDP figures. The negative slope in Figure 2 is especially meaningful as it implies that those states with high GDP growth rates tend to have much lower rates of inclusive wealth growth. This does not imply that any state is currently on an unsustainable path as all have positive inclusive investment per capita. However, the negative slope in Figure 2 does

imply that high GDP growth states are investing at much lower rates than low GDP growth states on average.

There are significant data challenges which limit applying the inclusive wealth theory empirically, even in the U.S. where data reliability and available are quite good. Data limitations, particularly in the number of capital types considered in the analysis and in the aggregation of capital assets into broad categories, are described in the paper. One important policy recommendation is for state governments to collect capital stock data in order to perform this type of inclusive wealth accounting. This would enable states to measure their rate of inclusive investment. Easy access to this type of data would make it clear to policy-makers if current GDP growth rates are sustainable in the long-run.

Despite the data challenges, this exercise produced empirical estimates of inclusive wealth growth rates that provide meaningful insights. The most important implication is that states with an inclusive wealth per capita annual growth rate that is less than their GDP per capita annual growth rate should increase inclusive investment in order to sustain higher GDP growth rates in the long-run. State governments could increase inclusive investment by encouraging education, reducing the extraction of natural resources, and increasing the construction of public infrastructure.

It is hoped that other researchers will make improvements to the methods used here by including additional forms of capital, disaggregating the forms of capital considered here, and by using more micro-data with the potential to reduce the need for broad aggregation over individuals. That the annual growth rates using these inclusive wealth figures are so different from those using the GDP figures is an indication that there is great potential for important contributions in the area of growth accounting.

State	Real GDP Per Capita 1990	Real GDP Per Capita 2000	Real GDP Per Capita Change	Real GDP Per Capita Growth Rate
Alabama	$24,142	$29,794	$5,652	2.13%
Arizona	$24,315	$34,695	$10,380	3.62%
Arkansas	$22,330	$28,849	$6,518	2.59%
California	$34,654	$43,254	$8,600	2.24%
Colorado	$31,833	$45,089	$13,256	3.54%
Connecticut	$43,245	$54,302	$11,057	2.30%
Delaware	$52,008	$59,595	$7,587	1.37%
Florida	$28,377	$34,198	$5,821	1.88%
Georgia	$30,272	$40,062	$9,790	2.84%
Idaho	$20,349	$30,329	$9,980	4.07%
Illinois	$33,835	$43,186	$9,351	2.47%
Indiana	$27,309	$36,429	$9,119	2.92%
Iowa	$26,559	$35,957	$9,398	3.08%
Kansas	$29,203	$36,359	$7,156	2.22%
Kentucky	$25,253	$31,691	$6,438	2.30%
Louisiana	$34,264	$37,597	$3,333	0.93%
Maine	$27,092	$32,603	$5,511	1.87%
Maryland	$34,122	$39,486	$5,364	1.47%
Massachusetts	$35,288	$47,355	$12,067	2.98%
Michigan	$29,386	$37,282	$7,896	2.41%
Minnesota	$31,403	$42,801	$11,397	3.14%
Mississippi	$20,722	$26,679	$5,957	2.56%
Missouri	$28,675	$36,530	$7,855	2.45%
Montana	$24,353	$28,547	$4,193	1.60%
Nebraska	$29,558	$38,028	$8,469	2.55%
Nevada	$37,398	$43,630	$6,232	1.55%
New Hampshire	$26,578	$39,292	$12,713	3.99%
New Jersey	$39,714	$46,647	$6,934	1.62%
New Mexico	$20,669	$32,144	$11,475	4.51%
New York	$38,207	$45,438	$7,231	1.75%
North Carolina	$29,683	$39,155	$9,472	2.81%
North Dakota	$24,201	$33,130	$8,930	3.19%
Ohio	$29,153	$37,761	$8,608	2.62%
Oklahoma	$26,597	$31,937	$5,340	1.85%
Oregon	$23,155	$35,338	$12,183	4.32%
Pennsylvania	$29,543	$36,828	$7,285	2.23%
Rhode Island	$30,905	$36,504	$5,599	1.68%
South Carolina	$26,173	$32,512	$6,339	2.19%
South Dakota	$23,817	$35,533	$11,716	4.08%
Tennessee	$26,931	$34,735	$7,803	2.58%
Texas	$31,887	$41,659	$9,772	2.71%
Utah	$26,386	$35,488	$9,102	3.01%
Vermont	$26,273	$32,738	$6,465	2.22%
Virginia	$34,069	$41,977	$7,908	2.11%
Washington	$36,029	$43,839	$7,810	1.98%
West Virginia	$21,455	$27,422	$5,966	2.48%
Wisconsin	$28,088	$37,061	$8,973	2.81%
Wyoming	$39,314	$46,844	$7,530	1.77%

TABLE 1

Real GDP per capita growth rate by state

Notes: GDP is in chained 2005 dollars. Data from the BEA and the U.S. Census Bureau. Calculations by the author.

TABLE 2
Exhaustible natural capital

Notes: Data from the U.S. Energy Information Administration.
Oil is measured in millions of barrels; natural gas is measured
in billions of cubic feet; and coal is measured in millions of
short tons. Calculations by the author.

State	Oil 1990	Oil Extracted 1990–2000	Coal 1990	Coal Extracted 1990–2000	Natural Gas 1990	Natural Gas Extracted 1990–2000
Alabama	180	90	4,546	247	9,046	3,057
Arizona	0	0	327	119	0	0
Arkansas	169	79	102	1	15,280	1,819
California	8,116	2,899	50	1	7,985	2,539
Colorado	716	251	16,585	240	39,100	4,676
Florida	95	56	0	0	97	58
Georgia	0	0	50	0	0	0
Idaho	0	0	50	0	0	0
Illinois	288	134	9,967	491	0	0
Indiana	44	18	9,967	320	0	0
Iowa	0	0	2,200	0	0	0
Kansas	1,029	429	406	4	13,322	6,059
Kentucky	69	30	32,062	1,563	4,251	657
Louisiana	1,973	1,007	471	33	48,956	14,771
Maryland	0	0	480	37	0	0
Michigan	206	115	50	0	6,683	1,777
Mississippi	632	202	128	1	2,869	1,016
Missouri	0	0	6,016	12	0	0
Montana	755	160	119,796	394	2,427	497
Nebraska	73	41	0	0	0	0
New Mexico	1,913	636	12,532	262	43,172	13,097
North Carolina	0	0	50	0	0	0
New York	0	0	0	0	771	189
North Dakota	0	0	9,507	304	2,089	468
Ohio	156	74	23,628	290	2,838	1,145
Oklahoma	1,935	780	1,533	17	55,746	16,976
Oregon	0	0	50	0	0	0
Pennsylvania	40	13	28,329	660	10,046	1,353
South Dakota	0	0	50	0	0	0
Tennessee	0	0	471	42	0	0
Texas	13,977	5,330	13,179	538	184,707	47,230
Utah	719	170	5,688	244	12,073	1,570
Virginia	0	0	2,167	380	4,487	433
Washington	0	0	1,383	48	0	0
West Virginia	52	19	35,140	1,627	9,679	1,709
Wyoming	1,750	724	68,148	2,491	59,387	7,959

State	Rural Land Area 1990	Rural Land Area 2000	Average Value per Acre	Total Value of Change
Alabama	29,389.5	28,705.4	$1,613	–$1,103.2
Arizona	40,937.2	40,778.3	$1,075	–$170.9
Arkansas	28,799.3	28,434.4	$1,258	–$459.2
California	48,720.5	47,415.6	$282	–$367.5
Colorado	41,123.1	40,820.9	$666	–$201.1
Connecticut	2,157.6	2,064.5	$7,616	–$709.0
Delaware	1,030.2	980.8	$3,123	–$154.4
Florida	27,371.5	26,008.8	$2,701	–$3,680.5
Georgia	31,960.9	30,619.5	$1,613	–$2,163.5
Idaho	18,847.4	18,567.0	$1,075	–$301.5
Illinois	32,049.2	31,690.2	$2,330	–$836.3
Indiana	20,380.9	20,066.1	$2,074	–$652.8
Iowa	33,731.9	33,567.1	$1,728	–$284.9
Kansas	49,832.3	49,626.0	$685	–$141.3
Kentucky	22,706.8	22,175.0	$1,600	–$850.9
Louisiana	24,935.1	24,600.0	$1,382	–$463.2
Maine	18,940.7	18,751.8	$1,446	–$273.2
Maryland	4,967.6	4,685.1	$3,968	–$1,120.8
Massachusetts	3,607.4	3,273.3	$6,477	–$2,164.2
Michigan	29,812.5	29,102.7	$1,702	–$1,208.4
Minnesota	45,641.0	45,291.4	$1,216	–$425.1
Mississippi	26,768.1	26,304.2	$1,134	–$526.1
Missouri	39,596.8	39,166.0	$1,126	–$485.2
Montana	65,077.1	65,036.9	$355	–$14.3
Nebraska	47,377.0	47,270.2	$742	–$79.3
Nevada	10,214.1	10,049.9	$370	–$60.8
New Hampshire	4,451.8	4,316.9	$2,880	–$388.5
New Jersey	3,135.1	2,825.2	$8,960	–$2,777.2
New Mexico	50,556.9	50,129.7	$268	–$114.3
New York	26,897.9	26,349.9	$1,638	–$897.8
North Carolina	25,582.0	24,398.2	$2,240	–$2,651.7
North Dakota	41,601.0	41,444.4	$477	–$74.8
Ohio	22,486.1	21,847.6	$2,240	–$1,430.2
Oklahoma	41,004.2	40,701.6	$700	–$211.9
Oregon	29,079.4	28,796.3	$1,080	–$305.9
Pennsylvania	24,642.7	23,753.4	$2,816	–$2,504.3
Rhode Island	465.6	445.1	$8,320	–$170.6
South Carolina	16,483.8	15,823.5	$1,715	–$1,132.5
South Dakota	44,553.6	44,438.1	$387	–$44.6
Tennessee	22,959.3	22,218.2	$1,715	–$1,271.1
Texas	158,454.2	156,840.3	$672	–$1,084.5
Utah	17,549.4	17,618.0	$909	$62.4
Vermont	5,211.8	5,125.5	$1,856	–$160.2
Virginia	20,342.8	19,744.5	$2,202	–$1,317.2
Washington	28,791.7	28,318.7	$1,370	–$647.9
West Virginia	13,459.4	13,102.7	$1,178	–$420.0
Wisconsin	30,644.3	30,311.3	$1,331	–$443.3
Wyoming	32,855.9	32,784.5	$246	–$17.5

TABLE 3

Non–federal rural land value

Notes: Land is reported in thousands of acres. The value of the change in rural land is reported in millions of 2005 dollars.

TABLE 4

Physical capital

Notes: The value is measured in millions of 2005 dollars.

State	Housing Wealth 1990	Housing Wealth 2000	Stock Market Wealth 1990	Stock Market Wealth 2000
Alabama	$59,507.7	$84,224.8	$50,004.4	$133,836.4
Arizona	$77,664.9	$130,482.6	$90,729.0	$262,553.1
Arkansas	$28,330.7	$37,328.6	$31,520.7	$71,681.1
California	$1,327,167.8	$1,344,377.8	$742,211.8	$2,010,736.0
Colorado	$74,425.9	$159,984.6	$152,113.5	$522,204.7
Connecticut	$156,864.0	$141,777.2	$116,999.0	$423,787.2
Delaware	$20,286.8	$23,382.2	$27,625.1	$68,840.9
Florida	$285,305.0	$373,479.7	$351,464.3	$1,613,398.7
Georgia	$121,092.1	$194,106.5	$101,459.6	$276,799.1
Idaho	$14,933.9	$27,518.8	$22,017.6	$59,188.9
Illinois	$262,500.6	$345,320.9	$314,871.4	$836,122.2
Indiana	$88,394.7	$130,318.2	$103,464.3	$240,530.4
Iowa	$35,738.1	$49,749.5	$83,855.9	$229,912.3
Kansas	$37,551.2	$45,737.1	$90,522.1	$193,811.9
Kentucky	$48,844.9	$74,839.6	$53,536.9	$96,028.2
Louisiana	$60,281.6	$80,441.7	$59,790.1	$128,326.9
Maine	$25,562.8	$25,689.5	$25,411.6	$60,588.7
Maryland	$166,633.4	$186,286.0	$140,308.9	$326,424.2
Massachusetts	$219,328.2	$237,960.5	$226,781.6	$1,023,827.5
Michigan	$171,723.2	$252,387.7	$265,080.2	$721,585.0
Minnesota	$90,747.9	$138,077.0	$185,931.4	$620,933.4
Mississippi	$29,210.8	$41,121.3	$24,998.3	$81,407.9
Missouri	$86,748.6	$116,565.6	$176,251.2	$426,377.5
Montana	$10,185.0	$17,180.7	$22,388.0	$61,556.2
Nebraska	$21,758.5	$31,234.9	$55,940.1	$129,394.9
Nevada	$26,556.9	$51,321.9	$22,683.8	$88,132.4
New Hampshire	$32,676.0	$34,157.9	$30,355.3	$77,861.0
New Jersey	$318,604.7	$308,545.8	$577,153.3	$812,277.8
New Mexico	$26,209.0	$42,290.3	$28,859.4	$77,076.2
New York	$444,422.7	$442,301.0	$609,043.2	$1,996,242.9
North Carolina	$117,904.9	$172,848.3	$111,551.8	$282,736.7
North Dakota	$6,606.6	$8,403.9	$13,259.8	$53,275.0
Ohio	$205,327.7	$277,324.5	$287,050.9	$653,173.7
Oklahoma	$42,246.3	$53,825.9	$48,006.5	$118,799.3
Oregon	$51,798.4	$98,752.5	$74,811.3	$208,450.4
Pennsylvania	$273,139.5	$286,023.3	$314,506.8	$866,540.5
Rhode Island	$32,431.2	$29,258.3	$22,153.5	$61,670.1
South Carolina	$56,203.9	$80,698.6	$42,308.9	$104,826.6
South Dakota	$6,911.8	$10,245.6	$19,402.9	$49,856.8
Tennessee	$79,389.4	$118,926.5	$75,021.2	$198,577.0
Texas	$266,619.0	$365,907.7	$301,788.2	$694,792.7
Utah	$29,735.5	$69,962.9	$30,065.7	$83,887.6
Vermont	$11,600.7	$11,702.0	$26,638.2	$37,763.1
Virginia	$174,970.3	$194,299.9	$150,218.4	$324,737.7
Washington	$136,665.6	$214,529.6	$138,605.6	$368,360.6
West Virginia	$23,754.0	$30,513.2	$19,235.4	$47,028.6
Wisconsin	$81,210.5	$121,490.9	$140,439.7	$418,154.2
Wyoming	$6,315.1	$10,079.6	$16,364.8	$29,134.4

State	Housing Wealth 1990	Housing Wealth 2000	Stock Market Wealth 1990	Stock Market Wealth 2000
Alabama	2.79	2.87	$39,969	$22,925.8
Arizona	2.90	2.95	$43,551	$17,833.9
Arkansas	2.76	2.84	$36,382	$12,778.4
California	2.92	2.97	$56,101	$124,622.2
Colorado	3.01	3.09	$48,326	$30,984.5
Connecticut	2.99	3.07	$57,889	$27,353.3
Delaware	2.91	2.98	$48,695	$5,211.0
Florida	2.86	2.93	$42,837	$83,482.6
Georgia	2.85	2.95	$45,166	$62,943.0
Idaho	2.87	2.94	$39,480	$5,776.8
Illinois	2.90	2.98	$49,681	$93,822.0
Indiana	2.84	2.91	$41,514	$33,641.1
Iowa	2.86	2.94	$37,268	$15,957.5
Kansas	2.92	3.00	$40,806	$15,750.7
Kentucky	2.76	2.85	$39,475	$23,303.6
Louisiana	2.80	2.86	$39,758	$17,258.2
Maine	2.88	2.96	$39,600	$7,143.7
Maryland	2.98	3.07	$50,254	$39,998.9
Massachusetts	2.99	3.10	$54,686	$65,028.8
Michigan	2.86	2.94	$48,688	$70,336.0
Minnesota	2.93	3.02	$45,264	$41,342.2
Mississippi	2.77	2.83	$35,841	$10,145.8
Missouri	2.85	2.93	$42,288	$34,547.2
Montana	2.90	2.98	$35,529	$4,213.8
Nebraska	2.90	2.98	$38,743	$10,004.7
Nevada	2.84	2.88	$45,029	$7,072.3
New Hampshire	2.96	3.04	$43,828	$7,822.3
New Jersey	2.94	3.03	$54,963	$69,080.9
New Mexico	2.89	2.95	$39,850	$6,081.8
New York	2.92	3.00	$56,937	$129,579.0
North Carolina	2.82	2.92	$41,916	$59,764.1
North Dakota	2.86	2.93	$34,950	$3,297.5
Ohio	2.85	2.93	$43,822	$75,764.4
Oklahoma	2.85	2.91	$39,944	$12,523.7
Oregon	2.92	2.99	$43,573	$18,134.9
Pennsylvania	2.86	2.94	$45,092	$82,707.0
Rhode Island	2.88	2.96	$44,629	$6,346.2
South Carolina	2.81	2.89	$39,706	$22,745.3
South Dakota	2.85	2.94	$33,436	$3,942.4
Tennessee	2.79	2.88	$40,321	$34,681.3
Texas	2.87	2.92	$45,492	$80,703.3
Utah	2.95	3.01	$40,274	$9,166.4
Vermont	2.96	3.05	$39,112	$3,821.2
Virginia	2.93	3.03	$49,184	$58,633.1
Washington	2.95	3.03	$50,814	$37,676.8
West Virginia	2.75	2.82	$38,317	$7,804.1
Wisconsin	2.87	2.95	$40,726	$36,256.4
Wyoming	2.90	2.96	$39,080	$2,078.0

TABLE 5

Human capital

Notes: The value of the change in human capital is measured in millions of 2005 dollars.

TABLE 6

Change in comprehensive wealth (millions of 2005 dollars)

Notes: The value of the change in human capital is measured in millions of 2005 dollars.

State	Natural Capital 2000–1990	Land Capital 2000–1990	Physical Capital 2000–1990	Human Capital 2000–1990	Total Change 2000–1990	Annual Growth Rate
Alabama	−$1,629.8	−$1,103.2	$108,549.2	$22,925.8	$128,742.0	1.24%
Arizona	−$289.4	−$170.9	$224,641.9	$17,833.9	$242,015.5	1.81%
Arkansas	−$695.6	−$459.2	$49,158.2	$12,778.4	$60,781.8	1.07%
California	−$9,821.3	−$367.5	$1,285,734.3	$124,622.2	$1,400,167.7	1.25%
Colorado	−$2,517.6	−$201.1	$455,649.8	$30,984.5	$483,915.6	2.97%
Connecticut		−$709.0	$291,701.4	$27,353.3	$318,345.7	2.19%
Delaware		−$154.4	$44,311.2	$5,211.0	$49,367.8	1.72%
Florida	−$191.8	−$3,680.5	$1,350,109.0	$83,482.6	$1,429,719.3	3.19%
Georgia		−$2,163.5	$248,353.8	$62,943.0	$309,133.3	1.36%
Idaho		−$301.5	$49,756.2	$5,776.8	$55,231.5	1.77%
Illinois	−$1,619.4	−$836.3	$604,071.0	$93,822.0	$695,437.3	1.69%
Indiana	−$835.4	−$652.8	$178,989.6	$33,641.1	$211,142.5	1.28%
Iowa		−$284.9	$160,067.8	$15,957.5	$175,740.4	2.10%
Kansas	−$2,844.9	−$141.3	$111,475.7	$15,750.7	$124,240.2	1.56%
Kentucky	−$4,056.2	−$850.9	$68,486.1	$23,303.6	$86,882.6	0.86%
Louisiana	−$6,868.8	−$463.2	$88,696.9	$17,258.2	$98,623.1	0.97%
Maine		−$273.2	$35,303.9	$7,143.7	$42,174.4	1.22%
Maryland	−$90.0	−$1,120.8	$205,768.0	$39,998.9	$244,556.1	1.42%
Massachusetts		−$2,164.2	$815,678.2	$65,028.8	$878,542.8	3.20%
Michigan	−797.2	−$1,208.4	$537,169.3	$70,336.0	$605,499.7	1.93%
Minnesota		−$425.1	$482,331.0	$41,342.2	$523,248.1	2.86%
Mississippi	−$890.7	−$526.1	$68,320.1	$10,145.8	$77,049.1	1.39%
Missouri	−$29.2	−$485.2	$279,943.3	$34,547.2	$313,976.1	1.87%
Montana	−$1,586.9	−$14.3	$46,163.9	$4,213.8	$48,776.5	0.94%
Nebraska	−$130.1	−$79.3	$82,931.1	$10,004.7	$92,726.4	1.77%
Nevada		−$60.8	$90,213.6	$7,072.3	$97,225.1	1.68%
New Hampshire		−$388.5	$48,987.6	$7,822.3	$56,421.4	1.46%
New Jersey		−$2,777.2	$225,065.7	$69,080.9	$291,369.4	0.87%
New Mexico	−$5,841.0	−$114.3	$64,298.2	$6,081.8	$64,424.7	1.42%
New York	−$46.0	−$897.8	$1,385,078.0	$129,579.0	$1,513,713.2	2.19%
North Carolina		−$2,651.7	$226,128.3	$59,764.1	$283,240.7	1.33%
North Dakota	−$853.1	−$74.8	$41,812.3	$3,297.5	$44,181.9	2.18%
Ohio	−$1,218.6	−$1,430.2	$438,119.5	$75,764.4	$511,235.1	1.50%
Oklahoma	−$6,645.6	−$211.9	$82,372.3	$12,523.7	$88,038.5	1.10%
Oregon		−$305.9	$180,593.1	$18,134.9	$198,422.1	2.02%
Pennsylvania	−$1,975.4	−$2,504.3	$564,917.4	$82,707.0	$643,144.7	1.74%
Rhode Island		−$170.6	$36,343.7	$6,346.2	$42,519.3	1.42%
South Carolina		−$1,132.5	$87,012.4	$22,745.3	$108,625.2	1.15%
South Dakota		−$44.6	$33,787.7	$3,942.4	$37,685.5	1.96%
Tennessee	−$102.1	−$1,271.1	$163,093.0	$34,681.3	$196,401.1	1.37%
Texas	−$29,712.2	−$1,084.5	$492,293.3	$80,703.3	$542,199.9	0.98%
Utah	−$1,514.8	$62.4	$94,049.3	$9,166.4	$101,763.3	1.72%
Vermont		−$160.2	$11,226.2	$3,821.2	$14,887.2	0.84%
Virginia	−$1,029.5	−$1,317.2	$193,848.9	$58,633.1	$250,135.3	1.09%
Washington	−116.7	−$647.9	$307,619.0	$37,676.8	$344,531.2	1.80%
West Virginia	−4,432.8	−$420.0	$34,552.5	$7,804.1	$37,503.8	0.82%
Wisconsin		−$443.3	$317,995.0	$36,256.4	$353,808.1	2.18%
Wyoming	−$10,291.7	−$17.5	$16,534.2	$2,078.0	$8,303.0	0.26%

TABLE 7

Change in comprehensive wealth per capita (2005 dollars)

State	Natural Capital 2000–1990	Land Capital 2000–1990	Physical Capital 2000–1990	Human Capital 2000–1990	Total Change 2000–1990	Annual Growth Rate	TFP Growth Rate
Alabama	–$676	–$1,309	$21,932	$11,871	$31,819	1.24%	1.45%
Arizona	–$118	–$3,478	$30,300	$7,952	$34,656	0.99%	0.25%
Arkansas	–$491	–$2,033	$15,280	$11,029	$23,785	0.99%	0.99%
California	–$399	–$65	$29,601	$8,602	$37,738	1.02%	1.56%
Colorado	–$4,315	–$2,007	$89,052	$13,996	$96,726	2.04%	0.72%
Connecticut		–$387	$82,506	$16,155	$98,273	2.22%	1.08%
Delaware		–$914	$45,660	$12,392	$57,139	1.35%	2.14%
Florida	–$17	–$1,301	$74,902	$11,809	$85,393	2.55%	1.52%
Georgia	–$4	–$1,922	$23,013	$15,938	$37,025	1.07%	1.08%
Idaho	–$27	–$4,665	$30,204	$10,323	$35,835	1.19%	0.06%
Illinois	–$305	–$587	$44,550	$15,521	$59,180	1.65%	1.13%
Indiana	–$524	–$777	$26,341	$11,214	$36,254	1.22%	0.96%
Iowa	–$98	–$1,160	$52,484	$10,794	$62,020	2.07%	1.14%
Kansas	–$1,294	–$1,136	$37,330	$11,701	$46,601	1.45%	1.39%
Kentucky	–$2,890	–$1,076	$14,475	$12,754	$23,263	0.85%	1.00%
Louisiana	–$1,793	–$560	$18,257	$8,999	$24,903	1.03%	2.54%
Maine		–$1,014	$26,153	$11,837	$36,976	1.31%	1.84%
Maryland	–$40	–$608	$32,565	$16,292	$48,208	1.34%	1.80%
Massachusetts		–$550	$124,179	$19,532	$143,161	3.14%	0.61%
Michigan	–$97	–$474	$50,919	$15,041	$65,389	1.94%	1.74%
Minnesota		–$1,488	$90,770	$15,398	$104,680	2.55%	0.93%
Mississippi	–$424	–$1,305	$21,986	$8,796	$29,053	1.35%	1.26%
Missouri	–$249	–$831	$45,546	$12,569	$57,034	1.76%	1.42%
Montana	–$43,909	–$3,320	$46,441	$10,769	$9,981	0.16%	1.37%
Nebraska	–$87	–$1,769	$44,596	$10,986	$53,725	1.64%	0.90%
Nevada		–$1,258	$28,691	$6,887	$34,320	0.75%	1.35%
New Hampshire		–$1,509	$33,614	$12,576	$44,681	1.30%	–0.17%
New Jersey		–$619	$17,467	$17,294	$34,142	0.79%	1.23%
New Mexico	–$8,323	–$1,533	$29,326	$8,166	$27,635	0.94%	–0.73%
New York	–$3	–$175	$69,841	$15,001	$84,664	2.21%	1.18%
North Carolina	–$3	–$1,844	$21,920	$15,265	$35,338	1.12%	0.56%
North Dakota	–$1,552	–$303	$65,023	$10,063	$73,230	2.30%	1.01%
Ohio	–$346	–$331	$36,551	$13,470	$49,345	1.57%	1.29%
Oklahoma	–$2,585	–$872	$21,301	$8,460	$26,304	1.04%	1.48%
Oregon	–$7	–$1,922	$45,249	$11,210	$54,529	1.62%	–0.15%
Pennsylvania	–$351	–$389	$44,415	$14,532	$58,206	1.86%	1.27%
Rhode Island		–$331	$32,206	$13,313	$45,187	1.51%	0.78%
South Carolina		–$1,335	$17,956	$12,228	$28,849	1.07%	1.44%
South Dakota	–$14	–$1,990	$41,760	$10,432	$50,189	1.83%	0.83%
Tennessee	–$51	–$1,370	$24,098	$12,709	$35,385	1.22%	1.15%
Texas	–$2,744	–$1,215	$17,292	$8,557	$21,889	0.68%	1.30%
Utah	–$3,200	–$2,086	$33,979	$8,524	$37,215	1.12%	0.87%
Vermont		–$1,537	$13,367	$12,793	$24,622	0.79%	1.39%
Virginia	–$273	–$1,089	$20,722	$16,674	$36,033	0.98%	1.70%
Washington	–$137	–$1,485	$42,440	$13,896	$54,714	1.43%	1.34%
West Virginia	–$2,847	–$303	$18,930	$10,606	$26,386	1.02%	0.92%
Wisconsin		–$813	$55,199	$12,794	$67,180	2.04%	1.13%
Wyoming	–$54,470	–$1,498	$29,366	$8,684	–$17,918	–0.26%	1.55%

TABLE 8

Annual growth rates

State	Inclusive Wealth			GDP Per
	Total (1)	Per Capita (2)	+TFP (3)	Capita (4)
Alabama	1.24%	1.24%	2.69%	2.13%
Arizona	1.81%	0.99%	1.24%	3.62%
Arkansas	1.07%	0.99%	1.98%	2.59%
California	1.25%	1.02%	2.58%	2.24%
Colorado	2.97%	2.04%	2.76%	3.54%
Connecticut	2.19%	2.22%	3.30%	2.30%
Delaware	1.72%	1.35%	3.49%	1.37%
Florida	3.19%	2.55%	4.07%	1.88%
Georgia	1.36%	1.07%	2.15%	2.84%
Idaho	1.77%	1.19%	1.25%	4.07%
Illinois	1.69%	1.65%	2.78%	2.47%
Indiana	1.28%	1.22%	2.18%	2.92%
Iowa	2.10%	2.07%	3.21%	3.08%
Kansas	1.56%	1.45%	2.84%	2.22%
Kentucky	0.86%	0.85%	1.85%	2.30%
Louisiana	0.97%	1.03%	3.57%	0.93%
Maine	1.22%	1.31%	3.15%	1.87%
Maryland	1.42%	1.34%	3.14%	1.47%
Massachusetts	3.20%	3.14%	3.75%	2.98%
Michigan	1.93%	1.94%	3.68%	2.41%
Minnesota	2.86%	2.55%	3.48%	3.14%
Mississippi	1.39%	1.35%	2.61%	2.56%
Missouri	1.87%	1.76%	3.18%	2.45%
Montana	0.94%	0.16%	1.53%	1.60%
Nebraska	1.77%	1.64%	2.54%	2.55%
Nevada	1.68%	0.75%	2.10%	1.55%
New Hampshire	1.46%	1.30%	1.13%	3.99%
New Jersey	0.87%	0.79%	2.02%	1.62%
New Mexico	1.42%	0.94%	0.21%	4.51%
New York	2.19%	2.21%	3.39%	1.75%
North Carolina	1.33%	1.12%	1.68%	2.81%
North Dakota	2.18%	2.30%	3.31%	3.19%
Ohio	1.50%	1.57%	2.86%	2.62%
Oklahoma	1.10%	1.04%	2.52%	1.85%
Oregon	2.02%	1.62%	1.47%	4.32%
Pennsylvania	1.74%	1.86%	3.13%	2.23%
Rhode Island	1.42%	1.51%	2.29%	1.68%
South Carolina	1.15%	1.07%	2.51%	2.19%
South Dakota	1.96%	1.83%	2.66%	4.08%
Tennessee	1.37%	1.22%	2.37%	2.58%
Texas	0.98%	0.68%	1.98%	2.71%
Utah	1.72%	1.12%	1.99%	3.01%
Vermont	0.84%	0.79%	2.18%	2.22%
Virginia	1.09%	0.98%	2.68%	2.11%
Washington	1.80%	1.43%	2.77%	1.98%
West Virginia	0.82%	1.02%	1.94%	2.48%
Wisconsin	2.18%	2.04%	3.17%	2.81%
Wyoming	0.26%	-0.26%	1.29%	1.77%

REFERENCES

ARROW, K.J., DASGUPTA, P. & MÄLER, K.G. (2003). The genuine savings criterion and the value of population. *Economic Theory, 21*(2), 217-225.

ARROW, K., DASGUPTA, P., GOULDER, L., DAILY, G., EHRLICH, P., HEAL, G.,...WALKER, B. (2004). Are we consuming too much? *The Journal of Economic Perspectives, 18* (3), 147-172.

ARROW, K.J., DASGUPTA, P., GOULDER, L.H., MUMFORD, K. & OLESON, K. (2010). China, the U.S., and sustainability: Perspectives based on comprehensive wealth. In G. Heal (Ed.) *Is economic growth sustainable?* London: Palgrave Macmillan.

ARROW, K.J., DASGUPTA, P., GOULDER, L.H., MUMFORD, K.J. & OLESON, K. (2010). Sustainability and the measurement of wealth. *NBER Working Paper No 16599.*

BOVER, O. (2010). Wealth inequality and household structure: U.S. vs. Spain. *Review of Income and Wealth, 56*(2), 259-290.

CASE, K.E., QUIGLEY, J.M. & SHILLER, R.J. (2005). Comparing wealth effects: The stock market versus the housing market. *Advances in Macroeconomics, 5*(1), 1.

DASGUPTA, P. (2001). *Human well-being and the natural environment.* Oxford: Oxford University Press.

DASGUPTA, P. & HEAL, G. (1974). The optimal depletion of exhaustible resources. *Review of Economic Studies, 41*(1), 3-28.

HAMILTON, K. & CLEMENS, M. (1999). Genuine savings in developing countries. *The World Bank Economic Review, 13* (2), 333-56.

KLENOW, P.J. & RODRÍGUEZ-CLARE, A. (1997). The neoclassical revival in growth economics: Has it gone too far? In B. Bernanke & J. Rotemberg (Eds.) *NBER macroeconomics annual 1997.* Cambridge, MA: MIT Press.

SHARMA, S.C., SYLWESTER, K. & MARGONO, H. (2007). Decomposition of total factor productivity growth in U.S. states. *Quarterly Review of Economics and Finance, 47*(2), 215-241.

WORLD BANK. (2006). *Where is the wealth of nations?* Washington, DC: World Bank.

WORLD BANK. (2011). *The changing wealth of nations: Measuring sustainable development in the new millennium.* Washington, DC: World Bank.

Are national economies (virtually) sustainable?: an empirical analysis of natural assets in international trade

Giles Atkinson, Matthew Agarwala and Pablo Muñoz

KEY MESSAGES

This chapter explores the impact of international trade on sustainable development and the measurement of genuine (or adjusted net) savings at both the global and domestic levels.

The chapter draws crucial distinctions between production- and consumption-based approaches to measuring changes in inclusive wealth, as well as between the notions of domestic and global sustainability, where the latter is defined in terms of the global genuine savings rate.

By looking only at per–country inclusive wealth accounting, we potentially weaken our understanding of global performance. The chapter addresses this by examining how changes in resource wealth are embodied in internationally traded goods and services.

Specifically, the chapter uses a disaggregated multi-regional input-output model (MRIO) to measure the value of resource depletion and the social costs of carbon emissions in the context of international trade.

The term "virtual sustainability" is introduced here as a way to consider the implications of trade and the role of consumption in understanding a country's contribution to global sustainability.

Our empirical findings indicate that the magnitudes of the (change in) natural assets embodied in trade can be substantial, both in dollar value terms and in relation to national economies. This could challenge both the conventional thinking on sustainability and the claims of progress made on this front by individual countries.

1 Introduction

The proposition that an extended net – or genuine – saving has a central place in any portfolio of indicators purporting to measure the sustainability of development appears now to be firmly established (UNECE 2007; STIGLITZ, SEN AND FITOUSSI 2009; WORLD BANK 2010). Nevertheless, a number of outstanding issues remain. Chief among these is a question as to whether (or how) international trade affects the way in which we should think about measuring the development prospects of individual (but open) economies.

There are several candidate mechanisms whereby trade might influence sustainable development (DUPUY 2011; OLESON 2011). These include: the capital gains (or changing terms of trade more generally) on traded extracted natural resources (VINCENT, PANAYOTOU AND HARTWICK 1997) as well as remaining resource stocks (ARROW ET AL. 2010); and the possibility of trade in resources at prices which are "too low" (OLESON 2011) perhaps because trade encourages resource depletion to be "too fast" (e.g., KLEPPER AND STÄHLER 1998). In addition, considerations about "openness" also includes transboundary pollution where countries impose burdens on each other and this, in turn, has implications for the distribution of (comprehensive) wealth (HAMILTON AND ATKINSON 1996; ARROW ET AL. 2010).

Common to all of these concerns is the impression that these interactions alter in some way the comprehensive wealth accounting problem for individual countries. Reflecting on these implications is important for at least two reasons. First, the sustainability prospects for an *individual* country might be misjudged if its own wealth accounting neglects these concerns. Secondly, this neglect could misrepresent the way in which an individual country contributes to *global* sustainability. In the words of the recent authoritative report by Stiglitz et al. (2009) in focusing exclusively on per country measurement "... we miss the global nature of sustainability" (P.69).

It is this contribution of countries and regions to this global sustainability that is primarily the focus of this chapter. We develop this theme through an extension of the growing literature that uses input-output approaches to model the way in which (changes in) resource wealth and environmental liabilities are embodied in goods and services traded across national boundaries. Our specific contribution is two-fold:

First, we investigate the value of resource depletion (such as the extraction of sub-soil assets) as well as the social costs of carbon dioxide emissions within a relatively disaggregated multi-regional input-output model (MRIO). Previously, much of this literature has either focused upon the quantities of carbon emissions only (or some other pollutant) (see, for a review, WIEDMANN [2009]) or has resorted to relatively highly aggregated models in the case of natural resources (ATKINSON AND HAMILTON 2002).

Second, we use our results to comment on the contribution of individual countries (and regions) to global sustainability, where the latter can be estimated as the global genuine saving rate in a particular year. We argue that examining the magnitudes of the values of natural assets that countries consume tells us something distinct about their "virtual sustainability." There are clear parallels between the notion of virtual sustainability and the recent literature (e.g., DAVIS AND CALDEIRA 2010; ATKINSON ET AL. 2011) on virtual carbon (i.e., embodied carbon). However, the links to concerns about the influence of trade on the sustainability of development represent a useful extension of this thinking.

Our results show that taking account of these trade interactions gives a rather different perspective on the "over-consumption" of individual countries in relation to global sustainability. Moreover, the empirical magnitude of the natural resource flows or environmental liabilities in international trade appears to be substantial. We also find that the notion of embodied – that is, virtual – (un)sustainability may shed a cautionary light on economies claiming to have made progress on this front, particularly if this progress is due to changes in trade patterns. The introduction of the term "virtual sustainability" here, we argue, offers a potentially valuable lens through which the relationship between trade and sustainability can be explored.

The rest of this chapter is organized as follows. The next section reviews a broad range of literature on which our more specific contribution is premised. Section 3 discusses virtual sustainability *vis-à-vis* international trade. Section 4 sets out our methodological framework, including a description of the model and the data that we use. Section 5 presents and critically reflects on our results. Section 6 concludes.

2 Literature review

At the heart of most definitions of sustainable development is a common concern about the way in which the fruits of development are shared across generations. For example, Pezzey (1989) states that development is sustained along a development path if welfare does not decrease at any point along the path. Moreover, there is increasing evidence of a consensus around the idea that the sustainability of development can be understood through an emphasis on wealth and what is happening to wealth, broadly construed to include natural assets (see, for example, UNECE [2007]; STIGLITZ ET AL. [2009]; AND WORLD BANK [2010]). The question of measurability has long been central to this focus. In particular, there is concern about the degree to which current systems of economic indicators fail to signal clearly that the economy is on an unsustainable path. It follows that if these indicators are lacking in this vital respect, then the result is that potentially misleading signals may be translated into policy errors.

An integral element of this measurement debate has been the way in which current decisions about consumption and saving have an impact upon future welfare and, in particular, how novel but measurable indicators (of what

is happening in the "here and now") can shed light on prospects for future welfare. Pearce and Atkinson (1993) were among the first to posit a practical linkage between sustainable development and a measure of national wealth that was expanded to include natural assets. If sustainability is a matter of maintaining levels of welfare, then Pearce and Atkinson proposed that this was in turn a question of maintaining total wealth and this could be measured by savings rates adjusted to reflect depletion and environmental degradation.

Subsequently, Atkinson et al. (1997) and Hamilton and Clemens (1999) have updated both the theoretical argument linking savings and sustainability and the empirical estimation of adjusted net savings rates – dubbed "genuine" saving to distinguish it from traditional national accounting measures of net saving – for a wide range of countries. The World Bank has been publishing estimates of genuine saving as part of its *World Development Indicators* since 1999 (see, in addition, WORLD BANK [2010]).[1] As a practical matter, genuine saving is defined in these publications as gross saving plus investments in human capital (proxied by education expenditures) minus the depreciation of produced capital as well as changes in certain natural assets. The latter specifically include natural resource depletion and liabilities caused by emissions of greenhouse gases and particulate matter.

Important contributions by Dasgupta and Mäler (2000) and Asheim and Weitzman (2001) have also established further theoretical foundations to this focus on genuine saving and, more broadly, comprehensive wealth accounting.[2] The link to sustainability here is that an economy should avoid negative genuine saving

---

1   In fact, *World Development Indicators* (and other World Bank publications) refers to this indicator as "adjusted net saving." However, we retain the term "genuine saving" throughout given that this is the predominant terminology in the broader literature.

2   Dasgupta and Mäler (2000), for example, show that net investment is equal to the change in social welfare in a non–optimizing framework where a resource allocation mechanism is used to specify initial capital

if development is to be sustained: if future declines in well-being are to be circumvented. Hamilton and Hartwick (2005) and Hamilton and Withagen (2005) establish a general policy rule for sustainability. If genuine saving is always positive and not growing too quickly then a development path is sustainable.[3]

While the importance of this savings indicator appears now to be firmly established, the process of getting to this point has also been accompanied by a significant debate. Importantly, the crucial issue of resource substitutability remains largely unanswered. Put simply, we still know little about the extent to which sustainability requires that a general portfolio of assets be managed sensibly or a more specific focus on sustaining stocks of certain (critical) resources (although see, for example, KRAUTKRAEMER [2005] and MARKANDYA AND PEDROSO-GALINATO [2007]). In addition, a variety of extensions and caveats in measuring genuine saving (and in wealth accounting) have been developed to address changing populations (DASGUPTA 2001; HAMILTON 2003), technological progress (WEITZMAN AND LÖFGREN 1997), and international trade. It is this last issue that is the focus of this chapter.

A comprehensive review of the possible relationships between trade and sustainability is provided by Dupuy (2011). While this indicates a number of candidate linkages, the focus within the wealth accounting literature has been far narrower. Much of the discussion has focused on assessment of how future capital gains arising from resources affect the way in which income or genuine saving should be measured now (see, for example, SEFTON AND WEALE [1996] and HARTWICK [1994]). That is, if resource prices are increasing (decreasing) then this has

the effect of boosting (shrinking) the genuine saving rate of a resource exporter (VINCENT, PANAYOTOU AND HARTWICK 1997) and vice versa for importers. Hamilton and Bolt (2004) estimate these capital gains for a large cross-section of resource exporting countries and, in doing so, indicate that these magnitudes tend not be large (i.e., less than 1 percent of gross national income or GNI) although, in some part, this is explained by the apparent lack of a statistically significant price trend for oil resources. Arrow et al. (2010) add further empirical insight to this work by estimating the capital gains "earned" by resource stocks in the ground.

This emphasis on capital gains (or losses) is a somewhat different focus than that implicit in the question posed by, for example, Martinez-Alier (1995) in his initial observation that estimates of genuine saving tended to suggest that unsustainable countries were located (for the most part) in the developing world. The link to trade, in turn, arose from Martinez-Alier's later speculation about whether an "ecological balance of payments" analysis would show that developed countries were actually unsustainable because those economies are relatively dependent on the import of resources from developing nations. Proposals for adjusting the saving rates of importing and exporting countries to take account of these international flows, however, need to be treated with care. Atkinson and Hamilton (2002), for example, express reservations at this interpretation in arguing that the onus is on resource extracting countries to make provision for the loss of their domestic natural assets whether for export or not.

This is not to say, however, that there is no rationale for adjusting saving rates in the presence of international trade. Stiglitz et al. (2009), for example, note the potential for a disparity between the (market) price at which some natural resources are traded and the actual scarcity value of these resources. What this means is that if no such mismatch exists then the fact that a resource is traded implies no further insights about how depletion should be accounted for in the genuine saving of either exporter or

---

stocks can be mapped to future stocks and flows in this economy.

3   Specifically, this means that genuine saving must grow at a percentage rate less or equal to the interest rate over a development path. Thus, for example, a constant and positive rate of genuine saving will ensure that both current utility and the present value of utility are increasing everywhere along the path.

importer. The genuine saving of the exporter should be measured to reflect the fact that the value of an asset that it owns has declined. For the importer, the value of resource imports already appears as a negative entry in the country's net foreign balance. Nevertheless, if the resource is traded at a price below its actual scarcity value then, by implication, the importer has not fully compensated the exporter in making this exchange.

There has been some discussion of the reasons why such disparities might occur (see, for a review, DUPUY [2011]). Explanations have been attributed to the nature of trade itself in perhaps giving rise to incentives which quicken the pace of resource depletion (KLEPPER AND STÄHLER 1998) or policy failures within, for example, the exporting country (ARROW ET AL. 2004; MYERS AND KENT 2000) or perhaps some combination of these two factors (see, for a discussion, COPELAND AND GULATI [2006], WTO [2010], and OLESON [2011]). It is this divergence that underpins claims that importers of (underpriced) resources are "buying sustainability" at the expense of exporters. In such cases, there might be arguments for imputing a liability to importers in recognition of their consumption of "under-valued" resources. Any such liability is, however, *notional* in the sense that this does not correspond to an actual transaction. Nevertheless, it seems useful to consider the nature of these international linkages in sustainability indicator construction as a supplement to existing efforts.[4]

A handful of contributions have sought to quantify these natural resource links including PROOPS ET AL. (1999), BAILEY AND CLARKE (2000), ATKINSON AND HAMILTON (2002) and, more recently, OLESON (2011). Of course, a growing and parallel literature has also emerged to examine the "embodied" or "virtual carbon" in international trade. Under the Kyoto Protocol, Annex B (developed) countries are committed to greenhouse gas emissions restrictions (including carbon dioxide, CO_2) while in an attempt to take account of historical responsibility and development concerns, developing countries are not (PETERS ET AL. 2011). Numerous authors have noted that trade in "virtual" carbon allows developed countries (in effect) to "offshore" their emissions by importing carbon intensive goods (PETERS AND HERTWICH 2008).[5]

Studies that have sought to measure the virtual carbon that are embodied in flows of goods and services traded across national boundaries include Lenzen et al. (2007), Peters and Hertwich (2008), Wiedmann et al. (2010), and Atkinson et al. (2010). Davis and Caldeira (2010) and Peters et al. (2011) find that carbon embodied in internationally traded goods and services accounted for 23 percent (6.2 gigatons) of total CO_2 emissions in 2004, and 26 percent (7.8 gigatons) for 2008, respectively. Both studies indicate that the majority of embodied carbon flows as exports from developing countries

4   Resource security concerns of importers reliant on particular exporting countries or particular strategically critical resources might also motivate further empirical examination of these trade linkages. Oleson (2011) stretches this point further by asserting that this security of importers might also be compromised potentially by relying on resources from countries which have negative genuine saving. While this seems an intriguing claim, it would be interesting to add further substance to this assertion and the nature of the linkages it implies. If, however, importers are altruistic then they have concern about resource depletion or even perhaps negative genuine saving in exporting countries (Atkinson and Hamilton 2002; Oleson 2011). So while such findings could form the basis of policies

to assist exporters in adopting prudent resource and public investment policies. This suggests, once more, the need for complementary and additional indicators rather than say an alternative method for calculating genuine saving.

5   For these reasons, MRIO has been employed to address questions such as the difference between the production and consumption emissions of countries. Baiocchi and Minx (2010) and Wiedmann et al. (2010), for example, confirm the insights drawn from the more rudimentary analysis in Helm et al. (2007) and thus recast the story of U.K. carbon emissions over the past two decades or so. Critically, it appears, while the U.K. has had relative success in reducing its production emissions within its own borders, there is evidence of an ever growing reliance on virtual carbon produced elsewhere.

to the developed world. Wiedmann (2009) and Wiedmann et al. (2007) provide extensive reviews of this growing literature.

A key distinction here is between production emissions (of carbon dioxide) and consumption emissions. The former are simply those CO_2 emissions generated domestically (i.e., in the production of a country's gross domestic product). The latter are flows of virtual carbon and specifically the CO_2 implicitly consumed in order to satisfy a country's domestic final demand. Multiple techniques have been developed in an attempt to track such emissions flows, both direct and indirect, at the global, regional, and national levels of analysis. This includes life cycle assessments (OLESON 2011), material flow analysis, ecological footprints (WACKERNAGEL ET AL. 2000), and bilateral analysis (SATO AND MARTIN 2011). The most prominent approach, however, appears to be variants of input-output analysis particularly utilizing multi-regional models. These MRIO approaches contain considerable detail about trade links between economic sectors across countries or regional groupings.[6]

While some of this carbon accounting literature has begun to turn to important policy questions, there has been little if any emphasis on the links to earlier contributions which

highlighted questions about sustainability and resource trade. However, these parallels are not only worth making once again but also are sufficiently interesting to explore further. The case of carbon emissions relates naturally to our previous discussion about accounting for (notional) liabilities. That is, these emissions contribute to the accumulation of a global liability. In this way, CO_2 emissions contribute negatively to genuine saving. The relevant question is how individual countries should account for this liability. This question, however, appears to have at least two plausible (but different) answers.

First, Arrow et al. (2010) estimate the deduction to be the climate change damage that will arise in a particular country as a result of global emissions in a given year. Put another way, if any economy wishes to stay on a sustainable path then it must, other things being equal, save enough to cover the value of damages that occur within its national boundaries *regardless* of the geographical origin of the (current) emission source that gives rise to this damage.

Second, World Bank (VARIOUS YEARS)[7], Hamilton and Atkinson (1996), and Hamilton and Clemens (1999) estimate the deduction as the social cost of a country's CO_2 emissions. Put another way, this country is accounting for the liability it accumulates in the form of total damages that its own emissions cause, *regardless* of the geographical destination in which these damages are felt.

The critical distinction in these alternative approaches is the assumption that these make about responsibility (ATKINSON AND HAMILTON 2007). If we assume that countries are individually responsible for bearing the burden of environmental damages that occur within their borders (and that polluters hold no liability for damages caused abroad) then the former method obviously would be the most appropriate. By contrast, the latter method involves an assumption about the suitability of extending

---

6   The chief benefit of the MRIO approach lies in its ability to capture the entire production process so that the full environmental impact of a traded good or service can be attributed to a final consumption good or service. Life cycle approaches (LCAs) are capable also of providing such information. Indeed, LCAs trace these impacts for specific goods and so permit a much more finely grained detail than in the MRIO approach. This makes the former particularly useful for developing industry and eco-labeling standards for product life cycle impact and attributing responsibility for the environmental impact of specific goods. However, the finer detail of LCA comes at the expense of aggregative capacity, making these methods less applicable to questions concerning global trade and systems of national accounts which involve greater product heterogeneity (Rebitzer et al. 2004; Lutter et al. 2008; Wiedmann et al. 2009). By contrast, in measuring sectoral flows rather than tracking individual products, MRIO permits a level of aggregation that facilitates analysis at the global level (Wiedmann et al. 2009).

7   We refer here to the World Bank's annual *World Development Indicators* reports which follow the manual produced by Bolt et al. (2002).

the *polluter pays principle* to the domain of national accounting. This requires that some portion of an economy's total savings should, at least notionally, be set aside in order to compensate the recipients of damage arising from carbon emissions.

Unfortunately, scrutiny of these competing assumptions is unlikely to lead to an unequivocal answer. On the one hand, if there were meaningful international treaties for managing emissions of a transboundary pollutant along with suitable control measures (such as emission taxes) that placed an explicit price on pollution liabilities then the latter accounting approach would unambiguously be the correct one. On the other hand, if there was little or no prospect of international action then the former accounting approach is an apt description of actual future prospects. Neither case seems to be an unequivocally satisfactory description of the real world.

Arguably, therefore, both approaches have their place in framing thoughts about the sustainability of development and it is important to acknowledge explicitly what is being assumed about responsibilities and liabilities in any particular approach. As a practical matter, however, data limitations may hamper empirical application in particular where detailed valuation is needed on estimated damage within individual countries. In addition, the recent literature on virtual carbon[8] potentially adds another twist.

That is, the social cost approach has involved estimating the (notional) liabilities arising from production emissions and deducting that from measures of genuine saving. It seems interesting to ask also what this savings analysis (in terms of the contribution of countries to global sustainability) would look like if instead we measured "responsibility" and (notional) "liabilities" with reference additionally to the social costs of *consumption emissions*.

3   Virtual sustainability and international trade

We take as the motivation for our empirical analysis the proposition that in terms of accounting for (changes in) comprehensive or inclusive wealth, the starting point for any country should be to account – first and foremost – for the assets that it owns. The reason for this is straightforward. It is the prudent management of these assets that is likely to determine primarily the sustainability of development. Nevertheless, there are a number of reasons for considering further how relationships between countries might be quantified within this framework for wealth accounting. Two such relationships are of interest in this chapter. The first concerns trade in depletable natural resources (including a range of non-living and living resources). The second concerns the liabilities or burdens

---

8   Arrow et al. (2010) estimate the putative damage that might occur in a country as a result of global carbon emissions in an accounting year. The specific method calculates the global damage that will arise from emissions of greenhouse gases in a given year: that is, the product of the quantity of (carbon–equivalent) emissions and the social cost of (a unit of) carbon. It then allocates this global damage to each country based on the assumed share of each country of that burden. The issue here is the evidence base simply does not exist and so, through necessity, practitioners must fall back on simplifying assumptions. Nordhaus and Boyer (2000), however, provide some disaggregation for 13 regions including five individual countries and eight country groupings. The latter is a mixture of geographically (broadly) similar countries (e.g., OECD Europe) and economic groupings. For example, those

countries belonging to the category "Other High Income" on average appear to benefit from a 2.5°C degree warming, although the group is comprised of a diverse mix of countries including Australia, Israel, and Canada. The category of "Lower Middle Income" includes countries such as Venezuela, South Africa, Iran, and Thailand. The point here is not a critique of Nordhaus and Boyer, which represents a useful extension of the highly aggregated single–world economy of much of the literature on the social costs of carbon. Moreover, the point made by Arrow et al. (2010) is a good one. It seems sensible to account for both the damage that a country bears from global emissions as well as the burden for which this same country is responsible. However, as things stand, we arguably lack the data to be able to do this accounting satisfactorily across a wide range of countries.

that countries impose burdens on one another because of transboundary pollution (specifically here arising from carbon emissions).

We must interpret the results of such quantification with care. In particular, we do not consider further those trade linkages which may actually affect the "bottom line" of exporters and importers. The correct accounting for capital gains and losses on traded resources would be one example of this. Our focus, in what follows, is (changes in) natural assets and trade flows which might be thought of as being, in some senses, *notional* liabilities. The nature of the liability for which we must account is determined by the interpretation of responsibility (for resource depletion or carbon emissions) that we take.

For resource depletion, conventionally we might think of the country producing the resource (e.g., through its domestic extraction activities) as being responsible for this depletion. The liability arising from the (negative) change in the resource stock arising from this depletion should be attributed to the accounts of the producing country. Alternatively, we might conceive of responsibility as residing with the country that ultimately consumes the resource (in order to satisfy its final demand). In this case, the liability reflecting the change in resource stock should be attributed to the accounts of the consuming country (or countries).

For carbon emissions, assuming a case can be made for saying that polluters should pay (and thus account) for the climate change damage they cause, a question also arises about where this liability should be charged. Typically, this has been thought of as "belonging" to the country that produced the emissions. However, responsibility (and hence liability) could instead be argued to lie with the country consuming the goods in which these emissions are embodied.[9]

In what follows, we define "virtual sustainability" as the quantification of aspects of these linkages between countries where responsibility is defined in terms of the value of the resources and carbon that a country consumes. Put another way, these linkages can be thought of as providing a somewhat different picture of a particular country's contribution to global sustainability. That is, for a country with very few domestic natural resources that relies on significant imports of resources from other countries, we say that this country's contribution to global sustainability is diminished by this consumption of resources (relative to its contribution taking into account its depletion of its own resources).

Before we proceed to describe our method for calculating the empirical magnitudes of these responsibilities, one final word of caution is needed in interpreting our results. We argue, in what follows, that taking account of trade linkages – and distinguishing between responsibility in terms of production and consumption of natural assets in the way we outline here – is useful for thinking about contributions to global sustainability. However, measures of resource consumption, for example, do not translate directly into a prescription about how much a resource-consuming country should actually save to ensure the sustainability of its own development. In other words, the emphasis on the term "virtual sustainability" here is important.

4 Methods and data

Multi-regional input-output (MRIO) models are well established as a popular tool of IO (input-output) practitioners (ISARD 1951; LEONTIEF AND

---

9 There are other perspectives on this issue of responsibility. We are grateful to an anonymous reviewer for suggesting that "source responsibility" might also be a candidate proposition. On this view, the responsibility for the climate liability might be said to reside (in some part) with the country that initially

depleted and traded, for example, fossil fuel resources. There are certainly policy contexts where this understanding of responsibility is articulated either implicitly or explicitly. Clearly, the debate between production, consumption perspectives, and alternatives would benefit greatly from the further contributions of environmental ethicists.

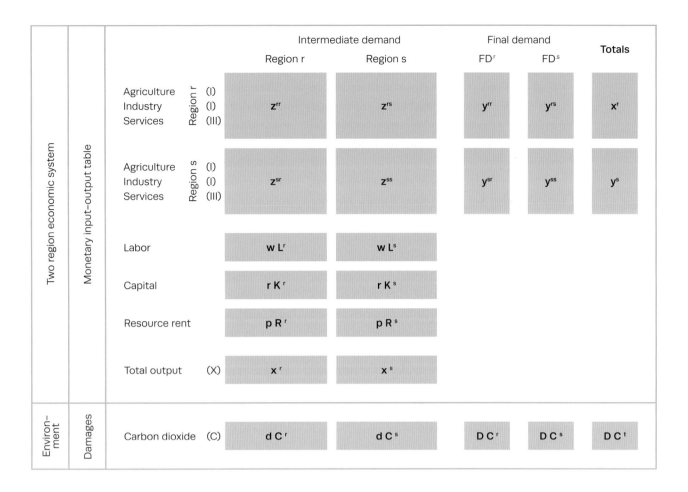

| | | | | Intermediate demand | | Final demand | | Totals |
				Region r	Region s	FD^r	FD^s	
		Agriculture	(I)					
		Industry	(I)	z^{rr}	z^{rs}	y^{rr}	y^{rs}	x^r
		Services	(III)					
		Agriculture	(I)					
		Industry	(I)	z^{sr}	z^{ss}	y^{sr}	y^{ss}	y^s
		Services	(III)					
		Labor		$w\,L^r$	$w\,L^s$			
		Capital		$r\,K^r$	$r\,K^s$			
		Resource rent		$p\,R^r$	$p\,R^s$			
		Total output	(X)	x^r	x^s			
		Carbon dioxide	(C)	$d\,C^r$	$d\,C^s$	$D\,C^r$	$D\,C^s$	$D\,C^t$

FIGURE 1

Schematic representation of
an extended multi–regional
input–output (MRIO) table

FORD 1971). Indeed, the number of studies applying MRIO models to environmental problems has increased substantially over the past two decades (for a literature review, see WIEDMANN [2009]). The MRIO modeling competency lies primarily in its ability to trace environmental impacts along the entire production chain, from the consumer country back to the producer country, considering both the direct and indirect effects (or embodied resources) in the commodity traded. Thus, by use of this technique it is possible to show how production and consumption are interconnected across regions and sectors. Revealing a nation's global resource needs provides the potential for a very different picture of its environmental responsibilities to emerge (MUNKSGAARD AND PEDERSEN 2001). For some applications of MRIO models applied

to environmental studies see for example: Andrew, Peters, and Lennox (2009); Atkinson et al. (2010); Davis and Caldeira (2010); Lenzen, Pade, and Munksgaard (2004); and Muñoz and Steininger (2010).

In this section, we describe the MRIO method as a tool for measuring the natural asset demands from a consumption perspective, as opposed to conventional accounting based on a production perspective. These two approaches, or accounting practices, are also known as the consumption-based principle (CBP) and the production-based principle (PBP), respectively (MUNKSGAARD AND PEDERSEN 2001). PBP means that indicators only capture the domestic environmental or resource pressures that are linked to the production of domestic consumption and exports within the geographical borders of a country. By contrast, CBP re-allocates these same environmental or resource pressures associated with exports to foreign countries and, in addition, domestic responsibilities are complemented by "responsibility" for impacts that take place abroad, that is those that are embodied in imports.

The two components of the genuine saving indicator that we focus upon from a CBP perspective are *natural resource depletion* and the social costs caused by *carbon production* or emissions. Thus, for example, while gross saving and investments in human capital boost genuine saving, natural resource depletion and liabilities caused by emissions of greenhouse gases, as well as the depreciation of produced capital, shrink genuine saving. More precisely, in the current context, natural resource depletion considered here comprises the following categories: fisheries; forest; energy resources (mainly oil, gas, and coal); and mineral extraction.[10]

Practical steps in measuring changes in natural wealth from a *consumption perspective* can be found, for instance, in the works of Proops and Atkinson (1998) and Proops et al. (1999), as well as in the study of Atkinson and Hamilton (2002). These first efforts found in the literature share a similar empirical level of analysis, in the sense that both studies use an MRIO model for the global economy at a "macro" level, representing the regional (or national) variables in the model by the total aggregated value of the region under study: that is, these models assumed each country, in effect, has a single economic sector trading with the rest of the world. As concerns the number of regions included in the model, this has been continuously increasing: while Proops et al. (1999) referred to 28 world regions, Atkinson and Hamilton (2002) augmented the number of regions up to 95. Furthermore, both

studies focus on various years between 1980 and 1990.

The ability to aggregate across resource sectors is due to the convention of tracing monetary (instead of physical) flows within the input-output framework (MILLER AND BLAIR 2009). There are several reasons that we take this approach in this chapter. The primary reason is that this approach provides us with a clear link to comprehensive wealth accounting. In addition, this facilitates inter- and intra-industry comparisons (WIEDMANN ET AL. 2009). First, outputs within a given sector are heterogeneous (fisheries produce anchovies and tuna), and aggregating across them is made easier by measuring monetary flows. Similarly, monetary terms permit the consolidation of diverse resource categories into a measure of natural resource depletion in a more intuitive way than one which requires adding tons of fish to tons of coal. While physical and hybrid input-output models are possible, and yield different results from monetary input-output analyses (see HUBACEK AND GILJUM [2003]), our approach accepts convention and makes use of monetary input-output techniques.[11] In the following subsection we take a closer look at the multi-regional accounting system that we use.

4.1 Model description

In Figure 1 we present an elaboration of a two-region accounting system extended to

---

10 A notable exception here is any robust treatment of the value of biodiversity or ecosystem services embodied in international trade. The reasons for this omission are readily apparent, and include difficulties in measurement and the reliability of data. The authors are grateful to Dr. Zafar Adeel of UNU–INWEH for this insightful comment.

11 We accept the loss of detail and exposure to monetary phenomena that this approach entails. Miller and Blair (2009) and Wiedmann et al. (2009) note that the use of monetary input–output tables can lead to skewed results when changes in price and exchange rate do not reflect actual changes in physical trade flows. This challenge may be especially pertinent for an analysis of resource sectors given their notoriously volatile prices (and even more so for year–to–year comparisons). However, given that our study reports on a 'snapshot' of trade flows in 2004, we are able to avoid at least some of this 'skew'. For an extensive review of these and other methodological issues, see Wiedmann et al. (2009).

resources and the environment, which underpins the development of the MRIO model. This figure provides a comprehensive overview of the consumption and production structure of two trading regions at an industry level. This is constructed on the basis of the System of National Accounts (SNA), input-output tables (IOTs), trade statistics, and the extensions of the system to environmental accounts such as – in the current context – CO_2 emissions. More specifically, 'x^j_i' (with j= 'r' and 's') is the vector of outputs domestically produced by industry 'i' (with $i=1,...,n$). Output production additionally needs primary inputs of labor (L^j_i), capital (K^j_i) and natural resources (R^j_i), while the monetary compensation per unit (or the price) of those production factors is given by 'w^j', 'r^j' and 'p^j' respectively.

In addition, production of this output in the domestic territory of region 'j' induces pollution and waste although, in this chapter, this is represented only by carbon dioxide emissions, 'C^j_i', with 'd' being the corresponding damage caused per ton of CO_2 emitted into the atmosphere by different sectors and households. Under the conventional PBP, the corresponding emissions and natural resource depletion are purely allocated to region 'j' even though some part of this production may be for exports to other regions. As regards commodity trade between both regions, exported commodities for final consumption from, for instance, region 'r' to region 's' are represented by vector '$\mathbf{y}^{rs}_i$', embodying the emissions and natural resource use that occurred in the exporting region, 'r'. In a similar way, the vector of exported commodities from region 's' for final demand in 'r' is denoted by '$\mathbf{y}^{sr}_i$'. The other component of the final demands comprises the commodities domestically produced, '$\mathbf{y}^{jj}_i$'.

Finally, domestically produced goods and services, 'x^j_i', necessarily need one or more commodities as inputs, whether these are "imported" or produced within the economy. These intra- and inter-industry intermediate products are indicated in Figure 1 by two groups of matrices: (1) 'Z^{sr}_{hi}' denotes exported commodity inputs of industry 'h' (with $h=1,..,n$) in region 's' to industry 'i' of region 'r' (and vice versa for 'Z^{rs}_{hi}'); (2) whereas 'Z^{jj}_{hi}' represents intra- and inter-industry deliveries within a region. These intermediate transaction matrices provide the key for understanding the relationship between consumption and production between regions and for assigning environmental responsibilities from a consumption-based perspective. On the basis of the accounting system described above, it is possible to develop the MRIO model with full linkages. We do not present in detail the equations underlying the model since they have been already widely described in recent years. For an explicit treatment of this, see Peters (2008), Atkinson et al. (2010), Davis and Caldeira (2010), Lenzen, Pade, and Munksgaard (2004), and Muñoz and Steininger (2010). The model formulations primarily allow tracing all the inputs required along the production chain, from final demand[12] upstream to the extraction phase, and the corresponding resource depletion and emissions damages.

4.2 Data description

Establishing an MRIO-model requires that a variety of data are sought. For the monetary side, the database of the Global Trade Analysis Project (GTAP) was used to construct an MRIO model with full linkages. In this chapter we have used GTAP V7 (NARAYANAN AND WALMSLEY 2008) for the year 2004. GTAP V7 provides harmonized input-output tables for 113 countries and country groups (multi-country regions in this case), representing the entire world economy. Moreover, the GTAP database (a) presents harmonized sectoral disaggregation across regions, which consists of 57 industries per region; and (b) is already balanced at the different scales of analysis (meso, macro and global level). For further details regarding the construction of

---

12 Here defined as household, government expenditures, and investment.

the MRIO model using the GTAP database, see Muñoz and Steininger (2010).

Valuing resource depletion: Consistent with Narayanan and Walmsley (2008) we have used data on resource rents supplied by GTAP v7. Natural resource rent comprised in GTAP is provided at a sectoral level for the following six industries: forestry; fishery; coal; oil; gas; and minerals. GTAP's resource rents are indirectly derived by estimating the cost share of the natural resource input in the total industrial output (for further details see HERTEL ET AL.). This procedure also ensures that sectoral rents in GTAP (or '$p.R$' in Figure 1) are harmonized with the other components of the economic system as well – regional value-added across industries, intermediate inputs, and domestic output data. However, it would be useful to explore further the links between the valuation of resource depletion that is implied within the GTAP *vis-à-vis* the more direct methodologies for estimating resource depletion values used in the sustainability and resource accounting literatures (see, for example, VINCENT, PANAYOTOU, AND HARTWICK [1997], ATKINSON AND HAMILTON [2007], and HAMILTON AND RUTA [2009]).

Carbon emissions: With regard to CO_2 emissions, GTAP provides data by sector and region, satisfying the physical data requirements presented in the previous section. It is important to mention, however, that GTAP v7 CO_2 data only refer to CO_2 emissions from fuel combustion. We have therefore also included CO_2 emissions stemming from industrial processes of the following sectors: mineral products; chemical industry; and metal production for all countries reported by UNFCCC (2009). Nevertheless, some countries do not report industrial process emissions for the specific years under study. In those cases, we updated the last year available by using indicators related to the industrial process. For mineral products and metal production we used the changes in cement production and steel in the respective country as a proxy variable for updating the CO_2 emissions in these industrial processes. Cement and steel data were obtained from the United States Geological Survey (USGS).

In the case of the chemical industry, we use the sectoral value-added of the examined country.

In this chapter, in order to value these flows of carbon, we need to make an assumption about the social costs of carbon: that is, the present value of future damages resulting from an additional unit of carbon emissions in a given year (FANKHAUSER 1994). Estimating this social cost is inherently complex and uncertain and our selection of this parameter will have a significant impact on our findings.

For our purposes, there are three candidate strategies for selecting a social cost of carbon. First, we could adopt a price as determined by an already existing carbon market, such as the EU Emissions Trading System. While this may be a valid approach in the future, it is at present limited by the infancy of current carbon markets. As Dellink et al. (2010) suggest, carbon markets are incomplete, closed, and, for most countries, non-existent. Furthermore, there is no guarantee that market prices would capture the full social cost of carbon (SCC) and, because markets are unlinked, there is no convergence to a common world price for us to adopt (DELLINK ET AL. 2010). Alternatively, we could adopt a price which is already in use such as the World Bank's long standing use of 20 \$/tC[13] (WORLD BANK 2010) or Australia's recent carbon tax of 23 \$/tC (COMMONWEALTH OF AUSTRALIA 2011). The chief value of this approach is that, to the extent that one exists, it entails the use of a standard and facilitates comparisons with existing literature. However, this too, fails to account for Dellink's objections, and for various reasons, may not properly reflect carbon's social costs. Finally, our third option is to adopt an estimated value for this parameter. This approach is in accordance with Stern (2006), and is adopted here.

The debate that followed the Stern Review indicated the central importance of discounting (TOL 2008; WEITZMAN 2007; STERN 2006). Additionally, the estimation of the social cost of current emissions is not independent of the

---

13 All monetary values in this chapter are expressed in USD.

TABLE 1

Resource depletion for selected economies

Country name	GNI (in million of US$)	Total resource depletion (in millions, US$)				
		Production		Consumption		Ratio
		Value	%GNI	Value	%GNI	Prod/ Cons.
United States	11.687.900	35.611	0.30	78,387	0.67	0.45
Japan	4.694.853	4.601	0.10	27,522	0.59	0.17
Germany	2.764.179	3.735	0.14	15,597	0.56	0.24
United Kingdom	2.215.020	8.444	0.38	11,276	0.51	0.75
France	2.077.657	2.059	0.10	9,902	0.48	0.21
China	1.928.118	34.308	1.78	36,819	1.91	0.93
Canada	971.963	14.505	1.49	7,827	0.81	1.85
India	695.941	7.047	1.01	13,026	1.87	0.54
Rest of West Asia	634.214	60.593	9.55	10,347	1.63	5.86
Russian Federation	578.971	29.586	5.11	10,948	1.89	2.70
Norway	259.079	14.351	5.54	1,233	0.48	11.64
Indonesia	225.214	9.142	4.06	6,256	2.78	1.46
South Africa	211.700	1.936	0.91	2,058	0.97	0.94
Portugal	176.127	371	0.21	1,460	0.83	0.25
Iran	160.332	14.611	9.11	4,924	3.07	2.97
Venezuela, RB	108.779	8.424	7.74	1,421	1.31	5.93
Singapore	103.199	41	0.04	1,022	0.99	0.04
Nigeria	78.110	9.354	11.98	931	1.19	10.05
Nicaragua	4.266	30	0.70	93	2.17	0.32
Eastern Europe	2.935	3	0.12	93	3.17	0.04
World	41272071	349294	0.85	349294	0.85	1.00

Raw data from GTAP v7. See Narayanan and Walmsley (2008) available online at

http://www.gtap.agecon.purdue.edu/databases/v7/v7_doco.asp

predicted path for future emissions, complicating further the asset valuation problem (STERN 2006). Further challenges include uncertainty in forecasting the frequency, intensity, and location of catastrophic climate events (NEWBOLD ET AL. 2010; PYCROFT ET AL. 2011; LEMOINE AND TRAEGER 2010; WEITZMAN 2007; STERN 2006).

These complexities notwithstanding, a number of empirical studies have sought to estimate the social cost of CO_2 emissions which, in turn, have been used to inform past wealth accounting work. Notably, World Bank (2010) uses a value of $20/tC. Arrow et al. (2010) and Atkinson et al. (2010), however, arrive at a value of $50/tC; a magnitude that can be justified with reference to the work of the Stern Review, market prices for EU emissions permits, and by recognizing the general trend in the field (GUO ET AL. 2006; TOL 2008; CLARKSON AND DEYES 2002).

TABLE 1

Continued

Country name	Per capita resource depletion and comparison to global average (GA) (in US$)				CO₂ emissions (in millions, US$) $50/tC			
	Production		Consumption		Production		Consumption	
	Value	P/GA	Value	C/GA	Value	%GNI	Value	%GNI
United States	120.55	2.30	265.35	4.88	85,421	0.73	95,467	0.82
Japan	35.96	0.69	215.15	3.96	15,704	0.34	20,140	0.43
Germany	45.19	0.86	188.71	3.47	12,131	0.44	14,878	0.54
United Kingdom	141.96	2.71	189.58	3.49	8,336	0.38	11,891	0.54
France	34.17	0.65	164.32	3.02	5,414	0.26	7,953	0.38
China	26.23	0.50	28.15	0.52	69,055	3.58	54,093	2.81
Canada	453.84	8.67	244.89	4.51	8,190	0.84	7,707	0.79
India	6.48	0.12	11.98	0.22	17,116	2.46	15,856	2.28
Rest of West Asia	511.76	9.78	87.39	1.61	14,409	2.27	11,403	1.80
Russian Federation	205.60	3.93	76.08	1.40	23,517	4.06	18,180	3.14
Norway	3,119.74	59.62	268.10	4.94	888	0.34	782	0.30
Indonesia	41.54	0.79	28.43	0.52	5,232	2.32	4,763	2.12
South Africa	41.00	0.78	43.60	0.80	5,363	2.53	3,598	1.70
Portugal	35.49	0.68	139.86	2.57	934	0.53	1,141	0.65
Iran	212.37	4.06	71.57	1.32	6,663	4.16	6,728	4.20
Venezuela, RB	320.54	6.13	54.06	1.00	2,178	2.00	1,661	1.53
Singapore	9.67	0.18	239.36	4.41	557	0.54	962	0.93
Nigeria	72.67	1.39	7.23	0.13	785	1.00	793	1.01
Nicaragua	5.54	0.11	17.21	0.32	64	1.51	80	1.88
Eastern Europe	0.83	0.02	22.04	0.41	109	3.70	158	5.37
World	54.54	1	54.54	1	384358	0.93	384358	0.93

An important study is Tol (2008) which offers an extensive meta-survey of over 200 estimates, ranging from -6.6 $/tC to 2,400 $/tC with variations due largely to differences in discount rates, assumptions about economic growth and adaptive behavior, the degree of equity rating, scientific uncertainties, and the treatment of tipping points (LEMOINE AND TRAEGER 2010; GUO ET AL. 2006; TOL 2008). Clearly, this is a wide range. In reflecting on how to narrow this range, however, Tol (2008) argues that under conservative

assumptions the mean value is $23/tC (and a certainty equivalent value is $25/tC) and that, furthermore, there is a 1 percent probability that the social cost of carbon exceeds $78/tC. In a recent paper, Tol (2009) suggests that $50/tC could be used for policies such as carbon taxes under plausible assumptions about governments' assessment of key parameters (such as the social discount rate). This corresponds to the value used, for example, by Arrow et al. (2010) and Atkinson et al. (2010) and for

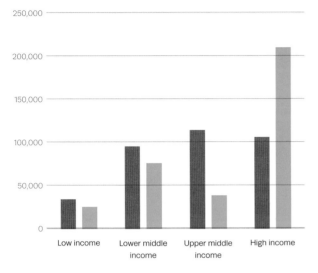

Income group classifications are consistent with World
Bank guidelines: low income (GNI/capita < $1,005), lower
middle income ($1,006<GNI/capita<$3,975), upper middle
income ($3,976<GNI/capita<$12,275), and high income (GNI/
capita>$12,276).

Raw data from GTAP v7. See Narayanan and Walmsley
(2008) available online at http://www.gtap.agecon.purdue.
edu/databases/v7/v7_doco.asp

FIGURE 3

Average per capita resource depletion
(US$)

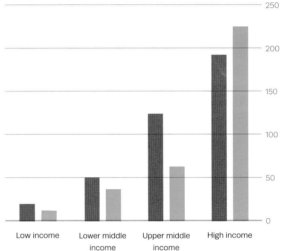

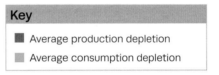

Income group classifications are consistent with World
Bank guidelines: low income (GNI/capita < $1,005); lower
middle income ($1,006<GNI/capita<$3,975); upper middle
income ($3,976<GNI/capita<$12,275); and high income (GNI/
capita>$12,276).

Raw data from GTAP v7. See Narayanan and Walmsley
(2008) available online at http://www.gtap.agecon.purdue.
edu/databases/v7/v7_doco.asp

illustrative purposes we use this value of $50/tC
in what follows (or just under $14/tCO$_2$).

Other data: We also make use of data on
gross savings, consumption of fixed capital and
education expenditure for the year 2004 and
published in World Bank (2011).

5 Empirical results

We divide our discussion of results into two
parts. First, we discuss – using our input-output
methodology – how our analysis highlights the
gap between the production and consumption
perspectives on resource depletion and carbon

emissions. Second, we explore, from the two
accounting perspectives, the virtual sustainability of individual countries (or regions), and thus
their contributions to global sustainability.

5.1 Production and consumption per-
spectives: comparisons and contrasts

Table 1 illustrates production and consumption
based resource depletion (total and per capita)
and CO$_2$ emissions for a select group of economies. Column 7 reports the ratio of produc-
tion/consumption based depletions, while columns 4 and 6 show each as a percentage of GNI.

FIGURE 4

Production – minus consumption–based resource depletion (in millions, US$)

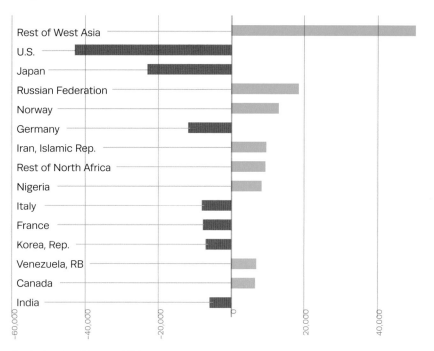

Depletion in millions of US$

Figure 4 lists the economies with the greatest difference between production- and consumption-based resource depletions. Definitions for regional aggregations are consistent with World Bank classifications and are available in Appendix A1.

Raw data from GTAP v7. See Narayanan and Walmsley (2008) available online at http://www.gtap.agecon. purdue.edu/databases/v7/v7_doco.asp

Depletion ratios greater (less) than one reflect net resource exporters (importers). Columns 8–11 describe per capita resource depletion. A comparison of each economy's (per capita) production and consumption based depletions to the global average is given in columns 9 and 11, respectively. Here, values that are greater than one indicate above average depletion while values less than one indicate the reverse. All CO_2 emissions reported here (including those used to calculate genuine savings) assume an scc of $50/tC.

Do rich economies use more resources from a production or consumption perspective? Clearly, the answer to this question will start to shed light on whether empirical thinking about virtual sustainability confirms the assertions of some commentators starting with Martinez-Alier (1995). Thus, Figures 2 and 3 group countries by income[14] to show the total and average per capita dollar value difference in production- and consumption-based resource depletion. When aggregated at this level the data appear to show a clear trend. However, the question remains as to how well this holds for individual economies.

Figure 4 thus examines the question of country level resource depletion. Shown here are the individual economies with the greatest disparity between production- and consumption-based depletion. Positive values (net exporters) show production based depletion in excess of consumption-based depletion, while negative values (net importers) indicate the reverse. That is, although economic activity in the Rest of West Asia entails significant resource depletion, a large portion of this is then traded abroad. Similarly, u.s. resource depletion entails significant imports. It is interesting to note that low- and high-income countries each appear on both sides of Figure 4.

For examining contributions to sustainability on a global level, it is instructive to see which individual economies entail the greatest resource depletion, and how this relates to the global average. Figures 5 and 6 rank the top 15 economies in terms of their per capita production- and consumption-based depletions relative to the global average. Ratios greater than one indicate

14 Income group classifications are consistent with World Bank guidelines: low income (GNI/capita < $1,005); lower middle income ($1,006<GNI/capita<$3,975); upper middle income ($3,976<GNI/capita<$12,275); and high income (GNI/capita>$12,276).

above average per capita resource depletion, while ratios less than one indicate the reverse. For a complete list, please see the complete table (columns 9 and 11) in Appendix A2.

Taking stock of these findings "in the round" leads to a number of reflections:

The ratio of production- to consumption-based resource depletion in Table 1 shows that in some economies (notably Norway, Nigeria, Venezuela, and West Asia), production entails far greater resource depletion than consumption. That is, for these economies, production-based accounting of resource depletion overstates the value of resources required by the domestic economy (i.e., to satisfy domestic final demand). Though in general, lower-income, resource-rich economies have higher ratios, it is important to note that this is not exclusively the case: developed (Norway and Canada) as well as developing (Nigeria and Venezuela) countries can maintain high ratios of production- to consumption-based depletions.

Alternatively, resource depletion ratios of less than one suggest that the economy requires more resources to satisfy consumption than production. This is particularly the case for several high-income countries such as Japan, France, Germany, the U.S., and the U.K. One way of interpreting this result is that developed economies with high per capita income tend to import resource intensive goods while their domestic production focuses on non-resource intensive services.[15] Though the list of countries with depletion ratios of less than one is primarily populated by developed countries, this too, is not exclusively the case (see, for example India, Eastern Europe, and Nicaragua).

One of the results from Chapter 3 relates to Japan as one of the few countries in which natural capital has been increasing over time. However, examining natural assets in international trade for the year 2004, it is further revealed that Japan's domestic resource

FIGURE 5

Ratio of per capita production–based resource depletions to the global average

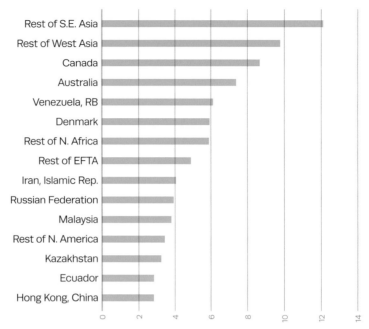

Ratio of per capita production–based depletions to global average

Figure 5 shows economies with the highest ratios of per capita production–based resource depletions/global average. Definitions for regional aggregations are consistent with World Bank classifications and are available in Appendix A1.

*Note that Norway's ratio of per capita production–based depletions to the global average was 59.62 and that for readability and scale it has been omitted from this chart as an outlier.

Raw data from GTAP v7. See Narayanan and Walmsley (2008) available online at http://www.gtap.agecon.purdue.edu/databases/v7/v7_doco.asp

extraction during constituted only 17 percent of the natural resource depletion induced worldwide by its consumption (see Table 1). This implies that if Japan had to produce all consumed goods and services in autarky, its figures with respect to natural capital would very likely be different.[16] Chapter 3 also reports a decrease

---

15   There is an analogy here to the literature on carbon leakage, although in other respects there are possibly key differences between these notions.

16   This hypothetical situation is not equivalent to (and is likely to be less than) simply adding the amount of imported resources to domestic depletion. This result is due to variations in production technologies, resource endowments, and efficiency of use between countries. Moreover, in such a situation, it is likely that significant substitution effects would come into play.

FIGURE 6

Ratio of per capita consumption–based resource depletions to the global average

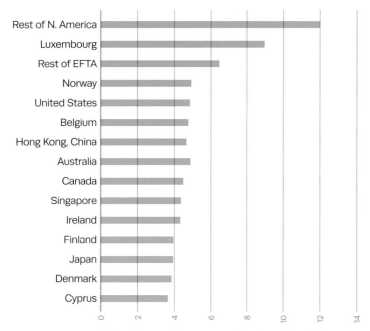

Ratio of per capita consumption–based depletions to global average

Figure 6 shows economies with the highest ratios of per capita consumption-based resource depletions/global average. Definitions for regional aggregations are consistent with World Bank classifications and are available in Appendix A1.

Raw data from GTAP v7. See Narayanan and Walmsley (2008) available online at http://www.gtap.agecon.purdue.edu/databases/v7/v7_doco.asp

broadly consistent with this. Second, the figures highlight not only the direction of these flows, but also their magnitude. Whether in terms of total dollar value, or average per capita value, these figures clearly show that production depletions exceed consumption depletions for low-, lower-middle-, and upper-middle-income countries. The reverse is true for high-income economies. The results also indicate that the disparity rises with income, suggesting that for rich (poor) countries, production-focused indicators understate (overstate) resource demand.

Figure 4 takes the analysis to the level of individual economies, showing that despite the trends implied by Figures 2 and 3, there is no steadfast rule regarding the relationship between income and production or consumption depletions. This is particularly interesting when considering adopting production-based versus consumption-based wealth accounting: the disparity between the two can be large for both developed and developing countries. The value of this difference, as we discuss in further detail below, can be interpreted as the (virtual) change in the contribution to global sustainability.

Figures 5 and 6 are particularly useful for assessing contributions to global sustainability by individual economies. Interestingly, several economies (Denmark, Canada, Australia, Hong Kong – China, Norway, the Rest of EFTA, and the Rest of North America) appear in both of these figures, suggesting that both their production and consumption patterns require greater than average resource depletions. Notably, however, both Canada and Norway also appear with positive values in Figure 4 suggesting that they are still net exporters of resources.

Results from our MRIO model can be further disaggregated to explore what lies beneath particular findings. For instance, our analysis indicates that the China's CO_2 responsibility is lower from a consumption perspective than from the production perspective. This is consistent with the findings elsewhere in the literature. However, if we look instead at total resource depletion for China, the opposite is found. That

in natural capital of, for example, Nigeria that is largely triggered by fossil fuel extractions. As this country is a net exporter of natural resources, with a production-consumption ratio of 10 (see Table 1), the opposite situation with respect to natural capital would potentially happen if this nation had a closed economy. Thus, the analysis of natural assets in international trade offers important insights into understanding the drivers of natural capital change presented in the previous chapter.

Figures 2 and 3 show global trends in resource depletion by gross national income and are important for two reasons. First, our results seem broadly consistent with the proposition that resources tend to flow from poor to rich countries. It is worth noting that our results are is, China's consumption of global resources and its resource depletion (or production) was $36,819 million and $34,408 respectively. This suggests a production-consumption ratio of 0.93 (see Table 1).

This finding is largely due to Chinese imports of oil. This oil, in turn, mainly originates (in terms of where it was depleted or produced) in the Middle East which is subsumed under the "Rest of Western Asia" region in our model. Thus, for the Rest of Western Asia, our model suggests that oil depletion from a consumption perspective was $15,172 million which is significantly greater than this region's resource consumption (of $8,586 million).

Turning our attention back to China, important sectoral drivers of its resource consumption are: Construction, petroleum and coal products, public administration, and machinery and equipment. A similar finding emerges if we look only at natural gas as again China appears to be a net importer of this resource. However, for coal, the results are different. China is a net exporter of this resource. In consumption terms, its responsibility amounts to $9,224 million. In production terms, depletion of coal within China was $12,486 million. The overall effect,

TABLE 2

Percentage contribution to global sustainability by region (percentage of gross world income)

| | | Genuine saving components | | | Virtual sustainability | | | | | |
| | Genuine saving | Gross saving | Depreciation of produced capital | Education expenditures | Change in natural assets: production perspective | | | Change in natural assets: consumption perspective | | |
					Carbon emissions	Natural resources	Total	Carbon emissions	Natural resources	Total
Aus./NZ/ Oceania	0.22	0.43	−0.27	0.09	−0.01	−0.02	−0.03	−0.01	−0.01	−0.02
China	1.53	2.18	−0.48	0.08	−0.17	−0.08	−0.25	−0.13	−0.09	−0.22
Japan	0.93	2.96	−2.34	0.36	−0.04	−0.01	−0.05	−0.05	−0.07	−0.12
East Asia	0.71	0.97	−0.36	0.13	−0.02	−0.01	−0.03	−0.03	−0.03	−0.06
South East Asia	0.31	0.54	−0.21	0.06	−0.03	−0.05	−0.08	−0.03	−0.04	−0.07
India	0.38	0.54	−0.17	0.07	−0.04	−0.02	−0.06	−0.04	−0.03	−0.07
South Asia	0.08	0.12	−0.04	0.01	−0.01	0.00	−0.01	−0.01	−0.01	−0.02
Canada	0.31	0.55	−0.31	0.12	−0.02	−0.03	−0.05	−0.02	−0.02	−0.04
United States	1.49	3.75	−3.32	1.35	−0.20	−0.09	−0.29	−0.23	−0.19	−0.42
Mexico	0.36	0.44	−0.16	0.10	−0.01	−0.01	−0.02	−0.02	−0.01	−0.03
South America	0.31	0.63	−0.35	0.11	−0.03	−0.05	−0.08	−0.02	−0.03	−0.05
Central America/ Caribbean	0.03	0.06	−0.03	0.01	−0.01	0.00	−0.01	−0.01	−0.01	−0.02
EU–15	3.40	6.18	−4.08	1.48	−0.12	−0.06	−0.18	−0.15	−0.17	−0.32
Russia	0.27	0.44	−0.09	0.05	−0.06	−0.07	−0.13	−0.04	−0.03	−0.07
EITs	0.16	0.45	−0.31	0.10	−0.05	−0.03	−0.08	−0.05	−0.03	−0.08
Other Europe	0.30	0.50	−0.25	0.09	−0.01	−0.03	−0.04	−0.01	−0.01	−0.02
North Africa/ Middle East	0.41	0.95	−0.41	0.16	−0.07	−0.22	−0.29	−0.06	−0.06	−0.12
Sub–Saharan Africa	0.08	0.23	−0.13	0.05	−0.02	−0.05	−0.07	−0.02	−0.02	−0.04
World	11.23	21.92	−13.32	4.41	−0.93	−0.85	−1.78	−0.93	−0.85	−1.78

Raw data from GTAP v7. See Narayanan and Walmsley (2008) available online at http://www.gtap.agecon.purdue.edu/databases/v7/v7_doco.asp

TABLE 3

Genuine saving and "virtual sustainability" by selected countries and regions

	Genuine saving		Change in natural assets (millions, US$)		
	% GNI	$ million	Production perspective	Consumption perspective	Difference
Rest of North America	−25.43	−407	75	163	−88
Rest of Europe	−12.42	−2,401	1,554	1,840	−286
Rest of South Central Africa	−10.24	−2,414	3,412	592	2,820
Rest of South America	−9.11	−192	62	81	−19
Former Soviet Union	−4.04	−565	4,863	3,175	1,688
Zimbabwe	−2.49	−112	203	166	37
Malawi	−2.18	−56	66	60	6
Senegal	−1.75	−139	153	282	−128
Rest of South Asia	−1.53	−224	423	593	−170
Malta	−0.67	−37	51	116	−65
Rest of EFTA	0.66	102	168	210	−42
Bulgaria	1.11	278	1,121	1,234	−113
Indonesia	2.59	5,841	14,374	11,020	3,355
Cambodia	2.68	137	176	191	−15
Mozambique	2.85	159	78	144	−66
Madagascar	3.59	154	223	146	76
Portugal	3.86	6,801	1,305	2,601	−1,296
South Africa	3.94	8,337	7,299	5,656	1,643
Nicaragua	4.42	188	94	173	−79
Lao PDR	4.79	115	90	109	−19

Raw data from GTAP v7. See Narayanan and Walmsley (2008) available online at http://www.gtap.agecon.purdue.edu/databases/v7/v7_doco.asp

reported in Table 1, however, is dominated by China's consumption of oil.

5.2 Contribution to Global Sustainability

Table 2 describes contributions to global sustainability defined as global genuine saving: that is the world's gross saving plus educational expenditures minus produced capital depreciation and the values of natural resource depletion and carbon emissions. That is, the final row indicates the global rate of genuine savings (i.e., genuine saving as a percentage of gross world income) as well as its (global) components. To simplify this exposition of "contribution" for the moment, we aggregate our 113 countries and regions to a smaller group of 18 regional units. For each of these units, the specific contribution to global sustainability overall is indicated in the initial column of results.

This indicates that China's genuine saving is such that overall it increases global sustainability – that is, the global rate of genuine saving – by 1.09 percent. For the components of genuine saving, the effect of each component is either to boost the (global) genuine saving rate, in the case of gross saving and education expenditures or to shrink this rate in the case of depreciation of produced capital, natural resource depletion, and (notional) liabilities arising from carbon emissions. Again, to use the example of China, the contribution of its gross saving rate is – other things being equal – to increase global sustainability by 2.18 percent while depreciation of produced capital decreases global sustainability by 0.48 percent.

We are particularly interested in how our assessment of the contribution of these regions to global sustainability shifts when we move to consider virtual sustainability. That is, when we look at the implied contributions from taking a consumption-based rather than a production-based perspective on both climate change liabilities and resource depletion. Column 10 of Table 2 illustrates the total contribution for the former approach while column 7 describes the latter. Given that these data are defined as percentages of gross world income, the magnitudes in the table tend to look small. Thus it should be borne in mind that these percentages correspond to substantial monetary magnitudes as the earlier discussion of our findings indicated.

Reference to columns 6 and 9 also make it clear that most of these total contributions (for the changes in natural assets that we consider) are due to the carbon emissions component. The region "other Europe" (which includes Norway) is the only exception, although for North Africa and Middle East as well as Sub-Saharan Africa, the components are less far apart (in percentage contribution terms). With regards to the differences between columns, the effect of taking the consumption-based perspective is to decrease the virtual sustainability of countries or regions such as Japan, the European Union (15), and the U.S. Thus, the decrease in virtual sustainability is 0.24 percent (of gross world income), 0.73 percent, and 1.03 percent, respectively. Under the production-based perspective, by contrast, these contributions are 0.15 percent, 0.49 percent, and 0.84 percent, respectively.

These results are not a surprise and confirm the earlier intuitions of Martinez-Alier (1995) and subsequent commentators about the contributions to sustainability of developed countries. Nevertheless, it is also the case that a number of countries and regions that are comprised of less-developed countries exhibit a decreased contribution to global sustainability including India, East Asia, South Asia, Mexico, and Central America and the Caribbean. Those regions that receive a boost to their (virtual) sustainability on this consumption perspective include North Africa and Middle East, Sub-Saharan Africa, Australia and New Zealand, Canada, and Russia.

Again this seems to indicate that it is far from straightforward to validate the view that richer countries "import sustainability" from poorer countries. However, at least two additional considerations are worth noting. The first is that our coverage of (changes in) natural assets here is limited. Second, there are a variety ways of looking at this issue of contributions to global sustainability. An appendix to this chapter describes the results (in Table A.2) in per capita terms to take account of different population levels. This indicates that although the virtual sustainability shrinks, for example, in India, South Asia, and Mexico, as well as Central America and the Caribbean, in *per capita* terms

the picture seems rather different. Thus, the (negative) contribution of the average citizens to (virtual) sustainability in these countries and regions is below the global (per capita) consumption level, whereas the opposite is true for Canada and Russia, for example. Put another way, while the consumption perspective means that contribution of both of these countries to global sustainability is boosted, in per capita terms, natural asset *consumption* remains well above the global (per capita) average.

Finally, Table 3 illustrates those countries or regions in our sample which appear to exhibit negative genuine saving (in 2004). The first column of data indicates this negative saving as a percentage of that country or region's GNI while the second column gives the corresponding dollar value. The two columns immediately adjacent give respectively the dollar value of the change in natural assets (i.e., carbon emissions and resource depletion) from the production and consumption perspectives. The final column is the dollar difference between these magnitudes.

It is evident that for some of these countries or regions, taking account of virtual sustainability (i.e., the resources that these areas implicitly consumed) worsens our assessment of their contribution to global sustainability. This includes Senegal, Bulgaria, and Portugal as a number of composite regions (such as the "Rest of South Asia"). For a number of other areas, the opposite is true. That is, virtual sustainability for these other countries or regions gives a more favorable impression given that it appears that significant amounts of resource depletion or domestic carbon emissions can be attributed to satisfying final demand in other parts of the world. Notable regions or countries in this respect appear to be Indonesia and South Africa. Indeed, for the Former Soviet Union (which comprises Tajikistan, Turkmenistan, and Uzbekistan) and the Rest of South Central Africa (which comprises Angola and the Democratic Republic of the Congo), the difference between natural asset depletion and consumption is greater than the estimated negative genuine saving level.

Conclusions

The real value of global resource trade increased more than six-fold between 1998 ($613 billion) and 2008 ($3.7 trillion) (WTO 2010). Given this context, it is perhaps not surprising that the way in which relationships between trade and sustainability should guide comprehensive wealth accounting has been a pervasive question since the genesis of current interest in sustainability indicators more than two decades ago. While some progress has been made in answering this question, it is also arguable that there has been no satisfactory resolution. While we do not claim to have solved this conundrum in this chapter, we hope to have provided additional empirical insights. We have done this by augmenting an approach that has been much used recently to examine questions about carbon footprints and carbon leakage and, specifically, the carbon emissions that are embodied in the goods and services traded across national economies (i.e., virtual carbon).

Our extension here has been to consider in a fuller way how natural resources and the value of (notional) liabilities arising from carbon emissions are embodied in international trade flows. Furthermore, we have related this discussion to concerns about the sustainability of development. The key distinction here has been that of looking at use of natural resources and carbon emissions from a production perspective or a consumption perspective. In the former, we are interested only in accounting for resources depleted or carbon emitted by a national economy. In the latter, we are interested in the resources or carbon that an economy consumes to satisfy its final demand. We have argued that moving from the former perspective to the latter gives additional insights concerning the contribution of national economies to global sustainability (where sustainability here has been defined in terms of genuine saving). This can be best conceived of as telling

us something about the virtual sustainability of a national economy (i.e., rather than offering concrete prescriptions about how much that economy should actually save).

The empirical findings presented in this chapter appear to indicate that the magnitudes of the (change in) natural assets embodied in trade are substantial, both in dollar value terms and in relation to national economies. Moreover, our results seem to confirm the assertions of those who have argued that such resources flow from poor to rich nations. Nevertheless, there are nuances and caveats here, and whether such empirical patterns are sufficiently concrete as to draw strong conclusions about the virtual unsustainability of certain countries is another matter.

Of course, a large number of extensions and further work suggest themselves. In particular, in the context of further development of the current chapter, the following issues seem especially important:

First, it would be desirable to link our valuation of natural resource depletion to discussions elsewhere about the measurement of scarcity rents. For example, the latest estimates of resource use published in World Bank (2010) provide a clear link to the correct valuation of the change in natural assets in terms of comprehensive wealth accounting and sustainability.

Second, we have focused here on the total value of (rents in) resource trade. But given that the clearest link to thinking about this trade in relation to global sustainability is based on the possible mismatch between these magnitudes and their true scarcity values. Introducing further reflections on this into our empirical analysis seems worth considering.

Finally, our model here has focused on investigating the full links between where a resource is depleted and where it is finally consumed. There remain legitimate questions about where the limits of responsibility end. Such questions have clear relevance to thinking about virtual sustainability. Therefore, the examination of bilateral trade flows also seems relevant from this perspective.

World Bank Regional Classifications

Rest of Oceania XOC
- American Samoa
- Cook Islands
- Fiji
- French Polynesia
- Guam
- Island of Wallis and Futuna
- Kiribati
- Marshall Islands
- Micronesia, Federated States of
- Nauru
- New Caledonia
- Niue
- Norfolk Island
- Northern Mariana Islands
- Palau
- Papua New Guinea
- Samoa
- Solomon Islands
- Tokelau
- Tonga
- Tuvalu
- Vanuatu

Rest of East Asia XEA
- Korea, Democratic Republic of
- Macau
- Mongolia

Rest of Southeast Asia XSE
- Brunei Darussalam
- Timor-Leste

Rest of South Asia XSA
- Afghanistan
- Bhutan
- Maldives
- Nepal

Rest of North America XNA
- Bermuda
- Greenland
- Saint Pierre and Miquelon

Rest of South America XSM
- Falkland Islands (Malvinas)
- French Guiana
- Guyana
- Suriname

Rest of Central America XCA
- Belize
- El Salvador
- Honduras

Caribbean XCB
- Anguilla
- Antigua and Barbuda
- Aruba
- Bahamas
- Barbados
- Cayman Islands
- Cuba
- Dominica
- Dominican Republic
- Grenada
- Guadeloupe
- Haiti
- Jamaica
- Martinique
- Montserrat
- Netherlands Antilles
- Puerto Rico
- Saint Kitts and Nevis
- Saint Lucia
- Saint Vincent and the Grenadines
- Trinidad and Tobago
- Turks and Caicos
- Virgin Islands, British
- Virgin Islands, U.S.

Rest of EFTA
- Iceland
- Liechtenstein

Rest of Europe XER
- Andorra
- Bosnia and Herzegovina

- Faroe Islands
- Gibraltar
- Macedonia, the former Yugoslav Republic of
- Monaco
- San Marino
- Serbia and Montenegro

Rest of Former Soviet Union
- Tajikistan
- Turkmenistan
- Uzbekistan

Rest of Western Asia XWS
- Bahrain
- Iraq
- Israel
- Jordan
- Kuwait
- Lebanon
- Oman
- Palestinian Territory, Occupied
- Qatar
- Saudi Arabia
- Syrian Arab Republic
- United Arab Emirates

Rest of North Africa XNF
- Algeria
- Libyan Arab Jamahiriya

Rest of Western Africa XWF
- Benin
- Burkina Faso
- Cape Verde
- Cote d'Ivoire
- Gambia
- Ghana
- Guinea
- Guinea-Bissau
- Liberia
- Mali
- Mauritania

- Niger
- Saint Helena
- Sierra Leone
- Togo

Rest of Central Africa XCF
- Cameroon
- Central African Republic
- Chad
- Congo
- Equatorial Guinea
- Gabon
- Sao Tome and Principe

Rest of South Central Africa XAC
- Angola
- Congo, Democratic Republic of the

Rest of Eastern Africa XEC
- Burundi
- Comoros
- Djibouti
- Eritrea
- Kenya
- Mayotte
- Reunion
- Rwanda
- Seychelles
- Somalia
- Sudan

Rest of South African Customs Union
- Lesotho
- Namibia
- Swaziland

Table A1: Resource Depletion and Carbon Emissions by Country.

Note: In some cases the sum column across countries may not add exactly to the total value of the 'World'. This is concretely due to the rounding in several values at the regional level. Raw data from GTAP v7. See Narayanan and Walmsley (2008) available online at http://www.gtap.agecon.purdue.edu/databases/v7/v7_doco.asp

Country Name	GNI (in millions of US$)	Total Resource Depletion (in millions, US$)					Per Capita Resource Depletion and Comparison to Global Average (GA) (in US$)				CO₂ Emissions (in millions, US$) $50/tC			
		Production		Consumption		Ratio	Production		Consumption		Production		Consumption	
		Value	(%GNI)	Value	(%GNI)	Production/Consumption	Value	(P/GA)	Value	C/GA	Value	% GNI	Value	% GNI
United States	11,687,900	35,611	0.30	78,387	0.67	0.45	121	2.30	265	4.88	85,421	0.73	95,467	0.82
Japan	4,694,853	4,601	0.10	27,522	0.59	0.17	36	0.69	215	3.96	15,704	0.34	20,140	0.43
Germany	2,764,179	3,735	0.14	15,597	0.56	0.24	45	0.86	189	3.47	12,131	0.44	14,878	0.54
United Kingdom	2,215,020	8,444	0.38	11,276	0.51	0.75	142	2.71	190	3.49	8,336	0.38	11,881	0.54
France	2,077,657	2,059	0.10	9,902	0.48	0.21	34	0.65	164	3.02	5,414	0.26	7,953	0.38
China	1,928,118	34,308	1.78	36,819	1.91	0.93	26	0.50	28	0.52	69,055	3.58	54,093	2.81
Italy	1,717,791	1,594	0.09	9,741	0.57	0.16	27	0.53	168	3.09	6,419	0.37	8,336	0.49
Spain	1,030,351	1,760	0.17	7,506	0.73	0.23	41	0.79	176	3.24	4,748	0.46	5,862	0.57
Canada	971,963	14,505	1.49	7,827	0.81	1.85	454	8.67	245	4.51	8,190	0.84	7,707	0.79
Mexico	749,084	4,197	0.56	4,210	0.56	1.00	40	0.76	40	0.73	6,140	0.82	6,533	0.87
Korea, Republic of	724,100	1,008	0.14	8,047	1.11	0.13	21	0.40	169	3.11	5,474	0.76	5,717	0.79
India	695,941	7,047	1.01	13,026	1.87	0.54	6	0.12	12	0.22	17,116	2.46	15,856	2.28
Brazil	647,037	4,901	0.76	5,055	0.78	0.97	27	0.51	27	0.51	4,374	0.68	4129	0.64
Rest of West Asia	634,214	60,593	9.55	10,347	1.63	5.86	512	9.78	87	1.61	14,409	2.27	11,403	1.80
Netherlands	626,189	1,272	0.20	2,188	0.35	0.58	33	0.63	57	1.04	3,970	0.63	3,635	0.58
Australia	581,527	7,707	1.33	5,053	0.87	1.53	386	7.39	253	4.66	5,091	0.88	5,036	0.87
Russian Federation	578,971	29,586	5.11	10,948	1.89	2.70	206	3.93	76	1.40	23,517	4.06	18,130	3.14
Switzerland	388,888	63	0.02	1,376	0.35	0.05	9	0.17	190	3.50	664	0.17	1,376	0.35
Turkey	387,401	974	0.25	3,628	0.94	0.27	13	0.26	50	0.92	3,035	0.78	3,571	0.92
Belgium	362,908	707	0.19	2,722	0.75	0.26	68	1.30	261	4.81	1,578	0.43	2,266	0.62
Sweden	356,409	548	0.15	1,775	0.50	0.31	61	1.16	197	3.63	729	0.20	1,235	0.36

Country Name	GNI (in millions of US$)	Total Resource Depletion (in millions, US$) Production Value	Production (%GNI)	Consumption Value	Consumption (%GNI)	Ratio Production/ Consumption	Per Capita Resource Depletion and Comparison to Global Average (GA) (in US$) Production Value	Production (P/GA)	Consumption Value	Consumption C/GA	CO₂ Emissions (in millions, US$) $50/tC Production Value	Production % GNI	Consumption Value	Consumption % GNI
Taiwan	329,838	590	0.18	3,458	1.05	0.17	26	0.50	152	2.80	3,370	1.02	2,796	0.85
Austria	290,517	307	0.11	1,552	0.53	0.20	38	0.72	190	3.50	1,085	0.37	1,559	0.54
Norway	259,079	14,351	5.54	1,233	0.48	11.64	3,120	59.62	268	4.94	888	0.34	782	0.30
Denmark	245,851	1,680	0.68	1,144	0.47	1.47	310	5.93	212	3.89	757	0.31	1,069	0.43
Poland	244,566	1,641	0.67	3,193	1.31	0.51	101	1.93	197	3.62	3,051	1.25	3,369	1.38
Greece	227,323	560	0.25	1,826	0.80	0.31	50	0.96	165	3.03	1,377	0.61	1,701	0.75
Indonesia	225,214	9,142	4.06	6,256	2.78	1.46	42	0.79	28	0.52	5,232	2.32	4,763	2.12
South Africa	211,700	1,936	0.91	2,058	0.97	0.94	41	0.78	44	0.80	5,363	2.53	3,598	1.70
Finland	190,495	504	0.26	1,135	0.60	0.44	96	1.84	217	3.99	950	0.50	1,075	0.56
Portugal	176,127	371	0.21	1,460	0.83	0.25	35	0.68	140	2.57	934	0.53	1,141	0.65
Hong Kong – China	168,892	1,037	0.61	1,769	1.05	0.59	148	2.85	254	4.68	806	0.48	1,499	0.89
Iran, Islamic Republic of	160,332	14,611	9.11	4,924	3.07	2.97	212	4.06	72	1.32	6,663	4.16	6,728	4.20
Ireland	157,376	275	0.17	963	0.61	0.29	67	1.29	236	4.35	668	0.43	848	0.54
Thailand	154,104	1,752	1.14	3,179	2.06	0.55	28	0.53	50	0.92	3,218	2.09	2,596	1.69
Argentina	144,211	2,338	1.62	1,184	0.82	1.97	61	1.16	31	0.57	2,170	1.51	1,721	1.19
Malaysia	118,328	4,947	4.18	1,769	1.50	2.80	199	3.80	71	1.31	2,085	1.76	1,336	1.13
Rest of North Africa	114,553	11,754	10.26	2,273	1.98	5.17	308	5.90	60	1.10	2,300	2.01	2,099	1.83
Colombia	109,496	2,498	2.28	1,122	1.02	2.23	56	1.06	25	0.46	859	0.79	900	0.82
Venezuela, RB	108,779	8,424	7.74	1,421	1.31	5.93	321	6.13	54	1.00	2,178	2.00	1,661	1.53
Czech Republic	103,508	405	0.39	836	0.81	0.48	40	0.76	82	1.50	1,734	1.67	1,404	1.36
Singapore	103,199	41	0.04	1,022	0.99	0.04	10	0.18	239	4.41	557	0.54	962	0.93
Pakistan	100,140	456	0.46	1,548	1.55	0.29	3	0.06	10	0.18	2,158	2.15	2,374	2.37
Hungary	96,864	187	0.19	702	0.72	0.27	18	0.35	69	1.28	844	0.87	1,009	1.04
New Zealand	93,907	523	0.56	737	0.78	0.71	131	2.50	185	3.40	527	0.56	613	0.65
Philippines	93,649	790	0.84	1,856	1.98	0.43	10	0.19	23	0.42	1,208	1.29	1,263	1.35

| Country Name | GNI (in millions of US$) | Total Resource Depletion (in millions, US$) | | | | | Per Capita Resource Depletion and Comparison to Global Average (GA) (in US$) | | | | CO₂ Emissions (in millions, US$) $50/tC | | | |
| | | Production | | Consumption | | Ratio | Production | | Consumption | | Production | | Consumption | |
		Value	(%GNI)	Value	(%GNI)	Production/Consumption	Value (P/GA)		Value	C/GA	Value	% GNI	Value	% GNI
Chile	87,815	1,046	1.19	931	1.06	1.12	65	1.24	58	1.06	929	1.06	800	0.91
Egypt, Arab Republic of	78,757	2,976	3.78	2,207	2.80	1.35	41	0.78	30	0.56	1,977	2.51	1,770	2.25
Nigeria	78,110	9,354	11.98	931	1.19	10.05	73	1.39	7	0.13	785	1.00	793	1.01
Romania	73,910	505	0.68	781	1.06	0.65	23	0.44	36	0.66	1,476	2.00	1,269	1.72
Peru	66,037	903	1.37	938	1.42	0.96	33	0.63	34	0.63	575	0.87	604	0.92
Ukraine	64,084	633	0.99	1,301	2.03	0.49	13	0.26	28	0.51	5,021	7.84	2,812	4.39
Bangladesh	59,542	958	1.61	1,297	2.18	0.74	7	0.13	9	0.17	541	0.91	736	1.24
Morocco	55,961	270	0.48	743	1.33	0.36	9	0.17	24	0.44	580	1.04	686	1.23
Slovak Republic	55,490	97	0.18	389	0.70	0.25	18	0.35	72	1.33	473	0.85	500	0.90
Rest of Caribbean	53,616	1,061	1.98	1,952	3.64	0.54	28	0.53	51	0.93	2,465	4.60	2,415	4.50
Rest of Western Africa	50,191	1,081	2.15	921	1.83	1.17	9	0.18	8	0.14	361	0.72	599	1.19
Vietnam	44,554	1,897	4.26	1,152	2.59	1.65	23	0.44	14	0.26	1,197	2.69	1,237	2.78
Kazakhstan	40,289	2,529	6.28	805	2.00	3.14	170	3.26	54	1.00	2,447	6.07	2,045	5.08
Rest of East Africa	39,926	1,643	4.11	1,117	2.80	1.47	16	0.31	11	0.21	381	0.95	607	1.52
Croatia	39,891	115	0.29	381	0.95	0.30	25	0.48	84	1.54	320	0.80	382	0.96
Slovenia	33,334	73	0.22	269	0.81	0.27	37	0.71	137	2.52	233	0.70	284	0.85
Rest of Central Africa	31,819	2,582	8.12	496	1.56	5.21	73	1.40	14	0.26	160	0.50	219	0.69
Ecuador	30,740	1,947	6.33	734	2.39	2.65	149	2.85	56	1.04	324	1.06	389	1.27
Luxembourg	29,593	9	0.03	222	0.75	0.04	20	0.37	490	9.01	200	0.68	232	0.79
Tunisia	26,895	392	1.46	464	1.72	0.85	39	0.75	46	0.85	355	1.32	339	1.26
Bulgaria	24,953	434	1.74	608	2.44	0.71	56	1.07	78	1.44	687	2.75	627	2.51
Rest of Central America	24,610	156	0.63	410	1.67	0.38	11	0.21	29	0.54	213	0.87	301	1.22
Guatemala	23,627	101	0.43	279	1.18	0.36	8	0.16	23	0.42	165	0.70	242	1.02
Rest of South Central Africa	23,571	3,258	13.82	352	1.49	9.25	46	0.87	5	0.09	154	0.65	240	1.02
Belarus	23,167	497	2.14	500	2.16	0.99	51	0.97	51	0.94	828	3.57	766	3.31
Lithuania	21,937	62	0.28	281	1.28	0.22	18	0.35	82	1.50	188	0.86	263	1.20

Country Name	GNI (in millions of US$)	Total Resource Depletion (in millions, US$) — Production Value	Production %GNI	Consumption Value	Consumption %GNI	Ratio Production/Consumption	Per Capita Resource Depletion vs GA (in US$) — Production Value	Production P/GA	Consumption Value	Consumption C/GA	CO_2 Emissions (in millions, US$ $50/tC) — Production Value	Production %GNI	Consumption Value	Consumption %GNI
Sri Lanka	20,458	187	0.91	495	2.42	0.38	9	0.17	24	0.44	187	0.91	271	1.32
Rest of Europe	19,329	454	2.35	762	3.94	0.60	32	0.61	53	0.98	1,100	5.69	1,078	5.58
Costa Rica	17,818	41	0.23	152	0.85	0.27	10	0.18	36	0.66	90	0.50	122	0.68
Rest of EFTA	15,551	83	0.53	115	0.74	0.72	255	4.88	354	6.52	85	0.55	95	0.61
Cyprus	15,135	13	0.09	165	1.09	0.08	16	0.30	199	3.67	110	0.73	148	0.98
Rest of South Asia	14,605	275	1.88	341	2.34	0.81	5	0.09	6	0.11	148	1.01	252	1.72
Former Soviet Union	13,980	1,907	13.64	844	6.04	2.26	51	0.97	23	0.42	2,957	21.15	2,331	16.67
Latvia	13,499	51	0.37	174	1.29	0.29	22	0.42	75	1.38	111	0.82	215	1.59
Panama	13,137	104	0.79	168	1.28	0.62	33	0.63	53	0.97	90	0.69	133	1.01
Uruguay	13,095	20	0.15	139	1.06	0.14	6	0.11	40	0.74	79	0.61	117	0.89
Rest of East Asia	11,483	563	4.90	458	3.99	1.23	22	0.42	18	0.33	1,067	9.29	817	7.11
Estonia	11,350	49	0.43	127	1.12	0.38	36	0.69	95	1.75	231	2.03	223	1.96
Tanzania	11,153	149	1.34	225	2.02	0.66	4	0.08	6	0.11	74	0.66	127	1.14
Rest of SACU	10,573	162	1.53	89	0.85	1.81	0.64	18	0.34	62	0.58	111		1.05
Ethiopia	9,989	64	0.64	180	1.81	0.35	1	0.02	2	0.04	92	0.92	141	1.41
Botswana	8,869	211	2.38	68	0.77	3.10	119	2.27	38	0.71	63	0.71	108	1.22
Bolivia	8,388	295	3.52	150	1.78	1.97	33	0.63	17	0.31	165	1.97	164	1.96
Uganda	8,338	233	2.79	98	1.18	2.37	8	0.16	4	0.07	49	0.58	69	0.83
Rest of South East Asia	8,323	818	9.83	48	0.58	17.03	634	12.12	37	0.69	109	1.31	70	0.84
Rest of Oceania	8,144	425	5.22	300	3.69	1.42	49	0.93	34	0.63	266	3.27	286	3.51
Azerbaijan	7,980	976	12.23	375	4.69	2.60	117	2.23	45	0.83	479	6.00	542	6.79
Rest of North America	1,600	23	1.44	84	5.25	0.27	180	3.44	656	12.07	52	3.27	80	4.97
Myanmar	-	287	-	188	-	1.53	6	0.11	4	0.07	135	-	172	-
World	41,272,071	349,294	0.8463205	349,294	0.8463205	1	54.54	1	54.54	1	384,358	0.93	384,358	0.93

Table A2: Per Capita Contribution to Global Sustainability by Region

Raw data from GTAP v7. See Narayanan and Walmsley (2008) available online at http://www.gtap.agecon.purdue.edu/databases/v7/v7_doco.asp

| | Genuine saving (millions, US$) | Genuine saving components | | | | | | "Virtual sustainability" | | |
| | | Gross saving | Depreciation of produced capital | Education expenditures | Change in natural assets: production perspective | | | Change in natural assets: consumption perspective | | |
					Carbon emissions	Natural resources	Total	Carbon emissions	Natural resources	Total
Aus./NZ/ Oceania	2,539	5,344	-3,434	1,069	-178	-262	-440	-179	-184	-363
China	480	682	-150	26	-52	-26	-78	-41	-28	-69
Japan	2,997	9,495	-7,492	1,150	-121	-35	-156	-155	-212	-367
East Asia	2,796	3,874	-1,446	502	-103	-31	-134	-104	-132	-236
South East Asia	223	402	-160	42	-25	-36	-61	-22	-28	-50
India	143	203	-66	28	-16	-6	-22	-14	-12	-26
South Asia	86	133	-43	9	-8	-5	-13	-10	-10	-20
Canada	3,834	6,983	-3,993	1,544	-253	-447	-700	-239	-243	-482
United States	2,060	5,207	-4,612	1,869	-285	-119	-404	-319	-262	-581
Mexico	1,342	1,702	-636	372	-57	-39	-96	-61	-39	-100
South America	349	698	-385	127	-31	-60	-91	-28	-31	-59
Central America/ Caribbean	156	341	-184	57	-39	-19	-58	-42	-39	-81
EU-15	3,440	6,247	-4,121	1,492	-120	-58	-178	-155	-168	-323
Russia	766	1,250	-261	141	-161	-203	-364	-125	-75	-200
EITs	281	780	-535	175	-94	-45	-139	-82	-53	-135
Other Europe	9,484	15,463	-7,682	2,905	-132	-1,070	-1,202	-181	-217	-398
North Africa/ Middle East	408	952	-411	157	-70	-220	-290	-64	-59	-123
Sub-Saharan Africa	44	129	-71	26	-11	-29	-40	-10	-10	-20
World	720	1,404	-853	282	-59	-54	-113	-59	-54	-113

REFERENCES

ANDREW, R., PETERS, G.P. & LENNOX, J. (2009). Approximation and regional aggregation in multi-regional input-output analysis for national carbon footprint accounting. *Economic Systems Research, 21,* 311-335.

ARROW, K., DASGUPTA, P., GOULDER, L., DAILY, G., EHRLICH, P., HEAL, G.,...WALKER, B. (2004). Are we consuming too much? *The Journal of Economic Perspectives, 18* (3), 147-172.

ARROW, K.J., DASGUPTA, P., GOULDER, L.H., MUMFORD, K.J. & OLESON, K. (2010). Sustainability and the measurement of wealth. *NBER Working Paper No 16599.*

ASHEIM, G. & WEITZMAN, M. (2001). Does NNP growth indicate welfare improvement? *Economics Letters, 73,* 233-239.

ATKINSON, G., DUBOURG, R., HAMILTON, K. & MUNASINGHE, M. (1997). *Measuring sustainable development: macroeconomics and the environment.* Cheltenham, UK: Edward Elgar.

ATKINSON, G. & HAMILTON, K. (2002). International trade and the 'ecological balance of payments'. *Resources policy, 28* (1-2), 27-37.

ATKINSON, G. & HAMILTON, K. (2007). Progress along the path: evolving issues in the measurement of genuine saving. *Environmental Resource Economics, 37* (1), 43-67.

ATKINSON, G., HAMILTON, K., RUTA, G. & VAN DER MENBRUGGHE, D. (2010). Trade in 'virtual carbon': Empirical results and implications for policy. *Global Environmental Change, 21* (1), 563-574.

BAILEY, R.W. & CLARKE, R. (2000). Global macroeconomic sustainability: A dynamic general approach. *Environment and Development Economics, 5,* 177-194.

BAIOCCHI, G. & MINX, J.C. (2010). Understanding changes in the UK's CO2 emissions: A global perspective. *Environmental Science and Technology, 44* (4), 1177-1184.

BOLT, K., MATETE, M. & CLEMENS, M. (2002). *Manual for calculating adjusted net savings.* Washington, D.C.: Environment Department, World Bank.

CLARKSON, R. & DEYES, K. (2002). Estimating the social cost of carbon emissions. *Government Economic Service Working Paper 140,* DEFRA.

COMMONWEALTH OF AUSTRALIA. (2011). *Securing a clean energy future: The Australian government's climate change plan.* Licensed from the Commonwealth of Australia under a Creative Commons Attribution 3.0 Australia Licence.

COPELAND, B. & GULATI, S. (2006). Trade and the environment in developing countries. In R.E. Lopez & M.A. Toman (Eds.) *Economic development and environmental sustainability: New policy options, the initiative for policy dialogue series.* New York: Oxford University Press.

DASGUPTA, P. (2001). *Human well-being and the natural environment.* Oxford: Oxford University Press.

DASGUPTA, P. & MÄLER, K.G. (2000). Net national product, wealth, and social well-being. *Environment and Development Economics, 5* (1-2), 69-93.

DAVIS, S.J. & CALDEIRA, K. (2010). Consumption-based accounting of CO2 emissions. *Proceedings of the National Academy of Sciences of the United States of America, 107* (12), 5687-92.

DELLINK, R., JAMET, S., CHATEAU, J. & DUVAL, R. (OECD). (2010). Towards global carbon pricing: Direct and indirect linking of carbon markets. *OECD Environmental Working Paper No. 20.*

DUPUY, L. (2011). *International trade and sustainability: A survey.* Universite Montesquieu Bordeaux IV.

FANKHAUSER, S. (1994). The social costs of greenhouse gas emissions: An expected value approach. *The Energy Journal, 15* (2), 157-184.

GUO, J., HEPBURN, C.J., TOL, R.S.J. & ANTHOFF, D. (2006). Discounting and the social cost of carbon: a closer look at uncertainty. *Environmental Science & Policy, 9* (3), 205-216.

HAMILTON, K. (2003). Sustaining economic welfare: Estimating changes in total and per capita wealth. *Environment, Development and Sustainability, 5,* 419-36.

HAMILTON, K. & ATKINSON, G. (1996). Air pollution and green accounts. *Energy Policy, 24* (7), 16-44.

HAMILTON, K. & BOLT, K. (2004). Resource price trends and development prospects. *Portuguese Economic Journal (Special Issue on Environmental Economics), 3,* 85-97.

HAMILTON, K. & CLEMENS, M. (1999). Genuine savings in developing countries. *The World Bank Economic Review, 13* (2), 333-56.

HAMILTON, K. & HARTWICK, J. (2005). Investing exhaustible resource rents and the path of consumption. *Canadian Journal of Economics, 38* (2), 615-621.

HAMILTON, K. & RUTA, G. (2009). Wealth accounting, exhaustible resources and social welfare. *Environmental & Resource Economics, 42,* 53-64.

HAMILTON, K. & WITHAGEN, C. (2005). *Savings, welfare and rules for sustainability.* Washington, D.C.: The World Bank.

HARTWICK, J.M. (1994). National wealth and net national product. *The Scandinavian Journal of Economics, 96* (2), 253-256.

HELM, D.R., SMALE, R. & PHILLIPS, J. (2007). *Too good to be true? The UK's climate change record.* Oxford: OXERA.

HUBACEK, J. & GILJUM, S. (2003). Applying physical input/output analysis to estimate land appropriation (ecological footprints) of international trade activities. *Ecological Economics, 44,* 137-151.

ISARD, W. (1951). Interregional and regional input-output analysis: A model of space-economy. *The Review of Economics and Statistics, 33,* 318-328.

KLEPPER, G. & STÄHLER, F. (1998). Sustainability in closed and open economies. *Review of International Economics, 6* (3), 488-506.

KRAUTKRAEMER, J.A. (2005). The economics of natural resource scarcity: The state of the debate. In R.D. Simpson, M.A. Toman & R.U. Ayres (Eds.) *Scarcity and growth revisited.* Washington, D.C.: RFF Press.

LEMOINE, D.M. & TRAEGER C. (2010). Tipping points and ambiguity in the integrated assessment of climate change. *CUDARE Working Papers: Paper 1111.*

LENZEN, M., MURRAY, J., SACK, F. & WIEDMANN, T. (2007). Shared producer and consumer responsibility — Theory and practice. *Ecological Economics, 61* (1), 27-42.

LENZEN, M., PADE, L.L. & MUNKSGAARD, J. (2004). CO2 multipliers in multi-region input-output models. *Economic Systems Research, 16,* 391-412.

LEONTIEF, W. & FORD, D. (1971). Air pollution and the economic structure: Empirical results of input-ouput computations. In A. Brody & A. Carter (Eds.) *Input-Output Techniques*. Amsterdam: North-Holland.

LUTTER, S., WILTING, H., WIEDMANN, T., PALM, V. & GILJUM, S. (2008). Interim-report on the results of the evaluation of methodologies assessed with the RACER framework. *ERA-NET SKEP Project EIPOT*.

MARKANDYA, A. & PEDROSO-GALINATO, S. (2007). How substitutable is natural capital? *Environmental Resource Economics, 37* (1), 297-312.

MARTINEZ-ALIER, J. (1995). The environment as a luxury good or "too poor to be green"? *Ecological Economics, 13* (1), 1-10.

MILLER, R.E. & BLAIR, P.D. (2009). Foundations of input-output analysis. In *Input-Output Analysis: Foundations and Extentions*. Cambridge: Cambridge University Press.

MUNKSGAARD, J. & PEDERSEN, K.A. (2001). CO₂ accounts for open economies: producer or consumer responsibility. *Energy Policy, 29*, 327-334.

MUÑOZ, P. & STEININGER, K. (2010). Austria's CO₂ responsibility and the carbon content of its international trade. *Ecological Economics, 69* (10), 2003-2019.

MYERS, N. & KENT, J. (2000). *Perverse subsidies: how tax dollars undercut the environment and the economy*. Washington, D.C.: Island Press.

NARAYANAN, B.G. & WALMSLEY, T.L. (EDS.) (2008). Global trade, assistance, and production: The GTAP 7 data base. Retrieved from www.gtap.agecon.purdue.edu/databases/v7/v7_doco.asp

NEWBOLD, S., GRIFFITHS, C., MOORE, C., WOLVERTON, A. & KOPITS, E. (2010). *The "social cost of carbon" made simple*. Washington, D.C.: United States Environmental Protection Agency.

NORDHAUS, W.D. & BOYER, J. (2000). *Warming the world: economic models of global warming*. Cambridge, MA: MIT Press.

OLESON, K.L.L. (2011). Shaky foundations and sustainable exploiters: Problems with national weak sustainability measures in a global economy. *Journal of Environment and Development, 20* (3), 329-349.

PEARCE, D. & ATKINSON, G. (1993). Capital theory and the measurement of sustainable development: an indicator of "weak" sustainability. *Ecological Economics, 8* (2), 103-108.

PETERS, G.P., MINX, J.C., WEBER, C.L. & EDENHOFER, O. (2011). Growth in emission transfers via international trade from 1990 to 2008. *Proceedings of National Academy of Sciences USA, 108* (21), 8903-8.

PETERS, G. & HERTWICH, E. (2008). CO2 embodied in international trade with implications for global climate policy. *Environmental Science and Technology, 42* (5), 1401-1407.

PETERS, G.P. (2008). From production-based to consumption-based national emission inventories. *Ecological Economics, 65* (1), 13-23.

PEZZEY, J. (1989). Economic analysis of sustainable growth and sustainable development. *Environment Department Working Paper No. 15*. Washington, D.C: The World Bank.

PROOPS, J.L.R. & ATKINSON, G. (1998). A practical sustainability criterion when there is international trade. In S. Faucheux, M. O'Connor & J. van der Straaten (Eds.) *Sustainable development: concepts, rationalities and strategies*. Dordrecht, The Netherlands: Kluwer Academic Publishers.

PROOPS, J.L.R., ATKINSON, G., SCHLOTHEIM, B.F. & SIMON, S. (1999). International trade and the sustainability footprint: A practical criterion for its assessment. *Ecological Economics, 28* (1), 75-97.

PYCROFT, J., VERGANO, L., HOPE, C., PACI, D. & CISCAR, J.C. (2011). A tale of tails: Uncertainty and the social cost of carbon dioxide. *Economics: The Open-Access, Open-Assessment E-Journal*. Retrieved from www.economics-ejournal.org/economics/journalarticles/2011-22

REBITZER, G., EKVALL, T., FRISCHKNECHT, R., HUNKELER, D., NORRIS, G., RYDBERG, T.,...PENNINGTON, D.W. (2004). Life cycle assessment part I: Framework, goal and scope definition, inventory analysis, and applications. *Environment International, 30* (5), 701-720.

SATO, M. & MARTIN, R. (2011). Embodied carbon flows in global supply chains: A study drawing on bilateral trade data. In *European Association of Environmental and Resource Economists 18th Annual Conference, 29 June – 2 July 2011*. Rome.

SEFTON, J.A. & WEALE, M.R. (1996). The net national product and exhaustible resources: The effects of foreign trade. *Journal of Public Economics, 61*, 21-47.

STERN, N. (2006). *The Stern review: The economics of climate change*. Cambridge, UK: Cambridge University Press.

STIGLITZ, J.E., SEN, A. & FITOUSSI, J.P. (2009). *Report by the Commission on the measurement of economic performance and social progress*. Retrieved from www.stiglitz-sen-fitoussi.fr/documents/rapport_anglais.pdf

TOL, R.S.J. (2008). The social cost of carbon: Trends, outliers, and catastrophes. *Economics: The Open-Access, Open-Assessment E-Journal, 2* (2008-25), 1-25.

UNECE. (2007). Measuring capital – Beyond the traditional measures. Paper read at Seminar session of the 2007 conference of European statisticians.

UNFCCC. (2009). Greenhouse gas inventory data. *United Nations Framework Convention on Climate Change*. Downloads Retrieved September 2009, from http://unfccc.int/ghg_data/items/3800.php

VINCENT, J.R., PANAYOTOU, T. & HARTWICK, J.M. (1997). Resource depletion and sustainability in small open eonomies. *Journal of Environmental Economics and Management, 33* (3), 274-286.

WACKERNAGEL, M., ONISTO, L., BELLO, P., LINARES, A., FALFAN, I., GARCIA, J.,...GUERRERO, G. (2000). Natural capital accounting with the ecological footprint concept. *Ecological Economics, 29*, 375-390.

WEITZMAN, M.L. & LÖFGREN, K.G. (1997). On the welfare significance of green accounting as taught by parable. *Journal of Environmental Economics and Management, 32*, 139-153.

WEITZMAN, M.L. (2007). The role of uncertainty in the economics of catastrophic climate change. *AEI-Brookings Joint Center for Regulatory Studies Working Paper Series: Working Paper 07-11*.

WIEDMANN, T. (2009). A review of recent multi-region input–output models used for consumption-based emission and resource accounting. *Ecological Economics, 69* (2), 211-222.

WIEDMANN, T., LENZEN, M., TURNER, K. & BARRETT, J. (2007). Examining the global environmental impact of regional consumption activities — Part 2: Review of input–output models for the assessment of environmental impacts embodied in trade. *Ecological Economics, 61* (1), 15-26.

WIEDMANN, T., WILTING, H., LUTTER, S., PALM, V., GILJUM, S., WADESKOG, A. & NIJDAM, D. (2009). Development of a methodology for the assessment of global environmental impacts of traded goods and services. In *SKEP ERA-NET Project EIPOT: Scientific Knowledge for Environmental Protection*.

WIEDMANN, T., WOOD, R. & MINX, J.C. (2010). A carbon footprint time series of the UK - Results from a multi-region input-output model. *Economic Systems Research, 22* (1), 19-42.

WORLD BANK. (2010). *World development indicators*. Washington, D.C.: The World Bank.

WORLD BANK. (2011). *The changing wealth of nations*. Washington, D.C.: The World Bank.

WTO. (2010). *World trade report 2010: Trade in natural resources*. Geneva: World Trade Organization.

CHAPTER 6

Natural capital as economic assets: a review

Partha Dasgupta

KEY MESSAGES

In calculating total wealth, depleting a type of natural capital and substituting it with another form of natural capital or with manufactured capital is frequently uneconomical in most countries. The assumption of absolute substitutability is not a realistic one.

Externalities are the effects of activities on the well-being of people who have not been parties to the negotiations that led to those activities. An example is the impact of upstream deforestation on downstream farmers. Without correction, the use of natural capital is implicitly subsidized by people who suffer from the externalities.

A large part of what nature offers is a necessity and not a luxury. There are options for some level of substitutability, but in consideration, caution must be taken for irreversible processes that might cause a decrease in well-being.

The social worth of natural resources can be divided into three parts: use value, intrinsic value, and option value – in varying proportions.

Property rights are currently focused on individual ownership. However, many of nature's services are public and therefore it is difficult to assign property rights to them. Moreover, if those rights are assigned, they are typically assigned without due accord to social justice. Ill-specified or unprotected property rights typically prevent markets from forming or make markets function wrongly when they do.

1. Introduction

Natural capital can be consumed directly (e.g., fruit and honey), used indirectly as inputs into production (e.g., fossil fuels and microbes that regulate diseases), or used directly and indirectly at the same time (e.g., clean air and fresh water). The value of natural capital could be *utilitarian* (e.g., a source of food or a keystone species) – economists call that its *use-value*; it could be *aesthetic* (e.g., places of scenic beauty); it could be *intrinsic* (e.g., primates and sacred groves); or it could be all those things together – in a word, biodiversity.

Natural capital often possesses yet another kind of value. It arises from a combination of two things: uncertainty in the future use-value of a resource (Box I); and irreversibility in its use. Genetic material in tropical forests is a prime example. The twin presence of uncertainty and irreversibility implies that preservation of its stock has the benefit of offering society flexibility regarding the future. Future options have additional value because, with the passage of time, more information should be forthcoming about the resource's use-value. That additional worth is often called an *option value*.[1]

Natural capital's worth to us could be from the product flows we are able to extract from it (e.g., timber, gum, honey, leaves, and bark), or from its presence as a stock (e.g., forest cover), or from both (e.g., watersheds). The stock could be an index of quality (e.g., air quality) or quantity. Quantity is sometimes expressed as a pure number (e.g., population size); in various other cases it is, respectively, (bio)mass, area, volume, or depth. But even quality indices are often based on quantity indices, as in "parts per cubic centimeters" for measuring atmospheric haze.

We view natural capital here in an inclusive way. At one extreme are fossil fuels. Economists call them "exhaustible resources" because each

unit of a fossil fuel used in production is lost forever. More broadly, economists sometimes refer to natural capital as "environmental resources," sometimes as "natural resources," and at other times as "environmental natural resources," the double adjective being a way to ensure that readers take their minds off dams, tarmacs, bulldozers, chain-saws, and automobiles.

However, when economists speak of environmental resources, they have regenerative resources in mind (e.g., water, timber, pollination). Handled with care, it can be put to use in a sustained way, but gets depleted if it is exploited at rates exceeding its ability to regenerate itself. The central problem in sustainability science is to uncover ways by which a literally indeterminate number of interlocking natural processes that shape regenerative resources can be managed so as to enable humanity to flourish indefinitely.

The Millennium Ecosystem Assessment (MA) (2005) was a pioneering study of the services humanity enjoys from *ecosystems*. Ecosystems are a mesh of humans and natural resources interacting with one another at a multitude of speeds and across often overlapping spatial scales. What constitutes an ecosystem is therefore dictated by the scope of the environmental problem. A number of ecosystems have a global reach (e.g., the deep oceans); others extend over large land masses (e.g., "biomes," such as the Savannah and the tundra); some cover entire regions (e.g., river basins); many involve clusters of villages (e.g., micro-watersheds); while others are confined to the level of a single village (e.g., the village pond).

MA (2005) offered a four-way classification of ecosystem services: (i) provisioning services (e.g., food, fiber, fuel, fresh water); (ii) regulating services (e.g., protection against natural hazards such as storms; the climate system); (iii) supporting services (e.g., nutrient cycling, soil production); and (iv) cultural services (e.g., recreation, cultural landscapes, aesthetic or spiritual experiences).In Sections 6 and 7 where we review various methods that have been devised to value natural capital, we will observe

---

1 The pioneering works on option values are Weisbrod (1964), Arrow and Fisher (1974), and Henry (1974). Option values are discussed in Section 7.3 and Box 4.

that the MA classification can be unified for the purposes of quantitative reasoning. Here it is also useful to note that cultural services and a variety of regulating services (such as disease regulation) contribute directly to human well-being, whereas others like soil production, for example, contribute indirectly by providing the means to grow food crops.

2. Nature as a capital asset

Viewing natural capital in an inclusive way allows us to develop a comprehensive language for sustainability science. We begin by studying five related issues that appear regularly in public discussions on the state of the environment: pollution and conservation; economic growth and the environment; necessities vs. luxuries; irreversible uses; and substitution possibilities.

2.1 Pollution and conservation

There is no conceptual difference between pollution and conservation. Environmental pollutants are the other side of environmental natural resources. In some cases, the emission of pollutants leads directly to a degradation of ecosystems (e.g., the effect of acid rains on forests); in others (e.g., wastes from pulp and paper mills), it means a reduction in environmental quality (deterioration of water quality in nearby streams), which also amounts to degradation of ecosystems (watersheds); in still others, it means depreciation of manufactured capital (e.g., the corrosion of buildings and structures). Thus, for analytical purposes there is no reason to distinguish resource management from pollution management. Roughly speaking, "resources" are "goods," while "pollutants" (the degrader of resources) are "bads." Pollution is the reverse of conservation.[2]

The mirror symmetry between conservation and pollution is illustrated by the atmosphere, which serves as both a source of nourishment and a sink for pollutants. The atmosphere is a *public good*: if the quality of the open atmosphere is improved, we all enjoy the benefits, and no one is excluded from enjoying those benefits.[3] However, unless public legislation says otherwise, the atmosphere is also a *common pool* for pollution. It's a pool into which everyone can discharge pollutants without having to pay. As the atmosphere is a public good, the private benefit from improving air quality is less than the social benefit. It follows that in the absence of collective action (e.g., public investment or public subsidy in cleaner technologies), there is under-investment in air quality.

Now look at the reverse side of the coin. As the atmosphere is a pool into which pollutants (e.g., carbon compounds) can be deposited by us all at no charge, the private cost of pollution is less than the social cost. It follows that without collective action (the imposition of a pollution tax; quantity restriction per user; or "cap-and-trade," which continues to be a much-discussed social mechanism for controlling carbon emissions), there is excessive use of the pool as a sink for pollutants. Either way, the atmosphere suffers from "the tragedy of the commons," which is a dramatic way of characterizing a wedge between private incentives and collective aspirations that is created by inadequate or ineffective property rights.[4]

---

2   This dual structure was developed in Dasgupta (1982).

3   The two characteristics of the atmosphere mentioned here define "public goods": such goods have the properties that (i) they are jointly consumable; and (ii) no one can be excluded from consuming them. What makes public goods "public" is an extreme feature of commodities whose use involves externalities, which are defined in Section X.

4   The metaphor is due to Hardin who coined the term "The Tragedy of the Commons" to explain the overexploitation of resources with no well established rules of use and governance (1968).

The theory

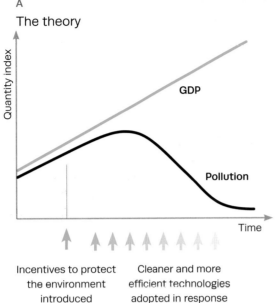

Incentives to protect
the environment
introduced

Cleaner and more
efficient technologies
adopted in response

B

The practice: GDP and emissions in OECD
countries

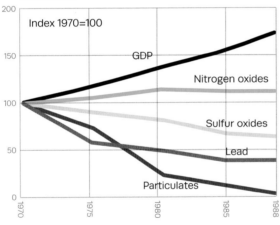

FIGURE 1

The theory and the prac-
tice: GDP and emissions in
OECD countries

2.2 Economic growth and the environment[5]

Ecosystem services are not only intrinsically valuable, they also have functional worth. But scratch an economist and you are likely to find someone who regards natural capital as a luxury. It is commonly thought that, to quote an editorial in the U.K.'s *The Independent* (DECEMBER 4, 1999), "... (economic) growth is good for the environment because countries need to put poverty behind them in order to care," or, to quote *The Economist* (DECEMBER 4, 1999: 17), "... trade improves the environment, because it raises incomes, and the richer people are, the more willing they are to devote resources to cleaning up their living space."

The idea is illustrated in the upper panel of Figure 1 and is given credence in the lower panel, where *emissions* of nitrous oxides (NO$_x$), sulfur oxides (SO$_x$), particulates, and lead were all found to have declined since 1970 in OECD countries even while gross domestic product (GDP) increased. Figure 1 is taken from World Bank (1992). Figure 2, also taken from World Bank (1992), shows that among countries where *per capita* income was under US$1,200 per year, the less poor suffered from greater *concentrations* of sulfur dioxide, but that among countries enjoying *per capita* income in excess of US$1,200, those that were richer suffered from lower concentrations. In short, the relationship between income *per capita* and concentration has the shape of an inverted-U. Among environmental economists, the curve in Figure 2 was promptly christened the "environmental Kuznets curve" because a similar relationship between GDP per capita and income inequality had been found decades ago by the economist Simon Kuznets. Figure 2 is based on inter-country data, not time series. Nevertheless, when taken in conjunction with Figure 1, it was found natural to interpret the evidence in such terms as the following:

5   This section draws heavily from Arrow et al. (1995), which was republished, with comments by a number of experts, in *Environment and Development Economics (1996)*, Vol. 1, No. 1.

"People in poor countries can't afford placing a weight on the natural environment over material well-being. So, in the early stages of economic development pollution is taken to be an acceptable, if unfortunate, side-effect of growth in GDP per capita. However, when a country has attained a sufficiently high standard of living, people care more about the natural environment. This leads them to pass environmental legislation and create new institutions to protect the environment."

The argument has been invoked in the main for amenities. Even within this class of goods, the environmental Kuznets curve has been uncovered for a very limited number of pollutants. Nevertheless, because it is consistent with the notion that as their incomes rise people spend proportionately more on environmental quality, it has proved tempting to believe that Figures 1 and 2 apply to environmental quality generally.

The temptation should be resisted. For example, if the degradation of natural capital were irreversible, economic growth itself would be at risk. And there are other reasons we should reject the use of Figure 1 as a general metaphor for the relationship between GDP and the state of the natural environment. Here are four reasons:

First, the inverted-U has been shown to be valid for pollutants involving local, short-term damages (sulfur, particulates, fecal coliforms), not for the accumulation of waste, nor for pollutants involving long-term and more dispersed costs, such as carbon dioxide, which typically have been found to increase continuously with income (WORLD BANK 1992; STERN 2006).

Second, the relationship between income per capita and environmental pollution cannot be the inverted-U if the feedback from pollution to the state of ecosystems is positive.

Third, the inverted-U hides system-wide consequences of emissions. Reductions in one pollutant in one country, for example, could involve increases in other pollutants in the same country or transfers of those same pollutants to other countries (transfer of dirty to dirty technology from rich to poor countries).

And fourth, in most cases where pollution concentrations have declined with rising income, the reductions have been due to local institutional reforms, such as environmental legislation and market-based incentives to reduce environmental impacts. Such reforms may ignore their possible adverse side effects on the poor and future generations. Where the environmental costs of economic activity are borne by those under-represented in the political process, the incentives to correct environmental problems are likely to be weak. The upper panel of Figure 1 is something of a mirage.

The solution to environmental degradation lies in such institutional reforms as would offer incentives to private users of resources to take account of the social costs of their actions. The inverted-U curve suggests this can happen only in *some* cases. Moreover, as we have already deduced, growth in GDP per capita is a wrong objective, we should instead be studying movements in wealth, not GDP.

2.3 Necessities vs. luxuries

Contrary to the views expressed in our quotes from newspapers, a large part of what nature offers us is a necessity, not a luxury. Many

FIGURE 2

Concentrations of sulfur dioxide

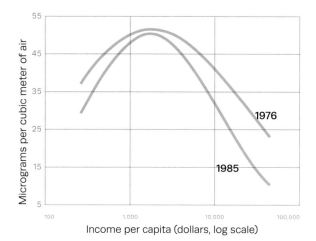

of the services we obtain from natural capital are "basic needs." Among the visible products are food, fibers, fuel, and fresh water – provisioning services (MA 2005). But many are hidden from view. Ecosystems, for example, maintain a genetic library, preserve and regenerate soil, fix nitrogen and carbon, recycle nutrients, control floods, mitigate droughts, filter pollutants, assimilate waste, pollinate crops, operate the hydrological cycle, and maintain the gaseous composition of the atmosphere – regulating services (MA 2005). A number of services filter into a global context, but many are geographically confined. Human well-being and the state of our natural environment are closely linked (DURAIAPPAH ET AL. 2005).

Natural capital offers joint products. Circulation of material (e.g., ocean currents and the wind system) transfers energy around the globe (e.g., influences precipitation) and dilutes pollutants; wetlands recycle nutrients and produce purified water; mangrove forests protect coastal land from storms and are spawning grounds for fish; and so on. Unhappily, social tensions arise in those many cases where an ecosystem has competing uses (farms versus forests versus urban development; forests versus agro-ecosystems; coastal fisheries versus aquaculture[6]). Dasgupta (1982, 1993) and Sachs, Gallup, and Mellinger (1998) traced the location of world poverty in part to the fact that the tropics harbor some of the most fragile ecosystems, including those that regulate disease. Carpenter et al. (2005) and Hassan, Scholes, and Ash (2005), which contain the first two sets of technical reports accompanying the Millennium Ecosystem Assessment, found that 15 out of the 24 major ecosystem services that the MA examined are either already degraded or are currently subject to unsustainable use.

A resource can be a luxury for others even while it is a necessity for some. Consider watersheds, which nurture commercial timber, agricultural land, recreational opportunities, and both market and non-market products (e.g., gums, resin, honey, fibers, fodder, fresh water, timber, and fuelwood). Watershed forests purify water and protect downstream farmers and fishermen from floods, droughts, and sediments. In tropical watersheds, forests house vast quantities of carbon and are the primary home of biodiversity. A number of products from watersheds are necessities for local inhabitants, including forest dwellers, downstream farmers, and fishermen; some are sources of revenue for commercial firms (e.g., timber companies), while others are luxuries for outsiders (eco-tourists). Some benefits accrue to nationals (agricultural products and fibers), while others spill over geographical boundaries (carbon sequestration). So, while watersheds offer joint products (e.g., protection of biodiversity, flood control, carbon sequestration, and household necessities), they also provide potential services that compete against one another (commercial timber, agricultural land, and biodiversity). Competition for nature's services has been a prime cause of the transformation of ecosystems. Politics often intervenes to ensure that commercial demand trumps local needs, especially under non-democratic regimes. Governments in poor countries have been known to issue timber concessions in upstream forests to private logging firms, even while evicting forest dwellers and increasing siltation and the risk of downstream flooding. Nor can the international community be depended upon to apply pressure on governments. When biodiversity is lost at a particular site, eco-tourists go elsewhere that has rich biodiversity to offer. So, international opinion is often at best tepid. In both examples, local needs are outflanked by outsiders' demands.

2.4 Irreversible uses

Ecosystems are driven by interlocking non-linear processes that run at various speeds and operate at different spatial scales (STEFFEN ET AL. 2004). That is why ecosystems harbor multiple basins

---

6 See Tomich et al. (2004), Tomich et al. (2005), and Palm et al. (2005); and Hassan, Scholes, and Ash (2005), respectively, on those tensions.

of attraction. The global climate system is now a well-known example, but small-scale ecosystems also contain multiple basins of attraction, and for similar reasons. For example, so long as phosphorus runoff into a fresh water lake is less than the rate at which the nutrient settles at the bottom, the water column remains clear. But if over a period of time the runoff exceeds that rate, the lake collapses into a eutrophic state. Usually the point at which the lake will collapse is unknown. That means the system is driven by non-linear stochastic processes (as discussed in Box 1 in Chapter 1).

When wetlands, forests, and woodlands are destroyed (for agriculture, mining, timber extraction, urban extension, or other uses), traditional dwellers suffer. For them, and they are among the poorest in society, there are no substitutes. For others, there is something else, often somewhere else, which means there are substitutes. Degradation of ecosystems is like the depreciation of roads, buildings, and machinery – but with three big differences: (1) depreciation of natural capital is frequently irreversible (or at best the systems take a long time to recover); (2) except in a very limited sense, it isn't possible to replace a depleted or degraded ecosystem with a new one; and (3) ecosystems can collapse abruptly, without much prior warning. Imagine what would happen to a city's inhabitants if the infrastructure connecting it to the outside world was to break down without notice. Vanishing water holes, deteriorating grazing fields, barren slopes, and wasting mangroves are spatially confined instances of corresponding breakdowns for the rural poor in poor countries. In recent years we have also seen how an ecological collapse accompanying high population growth, such as the one that has been experienced in recent years in the Horn of Africa and the Darfur region of Sudan, can trigger rapid socio-economic decline (HOMER-DIXON 1999; DIAMOND 2005; COLLIER 2007). The range between a need and a luxury is thus enormous and dependent on context. Macroeconomic reasoning glosses over the heterogeneity of earth's resources and the diverse uses to which they are put, by people residing at the site and those elsewhere.

2.5 Substitution possibilities

Environmental debates are often over the extent to which people are able to substitute one thing for another. Many believe that problems arising from the depletion of natural capital can always be overcome by the accumulation of manufactured capital, knowledge, and skills.[7] Others argue that humanity has reached the stage where there are severe limits to further substitution possibilities among large numbers of natural resources and among environmental resources and other forms of capital assets (EHRLICH AND GOULDER 2007).

Four kinds of substitution help to ease resource constraints, be they local or global. First, there can be substitution of one thing for another in consumption (e.g., nylon and rayon substituting for cotton and wool; pulses substituting for meat). Second, manufactured capital can substitute for labor and natural capital in production (the wheel and double-glazing are two extreme examples). Third, novel production techniques can substitute for old ones.[8] Fourth, and most important in the context of this chapter, natural resources themselves can substitute for one another (e.g., renewable energy sources could substitute for non-renewable ones). These examples point to a general idea: as each resource is depleted, there are close substitutes lying in wait, either at the site or elsewhere. The thought that follows is that even as constraints increasingly bite on any one resource base, humanity should be able move

---

7 Lomborg (2001) is an example. Macroeconomic growth theories are mostly built on economic models in which Nature makes no appearance.

8 For example, the discovery of effective ways to replace the piston by the steam turbine (i.e., converting from reciprocating to rotary motion) was introduced into power plants and ships a little over 100 years ago. The innovation was an enormous energy saver in engines.

Timber export and wealth transfers

An easy way for governments in countries that are rich in forests to earn revenue is to issue timber concessions to private firms. Often, concessions are awarded in forests in upstream watersheds. However, deforestation gives rise to soil erosion and increases fluctuations in water supply downstream. If the law recognizes the rights of those who suffer damage from deforestation, the timber firm would be required to compensate downstream farmers. But compensation is unlikely because (a) the cause of damage is many miles away, (b) the concession has been awarded by the state, and (c) the victims are scattered groups of farmers. Problems are compounded because the damage is not uniform across farms: location matters. It can also be that those who are harmed by deforestation don't know the underlying cause of their deteriorating circumstances. As the timber firm isn't required to compensate farmers, its operating cost is less than the social cost of deforestation (the latter, as a first approximation, being the firm's logging costs and the damage suffered by all who are adversely affected). The export therefore contains an implicit subsidy, paid for by farmers downstream. And we haven't included forest inhabitants, who now live under even more straightened circumstances; or worse, are evicted without compensation. The subsidy is hidden from public scrutiny, but it amounts to a transfer of wealth from the exporting country to the importing country. Some of the poorest people in a poor country subsidize the incomes of the average importer in what could well be a rich country. That doesn't feel right.

(BASED ON DASGUPTA ([1990]))

to other resource bases, either at the same site or elsewhere. The enormous additions to the sources of industrial energy that have been realized (successively, human and animal power, wind, timber, water, coal, oil and natural gas, and, most recently, nuclear power) are a prime historical illustration of this possibility.[9]

Humanity has been substituting one thing for another since time immemorial. Even the final conversion of forests into agricultural land in England in the Middle Ages was a form of substitution: large ecosystems were transformed to produce more food.[10] But both the pace and scale of substitution in recent centuries have been unprecedented. Landes (1969) has argued that the discovery of vast numbers of ways of substituting resources among one another characterized the Industrial Revolution in late eighteenth century. The extraordinary economic progress in Western Europe and North America since then, and in East Asia more recently, has been another consequence of finding new ways to substitute goods and services among one another and to bring about those substitutions. That ecosystems are spatially dispersed has enabled this to happen. The ecological transformation of rural England in the Middle Ages probably reduced the nation's biodiversity, but it increased income without any direct effect on global productivity.

But that was then and there, and we are in the here and now. The question is whether it is possible for the scale of human activity to increase substantially beyond what it is today without placing undue stress on the major ecosystems that remain. The cost of substituting manufactured capital for natural resources can be high. Low-cost substitutes could turn out to be not so "low-cost" if the true costs are used in the accounting, rather than the costs recorded in the marketplace (see below). Depleting one

---

9 But these shifts have not been without unintended consequences. Global climate change didn't feature in economic calculations until very recently.

10 Forests in England had begun to be denuded earlier, by Neolithic Britons and the Romans.

type of natural capital and substituting it with another form of natural capital or with a manufactured capital is frequently uneconomical.

3. Property rights

If natural capital is being degraded and depleted at unacceptable rates, wouldn't their market prices have risen? Aren't price increases the only reliable sign of growing scarcity?

The answer is "no." It could be that various kinds of natural capital are becoming scarcer even while prices in the market don't register that. So, in the presence of externalities – the effects of activities on the well-being of people who have not been parties to the negotiations that led to those activities – markets don't provide us with the right incentives to economize on our use of nature's services.

The question arises: Why don't market prices reflect nature's scarcity value? A common reason is that the institutions mediating the use of natural resources harbor externalities.

The presence of externalities in the use of natural capital means that their markets not only don't function well, they often don't even exist. In some cases markets don't exist because relevant economic interactions take place over large distances, making the costs of negotiation among interested parties too high (e.g., the effects of upland deforestation on downstream farming and fishing activities – see Box 1). In other cases, they don't exist because the interactions are separated by large temporal distances (the effect of carbon emissions on climate in the distant future, in a world where forward markets don't exist because future generations are not present today to negotiate with us). But the overarching reason is that private property rights to natural capital are frequently impossible to define, let alone enforce. And a common reason for the latter is that many "species" of natural capital are mobile. Birds and insects fly, rivers flow, fish swim, the winds carry, gases and particulates diffuse in air and water, and even earthworms are known to travel. The migratory

character of natural resources prevents markets from being formed because it isn't possible for people acting singly to lay claim to them.[11] The atmosphere and the open seas are prominent examples of resources whose markets don't exist. They are open to all, which is why they are called "open access" resources. As people are able to "free-ride," they collectively experience the "tragedy of the commons" (HARDIN 1968). Admittedly, private monopoly of a self-contained ecosystem would avoid free-riding, but it would grant far too much power to one person in the community.

That the constituents of ecosystems are mobile is related to the fact that ecosystem dynamics are non-linear, and involve positive feedback. And because the whole is frequently greater than the sum of its spatial parts, ecosystems are indivisible. If you slice off a portion for some other purpose, the productivity (e.g., biomass production) per unit area of what remains is reduced. Even if it were decreed that no portion could be converted for another use, parceling ecosystems into private bits would be inefficient because of the influences the mobile components would have on the parcels.

Agricultural land, especially in densely populated areas, is a different matter. Both labor and capital are critical inputs in production. Investment can increase land's productivity enormously. If agricultural land were to be decreed to be common property, it would be subject to serious management problems: temptations to free-ride on investment costs would be immense. The lack of incentives to invest and innovate would lead to stagnation, even decay. The fate of collective farms in the former Soviet Union testifies to that. Those regions of Sub-Saharan Africa where land is, or was until recently, held by the kinship, were exceptions, but in that region land was plentiful

---

11   Aquifers and oil reserves could be thought to be prominent counter examples. But rival extracters are able to siphon the resources from one another. Unless the extracter is a monopoly, enforcing property rights to mobile resources underground is a very difficult matter.

in the past and poor soil quality meant that land had to be kept fallow for extended periods. Of course, it may be that agricultural productivity remained low there *because* land was held by the kinship, not by individuals. As elsewhere in the social sciences, causation typically works in both directions.

Each of the above examples points to a failure to have secure *private* property rights to natural capital. We can state the problem in the following way: ill-specified or unprotected property rights prevent markets from forming or make markets function wrongly when they do form.

What about non-market institutions? In order to study these, we enlarge the notion of property rights to include *communal* rights over resources such as coastal fisheries, local woodlands, and village tanks; and *public* or state property rights (over forest lands, park, and inland lakes, for example). At the extreme are *global* property rights, a concept that is implicit in current discussions on climate change. But the idea isn't new, not even in the modern era. That humanity has collective responsibility over the state of the world's oceans used to be explicit in the 1970s, when politicians maintained that the oceans are a "common heritage of mankind."

The reasons markets don't function well also apply to non-market institutions. Environmental degradation is a consequence of *institutional failure*. The failure could be an absence of markets for ecological services; but it could be the inability of a group of nations to agree on a common fisheries policy in the seas, or it could be the state and private industry riding roughshod over forest inhabitants; it could be the local community, whose norms of behavior over the use of their local commons have collapsed; or it could be failure within the household, where the dominant male insists on growing fruit trees (the fruit can be sold in the market to which the female doesn't have easy access), rather than trees that would supply the woodfuel the female is expected to gather from the receding woodlands. To identify environmental problems as "market failure," as is commonly done in environmental economics, is a mistake.

4. Types of externalities

As institutional failure with regard to the use of environmental resources is commonly associated with the presence of externalities, let us remind ourselves that by an *externality* we mean the effects of human activities on people who weren't party to the decisions that led to those activities. Our definition relates directly to the observation that externalities are a symptom of institutional failure. Logging in the upland forests of watersheds can cause water runoff and inflict damage on farmers and fishermen downstream. If those who suffer damage are not compensated by mutual agreement, the damage is an externality. Free-riding on common property resources (CPRs) is another example of behavior that gives rise to externalities. Two broad types of externalities may be contrasted: *unidirectional* and *reciprocal* (DASGUPTA 1982). We discuss them here.

4.1 Unidirectional vs. reciprocal externalities

Unidirectional externalities are just that – unidirectional – where one agent (or a group of agents) inflicts or confers an externality on another (or others). Upstream deforestation damaging downstream farmers and fishermen is an example. Under reciprocal externalities each party confers or inflicts an externality upon all others, as in the private production of public goods or in the use of unmanaged CPRs.

The examples we have cited so far display "external dis-benefits." In contrast, when someone becomes literate at his own cost, he no doubt enjoys a benefit, but he also bestows benefits on those others who now are able to correspond with him. This is an example of an "external benefit." Meade (1952) famously studied the example of the apple grower and the neighboring beekeeper. As each person's activity confers a benefit on the other, the externalities are reciprocal. If the pair were to act without mutual consultation and negotiation, neither would take into account the beneficial effect of his investment on the other: the apple grower would invest in fewer trees and the beekeeper would keep fewer bees than would be in their mutual interest. The private production of public goods also involves external benefits.

The present definition of externalities is rough and not absolute. In many circumstances there would be people who would not be actual parties to agreements, but whose interests would be taken into account by those seeking to reach agreements with others. Accumulating funds in a bank for one's children's education is an obvious example; international agreements on carbon emissions to protect future generations from undue harm would be another. So we extend the notion of externalities to include cases where the interests of some of the affected parties were not adequately reflected in the agreements that underwrote the transactions.

Externalities are symptoms of institutional failure. Malfunctioning institutions sustain inefficient allocations of resources among contemporaries, across contingencies, and across time. They create a wedge between private and social rates of discount. Humanity's dealings with natural capital are riddled with externalities. So, a fruitful way to evaluate institutions is to study the extent to which they *don't* harbor externalities. What kind of institutions would they be?

4.2 Eliminating externalities

In the case of the upstream firm and downstream farmers, the state could tax the firm for felling trees (PIGOU 1920). The firm in this case would be the "polluter," the farmers the "pollutees." Pigovian taxes therefore invoke the *polluter-pays-principle* (PPP). The efficient rate of taxation would be the damage suffered by farmers. What the state does with the tax revenue is a distributional matter. Here we are concerned

with the efficiency of resource allocations. Pollution taxes are known today as *green taxes*.

But there is also a "market-friendly" way to eliminate externalities. The work of Lindahl (1958 [1919]) – and subsequently Meade (1953, 1972) and Coase (1960) – suggested that the state (or the community) could introduce private property rights on natural capital, the thought being that markets would emerge to eliminate the externalities. A problem with the proposal, at least as it is presented it here, is that it isn't clear who should be awarded property rights. In our example of the upstream firm and downstream farmers, the sense of natural justice might suggest that the rights should be assigned to farmers, who can be regarded as the pollutees. Under a system of "pollutees'-rights," the upstream timber firm would be required to compensate farmers for the damage it inflicts on them. Such a property-rights regime also invokes PPP.

Of course, the rights could be awarded to the timber firm instead. In that case it would be the farmers who would have to compensate the firm for not felling trees. The latter system of property rights invokes the *pollutee-pays-principle* (a reverse PPP, as it were), which for many people would seem repellent. But from an efficiency point of view, it's a matter of indifference as to which system of private property rights is introduced, so long, that is, as the prices that emerge (including those in the markets for externalities) are competitive prices (STARRETT 1972). Arrow (1971) pointed to a problem with Lindahl's proposal. Markets for externalities would be "thin." In our example, each market would involve precisely two parties: the timber firm and one farmer. It is hard to imagine that competitive prices could emerge in such circumstances. Nevertheless, markets for externalities have attracted much attention among ecologists and development experts in recent years, under the label *payment for ecosystem services*, or PES (see PAGIOLA ET AL. 2002, for a sympathetic review of a market-based PES).

A PES system, in which the state plays an active role, is attractive for wildlife conservation and habitat preservation. In poor countries property rights to grasslands, tropical forests, coastal wetlands, mangroves, and coral reefs are often ambiguous. The state may lay claim to the assets ("public" property being the customary euphemism), but if the terrain is difficult to monitor, inhabitants will continue to reside there and live off its products. Inhabitants are therefore key stakeholders. Without their engagement, the ecosystems couldn't be protected. Meanwhile flocks of tourists visit the sites on a regular basis. An obvious thing for the state to do is to tax tourists and use the revenue to pay local inhabitants for protecting their site from poaching and free-riding. Local inhabitants would then have an incentive to develop rules and regulations to protect the site. Box 2 offers an account of recent work on PES arrangements.

5. Quantifying externalities

Institutional failure is a prime reason why natural resources are underpriced in the market. Tracking time series of the market prices of minerals and fossil fuels in order to judge whether we face increasing resource scarcity is a bad move. Mining, smelting, and transporting minerals and ores involve the use of other types of natural capital (rivers, land, and the atmosphere, into which industrial effluents are deposited) for which payment is usually not made. So, mining, smelting, and transporting minerals and ores create externalities (MALER AND WYZGA 1972). The social cost (or *shadow cost*) of those industrial operations could be rising even while market prices for minerals remain flat or perhaps even decline. Under such institutional failure, the use of natural capital is implicitly subsidized by people who suffer from the externalities.[12]

5.1 External harms

At the global level, what is the annual subsidy of natural capital use? One calculation suggested that it is 10 percent of annual global income (MYERS AND KENT 2000). The margin of error in that estimate is very large, but until recently it's the only global estimate we have had. A recent study of The Economics of Ecosystems and Biodiversity (TEEB) puts the annual loss in ecosystem services at 1–2 percent of global income. That figure, too, is subject to a large margin of error. Many of the most reliable studies are those that look at "small" problems (households or industries exploiting fisheries, wetlands, coral reefs, water holes, mangroves, grazing fields, woodlands, etc.). The most promising route to a better understanding of the socio-ecological processes that shape our macroeconomies is to aggregate those small problems. From the global perspective, each of those many problems is small, but when added up, the sum would be significant (REPETTO 1989; MA 2005).

The spatial character of unidirectional externalities is self-evident, but getting a quantitative feel involves hard work. So the literature is sparse. As elsewhere in sustainability science, some of the best advances have been made in studies of involving multi-disciplinary expertise. Repetto et al. (1989) and Vincent and Ali (1997) estimated the decline in forest cover in Indonesia and Malaysia, respectively, owing to logging. Their investigation was at an intermediate spatial scale. The authors found that when deforestation is included, national accounts look quite different: net domestic saving rates are some 20–30 percent lower than recorded saving rates. In their work on the depreciation of natural resources in Costa Rica, the World Resources Institute some years ago found that the depreciation of three resources – forests, soil, and fisheries – amounted to 10 percent of

---

12   That is why the infamous bet between Paul Ehrlich and the late Julian Simon on the future trajectory of mineral and metal prices was a case of misplaced theorizing. Being an ecologist, Ehrlich should not have been expected to know that he had shadow prices in

mind, not market prices. And Simon, being an economist, should have told Ehrlich that it is shadow prices, not market prices, that reflect social scarcities. The bet was unfair.

GDP and over a third of capital accumulation. The findings suggest that an economy could in principle enjoy growth in GDP per capita and improvements in the United Nations' Human Development Index (HDI) for a long period even while its productive base shrinks.

5.2 External benefits

It was the point of Meade's (1952) example that in the absence of an agreement between the apple grower and beekeeper, pollination involves reciprocal externalities. But it is only recently that quantitative estimates have been made. There are several credible estimates at the local level. In a study in Costa Rica on pollination services, Ricketts et al. (2004) found that forest-based pollinators increase the annual yield in nearby coffee plantations by as much as 20 percent. Subsequently, Ricketts et al. (2008) analyzed the results of some two dozen studies, involving 16 crops in five continents, and discovered that the density of pollinators and the rate at which a site is visited by them declines at rapid exponential rates with the site's distance from the pollinators' habitat. At 0.6 km (resp. 1.5 km) from the pollinators' habitat, for example, the visitation rate (resp. pollinator density) drops to 50 percent of its maximum.

Pattanayak and Kramer (2001) reported that the drought mitigation benefits farmers enjoy from upstream forests in a group of Indonesian watersheds are 1–10 percent of average agricultural incomes. In another exemplary work, Pattanayak and Butry (2005) studied the extent to which upstream forests stabilize soil and water flow in Flores, Indonesia (see also PATTANAYAK 2004). Downstream benefits were found to be 2–3 percent of average agricultural incomes.

6. Estimating shadow prices

How should shadow prices be estimated? The term "externalities" is a catchword for a wide class of institutional failures that are translated into gaps between market prices and shadow prices. So, if at time t, $P(t)$ is the shadow price of asset i, $R(t)$ its market price, and $E(t)$ the social value of the net externalities its presence creates, then

EQUATION 1

$$P_i(t) = R_i(t) + E_i(t)$$

6.1 A general formulation

There is a utopian scenario where market prices equal shadow prices. The state of affairs prevailing utopia is called the full optimum. There are no externalities at a full optimum (i.e., $E_i(t)=0$), because what externalities there could have been have been internalized via institutional reforms and policy changes. Elsewhere, depending on the circumstances, market prices are reasonable approximations for some goods and services, while for others they are not.

For public goods and bads, $R_i(t)=0$ in Equation 1, which means that $P_i(t)=E_i(t)$. Fisheries in the open seas, carbon concentrations in the atmosphere, and such localized resources as mangroves, coral reefs, streams, and ponds are examples of the latter.

Assets are stocks. Recalling Definition 2 from Chapter 1, which states: *The shadow price of a capital asset is the contribution a marginal unit of it is forecast to make to human well-being,* we have

Proposition 1 $P_i(t)$ is the present discounted value of the flow of benefits society enjoys from a marginal unit of i.[13]

By the same token as Proposition 1, we have

Proposition 2. $E_i(t)$ is the present discounted value of the flow of the externalities associated with the presence of a marginal unit of i.

In estimating shadow prices of environmental resources, it is safest to return to the formal definition of shadow prices, which is provided by Equations (1) and (2). Recalling Equation (1) from Chapter 1 where

EQUATION 2

$$V(t) = V(\mathbf{K}(t),\mathbf{M},t)$$

V is intergenerational well-being, K are the capital assets and M is the evolving political economy (see Chapter 1 for a more detailed analysis of these equations)

Equation 2 tells us that in order to estimate the shadow price of any capital asset we need:

(a) A descriptive model of the economy.

(b) The size and distribution of the economy's capital assets at the date the evaluation is undertaken.

(c) A conception of intergenerational well-being.

Recall that natural capital can be consumed directly (e.g., fruit and honey), used indirectly as inputs into production (e.g., fossil fuels and microbes that regulate diseases), or used directly and indirectly at the same time (e.g., clean air and fresh water). Ingenious techniques for estimating shadow prices have been developed for those types of natural capital that are used directly, but are public goods (e.g., amenities such as places of scenic beauty and recreational areas, and such sites that are thought to possess intrinsic value [e.g., sacred groves]).[14] Unfortunately, ecosystem services and other inputs in production activities have not been studied much, so there is still no comprehensive text. The February 2011 issue of the journal, Environmental & Resource Economics (VOL. 48, NO. 2), containing a Symposium on "Conservation and Human Welfare: Economic Analysis of Ecosystem Services," is a rare exception in the prevailing literature on the valuation of ecosystem services (see especially, BALMFORD ET AL. 2011; and BATEMAN ET AL. 2011).

---

13 The discount rate to be used in estimating the present values are social rates of discount.

14 Freeman (1992) and Smith (1997) are fine expositions of the methods.

6.2 Asking questions and observing behavior

For environmental amenities, an appeal to Definition 1 in Chapter 1 (*By sustainable development we mean a pattern of societal development along which (intergenerational) well-being does not decline*) directly is problematic because of the enormous quantity of information demanded by requirements (*a*)–(*c*). So environmental and resource economists have devised two indirect methods. In one method, investigators ask people to place a value on ecological resources. This is often called contingent valuation. The other method has investigators study behavior and the consequences of that behavior to infer the value individuals place on those assets. This method is frequently called the revealed preference approach. It has been put to wide use in valuing subtle characteristics of capital assets that are hard to unscramble from their overall value. As an example, consider an asset that has multiple characteristics, such as land. The "hedonic price method" uses the market price of a piece of land to uncover the shadow price of one of its characteristics, for example, the value of its aesthetic qualities.

The hedonic price method has been much used to value real estate. In their work on inland wetlands in eastern North Carolina (U.S.), Bin and Polasky (2004) found that, other things being equal, proximity to wetlands reduced property values. Wetlands have many virtues, associated with the services they provide in decomposing waste, purifying water, and providing a sanctuary for birds and other animals. What Bin and Polasky (2004) discovered is that they may also possess a negative feature, namely bad odor!

As noted previously, the valuation methods that have become most popular were devised for environmental amenities, such as places of scenic beauty or cultural significance. The cost of travel to a site takes "revealed preference" to be the basis for valuing the site. Englin and Mendelsohn (1991), for example, is a well-known application of the method for estimating the recreation value of forests.

In contrast, the contingent valuation method (CVM) has proved to be extremely popular in those cases where there is no observed behavior (see CARSON [2004] for an extensive bibliography). The idea is to ask people how much they would be willing to pay for the preservation of an environmental amenity (e.g., flood control) or a resource of intrinsic worth (e.g., an animal or bird species).

Each of the above methods is of limited use for valuing the local natural resource base in the poor world. Moreover, one can question whether requirements (a)–(c) can be met adequately by studying people's behavior or analyzing their responses even to well-designed questions. One reason for being cautious about those methods (there are many other reasons) is that people often aren't aware of environmental risks. Jalan and Somanathan (2008) conducted an experiment among residents of a suburb of New Delhi. The aim was to determine the value of information on the health risks that arise from drinking water containing bacteria of fecal origin. Without purification, the piped water in 60 percent of the households were found to be contaminated. Among households in the sample that had not been purifying their piped water, some were informed by the investigators that their water was possibly contaminated, while the rest were not informed. The authors report that the former group of households was 11 percent more likely to invest in purification within the following eight weeks than the latter group. An additional year of schooling of the most educated male in the household was associated with a 3 percent increase in the probability that its piped water was being treated. The finding is noteworthy because the wealth and education levels of households in the sample were above the national average. If ignorance of environmental risks is pervasive, estimates of the demand for environmental quality that assume full information must be misleading.[15]

7. Using nature's production functions

So we return to requirements (a)–(c) as the basis for estimating shadow prices.

7.1 Carbon concentration

The welfare economics of climate change requires carbon in the atmosphere to be priced. It has been customary in that literature (e.g., CLINE 1992; STERN 2006) to place a global price for carbon concentration. A figure of US$20 per ton for carbon's global shadow price was suggested by Fankhauser (1995) and Pearce et al. (1996), with but scant justification. That figure was however used in the World Bank's work on sustainable development. But there are likely to be enormous regional variations in the impact of global climate change on economic activity (ROSENZWEIG AND HILLEL 1998; MENDELSOHN ET AL. 2006; DINAR ET AL. 2008). Agriculture in semi-arid tropical countries is expected to suffer from warming, while in temperate regions it will probably benefit. If we apply distributional weights to the losses and gains, the disparity is bigger than the nominal figures that have been suggested, because the former group of countries are almost all poor while the latter are middle-income to rich. Using a range of climate models, Mendelsohn et al. (2006) have published estimates of losses and gains in year 2100. The authors aggregated five sectors: agriculture, water, energy, timber, and coasts. Depending on the scenario, they found that the poorest countries (almost all in Africa) are likely to suffer damages from 12 percent to 23 percent of their GDP, while the range of impacts on the richest countries (North America and northern Europe)

is from damages of 0.1 percent to a gain of 0.9 percent of their GDP. Dinar et al. (2008) fear that with warming, the agricultural income in the semi-arid tropics could be more than halved in 2100 from its projected value in the case where there is no warming. But these estimates are based on market prices. If distributional weights are applied to obtain a global shadow price of carbon, it would be a lot higher than if we were merely to add the regional gains and losses. It should also be noted that the effects of climate change on health and the environment (e.g., loss of species) were not included in those estimates.

7.2 Ecosystem services

Several recent valuation studies have met requirement (a) by estimating the production function for nature's service (e.g., pollination as a function of the distance to a forest; primary productivity as a function of biodiversity; net reproduction rate of a species), but have otherwise assumed that market data are more or less sufficient to meet the other requirements.[16] Pattanayak and Kramer (2001) and Pattanayak and Butri (2005), for example, constructed a hydrological model to measure the contribution of upland forests to farm productivity downstream. Hassan (2002) used quantitative models of woody land resources in South Africa to estimate the value to rural inhabitants of (among other resources) the Fynbois Biome, which dominates sandy soils there. Barbier (1994) and Gren et al. (1994) used formal ecological models to compile a catalogue of the various services that are provided by wetlands, while Duraiappah (2003) developed a range of dynamic optimization coupled socioeconomic-ecological models to capture a variety of ecosystem services including tidal flushing, water

---

15 Determining the "willingness to pay" for changes in risk involves additional problems. See Smith and Desvouges (1987).

16 See Dobson et al. (1997), Barbier (2000), Turner et al. (2000), and Tilman et al. (2005) for illustrations of ecosystem production functions and the corresponding dynamics of the socio–ecological systems.

purification, and biomass evolution. In their study of wetlands in northern Nigeria, Acharya (2000) and Acharya and Barbier (2000) applied models of ground water recharge to show that the contribution wetlands make to recharging the basins is some 6 percent of farm incomes.

7.3 Option value

Economists as a general rule encourage decision-makers to maximize the expected value of well-being (Box 1) whereas environmentalists urge them to keep future options open. There is a sound intuitive basis for the latter. The use of environmental resources can have effects that are irreversible, implying that decisions today may constrain choices in the future. But that alone is not a reason for concern because if the future is known with certainty, then there is no cost to forgoing one's future options. It is the twin presence of uncertainty and irreversibility that makes flexibility an attractive feature of a planned course of action. An option value reflects the social worth of flexibility in a world where the social evaluator evaluates on the basis of the expected value of well-being.

Nowhere has the desirability of keeping future options open been advanced as vociferously as in discussions of the need for the on-site preservation of genetic diversity of plants and crops. Tropical forests are particularly noted for providing a habitat for a rich genetic pool, most of which is so far untapped for direct use, but some of which provides ingredients for pharmaceutical products. Much attention has been drawn to the continued decay of the genetic variability of crops resulting from an increased reliance on a few high-yield varieties in large parts of the world. As new varieties of crop pests and diseases appear, the chance of locating crop varieties that are resistant to them will be that much lower if genetic reserves are small. The genetic pool is a public good whose value becomes more and more sharply etched with the passage of time. Box 3 presents a numerical

example to show how option values ought to be determined.

7.4 Biases in estimates

What is the point of basing shadow prices solely on one particular use value when we know that natural capital often possesses other values too? The answer is that the method provides us with biased estimates of shadow prices. That can be useful information. For example, in a beautiful paper on the optimal rate of harvest of blue whales, Spence (1974) took the shadow price of whales to be the market value of their flesh, a seemingly absurd and repugnant move. But on estimating the population growth functions of blue whales and the harvest-cost functions, he found that under a wide range of plausible parameter values it would be most profitable commercially for the international whaling industry to agree to a moratorium until the desired long-run population size was reached, and for the industry to subsequently harvest the whales at a rate equal to the population's optimal sustainable yield.[17] In Spence's analysis, preservation was recommended solely on commercial grounds. But if preservation is justified when the shadow price of blue whales is estimated from their market price, the recommendation would, obviously, be reinforced if their intrinsic worth were to be added. This was the point of Spence's exercise.

8. Conclusion

The social worth of natural resources can be divided into three parts: *use value*, *intrinsic value*, and *option value*. The proportions differ. Oil and natural gas aren't usually thought to possess intrinsic value, nor perhaps an option value,

---

17 During the moratorium the whale population grows at the fastest possible rate. In Spence's numerical computations, the commercially most–profitable duration of the moratorium was found to be some 10–15 years.

BOX 3
Valuing Options

Section 7.3 introduced a component of environmental shadow prices that goes by the name "option value." Option values arise from the twin presence of *uncertainty* about an asset's future worth and *irreversibility* of decisions in case the asset is degraded. An option value measures the social worth of the *flexibility* that a society would enjoy by keeping options open for the future, when new information about the worth of existing assets is expected to be forthcoming. Here we study the idea by means of an extreme example.

We suppose the decision-maker is risk-neutral. Because under normal circumstances a risk-neutral decision-maker can replace random variables by their expected values, we will be able to compute the value of flexibility relatively easily.

There are two periods, $t=0$ and 1. A forest, in area K, harbors a genetic pool. We assume that off-site preservation of the genetic material is prohibitive and that the forest land has alternative uses, say, urban development. However, deforestation would mean a loss of genetic diversity. That's the trade-off: genetic diversity vs. urban development. For simplicity, it is assumed that genetic diversity is proportional to forest size.

The social benefit from developing a marginal unit of forest land at $t=0$ is known to be $B(0)$. By definition, $B(0)$ would be the increase in well-being if an additional bit of the forest were developed for its alternative use. At $t=0$ there is uncertainty regarding the social losses from deforestation. In regards to that uncertainty, there are two possibilities, s_1 and s_2, with probabilities π and $(1-\pi)$ respectively. Following the established terminology of decision theory, we call the possibilities "states of nature." The state of nature will be revealed at $t=1$ (the future). If s_1 were to prevail, net social benefit at $t=1$ from

developing a marginal bit of the forest would be $B_1(1)$; if s_2 were to prevail, the net social benefit at $t=1$ from developing a marginal bit of the forest would be $B_2(1)$. We assume that if the entire forest is not developed at $t=0$, there will be a further option of how much of the forest to develop at $t=1$, once the state of nature is revealed. In short, the decision to develop the forest can be made at both periods. It's only if the entire forest is converted that future options are closed.

Let $D(0)$ be the area that is developed at $t=0$. Naturally, $0 \leq D(0) \leq K$. Now let $D_1(1)$ and $D_2(1)$ be the areas developed at $t=1$ under s_1 and s_2, respectively. Finally, let r be the rate at which social costs and benefits are discounted. It follows that expected value of the proposed development policy is

EQUATION B.4.1

$$V = \frac{B(0)D(0) + \left[\pi B_1(1) D_1(1) + (1-\pi) B_2(1) D_2(1)\right]}{(1+r)}$$

To have an interesting problem, we imagine that $B_1(1) < 0$, $B_2(1) > 1$, and $\left[\pi B_1(1) D_1(1) + (1-\pi) B_2(1) D_2(1)\right] > 0$; the latter of which says that at $t=0$, it is expected that at $t=1$ further development will be a good thing.

To formalize option values in this example, we begin by imagining that the loss of genetic diversity is fully reversible, that is, the area deforested at $t=0$ can be re-established without cost at $t=1$ should that be desired. The social evaluator's problem is to maximize equation B4.1 by choosing $B(0)$, $B_1(1)$, $B_2(1)$ subject to the constraints:

EQUATION B.4.2

$$0 \leq D(0), D_1(1), D_2(1) \leq K$$

The optimum decision rule is simple:

$D(0) = K$ if $B(0) > 0$ and $D(0) = 0$ if $B(0) < 0;$[1]

and $D_1(1) = 0$ and $D_2(1) = K$

Now suppose the other extreme, that genetic loss is irreversible. Irreversibility means that in place of constraint (B4.2), the social evaluator faces the constraint

EQUATION B.4.4

$$0 \leq D(0) \leq D_1(1), D_2(1) \leq K$$

The social evaluator's problem is to maximize (B4.1) subject to constraint (B4.4). The way to solve the problem is to work backward, from $t=1$ to $t=0$. If, at $t=1$, the true state of nature is revealed to be s1 then the social evaluator would choose $D_1(1) = D(0)$; if instead it turns out to be s_2, the social evaluator would choose $D_2(1) = K$. Thus, at $t=0$ the problem facing the social evaluator is to choose $D(0)$ so as to maximize

EQUATION B.4.5

$$V = \frac{\left[B(0) + \pi\, B_1(1)\big/(1+r)\right]D(0) + (1-\pi)B_2(1)K}{(1+r)}$$

The decision rule is clear:

EQUATION B.4.6

$D(0) = K$ if and only if $B(0) + \pi B_1(1)\big/(1+r) > 0$

Uncertainty and irreversibility, taken together, require a stiffer criterion for development than in their absence, because

EQUATION B.4.7

$$\frac{B(0) > B(0) + \pi B_2(1)}{(1+r)}$$

The difference between the two figures, namely, the absolute value of $\pi B1\big/(1+r)$, is the option value. Development has to be that much more valuable today if the forest is to be cleared for it.

---

[1] If B(0) = 0, then the choice of D(0) is a matter of indifference.

but they do have use value. The great apes are intrinsically valuable; some would say they should have no other value, that they are an end in themselves, not a means to anything. Option value is the value we apportion to a natural resource which could prove to be have a social worth *beyond* its known use value or intrinsic value. Biodiversity possesses all three types of value. Although there are several excellent treatises on valuation methods (e.g., FREEMAN 1992), they are altogether too limiting for the task in hand. MA (2005) has drawn our attention to the plight of the world's ecosystems. Yet, in comparison with the number of studies we currently have at our disposal on the valuation of environmental amenities, the size of the literature on the valuation of ecosystems is pitifully small. This paper has sketched a formulation that tells us the steps that are necessary to value ecosystem services. Valuation in practice requires a multi-disciplinary effort. At a minimum, economists need to get together with environmental scientists to devise methods for implementing steps (a)-(c), which provide the basis for understanding the shadow prices and, thereby, valuing ecological systems.

The valuation techniques we have enumerated here are built around the idea that preferences and demands, as they stand, should be respected. There is an enormous amount to be said for this, reflecting as it does a democratic viewpoint. But even when commending it, we shouldn't play down the strictures of those social thinkers who have urged the rich, whether in rich countries or in poor ones, to curb their material demands, to alter their ways so as to better husband earth's limited resources. Their thought is that we deplete resources without trying to determine the consequences of depleting them, sometimes because we haven't the time to find out, but sometimes because we may not wish to know, since the answer may prove to be unpalatable to us. Being sensitive to ecological processes requires investment in early education on the connection between human well-being and the natural environment. If such strictures as we are alluding to seem quaint today, it may be because we are psychologically uncomfortable with the vocabulary. But that isn't an argument for not taking them seriously.

REFERENCES

ACHARYA, G. (2000). Approaches to valuing the hidden hydrological services of wetland ecosystems. *Ecological Economics, 35*(1), 63-74.

ACHARYA, G. & BARBIER, E.B. (2000). Valuing ground water recharge through agricultural production in the Hadejia'Jama'are wetlands in Northern Nigeria. *Agricultural Economics, 22*, 247-259.

ARROW, K.J. (1971). Political and economic evaluation of social effects of externalities. In M. Intriligator (Ed.) *Frontiers of quantitative economics, Vol. 1*. Amsterdam: North Holland.

ARROW, K.J. & FISHER, A. (1974). Preservation, uncertainty and irreversibility. *Quarterly Journal of Economics, 88*, 312-19.

ARROW, K.J., BOLIN, B., COSTANZA, R., DASGUPTA, P., FOLKE, C., HOLLING, C.S.,...PIMENTEL, D. (1995). Economic growth, carrying capacity, and the environment. *Science, 268*(5210), 520-1. (Reprinted in *Environment and Development Economics*, 1996, 1.)

ARROW, K.J., SOLOW, R.M., PORTNEY, P., LEAMER, E., RADNER, R. & SCHUMAN, H. (1993). Report of NOAA panel on contingent valuation. *Federal Register, 58*, 4601-14.

BALMFORD, A., FISHER, B., GREEN, R.E., NAIDOO, R., STRASSBURG, B., KERRY TURNER, R. & RODRIGUES, A.S.L. (2011). Bringing ecosystem services into the real world: An operational framework for assessing the economic consequences of losing wild nature. *Environmental & Resource Economics, 84*(2), 161-175.

BARBIER, E.B. (2000). Valuing the environment as an input: Review of mangrove fishery linkages. *Ecological Economics, 35*(1), 47-61.

BATEMAN, I.J., MACE, G.M., FEZZI, C., ATKINSON, G. & TURNER, K. (2011). Economic analysis of ecosystem service assessments. *Environmental & Resource Economics, 84*(2), 177-218.

BIN, O. & POLASKY, S. (2005). Evidence on the amenity value of wetlands in a rural setting. *Journal of Agricultural and Applied Economics, 37*(3), 589-602.

BULTE, E.H., LIPPER, L., STRINGER, R. & ZILBERMAN, D. (2008). Payments for ecosystem services and poverty reduction: Concepts, issues, and empirical perspectives. *Environment and Development Economics, 13*(3), 245-254.

CARPENTER, S.R., PINGALI, P.L., BENNET, E.M. & ZUREK, M.B. (2005). *Ecosystems and human well-being, Vol. 2: Scenarios*. Washington, DC: Island Press.

CARSON, R.T. (2004). *Contingent valuation: A comprehensive bibliography and history*. Northampton, MA: Edward Elgar.

CLINE, W.R. (1992). *The economics of global warming*. Washington, DC: Institute for International Economics.

COASE, R. (1960). The problem of social cost. *Journal of Law and Economics, 3*(1), 1-44.

COLLIER, P. (2007). *The bottom billion*. Oxford: Oxford University Press.

DAILY, G. & ELLISON, K. (2002). *The new economy of nature: The quest to make conservation profitable*. Washington, DC: Island Press.

DASGUPTA, P. (1982). *The control of resources*. Cambridge, MA: Harvard University Press.

DASGUPTA, P. (1990). The environment as a commodity. *Oxford Review of Economic Policy, 6*(1), 51-67.

DASGUPTA, P. (1993). *An inquiry into well-being and destitution*. Oxford: Clarendon Press.

DASGUPTA, P. & HEAL, G.M. (1979). *Economic theory and exhaustible resources*. Cambridge: Cambridge University Press.

DIAMOND, J. (2005). *Collapse: How societies choose to fail or survive*. London: Allen Lane.

DINAR, A., HASSAN, R., MENDELSOHN, R., BENHIN, J. ET AL. (2008). *Climate change and agriculture in Africa: Impact assessment and adaptation strategies*. London: Earthscan.

DOBSON, A.P., BRADSHAW, A.D. & BAKER, A.J.M. (1997). Hope for the future: Restoration ecology and conservation biology. *Science, 277*, 515-522.

DURAIAPPAH, A.K, NAEEM, S., AGARDY, T., ASH, N.J., COOPER, H.D., DÍAZ, S., FAITH, D.P., MACE, G. MCNEELY, J.A., MOONEY, H.A., OTENG-YEBOAH, A.A., PEREIRA, H.M., POLASKY, S. PRIP, C., REID, W.V., SAMPER, C., SCHEI, P.J., SCHOLES, R., SCHUTYSER, F., JAARSVELD, A.J. (2005). *Ecosystems and human well-being. Biodiversity synthesis. A report of the millennium ecosystem assessment*. Washington, DC: World Resources Institute.

DURAIAPPAH, A.K. (2003). *Computational models in the economics of environment and development*. Dordrecht, Holland: Kluwer Academic Publishers.

EHRLICH, P.R. & GOULDER, L.H. (2007). Is current consumption excessive? A general framework and some indications for the United States. *Conservation Biology, 21*(5), 1145-1154.

ENGLIN, J. & MENDELSOHN, R. (1991). A hedonic travel cost analysis for valuation of multiple components of site quality: The recreation value of forest management. *Journal of Environmental Economics and Management, 21*, 275-90.

FANKHAUSER, S. (1995). *Valuing climate change: The economics of the greenhouse*. London: Earthscan.

FREEMAN III, A.M. (1993). *The measurement of environmental and resource values: Theory and methods*. Washington, DC: Resources for the Future.

GOLDSTEIN, J., DAILY, G.C., FRIDAY, J.B., MATSON, P.A., NAYLOR, R.L. & VITOUSEK, P.M. (2006). Business strategies for conservation on private lands: Koa forestry as a case study. *Proceedings of the National Academy of Sciences, 103*(26), 10140-10145.

GREN, I.M., FOLKE, C., TURNER, R.K. & BATEMAN, I. (1994). Primary and secondary values of wetland ecosystems. *Environmental and Resources Economics, 4*(1), 55-74.

HARDIN, G. (1968). The tragedy of the commons. *Science, 162*, 1243-8.

HENRY, C. (1974). Investment decisions under uncertainty: The irreversibility effect. *American Economic Review, 64*, 1006-12.

HOMER-DIXON, T.E. (1999). *Environment, scarcity, and violence*. Princeton, NJ: Princeton University Press.

JACK, B.K., KOUSKY, C. & SIMS, K.R.E. (2008). Designing payment for ecosystem services: Lessons from previous experience with incentive-based mechanisms. *Proceedings of the National Academy of Sciences, 105*(28), 9465-9470.

JALAN, J. & SOMANATHAN, E. (2008). The importance of being informed: Experimental evidence on demand for environmental quality. *Journal of Development Economics, 87*(1), 14-28.

LANDES, D. (1969). The unbound Prometheus. Cambridge: Cambridge University Press

LINDAHL, E. (1928). Some controversial questions in the theory of taxation. In R.A. Musgrave & A.T. Peacock (Eds.) *Classics in the theory of public finance*. London: MacMillan.

LOMBORG, B. (2001). *The skeptical environmentalist.* Cambridge: Cambridge University Press.

MÄLER, K.G. & WYZGA, R.E. (1976). *Economic measurement of environmental damage.* Paris: OECD.

MEADE, J.E. (1952). External economies and diseconomies in a competitive situation. *Economic Journal, 62*(1), 54-67.

MEADE, J.E. (1973). *The theory of externalities.* Geneva: Institute Universitaire de Hautes Etudes Internationales.

MENDELSOHN, R., DINAR, A. & WILLIAMS, L. (2006). The distributional impact of climate change in rich and poor countries. *Environment and Development Economics, 11*(2), 159-178.

MILLENNIUM ECOSYSTEM ASSESSMENT (2005). *Ecosystems and human well being.* World Resources Institute, Washington, DC: Island Press.

MYERS, N. & KENT, J. (2000). *Perverse subsidies: How tax dollars undercut our environment and our economies.* Washington, DC: Island Press.

PAGIOLA, S., LANDELL-MILLS, N. & BISHOP, J. (2002). Making market-based mechanisms work for forests and people. In S. Pagiola, J. Bishop & N. Landell-Mills (Eds.) *Selling forest environmental services: Market-based mechanisms for conservation and development.* London: Earthscan.

PAGIOLA, S., RIOS, A.R. & ARCENAS, A. (2008). Can the poor participate in payments for environmental services? Lessons from the silvopastoral project in Nicaragua. *Environment and Development Economics, 13*(3), 299-326.

PALM, C.A., VOSTI, S.A., SANCHEZ, P.A. & ERICKSON, P.J. (2005). *Slash-and-burn agriculture: The search for alternatives.* New York: Columbia University Press.

PATTANAYAK, S.K. (2004). Valuing watershed services: Concepts and empirics from Southeast Asia. Agriculture, *Ecosystems & Environment, 104*(1), 171-184.

PATTANAYAK, S.K. & BUTRY, D.T. (2005). Spatial complementarity of forests and farms: Accounting for ecosystem services. *American Journal of Agricultural Economics, 87*(4), 995-1008.

PATTANAYAK, S.K. & KRAMER, R.A. (2001). Worth of watersheds: A producer surplus approach for valuing drought mitigation in Eastern Indonesia. *Environment and Development Economics, 6*(1), 123-146.

PEARCE, D., CLINE, W., ACHANTA, A., FANKHAUSER, A., PACHAURI, R., TOL, R. & VELLINGA, P. (1996). The social cost of climate change: Greenhouse damage and the benefits of control. In J. Bruce, H. Lee & E. Haites (Eds.) *Climate change 1995: Economic and social dimensions of climate change.* Cambridge: Cambridge University Press, pp. 179-224

PIGOU, A.C. (1920). *The economics of welfare.* London: Macmillan.

REPETTO, R., MAGRATH, W., WELLS, M., BEER, C. & ROSSINI, F. (1989). *Wasting assets: Natural resources and the national income accounts.* Washington, DC: World Resources Institute.

RICKETTS, T.H., DAILY, G.C., EHRLICH, P.R. & MICHENER, C. (2004). Economic value of tropical forests in coffee production. *Proceedings of the National Academy of Sciences, 101,* 12579-12582.

RICKETTS, T.H., REGETZ, J., STEFFAN-DEWENTER, I., CUNNINGHAM, S.A., KREMEN, C., BOGDANSKI, A.,...VIANA, B.F. (2008). Landscape effects on crop pollination services: Are there general patterns? *Ecology Letters, 11,* 499-515.

ROSENZWEIG, C. & HILLEL, D. (1998). *Climate change and the global harvest: Potential impacts of the greenhouse effect on agriculture.* New York: Oxford University Press.

SACHS, J.D., GALLUP, J.L. & MELLINGER, A. (1998). Geography and economic development. In B. Pleskovic & J.E. Stiglitz (Eds.) *Annual World Bank conference on development economics.* Washington, DC: World Bank.

SAFRIEL, U. & ADEEL, Z. (2005). Dryland systems. In R. Hassan, R. Scholes & N. Ash (Eds.) Ecosystems and human well-being: Current state and trends. Findings of the condition and trends working group (pp. 623–662). *The Millennium Ecosystem Assessment Series, Volume 1.* Washington, DC: Island Press.

SCHEFFER, M. (2009). *Critical transitions in nature and society.* Princeton, NJ: Princeton University Press.

SMITH, V.K. (1997). Pricing what is priceless: A status report on non-market valuation of environmental resources. In H. Folmer & T. Tietenberg (Eds.) *The international yearbook of environmental and resource economics 1997/1998.* Cheltenham: Edward Elgar, pp. 156-204.

SMITH, V.K. (2004). Fifty years of contingent valuation. In H. Folmer & T. Tietenberg (Eds.), *The international yearbook of environmental and resource economics 2004/2005: A survey of current issues.* Cheltenham: Edward Elgar.

SMITH, V.K. & DESVOUSGES, W.H. (1987). An empirical analysis of the economic value of risk changes. *Journal of Political Economy, 95*(1), 89-114.

SPENCE, A.M. (1974). Blue whales and optimal control theory. In H. Göttinger (Ed.) *Systems approaches and environmental problems.* Gottingen: Vandenhoek and Ruprecht.

STARRETT, D. (1972). Fundamental non-convexities in the theory of externalities. *Journal of Economic Theory, 4,* 180-199.

STEFFEN, W., SANDERSON, A., TYSON, P.D., JÄGER, J., MATSON, P.A., MOORE III, B.,...WASSON, R.J. (2004). *Global change and the earth system.* Berlin: Springer.

STERN, N.H. (2006). *The Stern review of the economics of climate change.* Cambridge: Cambridge University Press.

TILMAN, D., POLASKY, S. & LEHMAN, C. (2005). Diversity, productivity and temporal stability in the economics of humans and nature. *Journal of Environmental Economics and Management, 49*(3), 405-426.

TOMICH, T.P., VAN NOORDWIJK, M. & THOMAS, D.E. (2004). Environmental services and land use change: Bridging the gap between policy and research in Southeast Asia. *Agriculture Ecosystems & Environment, 104*(1), 229-244.

TOMICH, T.P., PALM, C.A., VELARDE, S.J., GEIST, H., GILLISON, A.N., LEBEL, L.,...WHITE, D. (2005). *Forest and agroecosystem tradeoffs in the humid tropics.* Nairobi: Alternatives to Slash-and-Burn Programme.

TURNER, R.K., VAN DEN BERGH, C.J.M., SODERQVIST, T., BARENDREGT, A., VAN DER STRAATEN, J., MALTBY, E. & IRELAND, E.C. (2000). Ecological-economics of wetlands: Scientific integration for management and policy. *Ecological Economics, 35*(1), 7-23.

VINCENT, J.R., ALI, R.M. & ASSOCIATES (1997). *Environment and development in a resource-rich economy: Malaysia under the new economic policy.* Cambridge, MA: Harvard Institute for International Development.

WEISBROD, B.A. (1964). Collective consumption services of individual consumption goods. *Quarterly Journal of Economics, 77,* 71-7.

WORLD BANK. (1992). *World development report.* New York: Oxford University Press.

ZILBERMAN, D., LIPPER, L. & MCCARTHY, N. (2008). When could payments for environmental services benefit the poor? *Environment and Development Economics, 13*(3), 255-278.

CHAPTER 7

The road to wealth accounting

Charles Perrings

KEY MESSAGES

It is clear that human activity has had a profound effect on our environment, and that these effects, in turn, have had an impact on human well-being. While the importance of this relationship is appreciated, there are still few reliable indicators of the value to people of biosphere change.

The Millennium Ecosystem Assessment was able to quantify the physical changes in ecosystem services that had occurred in the previous half century, but it was unable to assign a value to the loss of non-marketed ecosystem services.

This chapter considers the issues involved in developing metrics of the social importance of biosphere change. What is needed is a measure of the impact of biosphere change on wealth and wealth distribution. The chapter discusses the welfare-theoretic foundations of wealth accounting, and the steps taken so far to build wealth accounts. It then considers what is required to evolve wealth accounts from the current system of national accounts (SNA).

The SNA provides an incomplete picture of wealth because it includes only property that generates private claims to future benefits. It therefore excludes parts of natural capital that is essential to human well-being but cannot be privately held (e.g., the atmosphere or the open oceans).

Two major efforts to advance our understanding of wealth are discussed here: the World Bank's idea of adjusted net savings, and the System of Environmental and Economic Accounts (SEEA). Both are important steps on the road to wealth accounting, but neither fully address the issues of what environmental stocks should be included, and how they should be measured and valued (the double counting caused by the SEEA's inclusion of ecosystems is particularly problematic).

Ultimately, country wealth measurements should include all natural assets that are under a country's jurisdiction and that contribute to human well-being, whether those assets are privately owned or not.

1. Posing the problem

There is accumulating evidence that human "management" of the biosphere is having a major effect on the abundance and diversity of other species, on ecological functioning, and on ecosystem processes. The most heralded impact of the conversion of land to human use is the extinction of other species, but anthropogenic environmental change has many other dimensions. Emissions into the air, soil, and water are affecting ecosystem processes at many different scales, extending from the global effect of greenhouse gas emissions on climate, to the local effects of nitrate emissions on groundwater. Two global assessments have documented the effect of people's use of terrestrial and marine resources on biodiversity change, and have offered some evidence for why it matters (HEYWOOD AND WATSON 1995; MILLENNIUM ECOSYSTEM ASSESSMENT 2005A). More recently, the TEEB (The Economics of Ecosystems and Biodiversity) report has summarized what is currently known about the value of biodiversity and non-marketed ecosystem services (KUMAR 2010). The problem remains, however, that there are few reliable indicators of the importance of biosphere change for human well-being.

The Millennium Ecosystem Assessment (MA) attempted to relate changes in biodiversity to human well-being through the identification of a set of "ecosystem services," defined as "the benefits that people get from ecosystems." These comprised provisioning services (production of foods, fuels, fibers, water, and genetic resources); cultural services (recreation, spiritual and aesthetic satisfaction, and scientific information); regulating services (controlling variability in production, pests and pathogens, environmental hazards, and many key environmental processes); and supporting services (the main ecosystem processes). The MA was not, however, able to do more than say whether the physical flows of these services had been enhanced or degraded in the previous half century. It was unable to assign a value to the loss of, for example, cultural or regulating services

relative to provisioning services. It was not, therefore, able to say whether the trade-offs being made between ecosystems services were warranted in terms of either their efficiency or fairness. Nor was it able to say whether the investments people had made in the conversion of ecosystems for the production of valued goods and services left society collectively richer or poorer – whether those investments were sustainable. Without information on the value of the ecosystem services forgone through land-use change, it is difficult for us to know whether land-use change is socially efficient, equitable, or sustainable. The TEEB project has subsequently summarized at least the range of value estimates reported in the economic literature (KUMAR 2010). But point estimates of the value of specific services are of little help in monitoring biosphere change.

This chapter considers the issues involved in developing metrics of the social importance of biosphere change. Whether society is concerned with inter-country comparisons, with tracking its own performance over time, or with understanding the distributional effects of biosphere change, the informational requirements are the same. What is needed is a measure of the impact of biosphere change on wealth and wealth distribution. The chapter discusses the implications of this requirement, first in terms of the welfare-theoretic foundations of wealth accounting, and then in terms of the steps required to evolve wealth accounts from the current system of national accounts.

2. Environmental change and environmental assets

2.1 Measuring environmental assets

The weaknesses of gross domestic product (GDP) or gross national income (GNI) as a measure of well-being have been often rehearsed and are well understood. Adjusting for transboundary flows and for the depreciation of assets to yield net national product (NNP) or net national income (NNI) addresses two of the main reasons why the measure is flawed. However, there still remain a number of fundamental problems including the exclusion of most non-marketed production and consumption, externalities, environmental deterioration and public lands, and the inclusion of defensive or remedial expenditures (repairing depreciation). Most importantly, NNP or NNI remain measures of a current flow of production or income. It is not a measure of the sustainability of that income. In other words, it does not test whether NNP is greater than, less than, or equal to income in the sense of Lindahl (1933) or Hicks (1939), and hence whether it increases, decreases, or has no effect on wealth. While a large number of alternative indices have been proposed in the literature[1] (GOOSSENS ET AL. 2007), we consider only those that address these specific weaknesses of NNP or NNI.

The MA classified the benefits obtained from ecosystems as belonging to one of four types: provisioning, cultural, regulating, and supporting.

- Provisioning services covered the products of renewable resources including foods, fibers, fuels, water, biochemicals, medicines, pharmaceuticals, and genetic material.
- Cultural services comprised a range of largely non-consumptive uses of the environment. In the MA they were defined to include the spiritual, religious, aesthetic, and inspirational well-being that people derive from the "natural" world; the value to science of the opportunity to study and learn from that world; and the market benefits of recreation and tourism.

- The regulating services included the moderation of air quality, climate, water flows, soil erosion, pests and diseases, and natural hazards. More generally, they comprise the benefits of biodiversity in regulating the effects of environmental variation on the production of the provisioning and cultural services, or the healthiness of the environment – in other words, benefits that people care about directly. They limit the effect of stresses and shocks to the system.
- Supporting services comprised the main ecosystem processes that underpin all other services such as soil formation, photosynthesis, primary production, and nutrient and water cycling (MILLENNIUM ECOSYSTEM ASSESSMENT 2005B).

Many provisioning services and some cultural services are supplied through well-functioning markets, and enter the national accounts through the product accounts for agriculture, industry, and services (SYSTEM OF NATIONAL ACCOUNTS [SNA] 2009). The prices of many may be distorted through the effects of government policy such as agricultural subsidies, but they are at least directly registered in the national income accounts. There are, however, a number of services that are not supplied through the market, and that are therefore unpriced and not currently captured in the national income accounts.

Note that this does not include all ecosystem services for which there are no functioning markets. Why? Consider a tract of land in private property that comprises a particular water sub-catchment, and that is used for the production of food crops. The production of food is one of the main MA provisioning services, but it depends on several other MA ecosystem services including the regulation of soil and water flows, pest and disease regulation, pollination, nutrient cycling, and so on. These services, and the biotic and abiotic conditions that support them, are what determine the productivity of the land. They are therefore also what determine its price – along with the land's location relative

---

1   These include Nordhaus and Tobin's Measure of Economic Welfare (MEW); the Index of Sustainable Economic Welfare (ISEW); the Genuine Progress Indicator (GPI); the UNDP's Human Development Index (HDI); the Gender–related Development Index (GDI); the Ecological Footprint (EF); the Happy Planet Index (HPI); the Environmental Sustainability Index (ESI); and the Environmental Performance Index (EPI) (Goossens et al. 2007).

to transport networks, markets, the characteristics that make it suitable as a place to live, and so on.

Variants of the MA classification have been proposed to address the potential for double counting (BOYD AND BANZHAF 2007; JOHNSTON AND RUSSELL 2011). It may be more useful simply to identify where double counting is likely to occur. To the extent that the regulating and supporting ecosystem services needed for agricultural production are reflected in the price of the land, they will be appropriately measured in the system of national accounts. Indeed, if all services are contained within the catchment, they will be fully accounted for. It is only the off-site benefits or costs of land management within the sub-catchment that are missing. Off-site flows of nutrients, pests and pesticides, siltation of rivers, and the like are externalities of land management that should be valued and accounted for wherever they have significant effects on well-being.

The task is not therefore to account for all ecosystem services. It is to account for ecosystem services that are not already explicitly or implicitly priced (and so reflected in the national income accounts), and that have a significant impact on well-being. Using the welfare theoretic basis for wealth accounting described in the appendix of this chapter as well as in Chapter 1 of this report, we are interested in changes in wealth due to changes in one or other of the principal stocks in the system: produced capital, $K_i(t)$, human capital, $L_i(t)$, and natural capital, $N_i(t)$. Wealth in country i is defined to be a function of these stocks:

EQUATION 1

$$V_i(S_i(t)) = V_i(K_i(t), L_i(t), N_i(t))$$

It follows that the change in wealth in any small interval of time is simply the net effect of changes in individual stocks. If there is no change in total factor productivity this is precisely equal to investment:

EQUATION 2

$$\frac{dV_i(S_i(t))}{dt} = \frac{\partial V(S_i(t))}{\partial K_i(t)} \frac{dK_i(t)}{dt}$$

$$+ \frac{\partial V_i(S_i(t))}{\partial L_i(t)} \frac{dL_i(t)}{dt} + \frac{\partial V_i(S_i(t))}{\partial N_i(t)} \frac{dN_i(t)}{dt} = I_i(t)$$

If there is a change in total factor productivity, and if that change depends upon the state of some global environmental public good, $G(t)$, then for the ith country:

EQUATION 3

$$\frac{dV_i(S_i(t), G(t))}{dt} = I_i(t) + \frac{\partial V_i(S_i(t))}{\partial G(t)}$$

$$\left(\frac{dG_i(t)}{dt} + \sum_{j \neq i} \frac{dG_j(t)}{dt} \right)$$

If $G_i(t) = G_i(N_i(t))$, that is to say if the contribution made by the ith country to a public good that influences total factor productivity, then there are two ways in which unpriced natural capital might influence national wealth. One is direct, the other indirect. The direct effect is the discounted value of a change in ecosystem services associated with a change in the physical quantity or quality of the country's natural capital. The indirect effect is the discounted value of the change in total factor productivity caused by the impact of a change in natural capital on environmental public goods.

It follows that conservation of natural capital in the ith country may confer benefits on other countries via an impact on total factor productivity:

EQUATION 4

$$\sum_{j \neq i, j=1}^{n} \frac{\partial V_j(S_j(t))}{\partial G(t)} \frac{\partial G(t)}{\partial G_i(t)} \frac{dG_i(t)}{dt}$$

Such effects will typically show up in changes in total factor productivity growth in other countries, and should properly be recorded in measures of net national product or income.

2.2 Environmental assets and total factor productivity growth (TFPG)

Vounaki and Xepapadeas (2009) have explored this effect (Table 1). They found that unaccounted contributions of the environment may be an important driver of estimates of total factor productivity growth (TFPG), and that explicitly accounting for environmental contributions can reduce it by a significant margin – potentially driving it into the negative range. In particular, they consider energy as an environmental factor of production in the aggregate production function that is priced, but that also generates an unpriced or uninternalized externality in the form of greenhouse gas emissions.

They ask how significant the effect of this has been on total factor productivity in a group of OECD countries, and what options exist to internalize their cost and thus to use them efficiently. The correction involves adjusting traditional total factor productivity growth measures by estimating an aggregate production function for a panel of 23 OECD countries, and subtracting the contribution of the unpriced or uninternalized part of energy costs, the CO_2 emissions, from output growth.

What is striking about their results is the number of cases in which total factor productivity growth has been driven into the negative range. The reason that this may happen is that if ecosystem services are an unpriced factor of production, their use may not be subject to the same discipline as priced factors, and so they may be used inefficiently. Negative total factor productivity growth would then be a measure of this inefficiency, its causes potentially lying in institutional conditions that "authorize" the externality in the first place (BAIER ET AL. 2006). The net effect is that the potential growth in national wealth is compromised.

2.3 Adjusted net savings

Adjusted net savings, as a measure of change in wealth, grew out the work of Pearce, Hamilton,

and Atkinson in the 1990s (PEARCE AND ATKINSON 1993; PEARCE ET AL. 1996; HAMILTON AND CLEMENS 1999; FERREIRA ET AL. 2008). It is a direct attempt to measure net change in the value of a country's capital stocks, where that includes produced, human, and at least some stocks of natural capital (HAMILTON AND CLEMENS 1999). If wealth is the value of the stock of all assets plus net investment, then the propositions in Section 2 imply that a necessary

TABLE 1

Traditional and externality–adjusted TFPG for 23 OECD countries

Countries	Traditional TFPG	Externality–adjusted TFPG
Canada	0.670	–1.979
U.S.A.	0.275	–2.206
Austria	0.635	–0.779
Belgium	1.079	–1.039
Denmark	0.321	–1.289
Finland	1.144	–1.107
France	0.705	–0.778
Greece	0.831	–0.479
Italy	1.537	0.387
Luxembourg	1.699	–2.580
Portugal	1.690	0.649
Spain	0.415	–0.695
Sweden	–0.040	–2.028
Switzerland	–0.059	–1.122
U.K.	0.859	–0.896
Japan	1.646	0.235
Iceland	0.473	–2.533
Ireland	1.638	–0.172
Netherlands	0.489	–1.414
Norway	1.564	–0.247
Australia	0.567	–1.226
Mexico	0.330	–0.814
Turkey	1.420	0.214
Average	0.865	–0.952

Source: Vouvaki and Xepapadeas (2009)

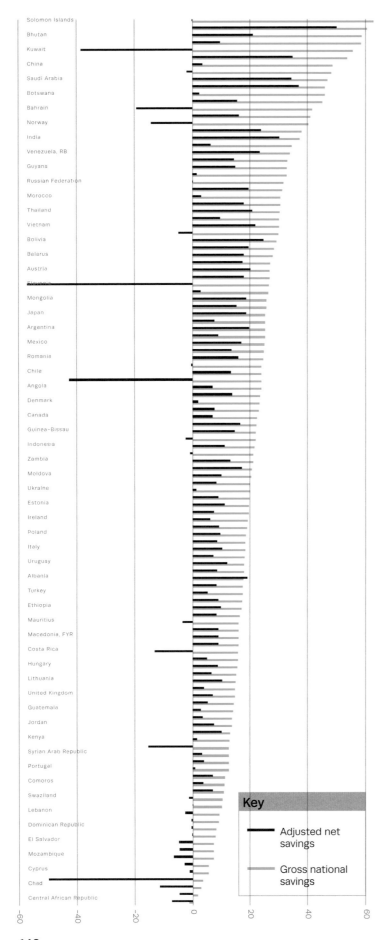

and sufficient condition for wealth to be increasing over time is that net investment be positive. That is, $dV(S(t))\big/dt > 0$. This in turn requires that $U'(C(t))(dC(t)\big/dt) <$ net national product. Adjusted net savings is intended to be a measure of $dV(S(t))\big/dt$.

In practice, adjusted net savings estimates are based on a partial correction of the figures in the SNA. The adjustments to gross savings reported in the national income accounts involve: (a) subtraction of the depreciation of produced capital; (b) addition of expenditure on education as a proxy for investment in human capital; (c) subtraction of the rents on depleted resource stocks; and (d) subtraction of specific pollution damages. The resource stocks currently included comprise energy (oil, gas, and coal); minerals (non-renewable mineral resources); and forest (rent being calculated on timber extraction Figure 1: gross national savings and adjusted net savings rates, 2008, in excess of the "natural" increment in wood volume). Pollution damages currently recorded include carbon dioxide and particulate matter (PM-10) damages.

Even though the correction is partial – including only some exploited natural resources, and a limited set of off-site external environmental effects – the impact on wealth assessments is substantial. Figure 1 shows the World Bank's estimates of gross national saving (GNS) and adjusted net savings (ANS) rates, using this method. In almost every case, GNS>ANS, and in many cases strongly positive GNS are associated with strongly negative ANS rates. Taking account of the depletion of valuable non-renewable assets and the environmental cost of industrial production in these cases implies that the value of aggregate capital stocks is declining, not increasing.

FIGURE 1

Gross national savings and adjusted net savings rates, 2008

Source: World Bank (2010)

While negative ANS in any one year provides a test of the sustainability of investment/consumption decisions in that year, to see whether a development program is sustainable requires evaluation over a longer period of time. Figure 2 reports ANS rates for four groups of countries over the period 1970–2005. The groups of countries are high-, middle- and low-income countries, shown together with the subset of low-income countries in the International Monetary Fund's Heavily Indebted Poor Country (HIPC) Program. Within that period all except the high-income countries had periods during which their adjusted net savings were negative – they were depleting aggregate capital stocks. However, for the most part, the adjusted net savings of most countries were positive. The exception is the HIPC countries, largely in Sub-Saharan Africa.

The group of countries in the HIPC program had negative adjusted net savings rates for most of this period. Since these countries are also characterized by high rates of population growth, the implication is that per capita wealth declined at an even faster rate.

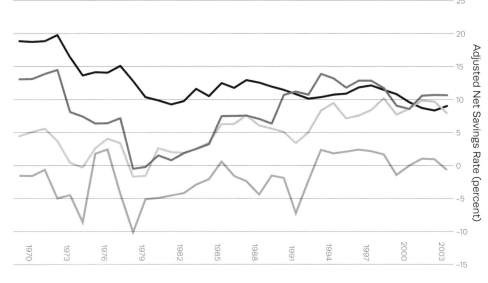

FIGURE 2

Adjusted net savings rates: high-, middle- and low-income countries plus heavily indebted poor countries, 1970–2005

Sources: Data from World Bank

Adjusted Net Savings (World Bank

2010), http://search.worldbank.org/data

Key

— High-income countries

— Heavily indebted poor countries

— Low-income countries

— Middle-income countries

3. Steps on the road to comprehensive wealth accounting

3.1 The World Bank's adjusted net savings indicators

The World Bank's report on global wealth and its distribution between countries in the year 2000, *Where is the Wealth of Nations?* (WORLD BANK 2006), and the update *The Changing Wealth of Nations* (WORLD BANK 2010) constitute the first attempts to understand the implications of such savings patterns for wealth and wealth creation. As such, they are critical steps on the road to global wealth accounting. They have, however, raised more questions than they have answered. These relate to four of the issues raised in the literature on the welfare theoretic foundations of wealth accounting:

- What is the role of environmental assets in the Solow residual and how does it affect changes in wealth?
- How should the off-site external environmental effects of resource use be reflected in asset values?
- What is the appropriate treatment of environmental assets that are public goods?
- What is the connection between environ-

mental wealth and poverty both within and across generations?

In the World Bank's approach there are two core stocks – "produced" and "natural" capital – and a balancing stock called "intangible" capital. Produced capital was defined as the sum of machinery, equipment, built structures, and built infrastructure together with the land on which such structures appear. The decision as to whether land was sufficiently modified to be classified as produced capital was based on existing land-use classifications. For example, urban land was considered sufficiently modified as not to be a "natural resource," and so was combined with produced capital in the wealth estimates. It was valued using the perpetual inventory method – that is by the aggregate value of gross investment less depreciation. Natural capital was defined as the sum of non-renewable resources occurring within the jurisdiction of a country such as oil, natural gas, coal, and minerals, together with arable lands, grazing lands, forested areas, and protected areas. It was valued by calculating the present value of resource rents over an arbitrary "lifetime" of 25 years at a discount rate of 4 percent.

Intangible capital was seen as a residual: the difference between total wealth and the sum of produced and natural capital. This included human capital (the knowledge, technical skills, cognitive capacities, physical attributes, etc. of the human population); the institutions of a country, sometimes referred to as social capital; and any produced and natural capital not explicitly accounted for in the produced and natural capital accounts (such as groundwater, diamonds, and fisheries), together with net foreign financial assets.

Not surprisingly, the World Bank found that intangible capital became increasingly significant as incomes rise, accounting for 81 percent of aggregate capital in high-income countries, 69 percent in middle-income countries, and 57 percent in low-income countries (WORLD BANK 2010). This reflects the greater importance of the service sector in high-income countries. It is partly accounted for by the fact that many more services fall within the market economy in high-income countries than in low-income countries, and partly by the concentration of skill-intensive services in high-income countries. To understand the relative importance of different factors in intangible capital, the World Bank (2006) modeled the residual in low- and middle-income countries as a function of domestic human capital (measured by per capita years of schooling of the working population); human capital abroad (measured by remittances from other countries); and governance/social capital (measured by the rule of law index). It found that most variation was explained by the rule of law, but that years of schooling were also important. While both are highly correlated with other things, it is a reasonable inference that human capital and social capital are both important components of intangible capital, and that these increase with per capita income.

Since intangible capital also includes environmental assets not recorded under natural capital and man-made assets not recorded under produced capital, and since it reflects factor prices that ignore external effects, this should be taken as a very rough guide only. While human capital and social capital are both important, is not possible to say much more. It is certainly not possible to draw conclusions about environmental assets beyond the traditional stocks recorded under natural capital.

One puzzle is that natural per capita wealth appears to rise with income. For example, per capita sub-soil assets were found to be an order of magnitude greater in high-income than in low-income countries. Since this does not correlate with the physical size of proven mineral reserves, the implication is that such resources are used more productively in high-income countries. At the same time, natural capital accounts for a greater share of per capita wealth in low-income countries than in high-income countries. This is frequently taken to mean that the poor are more dependent on environmental assets than the rich, and that they are consequently more affected by environmental degradation. Markandya's (2001) review of the literature on the relation between poverty, environmental change, and sustainable development suggested that to the question, "does poverty damage the environment?" the answer was broadly "no." To the question "does environmental degradation hurt the poor?" the answer was broadly "yes." Hence he concluded while poverty alleviation would not necessarily enhance environmental quality, and may in fact increase stress on the environment, environmental protection would generally benefit the poor (MARKANDYA 2001). This reflects the fact that a greater proportion of the labor force is employed in the resource sectors, and that agriculture, forestry, and fisheries account for a greater share of GNP in low-income countries than in high-income countries. But it also reflects the fact that property rights are frequently less well-defined in low-income countries, and that many natural assets are exploited under either open access regimes or as weakly regulated common pool resources.

What has not been resolved by the World Bank, and what needs to be resolved if we are to develop a full set of wealth accounts, is the identification of net changes in physical stocks, the value of ecosystem service flows that are external to the markets, and the problem of accounting for the environmental drivers of total factor productivity growth. Identification of net investment requires specification of net changes in both physical stocks and their shadow values.

3.2 Subtractions from and additions to natural resources

The first problem requires correct identification of physical stocks, along with additions to and subtractions from those stocks. A significant part of the problem with existing accounts is that the boundary between produced and natural assets is both ill-defined and shifting. A number of assets that deliver significant benefits are excluded. The only assets included in the accounts are those that are subject to well-defined property rights and an associated set of claims. This excludes human capital, social capital, and many natural resources.[2] Natural resources need both to be owned and capable of generating economic benefits for their owners, under "available technology, scientific knowledge, economic infrastructure, available resources and set of relative prices prevailing on the dates to which the balance sheet relates or expected to do so in the near future" (EUROPEAN COMMUNITIES ET AL. 2009). The SNA approach allows for forms of property other than strictly private property, in other words natural resources may be owned by groups of people, but it excludes resources that are not the property of either individuals or groups. Examples of excluded assets are the atmosphere, the open oceans, and uncultivated forests.

Whether investment in natural resources generates produced or natural capital in the SNA depends on the degree to which the resources are modified in the process. Natural resources are land, water, uncultivated forests, and mineral deposits. Their modification generally creates a produced asset, and is not regarded as affecting the value of the pre-existing natural resource (EUROPEAN COMMUNITIES ET AL. 2009). The problem with this approach is that the social value of the pre-existing assets rests in the discounted flow of the set of ecosystem services they deliver. In practice, what this means is that increasing land modification is assumed to build produced capital without impacting the flow of ecosystem services. Indeed, the value of changes in pre-existing ecosystem services is generally neglected. In *Where is the Wealth of Nations?*, for example, urban land is regarded as defined as produced capital – and valued as a proportion of the value of machinery and buildings.

This complicates the treatment of losses (depreciation) and gains (discoveries of non-

---

2   The SNA 2008 puts it as follows: "The coverage of assets is limited to those assets used in economic activity and that are subject to ownership rights; thus for example, consumer durables and human capital, as well as natural resources that are not owned, are excluded"

renewable natural resources, regeneration of renewable natural resources) in natural resource stocks. The major innovation of the World Bank's adjusted net savings estimate was the inclusion of the depletion of particular natural resources. It was limited to mineral deposits, forests, and water resources, and so did not capture changes in many other ecosystem services. Nor did it treat gains symmetrically. Nevertheless, it was a significant step in the development of wealth accounts.

At present, the SNA (2008) treats all gains and losses to natural resources as "other changes in the volume of assets account." These fall into a number of categories: changes in mineral stocks, the natural regeneration of biological resources, the effects of externalities and disasters, the assignment of property rights, monuments and valuables. In principle, natural regeneration is taken to be gross regeneration, but in practice it is recorded net. Depletion of forests, for example, was taken in World Bank (2006) to be depletion in excess of regeneration rates. In general, the SNA takes biological regeneration to be "produced" or "non-produced" depending on the degree of control exercised by the resource manager. Cultivation typically implies control, so the value of land in the SNA is exclusive of "any buildings or other structures situated on it or running through it; cultivated crops, trees, and animals; mineral and energy resources; non-cultivated biological resources and water resources below the ground. The associated surface water includes any inland waters (reservoirs, lakes, rivers, etc.) over which ownership rights can be exercised and that can, therefore, be the subject of transactions between institutional units" (EUROPEAN COMMUNITIES ET AL. 2009). By contrast, in non-cultivated systems, any increment in biomass is recorded as an "economic appearance" in "other changes in the volume of assets."

It follows that ecosystems, as entities that span distinct parcels of land, groundwater bodies, and the like, are not assets. Nor can they be recorded as assets in the accounts. The natural productivity and hence the value of a particular parcel of land in some economic use may reflect its place within an ecosystem. If a change in the ecosystem changes the productivity of the land, it will (in principle) appear in "other changes in the volume of assets." However, if the interactions between the biotic and abiotic elements of an ecosystem involve flows across property boundaries, and if these are external to the market, they will not be recorded.

3.3 Externalities

Calculation of the shadow value of the different capital stocks effectively demands that the rents on assets be calculated net of externalities. These are not currently accounted for in the SNA, although they may in principle be recorded in "other changes in the volume of assets." A discussion of the options for including externalities in the accounts by Nordhaus (2006) identifies two major issues: one being the adjustments to the accounts necessary to accommodate non-market activities; the other being the boundary of non-market accounts.

For non-market activities, the real problem concerns activities that generate public externalities. If non-market activities do not generate public externalities, they can be treated in a parallel fashion to private market activities. If there is, for example, a parallel market activity producing the same or a similar product, the "pricing" of the non-market activity by the market good through the "third-party rule" is adequate. If, however, production of some market good involves co-production of non-market effects, and there is no market analog to the non-market effect, "pricing" that effect is more problematic.

Nordhaus (2006) considers two cases. One is where externalities are already reflected in the accounts: where, for example, pollution damage inflicted by one activity on another increases the costs faced by the second activity. The advantage of measuring and accounting for such externalities lies in the efficiency gains that would occur if the costs incurred by the first activity fully reflected the damage inflicted on the second. The second case is where externalities cross the boundary between market and non-market activity. In this case they are not already reflected in the accounts, and estimating them would change value added in both the market and non-market accounts. He argues that it is more important to correct for the second case than the first.

The off-site externalities of many land uses may be characterized as ecosystem services/disservices. While most land uses are undertaken to provide benefits from the production of marketed goods and services – foods, fuels, fibers, recreation, etc. – they typically generate other benefits or costs. It is worth repeating that the ecosystem services we need to measure and account for are these same off-site effects. In the absence of off-site costs or benefits, the rents to some land use should capture the net effect of the full set of ecosystem services generated by that use. If there are off-site costs or benefits it will not.

As a general observation, it will seldom make sense to try to estimate the value of every off-site effect of some land use. It will only make sense to address effects that are sufficiently large that they lead to significant inefficiencies if neglected. For example, the importance of water regulation in the Catskills – a poster child for ecosystem services – lies in the fact that the catchment serves a city of 17 million people. Off-site hydrological effects in many other catchments might not warrant the same effort. What is needed is a system of triage to identify which ecosystem service flows would warrant attention and where.

3.4 Productivity growth

The third major problem still to be addressed in the development of wealth accounts concerns the Solow residual. Total factor productivity growth has a number of drivers, few of which are explicitly accounted for in the national income accounts. Among these are public sector research and development, and the efficiency of resource allocation. The efficiency of resource allocation in turn depends on the effectiveness of markets and regulatory institutions, the rule of law, and the trust that people have in the rule of law – or social capital. Knowing what drives total factor productivity growth in an economy is extremely important for the management of economic growth. The World Bank's wealth estimates found that a residual comprising human capital along with many of the drivers of total factor productivity growth was the primary correlate of income (WORLD BANK 2006). Currently, the SNA recognizes the need to include research and development as capital formation, and acknowledges that it should be valued at expected future benefits (EUROPEAN COMMUNITIES ET AL. 2009). However, most of the drivers of total factor productivity growth are not directly measured in the accounts.

The reason to focus on this problem here is that it is likely that environmental factors are an important element of total factor productivity growth. While this is intuitive in the case of renewable resource-based sectors such as agriculture, forestry, fisheries, conservation, ecotourism, water supply, and so on, it also applies to sectors in which productivity may be related to health conditions. For renewable resource-based sectors, improvements in ambient animal and plant health, water quality, soil loss, and the like would be expected to lead to productivity growth. But it is also the case that improvements in ambient human health are likely to have positive effects on productivity growth in many other sectors. Moreover, there are likely to be interactions between the drivers of total factor productivity growth.

The very high rates of productivity growth achieved in agriculture, for example, are generally assigned to research and development, the rate of return on agricultural R&D investment being estimated to lie between 45 percent and 55 percent (ALSTON ET AL. 2009; ALSTON ET AL. 2010). This depends on the impact improvements have on crop yields, but it also depends on the rate at which the material becomes available, the extent to which it is diffused – including the rate at which it is allowed to spill over into other jurisdictions – and the capacity of users to exploit it (PIESSE AND THIRTLE 2010). Projections of future total factor productivity growth in agriculture are much less optimistic, however. In the U.S., for example, total factor productivity growth over the period 2000–2025

TABLE 2
SNA environmental assets

AN.1	Produced assets
AN.11	Fixed assets
AN.111	Tangible fixed assets
AN.1114	Cultivated assets
AN.11141	Livestock for breeding, dairy, draught, etc.
AN.11142	Vineyards, orchards and other plantations
AN.112	Intangible fixed assets
AN.1121	Mineral exploration
AN.12	Inventories
AN.122	Work in progress
AN.1221	Work in progress on cultivated assets
AN.2	Non-produced assets
AN.21	Tangible non-produced assets
AN.211	Land
AN.2111	Land underlying buildings and structures
AN.2112	Land under cultivation
AN.2113	Recreational land and associated surface water
AN.2119	Other land and associated surface water
AN.212	Subsoil assets
AN.2121	Coal, oil and natural gas reserves
AN.2122	Metallic mineral reserves
AN.2123	Non-metallic mineral reserves
AN.213	Non-cultivated biological resources
AN.214	Water resources
AN.22	Intangible non-produced assets
AN.222	Leases and other transferable contracts

Source: SEEA (2003)

is expected to be less than half the rate achieved between 1975 and 2000 (GOETTLE ET AL. 2007). One consequence of this is that the growth in food production needed to meet the needs of the growing world population will increase the rate at which land is converted from other uses to agriculture, with all the consequences that has for biodiversity and ecosystem services.

The solution both to the problem of constructing wealth accounts, and to the management of interactions between assets not currently accounted for, is to quantify and value the capital stocks that do affect total factor productivity growth. That is the motivation for adding such stocks as explicit factors of production (VOUVAKI AND XEPAPADEAS 2009).

4. Satellite accounts and the capital accounts in the SNA

The consensus is that changes to the national income accounts needed to address these issues should appear first in satellite accounts. In practice, changes in both natural capital stocks and environmental externalities are addressed via the satellite *System of Environmental and Economic Accounts* (SEEA), still under development by the UN, the EC, the OECD, the IMF, and the World Bank. The SEEA (2003) includes measures of the effect of environmental change on capital stocks. Since the SEEA has a capital focus it is, in principle, consistent with the welfare-theoretic approach adopted by Dasgupta et al. (2000) That is, it takes changes in aggregate capital as a test of sustainability. Development is regarded as unsustainable if it relies on stocks of natural capital, and these are degraded to the point where they are no longer able to adequately provide what are referred to in the SEEA as "resource," "service," or "sink" functions (loosely corresponding to the MA provisioning, cultural, and regulating/supporting services). The SEEA comprises four accounts:

- Flow accounts for pollution, energy, and materials, recording industry level use of energy and materials as inputs to production along with the generation of pollutants and solid waste.

- Environmental protection and resource management expenditure accounts identifying expenditures incurred by industry, government, and households to protect the environment or to manage natural resources (already recorded in the SNA).
- Natural resource asset accounts recording changes in traditional natural resource stocks such as land, fish, forest, water, and minerals.
- Valuation of non-market flow and environmentally adjusted aggregates which adjusts aggregates for depletion and degradation costs, and defensive expenditures.

In contrast with the definition of natural resources in the SNA (Table 2), environmental assets in the SEEA are defined in Table 3.

Two aspects of these assets are worth noting.

First, aside from the intangible assets, these are all place-based and involve the conversion and management of, or impact on, ecosystem services associated with a particular place. *In situ* subsoil resources are not generally associated with biological activity, but their extraction involves production, processing, and waste disposal on the surface that frequently has extensive direct and indirect off-site impacts on ecosystem services. Surface "land" and "land-based" or "water" resources are more immediately used to enhance the flow of particular ecosystem services, though this may be at a cost to other services.

Second, there may be a range of property rights applying to environmental assets extending from private ownership (freehold), through time-limited use rights (leasehold), common property (common pool resources and public lands), to undefined rights (open access). Within the SNA, only assets subject to well-defined property rights are included, and most changes in environmental assets recorded in the SNA occur as "other changes in the volume of assets." The

TABLE 3

SEEA environmental assets

EA.1	Natural resources
EA.11	Mineral and energy resources (cubic meters, tonnes, tonnes of oil equivalents, joules)
EA.12	Soil resources (cubic meters, tonnes)
EA.13	Water resources (cubic meters)
EA.14	Biological resources
EA.141	Timber resources (cubic meters)
EA.142	Crop and plant resources, other than timber (cubic meters, tonnes, number)
EA.143	Aquatic resources (tonnes, number)
EA.144	Animal resources, other than aquatic (number)
EA.2	Land and surface water (hectares)
EA.21	Land underlying buildings and structures
EA.22	Agricultural land and associated surface water
EA.23	Wooded land and associated surface water
EA.24	Major water bodies
EA.25	Other land
EA.3	Ecosystems
EA.31	Terrestrial ecosystems
EA.32	Aquatic ecosystems
EA.33	Atmospheric systems
Memorandum items	Intangible assets related to environmental issues (extended SNA codes)
AN.1121	Mineral exploration
AN.2221	Transferable licenses and concessions for the exploitation of natural resources
AN.2222	Tradable permits allowing the emission of residuals
AN.2223	Other intangible non–produced environmental assets

Source: SEEA (2003)

SEEA, by contrast, focuses not on property rights but on the physical attributes of assets, and so includes a wider and less well-defined range of environmental assets. The SEEA asset boundary includes not just all land and natural resources, for example, but also ecosystems.

The inclusion of ecosystems is the biggest difference between the SNA and SEEA. It is also quite problematic. The SEEA's ecosystem assets deliberately introduce an element of double counting in the interests of recording each of a number of distinct ecosystem services.[3] Three types of systems are recognized: terrestrial, aquatic, and atmospheric. Each is recognized to deliver multiple services. An asset identified as EA1 or EA2 can also appear in EA3, if it is associated with any of the services of EA3. As long as ecosystem services are recorded in physical terms the double counting is not an issue, but when the assets are valued, this does not make as much sense.

The designation of ecosystems as assets is motivated by a desirable goal – the inclusion of valuable ecosystem services in the system of national income accounts. However, this may not be the best option for capturing currently non-marketed ecosystem services. Any piece of land will jointly produce a number of goods and services, some of which may generate off-site benefits/costs. The social value of the land as an asset is the discounted flow of all the services it yields, whether marketed or not and whether on-site or not. The on-site benefits should be captured in land prices (where these exist), so the task of the SEEA is to identify the off-site services. The justification provided in SEEA (2003) for citing ecosystems as the source of such services is that "it is not generally the components of ecosystems that benefit humans, but the systems as a whole." But this is simply not correct. The value of any piece of land committed to some use derives from the marginal impact of that use on the flow of all the goods and services from the land. If the service providing benefits is a public good, then the marginal value of actions by the ith provider that change the flow of the public good should be recorded in the accounts. The contributions of all other providers (the grey terms) affect the value of their own assets. Of course, there may well be assets (defined in terms of property rights) that extend over whole ecosystems. The SEEA water assets, for example, include the exclusive economic zones of countries, and so cover a number of large marine ecosystems. However, in general, asset values derive from the marginal contribution that individual properties make to the flow of all economically relevant ecosystem services.

The SEEA approach to estimating asset values is summarized in Table 4.

As in the SNA, multiple methods are used including both perpetual inventory methods and direct estimation of resource rents. For most environmental assets, the resource rent is derived by deducting costs from the market price received for marketed products, the value of the stock being calculated as the net present value of rents. The SEEA suggests that non-market valuation techniques be used for services that do not have a market price. To capture the effect of non-marketed off-site ecosystem services flows, what is needed is a measure of the externality involved, and not the addition of ecosystems as an extra category of assets.

---

3   With the exception of natural resources that provide direct use benefits, the individual organisms and physical features that make up ecosystems are not classified as unique assets in the SEEA. This reflects the fact that it is not generally the components of ecosystems that benefit humans, but the systems as a whole. However, because natural resources are recognized as specific assets, some elements of the environment appear twice in the SEEA asset classification, once as natural assets and again as components of ecosystems. Thus, forests that are used as a source of timber are classified as natural resource assets. Since these same forests provide other benefits as well (carbon absorption for example), they are also classified as ecosystem assets. This reflects the fact that these forests provide more than one kind of benefit. As natural resources, they provide direct use benefits, while as components of ecosystems they provide indirect use benefits. It is necessary to recognize both roles of forests and other biological resources if a complete picture of the benefits provided to humans by the environment is to be captured in the SEEA. Note, though, that the inclusion of ecosystems as a separate category, like that of the inclusion of soil, means that there is an element of double counting in the SEEA classification, deliberately introduced to enable different environmental aspects to be examined. (SEEA 2003: 7.74).

What is needed to correct the wealth accounts in the SNA (or the National Income and Product Accounts [NIPAS] in the U.S.) is both the extension of the set of stocks measured to comprise all relevant sources of wealth, and the inclusion of the non-marketed impacts of asset use on third parties. The most important single addition to make to the set of stocks measured is undoubtedly human capital. The findings of World Bank (2006) along with numerous studies of total factor productivity growth indicate that the most important driver of wealth creation is the skills and know-how of the population. This is excluded from both the NIPA and the SNA (JORGENSON AND LANDEFELD 2006; EUROPEAN COMMUNITIES ET AL. 2009). The most important *environmental stocks* to add are those currently excluded on grounds that they lack sufficiently well-defined property rights. These are not ecosystems as such, but the many public lands, open access resources, and sea areas within the exclusive economic zone that are important components of national wealth, but that do not currently appear in the accounts.

The most important non-marketed impacts of asset use on third parties are off-site ecosystem service flows: environmental externalities. There are four main categories of off-site ecosystem service flows that are currently neglected in the national accounts.

- Hydrologically mediated flows include water pollution, siltation, soil loss, flooding, and so on.
- Atmospherically mediated flows include emissions with local (PM-10, photochemical smog); regional (sulfur dioxide); and global (carbon dioxide, nitrous oxide, methane) consequences.
- Human travel and transport-mediated flows include the transmission of pests and pathogens through local, regional, and global goods transport and travel networks.
- Access mediated flows include changes in on-site benefits accessed by people elsewhere. Examples include the external benefits or costs to others of on-site

TABLE 4

Methods used to estimate asset values in the SEEA

Data needed for estimating stock values:
Resource rent
Stock of the resource
Life–length or rate of extraction of the resource
Decision on how to record renewals/discoveries
Discount rate for future income

Data needed for estimating resource rent:
1. Appropriation method
direct observation
2. PIM–based method
stock of produced capital (estimated from price decline)
net operating surplus
rate of return to produced capital
3. Capital service–based method
stock of produced capital (estimated from efficiency decline)
gross operating surplus
capital services rendered by produced capital

Source: SEEA (2003)

biodiversity conservation/loss. Such flows may involve either information or physical (e.g., travel) movements.

Many local flows might fall into Nordhaus's category of external effects whose impact on asset values are already included in the accounts (NORDHAUS 2006). However, many regional and all global flows are international, and are currently not recorded anywhere in the accounts. Since many of these flows are non-exclusive and non-rival in their effects (they are public goods), whether they are significant enough to be measured and recorded depends on the extent of the public interest affected – the per capita benefits conferred or costs imposed and the size of the affected population. Indeed, this is why a system of triage is needed. Capturing important off-site ecosystem service flows is, however, critical to the correct estimation of the value of the assets involved.

5. Conclusion

The capital accounts in the existing national income accounts do a poor job of tracking changes in wealth. This is partly because of their focus on "tangible" assets and hence their neglect of human and social capital, but it is also because of the way in which environmental assets are currently recorded. The weaknesses of the approach to environmental assets in the SNA have long been recognized (REPETTO ET AL. 1989; PEARCE AND WARFORD 1993). The World Bank's adjusted net savings measure is an attempt to estimate the errors involved (WORLD BANK 2006, 2010). The SEEA (2003) is an attempt to generate the environmental data needed to measure environmental wealth. While both move the agenda forward, neither resolves the questions of what environmental stocks are important to include, how they should be measured and how they should be valued.

A very large part of the problem lies in the exclusions implied by the property rights focus of the SNA. Since the only admissible assets are those that generate claims to future benefit streams, the SNA excludes a number of natural resources that are important to human well-being, but that cannot be privately co-opted. The list of excluded resources includes many in public ownership or that lie beyond national jurisdiction. From a global perspective, it is important that the set of accounts used to measure the growth, equity, and sustainability of resource use covers all assets on which human well-being depends, including those beyond national jurisdiction. Three points are important.

First, the stocks of "environmental" assets that need to be recorded comprise all lands that generate off-site benefits or costs as a result of environmental flows, noting that "land" in this context defines a surficial area associated with the off-site ecosystem service flows described above, that is it comprises both terrestrial and aquatic properties. Note that this is not the same as the "ecosystems" referred to in the SEEA. Surficial assets should be defined by ownership.

They should cover the full extent of the surface over which the country has rights, and should include all forms of property, whether or not they yield marketed products. If a parcel of land genuinely makes no contribution to human well-being, then its shadow value will be zero. But it should be on the list of assets.

Second, the lands that generate off-site ecosystem service flows are not restricted to the natural resource categories in either the SNA or the SEEA. There is an increasing appreciation that built environments – urban and industrial areas – create ecosystems that generate benefits and costs to people that are sometimes similar and sometimes different from ecosystems in other areas. They also involve off-site flows that affect well-being. For example, urban environments play a critical role in the transmission of infectious diseases, even if the origins of those diseases might lie elsewhere. Urban systems tend to have different thermal properties than other systems. The heat island effect, for example, is an urban phenomenon. They also play a critical role in stimulating demand for ecosystem services within the urban hinterland. Whether assets are classified in the national accounts as natural resources or something else is not important. What is important is that if assets in other classifications have significant off-site environmental effects, then that should impact their value in the accounts.

Third, it is worth repeating that the non-marketed ecosystem services that should be recorded in the accounts are those generating costs or benefits not currently reflected in the rents to asset holders. Specifically, off-site externalities that affect the value of other assets should be recorded. Such externalities can generally be associated with particular types of ecosystem services. So, for example, changes in on-site characteristics that affect the access that others have will frequently be cultural services. Off-site flows, including water pollution, soil loss, siltation, disease transmission, and so on, will frequently be regulating services. From an accounting point of view, however, it is the effect on the value of other assets and not the classification of the service that matters.

The relationship between asset holdings, externalities, and poverty is important to unravel. The dependence of many people on the non-market exploitation of natural resources in open- or weakly-regulated access common pool resources is not reflected in the national accounts as they now exist. This is partly because of the SNA rules on assets not subject to well-defined property rights, and partly because of the exclusion of environmental externalities. The evidence from the adjusted net savings estimates suggests that the poorest countries have, on average, reduced the value of their assets over the last four decades. In the absence of comprehensive wealth estimates it is, however, difficult to confirm this.

The welfare–theoretic foundations of wealth accounting

Fifty years ago, Samuelson (1961) suggested that the appropriate measure for making intergenerational well-being comparisons is wealth, as distinct from the income measures commonly reported in the system of national income accounts. It was not until the 1990s, however, that progress was made in formalizing the notion in ways that made it possible to begin constructing wealth accounts and to adjust the system of national accounts to take account of the depreciation of environmental assets (HARTWICK 1990; PEARCE AND ATKINSON 1993; HAMILTON 1994; HARTWICK 1994; PEARCE ET AL. 1996; HAMILTON AND CLEMENS 1999; HARTWICK 2000). Much of this work was stimulated by the Brundtland Report, published in 1987, which defined sustainable development in terms of intergenerational changes in wealth: "Sustainable development is development that meets the needs of the present without compromising the ability of future generations to meet their own needs" (WORLD COMMISSION ON ENVIRONMENT AND DEVELOPMENT 1987). From a welfare-theoretic standpoint, the central requirement of a sustainable consumption program for the current generation is that it should not reduce the consumption possibilities available to future generations. This idea was first introduced by Lindahl in the 1930s (LINDAHL 1933) who defined "income" to be the maximum amount that could be consumed without reducing the value of the capital stocks available to future generations. Income in the Lindahl sense is equivalent to the SNA concepts of net national product or net national income.

To see what it contains, and how it relates to changes in the value of capital stocks, consider the simplest representation of the economy. In this we adapt an argument from Dasgupta (2009) that builds on Dasgupta and Maler (2000) and Arrow et al. (2003). Define Y(t), or gross national product at time t, to be a measure of the output achievable given the produced capital stock, $K(t)$, the human capital stock, $L(t)$, and a stock "natural resources" which may be thought about as an area of land or sea, along with the biotic and abiotic elements that area contains, $N(t)$, together with the technology, institutions, and environmental conditions that collectively determine total factor productivity, $A(t)$. Total factor productivity measures the proportion of output not explained by the amount of inputs used in production, and captures the effect of technical progress, the efficiency with which inputs are used, institutional conditions, and the impact of environmental factors such as climate. If we ignore the sensitivity of total factor productivity to investment in produced and human capital, and to the rate at which natural resources are extracted, GNP can be described by the function:

EQUATION A.1

$$Y(t) = A(t)f\big(K(t)L(t)N(t)\big)$$

Suppose that the depreciation rate corresponding each type of capital stock is δ_K, δ_L, and δ_N respectively, and that investment in each type of capital is I_K, I_L, and I_N. In addition to the effects of investment, natural resources may be expected to regenerate through some set of biogeochemical process according to the function $g\big(N(t),I_N(t)\big)$.

The growth rate for each of the capital stocks may be written as

EQUATION A.2

$$\frac{dK}{dt} = A(t)f\big(K(t)L(t)R(t)\big)-C(t)-I_L(t)-I_N(t)-\delta_K K(t)$$

EQUATION A.3

$$\frac{dL}{dt} = I_L(t)-\delta_L L(t)$$

EQUATION A.4

$$\frac{dN}{dt} = g\big(N(t)\big)-\delta_N N(t)$$

That is, net investment in produced capital is just the difference between gross national product and the sum of consumption, investment in human and natural capital, and the depreciation of produced capital. Net investment in human and natural capital is measured by the difference between additions and subtractions – where additions include investment and/or natural regeneration in the case of natural capital.

Aggregate consumption at time t is denoted $C(t)$. It is assumed that intergenerational well-being, $V(t)$ depends on aggregate consumption via the relation:

EQUATION A.5

$$V(t) = \int_t^\infty U\big(C(t)\big)e^{-r(t-\tau)}d\tau$$

in which $U\big(C(t)\big)$ is instantaneous well-being measured at time t, and is assumed to be a concave function – to have positive first and negative second derivatives.

The feature of Dasgupta's approach that makes it particular helpful to the implementation of wealth accounting is that no assumption is made about the optimality of $V(t)$, $C(t)$, or the time paths of the various capital stocks. Denote the state of the system at time t by:

EQUATION A.6

$$S(t) = \big(K(t),L(t),N(t)\big)$$

An economic program is then a consumption and investment path from t onwards, $\big\{E(\tau)\big\}_t^\infty = \big\{C(\tau),K(\tau),L(\tau),N(\tau),I_L(\tau),R(\tau)\big\}_t^\infty$, that satisfies the equations of motion of the capital stocks, (INNES ET AL. 1998). Dasgupta (2009) defines a resource allocation mechanism to be a mapping from the state of the system to an economic program: $\alpha:\big\{S(t),t\big\}\rightarrow\big\{E(\tau)\big\}_t^\infty$, making the point that there is no requirement that the program be efficient. This is particularly relevant if some of the services associated with the capital stocks are public goods, having benefits or costs beyond the jurisdiction of the country concerned. Institutions having responsibility for the domestic allocation of international environmental public goods have little incentive to satisfy the Samuelson condition for the efficient allocation of public goods.

The intergenerational measure of well-being corresponding to a particular economic program is thus:

EQUATION A.7

$$V(S(t),t) = \int_t^\infty U\big(C(t)\big)e^{-r(t-\tau)}d\tau$$

and the shadow or accounting prices of the capital stocks are simply the partial derivatives of this function with respect to those stocks. For assets for which there are well-functioning markets and few externalities, shadow prices and market prices should be reasonably closely aligned. For assets for which there are no markets, or for which there are significant externalities, shadow prices would be expected to deviate substantially from market prices. Dasgupta (2009) offers a number of propositions that follow from such a formulation of the problem.

1. In the special case where total factor productivity is constant, the time derivative of $V(S(t))$ is simply the sum of the change in each of the capital stocks evaluated at the shadow price of those stocks. That is,

EQUATION A.8

$$\frac{dV(S(t))}{dt} = \frac{\partial V(S(t))}{\partial K(t)}\frac{dK(t)}{dt} +$$

$$\frac{\partial V(S(t))}{\partial L(t)}\frac{dL(t)}{dt} + \frac{\partial V(S(t))}{\partial N(t)}\frac{dN(t)}{dt}$$

Since the equations of motion for each of the capital stocks record the net effect of investment and depreciation, together with the regeneration of natural capital stocks, this is a measure of aggregate net investment – what Dasgupta refers to as comprehensive investment. Aggregate net investment, evaluated at the shadow or accounting prices of assets, is a measure of the rate at which marginal intergenerational well-being changes over time.

2. Aggregate net investment is also a measure of the discounted stream of consumption that it induces.

3. An economic program is sustainable if and only if aggregate net investment is positive.

4. Aggregate wealth is the shadow value of the stocks of all assets available to the economy.

5. An economic program at time t is sustainable if and only if, holding shadow prices constant, aggregate wealth is non-declining at t.

6. $dV(S(t))/dt > 0$ if and only if $U'(C(t)) dC(t)/dt$ < net national product. That is, Lindahl's condition on "income" holds. Intergenerational well-being is growing if and only if consumption is less than net national product.

7. Intergenerational well-being in a country is higher/lower than in another country if its wealth, evaluated in terms of its shadow prices, is greater/less.

Note that these propositions hold whether or not the allocation mechanism is efficient. They imply that if we wish to understand changes in intergenerational well-being, we need to understand changes in wealth, and to do this we need to track changes in aggregate net investment.

Now consider the more general case where total factor productivity is not constant. In a closed economy, if all factors of production were fully accounted for, and if all effects of new technical knowledge, institutions, and so on were captured in investment in those factors of production, then the residual would be equal to zero: $(dA(t)/dt)(1/A(t)=0$. In practice, not all factors of production are fully accounted for. In particular, many natural resources lie outside the market and are not taken into account in production decisions. The effects of changes in technical knowledge – especially technical knowledge due to publicly funded R&D – are not captured in factor prices. Nor are changes in the efficiency of the allocation mechanism, or environmental conditions. So even in a closed economy, the residual will not be zero. In an open economy there are, in addition, the effects of international technology transfers and the effects of transboundary environmental externalities. All of these have the capacity to change total factor productivity.

Suppose, for example, that total factor productivity depends on a global public good, G, which is influenced by the natural resource use decisions of all countries. To fix ideas, it might be thought of as a public good characterized by an additive supply technology, such as climate change mitigation through carbon sequestration. So the size of the public good at time t would be $G(t)=\sum_{i=1}^{n}G(t)_i$, that is the sum of the contributions of all n countries. If total factor productivity in country i is $A_i(t)=A_i(G(t),t)$, $i = 1,...,n$, and if $dV_i(S(t))/dG_i(t)=[\partial V_i(S_i(t))/\partial A_i(t)][dA_i(t)/dG_i(t)]$, the ith county is able to affect its GDP through its own carbon sequestration efforts, $G_i(t)$, it will internalize that impact. However, it will ignore any effects it has on total factor productivity in other countries. Intergenerational well-being in country i is now a function of the allocation mechanism in that country, the state of its capital assets, and the global public good:

EQUATION A.9

$$V_i(t)=V_i(\alpha_i,S_i(t),G(t),t)$$

and the rate at which it changes is given by:

EQUATION A.10

$$\frac{dV_i(\alpha_i,S_i(t),G(t))}{dt} = I_i(t)+ \frac{\partial V_i(S_i(t))}{\partial G(t)}$$

$$\left(\frac{dG_i(t)}{dt} + \sum_{j \neq i} \frac{dG_j(t)}{dt} \right)$$

where

EQUATION A.11

$$I(t) = \frac{\partial V_i(S_i(t))}{\partial K_i(t)} \frac{dK_i(t)}{dt} + \frac{\partial V_i(S_i(t))}{\partial L_i(t)} \frac{dL_i(t)}{dt}$$

$$+ \frac{\partial V_i(S_i(t))}{\partial N_i(t)} \frac{dN_i(t)}{dt}$$

Only the quantity $[\partial V_i(S_i(t))/\partial G(t)][dG_i(t)/dt]$ is part of the ith country's decision. The contribution of all other countries to the well-being of country i, given by $[\partial V_i(S_i(t))/\partial G(t)]$ $[\sum_{j \neq i}dG_j(t)/dt]$ is taken as given, and the contribution of country i to all other countries, $\sum_{j \neq i, j=1}^{n}$ $[\partial V_j(S_j(t))/\partial G(t)][\partial G(t)/\partial G_i(t)][dG_i(t)/dt]$, is ignored. But these impacts have a potentially important effect on the performance of other countries (positive or negative) and should be accounted for.

REFERENCES

ALSTON, J.M., ANDERSEN, M.A., JAMES, J.J. & PARDEY, P.G. (2010). *Persistence pays: U.S. agricultural productivity growth and the benefits from public R&D spending.* Dordrecht: Springer.

ALSTON, J.M., BEDDOW, J.M, & PARDEY, P.G. (2009). Agricultural research, productivity, and food prices in the long run. *Science, 325,* 1209-1210.

ARROW, K.J., DASGUPTA, P. & MÄLER, K.G. (2003). The genuine savings criterion and the value of population. *Economic Theory, 21*(2), 217-225.

BOYD, J. & BANZHAF, S. (2007). What are ecosystem services? The need for standardized environmental accounting units. *Ecological Economics, 63,* 616-626.

DASGUPTA, P. (2009). The welfare economic theory of green national accounts. *Environmental and Resource Economics, 42*(1), 3-38.

DASGUPTA, P. & MÄLER, K.G. (2000). Net national product, wealth, and social well being. *Environment and Development Economics, 5*(1), 69-93.

EUROPEAN COMMUNITIES, INTERNATIONAL MONETARY FUND, ORGANISATION FOR ECONOMIC CO-OPERATION AND DEVELOPMENT, UNITED NATIONS & WORLD BANK. (2009). *System of national accounts 2008.* New York: United Nations.

FERREIRA, S., HAMILTON, K. & VINCENT, J.R. (2008). Comprehensive wealth and future consumption: Accounting for population growth. *The World Bank Economic Review, 22,* 233–248.

GOETTLE, R.J., HO, M.S., JORGENSON, D.W., SLESNICK, D.T. & WILCOXEN, P.J. (2007). *IGEM, an inter-temporal general equilibrium model of the U.S. economy with emphasis on growth, energy and the environment.* Washington, DC: U.S. Environmental Protection Agency, Office of Atmospheric Programs Climate Change Division.

GOOSSENS, Y., MÄKIPÄÄ, A., SCHEPELMANN, P., VAN DE SAND, I., KUHNDTAND, M. & HERRNDORF, M. (2007). *Alternative progress indicators to gross domestic product (GDP) as a means towards sustainable development.* Brussels: European Parliament: Policy Department, Economic and Scientific Policy.

HAMILTON, K. (1994). Green adjustments to GDP. *Resources Policy, 20,* 155-168.

HAMILTON, K. & CLEMENS, M. (1999). Genuine savings in developing countries. *The World Bank Economic Review, 13* (2), 333-56.

HARTWICK, J.M. (1990). Natural resources, national accounting and economic depreciation. *Journal of Public Economics, 43,* 291-304.

HARTWICK, J.M. (1994). National wealth and net national product. *The Scandinavian Journal of Economics, 96* (2), 253-256.

HARTWICK, J. (2000). *National accounting and capital.* Cheltenham: Edward Elgar.

HEYWOOD, V. & WATSON, R. (1995). *Global biodiversity assessment.* Cambridge: Cambridge University Press.

HICKS, J.R. (1939). *Value and capital.* Oxford: Clarendon Press.

INNES, R., POLASKY, S. & TSCHIRHART, J. (1998). Takings, compensation and endangered species protection on private lands. *Journal of Economic Perspectives, 12,* 35-52.

JOHNSTON, R.J. & RUSSELL, M. (2011). An operational structure for clarity in ecosystem service values. *Ecological Economics, 70,* 2243-2249.

JORGENSON, D.W. & LANDEFELD, J.S. (2006). Blueprint for expanded and integrated U.S. accounts: Review, assessment and next steps. In D.W. Jorgenson, J.S. Landefeld & W.D. Nordhaus (Eds.) *A new architecture for the U.S. national accounts* (pp. 13-112). Chicago: Chicago University Press.

KUMAR, P. (2010). *The economics of ecosystems and biodiversity: Ecological and economic foundations.* London: Earthscan.

LINDAHL, E. (1933). The concept of income. In G. Bagge (Ed.) *Economic essays in honor of Gustav Cassel* (pp. 399–407). London: Allen and Unwin.

MARKANDYA, A. (2001). *Poverty alleviation and sustainable development implications for the management of natural capital.* Washington, DC: World Bank.

MILLENNIUM ECOSYSTEM ASSESSMENT. (2005A). *Ecosystems and human well-being: Biodiversity synthesis.* Washington, DC: World Resources Institute

MILLENNIUM ECOSYSTEM ASSESSMENT. (2005B). *Ecosystems and human well-being: Current state and trends.* Washington, DC: Island Press.

NORDHAUS, W.D. (2006). Principles of national accounting for non-market accounts. In D.W. Jorgenson, J.S. Landefield & W.D. Nordhaus (Eds.) *A new architecture for the U.S. national accounts* (pp. 143-160). Chicago: University of Chicago Press.

PEARCE, D. & ATKINSON, G. (1993). Capital theory and the measurement of sustainable development: an indicator of "weak" sustainability. *Ecological Economics, 8* (2), 103-108.

PEARCE, D., HAMILTON, K. & ATKINSON, G. (1996). Measuring sustainable development: Progress on indicators. *Environment and Development Economics, 1,* 85-101.

PEARCE, D.W. & WARFORD, J.J. (1993). *World without end: Economics, environment, and sustainable development.* Oxford: Oxford University Press.

PIESSE, J. & THIRTLE, C. (2010). Agricultural R&D, technology and productivity. *Philosophical Transactions of the Royal Society B: Biological Sciences, 365,* 3035-3047.

REPETTO, R., MAGRATH, W., WELLS, M., BEER, C. & ROSSINI, F. (1989). *Wasting assets: Natural resources and the national income accounts.* Washington, DC: World Resources Institute.

SAMUELSON, P.A. (1961). The evaluation of social income: Capital formation and wealth. In F.A. Lutz & D.C. Hague (Eds.) *The theory of capital* (pp. 32–57). New York: St Martins Press.

VOUVAKI, D. & XEPAPADEAS, A. (2009). Total factor productivity growth when factors of production generate environmental externalities. *Fondazione Eni Enrico Mattei Working Papers 281.*

WORLD BANK. (2006). *Where is the wealth of nations?* Washington, DC: World Bank.

WORLD BANK. (2011). *The changing wealth of nations.* Washington, DC: World Bank.

WORLD COMMISSION ON ENVIRONMENT AND DEVELOPMENT. (1987). *Our common future.* New York: Oxford University Press

CHAPTER 8

Ecosystem services and wealth accounting

Edward B. Barbier

KEY MESSAGES

Ecosystems should be treated as an important asset in an economy and, in principle, ecosystem services should be valued in a similar manner as any other form of wealth. Quantifying these services is very challenging.

The purpose of this chapter is to review progress in economics and ecology in assessing ecosystem services and their values, and to discuss the resulting implications for including such services in a wealth accounting framework.

Understanding the relationship between ecosystems, their structure and functions, and the ecological services they generate is essential to determining how the structure and functions of an ecosystem provide valuable goods and services to humans.

Since the purpose of new investment is to increase the quantity and quality of the economy's total capital stock, or wealth, adjusting gross domestic product (GDP) for depreciation in this stock would measure more accurately whether net additions to capital are occurring.

If net domestic product (NDP) is to serve as a true measure of the changes in an economy's wealth, it must include any appreciation or depreciation to human and natural capital as well.

The approach developed here requires, first, recognizing ecosystems as a component of natural capital, or ecological capital; and second, measuring these important assets in terms of the land area, or ecological landscape, which defines their boundaries.

1. Introduction

The growing scarcity of ecosystem goods and services, or ecological scarcity, indicates that an important source of economic wealth, the world's ecosystems, is being irreversibly lost or degraded (BARBIER 2011A). Over the past 50 years, ecosystems have been modified more rapidly and extensively than in any comparable period in human history, largely to meet rapidly growing demands for food, freshwater, timber, fiber, and fuel. The result has been a substantial and largely irreversible loss in biological diversity, ecosystems, and the ecological services that they provide. Approximately 15 out of 24 major global ecosystem services have been degraded or used unsustainably, including freshwater, capture fisheries, air and water purification, and the regulation of regional and local climate, natural hazards, and pests (MA 2005). Over the next 50 years, the rate of biodiversity loss is also expected to accelerate, leading to the extinction of at least 500 or the 1,192 currently threatened bird species and 565 of the 1,137 mammal species (DIRZO AND RAVEN 2003).

An important contribution of the Millennium Ecosystem Assessment was to define ecosystem goods and services as valuable "benefits" to humans and to highlight the deteriorating state of many global ecosystems and their key services (MA 2005). As a U.S. National Research Council Report points out, "the fundamental challenge of valuing ecosystem services lies in providing an explicit description and adequate assessment of the links between the structure and functions of natural systems, the benefits (i.e., goods and services) derived by humanity, and their subsequent values" (NRC 2005, P. 2). The main reason for this challenge is the "lack of multiproduct, ecological production functions to quantitatively map ecosystem structure and function to a flow of services that can then be valued" (POLASKY AND SEGERSON 2009, P. 422).

Despite these valuation problems, the consensus in the literature is that ecosystems are assets that produce a flow of beneficial goods and services over time.[1] For example, as Daily et al. (2000, P. 395) state, "the world's ecosystems are capital assets. If properly managed, they yield a flow of vital services, including the production of goods (such as seafood and timber), life support processes (such as pollination and water purification), and life-fulfilling conditions (such as beauty and serenity)." Ecosystems should therefore be treated as an important asset in an economy and, in principle, ecosystem services should be valued in a similar manner as any other form of wealth. That is, regardless of whether there exists a market for the goods and services produced by ecosystems, they make contributions to current and future well-being. The importance of this economic contribution of ecosystems has become the focal point of recent international and national studies, such as the Economics of Ecosystems and Biodiversity (TEEB 2010) and the U.K. National Ecosystem Assessment (2011).

As chapters in this report have stressed, accounting for the depreciation of ecological assets is essential to any inclusive wealth accounting framework (see, especially, 3, 6, 7, and 9). However, a major difficulty arising in treating ecosystems as economic assets is in quantifying this form of capital and in measuring the valuable benefits that it produces (BARBIER 2008, 2011A, 2011B; MÄLER ET AL. 2008; POLASKY AND SEGERSON 2009). The valuation challenge is further exacerbated by the difficulty in determining the ecological production of many ecosystem goods and services and in observing values for the myriad economic benefits, many of which are non-marketed. The purpose of this chapter is to review progress in economics and ecology in assessing ecosystem services and their values, and to discuss the resulting implications for including such services in a wealth accounting framework.

---

1   See, for example, Barbier (2008) and (2011a); Daily et al. (2000); EPA (2009); MA (2005); NRC (2005); Polasky and Segerson (2009); TEEB (2010); and WRI (2001).

The next section provides an overview of the wealth accounting method suggested for natural capital by Dasgupta and Perrings in this report and by Dasgupta (2009), and discusses how ecosystem services can be incorporated into this framework. Section 3 examines further how ecosystems can be characterized as economic by adopting ecological landscape – or land area – as the basic measuring unit. As Section 4 explains, understanding the relationship between ecosystems, their structure and functions, and the ecological services they generate is essential to determining how the structure and functions of an ecosystem provide valuable goods and services to humans. Section 5 discusses how the economic concept of a "benefit" should be applied to ecosystem goods and services as a guide to their correct economic valuation through integrating the "ecological production" of ecosystem goods and services with "economic valuation" of these benefits. Section 6 provides an overview of the substantial progress that has been made by economists working with ecologists and other natural scientists on this "fundamental challenge" to improve the application of environmental valuation methodologies to non-market ecosystem services. Section 7 focuses on the specific challenges that need to be overcome in correcting wealth accounts for ecological capital. To illustrate, Section 8 provides an example of inclusive wealth accounting with a case study from Thailand involving mangrove loss, based on Barbier (2007). The conclusion to this chapter offers some final remarks on how incorporating ecosystem services in wealth accounting can be further improved.

2. Wealth accounting and ecosystem services

Following the framework developed by Dasgupta (2009), previous chapters in this report suggest a common wealth accounting methodology for natural capital, including ecosystems (see Chapters 6 and 7). Such an accounting framework defines the aggregate wealth as the shadow value of the stocks of all the assets of an economy, and suggests that ecosystems should be included as an important form of "natural capital" in this wealth. Moreover, the aggregate wealth of the economy will increase over time only if current consumption is less than the net national (or domestic) product, provided that the latter correctly accounts for the economic contributions of all capital, including ecosystems. The next section summarizes the basic wealth accounting principles arising from this methodology, extends it to incorporate ecosystems and their valuable goods and services, and thus constructs an adjusted measure of net domestic product (NDP) that accounts for the additional contributions of ecological capital.

For most economies, the standard measure of economic progress is real per capita gross domestic product (GDP), the market value of all final goods and services produced within the economy.[2] The problem with GDP as an economic indicator, however, is that it does not reflect changes in the capital stock underlying the production of goods and services. GDP accounts for gross investment in an economy but not for any depreciation in existing capital. Since the purpose of new investment is to increase the quantity and quality of the economy's total capital stock, or wealth, adjusting GDP for depreciation in this stock would measure more accurately whether net additions to capital are occurring. And, as has been demonstrated, economic development is sustained if and only if such investment in overall wealth is non-negative over time (DASGUPTA 2009; DASGUPTA AND MÄLER 2000; HAMILTON AND CLEMENS 1999).

---

2 The alternative measure to gross domestic product is gross national product (GNP), which is the GDP of an economy plus net income from abroad. The latter net payments consist of the income that people and organizations resident in the domestic economy receive from abroad on account of property and other assets which they own in foreign countries less the income paid to non-residents from their holdings of property and assets in the domestic economy. Thus, GDP is the total income of an economy produced domestically, whereas GNP is the total gross income received by the residents of an economy.

The idea of deducting capital depreciation from GDP to obtain a "net" domestic product (NDP) measure is not new. Lindahl (1933) first provided the justification by suggesting that an economy's income should exceed current consumption, including any consumption of existing capital, to prevent the economy's total wealth from declining. However, the aggregate stock of economic assets should be much broader than conventional reproducible (or fixed) assets, such as roads, buildings, machinery, and factories. Investments in human capital, such as education and skills training, are also essential to sustaining development. Similarly, an economy's endowment of natural resources is an important form of "natural wealth." Thus, a better indicator of an economy's progress would be an expanded measure of NDP that is "adjusted" for real depreciation in reproducible and natural capital, as well as any net additions to human capital, such as through real education, health, and training expenditures in the economy.[3]

In economics, and in systems of national accounts, "capital" is conventionally defined as reproducible real assets, which includes roads, railways, buildings, private dwellings, factories, machinery, equipment, and other human-manufactured fixed assets. Thus, investment in the economy, or gross capital formation, is conventionally measured as outlays or additions to these reproducible assets plus net changes in the level of inventories and valuables. If allowance is made for any capital consumption, or depreciation, then the net changes in reproducible assets represent net investment in the economy.

However, the economy does not just depend on reproducible assets, but also human and natural capital. Traditionally, investment in human capital, which can be thought of the education, skills, and health per person, are not included in the national accounts. Similarly, additions to and depreciation of natural capital are excluded. In a true wealth accounting framework to estimate the NDP of an economy, both of these omissions need correcting. That is, the three basic assets comprising the overall wealth of an economy are reproducible, human and natural capital.

Clearly, natural capital must include those conventional natural resources that are the source of raw material, land, and energy inputs to the economy, such as fossil fuels, minerals, metals, forest resources, and arable land. But, in addition, natural capital should include those ecosystems that through their natural functioning and habitats provide important goods and services to the economy. As suggested by Barbier (2007), these benefits are wide-ranging, which in economics would normally be classified under three different categories:

(i) "goods" (products obtained from ecosystems, such as resource harvests, water, and genetic material),

(ii) "services" (e.g., recreational and tourism benefits or certain ecological regulatory and habitat functions, such as water purification, climate regulation, erosion control, and habitat provision), and

(iii) "cultural benefits" (e.g., spiritual and religious beliefs, heritage values).

It is clear that some of these ecosystem goods and services contribute directly to human well-being, for example through enhancing recreation and other direct enjoyment of the environment, augmenting our current and future natural heritage, or by reducing harmful pollution and assimilating waste. But some services, either on their own or combined with human inputs, also contribute indirectly to human welfare by supporting economic production (e.g., raw materials, food, and other harvested inputs; provision of freshwater, watershed protection, and coastal habitats for off-shore fisheries) or by protecting production activities, property, and lives (e.g., flood control, storm protection, managing climate). In other words, "ecosystem services are the direct or indirect contributions

---

3 See, for example, Aronsson and Löfgren (1996); Dasgupta (2009) and (2012); Hamilton and Clemens (1999); Hartwick (1990); Mäler (1991); Pearce and Barbier (2000); and Perrings (2012).

that ecosystems make to the well-being of human populations" (EPA 2009, p. 12).

However, as noted in the introduction to this chapter, ecosystems are under threat from degradation and loss globally. Global land use change has been a major cause of the alteration and loss of terrestrial ecosystems, especially in developing economies and tropical regions (BARBIER 2011A; DIRZO AND RAVEN 2003; FAO 2006; MA 2005). Coastal and marine ecosystems are also some of the most heavily used and threatened natural systems globally, such that 50 percent of salt marshes, 35 percent of mangroves, 30 percent of coral reefs, and 29 percent of seagrasses are either converted or degraded worldwide (FAO 2007B; MA 2005; ORTH ET AL. 2006; UNEP 2006; VALIELA ET AL. 2001; WAYCOTT ET AL. 2009). The major reason for this loss is land conversion, such as the transformation of forests and wetlands to crop and grazing land, expansion of aquaculture and agriculture in coastal areas, and the demand for land for urban and commercial development. In national accounting terms, the implication is that the depreciation of an important natural asset (ecosystems) is partly compensated for by the appreciation of another asset (more land for economic production and development). As Hartwick (1992) has illustrated with the example of agricultural conversion of tropical forests, such changes in the stock of an economy's wealth must be included as capital value adjustments in an accounting framework. In effect, the opportunity cost of holding on to ecosystems as natural capital is the foregone benefits of economic development based on converting ecological landscape (BARBIER 2008 and 2011A).

In sum, ecosystems can be considered a component of natural capital – or ecological capital for short – that affects current economic well-being, either directly or indirectly through supporting production and protecting human lives and property. However, ecological capital is unlikely to be intact, as many ecosystems continue to be converted to land for economic development and production.

The appendix of this chapter develops a formal model to show why accounting for the welfare contributions of reproducible human and natural capital – including ecological capital – is essential to determining the sustainability of an economy. The key accounting result of this model is also summarized and explained in Box 1. The model yields the following important insights concerning wealth accounting, ecosystem services, and sustainable economic development:

First, non-declining welfare is taken as the crucial criterion defining sustainable development of an economy.[4] Using this criterion, the model in the appendix confirms the result obtained by Dasgupta (2009) that investment in the aggregate capital stock of an economy, including ecological capital, determines changes in intergenerational well-being over time. That is, sustainable economic development is achieved if the aggregate wealth of the economy does not decline. Thus, the sustainability criterion that "welfare does not decline over time" essentially "requires managing and enhancing a portfolio of economic assets, the total capital stock, such that its aggregate value does not decline over time," but only if it is recognized that "the total stock of the economy available to the economy for producing goods and services, and ultimately well-being, consists not just of human and physical capital but also of natural capital" (PEARCE AND BARBIER 2000, PP. 20-21).

Second, as the appendix illustrates, the appropriate indicator for measuring the contribution of aggregate wealth to an economy is net domestic product (NDP). However, this indicator should not be conventionally defined NDP as currently measured in most national accounts of economies, that is the gross domestic product (GDP) of the economy less any depreciation (in value terms) of previously accumulated reproducible capital. Instead, as summarized in

---

4 For example, Pearce et al. (1989, p. 32) state: "the wellbeing of a defined population should be at least constant over time and, preferably, increasing for there to be sustainable development."

Box I, if NDP is to serve as a true measure of the changes in an economy's wealth, it must include any appreciation or depreciation to human and natural capital as well. In the case of non-renewable resources, such as fossil fuels and minerals, depletion of these resources should be deducted from NDP. For renewable resources, such as forests and fisheries, NDP must include any depreciation (appreciation) in natural resource stocks if current extraction rates are greater (lesser) than biological growth.

Finally, we should also adjust the NDP of the economy to include two contributions due to ecological capital:

- the value of the direct benefits provided by the current stock of ecosystems; and
- any capital revaluation as a result of conversion of ecosystems to other land uses, with the "price" of changes in ecological capital reflecting the present value of the future direct and indirect benefits of ecosystems.

As discussed previously, the direct ecosystem benefits might include the value of ecosystems in providing recreational, educational and scientific benefits, their value in terms of natural heritage or bequests to future generation or the value of ecosystems in reducing harmful pollution, assimilating waste, and managing climate. In addition, ecological capital protects or supports economic activity, property, and human lives. These indirect ecosystem benefits are broad ranging, and include raw materials, food, and other harvested inputs used in production activities, provision of freshwater, watershed protection, coastal habitats for off-shore fisheries, flood control, storm protection, climate stabilization, and similar services.

In the wealth accounting framework adopted here, the resource allocation mechanism of the economy may not be optimal or even efficient, so it is possible that ecosystem conversion may be taking place even though the capitalized value, or "price," of developed land is actually less than the capitalized value of ecosystems. This being the case, as we have discussed, NDP should be adjusted for the

depreciation in ecological capital that occurs as it is converted to less valuable developed land. But if ecosystems are an important component of natural capital, and if we want to adjust NDP to account for real depreciation in this form of natural wealth, then we need to find a way of, first, measuring such assets, and second, valuing the various benefit flows that they generate (BARBIER 2008, 2011A, and 2011B). The purpose of the next several sections is to discuss how best to overcome these measurement challenges. Later in the chapter, the example of mangrove loss in Thailand is used to illustrate the practical application of correctly adjusting NDP to account for the contributions of ecological capital.

3. Ecosystems as natural capital

If we are to view ecosystems as economic assets, and measure their economic depreciation in wealth accounting, then we need a way of measuring this form of "ecological wealth" (MÄLER ET AL. 2008). One barrier to such an approach is that, in ecology, the concept of an ecosystem has been difficult to define or to measure quantitatively (O'NEILL 2001; PICKETT AND CADENASSO 2002).

However, it is increasingly recognized that most ecological processes are influenced by the spatial extent, or landscape, that defines the boundary of the system.[5] Similarly, the various coastal and marine ecosystems that make up the land-sea interface located between watersheds, the coast, and oceans could be designated in terms of distinct seascapes that define the boundaries between each type of system (MOBERG AND RÖNNBÄCK 2003; SHACKEROFF ET AL. 2009). Thus, as shown by Barbier, (2008 and 2011a), through adopting ecological landscape, or land area, as the basic unit, characterizing the ecosystem as a natural asset is relatively straightforward. It also facilitates

---

5   See, for example, Bockstael (1996); O'Neill (2001); Perry (2002); Pickett and Cadenasso (1995) and (2002); Turner (2005); and Zonneveld (1989).

the examination of human transformation of an ecological landscape through land use conversion, leaving the residual land for ecological processes and habitat for species through relatively straightforward models of land use change. This then facilitates measurement of the physical depreciation of ecosystems, which is essential if we are to account for how stocks of such wealth change.

To illustrate why the landscape containing an ecosystem might serve as the basic unit for measuring changes in this natural asset, it is helpful to discuss a specific example, such as wetland ecosystems. These systems, which comprise coastal wetlands, freshwater swamps and marshes (including floodplains), and peatlands, amount to 6–8 million km² globally (MITSCH ET AL. 2009). The goods and services provided by wetlands are uniquely related to hydrological processes. For example, seasonal soil-water regimes, surface inundation, and maintenance of water quality, critically determine wetland ecosystem structure and function, and thus influence the type ecosystem goods and services provided. Similarly, changes in water regime will affect different wetland services significantly, resulting in many possible trade-offs and synergies among these services within different wetland scenarios and water regimes. The consequence is that the ecosystem services provided by wetlands are driven by hydrology, and understanding how changes in hydrological processes affect the delivery of these services is critical to determining the impact on human welfare (BRAUMAN ET AL. 2007; BULLOCK AND ACREMAN 2003; EMERTON AND BOSS 2008; MITSCH ET AL. 2009).

Because the structure and functions of many wetlands can be uniquely defined by hydrological processes, it is possible to identify the spatial unit, or natural landscape, that is distinct to each type of wetland. In particular, different aspects of the hydrological system underlying wetlands and their services operate at different scales, for example surface inundation (flooding), water quality, and biodiversity. Thus, as a wetland landscape varies in scale, due perhaps to

conversion, draining, or other human-induced disturbances, the impact on the provision of and synergies between wetland services can be substantial. Such a landscape approach is being increasingly used for assessing the cumulative effects of wetland loss and degradation, characterizing wetland boundaries and identifying restoration or mitigation opportunities (BEDFORD 1996 and 1999; GWIN ET AL. 1999; MITSCH AND GOSSELINK 2000; NRC 1995; SIMENSTAD ET AL. 2006). It follows that the various goods and services provided by a wetland will also be tied to, and thus defined by, its landscape extent; that is, "wetland values depend on the hydrogeomorphic location in which they are found" (MITSCH AND GOSSELINK 2000, P. 27).

If the hydrological services of wetlands are related to their landscape extent, then characterizing wetland ecosystems as natural assets is straightforward. In other words, as there are "reciprocal interactions between spatial pattern and ecological processes" (TURNER 2005, P. 319), it is the spatially heterogeneous area of a wetland landscape that is the fundamental to its ability to provide various goods and services. It follows that, if for each wetland ecosystem we can define its corresponding landscape in terms of a quantifiable "land unit," which is defined as "a tract of land that is ecologically homogeneous at the scale level concerned" (ZONNEVELD 1989, P. 68), then we have a representation of the wetland ecosystem as a natural asset in the form of this unit of land, or ecological landscape.

However, even with a well-defined ecological landscape one must be careful to account for heterogeneous units within such a landscape and to avoid problems of double counting. For example, large-scale forested ecosystems can also contain wetlands, freshwater channels and rivers. Similarly, qualitative features of the landscape may significantly influence the ecological production of benefits. For example, the timber benefits of a forested landscape may depend not only on the overall size of the system but also the spatial distribution of trees across the landscape in terms age, size and species as well as variations in soil quality and nutrients (MÄLER

ET AL. 2008). The ability of vegetated coastal landscapes to attenuate storm surges and protect against damages not only varies considerably at the seaward edge as opposed to further inland but also is affected by coastal geomorphology, elevation and topography (KOCH ET AL. 2009). Finally, in a "mixed" ecological landscape, then it may be difficult to determine how a particular ecosystem benefit arises from the landscape and to avoid problems of double counting. For example, outdoor recreation values may be enhanced by the diverse ecological features of a mixed landscape, including the presence of wetlands, forests, and river channels. How to separate out the specific contribution to the value of recreation provided by each ecological component of the landscape may be problematic. Nor would it be correct to attribute the full recreational value to each of the wetland, forest and river components of the landscape.

4. Ecosystems and ecosystem services

There is much confusion over the relationship between ecosystems, their structure and functions, and the ecological services they generate that contribute to human welfare. Understanding such a relationship is essential in order to determine how the structure and functions of an ecosystem provide valuable goods and services to humans.

An ecosystem has the characteristics of a "system," in the sense that it includes an assemblage of organisms interacting with its associated physical environment in a specific place (O'NEILL 2001; PICKETT AND CADENASSO 2002). Thus, within its prescribed area or location, an ecosystem comprises its abiotic (non-living) environment and the biotic (living) groupings of plant and animal species, or communities. The biotic and abiotic components, and the interactions between them, are often referred to as the ecosystem structure.

Two important ecosystem functions are carried out in every ecosystem: biogeochemical cycling; and flow of energy. Important processes of biogeochemical cycling include primary production (photosynthesis), nutrient and water cycling, and materials decomposition. The flow, storage and transformation of materials and energy through the system are also influenced by processes that link organisms with each other, such as the food web, which is made up of interlocking food chains. These food chains are often characterized by other important functions, such as pollination, predation, and parasitism.

The structure and functions of an ecosystem provide valuable goods and services to humans. For example, some of the living organisms found in an ecosystem might be harvested or hunted for food, collected for raw materials, or simply valued because they are aesthetically pleasing. Some of the ecosystem functions, such as nutrient and water cycling, can also benefit humans through purifying water, controlling floods, recharging aquifers, reducing pollution, or simply by providing more pleasing environments for recreation. These various benefits provided by an ecosystem via its structure and functions are now referred to as ecosystem services. As summarized in Box 2, the structure and functions of an ecosystem are not the same as its services. Ecosystem structure and functions describe the components of an ecosystem and its biophysical relationship regardless of whether humans benefit from them. Only if they contribute to human well-being do these components and relationships generate an "ecosystem service."[6]

5. Assessing the value of ecosystem goods and services

The idea that ecosystems provide a range of "services" that have value to humans is an important step in characterizing these systems as "natural capital." In order to view ecosystems as a special type of capital asset – a form

---

6   For more discussion, see Barbier (2011a and 2011b); Bockstael et al. (2000); Boyd and Banzhof (2007); EPA (2009); and Polasky and Segerson (2009).

of "ecological wealth" – then just like any other asset or investment in the economy, ecosystems must be capable of generating current and future flows of income or benefits. It follows that, in principle, ecosystems can be valued just like any other asset in an economy. Regardless of whether there exists a market for the goods and services produced by ecosystems, their social value must equal the discounted net present value (NPV) of these flows. However, for economists, the term "benefit" has a specific meaning. This section discusses how this concept of economic benefit should be applied to ecosystem goods and services as a guide to their correct economic valuation. In addition, the section outlines the main approach that is required to integrate the "ecological production" of ecosystem goods and services with "economic valuation" of these benefits.

As noted previously, the literature on ecological services implies that ecosystems are assets that produce a flow of beneficial goods and services over time. For example, a common practice in this literature is to adopt the broad definition of the MA (2005) that "ecosystem services are the benefits people obtain from ecosystems." However, according to Mendelsohn and Olmstead (2009, P. 326), "(t)he economic benefit provided by an environmental good or service is the sum of what all members of society would be willing to pay for it." Consequently, some economists argue that it is misleading to characterize all ecosystem services as "benefits." As explained by Boyd and Banzhaf (2007, P. 619), "as end-products of nature, final ecosystem services are not benefits nor are they necessarily the final product consumed. For example, recreation is often called an ecosystem service. It is more appropriately considered a benefit produced using both ecological services and conventional goods and services." To illustrate this point, they consider recreational angling. It requires certain ecosystem services, such as "surface waters and fish populations" but also "other goods and services including tackle, boats, time allocation, and access" (BOYD AND BANZHAF 2007, P. 619). But other economists still prefer the broader

perspective of the MA (2005), which equates ecosystem services with benefits. For example, Polasky and Segerson (2009, P. 412) state: "We adopt a broad definition of the term ecosystem services that includes both intermediate and final services," which they justify by explaining that "supporting services, in economic terms, are akin to the infrastructure that provides the necessary conditions under which inputs can be usefully combined to provide intermediate and final goods and services of value to society." Thus, unlike Boyd and Banzhaf (2007), Polasky and Segerson (2009) consider recreation to be an ecosystem service.

Economists do agree that, in order to determine society's willingness to pay for the benefits provided by ecosystem goods and services, one needs to measure and account for their various impacts on human welfare. Or, as Bockstael et al. (2000, P. 1385) state: "In economics, valuation concepts relate to human welfare. So the economic value of an ecosystem function or service relates only to the contribution it makes to human welfare, where human welfare is measured in terms of each individual's own assessment of his or her well-being." The key is determining how changes in ecosystem goods and services affect an individual's well-being, and then determining how much the individual is either willing to pay for changes that have a positive welfare impact or, conversely, how much the individual is willing to accept as compensation to avoid a negative effect.

The starting point in identifying ecosystem services and their values is the consensus economic view outlined above. As long as nature makes a contribution to human welfare, either entirely on its own or through joint use with other human inputs, then we can designate this contribution as an "ecosystem service." In other words. as stated in Box 2, "ecosystem services are the direct or indirect contributions that ecosystems make to the well-being of human populations." Although it is acceptable to use "the term ecosystem service to refer broadly to both intermediate and final end services," "in specific valuation contexts...it is important to identify whether the service being valued is an intermediate or a final service" (EPA 2009, PP. 12-3).

Following this approach, for example, recreation can be considered the product of an ecosystem service. But, as pointed out by Boyd and Banzhaf (2007, P.619), the ecosystem provides only an "intermediate service" (along with "conventional goods and services") in the production of the final benefit of recreation and tourism. In estimating the value of this intermediate ecosystem service in producing recreational benefits, it is therefore important to assess only the effects of changes in the ecosystem on recreation, and not the additional influence of any human inputs. The same approach should be taken for those "final" ecosystem services, such as coastal protection, erosion control, nutrient cycling, water purification, and carbon sequestration, which may benefit human well-being with or without any additional human-provided goods and services. Valuation should show how changes in these services affect human welfare, after controlling for the influence of any additional human-provided goods and services.

Although valuing ecosystem goods and services seems straightforward, in practice there are a number of challenges to overcome. These difficulties are key to understanding why there are still a large number of ecosystem goods and services that have yet to be valued or have very unreliable valuation estimates.

The most significant problem is that very few are marketed. Some of the products provided by ecosystems, such as raw materials, food, and fish harvests, are bought and sold in markets. Given that the price and quantities of these marketed products are easy to observe, there are numerous value estimates of the contribution of the environmental input to this production. However, this valuation can be more complicated than it appears. Market conditions and regulatory policies for the commodity bought and sold will influence the values imputed to the environment input. For example, one important service of many estuarine and coastal ecosystems is that they serve as coastal breeding and nursery habitat for offshore fisheries. As many fisheries are exploited commercially, the inability to control fishing access and the presence of production subsidies and other market distortions can impact harvests, the price of fish sold, and ultimately, the estimated value of coastal habitats in supporting these fisheries (BARBIER ET AL. 2002; BARBIER 2007; FREEMAN 1991; SMITH 2007).

However, the majority of ecosystem goods and services are not marketed. These include many services arising from ecosystem processes and functions that benefit human beings largely without any additional input from them, such as coastal protection, nutrient cycling, erosion control, water purification, and carbon sequestration. In recent years, substantial progress has been made by economists working with ecologists and other natural scientists in applying environmental valuation methodologies to assess the welfare contribution of these services. The various non-market valuation methods employed for ecosystem services are essentially the standard techniques that are available to economists.[7] Later in this chapter, we discuss these issues further. Nevertheless, what makes applying these methods to estimate the value of a non-marketed ecosystem service especially difficult is that it requires three important and interrelated, steps (BARBIER 1994, 2011A, AND 2011B; EPA 2009; FREEMAN 2003; NRC 2005; POLASKY AND SEGERSON 2009).

The first step involves determining how best to characterize the change in ecosystem structure, functions and processes that gives rise to the change in the ecosystem service. For example, the change could be in the spatial area or quality of a particular type of ecosystem, such as a mangrove forest, marsh vegetation or watershed extent. It could also be a change in a

---

7   For example, Barbier (2007, 2011a, and 2011b); Bateman et al. (2011); EPA (2009); Freeman (2003); Hanley and Barbier (2009); Mendelsohn and Olmstead (2009); NRC (2005); and and Pagiola et al. (2004) discuss how these standard valuation methods are best applied to ecosystem services, emphasizing in particular both the advantages and the shortcomings of the different methods and their application.

key population, such as fish or main predator. Alternatively, the change could be due to variation in the flow of water, energy, or nutrients through the system, such as the variability in tidal surges due to coastal storm events or the influx of organic waste from pollution upstream from estuarine and coastal ecosystems.

The second step requires tracing how the changes in ecosystem structure, functions and processes influence the quantities and qualities of ecosystem service flows to people. Underlying each ecosystem service is a range of important energy flow, biogeochemical, and biotic processes and functions. For example, water purification by seagrass beds is linked to the ecological processes of nutrient uptake and suspended particle deposition (KOCH ET AL. 2006; RYBICKI 1997). However, the key ecological process and functions that generate an ecosystem service are in turn controlled by certain abiotic and biotic components that are unique to each ecosystem's structure. The various controlling components that may affect nutrient uptake and particle deposition by seagrass ecosystems include seagrass species and density, nutrient load, water residence time, hydrodynamic conditions, and the availability of light. Only when these first two steps are completed is it possible to conduct the final step, which involves using existing economic valuation method to assess the impact on human well-being that results from the change in ecosystem goods and services.

Figure 1 provides a visual summary of the key elements of this three-step approach. Human drivers of ecosystem change affect important ecosystem processes and functions and their controlling components. Assessing this change is crucial yet difficult. However, as NRC (2005, PP. 2-3) points out, "making the translation from ecosystem structure and function to ecosystem goods and services (i.e., the ecological production) is even more difficult" and "probably the greatest challenge for successful valuation of ecosystem services is to integrate studies of the ecological production function with studies of the economic valuation function." Similarly,

FIGURE 1

Key interrelated steps in valuing ecosystem goods and services

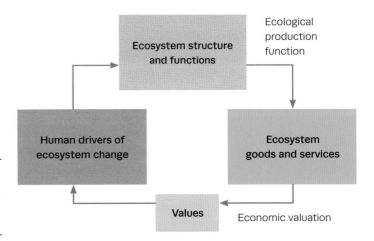

Source: Adapted from NRC (2005, Figure 1–3)

Polasky and Segerson (2009, P. 422) maintain that "among the more practical difficulties that arise in either predicting changes in service flows or estimating the associated value of ecosystem services" include the "lack of multiproduct, ecological production functions to quantitatively map ecosystem structure and function to a flow of services that can then be valued."

6. Valuing non-market ecosystem goods and services

One of the fundamental challenges is that many important ecosystem goods and services are non-marketed. These include many important services arising from ecosystem processes and functions, such as coastal protection, nutrient cycling, erosion control, water purification, and carbon sequestration. In recent years substantial progress has been made by economists working with ecologists and other natural scientists on this "fundamental challenge" to improve the application of environmental valuation methodologies to non-market ecosystem services. Nevertheless, a number of important challenges arise in applying these methods, which are reviewed in this section.

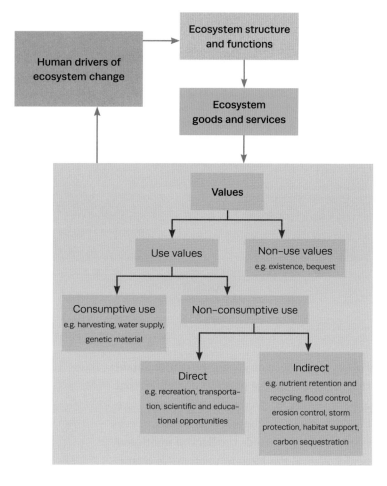

FIGURE 2

Economic valuation of ecosystem goods
and services

Source: Adapted from NRC (2005, Figure 7-1)

In the previous section, we discussed the three-step approach that is required to integrate the "ecological production" of ecosystem goods and services with "economic valuation" of these benefits, which was summarized visually by Figure 1. In recent years, substantial progress has been made by economists working with ecologists and other natural scientists on this "fundamental challenge" to improve the application of environmental valuation methodologies to non-market ecosystem services. Nevertheless, a number of important challenges arise in applying these methods. To help our subsequent discussion of valuation issues, it is useful to look at a more detailed version of

Figure 1 that emphasizes the economic valuation component of the Figure 2.

As indicated in Figure 2, there are a number of different ways in which humans benefit from, or value, ecosystem goods and services. The first distinction is between the use values as opposed to non-use values arising from these goods and services. Typically, use values involve some human "interaction" with the environment whereas non-use values do not, as they represent an individual valuing the pure "existence" of a natural habitat or ecosystem or wanting to "bequest it to future generations." Direct use values refer to both consumptive and non-consumptive uses that involve some form of direct physical interaction with environmental goods and services, such as recreational activities, resource harvesting, drinking clean water, breathing unpolluted air, and so forth. Indirect use values refer to those ecosystem services whose values can only be measured indirectly, since they are derived from supporting and protecting activities that have directly measurable values. For example, for wetlands, the indirect use values associated with ecosystems services include coastal protection, erosion control, flood protection, water purification, carbon sequestration, maintenance of temperature and precipitation, and habitat support for fishing, hunting, and foraging activities outside the wetlands (BARBIER 2007).[8]

Table 1 indicates the various non-market methods that can be used for valuing ecosystem goods and services. As shown in this table, the methods employed are essentially the standard non-market valuation techniques that are available to economists. However, the application of non-market valuation to ecosystem goods and services is not without difficulties. Here, we simply summarize some of the key issues.

---

8 Another component of value, *option value*, is commonly referred to as a non-use value in the literature. However, option value arises from the difference between valuation under conditions of certainty and uncertainty, and is a numerical calculation, not a value held by people *per se*. See NRC (2005, ch. 6) for further discussion.

First, the application of some of the valuation methods listed in Table 1 is often limited to specific types of ecological goods and services. For example, the travel cost method is used principally for those environmental values that enhance individuals' enjoyment of recreation and tourism, averting behavior models are best applied to the health effects arising from environmental pollution. Similarly, hedonic wage and property models are used primarily for assessing work-related environmental hazards and environmental impacts on property values, respectively.

In contrast, stated preference methods, which include contingent valuation methods and choice modeling, have the potential to be used widely in valuing ecosystem goods and services. These valuation methods share the common approach of surveying individuals who benefit from an ecological service or range of services, in the hope that analysis of these responses will provide an accurate measure of the individuals' willingness to pay for the service or services. In addition, stated preference methods can go beyond estimating the value to individuals of single and even multiple benefits of ecosystems and in some cases elicit non-use values that individuals attach to ensuring that a preserved and well-functioning system will be around for future generations to enjoy. For example, a study of mangrove-dependent coastal communities in Micronesia demonstrated through the use of contingent valuation techniques that the communities "place some value on the existence and ecosystem functions of mangroves

over and above the value of mangroves' marketable products" (NAYLOR AND DREW 1998, P. 488). Similarly, choice modeling has the potential to elicit the relative values that individuals place on different ecosystem services. A study of wetland restoration in southern Sweden revealed through choice experiments that individuals' willingness to pay for the restoration increased if the result enhanced overall biodiversity but decreased if the restored wetlands were used mainly for the introduction of Swedish crayfish for recreational fishing (CARLSSON ET AL. 2003).

However, as emphasized by NRC (2005), to implement a stated-preference study two key conditions are necessary:

TABLE 1

Various non–market valuation methods applied to ecosystem services

Valuation method[a]	Types of value estimated	Common types of applications	Ecosystem services valued
Travel cost	Direct use	Recreation	Maintenance of beneficial species, productive ecosystems and biodiversity
Averting behavior	Direct use	Environmental impacts on human health	Pollution control and detoxification
Hedonic price	Direct and indirect use	Environmental impacts on residential property and human morbidity and mortality	Storm protection; flood mitigation; maintenance of air quality
Production function	Indirect use	Commercial and recreational fishing; agricultural systems; control of invasive species; watershed protection; damage costs avoided	Maintenance of beneficial species; maintenance of arable land and agricultural productivity; prevention of damage from erosion and siltation; groundwater recharge; drainage and natural irrigation; storm protection; flood mitigation
Replacement cost	Indirect use	Damage costs avoided; freshwater supply	Drainage and natural irrigation; storm protection; flood mitigation
Stated preference	Use and non-use	Recreation; environmental impacts on human health and residential property; damage costs avoided; existence and bequest values of preserving ecosystems	All of the above

Notes: [a]See Barbier (2007); Bateman et al. (2011); EPA (2009); Freeman (2003); Hanley & Barbier (2009); Mendelsohn & Olmstead (2009); NRC (2005); and Pagiola et al. (2004) for more discussion of these various non–market valuation methods and their application to valuing ecosystem goods and services.

Source: Adapted from NRC (2005), Table 4–2.

(1) the information must be available to describe the change in an ecosystem in terms of the goods and services that people care about, in order to place a value on those goods and services; and

(2) the ecosystem change must be explained in the survey instrument in a manner that people will understand while not rejecting the valuation scenario.

For many of the specific ecosystem goods and services listed in Table 1, one or both of these conditions may not hold. For instance, it has proven very difficult to describe accurately through the hypothetical scenarios required by stated-preference surveys how changes in ecosystem processes and components affect ecosystem regulatory and habitat functions and thus the specific benefits arising from these functions that individuals value. If there is considerable scientific uncertainty surrounding these linkages, then not only is it difficult to construct such hypothetical scenarios, but also any responses elicited from individuals from stated-preference surveys are likely to yield inaccurate measures of their willingness to pay for ecological services (BATEMAN ET AL. 2009). Valuation workshop methods may, however, help in terms of conveying information about complex ecological goods, and investigating the effects on people's values of scientific uncertainty about linkages within the system (see, for example, CHRISTIE ET AL. 2006).

In contrast to stated preference methods, the advantage of production function (PF) approaches is that they depend on only the first condition, and not both conditions, holding (see BARBIER 1994 and 2007; MCCONNELL AND BOCKSTAEL 2005). That is, for those ecological functions where there is sufficient scientific knowledge of how these functions link to specific ecological services that support or protect economic activities, then it may be possible to employ the PF approach to value these services. The basic modeling approach underlying PF methods – also called "valuing the environment as input" – is similar to determining the additional value of a change in the supply of any factor input. If changes in the structure and functions of ecosystems affect the marketed production activities of an economy, then the effects of these changes will be transmitted to individuals through the price system via changes in the costs and prices of final good and services. This means that any resulting "improvements in the resource base or environmental quality" as a result of enhanced ecosystem services, "lower costs and prices and increase the quantities of marketed goods, leading to increases in consumers' and perhaps producers' surpluses" (FREEMAN 2003, P. 259).

An adaptation of the PF methodology is required in the case where ecological regulatory and habitat functions have a protective value, through various ecological services such as storm protection, flood mitigation, prevention of erosion and siltation, pollution control, and maintenance of beneficial species (BARBIER 2007; MCCONNELL AND BOCKSTAEL 2005). In such cases, the environment may be thought of producing a non-marketed service, such as "protection" of economic activity, property, and even human lives, which benefits individuals through limiting damages. Applying PF approaches requires modelling the "production" of this protection service and estimating its value as an environmental input in terms of the expected damages avoided by individuals. However, PF methods have their own measurement issues and limitations when they are employed to value ecosystem goods and services.

For instance, applying the PF method raises questions about how changes in the ecological service should be measured, whether market distortions in the final goods market are significant, and whether current changes in ecological services may affect future productivity through biological "stock effects." A common approach in the literature is to assume that an estimate of ecosystem area may be included in the "production function" of marketed output as a proxy for the ecological service input. For example, this is the standard approach adopted in coastal habitat-fishery PF models, as allowing wetland area to be a determinant of fish catch is thought

Adjusting net domestic product (NDP) for the contributions of ecological capital

The formal model in the Appendix derives the following expression for net domestic product (NDP), which illustrates the importance of measuring explicitly the economic contributions of natural capital, and especially that of ecological capital.

EQUATION 1

$$NDP = v^K[Y - \omega K] + v^K\left(\frac{h(E)}{h'} - E\right) + v^K AF_R$$
$$[G(S) - R] + U_N N + (v^D - v^N)c$$

In the above expression $v^K(t)[Y(t) - \omega K(t)]$ is conventionally defined net domestic product (NDP), that is the gross domestic product of the economy, Y, less any depreciation (in value terms) of previously accumulated reproducible capital, ωK. This is NDP as currently measured in most national accounts of economies, although of course it is usually valued at market prices rather than in terms of the shadow price of reproducible capital, v^K. However, if NDP is to serve as a true measure of the changes in an economy's wealth, it must include any appreciation or depreciation to human and natural capital as well. For instance, $v^K(t)(h(E(t))/h' - E(t))$ is the net appreciation (in value terms) in human capital, and $v^K(t)A(t)$ $F_R[G(S(t)) - R(t)]$ represents the net changes (in value

terms) in natural resource stocks. In the case of non-renewable resources, such as fossil fuels and minerals, $G(S) = 0$ and so $-v^K AF_R R$ measures the deduction from NDP of resource depletion. For renewable resources, such as forests and fisheries, NDP must include any depreciation in natural resource stocks if $G(S) < R$. The expression $U_N N(t) + [v^D(t) - v^N(t)]c(t)$ includes both the benefits to current well-being provided by ecosystems, $U_N N$, and any capital revaluation that occurs as ecosystems are converted by land use change for development, $(v^D - v^N)c$, where $v^D(t)$ and $v^N(t)$ are the capitalized values, or *prices*, of development and ecosystem land, respectively. As ecosystems are converted by land use change for development, $(v^D - v^N)c$ is the capital appreciation (depreciation) in land that occurs if $v^D > v^N$ ($v^D < v^N$). In other words, we should also adjust the NDP of the economy to include two contributions due to ecological capital:

- the value of the *direct benefits* provided by the current stock of ecosystems, $U_N N$; and
- any capital revaluation as a result of conversion of ecosystems to other land uses, $(v^D - v^N)c$, with the price of changes in ecological capital, $v^N(t)$, reflecting the present value of the future *direct and indirect benefits* of ecosystems.

---

by economists and ecologists to proxy some element of the productivity contribution of this important habitat function (BARBIER 2000, 2007; FREEMAN 2003, CH. 9; MCCONNELL AND BOCKSTAEL 2005). In addition, as pointed out by Freeman (1991), market conditions and regulatory policies for the marketed output will influence the values imputed to the environmental input. For instance, in the previous example of coastal wetlands supporting an offshore fishery, the fishery may be subject to open access conditions. Under these conditions, profits in the fishery would be dissipated, and price would be equated to average and not marginal

costs. As a consequence, producer values are zero and only consumer values determine the value of increased wetland area. Finally, a further measurement issue arises in the case where the ecological service supports a natural resource system, such as a fishery, forestry, or a wildlife population, which is then harvested or exploited through economic activity. In such cases, the key issue is whether the effects on the natural resource stock or biological population of changes in the ecological service are sufficiently large that these stock effects need to be modelled explicitly. In the production function valuation literature, approaches that ignore stock effects are referred to as "static models" of environmental change on a natural resource production system, whereas approaches that take into account the intertemporal stock effects of the environmental change are referred to as "dynamic models" (BARBIER 2000, 2007; FREEMAN 2003, CH. 9).

Finally, measurement issues, data availability and other limitations can prevent the application of standard non-market valuation methods to many ecosystem services. In circumstances where an ecological service is unique to a specific ecosystem and is difficult to value, then economists have sometimes resorted to using the cost of replacing the service or treating the damages arising from the loss of the service as a valuation approach. However, economists consider that the replacement cost approach should be used with caution (BARBIER 1994 and 2007; ELLIS AND FISHER 1987; FREEMAN 2003; MCCONNELL AND BOCKSTAEL 2005; SHABMAN AND BATIE 1978). For example, a number of studies that have attempted to value the storm prevention and flood mitigation services of the "natural" storm barrier function of mangrove and other coastal wetland systems have employed the replacement cost method by simply estimating the costs of replacing mangroves by constructing physical barriers to perform the same services (CHONG 2005). Shabman and Batie (1978) suggested that this method can provide a reliable valuation estimation for an ecological service, but only if the following conditions are met: (1) the alternative considered provides the same services; (2) the alternative should be the least-cost alternative; and (3) there should be substantial evidence that the service would be demanded by society if it were provided by that least-cost alternative. Unfortunately, very few replacement cost studies meet all three conditions.

However, one study that met these criteria for valuing an ecosystem service was the analysis of the policy choice of providing clean drinking water by the Catskills Mountains for New York City (CHICHILINSKY AND HEAL 1998; NRC 2005). Rather than value all the services of the Catskills watershed ecosystems; instead, it was sufficient simply to demonstrate that protecting and restoring the ecological integrity of the Catskills was less costly than replacing this ecosystem service with a human-constructed water filtration system. The total costs of building and operating the filtration system were in the range of US$6–8 billion, whereas it would cost New York City US$1–1.5 billion to protect and restore the natural ecosystem processes in the watershed, thus preserving the clean drinking water service provided by the Catskills. A second case study that also met the above criteria estimates the value of using wetlands for abatement of agricultural nitrogen load on the Baltic Sea coast of Sweden (BYSTRÖM 2000). In this study, the replacement value of wetlands was defined and estimated as the difference between two cost-effective reductions of agricultural nitrogen pollution: one that uses wetlands for nitrogen abatement, and one that does not. The study showed that the use of wetlands as nitrogen sinks can reduce by 30 percent the total costs of abating nitrogen pollution from agriculture in Sweden.

7. Correcting wealth accounts for ecological capital

Overcoming measurement issues and challenges to determine the value of non-market ecosystem goods and services is an important, but there are additional considerations in using these values to correct wealth accounts for ecological capital. This section focuses on two important issues: double counting; and accounting for special properties of ecosystems, such as ecological stability, resilience, and collapse.

Recall that, as Box 1 indicates, the net domestic product (NDP) of the economy should be adjusted for the value of the direct benefits provided by the current stock of ecosystem. But NDP should not be adjusted for any indirect benefits of this current stock through its support or protection of production in the economy. The reason for the latter omission is that it may

The value of ecosystem resilience in the Goulburn–Broken Catchment of southeast Australia

Using the inclusive wealth framework of Arrow et al. (2003), Mäler (2008) shows that it is possible to add a "resilience stock" to the measure of an economy's wealth. Resilience is interpreted as the probability of the system transitioning to another state (regime). That is, the closer to the threshold, the lower the stock of resilience, and the higher is the probability that the system will flip to the alternative regime. The real value, or shadow price, of the resilience stock is the expected change in future social welfare from a marginal change in resilience today. This value changes as the likelihood of crossing the threshold into the alternative regime increases.

Walker et al. (2010) apply this approach to the Goulburn–Broken Catchment (GBC) in Southeast Australia. The GBC includes 300,000 ha in irrigation, of which 80% is for dairy pasture. However, the removal of native vegetation for agriculture has led to rising water tables and increased soil salinity. Once the water table rises above 2 meters (m), however, pasture land is radically changed, and the agro-ecological system shifts to a different regime dominated by degraded and salinized soil. Thus, the resilience of the GBC system is measured by the distance from the water table to the 2 m threshold, and this indicator determines the probability that

the system will shift from the non-saline to saline regime. To demonstrate the impact of resilience on the inclusive wealth of the GBC, Walker et al. assume that all other economic assets are constant and only the stock of resilience changes. Between 1991 and 2001, they calculate that the resilience stock increased by 0.5 m due to a water table fall from 3,0 to 3.5 m. They estimate the value of this change in resilience under two different climate regimes: normal versus drier rainfall and evaporation conditions. The results are depicted in the table below. Under normal climate conditions, the 0.5 m change in ecosystem resilience is valued at about $23 million, or around 7% of the total wealth of the GBC in 1991. Under drier climatic conditions, resilience is worth $28 million, or 8.4% of total wealth.

Climate scenario	Change in wealth from 1991 to 2001 form 0.5 m change in the resilience stock	Share of 1991 inclusive wealth
Normal conditions	$22,852, 650	7.0%
Dry conditions	$28,558,360	8.4%

Source: Walker et al. (2010, Table 2).

create problems of double counting in the wealth accounts of an economy.

As discussed in the previous section and outlined in Table 1, the production function method is an important non-market valuation method of measuring the economic contribution of many ecosystem goods and services that affect human welfare indirectly through their support or protection of production activities, property, or human lives. In other words, ecosystem services that arise from the regulatory functions of ecosystems, such as waste management, habitat support, storm protection, flood mitigation, and groundwater recharge, often

serve as intermediate inputs in economic production activities, which are in turn often marketed. Similarly, goods or products from ecosystems, such as harvested raw materials, water supplies, food, fiber, and fuel, may themselves be marketed, or in turn are processed by industries into marketed products. But if these goods and services produced from the current stock of ecosystems serve as intermediate inputs into marketed production, then conventionally defined NDP will most likely already reflect their current contribution. To add to NDP the marginal value contribution to economic production of ecosystem goods and services that are intermediate

FIGURE 3

Estimated mangrove area, Thailand, 1961–2009

Sources: FAO (2007b) and Spalding et al. (2010).

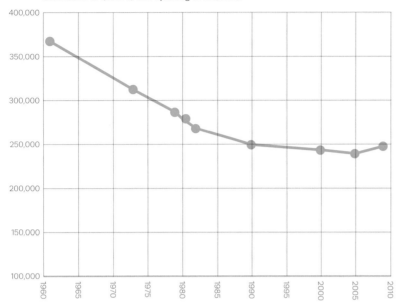

inputs would result in double counting (MÄLER 1991; MÄLER ET AL. 2008; VINCENT 2012).

For example, if a coastal marsh or mangrove serves as a nursery or breeding habitat for an off-shore commercial fishery, then this habitat will have an influence on current harvested and marketed output of the fishery. However, the harvested fish will already be included in conventional NDP of an economy, as it is a marketed product. Similarly, if the wetlands also protect coastal property from storm damages, the value of the latter assets already accounts for the storm protection value of the wetlands. In addition, if the wetlands themselves are a source of currently harvested food, fiber, and raw materials, which are in turn sold commercially, then the NDP will already include these marketed products. In contrast, if any harvested wetland products are not marketed but support the subsistence needs of harvesting households, then the value of these ecological goods will not appear in conventionally measured NDP. Because they are consumed and not marketed, these products are essentially direct benefits to households. Finally, coastal wetlands may generate many other non-marketed ecosystem

services that also directly influence welfare, such as filtering water pollution that affects human health, enhancing enjoyment of coastal areas and recreation, and providing cultural benefits. Again, these current values of the wetlands are unlikely to appear in conventional NDP.

To summarize, to avoid double counting, the NDP of an economy should not be adjusted by including the value of any goods and services provided currently by ecosystems, if they serve as intermediate inputs in the production of marketed final goods and services. However, if ecosystem goods and services affect current production activities that are not marketed, such as raw materials, food, fiber, and water that are consumed directly by households, then the value of these ecological contributions should be assessed and added to NDP.

However, as indicated in Box 1, this particular double counting problem does not arise when adjusting NDP to account for any capital revaluation in the economy that occurs when, say, ecosystems are converted to other land uses. In this case, the capitalized value of converted ecosystems must reflect the present value of all foregone future benefits of these ecosystems, whether they influence welfare directly or indirectly through production of marketed final goods and services.

Landscape losses and degradation of ecosystem processes and functions can also lead to unpredictable and sudden increases in the risk of ecological collapse, due to the presence of ecological thresholds and feedback effects. That is, large shocks or sustained disturbances to ecosystems lead to further interactions that can contravene ecological thresholds, causing the systems to "flip" irreversibly from one functioning state to another. Thus the resilience or robustness of an ecosystem – its ability to absorb large shocks or sustained disturbances and still maintain internal integrity and functioning – may be an important attribute determining the extent to which landscape conversion and ecosystem degradation affects the risk of ecological

Valuation estimates used in accounting for mangrove wealth, Thailand

As indicated in Box 1, the net domestic product (NDP) of an economy must be adjusted for the direct benefits to current well-being provided by ecosystems, $U_N N$, and any capital revaluation that occurs as ecosystems are converted by land use change for development, $(v^D - v^N)c$. Mangrove ecosystems in Thailand provide four essential goods and services. These are the role of mangroves as natural "barriers" to periodic damaging coastal storm events, their role as nursery and breeding habitats for offshore fisheries, their ability store carbon, and the exploitation of mangrove forests by coastal communities for a variety of wood and non-wood products. Estimates of the value of all four benefits exist for Thailand.

For example, the value of coastal protection from storms is based on a marginal value per ha of damages avoided (in 1996 US$) of $1,879; over a 20-year time horizon and a 10% discount rate this yields a net present value (NPV) of $15,997 per ha (Barbier, 2007). The value of habitat-fishery linkages is based on a net value per ha (in 1996 US$, assuming a price elasticity for fish of –0.5) of mangrove habitat of $249; over a 20-year time horizon and a 10% discount rate this yields a NPV of $2,117 per ha (Barbier, 2003). The value of wood and non-wood products is based on net income per has from mangrove forests to local community (updated to 1996 US$) of $101; over a 20-year time horizon and a 10% discount rate this yields a NPV of $864 per ha (Sathirathai & Barbier, 2001). Chmura et al. (2003) estimate permanent carbon sequestration by global mangroves of 2.1 metric tons per ha per year, and

World Bank (2011) values unit carbon dioxide damage at $20 per ton of carbon (1995 US$), which yields an annual value (in 1995 US$) of $42 per ha for carbon sequestration. Over a 20-year time horizon and a 10% discount rate this yields a net present value (NPV) of $413 per ha. These values are converted to 2000 US$ using the GDP deflator for Thailand (World Bank, 2011). As a result, mangroves in Thailand have a constant 2000 US$ capitalized value, v^N, of $21,443 per ha.

As the main activity responsible for mangrove conversion in Thailand has been shrimp aquaculture, the capitalized value of this activity is used for v^D. The net present value (NPV) per ha for the commercial net returns to shrimp farming over a 20-year time horizon and 10% discount rate is based on (Sathirathai & Barbier, 2001), which when updated to 1996 US$, amounts to a value of $9,632 per ha. However, many of the inputs used in shrimp pond operations are subsidized, below border-equivalent prices, thus increasing artificially the private returns to shrimp farming. Without these subsidies, the resulting economic net returns to shrimp farming result in a NPV of $1,220 per ha. When converted to 2000 US$ using the GDP deflator for Thailand (World Bank, 2011), the capitalized value of mangroves converted to shrimp farms is $1,351 per ha. Because the capitalized value, or "price," of mangroves converted to shrimp farming is less than the capitalized value of mangroves, or $(v^N - v^N) < 0$, then the NDP of Thailand should be adjusted for this resulting capital depreciation in mangrove land.

---

collapse.[9] Thus, one approach to accounting for the resilience property of ecosystems is to

measure directly the wealth effects of resilience (MÄLER 2008; WALKER ET AL. 2010).

Box 2 summarizes the effort by Walker et al. (2010) to value ecosystem resilience for the Goulburn-Broken Catchment (GBC) in Southeast Australia. The GBC is prime agricultural land, most of which is used for dairy pasture. However, the agro-ecosystem is threatened by increased

---

9   See, for example, Dasgupta and Mäler (2003); Elmqvist et al. (2003); Folke et al. (2004); Levin (1999); Levin and Lubchenco (2008); Perrings (1998); Scheffer et al. (2001); and Walker et al. (2004).

soil salinity due to rising water tables from removal of native vegetation. At the 2 meter (m) water table threshold, the system is in danger of flipping to a different regime dominated by degraded and salinized pasture. The authors estimate resilience as the distance from the current water table to the 2 m threshold. Under normal climate conditions, a 0.5 m change in ecosystem resilience is valued at about US$23 million, or around 7 percent of the total wealth of the GBC in 1991. Under drier climatic conditions, resilience is worth US$28 million, or 8.4 percent of the total wealth of the GBC.

This example from Australia of valuing of ecosystem resilience suggests that this economic contribution can be considerable. In such highly productive ecosystems supporting economic activity, regime shift can be catastrophic. Or to put it differently, the value of avoiding regime shift by maintaining or enhancing the resilience of ecosystems can be a sizable component of the total economic wealth generated by these systems.

8. A case study: adjusted NDP and mangrove loss in Thailand

Although the previous sections discuss the important issues and challenges that arise when attempting to value ecosystem services and account for their contributions to wealth, significant progress has been made in recent years. For some major ecosystems, we may be very close to implementing the methodology of adjusting NDP to reflect ecological values as well as the depreciation or appreciation in these key natural assets.

The purpose of this section is to provide an example of wealth accounting with a case study from Thailand involving mangrove loss. Mangroves are various kinds of trees and shrubs that grow in saline coastal and estuarine habitats in the tropics and subtropics. The case study illustrates the two adjustments to NDP due to ecological capital: the value of the direct benefits provided by the current stock of ecosystems; and any capital revaluation that occurs as a result of ecosystem conversion to other land uses. Estimating the wealth effects of ecosystem resilience is beyond the scope of this case study.

Thailand is estimated to have lost around a third of its mangroves since the 1960s, mainly to shrimp farming expansion and other coastal development (FAO 2007A; SPALDING ET AL. 2010). During this period, real GDP per capita in Thailand has increased five-fold (World Bank 2011). A measure of the adjusted NDP, taking into account human and natural capital loss since 1970, is constructed. Based on estimates of four mangrove ecosystem benefits – collected products, habitat-fishery linkages, storm protection, and carbon sequestration – the methodol-

FIGURE 4

GDP and ANDP per capita, Thailand, 1970–2009

Sources: FAO (2007b) and Spalding et al. (2010).

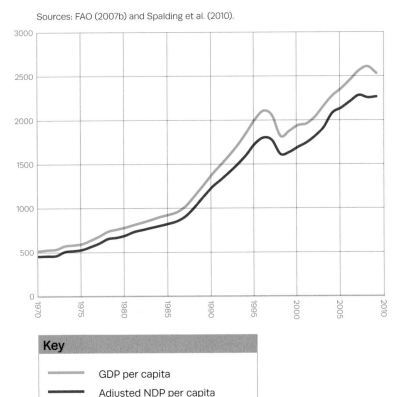

Key

— GDP per capita

— Adjusted NDP per capita

TABLE 2

Wealth accounting for mangrove capital, Thailand, 1970–2009

		Average annual values per capita (constant 2000 US$)						
	Average annual mangrove loss (ha)	Storm protection	Habitat–fishery linkage	Wood and non–wood products	Carbon sequestration	Total value of mangroves	Mangrove depreciation	Net value of mangroves
1970–79	4,676	–	0.11	0.10	0.36	18.59	2.26	–1.69
1980–89	2,980	–	0.08	0.07	0.25	13.00	1.16	–0.76
1990–99	610	–	0.06	0.06	0.20	10.47	0.21	0.11
2000–09	97	–	0.05	0.05	0.18	9.28	0.03	0.25

Notes: As storm protection value is based on expected damages to economic property, it is assumed that this benefit is already accounted for in the current market values of property. Current habitat–fishery linkages benefits are based only the imputed subsistence value, which based on a survey of four Thai coastal villages, is approximately 5.3 percent of total household income (Sarntisart and Sathirathai 2004, Tables 6.3 and 6.4). Current wood and non–wood product benefits are based only the imputed subsistence value, which based on a survey of four Thai coastal villages, is approximately 12.4 percent of total household income (Sarntisart and Sathirathai 2004, Tables 6.3 and 6.4).

ogy of adjusting NDP for the value of ecosystems is also included as an illustration.

In 1961, Thailand was estimated to have around 368,000 hectares (ha) of mangroves in 1961 (see Figure 3). Mangrove deforestation proceeded swiftly in the 1970s and 1980s, but since 2000, the area of mangroves seems to have stabilized around 240,000 to 250,000 ha. The main cause of mangrove loss in Thailand is attributed to conversion to shrimp aquaculture (AKSORNKOAE AND TOKRISNA 2004). The main reason for the slowdown in mangrove loss is that many of the suitable sites for establishing shrimp farms in the Gulf of Thailand have been deforested, whereas the mangrove areas on the Andaman Sea (Indian Ocean) coast are too remote and less suitable for shrimp farms (BARBIER AND COX 2004).

Box 3 outlines the valuation estimates that are used for accounting for the current benefits of mangroves as well as their capitalized values for Thailand over 1970 to 2009. The four principal ecosystem goods and services are the role of mangroves as natural "barriers" to periodic damaging coastal storm events, their role as nursery and breeding habitats for offshore fisheries, their ability store carbon, and the exploitation

of mangrove forests by coastal communities for a variety of wood and non-wood products. As outlined in Box 3, these four benefits of mangroves in Thailand have a constant 2000 US$ capitalized value of US$21,443 per ha. As the main activity responsible for mangrove conversion in Thailand has been shrimp aquaculture, the capitalized value (in 2000 US$) of this alternative use of mangrove ecosystems is US$1,351 per ha. Note that, because the capitalized value, or "price," of mangroves converted to shrimp farming is less than the capitalized value of mangroves, the NDP of Thailand should be adjusted for this depreciation in mangrove capital.

However, not all the current benefits of mangroves impact welfare directly, but may do so only through support or protection of economic activity and property. That is certainly the case for storm protection benefits of mangroves, which are estimated through an expected damage approach that determines their value in terms of protecting economic property (BARBIER 2007). As this benefit is already accounted for in the current market values of property, to avoid double counting, the NDP of the Thai economy should not be adjusted to include the benefit of storm protection provided by the current stock of mangroves. Similarly, a survey of four Thai villages from two coastal provinces indicates that only 12.4 percent of the value of collected wood and non-wood products from mangroves and 5.3 percent of the value of coastal fishery harvests can be attributed to subsistence production (SARNTISART AND SATHIRATHAI 2004).[10] Thus, the NDP should be adjusted only for these subsistence contributions of these two benefits of the mangroves in Thailand.

Using the data from Box 3, Table 2 depicts the per capita wealth accounting estimates for Thailand's mangroves from 1970 to 2009. Average annual mangrove loss has fallen steadily in every decade since the 1970s (see also Figure 3). Nevertheless, because around a third of the mangrove area has been deforested from 1970 to 2009, whereas Thailand's population has nearly

doubled over this period, the current per capita benefits of mangroves has halved since the 1970s, from US$0.57 to US$0.28 per person.[11] In the 1970s, when mangrove loss in Thailand was at its highest, mangrove depreciation amounted to US$2.26 per person, whereas by the 2000s, it had fallen to only US$0.03 per capita. The result is that the net value of mangroves per capita in Thailand, which is the total value less mangrove depreciation, was actually negative in the 1970s and 1980s, averaging -US$1.69 and -US$0.76 per person respectively. However, in the 1990s and 2000s, the net value was slightly positive, averaging US$0.11 and US$0.22 respectively.

Table 3 depicts an approximate estimate of adjusted net domestic product (ANDP) per capita for real changes in reproducible, human and natural capital for Thailand over 1970 to 2009. ANDP is GDP less consumption of fixed capital

---

10 The four villages are Ban Sam Chong Tai and Ban Bang Pat of Phang-nga Province, and Ban Gong Khong and Ban Bkhlong Khut in Nakhon Si Thammarat Province.

---

11 According to World Bank (2011), in 1970 Thailand's population was 36.9 million and grew steadily to 68.7 million in 2009.

TABLE 3

Wealth accounting, Thailand – 1970–2009

Average annual values per capita (constant 2000 US$)						
	GDP	ANDP	Consumption of fixed capital	Natural resource depletion	Education expenditure	Net value of mangroves
1970–79	617	544	89	13	30	–1.7
1980–89	956	852	130	19	46	–0.8
1990–99	1,793	1,563	296	20	86	0.1
2000–09	2,291	2,041	280	79	109	0.3

Notes: GDP = Gross Domestic Product

ANDP = Adjusted Net Domestic Product, or GDP less consumption of fixed capital and natural resource depletion, plus education expenditure and the net value of mangroves (estimated in Table 2).

Natural resource depletion is the sum of net forest depletion, energy depletion, and mineral depletion. Net forest depletion is unit resource rents times the excess of roundwood harvest over natural growth. Energy depletion is the ratio of the value of the stock of energy resources to the remaining reserve lifetime (capped at 25 years). It covers coal, crude oil, and natural gas.

Mineral depletion is the ratio of the value of the stock of mineral resources to the remaining reserve lifetime (capped at 25 years). It covers tin, gold, lead, zinc, iron, copper, nickel, silver, bauxite, and phosphate.

Source: World Bank (2011), except for net value of mangroves, which is from Table 2.

and natural resource depletion, plus education expenditure and net values of mangrove depletion. The latter estimate is based on the net value of mangroves from Table 2. Since the 1970s, both consumption of fixed capital and natural resource depreciation have increased significantly in Thailand. The value of expanding human capital, as proxied by education expenditures, has also increased, and because of the slowdown in mangrove loss, the net value of this ecological capital has gone from a negative to a positive contribution to NDP. Overall, the value of mangroves and expanding human capital has not kept pace with reproducible capital depreciation and natural resource depletion in Thailand. As a consequence, adjusted net domestic product per capita in Thailand has remained consistently below GDP per capita since the 1970s. As shown in Figure 4, since 1990 the gap between GDP and ANDP per capita in Thailand has widened significantly.

To summarize, because many of the benefits provided by the current stock of mangroves in Thailand arise through supporting or protecting marketed production and property, these benefits should already be included in the GDP estimates for Thailand. However, any adjusted NDP measure does need to take into account the current direct benefits provided by mangroves in the form of carbon sequestration, habitat and breeding ground services that support any fishery harvests consumed by coastal households and mangrove products that also comprise subsistence consumption. On the other hand, all future mangrove benefits are lost as a result of mangrove conversion, which has been substantial in Thailand since the 1970s. The substantial mangrove depreciation that occurred in the 1970s and 1980s meant that the net value of mangroves was actually negative in these decades. Although mangrove deforestation and thus its capital depreciation has slowed since, the net value of mangroves per capita, as an indicator of its contribution to the wealth of Thailand, is still extremely low. Thus, the Thailand mangrove case study not only provides an illustration of the adjusted NDP methodology

for ecological capital but also illustrates how significant loss of this capital can influence its net value in wealth accounts.

9. Conclusion

This chapter has explored the methodology and the challenges of including ecosystem goods and services in a wealth accounting framework. Following the approach developed by Dasgupta (2009), which is elaborated further in the chapters by Dasgupta (2012) and Perrings (2012), it is shown how this framework can be extended to incorporate ecosystem and their valuable goods and services. The approach developed here requires, first, recognizing ecosystems as a component of natural capital, or ecological capital, and second, measuring these important assets in terms of the land area, or ecological landscape, which defines their boundaries.

Such an approach clarifies how we should value and include changes in ecological capital in wealth accounting, which can be proxied by the net domestic product (NDP) of an economy provided that this indicator accounts for the depreciation of all forms of capital – reproducible, human, and natural capital. There are two main adjustments to NDP of the economy that result, if ecological capital is also to be considered.

First, we should adjust NDP to include the value of the various goods and services provided by the current stock of ecosystems that derives from direct impacts on welfare. These direct ecosystem benefits might include the value of ecosystems in providing non-market recreational, educational, and scientific benefits, their value in terms of natural heritage or bequests to future generation or the value of ecosystems in reducing harmful pollution and assimilating waste that affect human welfare and health directly. In addition, ecological capital protects or supports current economic activity and property. These indirect ecosystem benefits are broad ranging, and include raw materials, food, and other harvested inputs used in production activities, provision of freshwater, watershed protection, coastal habitats for off-shore fisheries, flood control, storm protection, and managing climate. However unlike direct benefits to current well-being, these indirect benefits should not be included as additional values in any measure of an economy's NDP, as they are likely to already be reflected in the prices of final marketed goods and services.

Second, conversion of ecological capital to other land uses requires a further adjustment to GDP to reflect any capital revaluation as a result of this land use change. As the resource allocation mechanism of the economy may not be optimal or even efficient, ecosystem conversion may be taking place even though the capitalized value, or "price," of developed land is actually less than the capitalized value of ecosystems. In which case, GDP should be adjusted for the depreciation in ecological capital that occurs as it is converted to less valuable developed land. The capitalized value of converted ecosystems must reflect the present value of all foregone future benefits of these ecosystems, whether they influence welfare directly or indirectly through production of marketed final goods and services.

The main challenges of applying such an approach is that there are still a large number of non-makreted ecosystem goods and services that have yet to be valued or have very unreliable valuation estimates. Measurement issues, data availability, and other limitations can prevent the application of standard non-market valuation methods to many ecosystem services. Fortunately, some progress is being made, due to the growing collaboration between economists, ecologists and other natural scientists in determining how the ecological production of key goods and services translate into economic valuation of these benefits.

For some major ecosystems, we may be very close to implementing the methodology advocated in this chapter of adjusting GDP to reflect ecological values as well as the depreciation or appreciation in these key natural assets. Using the example of mangroves in Thailand, this chapter illustrates how such an approach might be applied. The case study is able to show how valuation estimates from existing studies could be used for accounting for the current direct benefits of mangroves as well as their capitalized values for Thailand over 1970 to 2009. The per capita value of mangroves net of depreciation in Thailand was actually negative in the 1970s and 1980s due to mangrove conversion to development activities, and principally shrimp aquaculture. The net value of the wealth contribution of mangroves per person was positive but very small in the 1990s and 2000s, only US$0.11 and US$0.25 respectively. In comparison, in the 2000s, reproducible capital depreciation was US$280 per person, natural resource depletion of energy, minerals, and forest was US$79 per capita, and human capital increased by US$109 per person. Thus, the case study demonstrates that accounting for the economic contributions and deprecations of mangrove capital is an important, albeit relatively small, component of the key capital adjustments that occur in Thailand's economy.

But perhaps the more important lesson to be learned from the example of adjusting Thailand's wealth accounts for mangrove current benefits and depreciation is that it illustrates that the challenges of including ecosystem services in a wealth accounting framework can be overcome.

Formal model of wealth accounting and ecosystem services

Assume a closed economy with a constant population that is normalized to one.[1] At time t, let $K(t)$ be a numerical index of the economy's stock of reproducible capital assets, and $H(t)$ be a numerical index of the total quantity of human capital, that is the level of health, education and skills per person. Reproducible capital depreciates at the constant rate $\omega > 0$, and assume that $E(t)$ is investment in human capital (e.g., current education, health, and training expenditures). Denoting the real GDP of the economy at time t as $Y(t)$ and aggregate consumption of goods and services as $C(t)$, then net accumulation of reproducible capital is

EQUATION 1

$$\dot{K} = Y(t) - C(t) - \omega K(t) - E(t), \ \dot{K} = dK(t) \big/ dt$$

Following Hamilton and Clemens (1999), letting represent the rate at which education, health, and training investments are transformed into human capital, then the latter accumulates according to

EQUATION 2

$$\dot{H} = h(E(t)), \ h' > 0, \ \dot{H} = dH(t) \big/ dt$$

Along with human and reproducible capital, the aggregate stock of natural capital available at time t is also important as the source of raw material, land, and energy inputs to the economy, such as fossil fuels, minerals, metals, forest resources, and arable land. If we represent these natural resource stocks as $S(t)$, then

EQUATION 3

$$\dot{S} = G(S(t)) - R(t), \ \dot{S} = dS(t) \big/ dt$$

where the function G represents the natural growth rate for any renewable resources, and

$R(t)$ is the use of any natural resource inputs by the economy.

But, in addition to $S(t)$, natural capital should include those ecosystems that through their natural functioning and habitats provide important goods and services to the economy. However, ecological capital is unlikely to be intact, as many ecosystems continue to be converted to land for economic development and production. It follows that the aggregate stock of developed land, $D(t)$, increases at the expense of ecological capital $N(t)$

EQUATION 4

$$\dot{D} = c(t) = -\dot{N}, \ \dot{D} = dD(t) \big/ dt, \ \dot{N} = dN(t) \big/ dt$$

where $c(t) \geq 0$ represents any ecosystem conversion to developed land at time t.

Following Dasgupta (2009), let $A(t)$ be a combined index of publicly known ideas and the effectiveness of the economies institutions, which can be interpreted as *total factor productivity* in the economy at time t. Given equations (1)–(4), the economy's real GDP, denoted as $Y(t)$, can be stated as

EQUATION 5

$$Y(t) = A(t)F\big(K(t), H(t), R(t), D(t), N(t)\big)$$

where F is a non-decreasing and twice differentiable function, and $F = 0$ if any of its arguments are zero.[2] Note that the production function of the economy should include ecological capital, $N(t)$, given that many ecosystem services support and protection production activities.

Letting $V(t)$ denote intergenerational well-being at time t, which takes the form

EQUATION 6

$$V(t) = \int_{t}^{\infty} U\big(C(\tau), N(\tau)\big) e^{-\delta(\tau-t)} d\tau$$

where $\delta > 0$ is the social rate of discount. Note that intergenerational welfare depends not only on aggregate consumption but also on the direct benefits of ecosystems, which are represented

---

1 As shown by Arrow et al. (2003) and Dasgupta (2009), the following model could accommodate population growth, but it is conceptually more difficult to do so.

2 As Dasgupta (2009) points out, unlike a standard neo-classical production function, F is not necessarily concave. As Dasgupta (2009) points out, unlike a standard neo–classical production function, F is not necessarily concave.

by the inclusion of $N(t)$ in the function for instantaneous well-being, or "utility," $U(t)$. It is assumed that the latter function is twice differentiable, additively separable and concave with respect to its two arguments.

As Dasgupta (2009) proves, regardless of whether the resource allocation mechanism of the economy is optimal or even efficient, given (1)–(6), for any such mechanism it is possible to define a set of shadow prices at time t for the various assets of the economy

EQUATION 7

$$v^i(t) = \partial V(t) \Big/ \partial i(t), \; i = K,H,S,N,D$$

Given these shadow prices, the economy's aggregate, or inclusive, wealth $W(t)$ and investment $I(t)$ at time t are, respectively

EQUATION 8

$$W(t) = v^K(t)K(t)+v^H H(t)+v^S S(t)+v^N N(t)+v^D D(t)$$

and

EQUATION 9

$$I(t) = v^K(t)\dot{K}+v^H\dot{H}+v^S\dot{S}+v^N\dot{N}+v^D\dot{D}$$

The current-value Hamiltonian that ensures intergenerational well-being (6) is at a maximum for any given resource allocation mechanism of the economy is therefore

EQUATION 10

$$H(t) = U\big(C(t),N(t)\big)+I(t) = \delta V(t)$$

The current-value Hamiltonian as specified in (10) is therefore an indicator of the return on intergenerational well-being, regardless of whether the resource allocation mechanism of the economy is efficient or optimal.[3]

By expressing the utility function $U(t)$ as $U\big(C(t),N(t)\big)=U_C C(t)+U_N N(t)$, equation (10) can be used to define aggregate or inclusive NDP of the economy at time t in "utils"

EQUATION 11

$$NDP(t) = U_C C(t)+U_N N(t)+I(t)$$

Equation (11) depicts NDP as the sum of investment in the aggregate capital stocks of an economy plus the value of consumption and ecosystem goods and services. Following an approach analogous to Dasgupta (2009), NDP as defined by (11) can also be used as an indicator for measuring whether intergenerational well-being in an economy is improving over time.

Differentiating (6) with respect to time yields $dV(t)\big/dt = \delta V - U\big(C(t),N(t)\big)$. Using the latter expression in (10), one obtains

EQUATION 12

$$\frac{dV(t)}{dt} = I(t)$$

Condition (12) states that investment in the aggregate capital stock of an economy determines changes in intergenerational well-being over time, and as a result, NDP as defined by (11) is an exact measure of these welfare changes. That is, (11) and (12) yield a condition akin to Proposition 9 in Dasgupta (2009): $dV(t)\big/dt \geq 0$ if and only if $NDP(t) \geq U_C C(t)+U_N N(t)$. As long as NDP exceeds the value of consumption and ecosystem goods and services, intergenerational welfare will not decline. Given that $dV(t)\big/dt \geq 0$ also implies $I(t) \geq 0$, then it follows from (8) that sustainable economic development will occur at time t if the aggregate wealth of the economy $W(t)$ does not decline.

To understand the importance of measuring explicitly the contributions of natural capital, and especially that of ecological capital, it is necessary to decompose NDP as defined by (11). Using the first-order conditions for maximizing the current-value Hamiltonian (10) with respect to $C(t)$ and $E(t)$, (11) can be rewritten (suppressing the time arguments) as

EQUATION 13

$$NDP = v^K\Big[C+\dot{K}+\frac{h(E)}{h'}\Big]+U_N N+v^S\dot{S}+v^N\dot{N}+v^D\dot{D}$$

$$= v^K[Y+\omega K]+ v^K\left(\frac{h(E)}{h'}-E\right)+ v^K AF_R$$

$$[G(S)-R]+U_N N+(v^D-v^N)c$$

---

3   $H(t)=\delta V(t)$ can be found by integrating the current–value Hamiltonian $H(t)=U(C(t),N(t))+I(t)$. See Dasgupta (2009).

In (13), the expression $v^K(t)[Y(t)+\omega K(t)]$ is conventionally defined net domestic product (NDP), that is the GDP of the economy less any depreciation (in value terms) of previously accumulated reproducible capital. This is NDP as currently measured in most national accounts of economies, although of course it is usually valued at market prices rather than in terms of the shadow price of reproducible capital. It is clear from (13) that, if NDP is to serve as a true measure of the changes in an economy's wealth, it must include any appreciation or depreciation to human and natural capital as well. For instance, $v^K(t)(h(E(t))/h'-E(t))$ is the net appreciation (in value terms) in human capital, and $v^K(t)A(t)F_R[G(S(t))-R(t)]$ represents the net changes (in value terms) in natural resource stocks.[4] In the case of non-renewable resources, such as fossil fuels and minerals, $G(S) = 0$ and so $-v^KAF_RR$ measures the deduction from NDP of resource depletion. For renewable resources, such as forests and fisheries, NDP must include any depreciation in natural resource stocks if $G(S)<R$. The expression $U_NN(t)+[v^D(t)-v^N(t)]$ $c(t)$ includes both the benefits to current well-being provided by ecosystems, U_NN, and any capital revaluation that occurs as ecosystems are converted by land use change for development, $(v^D-v^N)c$.[5] To interpret the latter term, it is helpful to explore further the shadow value of

ecological capital $v^N(t)$ and developed land $v^D(t)$, respectively.

By definition, from (10), $v^N(t) = \int_t^\infty (\partial H/\partial N)$ $(\tau)e^{-\delta(\tau-t)}d\tau$ and $v^D(t) = \int_t^\infty (\partial H/\partial D)(\tau)e^{-\delta(\tau-t)}d\tau$. It follows that

EQUATION 14

$$v^D(t)-v^N(t)= \int_t^\infty e^{-\delta(\tau-t)} v^K(\tau)A(t)F_D(\tau)d\tau$$

$$-\int_t^\infty e^{-\delta(\tau-t)} [U_N(\tau)+v^K(\tau)A(\tau)F_N(\tau)]d\tau$$

Thus, $v^D(t)$ is the present value of any additional production resulting from any increase in land for economic development land, whereas $v^N(t)$ is the present value of any additional eco-system benefits due to increases in ecosystem land. That is, $v^D(t)$ and $v^N(t)$ are the capitalized values, or *prices*, of development and ecosystem land, respectively. As ecosystems are converted by land use change for development, $(v^D-v^N)c$ is the capital appreciation (depreciation) in land that occurs if $v^D > v^N(v^D< v^N)$. As land is a durable and capital good, condition (13) indicates that NDP must be adjusted for any such capital revaluation.

To summarize, although conditions (13) and (14) seem complicated, they help clarify how we should value and include changes in ecological capital in wealth accounting. First, we should adjust the NDP of the economy to include two contributions due to ecological capital:

- the value of the *direct benefits* provided by the current stock of ecosystems, U_NN, and
- any capital revaluation as a result of conversion of ecosystems to other land uses, $(v^D-v^N)c$, with the price of changes in ecological capital, $v^N(t)$, reflecting the present value of the future *direct and indirect benefits of ecosystems*.[6]

---

4   In (13), it is assumed that v^S accounts for the marginal cost of resource extraction or harvesting. For example, suppose that such costs can be represented by the function $f(R)$, $f_R>0$, which are in turn paid out of an economy's gross domestic product, Y. It follows from the first-order condition for maximizing the current-value Hamiltonian (10) $\partial H/\partial R=0$ that $v^S=v^K[AF_R-f_r]$, or equivalently, $v^KAF_R=v^S+v^Kf_r$

5   In (13), it is assumed that v^D accounts for the marginal costs of converting ecosystems to land for development. For example, if such costs are represented by $g(c)$, $g_c>0$ and deducted from the economy's gross domestic product, Y, then it follows from the first-order condition of maximizing (10) $\partial H/\partial c=0$ that $v^D=v^N+v^Kg_c$, or equivalently $v^D-v^N=v^Kg_c$. However, as will be discussed presently, as the resource allocation mechanism of the economy may not be optimal or even efficient, ecosystem conversion may not take place so that the difference between the price of developed land and the capitalized value of eco-systems is just equal to marginal cost of conversion.

6   These adjustments to NDP for ecological capital are similar to those for environmental resource stocks derived by Mäler (1991). It appears that, although ecosystems generate a wide variety of complex goods and services, the actual rules for determining how the direct and indirect benefits of eco-logical capital should be accounted for in NDP are no different than for any stock that generates both affects human welfare directly or indirectly via supporting or protecting economic production.

REFERENCES

AKSORNKOAE, S. & TOKRISNA, R. (2004). Overview of shrimp farming and mangrove loss in Thailand. In E.B. Barbier & S. Sathirathai (Eds.) *Shrimp farming and mangrove loss in Thailand* (pp. 37-51). London: Edward Elgar.

ARONSSON, T. & LÖFGREN, K.G. (1996). Social accounting and welfare measurement in a growth model with human capital. *Scandinavian Journal of Economics, 98*, 185-201.

ARROW, K.J., DASGUPTA, P. & MÄLER, K.G. (2003). The genuine savings criterion and the value of population. *Economic Theory, 21*(2), 217-225

BARBIER, E.B. (1994). Valuing environmental functions: Tropical wetlands. *Land Economics, 70*, 155-173.

BARBIER, E.B. (2000). Valuing the environment as an input: Review of mangrove fishery linkages. *Ecological Economics, 35*(1), 47-61.

BARBIER, E.B. (2003). Habitat-fishery linkages and mangrove loss in Thailand. *Contemporary Economic Policy, 21*, 59-77.

BARBIER, E.B. (2007). Valuing ecosystem services as productive inputs. *Economic Policy, 22*, 177–229.

BARBIER, E.B. (2008). Ecosystems as natural assets. Foundations and Trends in Microeconomics, 4, 611-681.

BARBIER, E.B. (2011A). Capitalizing on nature: Ecosystems as natural assets. Cambridge: Cambridge University Press.

BARBIER, E.B. (2011B). Pricing nature. *Annual Review of Resource Economics, 3*, 337-353.

BARBIER, E.B. & COX, M. (2004). An economic analysis of shrimp farm expansion and mangrove conversion in Thailand. *Land Economics, 80*(3), 389-407.

BARBIER, E.B., STRAND, I. & SATHIRATHAI, S. (2002). Do open access conditions affect the valuation of an externality? Estimating the welfare effects of mangrove-fishery linkages in Thailand. *Environmental and Resource Economics, 21*, 343-367.

BATEMAN, I.J., DAY, B.H., JONES, A.P. & JUDE, S. (2009). Reducing gain-loss asymmetry: a virtual reality choice experiment valuing land use change. *Journal of Environmental Economics and Management, 58*, 106-118.

BATEMAN, I.J., MACE, G.M., FEZZI, C., ATKINSON, G. & TURNER, K. (2011). Economic analysis of ecosystem service assessments. Environmental & *Resource Economics, 84*(2), 177-218.

BEDFORD, B.L. (1996). The need to define hydrological equivalence at the landscape scale for freshwater wetland mitigation. *Ecological Applications, 6*(1), 57-68.

BEDFORD, B.L. (1999). Cumulative effects on wetland landscapes: Links to wetland restoration in the United States and Southern Canada. *WETLANDS, 19*(4), 775-788.

BOCKSTAEL, N.E. (1996). Modeling economics and ecology: The importance of a spatial perspective. *American Journal of Agricultural Economics, 78*, 1168-1180.

BOCKSTAEL, N.E., FREEMAN III, A.M., KOPP, R.J., PORTNEY, P.R. & SMITH, V.K. (2000). On measuring economic values for nature. *Environmental Science and Technology, 34*, 1384-1389.

BOYD, J. & BANZHAF, S. (2007). What are ecosystem services? The need for standardized environmental accounting units. *Ecological Economics, 63*, 616-626.

BRAUMAN, K.A., DAILY, G.C., DUARTE, T.K. & MOONEY, H.A. (2007). The nature and value of ecosystem services: An overview highlighting hydrologic services. *Annual Review of Environment and Resources, 32*, 67-98.

BULLOCK, A. & ACREMAN, M.C. (2003). The role of wetlands in the hydrological cycle. *Hydrology and Earth System Sciences, 7*(3), 75-86.

BYSTRÖM, O. (2000). The replacement value of wetlands in Sweden. *Environmental and Resource Economics, 16*, 347-362.

CARLSSON, F., FRYKBLOM, P. & LILIJENSTOLPE, C. (2003). Valuing wetland attributes: an application of choice experiments. *Ecological Economics, 47*, 95-103.

CHICHILNISKY, G. & HEAL, G.M. (1998). Economic returns from the biosphere. *Nature, 391*, 629-630.

CHMURA, G.L., ANISFELD, S.C., CAHOON, D.R. & LYNCH, J.C. (2003). Global carbon sequestration in tidal, saline wetlands. *Global Biogeochemical Cycles, 17*, 1111-1123.

CHRISTIE M., HANLEY, N., WARREN, J., MURPHY, K., WRIGHT, R. & HYDE, T. (2006). Valuing the diversity of biodiversity. *Ecological Economics, 58*(2), 304-317.

DAILY, G.C., SÖDERQVIST, T., ANIYAR, S., ARROW, K., DASGUPTA, P., EHRLICH, P.R., WALKER, B. (2000). The value of nature and the nature of value. *Science, 289*, 395-396.

DASGUPTA, P. (2009). The welfare economic theory of green national accounts. *Environmental and Resource Economics, 42*(1), 3-38.

DASGUPTA, P. & MÄLER, K.G. (2000). Net national product, wealth, and social well being. *Environment and Development Economics, 5*(1), 69-93.

DASGUPTA, P.S. & MÄLER, K.G. (2003). The economics of non-convex ecosystems: An introduction. *Environmental and Resource Economics, 26*, 499-525.

DIRZO, R. & RAVEN, P.H. (2003). Global state of biodiversity and loss. *Annual Review of Environment and Resources, 28*, 137-167.

ELLIS, G.M. & FISHER, A.C. (1987). Valuing the environment as input. *Journal of Environmental Management, 25*, 149-156.

ELMQVIST, T., FOLKE, C., NYSTRÖM, M., PETERSON, G., BENGTSSON, J., WALKER, B. & NORBERG, J. (2003). Response diversity, ecosystem change, and resilience. *Frontiers in Ecology & Environment, 1*, 488-494.

EMERTON, L. & BOSS, L. (2008). *Value: Counting ecoservices as water infrastructure.* Gland, Switzerland: IUCN.

ENVIRONMENTAL PROTECTION AGENCY (EPA). (2009). *Valuing the protection of ecological systems and services.* Washington, DC: EPA.

FOLKE, C., CARPENTER, S., WALKER, B., SCHEFFER, M., ELMQVIST, T., GUNDERSON, L. & HOLLING, C.S. (2004). Regime shifts, resilience, and biodiversity in ecosystem management. *Annual Review of Ecology, Evolution, and Systematics, 35*, 557-581.

FOOD AND AGRICULTURAL ORGANIZATION OF THE UNITED NATIONS (FAO). (2006). Global forest resources assessment 2005, main report. Progress towards sustainable forest management. *FAO Forestry Paper 147.* Rome: FAO.

FOOD AND AGRICULTURAL ORGANIZATION OF THE UNITED NATIONS (FAO). (2007a). Mangroves of Asia 1980-2005: Country reports. *Forest resource assessment working paper no 136.* Rome: FAO.

FOOD AND AGRICULTURAL ORGANIZATION OF THE UNITED NATIONS (FAO). (2007b). The world's mangroves 1980-2005. *FAO forestry paper 153.* Rome: FAO.

FREEMAN, A.M. III. (1991). Valuing environmental resources under alternative management regimes. *Ecological Economics, 3*, 247-256.

FREEMAN, A.M. III. (2003). *The measurement of environmental and resource values: Theory and methods (2nd ed)*. Washington, DC: Resources for the Future.

GWIN, S.E., KENTULA, M.E. & SHAFFER, P.W. (1999). Evaluating the effect of wetland regulation through hydrogeomorphic classification and landscape profiles. *WETLANDS, 19*(3), 477-489.

HAMILTON, K. & CLEMENS, M. (1999). Genuine savings in developing countries. *The World Bank Economic Review, 13* (2), 333-56.

HARTWICK, J.M. (1990). Natural resources, national accounting and economic depreciation. *Journal of Public Economics, 43*, 291-304.

HARTWICK, J.M. (1992). Deforestation and national accounting. *Environmental and Resource Economics, 2*, 513-521.

KOCH, E.W., ACKERMAN, J., VAN KEULEN, M. & VERDUIN, J. (2006). Fluid dynamics in seagrass ecology: from molecules to ecosystems. In A.W.D. Larkum, R.J. Orth & C.M. Duarte (Eds.) *Seagrasses: Biology, ecology and conservation* (pp. 193-225). Heidelberg, Germany: Springer-Verlag.

KOCH, E.W., BARBIER, E.B., SILLIMAN, B.R., REED, D.J., PERILLO, G.M.E., HACKER, S.D.,...WOLANSKI, E. (2009). Non-linearity in ecosystem services: temporal and spatial variability in coastal protection. *Frontiers in Ecology and the Environment, 7*, 29-37.

LEVIN, S.A. (1999). *Fragile dominion: Complexity and the commons*. Reading, MA: Perseus Books.

LEVIN, S.A. & LUBCHENCO, J. (2008). *Resilience, robustness, and marine ecosystem-based management*. BioScience, 58, 27-32.

LINDAHL, E. (1933). The concept of income. In G. Bagge (Ed.) *Economic essays in honor of Gustav Cassel* (pp. 399–407). London: Allen and Unwin.

MÄLER, K.G. (1991). National accounts and environmental resources. *Environmental and Resource Economics, 1*, 1-15.

MÄLER, K.G. (2008). Sustainable development and resilience in ecosystems. *Environmental and Resource Economics, 39*,17-24.

MÄLER, K.G., ANIYAR, S. & JANSSON, A. (2008). Accounting for ecosystem services as a way to understand the requirements for sustainable development. *Proceedings of the National Academy of Sciences, 105*, 9501-9506.

MCCONNELL, K.E. & BOCKSTAEL, N.E. (2005). Valuing the environment as a factor of production. In K.G. Mäler & J.R. Vincent (Eds.) *Handbook of environmental economics, vol. 2* (pp. 621-669). Amsterdam: Elsevier.

MENDELSOHN R. & OLMSTEAD, S. (2009). The economic valuation of environmental amenities and disamenities: Methods and applications. *Annual Review of Environment and Resources, 34*:325-347.

MILLENNIUM ECOSYSTEM ASSESSMENT (MA). (2005). *Ecosystems and human well-being: Synthesis*. Washington, DC: Island Press.

MITSCH, W.J. & GOSSELINK, J.G. (2000). The value of wetlands: importance of scale and landscape setting. *Ecological Economics, 35*, 25-33.

MITSCH, W.J., GOSSELINK, J.G., ZHANG, L. & ANDERSON, C.J. (2009). *Wetland ecosystems*. New York: John Wiley.

MOBERG, F. & RÖNNBÄCK, P. (2003). Ecosystem services of the tropical seascape: interactions, substitutions and restoration. *Ocean and Coastal Management, 46*, 27-46.

NATIONAL RESEARCH COUNCIL (NRC). (1995). *Wetlands: Characteristics and boundaries*. Washington, DC: National Academies Press.

NATIONAL RESEARCH COUNCIL (NRC). (2005). *Valuing ecosystem services: Towards better environmental decision-making*. Washington, DC: National Academies Press.

NAYLOR, R. & DREW, M. (1998). Valuing mangrove resources in Kosrae, Micronesia. *Environment and Development Economics, 3*, 471–490.

O'NEILL, R.V. (2001). Is it time to bury the ecosystem concept? (With full military honors, of course!) *Ecology, 82*, 3275-3284.

ORTH, R.J., CARRUTHERS, T.J.B., DENNISON, W.C., DUARTE, C.M., FOURQUREAN, J.W., HECK JR., K.L.,...WILLIAMS, S.L. (2006). A global crisis for seagrass ecosystems. *BioScience, 56*, 987-996.

PAGIOLA, S., VON RITTER, K. & BISHOP, J. (2004). *How much is an ecosystem worth? Assessing the economic value of conservation*. Washington, DC: The World Bank.

PEARCE, D.W. & BARBIER, E.B. (2000). *Blueprint for a sustainable economy*. London: Earthscan.

PEARCE, D.W., MARKANDYA, A. & BARBIER, E.B. (1989). Blueprint for a green economy. London: Earthscan.

PERRINGS, C. (1998). Resilience in the dynamics of economic-environmental systems. Environmental and Resource Economics, 11, 503-520.

PERRY, G.L.W. (2002). Landscapes, space and equilibrium: Shifting viewpoints. Progress in Physical Geography, 26, 339-359.

PICKETT, S.T.A. & CADENASSO, M.L. (1995). Landscape ecology: Spatial heterogeneity in ecological systems. Science, 269, 331-334.

PICKETT, S.T.A. & CADENASSO, M.L. (2002). The ecosystem as a multidimensional concept: Meaning, model, and metaphor. Ecosystems, 5, 1-10.

POLASKY, S. & SEGERSON, K. (2009). Integrating ecology and economics in the study of ecosystem services: Some lessons learned. Annual Review of Resource Economics, 1, 409-434.

RYBICKI, N.B. (1997). Observations of tidal flux between submersed aquatic plant stand and the adjacent channel in the Potomac River near Washington, DC. Limnology and Oceanography, 42, 307-317.

SARNTISART, I. & SATHIRATHAI, S. (2004). Mangrove dependency, income distribution and conservation. In E.B. Barbier & S. Sathirathai (Eds.) Shrimp farming and mangrove loss in Thailand (pp. 96-114). Cheltenham, UK: Edward Elgar.

SATHIRATHAI, S. & BARBIER, E.B. (2001). Valuing mangrove conservation, Southern Thailand. Contemporary Economic Policy, 19, 109-122.

SCHEFFER, M., CARPENTER, S., FOLEY, J.A., FOLKE, C. & WALKER, B. (2001). Catastrophic shifts in ecosystems. Nature, 413, 591-596.

SHABMAN, L.A. & BATIE, S.S. (1978). Economic value of natural coastal wetlands: A critique. Coastal Zone Management Journal, 4(3), 231-247.

SHACKEROFF, J.M., HAZEN, E.L. & CROWDER, L.B. (2009). The oceans as peopled seascapes. In K.L. McLeod & H.M. Leslie (Eds.) Ecosystem-based management for the oceans (pp. 33-54). Washington, DC: Island Press.

SIMENSTAD, C., REED, D. & FORD, M. (2006). When is restoration not? Incorporating landscape-scale processes to restore self-sustaining ecosystems in coastal wetland restoration. Ecological Engineering, 26, 27-39.

SMITH, M.D. (2007). Generating value in habitat-dependent fisheries: The importance of fishery management institutions. Land Economics, 83, 59-73.

SPALDING, M., KAINUMA, M. & COLLINS, L. (2010). World atlas of mangroves. London: Earthscan.

THE ECONOMICS OF ECOSYSTEMS AND BIODIVERSITY (TEEB). (2010). The economics of ecosystems and biodiversity: Mainstreaming the economics of nature: A synthesis of the conclusions and recommendations of TEEB. Bonn, Germany: TEEB.

TURNER, M.G. (2005). Landscape ecology: What is the state of the science? Annual Reviews of Ecological and Evolutionary Systems, 36, 319-344.

UK NATIONAL ECOSYSTEM ASSESSMENT. (2011). The UK national ecosystem assessment: Technical report. Cambridge: UNEP-WCMC.

UNITED NATIONS ENVIRONMENT PROGRAMME (UNEP). (2006). Marine and coastal ecosystems and human wellbeing: A synthesis report based on the findings of the Millennium Ecosystem Assessment. Nairobi: UNEP.

VALIELA, I., BOWEN, J.L. & YORK, J.K. (2001). Mangrove forests: one of the world's threatened major tropical environments. BioScience, 51, 807-815.

VINCENT, J. (2012). Ecosystem services and green growth. Paper presented for the inaugural conference Green Growth Knowledge Platform, Mexico City, Mexico, January 12-13, 2012.

WALKER, B., HOLLING, C.S., CARPENTER, S.R. & KINZIG, A. (2004). Resilience, adaptability and transformability in social-ecological systems. Ecology and Society, 9(2), 5.

WALKER, B., PEARSON, L., HARRIS, M., MÄLER, K.G., LI, C.Z., BIGGS, R. & BAYNES, T. (2010). Incorporating resilience in the assessment of inclusive wealth: An example from South East Australia. Environmental and Resource Economics, 45, 183-202.

WAYCOTT, M., DUARTE, C.M., CARRUTHERS, T.J.B., ORTH, R.J., DENNISON, W.C., OLYARNIK, S.,...WILLIAMS, S.L. (2009). Accelerating loss of seagrasses across the globe threatens coastal ecosystems. Proceedings of the National Academy of Sciences, 106, 12377-12381.

WORLD BANK. (2011). World development indicators. Washington, DC: The World Bank.

ZONNEVELD, I.S. (1989). The land unit – A fundamental concept in landscape ecology, and its applications. Landscape Ecology, 3, 67-86.

CHAPTER 9

Inclusive wealth accounting for regulating ecosystem services

Heather Tallis, Stephen Polasky, Juan Sebastian Lozano, and Stacie Wolny

KEY MESSAGES

Studies that have sought to value natural capital have typically focused on "provisioning" services or natural resource stocks such as oil and natural gas, minerals, timber, and fisheries. Other than the cost of CO_2 emissions vis-à-vis climate regulation, regulating services have not been considered in any great depth.

Due to the high degree of uncertainty in estimating the value of regulating services, it will be useful for policy-makers to see a range of values with lower and upper bound estimates. We provide such uncertainty analyses for climate regulation through carbon sequestration.

The marginal net benefit of regulating services is large enough to justify undertaking future research in identifying servicesheds, unbundling regulatory services into explicit benefits, and producing value estimates for inclusion in wealth accounts.

An important first step for including regulating services in an inclusive wealth framework is to have well-defined individual services. The present typology of regulating services does not lend itself well to wealth accounts because multiple services are embedded within common regulating service category. Identifying individual services also simplifies the valuation process.

It is important to identify servicesheds in order to estimate the value of ecosystem services. A serviceshed is the area that provides a specific benefit to a specific individual or group of people. It is further characterized by three factors: (1) ecosystem supply; (2) institutions; and (3) physical access.

1. Introduction [1]

Concerns over the current trajectory of the global economy and sustainable development have led to high-profile calls for expanding the system of national accounts to include measures that better reflect natural capital and ecosystem services (e.g., STIGLITZ ET AL. 2010; WORLD BANK 2006). The current set of national accounts does a good job of measuring the value of benefits that flow through markets, but has done a poor job to date of capturing the value of benefits of most ecosystem services that largely do not flow through markets. Ignoring the value of natural capital and ecosystem services in national accounts and in benefit-cost assessment of specific projects causes a systematic imbalance in economic accounting. Without accurate pricing of natural capital and ecosystem services, decision-makers do not have an appropriate set of signals and decisions may result in excessive depletion of natural capital with a consequent decline in the flow of ecosystem services. The Millennium Ecosystem Assessment (MA) found that the majority of ecosystem services had declined over the past 50 years (MA 2005). The pattern of decline matches closely with the set of ecosystem services without market prices (KINZIG ET AL. 2011).

The inclusive wealth framework provides a theoretically grounded and comprehensive approach for the inclusion of natural capital, along with other forms of capital assets (manufactured capital, human capital), in assessing sustainable development (ARROW ET AL. 2004; DASGUPTA AND MÄLER 2000; PEARCE AND ATKINSON 1995). Sustainable development, interpreted as non-declining human well-being over time, is equivalent to non-declining value of inclusive wealth (or under certain conditions, non-declining value of inclusive wealth per capita, [ARROW ET AL. 2010]). The great advantage of valuing assets in the inclusive wealth framework is that the value of capital takes account of

the value of the present and future flow of services generated by the asset. Measures of current income like gross domestic product (GDP) only take into account the value of the current flow of services. This narrow accounting of the value of the current flow of services can give a distorted view of sustainability. For example, exploiting natural resources more intensively now can increase current income but at the expense of natural capital. These natural capital declines will lead to declines in the future flow of ecosystem services. Such unsustainable exploitation could register positively for current income but would register as a decline in inclusive wealth.

To implement an inclusive wealth accounting approach, we need to be able to account for the current and future value of all ecosystem services. Many systems have been created for categorizing ecosystem services (e.g., DE GROOT ET AL. 2002; BOYD AND BANZHAF 2007; FISHER AND TURNER 2008). The most widely accepted and applied categorization of ecosystem services is that which is laid out in the MA (2005), which differentiates among provisioning, regulating, supporting, and cultural services. In this chapter, we focus on regulating services. As defined by the MA, regulating services are benefits derived from regulating ecosystem processes and include: air quality regulation; climate regulation; water regulation; erosion regulation; water purification and waste treatment; disease regulation; pest regulation; pollination; and natural hazard regulation.

While there are a growing number of studies that compare the value of ecosystem services for alternative scenarios at the landscape level (e.g., NELSON ET AL. 2009; POLASKY ET AL. 2011), few studies have attempted to incorporate the value of ecosystem services into national accounts, or to incorporate the value of natural capital into measures of inclusive wealth. The studies that have attempted to do this mostly focus on the value of provisioning services or natural resource stocks such as oil and natural gas, minerals, timber, and fisheries (ARROW ET AL. 2004, 2010; WORLD BANK 1997, 2006, 2010).

1   This work was supported by the Gordon and Betty Moore Foundation.

Regulating services have not been included in these studies, with the exception of factoring in costs of CO_2 emissions as part of climate regulation (ARROW ET AL. 2010). There is more work on the value of particular regulating services in specific contexts such as natural hazard regulation (e.g., DAS AND VINCENT 2009) and pollination (e.g., RICKETTS ET AL. 2004; KREMEN ET AL. 2007). A recent book on the valuation of regulating services that provides an overview of issues and summary of empirical work on specific services highlights just how far we remain from rigorous, comprehensive measures of the value of regulating services (KUMAR AND WOOD 2010).

In this chapter, we discuss principles for including regulating services in measures of inclusive wealth, then focus on a few key services to show how we can track their provision and value in an inclusive wealth framework. Finally, we give examples of what is possible at the national scale today from two developing countries, Colombia and Ecuador.

2. Principles for including regulating services in inclusive wealth

Unlike the case for provisioning services, little progress has been made towards including regulating ecosystem services into measures of inclusive wealth. In large part, this stems from the greater conceptual difficulty in valuing regulating services and from significant data limitations. Here we review some of the challenges of valuing regulating services and provide principles for successful valuation and incorporation into an inclusive wealth framework.

2.1 Unbundling regulatory services for national accounts

Although the MA laid out useful distinctions among types of services (provisioning, regulating, cultural, and supporting), some regulating services such as erosion regulation or water regulation do not represent a single service. Rather, these general labels bundle together multiple services. For example, erosion control encompasses soil fertility benefits to farmers; extended infrastructure life benefits to reservoir managers and hydropower producers; and fish habitat benefits to commercial and recreational fishers. Water quality regulation includes regulation of bacteria and other impurities in drinking water and regulation of nutrients that affect eutrophication of surface waters with potential impacts on recreation, fishing, and drinking water quality. Natural hazard regulation includes protection of coastal property from storm surge and erosion, protection of inland property from river flooding, and protection of property from fire. Bundling together multiple services in a single name confuses issues and makes accounting for the value of services in an inclusive wealth context difficult or impossible. A necessary first step for inclusion of regulatory ecosystem service values into an inclusive wealth framework is to have well-defined individual services. This approach will help to provide a more complete accounting of all regulating services and will simplify and clarify the valuation process.

2.2 Clarifying the distinction between supply and service provision

The inclusion of regulating services in inclusive wealth estimation has two vital components: (1) calculating how much service is provided; and (2) identifying the value of those services to society in the form of improvement in human well-being. The first step has been hindered by the fact that most studies claiming to measure ecosystem services measure the potential of an ecosystem to provide the service (supply), but stop short of asking whether there is service demand (TALLIS AND POLASKY 2009; TALLIS AND POLASKY 2011; TALLIS ET AL. 2012B). Just as with other goods and services, it is the interaction of supply and demand that determines provision of the good or service. For example, consider two ecosystems that each filter pollutants and improve water quality downstream. One ecosystem lies in a watershed with cities and towns downstream that rely on the watershed for drinking water and recreational opportunities, while the other ecosystem lies in an uninhabited watershed that flows into the open ocean. Both ecosystems supply water purification, however only the inhabited ecosystem supplies ecosystem services related to water quality regulation. Analyzing provision requires assessing both ecosystem service supply and demand, a process that requires both ecological and economic approaches.

2.3 Servicesheds

An important challenge in ecosystem services is to identify who benefits from regulating services and how much benefit people actually receive. Addressing this challenge requires a clear understanding of where regulating services are produced in an area relative to people who might benefits from these services. To simplify the accounting of these connections, we introduce the concept of a "serviceshed." A serviceshed for an ecosystem service is simply the area where a specific benefit is provided to a specific individual or group of people. Servicesheds are characterized by three factors: (1) ecosystem service supply; (2) institutions; and 3) physical access. The configuration of servicesheds and the importance of these three factors vary by service and beneficiary. For example, the serviceshed for a coastal resident receiving benefits from inundation regulation is the nearshore area where natural capital (e.g., mangroves, coral reefs, etc.) can dampen waves and reduce flood frequency or intensity on their property. For climate regulation, the serviceshed is the entire globe because the atmosphere is well-mixed and there are no laws, social norms, or forms of infrastructure that limit the ability of anyone on the planet to enjoy the benefits of a well-regulated climate.

For water-related regulating services, servicesheds are often closely related to watersheds.

The serviceshed for drinking water quality regulation is the area upstream of a person's or a community's water extraction point (Figure 1). For a person or community to benefit from water quality regulation, they must be downstream of an area that has natural capital that can regulate water quality (supply) and have physical access (pipes, foot paths, wells, etc.) and institutional access (legal rights, informal rights) to that water. The importance of all three factors is illustrated aptly by water regulatory services. In cases where water supply is large (i.e., no physical scarcity) but where a group's access is limited by institutional arrangements (e.g., a water source is in a national protected area or poor rural farmers lack legal water rights for irrigation) or by a lack of physical access (e.g., no infrastructure), there will not be benefits generated for the group.

2.4 The public goods nature of regulatory ecosystem services

Even when the provision of a regulatory ecosystem service is clear, the second task of identifying the value of those services to society can be challenging. Many regulatory services have elements of public goods. For example, consider a watershed with two cities on the mainstem of the river that each rely on the river for drinking water. If landowners upriver of both cities undertake actions that result in more filtration and higher quality water downstream then both cities will benefit. Similarly, sequestering carbon and reducing atmospheric greenhouse gas concentrations yields climate regulation that may have global benefits. Public goods create two distinct challenges for understanding both the provision and value of ecosystem services: (1) it can be difficult to estimate the value of ecosystem service provision; and (2) it is not always clear *a priori* who the beneficiaries are.

Since many regulatory ecosystem services are public goods, are not traded in markets, and do not contribute directly to production of other marketed goods, methods of non-market valuation are needed. The difficulties

A

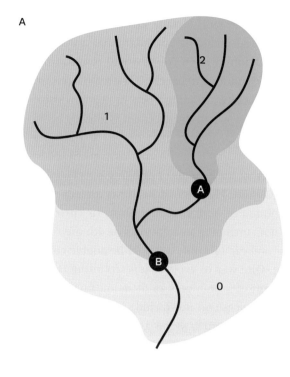

B

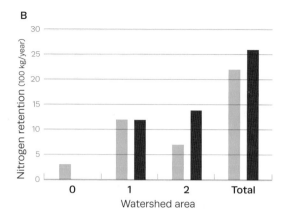

FIGURE 1

Hypothetical depiction of servicesheds for water–related regulating services. In watershed Area "0"

(a), there is supply, but no service in this hypothetical case because there are no beneficiaries (black dots) downstream of that region of the watershed to enjoy its benefits (b). In watershed Area "1" (a), City B enjoys the benefits of the area, so supply and

service are equal (b). In watershed Area "2" (a), supply is lower than watershed Area 1 (b) because the region is smaller, and biophysical processes provide less potential benefit, but service is higher than Area 1 because both City A and City B enjoy its benefits, doubling the amount of service Area 2 delivers. This relationship and outcome will only hold if City A enjoys the service non–consumptively, or does not extract all available water, thus making the benefit unavailable for City B.

of non-market valuation make the translation of biophysical estimates of service provision to human well-being impacts more challenging than it is for many provisioning services that are directly tied to marketed commodities. There are a number of non-market valuation approaches including both stated and revealed preference methods that can be used to estimate the value of regulatory ecosystem services (see NRC [2005] for a review of standard valuation methods). Regulatory services often reduce the impact of potential harms or damages. Therefore, estimates of harms or damages, or estimates of the cost of alternative methods of reducing harm or damages (avoided cost), can be useful in valuation. For example, the value of the regulatory services contributing to water quality for drinking water for a number of major metropolitan areas has been

estimated based on avoided water treatment costs. The value of natural hazard regulation is often estimated based on changes in the level of expected damages. For example, the value of mangroves or coastal wetlands for storm protection can be estimated by modeling the reduction in the probability of storm damage with that natural capital in place. The decision to use avoided cost or estimated damages should depend on what is actually done in each country. In developed countries, the appropriate approach for drinking water quality regulation is typically avoided costs because these countries will supply clean drinking water in one way or another (e.g., natural purification, water treatment plants, bottled water). In developing countries, it is less common for actions to be taken to avoid the damages from lost services so people will actually suffer losses in well-being. For example, loss of drinking water quality regulation will often lead to higher water-borne disease and loss of working days.

Because many regulatory services are public goods, there can be multiple groups benefiting from the supply of services. For example, consider drinking water quality regulation with two cities that both rely on the same river for drinking water, one in the upper part of the watershed (City A) and one in the middle part of the watershed (City B, Figure 1). The area upstream of both cities (Figure 1a, watershed area 2) provides water quality regulation benefits to both cities. The area downstream of both cities provides supply, but it does not provide any drinking water quality service, as there are no downstream beneficiaries (Figure 1b). Calculating benefits requires accurate determination of the serviceshed for services. In this case, summarizing the amount of service to be valued in an inclusive wealth account would show that service is higher than supply (Figure 1b, Total). As this example illustrates, accurate delineation of servicesheds is necessary to calculate regulating service delivery and value.

2.5 Providing complete accounting while avoiding double counting

Ecosystems provide a bundle of services, making it essential to provide as complete an accounting as possible. Leaving out important services can lead to poor decisions and inferior outcomes. In the current system, many provisioning services lead to production of commodities valued in markets, but most regulatory services lead to public goods not valued in markets. This situation has led to the undervaluing of regulatory services by decision-makers and a decline in most regulatory services over time (MA 2005).

The flip side, double counting of benefits, can also be a problem with incorporating ecosystem services into national accounts. For example, pollination services are important to improved crop production. However, since the value of crops is already included in national accounts, including an additional value for pollination in the account would result in the double counting of benefits. The main question to ask before including a benefit in an inclusive account is whether the benefit is already being captured in another part of the account. As another example, health metrics may be used to represent the benefits of drinking water quality regulation. However, if health is already well-captured in human capital terms (it currently is not), including an additional health metric in natural capital context would be double counting. One way to avoid double counting in the system of accounts is to focus on final goods and services and not include intermediate services (BOYD AND BANZHAF 2007).

2.6 Stocks and flows: the value of ecosystem services and natural capital

Any of the valuation methods described above has to be tailored for use in a wealth accounting context. In addition to the issues already raised, it is important to distinguish between valuing stocks and flows. Much of the discussion above (and in the literature in general) focuses on valuing ecosystem services rather than valuing natural capital. The value of ecosystem services is a measure of the flow of benefits and is more akin to measuring income rather than wealth. Natural capital is an asset (stock) and measuring the value of natural capital is an important component of measuring inclusive wealth. As stated in the introduction, the great advantage of measuring inclusive wealth, as compared to measuring current income, even inclusive income that includes the value of regulatory ecosystem services, relates to sustainability. Increases in the current value of services can be achieved by intensive use that degrades capital, which will lead to lower service provision in the future. To achieve a sustainable outcome, the proper goal for decision-makers is non-declining inclusive wealth rather than high current value of income. The value of natural capital and the value of ecosystem services are linked. The value of an asset is, in principle, determined by the flow of benefits generated by the asset. So, one way to measure the value of natural capital that provides regulatory services is to predict the value of the flow of services through time generated by the natural capital and compute a present value of these flows. In practice, predicting the future flow of services as a function of the presence of natural capital, the likely value of these services in the future, and how to properly discount future values of ecosystem services, are all problematic.

2.7 Marginal versus total value

Computing the total value of natural capital for inclusive wealth calculations is quite difficult and may go beyond what can currently be achieved. A more achievable goal might be to evaluate marginal value of natural capital, which is how a small change in natural capital will change the present value of the flow of services.

The general approach of capital accounts aims to identify the total value of capital assets. This value is usually defined as the amount of value generated by the existence of the capital asset. In other words, what would be lost in terms of benefits created if the capital assets were destroyed? In addition to reasons discussed above, this approach can be problematic for regulating ecosystem services, especially those that are crucial for life-support. The total value of some regulating services is extremely large (perhaps infinite if it truly is necessary for life-support). As services become scarcer their marginal value tends to rise. Using market prices or estimates of marginal value when the service is abundant and assuming that this price holds when the service is scarce can lead to serious underestimates of value.

In addition, many regulating services are hard to observe directly, so we will often need models to estimate the impact of changes in natural capital on the provision of ecosystem services and the consequent change in benefits. However, large changes in environmental conditions may lead to shifts in ecosystem processes that alter functional relationships. It may be difficult to correctly forecast the future provision of services when conditions are quite different from current conditions. Finally, regularly collected data are often inadequate to measure values at larger spatial scales necessary for national accounts. For example, water quality regulation cannot be observed through standard measures of water quality because the service is the amount of pollutant *retained* by the ecosystem, not the amount released (observed). Studies of actual pollutant cycling are often done at the plot or regional scale and are seldom connected to beneficiaries (e.g., CRUMPTON ET AL. 2008; DEEGAN ET AL. 2010) making it difficult to use this approach for the kind of annual, national scale observations needed for national accounts. Similarly, the value of keeping contaminants out of drinking water cannot be observed through water treatment costs or human health metrics since contaminant loads are only one factor of many affecting treatment costs and health conditions. These challenges exist for most regulating services. In these cases, we will need to identify the marginal contribution of the ecosystem to regulating services through modeling the core regulating processes under conditions with and without natural capital (TALLIS AND POLASKY 2009; TALLIS ET AL. 2012A).

3. Examples of the accounting process for key regulating services

The principles outlined above are relevant to inclusive wealth accounting for any regulating ecosystem service. In reality, countries will likely start such accounting with a short list of services to reduce assessment time and costs. Given these probable limitations, we outline the accounting process for a subset of services that are likely to be critical in all countries and whose assessment potential is relatively well-developed.

3.1 Climate regulation through carbon sequestration

Many atmospheric constituents interact with climate regulation including nitrous oxide, ozone, particulate matter, methane, and carbon dioxide (KARL AND TRENBERTH 2003). Vegetation and microbial organisms can regulate the flux of several of these, providing a suite of climate regulation services. The regulation of climate through carbon sequestration is the regulating service that has garnered the most international attention and the only climate regulation service that has any sort of market developed around its value. To account for the wealth benefits provided by a country's ecosystem service flows, we first need to be able to estimate carbon stocks and sequestration rates. We can observe stocks and sequestration rates directly through biomass and growth surveys, and many countries have developed rigorous protocols for measuring this process for the purpose of trading carbon credits in markets (BROWN 2002; PEARSON ET AL. 2007; PETROKOFSKY ET AL. 2011). Remote sensing protocols are rapidly developing that will continue to improve the feasibility of making annual above-ground carbon stock and sequestration measurements at the national scale (ASNER 2009). Fully accounting for carbon regulation will require more practical approaches for monitoring soil carbon storage and fluxes (CONANT ET AL. 2010). In cases where measurement at the national scale is not feasible, models can be used to estimate stocks and sequestration, with strong ground-truthing and validation. Many models exist for the estimation of carbon stocks and sequestration rates, ranging from very simple (look-up table-driven approaches like the Intergovernmental Panel on Climate Change [IPCC] tables or the INVEST model; CONTE ET AL. 2011a) to complex, dynamic process-based models (e.g., CENTURY, LPJml).

In the simplest approach, the value of the carbon stock would be calculated as the size of the stock (metric tons C) times the value of keeping one metric ton of carbon stored in the ecosystem and out of the atmosphere. In valuing the change in carbon stocks through time, we also need to account for how the value of carbon storage changes. One major issue with accounting for the value of carbon storage is that there is no consensus on what is the value for storing a metric ton of carbon. The value of the physical asset – the carbon stock – is equal to the value of reducing emissions as both lead to reductions in atmospheric concentration of carbon. Economists measure the value of reduced emissions by estimating the social cost of carbon, which is the damage to society, in terms of diminished economic output, health costs and other impacts, caused by more intense climate change resulting from an additional unit of atmospheric CO_2 (TOL 2009). Estimates of the social cost of carbon range widely, from near zero to well over US$1,000[2] per metric ton C depending on the model used, the assumed discount rate, atmospheric CO_2 concentration, and other factors (TOL 2009).

The existence of carbon markets, most notably the European Union Emissions Trading Scheme, has led some to advocate for using market prices rather than the social cost of carbon. However, existing market prices do not accurately reflect the social cost of carbon but rather the stringency of the cap under which trading in the market occurs. For example, in January 2008 the price for carbon in Europe was 21.03€ metric ton-1 (or US$30.86 metric ton-1) while the price for carbon in the United States on the Chicago Climate Exchange, a voluntary program allowing commitment to very modest emission reductions, was US$2.30 metric ton-1. Since then, the Chicago Climate Exchange has ceased to exist so the carbon price has dropped effectively to zero in the United States while future society clearly remains vulnerable to

2 All monetary values are expressed in US$, unless otherwise noted.

reductions in well-being from climate change. European emissions have the same potential for social damage as emissions from the United States and therefore should have the same value. The difference in market price was due to the difference in stringency of regulation not the value of reductions in carbon to the atmosphere. Given these imperfections in the market value of carbon, we currently strongly recommend the use of the social cost of carbon in estimates of carbon values until carbon markets more accurately represent the true change in human well-being from climate regulation.

Using the social cost of carbon has its own limitations. Calculations of the social cost of carbon represent the present value of damages from more intense climate change from emitting a unit of CO_2 into the atmosphere for the time that the unit would likely remain in the atmosphere. Because it is calculated for the lifetime of carbon in the atmosphere, the social cost of carbon will undervalue the service of permanent carbon storage in the ecosystem. If, however, carbon will be released because of land-use change, fire, or other disturbances – and so is not permanently stored – then this change in storage must be reflected as a change in the amount of the asset similar to loss of other forms of capital assets.

3.2 Nutrient retention for drinking water quality

Water quality regulation captures the effects of natural capital on the chemical form and concentration of many constituents that affect human well-being. The value of natural capital that provides a flow of benefits from improved water quality over time is equal to the present value of change in benefits over time. Nutrients, primarily nitrogen and phosphorus, can cause algal or cyanobacterial blooms that contaminate drinking water if not treated. These same blooms can damage fisheries by decreasing deeper water oxygen concentrations, leading to "dead zones" (DIAZ AND ROSENBURG 2008).

Vegetation and microbes in soils can transform these nutrients, turning them into gases that are then released to the atmosphere, or biomass that is locked away, at least for some period of time. These cycling and uptake processes reduce the concentration of nutrients in receiving waters, reducing water treatment costs or human health risk or increasing fisheries productivity and related nutrition or income. Other chemicals that affect human health and may be regulated to some degree by natural capital include agrochemicals, coliform bacteria, dissolved organic matter and many others. Here, we only discuss nutrients, but the general approach can be applied to any chemical form, with any associated benefit (see the next section for a treatment of sediment in drinking water).

The marginal contribution of natural capital to nutrient regulation cannot be measured directly at large enough scales for national wealth accounting. Therefore, we must rely on models to provide useful estimates. Many nutrient cycle or flux models have been developed including relatively simple ones, such as N-SPECT (NOAA 2004) and INVEST (CONTE ET AL. 2011B), and more complex models such as ANNAGNPS (YOUNG ET AL. 1989), SWAT (ARNOLD ET AL. 1998), and many others. Any of these models can be used to assess nutrient retention rates but most need to be altered to some degree to track the retention process (instead of export) and to account for the actual delivery of regulating services to people. Including the location and activities of beneficiaries allows the calculation of how much service is actually delivered, rather than capturing the full potential of the system to provide a given benefit as most of the listed models do. INVEST accounts for demand in a simple way by using extraction points and the watershed area contributing to each point to estimate actual service delivery.

An additional adjustment must be made in service estimation to represent any "allowed" or "safe" loads of nutrients. In many countries, drinking water quality standards establish an acceptable level of nutrient concentrations in drinking water. Retention of nutrients in a system where concentrations are below this threshold may not actually provide a service if there is no damage to human well-being for concentrations below the threshold. For example, annual phosphorous loading to Lake Okeechobee (Florida) was 498 metric tons y-1 from 1973 to 1999 (HAVENS ET AL. 2009). The established total maximum daily loads (TMDL) would be achieved with an annual loading rate of 140 metric tons y-1. Therefore, improvements in natural capital that increased phosphorous retention could provide a maximum service rate of 358 metric tons y-1 (the difference between the average annual load and the allowed annual load). Any further reductions in phosphorus loading would be below the TMDL and therefore not provide additional service value.

Nutrient regulation benefits are not commonly traded in markets. In lieu of market prices, we can use several methods to derive a monetary estimate of the value of changes in service provision. First, when water is treated before use in industry, drinking water or other uses, we can use the avoided treatment cost as an estimate of the value of nutrient retention. Avoided cost has been used to estimate the value watershed protection to provide clean water to municipal water systems such as in the case of New York City (NRC 2000, 2005). In cases where no treatment occurs before consumption, we can use non-market valuation techniques to estimate losses in benefits that people experience with lower quality water. A large number of studies have estimated losses in recreation, aesthetics, and other benefits in developed countries (e.g., CARSON AND MITCHELL 1993; VAN HOUTVEN ET AL. 2007) and some studies have estimated the losses associated with health and productivity consequences of poor quality water in developing countries (e.g., CHOE 1996; PATTANAYAK 2004).

3.3 Erosion regulation for drinking water quality or reservoir maintenance

The erosion regulation provided by natural capital can contribute to benefits in several ways. Keeping soil on crop fields increases soil fertility and crop yields. In addition, keeping sediment out of rivers can increase drinking water quality, lengthen the lifetime of infrastructure by avoiding abrasion and damage or reducing dredge costs, contribute to flood regulation or help maintain commercially, recreationally, or culturally important fish populations. Each of these benefits is supported by a different set of processes and is experienced at different locations by different groups of people. Here, we only address the role of erosion regulation in improving water quality and reservoir maintenance. Other methods would be needed to capture the many other benefits provided by erosion control.

As with water quality regulation, it is difficult to observe erosion regulation directly. Plot scale studies have been used extensively (MAGETTE ET AL. 1989, WHITE ET AL. 2007, ZHANG ET AL. 2010) but are difficult to replicate annually at large enough scales to contribute to national accounting. Again, models can be a powerful tool for assigning the marginal contribution of natural capital to erosion regulation processes (MUÑOZ-CARPENA ET AL. 1999). Several of the models noted above are also widely used to model key erosion processes (e.g., N-SPECT, INVEST, SWAT). To estimate the two focal service flows, these models need to be applied upstream of drinking water treatment facilities, direct drinking water extraction points, or reservoirs used for drinking water or hydropower production. When considering the contribution of erosion regulation to drinking water quality, the same allowed load principle introduced above for water quality regulation applies to sediment. If there are drinking water quality standards for suspended sediment loads, service is only provided by regulation of loads above that standard. Similarly, there is an allowed load for reservoirs equivalent to their engineered dead volume.

When building reservoirs, engineers plan for erosion and sedimentation that will reduce the volume, and therefore productive capacity of the reservoir over time. If sediment loads are at the rate considered in engineering the dead volume, additional erosion regulation does not provide a benefit.

As with the value of nutrient regulation, erosion control benefits are typically not traded in markets so there is no market price. The value of erosion regulation can be estimated using gains in productivity or avoided cost. For example, preventing sediment from entering a reservoir can enhance the productive life of the reservoir for hydropower generation or reduce dredging costs. The value of reduced sediment then can be estimated by valuing the additional hydropower generation or the costs of dredging. If erosion regulation improves water quality linked to recreation or health benefits then methods discussed above for nutrient regulation are also applicable. As with other benefits, the value of natural capital is equal to the present value of the flow of benefits it creates through time.

4. Applying principles to national accounting in Colombia and Ecuador

Here, we attempt to apply the methodology outlined above with readily available data in two countries: Colombia and Ecuador. This is a preliminary effort to explore the state of science and key limitations for implementing inclusive wealth accounting in each case. We emphasize that our findings should in no way be seen as official estimates as we conducted this work as a demonstrative, academic exercise, not as part of an official process with either country. We also used the most readily available data, which may not be the best official data. In both cases, we were not able to implement all of the principles discussed above, and highlight these limitations as a means of indicating where future research and data collection should be focused.

Colombia and Ecuador are developing countries in Latin America where inclusive wealth reporting could dramatically change the national view of development progress and influence natural resource management and poverty alleviation decisions. Their GDPs vary (Colombia GDP = US$288.8 billion in 2010; Departmento Nacional de Estadística, Ecuador GDP = US$108.4 billion in 2010) but both countries have high poverty rates (percentage of population below poverty line: Colombia = 45.5 percent in 2009, Ecuador = 33.1 percent in 2010) (CIA Factbook). The potential utility of a new accounting approach in the region has been recognized by the World Bank. They have chosen Colombia as one of five pilot countries for an effort to implement Wealth Accounting and Valuation of Ecosystem Services (WAVES). Here, we attempt to apply the INVEST models, as a demonstration of the components of the methodologies described above that are feasible with readily available data, to four regulating services in each country.

4.1 Colombia

4.1.1 Climate regulation through carbon sequestration

Carbon sequestration is the only regulating service we were able to value with readily available data. We used the INVEST carbon model, a simple look-up table of four carbon stocks per vegetation class (CONTE ET AL. 2011A). This approach mirrors the IPCC accounting approach, and we used stocks derived by Peralvo (2008A) via the IPCC methodology (IPCC 2006) for the land use and land cover in the country in the year 2000 (IDEAM ET AL. 2007). All four standard carbon stocks were represented (above-ground biomass, below-ground biomass, soil, and dead organic matter), but we did not account for the harvested wood product pool. Carbon stocks in 2000 were highest in primary forest regions, and heavily concentrated in the Amazon basin (Figure 2a, c), totaling 19.3 billion metric tons C in the country. Assuming static physical assets, the value of this stock using a US$50 metric ton

FIGURE 2

Projected land use change, carbon stocks and sequestration from 2000 to 2030 in Colombia and Ecuador.

Primary forest, especially in the Amazon basin, in the east of both countries (a) held large carbon stocks in the year 2000 (c, e). Areas likely to be converted from forest to some other land use between 2000 (a) and 2030 (b) show climate regulation loss (gray areas, d and f) and those that will sequester carbon over the same time period show climate regulation gains (green areas, c and d). The projected net change for the country over the 30-year period represents a significant loss in wealth. Pixels in Colombia are 250 m, pixels in Ecuador are 90 m.

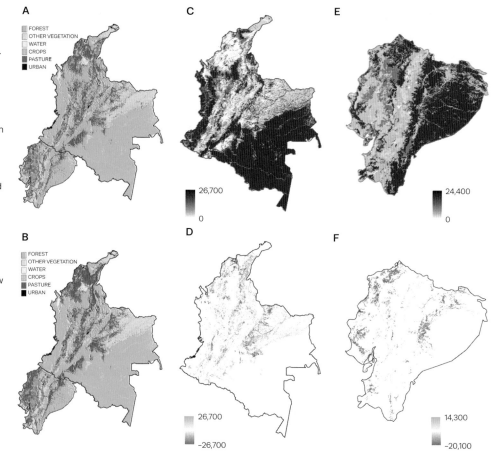

C-1 social cost of carbon (TOL 2009) was US$964.06 billion.

However, we know land conversion is likely to degrade this stock into the future, so we used a scenario for land use and land cover in 2030 generated using the CLUE-S model (GALINDO 2008) and assumed no climate change effects on vegetation distribution and no change in land use past that year. This scenario shows land use change patterns affecting carbon sequestration, primarily west of the Andes (Figure 2b). The net effect of these changes results in a national loss of carbon storage of approximately 507,308,000 metric tons over the 30-year time period. We assumed a linear loss rate, calculated the discounted value of the carbon stock lost each year, and deducted that value over the 30 years from the static asset estimate stated above. We also bounded our value estimate to represent the possibilities for high or low discount rates (three percent and one percent, respectively) and high or low annual changes in the social

cost of carbon (one percent increase and no change, respectively). With this approach, the present value of Colombia's national carbon stocks in 2000 is estimated to be between about US$942.1 billion and US$947.5 billion. The reduction in the value of carbon storage is the difference between these amounts and the value of US$964.06 billion assuming permanent storage, or US$16.6 to US$22 billion. Given the uncertainty in estimation of the social cost of carbon, we offer two other estimates. Using a lower estimate of $20 metric ton C-1, the rate commonly applied by the World Bank, the value of the 2000 carbon stock is between US$376.8 billion and US$379.0 billion. Using a higher estimate of US$205 metric ton C-1 (the 95th percentile value based on 232 published estimates of the social cost of carbon [TOL 2009]), the value of the 2000 carbon stock was between US$3.862 trillion and US$3.885 trillion.

This application of the INVEST carbon sequestration model has several limitations.

The INVEST Tier 1 carbon model does not represent sequestration by aging vegetation because carbon stocks only change if land use land cover types change. This means we have likely underrepresented the value of carbon stocks in the Amazon Basin and other forested regions and possibly overestimated the net loss of carbon nationwide over the 30-year future projection. However, while carbon stocks are high in old growth forests, carbon sequestration rates in old growth forests are generally low (PREGITZER AND EUSKIRCHEN 2004). Another major limitation to using this approach for national accounting is the lack of regularly updated national inventories of carbon stocks or national land use and land cover maps. As a case in point, the most recent land use and land cover map we could find for these analyses was developed in 2000. At least one of these data sources must be available to allow annual tracking of carbon sequestration and its value in an inclusive wealth accounting context. The lack of such data is a global problem and must be addressed by the remote sensing community before real progress can be made (TALLIS ET AL., IN REVIEW). Some efforts are underway, but must become standardized, efficient, and cost-effective before they can be applied in this context.

4.1.2 Nutrient retention for drinking water quality

We were able to estimate and map nutrient retention for drinking water quality supply and service delivery, but not value. We used the INVEST water purification: nutrient retention model (CONTE ET AL. 2011B; TALLIS ET AL. 2012A). This model estimates supply based on the export coefficient approach (first developed by RECKHOW ET AL. 1980), where each land use and land cover class exports a certain amount of nutrient. This export is influenced by runoff (calculated by the INVEST water yield model, a simple pixel-based water balance model), and retention by downslope vegetation and soils. Exported nutrients are routed across the landscape and each land use and land cover type retains nutrients in a constant, non-saturating

function. The model outputs the total amount of nutrients exported by the landscape in an average year, and the total amount of nutrients retained. These outputs can be calculated at the pixel scale, and summarized to any larger unit such as political boundaries or large basins. Summarizing retention for the whole country gives an estimate of supply, or the full potential for nutrient retention benefits. Summarizing retention for servicesheds upstream of drinking water extraction points gives an estimate of service delivery because it accounts for how much retention is actually providing benefit to a downstream user.

We applied the water purification model for total nitrogen (TN) and summarized retention to the national boundary (supply) and to servicesheds delineated for all population centers (INSTITUTO GEOGRÁFICO AGUSTÍN CODAZZI 2007) in the country (service). Maps of the locations of actual water extraction points or water treatment facilities should be used to identify beneficiaries and servicesheds, but such maps are not freely available for Colombia. For all cities, we assumed surface water use and identified the extraction point as the closest point on a river within five kilometers. We used a 250 m digital elevation model (FARR ET AL. 2007), soil depth (IGAC 2003; BATJES 2005), plant available water content (ESTRADA ET AL. 2007), annual precipitation according to WorldClim (HIJMANS ET AL. 2005), potential evapotranspiration (derived from WORLDCLIM data using Hargreaves method [DROOGERS AND ALLEN 2002]), and land use and land cover data (IDEAM ET AL. 2007). For each land use and land cover class we defined a root depth, evapotranspiration coefficient, export coefficient (total amount of TN exported ha-1 yr-1), and retention efficiency (percentage of TN retained yr-1) based on an extensive global and regional literature review (TALLIS 2012).

In the year 2000, TN retention rates were highest in the Andean valleys, where TN exports from agricultural and pasture lands are high and some natural vegetation remains along flowpaths to provide retention (Figure 3a). In general, retention is potentially higher in areas

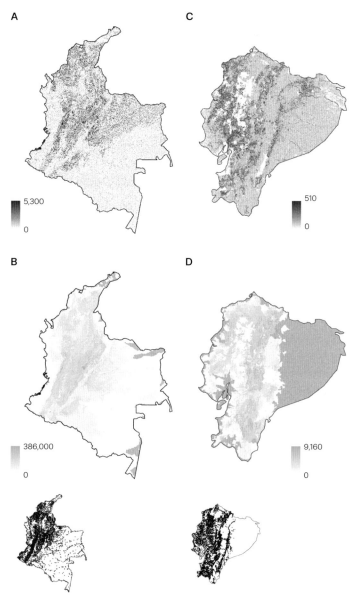

A

5,300

0

C

510

0

B

386,000

0

D

9,160

0

FIGURE 3

Nutrient regulation for drinking water quality in the year 2000

The magnitude of nutrient regulation supply (a, c) differs from service
delivery (b, d) because the populations
of Colombia and Ecuador are focused
in the western parts of the countries

(inset in b, d), amplifying the demand
in that region. In both countries,
maximum service delivery is higher
than maximum supply because of
overlapping servicesheds in densely
populated areas. Areas not included in
a serviceshed are shown in grey (b, d).
Pixels in Colombia are 250 m, pixels in
Ecuador are 90 m.

it up and provide a reduction in pollutant load.
This is somewhat counter-intuitive, but correct.
Pristine systems generally export little TN relative to productive areas (e.g., crops, pastures), so
there is little potential for downstream vegetation and soils to retain it. At the national level,
the total supply of nitrogen retention for drinking water in the year 2000 was ~785.8 million
kg TN. Summarizing this retention within servicesheds (Figure 3b) gives us a national service
delivery estimate of ~32.7 billion kg TN. The
national population of ~45 million people is distributed throughout the country and drinking
water servicesheds cover nearly the entire country (Figure 3b). Many servicesheds are overlapping, making service delivery much higher than
supply, especially in the area with the highest
density of population centers (Figure 3b inset).

For these ecosystem service estimates to
enter into an inclusive wealth account, we need
to value the well-being impact of service delivery
with a standard net present value approach using
any of the methods discussed above. Estimating
the future flows of service is straightforward: we
can simply run the INVEST model on the future
landscape as predicted in the 2030 land use and
land cover map (GALINDO 2008). However, data
and methods for valuation were limiting. Data
on water treatment costs are not readily available for all facilities in Colombia. The alternative
approach of estimating health and productive
losses would require another modeling effort to
extract the marginal contribution of nitrogen
regulation to these components of well-being.
Neither was feasible for this study, but can be
developed in the future.

4.1.3 Erosion regulation for drinking water qual-
ity and reservoir maintenance

Of the many benefits provided by erosion regulation, we were able to map and quantify the
supply and service delivery of two services: erosion regulation for drinking water quality and
for reservoir maintenance. The supply estimation process for these services is identical (and
would apply to estimation of any other erosion

where there are high nutrient inputs (fertiliz-
ers, fixation, etc.) because when there is more
nitrogen flowing across the landscape, there is
more potential for vegetation and soils to take

regulation benefit). In both cases, we used the INVEST sediment retention model (CONTE ET AL. 2011B, TALLIS ET AL. 2012A). This model is based on the Universal Soil Loss Equation (USLE; WISCHMEIER AND SMITH 1978), where soil loss is driven by slope, rainfall (erosivity), soil type (erodibility), vegetation type, and land use practices. In the INVEST model, the USLE approach is improved and retention is calculated as the combination of two retention processes; the regulation of erosion from a given pixel, and the ability of the vegetation and management on that pixel to retain sediment arriving from upslope parts of the watershed (run-on retention). On-pixel retention is calculated by internally comparing erosion on the current landscape to a "no-natural-capital" baseline. As such, this model does the necessary calculation to compare the current capital asset to its absence. Run-on retention is calculated by routing eroded sediment down flowpaths and applying a land use and land cover-specific retention efficiency (percentage retained) at each pixel. Sediment

accumulated by these two processes is simply added together on each pixel to estimate how much sediment is retained by natural capital.

We applied the sediment retention model for drinking water quality improvement as well as avoided reservoir sedimentation. We delineated servicesheds independently for each service since the services are enjoyed by different groups of people in different places. Servicesheds for drinking water quality were drawn as they were for nitrogen regulation (above). Servicesheds for reservoir maintenance were delineated as the contributing watershed area upstream of each known drinking water and hydropower production reservoir in the country (INSTITUTO GEOGRÁFICO AGUSTÍN CODAZZI 2007). We used the same digital elevation model, annual precipitation map, and land use and land cover map noted above. An erodibility map was developed by assigning erodibility values from Stone and Hilborn (2008) to textural soil classes and soil organic content identified by the USDA (2007). Erosivity was derived from annual WorldClim

FIGURE 4

Erosion regulation for drinking water quality and reservoir maintenance in 2000.

Erosion regulation supply is focused in the Andean valleys and foothills (a, d). Service delivery for drinking water quality (b, e) is much higher than supply. Service delivery for reservoir maintenance (c) is focused watersheds (servicesheds) upstream of the Colombia's few major reservoir The black outline in (b) identifies the expanded area in (c). Outlines in (c) delineate reservoir servicesheds. Pixels in Colombia are 250 m, pixels ir Ecuador are 90 m.

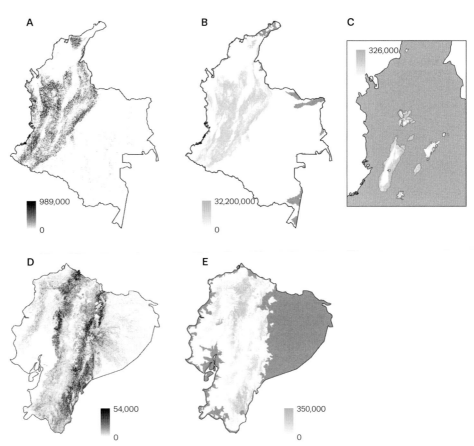

precipitation data using the method in Perez and Mesa (2002). For each land use and land cover class, we defined C (vegetation) and P (management) factors based on an extensive global and regional literature review (TALLIS 2012).

Following a pattern similar to nutrient retention, sediment retention in the year 2000 was highest in the Andean valleys (Figure 4a). At the national level, the total supply of sediment retention was ~25.9 billion tons of sediment. Considering demand at drinking water quality extraction points, this translated into a much higher service delivery estimate for drinking water quality regulation of ~1.1 trillion tons of sediment (Figure 4b). Again, many drinking water servicesheds are overlapping, making service delivery much higher than supply for this regulating service, especially in areas of high population density. Given the much lower number of demand points for major reservoirs (Figure 4c), the service delivery estimate for reservoir maintenance in 2000 was ~1.3 billion tons of sediment.

As with nutrient regulation, these ecosystem service estimates need to be valued in terms of their well-being impact before they can inform national accounts. We can again estimate the future flow of services by running the INVEST model on the future landscape as predicted in the 2030 land use and land cover map (GALINDO 2008). But as for nutrient retention, data and methods for valuation were limiting. For drinking water quality regulation value, data or models on water treatment costs or marginal health impacts are not readily available. For reservoir maintenance, production information (production and dredge costs, production practices, etc.) is generally proprietary. Additional systems of data collection or reporting must be developed before ready calculation of values can proceed on a regular basis.

4.2 Ecuador

The same INVEST modeling approaches were used in Ecuador. The land use and land cover map used in all analyses was produced by MAG

and others (2002) and represents the landscape in the year 2000. The land use and land cover map for 2030 was created by Peralvo (2008B). Other service-specific data sources and results are described below.

4.2.1 Climate regulation through carbon sequestration

Following the same approach and data sources described for Colombia, we estimate total carbon stock in 2000 of 3.9 billion metric tons C in Ecuador. Stocks are again concentrated in primary forest areas, especially in the Amazon basin on the eastern side of the country (Figure 2a, e). Using the same assumption of likely future loss of carbon from land conversion, and the estimation of that conversion by 2030 according to Peralvo (2008B), we estimate a loss of 211,137,000 metric tons of carbon over the 30-year period. Considering this likely future loss, we estimate the present value of carbon in Ecuador in 2000 to be between US$186.2 billion and US$188.5 billion. Again, considering the uncertainty in social cost of carbon estimates, we offer a lower bound estimate of US$74.5 billion to US$75.4 billion (using US$20 metric ton C-1), and an upper bound estimate of US$763.6 billion to US$772.8 billion (using US$205 metric ton C-1).

4.2.2 Drinking water quality regulation and erosion regulation for reservoirs

We were able to estimate supply and service for nutrient retention and erosion regulation for drinking water quality, and supply for erosion regulation for reservoirs in Ecuador. Data on the location of reservoirs were not accessible in the timeframe of this study, but can be added in the future. We applied the INVEST water purification model for TN using a 90-meter digital elevation model (FARR ET AL. 2007), soil depth (PRONAREG 1980), plant available water content (SAXTON AND RAWLS 2006), annual precipitation from WorldClim (HIJMANS ET AL. 2005), and potential evapotranspiration calculated from the WorldClim data using the Hargreaves method (DROOGERS AND ALLEN 2002). For each land use and land cover type, we defined a root depth, evapotranspiration coefficient, export coefficient and retention efficiency (TALLIS 2012). We also applied the Sediment Retention model with additional data on erosivity (ROOSE 1996) and erodibility (PRONAREG 1980; USDA 2007; STONE AND HILBORN 2008). Drinking water servicesheds were delineated as they were for Colombia, assuming surface water use and extraction from nearby river sources.

The areas of highest TN retention are again in the valleys and foothills of the Andes, and in the western region of the country (Figure 3c). At a national level, total TN retention supply in 2000 was approximately 221.5 million kg. Summarization to drinking water servicesheds showed a much higher level of service delivery, 1.2 billion kg for the country. Service delivery is focused and amplified in the heavily populated region west of the Andes (Figure 3d). We likely underestimated national service delivery as there are inhabited areas in the Amazon basin that are not captured in the population center data we were able to access.

Sediment retention was even more strongly focused in the Andean valleys and foothills (Figure 4d), offering a total national sediment retention supply of ~3.8 billion tons of sediment. Summarizing this supply to servicesheds again amplified the service estimate due to overlapping servicesheds. The national total sediment retention service in 2000 was ~24.5 billion tons of sediment. These contributions are much smaller than those seen in Colombia, but Ecuador is a much smaller country (~113 million ha vs ~25 million ha, respectively). Valuation of these services can be done by delineating servicesheds and following the same additional steps noted for Colombia. However, much more ready access to data sources is needed for this to be a replicable process.

5. Case studies vs. principles

The case studies provide a valuable opportunity to assess the state of the science to meet the principles we can define in theory. Although it may seem disappointing that we were unable to assign monetary value to three of the four regulating services we explored in Colombia and Ecuador, we were able to apply several of the core principles. In all cases, we were able to apply methods that allowed us to unbundle regulating services into explicit benefits to explicit groups. We were also able to differentiate between supply and service delivery for all services, and the resulting numbers emphasize how critical this step is in accurately accounting for the benefits received by people. We were able to delineate servicesheds for all services, but with some serious limitations. Without data on actual extraction points, and the ability to differentiate between users who rely on surface or groundwater, our estimates may be largely skewed in space, and in terms of the national totals for nutrient regulation and erosion regulation. Regular reporting and improved access to data such as land use and land cover maps, ecosystem service access points, water treatment practices and costs and reservoir management will be essential before we can regularly report on the wealth of this subset of regulating services.

6. The need to continue forward

The fundamental approach for including regulating services in inclusive wealth accounts has been detailed here and in previous works. We have taken the first steps towards implementing the approach and find many limitations in data availability, especially for inputs that must be updated annually to provide useful information to decision-makers at the national scale. However, the magnitude of wealth that these preliminary analyses demonstrate is large enough to have significant impacts on the national view of social status in these two countries. This suggests that, while difficult, the approach and principles we have proposed here should be pursued if we are to accurately track the real wealth of nations.

REFERENCES

ARNOLD, J.G., SRINIVASAN, R., MUTTIAH, R.S. & WILLIAMS, J.R. (1998). Large area hydrologic modeling and assessment. Part I: model development. *Journal of the American Water Resources Association, 34*, 73-89.

ARROW, K., DASGUPTA, P., GOULDER, L., DAILY, G., EHRLICH, P., HEAL, G.,...WALKER, B. (2004). Are we consuming too much? *The Journal of Economic Perspectives, 18* (3), 147-172.

ARROW, K.J., DASGUPTA, P., GOULDER, L.H., MUMFORD, K.J. & OLESON, K. (2010). Sustainability and the measurement of wealth. *NBER Working Paper No 16599.*

ASNER, G.P. (2009). Tropical forest carbon assessment: integrating satellite and airborne mapping approaches. *Environmental Research Letters, 4*, 1-11.

BATJES, N. (2005). *SOTER - based soil parameter estimates for Latin America and the Caribbean (Ver. 1.0).* Wageningen: ISRIC-World Soil Information.

BOYD, J. & BANZHAF, S. (2007). What are ecosystem services? The need for standardized environmental accounting units. *Ecological Economics, 63*, 616-626.

BROWN, S. (2002). Measuring, monitoring and verification of carbon benefits for forest-based projects. *Philosophical Transactions of the Royal Society of London, 360*, 1669-1683.

CARSON, R.T. & MITCHELL, R.C. (1993). The value of clean water: The public's willingness to pay for boatable, fishable, and swimmable water quality. *Water Resources Research, 29*, 245-254.

CHOE, K., WHITTINGTON, D. & LAURIA, D.T. (1996). The economic benefits of surface water quality improvements in developing countries: A case study of Davao, Philippines. *Land Economics, 72*, 519-537.

CONANT, R.T., OGLE, S.M., PAUL, E.A. & PAUSTIAN, K. (2010). Measuring and monitoring soil organic carbon stocks in agricultural lands for climate mitigation. *Frontiers in Ecology and the Environment, 9*, 169-173.

CONTE, M., NELSON, E., CARNEY, K., FISSORE, C., OLWERO, N., PLANTINGA, A.J.,...RICKETTS, T. (2011A). Terrestrial carbon sequestration and storage. In P.M. Kareiva, H. Tallis, T.H. Ricketts, G.C. Daily & S. Polasky (Eds.) *Natural capital: Theory and practice of mapping ecosystem services.* Oxford University Press.

CONTE, M., ENNAANAY, D., MENDOZA, G., WALTER, M.T., WOLNY, S., FREYBERG, D.,...SOLORZANO, L. (2011B). Retention of nutrients and sediment by vegetation. P.M. Kareiva, H. Tallis, T.H. Ricketts, G.C. Daily & S. Polasky (Eds.) *Natural capital: Theory and practice of mapping ecosystem services.* Oxford University Press.

CRUMPTON, W.G., KOVACIC, D.A., HEY, D.L. & KOSTEL, J.A. (2008). Potential of restored and constructed wetlands to reduce nutrient export from agricultural watersheds in the corn belt. In Final Report: Gulf Hypoxia and Local Water Quality Concerns Workshop, American Society of Agricultural and Biological Engineers.

DAS, S. & VINCENT, J.R. (2009). Mangroves protected villages and reduced death toll during Indian super cyclone. *Proceedings of the National Academy of Sciences, 106*, 7357–7360.

DASGUPTA, P. & MÄLER, K.G. (2000). Net national product, wealth, and social well being. *Environment and Development Economics, 5*(1), 69-93.

DEEGAN, L.A., NEILL, C., HAUPERT, C.L., BALLESTER, M.V.R., KRUSCHE, A.V., VICTORIA, R.L.,...DE MOOR, E. (2010). Amazon deforestation alters small stream structure, nitrogen biogeochemistry and connectivity to larger rivers. *Biogeochemistry, 105*, 53-74.

DE GROOT, R.S., WILSON, M.A. & BOUMANS, R.M.J. (2002). A typology for the classification, description, and valuation of ecosystem functions, goods and services. *Ecological Economics, 41*, 393-408.

DIAZ, R.J. & ROSENBERG, R. (2008). Spreading dead zones and consequences for marine ecosystems. *Science, 321*, 926-929.

DIXON, R.K., SOLOMON, A.M., BROWN, S., HOUGHTON, R.A., TREXIER, M.C. & WISNIEWSKI, J. (1994). Carbon pools and flux of global forest ecosystems. *Science, 263*, 185-190.

DROOGERS, P. & ALLEN, R. (2002). Estimating reference evapotranspiration under inaccurate data conditions. *Irrigation and Drainage Systems, 16*, 33-45.

ESTRADA, R., URIBE, N. & QUINTERO, M. (2007). Impacto del Uso de la Tierra en la Generación de Caudales y Sedimentos: El Caso de las Cuencas de los Ríos Cauca y Magdalena Santiago de Cali: Convenio Interinstitucional de Investigación y Desarrollo entre la OFN - Andina y el Centro Internacional de Agricultura Tropical (CIAT).

INTERGOVERNMENTAL PANEL ON CLIMATE CHANGE (IPCC). (2006). *2006 IPCC guidelines for national greenhouse gas inventories. Volume 4: Agriculture, forestry and other land use.* Hayama, Japan: Institute for Global Environmental Strategies (IGES).

FARR, T.G., ROSEN, P.A., CARO, E., CRIPPEN, R., DUREN, R., HENSLEY, S.,...ALSDORF, D. (2007). The shuttle radar topography mission. *Reviews of Geophysics, 45*(2).

FISHER, B. & TURNER, R.K. (2008). Ecosystem services: Classification for valuation. *Biological Conservation, 141*, 1167-1169.

GALINDO, G. (2008). *Implementation of the GLOBIO3 – CLUE methodology in Colombia.* Bogota, Colombia: Instituto Alexander von Humboldt.

HAVENS, K.E. & WALKER, W.W. JR. (2009). Development of a total phosphorus concentration goal in the TMDL process for Lake Okeechobee, Florida (USA). *Lake and Reservoir Management, 18*, 227-238.

HIJMANS, R., CAMERON, S., PARRA, J., JONES, P. & JARVIS, A. (2005). Very high resolution interpolated climate surfaces for global land areas. *International Journal of Climatology, 25*, 1965-78.

IDEAM, IAVH, IGAC, IIAP, INVEMAR, SINCHI. (2007). *Mapa de ecosistemas continentales, costeros y marinos de Colombia. Escala 1:500000.* Bogotá: Instituto de Hidrología, Meteorología y Estudios Ambientales (IDEAM), Instituto de Investigaciones de Recursos Biológicos Alexander von Humboldt (IAvH), Instituto Geográfico Agustín Codazzi (IGAC), Instituto de Investigaciones Ambientales del Pacífico John von Neumann (IIAP), Instituto de Investigaciones Marinas y Costeras José Benito Vives De Andréis (INVEMAR) e Instituto Amazónico de Investigaciones Científicas (SINCHI).

IGAC. (2003). *Mapa de suelos de Colombia. Escala 1:500000.* Bogotá: Instituto Geográfico Agustín Codazzi.

KARL, T.R. & TRENBERTH, K.E. (2003). Modern global climate change. *Science, 302*, 1719-1723.

KINZIG, A., PERRINGS, C., CHAPIN, F.S. III, PO-LASKY, S., SMITH, V. K., TILMAN, D. & TURNER, B.L. II. (2011). Paying for ecosystem services – promise and peril. *Science, 334*, 603-604.

KREMEN, C., WILLIAMS, N.M., AIZEN, M.A., GEMMILL-HARREN, B., LEBUHN, G., MINCKLEY, R.,... RICKETTS, T.H. (2007). Pollination and other ecosystem services produced by mobile organisms: a conceptual framework for the effects of land-use change. *Ecology Letters, 10*, 299-314.

KUMAR, P. & WOOD, M.D. (2010). *Valuation of regulating services of ecosystems.* New York: Routledge.

MAG, IICA & CLIRSEN. (2002). *Mapa de uso y cobertura del suelo del Ecuador. Escala 1:250000.* Quito: Ministerio de Agricultura y Ganadería del Ecuador (MAG), Instituto Interamericano de Cooperación para la Agricultura (IICA) y Centro de Levantamientos Integrados de Recursos Naturales por Sensores Remotos (CLIRSEN).

MAGETTE, W.L., BRINSFIELD, R.B., PALMER, R.E. & WOOD, J.D. (1989). Nutrient and sediment removal by vegetated filter strips. *American Society of Agricultural Engineers, 32*(2), 663-667.

MILLENNIUM ECOSYSTEM ASSESSMENT. (2005). *Ecosystems and human well-being.* Washington, DC: Island Press.

MUNOZ-CARPENA, R., PARSONS, J.E. & GIL-LIAM, J.W. (1999). Modeling hydrology and sediment transport in vegetative filter strips. *Journal of Hydrology, 214*, 111-129.

NATIONAL RESEARCH COUNCIL (NRC). (2000). *Watershed management for potable water supply: Assessing the New York City strategy.* Washington, DC: National Academies Press.

NATIONAL RESEARCH COUNCIL (NRC). (2005). *Valuing ecosystem services: Towards better environmental decision-making.* Washington, DC: National Academies Press.

NELSON, E., MENDOZA, G., REGETZ, J., POLASKY, S., TALLIS, H., CAMERON, D.R.,...SHAW, M.R. (2009). Modeling multiple ecosystem services, biodiversity conservation, commodity production, and tradeoffs at landscape scales. *Frontiers of Ecology and Environment, 7*, 4–11.

NOAA. (2004). *Nonpoint source pollution and erosion comparison technical guide (N-SPECT).* Charleston: NOAA Coastal Services Center.

PATTANAYAK, S.K. (2004). Valuing watershed services: Concepts and empirics from Southeast Asia. *Agriculture, Ecosystems & Environment, 104*(1), 171-184.

PEARCE, D. & ATKINSON, G. (1993). Capital theory and the measurement of sustainable development: an indicator of "weak" sustainability. *Ecological Economics, 8* (2), 103-108.

PEARSON, T.R.H., BROWN, S. & BIRDSEY, R.A. (2007). *Measurement guidelines for the sequestration of forest carbon.* Newtown Square, PA: US Department of Agriculture, Forest Service.

PERALVO, M. (2008A). *Impelmentacion de un modelo de evaluación del servicio ecosistémico de almacenamiento de carbono para Ecuador y Colombia.* Quito: Seearth Consulting Group.

PERALVO, M. (2008B). *Generación de un indicador global del estado de conservación de la biodiversidad en el Ecuador continental: Implementación de la metodología GLO-BIO3 – CLUE.* Quito, Ecuador: Fundación EcoCiencia.

PÉREZ, J. & MESA, O. (2002). *Estimación del factor de erosividad de la lluvia en Colombia.* Colombia: Simposio Latinoamericano de Control de Erosión.

PETROKOFSKY, G., HOLMGREN, P. & BROWN, N.D. (2011). Reliable forest carbon monitoring-systematic reviews as a tool for validating the knowledge base. *International Forestry Review, 13*, 56-66.

POLASKY, S., NELSON, E., PENNINGTON, D. & JOHNSON, K. (2011). The impact of land-use change on ecosystem services, biodiversity and returns to landowners: A case study in the State of Minnesota. *Environmental and Resource Economics, 48*, 219-242.

PREGITZER, K.S. & EUSKIRCHEN, E.S. (2004). Carbon cycling and storage in world forests: biome patterns related to forest age. *Global Change Biology, 10*, 2052-2077.

PRONAREG. (1980). *Mapa de suelos del Ecuador. Escala 1:1000000.* Quito: PRONAREG.

RECKHOW, K.H., BEAULAC, M.N. & SIMPSON, J.T. (1980). *Modeling phosphorus loading and lake response under uncertainty: A manual and compilation of export coefficients.* Washington, DC: U.S. Environmental Protection Agency.

RICKETTS, T.H., DAILY, G.C., EHRLICH, P.R. & MICHENER, C. (2004). Economic value of tropical forests in coffee production. *Proceedings of the National Academy of Sciences, 101*, 12579-12582.

ROOSE, E. (1996). *Land husbandry - components and strategy. 70 FAO soils bulletin.* Rome: Food and Agriculture Organization of the United Nations.

SAXTON, K.E. & RAWLS, W.J. (2006). Soil water characteristic estimates by texture and organic matter for hydrologic solutions. *Soil Science Society of America Journal, 70*(5), 1569-78.

STIGLITZ, J.E., SEN, A. & FITOUSSI, J.P. (2010). *Mismeasuring our lives: Why GDP doesn't add up.* New York: The New Press.

STONE, R. & HILBORN, D. (2008). *Universal soil loss equation (USLE).* Ontario: Ministry of Agriculture, Food & Rural Affairs.

TALLIS, H. (2012). Non-reviewed databases on export coefficients (https://docs.google.com/spreadsheet/ccc?key=0AqZtsmcgQETMdGlBU3JxWHF1YUdXVnRDNS1wNlVVR-FE); nutrient retention efficiencies (https://docs.google.com/spreadsheet/ccc?key=0AqZtsmcgQETMdEFBUnlhMXVFVDRXanlwbzBTYW9xa1E); sediment retention efficiencies (https://docs.google.com/spreadsheet/ccc?key=0AqZtsmcgQETMdFgzOUZWcjdpVmcoTlV0U3JPQmxYOGc); and C and P factors for use in the USLE equation (https://docs.google.com/spreadsheet/ccc?key=0AqZtsmcgQETMdFdhaDJkdGRwTGdPM3ItbC1lU19PRkE).

TALLIS H. & POLASKY, S. (2009). Mapping and valuing ecosystem services as an approach for conservation and natural-resource management. *Annals of the New York Academy of Sciences, 1162*, 265-283.

TALLIS H. & POLASKY S. (2011). Assessing multiple ecosystem services: An integrated tool for the real world. In P.M. Kareiva, H. Tallis, T.H. Ricketts, G.C. Daily & S. Polasky (Eds.) *Natural capital: Theory and practice of mapping ecosystem services.* Oxford University Press.

TALLIS, H.T., RICKETTS, T., GUERRY, A.D., WOOD, S.A., SHARP, R., NELSON, E.,...BERNHARDT, J. (2012A). *InVEST 2.2 beta user's guide.* The Natural Capital Project, Stanford University.

TALLIS, H., LESTER, S.E., RUCKELSHAUS, M., PLUMMER, M., MCLEOD, K., GUERRY, A.,... WHITE, C. (2012B). New metrics for managing and sustaining the ocean's bounty. *Marine Policy, 36*, 303-306.

TILMAN, D., FARGIONE, J., WOLFF, B., D'ANTONIO, C., DOBSON, A., HOWARTH, R.,... SWACKHAMER, D. (2001). Forecasting agriculturally driven global environmental change. *Science, 292*, 281-284.

TOL, R.S.J. (2009). The economic effects of climate change. *Journal of Economic Perspectives, 23*, 29–51.

USDA (UNITED STATES DEPARTMENT OF AGRICULTURE). (2007). *National soil survey handbook, title 430-VI*. Washington, DC: U.S. Department of Agriculture, Natural Resources Conservation Service.

VAN HOUTVEN, G., POWERS, J. & PATTANAYAK, S.K. (2007). Valuing water quality improvements in the United States using meta-analysis: Is the glass half-full or half-empty for national policy analysis? *Resource and Energy Economics, 29*, 206-228.

WHITE, W.J., MORRIS, L.A., PINHO, A.P., JACKSON, C.R. & WEST, L.T. (2007). Sediment retention by forested filter strips in the Piedmont of Georgia. *Journal of Soil and Water Conservation, 62*(6), 453-463.

WISCHMEIER, W.H. & SMITH, D. (1978). *Predicting rainfall erosion losses: a guide to conservation planning*. Washington, DC: USDA-ARS Agriculture Handbook.

WORLD BANK. (1997). *Expanding the measure of wealth: Indicators of environmentally sustainable development*. Washington, DC: World Bank.

WORLD BANK. (2006). *Where is the wealth of nations?* Washington, DC: World Bank.

WORLD BANK. (2011). *The changing wealth of nations: Measuring sustainable development in the new millennium*. Washington, DC: World Bank.

ZHANG, X., LIU, X., ZHANG, M. & DAHLGREN, R.A. (2010). A review of vegetated buffers and a meta-analysis of their mitigation efficacy in reducing nonpoint source pollution. *Journal of Environmental Quality, 39*, 76-84.

CHAPTER 10

Accounting for water: stocks, flows, and values

Chris Perry

KEY MESSAGES

As water becomes increasingly scarce, as sectoral competition for water intensifies, and as humanity increasingly interferes with nature's hydrological cycle, the need to measure and value water flows and stocks has increased.

Such evaluation must proceed in two discrete steps: first, the construction of physical water accounts, designed to figure out how much water there is, where it is, when it is available, how accessible it is, and with what reliability; and second, when the accounts are in place, the analysis can proceed towards placing a value on these resources.

The UN's System of Environmental–Economic Accounting for Water (SEEAW) is an important step forward in understanding the flows and stocks of water. The flows comprise abstraction, consumption, and return flows; the stocks, which are harder to assess, look at groundwater resources, lakes, snowpack, and the like.

SEEAW has important strengths. It is multi-sectoral; it clearly distinguishes between consumptive and non-consumptive uses of water; it is hydrologically consistent with the law of conservation of mass; and it can be applied at various scales (project, sector, region, country, and basin).

While SEEAW has been promoted for a few years, Australia is the only country for which detailed implementation plans and progress seem to be available. The process has been lengthy and detailed and has resulted in many reports, reviews, and studies.

SEEAW accounts should be expanded to include the "unmanaged" natural landscape; "managed" areas; and rainfed agriculture.

1. Introduction

Human, animal, and plant life all depend on water. Water is also an essential factor in most economic activities – a source of energy for hydro-power; the medium in which fish grow; a coolant for thermal power stations; a dilution agent for wastes and pollutants; and the critical constraint to food and fiber production in arid and semi-arid areas.

In the early years of human intervention in the hydrological cycle, diversions and impoundments affected a very small proportion of natural flows. Impacts, though real, were of no concern to the human actors. Over time, populations expanded, living standards rose, and dependence on water increased; interest developed in measurements and predictions of whether the year's flow was likely to be scarce, adequate, abundant or, indeed, dangerously overabundant. Thousands of years ago, as Egypt began to exploit the Nile as a key economic resource, the world's first significant hydrological measurement and prediction system began, based on the "Nilometer" where the depth of the Nile was continuously recorded and interpreted as a predictor of future flow patterns.

Today, ensuring water availability for drinking, sanitation, navigation, fisheries, recreation, irrigation, and commercial activities is accepted as a fundamental responsibility of governments, at least at the level of regulating resource allocation and use. Additionally, governments are seen to be responsible for ensuring that the environment is protected, or where necessary, restored.

When water is scarce, these various social, commercial and environmental interests intersect in many ways. Should water be released from dams during the summer for irrigation, or during the winter to generate power for heating? Should forests be replanted to sequester carbon and mitigate climate change, thus increasing upstream water consumption and decreasing river flows? Are golf courses, which generate substantial economic activity, a higher priority than low-value grain crops for food security? Should cities have unrestricted access to water for domestic and sanitation purposes? If some groups in society have historically been disadvantaged in access to water, should preferential entitlements be established? "The environment" often requires a great deal of water to remain healthy – but to what extent is "the environment" more important than feeding people or providing jobs? What are the relative rights of upstream countries, where the rain falls and the rivers are fed, compared to downstream countries that have depended for millennia on the water in those rivers?

These and many other scenarios of competition and conflict can be identified across the world – from high-income to the least-developed countries, in countries with extreme scarcity of water and countries with relatively plentiful supplies. Every water situation is a unique combination of history, climate, social and economic pressures, resource endowments, trading opportunities, and so on. To this extent, the solution to every problem must be uniquely designed, and be the result of political processes that allow local preferences and priorities to contribute to the allocation of the scarce resource.

How these conflicting demands are resolved fundamentally affects the individual, sectoral, and national benefits that a nation derives from its access to water. Underpinning these processes and the decisions that must be made lies the essential foundation of a system of water accounting that unambiguously reports both the current state of water use, and the impacts of proposed interventions that can change that pattern of use.

The prosperity of a nation is affected by the availability of water, and the contribution that water makes to national wealth and well-being – and the impact that changes in water availability might have on these parameters – appear to be legitimate components of any assessment of national wealth that goes beyond traditional constructs such as gross domestic product or capital formation.

Such an evaluation must necessarily proceed in two discrete steps: 1) the construction of physical water accounts – how much water is there, where, when, how accessible, with what reliability?; and 2) with the physical accounts in place, the analysis can proceed towards placing values on these resources.

In the following sections, some of the issues that arise in devising meaningful water accounts are described: first regarding the difficult distinction between stocks of water and flows; second, in reporting on water use. A brief history of water accounting is presented, focusing finally on the UN System of Environmental-Economic Accounting for Water (SEEAW), and identifying the extent to which that framework helps understand the role of water in the national economy, and the limitations of physical water accounts – even when linked to economic accounts – as a basis for estimating water wealth.

In Section 5, some experiences with applying SEEAW are presented, and the extent to which such analyses can be interpreted as measures of wealth at local or national levels is discussed.

2. Physical water accounting

Conflicting perspectives about water

The purpose of accounting is to provide information in a consistent format for further analysis. Any accounting system must be based on an agreed upon and appropriate numeraire (dollars, yen, barrels of oil). However, because the water-using sectors have operated independently when water was plentiful, each sector has evolved its own perspective, and the problem of selecting a numeraire crosses disciplinary boundaries.

The most critical (and most frequently misunderstood) attribute of a particular water use is whether it is consumptive or non-consumptive. For most inputs into economic processes – energy, perhaps, provides a useful comparator – the input is consumed in the process. Electrical energy is generated at a power station, distributed to consumers, and used for heating, lighting, or to power a motor. Once the purpose has been achieved, the electricity has been consumed (albeit converted into another form of energy), and if more is needed, more must be generated. Certainly the electricity originally supplied is not available for re-use. The meaning of "efficiency" (providing the same amount of heat or light with less electrical energy), and "savings" (reducing transmission losses, for example) are entirely clear. Using electricity is indistinguishable from consuming electricity.

With water, the picture is much more complex. Many uses of water – domestic use, generation of hydro-power, navigation, fisheries, and industrial processes – are predominantly non-consumptive. The quantity of water diverted for use is almost the same as the quantity of water returned to the hydrological system. For most household purposes (washing, cooking, bathing, wcs, etc.) the purpose is generally achieved with only minimal conversion of water into vapour; hydro-power plants are entirely non-consumptive, unless water storage leads to extra evaporation from the reservoir; and thermal plants only evaporate a small fraction of the vast quantities of water passed through the system for cooling.

Agriculture, which is often the major user of water in water-scarce countries, is different. Water is used in agriculture (rainfed and irrigated) to ensure that crops can transpire freely and grow vigorously. Biomass formation is a direct function of the rate of transpiration through the open stomata, which simultaneously allows the plant to assimilate carbon. If water supplies are inadequate, production is depressed. Transpired water (as well as evaporation from wet soil and leaves) re-enters the atmosphere as water vapour, and is consequently removed from the local hydrological cycle. In this sense, the water is "consumed" and available supplies for downstream users are reduced. This linkage between upstream use and consumption and downstream availability is the basis for the accepted need to plan water

TABLE 1

Global water distribution

Water source	Water volume in cubic km	Percentage of freshwater	Percentage of total water
Oceans, seas, and bays	1,338,000,000	--	96.5
Ice caps, glaciers, and permanent snow	24,064,000	68.6	1.74
Groundwater:	23,400,000	--	1.7
Fresh	10,530,000	30.1	0.76
Saline	12,870,000	--	0.93
Soil moisture	16,500	0.05	0.001
Ground ice and permafrost	300,000	0.86	0.022
Lakes:	176,400	--	0.013
Fresh	91,000	0.26	0.007
Saline	85,400	--	0.007
Atmosphere	12,900	0.04	0.001
Swamp water	11,470	0.03	0.0008
Rivers	2,120	0.006	0.0002
Biological water	1,120	0.003	0.0001

Table 1 shows the distribution of the world's total water resources. This is a statement of stocks – an instantaneous picture of where all the water is at any moment. The right-hand column indicates the dominance of the oceans. From the stock perspective, total water availability is dominated by the oceans; while freshwater availability is dominated by ice and snow, and groundwater. Rivers, from either perspective, are a tiny fraction of the water resource, amounting to only 350 m3 per capita – significantly less than Falkenmark's (1989) water stress indicator of 1,000 m3 per capita per year.

Viewed from a flow perspective the water resource looks rather different. Annual evaporation and transpiration from the earth's surface (land and oceans) is about 485 km3; precipitation on land is some 111,000 km3, of which 71,000 km3 evaporates or transpires *in situ*, and 40,000 km3 runs off to rivers. Thus, the *flow* in rivers is some 20 times larger than the water in a river at any moment, and on average the water availability per capita per year comfortably exceeds Falkenmark's stress indicator. The distribution of this average is of course highly skewed.

Given that some of water's contributions to human well-being depend on flows (power generation, irrigation) while others depend on stocks (fisheries, amenity value of lakes), and others depend on both (wetland health requires that water be present in abundance, *and* that it is continuously refreshed) we already see that water is rather more difficult to describe, account for, and value than most other natural resources. Sectoral perspectives add further complications.

Source: Igor Shiklomanov's chapter "World fresh water resources" in Peter H. Gleick (editor), 1993, Water in Crisis: A Guide to the World's Fresh Water Resources (Oxford University Press, New York).

use from a basin perspective – the basin being the integrating hydrological unit of account.

Planners wish to assess water consumption, losses, and efficiency, and to understand how water is currently allocated and how new allocations will impact on current use. Sectoral specialists, however, have a different understanding of water consumption.

Water utilities supplying households and commercial users pay attention to "unaccounted-for water," meaning either leakage, or unauthorized extraction from the delivery system. The consequences of addressing these quite separate issues are likely to be different. Leakage from pipes will typically contribute to recharge of any underlying aquifer if the leaking pipe is buried. If the pipe is at or near the surface, water may evaporate and is thus consumptively used. Repairing leaks may thus reduce total abstraction (to the benefit of downstream users), but reduce the rate of recharge of a local aquifer.

The consequences of reducing unauthorized abstraction, on the other hand, will be a mixture of increased revenues and decreased demand as previously unauthorized users decide whether to continue using and paying, or reduce their use. In sum, in the simple case where water supplied to households is collected, treated, and returned to the system for reuse downstream, the impact of demand-reduction measures on actual water consumption is small. The picture changes dramatically, of course, if the domestic or industrial user is located close to the coast where the potential for downstream use is minimal. Water supplies may not be "consumed," but are lost to further use in the system.

The impact of thermal power stations is also complex: stations that draw water from a river, pass it through the cooling system, and return it to the river use very large quantities of water – but typically only consume 2 percent or so of the water abstracted. On the other hand, closed-loop systems (where water is only abstracted to "top up" leakage and evaporation) use much less water but consume 2–3 times more water per unit of electricity generated. An "efficient" design for a power station would thus have to consider the quantity and continuity of water availability as well as its scarcity.

Turning now to agriculture, when an irrigation specialist aims to improve "efficiency," the first objective – as in the domestic sector – is to maximize the proportion of abstracted water that is delivered to the user (ultimately, the plant). But just as leaks from water supply pipes can contribute to aquifer recharge or to non-productive evaporation, so irrigation systems are often major sources of aquifer recharge. "Losses" must therefore be carefully evaluated at a broader scale than the field, canal, or project to fully understand the impact of interventions.

The second aim of improved irrigation efficiency is to maximize the proportion of water delivered that is consumed by the plant and converted from liquid water to water vapour by crop transpiration. Broadly speaking, biomass production (and hence yield) has a linear relationship with transpiration, so maximizing crop production implies maximizing transpiration. Here, and indeed in agriculture more generally, the implications of increased efficiency are quite different from most other sectors, directly implying a reduction in water availability for other users.

Water harvesting for rainfed agriculture provides another complex example: the objective is to minimize runoff so that local crops can transpire more and hence increase production. Without knowing whether the natural runoff would have evaporated unproductively, or reached a possibly more productive downstream use, it is impossible to be sure whether the harvesting was a net benefit, neutral, or a net loss to the economy.

As a final example, forestry and other forms of catchment protection and development present similar complexities. A thriving healthy forest will certainly transpire more water than a degraded catchment, but the reduced quantity of water that arrives downstream will be a more steady flow with less silt. Timing and quantity are of concern in assessing whether the impact is positive or negative.

TABLE 2

Water supply and use statement, Denmark

Physical use table (Million cubic metres)

		Industries by ISIC category								
		Ag., forestry and fisheries	Mining, constr'n	Power	Water supply	Sewerage	Waste collection other	TOTAL	Households	TOTAL
From the environment	**1. Total abstraction (= 1.a+1.b, =1.i+1.ii)**	108	115	404	429	100	2	**1,158**	11	**1,169**
	1.a Abstraction for own use	108	115	404	23	100	2	**752**	11	763
	1.b Abstraction for distribution				406			**406**		**406**
	1.i From water resources:	108	115	404	429	100	2	**1,158**	11	**1,169**
	1.i.1 Surface water	*55*	*80*	*301*	*5*			*441*		*441*
	1.i.2 Groundwater	*3*	*35*	*3*	*423*		*2*	*466*	*10*	*476*
	1.i.3 Soil water	*50*						*50*		*50*
	1.ii From other sources				100	1	100	*201*	1	*202*
	1.ii.1 Collection of precipitation					100		*100*	*1*	*101*
	1.ii.2 Abstraction from the sea				*100*	*1*		*101*		*101*
Within the economy	**2. Use of water received from other economic units,** *of which:*	51	86	4		427	51	**619**	240	859
	2.a Reused water	*12*	*41*					*53*		*53*
	3. Total use of water (=1+2)	159	201	408	429	527	53	**1,777**	251	**2,028**

Physical supply table

		Ag., forestry and fisheries	Mining, constr'n	Power	Water supply	Sewerage	Waste collection other	TOTAL	Households	TOTAL
Within the economy	**4. Supply of water to other economic units** *of which:*	18	128	6	380	43	49	**624**	236	860
	4.a Reused water		*10*			*43*		*53*		*53*
	4.b Wastewater to sewerage	*18*	*118*	*6*	*1*		*49*	*192*	*236*	*428*
	4.c Desalinated water				*1*			*1*		*1*
To the environment	**5. Total returns (=5.a+5.b)**	65	29	400	47	484	1	**1,026**	5	1,031
	5.a To water resources (=5.a.1+5.a.2+5.a.3)	65	23	300	47	228	1	**664**	5	669
	5.a.1 Surface water			*300*		*53*		*353*	*1*	*354*
	5.a.2 Groundwater	*65*	*23*		*47*	*175*	*1*	*311*	*4*	*315*
	5.a.3 Soil water									
	5.b To other sources (e.g. Seawater)		5	100		256		361		361
	6. Total supply of water (= 4+5)	83	157	406	427	527	50	**1,650**	241	**1,891**
	7. Consumption (=3–6)	76	44	2	2		3	**127**	10	**137**

These stylized examples demonstrate that losses, savings, and efficiency are not unambiguous, having different meanings in different sectors. None of this is to argue that reducing household demand (and consequently reducing the costs of water treatment, pumping, investment in capacity expansion, etc.) is not a good idea, nor that improving the delivery of water to crops so that yields increase is not a benefit, or that improving the forests does not stabilize catchments. Rather it is to point out that in conditions of scarcity and competition, the hydrological context is critical, and simplistic statements about saving water, reducing losses, and increasing efficiency do not translate across sectors. Each sounds desirable, because the terms are value-laden, but within the overall basin or aquifer context, actual physical flows and the law of conservation of mass must be the basis of any sound analysis.

3. Closing the inter–sectoral divide: attempts to "unify" terminology

The difficulties and contradictions surrounding the measurement of water stocks and flows have led to a number of attempts to establish a water accounting terminology that can be uniformly applied across sectors without confusion. The history is long. Irrigation efficiency was the topic of research in the 1940s (ISRAELSEN 1950), while in the 1960s a U.S. Inter-Agency Task force on water allocation noted that interventions that improved irrigation efficiency should be evaluated very carefully before assuming that water would actual be saved. But in the decades that followed, the dominant approaches to water scarcity continued to be dominated by a discourse based on value-laden, terminology of savings, losses, and efficiency.

Several authors and agencies have, in recent years, set out to address these issues. Specifically in the agricultural sector, Jensen (1967; 1993) and Willardson et al. (1994) led the way in addressing the confusion around "efficiency." The International Water Management Institute

(MOLDEN 2007) and the International Commission on Irrigation and Drainage (ICID) (PERRY 2007) made broadly similar recommendations, the last after an extensive process of consultation across ICID's international membership. The Food and Agriculture Organization (FAO), through a variety of publications related to agriculture in general and irrigation in particular, has developed a wide (and particularly well documented) set of terms. Most recently, the United Nations, following a lengthy consultation process, has adopted a System of Environmental-Economic Accounting for Water (SEEAW), and associated International Recommendations for Water Statistics.

SEEAW has important strengths. It is multisectoral; it clearly distinguishes between consumptive and non-consumptive uses; it is hydrologically consistent with the law of conservation of mass; and it can be applied at various scales (sector, region, country, and basin). Its approach to water quality is pragmatic – first proposing that the physical accounts (of volumes and flows) can usefully be constructed independently of quality, while noting that water quality is an important issue. The difficulty with water quality accounting (as also acknowledged in the ICID approach) is that the significance of any particular form of pollution depends entirely on the proposed use. E-coli bacteria have no relevance to hydro-power or navigation, but are exceptionally important for human uses. Quality accounting, in the current SEEAW document, is thus something to be further considered "at a later date."

The nomenclature of SEEAW is not immediately transparent for most sectoral specialists, which is unsurprising as this is where

NOTES TO TABLE 2

The water supply sector illustrates the key elements of how SEEAW works. In Denmark, total water abstraction is 429 Mm³ of which 23 Mm³ are for "own use" and the rest for distribution to customers. The actual quantity of water supplied to customers (Item 4) is only 380 Mm³, because 47 Mm³ are lost through leakage to groundwater (Item 5.a.2) while consumption (Item 7) accounts for the balance of 2 Mm³ – less than 0.5 percent of total abstraction. By comparison, in agriculture, forests, and fisheries, total water use is 159 units, of which 76 units are consumed (48 percent of the total supply) while the household sector consumes only 4 percent of the total supplied (10 units out of 251).

Source: based on SEEAW Table 3.3

compromises must be made. Four points are critical:

- "The environment" is simply the source from which water is abstracted (rivers and aquifers), and the sink to which some or all of the abstracted water returns as surface runoff or infiltration.
- In SEEAW, "the environment" has no particular connotation of a natural system requiring protection from intervention.
- SEEAW distinguishes between water abstracted for "own use" and water abstracted for distribution to other users – thus allowing proper analysis of utilities that withdraw, treat, and distribute water to consumers, and collect, treat, and return sewerage to "the environment."
- The accounts distinguish between water flows from and to "the environment," and water flows "within the economy." Thus utilities abstract water from the environment and deliver the water to households (a transaction "within the economy"); the household then returns the water to a sewage treatment agency (again, "within the economy") which in turn treats the effluent and returns it to "the environment."

3.1 SEEAW flow accounts

The sample tabulation of national annual flow data included in the SEEAW report is shown below (Table 2). The data refer to Denmark – a country for which comprehensive data were available, though even here some estimation was required to complete the tables.

The water supply sector illustrates the key elements of how SEEAW works. In Denmark, total water abstraction is 429 Mm³ of which 23 Mm³ are for "own use" and the rest for distribution to customers. The actual quantity of water supplied to customers (Item 4) is only 380 Mm³, because 47 Mm³ are lost through leakage to groundwater (Item 5.a.2) while consumption (Item 7) accounts for the balance of 2 Mm³ – less

than 0.5 percent of total abstraction. By comparison, in agriculture, forests, and fisheries, total water use is 159 units, of which 76 units are consumed (48 percent of the total supply) while the household sector consumes only 4 percent of the total supplied (10 units out of 251).

3.2 SEEAW stock accounts

Imbalances between inflows and outflows over a given time period cause a change in *stocks*. Some such changes are easily observed: river flows (and rainfall) enter a reservoir, and are released for power generation, irrigation, or other uses. In high-rainfall years, the inflows will be high, so that at the end of the hydrological reporting period the reservoir will contain more water than at the beginning. Observation of the depth of water in the reservoir allows estimation of the opening stock, the closing stock, and thus the change in stock. Such information is of great importance to water managers who must plan in advance to protect supplies if severe shortages are anticipated, or to guard against downstream flooding if high inflows are expected while the reservoir is full.

Other water stocks are much less easy to measure or monitor. In the case of snowpacks it is very difficult to estimate opening and closing stocks, because they rest on rock formations whose precise topography is hidden from view, but it is possible to monitor trends over time that indicate whether the stock is increasing, decreasing, or stable. Similarly, aquifers are complex structures, with varying porosity and poorly documented linkages between shallow and deep components – so that translating changes in depth at sample locations into volumes is difficult, though the trend is a clear indicator of whether the aquifer is gaining or losing storage over time.

Table 3 presents SEEAW's reporting format for stocks.

This example already has some obvious "round number" estimates – indeed all the opening stock items are rounded to one or two

TABLE 3

Statement of stocks (Mm³)

	Surface water			Snow, ice, glaciers	Ground water	Soil water	Total
	Reservoirs	Lakes	Rivers				
1. Opening stocks	1,500	2,700	5,000		100,000	500	109,700
Increases in stocks							
2. Returns	300		53		315		669
3. Precipitation	124	246	50			23,015	23,435
4. Inflows	1,054	339	20,137		437		21,967
4.a From upstream territories			17,650				17,650
4.b From other resources in the territory	1,054	339	2,487		437		4,317
Decreases in stock							
5. Abstraction	280	20	141		476	50	967
6. Evaporation/actual evapotranspiration	80	215	54			21,125	21,474
7. Outflows							
7.a To downstream territories			9,430				9,430
7.b To the sea			10,000				10,000
8. Other							
9. Closing stocks	1,618	2,950	4,272		100,189	553	109,583

Source: based on SEEAW table 6.1

significant figures, while the changes in stock are expressed with great precision (up to five significant figures).

Soil water (sw) is of some interest, and was contentious during the process of formulating SEEAW (K. FRENKEN, PERSONAL COMMUNICATION, AUGUST 15, 2011.)[1] We note first that the reported *change* in stock over the reporting period (53 Mm³, closing stock-opening stock in Table 3) is 0.22 percent of annual flow through the soil, or the typical flow for one day. Heavy rain the day before, or after, the time of evaluation of this variable would substantially affect the actual value of stock, but the facilities to record such data at the national level do not exist.

Technically, sw is that quantity of water stored in the upper profile of the soil that is available for crop transpiration, or can evaporate directly. This apparently simple definition is, however, complicated by several factors.

First, the quantity that can be stored depends on the soil type and depth, so the potential for sw storage must be mapped, and then converted to an actual level depending on previous precipitation and/or irrigation events.

Second, a deep-rooted plant can obviously draw on more water than a shallow-rooted plant – so the estimate of sw obtained in the first step, above must be further adjusted for actual plant cover.

Third, whether sw actually becomes evaporation, transpiration, or something else depends on factors totally outside the control of managers – in particular, whether it rains "on top of"

---

1   Karen Franken is Co-ordinator of the AQUASTAT Program and a Senior Water Resources Management Officer with the FAO.

the existing sw. For any given combination of current sw, soil type, and plant cover, additional rainfall or irrigation will result in some combination of: (a) additional infiltration to the groundwater if the soil profile exceeds its water-holding capacity; (b) additional runoff if the profile becomes saturated or the rate of delivery of additional water exceeds the maximum rate of infiltration for the soil type/topography; (c) additional evaporation if the soil surface was not fully wet; and/or (d) additional transpiration if the crop was water-stressed prior to the arrival of extra water.

Viewed from this perspective, sw has the characteristics of a *contingent asset*: an asset whose value will be determined by events outside the control of the owner of the asset. A specific volume of sw will contribute to one or another of the above outflows depending on subsequent rainfall events. Converting this already uncertain scenario from a physical to a financial indicator adds the dimension that the ultimate value of plant transpiration from today's soil moisture depends on future supplies to ensure that the crop reaches maturity.

3.3 SEEAW accounts: an evaluation

The SEEAW approach is an effective way to summarize hydrological flow data in a consistent format. The framework is hydrologically sound – distinguishing between consumptive and non-consumptive uses, and respecting the law of conservation of mass.

The stock accounts are problematic – not because of conceptual limitations, but rather because key data are unlikely ever to be available.

One aspect of the SEEAW accounts as presented in the manual relates directly to the question of valuing natural wealth: the manual does not address the traditional construct of "the environment" (i.e., the largely unmanaged collection of ecosystems, plant and animal life, habitats, etc., that both enrich life for all and provide crucial services for human well-being).

This issue is easily remedied by a simple extension of SEEAW's reporting format that does not conflict with the principles on which SEEAW is formulated. Additional columns for areas of interest (rainfed agriculture, natural forests, rangelands, wetlands, etc.) are added to the table, and the relevant flows are reported. The SEEAW accounts already include "households," which have no ISIC classification but are essential to documenting the financial flows in the economy. Adding columns for the main actors in the water economy is similarly consistent with SEEAW's logic.

These comments and suggested amendments to the physical accounts proposed in the SEEAW manual do not yet tackle valuation of those elements of the "natural" economy, or indeed deriving value-of-water estimates (financial, economic, and social) from the relationship between water flows and financial flows in the economic sectors.

4. From physical water accounting to valuing water

At the beginning of this chapter, some of the problems and challenges involved in describing physical water use consistently across sectors were identified. Valuing water is also problematic both for "water-specific" reasons and for reasons that apply to the valuation of any input into economic processes. The "water-specific" reasons are outlined below.

The fundamental role of water to human life – we die of thirst in its absence – suggests a near infinite value for the first few liters per capita per day. Since plants require water to grow, our next fundamental need, for food, is also extremely valuable and typically several orders of magnitude greater in terms of volume: a kilogram of grain typically involves transpiration of a metric ton of water, or one thousand liters. Further economic activities (as clearly set out in SEEAW) also involve water use and/or consumption, and what we can learn about value from those accounts will be discussed below. First, though, we should note that adding more water to "the economy" rather quickly progresses from high value (as scarcity is alleviated), to no value (excess rainfall that drains away naturally), to negative value when floods occur. Thus the value of water cannot be disaggregated from time, location, quantity, and the precedent conditions: it may rain heavily in one part of the country, causing floods and negative value added, while a few hundred kilometers away an area in drought would have benefited greatly from the incremental water supply; heavy rains after a period of drought bring relief, while the same quantity of rain following earlier rainfall brings floods.

Additionally, while most components of natural wealth exist predominantly as stocks that change slowly over time (forests, mineral reserves, ecosystems, etc.), water, except in the polar icecaps, is predominantly a flow. A nation's water assets are predominantly the rainfall that supports natural vegetation, and the associated river flows that can, to some extent at least, be harnessed for economic exploitation. The exception to this is groundwater stored in aquifers. Depletion of the aquifer occurs when abstractions exceed recharge, which may be an occasional aberration, or a long-term imbalance. In some countries, aquifers deposited over millennia are (rather like a coal deposit) being continuously depleted.

While it may be possible to estimate the value that can be derived from the storage in an aquifer (one kilogram of grain per cubic meter stored, for example), assessing the value of rainfall is a far more complicated and uncertain process – continuous rainfall for 80 percent of the cropping season will have no value at all if followed by complete drought for the final 20 percent; excess rainfall will damage crops, and so on. And to add to this complexity, when there is a widespread drought (as in 2008, for example) the prices of grains and other agricultural commodities rise sharply so that the total value of production may not change significantly. One interpretation of that phenomenon might be that the unit value of water increased while the total value remained constant. An alternative view is that water is such a fundamental input into life that it cannot be evaluated "locally" without knowing what is happening everywhere else.

Turning now to the general difficulties of placing a value on one input into an economic activity, even the fullest and most accurate set of SEEAW accounts gives only the most superficial indicator of the value of water. If, for example, we know that an industry uses x units of water and produces y units of economic activity, we still do not know whether adding or subtracting a unit of water *would proportionately impact* on the economic outcome. If the use is predominantly non-consumptive, such as household use, where consumption is say 4 percent of water supplied, then the water could, with suitable treatment, be recycled indefinitely and "water use" as measured by abstractions from the environment would fall by 96 percent without loss of economic benefit, but at the cost of investment in on-site treatment. Similarly, industries can often recycle water, and the case of alternative technologies for cooling thermal power plants has already been discussed above. Different technologies have vastly different coefficients of water use and consumption for the same economic result.

In agriculture particularly, the productivity of water (and hence the estimate of "water wealth") implied by the ratio of economic output to water use depends substantially on other factors of production. The green revolution effectively doubled grain yields per unit of water consumed. Did the "water wealth" of countries that benefited from the green revolution double during that period? How can the incremental production over the green revolution period be allocated among research into high yielding varieties, technology, management, increased use of chemicals, and the water, soil, and sunshine that nature provided? Only for producers who are at the production frontier can we be sure that reduced supplies of one input will impact on the economic outcome, and even there the marginal productivity is not equal to the average productivity implied by the simple division of output by total input.

Finally, there is the problem of aggregation in space and time. Most countries, even small, temperate ones such as the U.K., have areas that have enough rainfall that agricultural production and ecosystem stability are rarely constrained by water (the southwest), and other areas where precipitation is frequently excessive (Wales), or in deficit (East Anglia). In such circumstances, analysis at the regional/annual level will identify whether there is a problem, and perhaps point to regional solutions. However, aggregating the average water supply to a national level will reduce the information available because the surplus from Wales will offset the scarcity in East Anglia. Such variations are far more extreme in large countries, such as India, which includes both the wettest location in the world and some of the driest. These issues are recognized in SEEAW:

> Regarding problems of *spatial* aggregation:
>
> 9.51. Water availability and demand, as well as water quality, can vary a great deal over time and space. It is difficult to address sustainability on a national level when sustainability of water use is determined on a local or regional basis.
>
> Source: SEEAW, p.152.

And regarding *temporal* aggregation:

> 9.60. A first possibility is to reduce the duration of the accounting period: in many countries, quarterly national accounts are already built. Quarterly water accounts may be useful in some countries; for example, seasonal water accounts for Spain would reveal higher pressure on water in summer compared to winter.
>
> Source: SEEAW, p.154.

An alternative source of information about the value of water is evidence from financial transactions involving water. The potential of markets and water pricing to provide incentives for better allocation of water, and indicators of its value have attracted substantial interest in recent years. The number of theoretical demonstrations of the potential benefits of

such mechanisms exceeds the examples "on the ground" by at least one order of magnitude, and more likely by two or three. Representative examples of the evidence from the field include groundwater markets (e.g., Eastern India); rising block tariffs (e.g., Israel); and the water rights trading system in the Murray-Darling basin in Australia.

The first of these – groundwater markets – while widely reported and studied, offer little information about the value of water, because in fact the market is in pumping services drawing from a common pool resource. As newer, bigger, deeper, more efficient wells are installed, the price of water tends to be driven down towards the costs of the most efficient pumper, while telling us nothing about what the price of water would be if constrained to the sustainable supply.

Rising block tariffs, which allow provision of a basic supply at a low unit price with successive increments being progressively more expensive, might offer more insights, but even where used effectively, such as in Israel, additional factors conspire to obscure the prospect of deriving a comprehensive valuation of the water resource (S. ARLOSOROFF,[2] PERSONAL COMMUNICATION, FEBRUARY 25, 2003).

- The allocation of water among sectors is determined by government decree based on recent hydrological data.
- A market-based system has been discussed, but resisted by politicians and farmers. State lawyers objected strongly against this, arguing mainly that you cannot trade with a commodity that does not belong to you, and to do so would undermine the basis of the water law and the public ownership of water.
- Within agriculture, the rising block tariff is basically set so as to encourage water demand at a particular level: the price per unit is below the likely benefits of use up to the target demand level, and

---

2 Saul Arlosoroff is the former Chair of the Israeli Water Commission. Interpretations are the responsibility of the author.

substantially higher than that price for supplies in excess of the target demand.

The information about the value of water that can be derived from these data is limited – all we know is that the marginal value of water to a sector whose total allocation has been administratively set is between the two prices at the target consumption level. We learn nothing about the average productivity of water and nothing about the prices that would have prevailed if trade between sectors had been allowed, or trade within the sector (which happens, but informally), or the average benefits derived from water use.

5. Application of SEEAW

SEEAW has been actively promoted through workshops and training programs for some years, but Australia is the only country for which detailed implementation plans and progress seem to be available. The process has been lengthy and detailed and has resulted in many reports, reviews, and studies. This brief summary tries only to capture key issues that have arisen during that process, to document the current implementation of SEEAW, and to summarize ongoing advances in preparing water accounts in Australia.

The initial step was to review data availability nationwide, and test the extent to which water accounts could be formulated on a standardized basis. This "discovery phase" reported the following:[3]

> [A]s part of the Water Accounting Project, information was sought on the availability of the data that, desirably, would be used to construct the water balances. It was found that for several items either no data or limited data existed. These items were:
> — Volume of water in soil moisture store (no data);
> — Volume of water in snowpack (no data);

> — Volume of water in river channels (data available in New South Wales).

> Although these items continue to be shown in the water balance it is not expected that any data could be shown against them. They remain in the water balance sheet as a reminder of their existence and that in some instances they should not be overlooked. In all water balances the data components have been listed even when data was not available to highlight data availability issues and reliability of the water balances....

> Key areas of water diversion and use that are generally excluded from accounting of water resources [include] forestry. The afforestation of catchments has the potential to reduce catchment runoff, to reduce recharge to groundwater, and to extract water directly from groundwater. Many of the states and territories are aware of this impact, but none has considered increased forestry development in their water resource planning frameworks.

> South Australia has introduced a system of "water effecting permits" to account for the impact of plantation forestry on groundwater recharge in the south east of the state.

These observations – on the difficulty of estimating soil moisture and other elements of the asset accounts – and the impacts of changes in land use on runoff – are noteworthy.

The Australian Bureau of Statistics had already in 2006 issued guidelines referencing the UN-SEEAW system,[4] which was to be applied to the reporting of the 2004–05 national water accounts.

However, the following statement from the introduction to Chapter 4 of the 2004–05 National Water Accounts for Australia[5] is apparently at variance with one critical element of the SEEAW approach – namely the distinction between consumptive and nonconsumptive uses:

---

3   Australian National Water Commission 2005

4   Australian Bureau of Statistics (2006), Proposed Methodology for Producing Regional Water Use Estimates, 2004–05, cat. no. 4610.0.55.001, 1–4

5   National Water Accounts for Australia (2004–05)

TABLE 4

Water accounts for Australia, 2004–05

1. Australian Capital Territory
2. New South Wales
3. Northern Territory
4. Queensland
5. South Australia
6. Tasmania
7. Victoria
8. Western Australia

	Water Consumption in 2004–05 (GL)								
	ACT[1]	NSW[2]	NT[3]	QLD[4]	SA[5]	TAS[6]	VIC[7]	WA[8]	Australia
Agriculture	1	4,133	47	2,916	1,020	258	3,281	535	12,191
Forestry and fishing	<1	11	<1	3	<1	4	8	25	52
Mining	<1	63	17	83	19	16	32	183	413
Manufacturing	<1	126	6	158	55	49	114	81	589
Elec and gas	–	76	1	81	3	<1	99	13	271
Water supply	5	631	8	426	71	20	793	128	2,083
Other	17	310	30	201	52	18	262	168	1,059
Household	31	573	31	493	144	69	405	362	2,108
Total	56	5,922	141	4,361	1365	434	4,993	1495	18,767
Total resource consumption %	256	45,369	55,784	112,905	4,321	47,056	21,332	49,094	336,117

This chapter examines the use of water within the agriculture industry in Australia. Water used by this industry includes stock drinking water and water applied through irrigation to crops and pastures.... Since the agriculture industry does not use water in-stream, or supply water to other users, total water use is equal to water consumption. (emphasis added)

Nevertheless, the accounts produced by Australia are the most comprehensive available application of the SEEAW approach. Table 4, assembles data from the 2004–05 accounts.

This table shows the wide variation across the country in the pattern and intensity of resource use. The table is entirely based on abstracted water, and thus masks the important contribution that rainfall makes to rainfed agriculture and the natural environment.

It also demonstrates the uncertain impact of aggregating regional accounts into a national account – which applies to many large countries like Australia – where transfers of water between regions are not economically feasible. While the national picture shows that only 6 percent of

the annual water resource is consumed, this figure masks variations from less than 1 percent of the available resource (Northern Territories) to 32 percent in South Australia, which is a severely water-stressed area, and where extensive government interventions to restore ecosystem health are underway.

Underlying these summary tables are many more detailed reports – agriculture broken down by crop; regions by basin; resources broken down into surface and groundwater; etc.

In many countries, rainfed agriculture is often a much more significant water user than irrigated agriculture; forestry may be larger still, and some countries have vast areas of rainfed land that provide the basic resource for tourism and recreational activities (for example, game parks in Africa and wilderness areas in the United States).

Efforts to translate these physical data into financial information are quite limited. Data from the Murray-Darling show returns from various crops varying by a factor of almost 10 between rice and vegetables – confirming the difficulty of placing a value on "water" even in a single sector when divorced from the associated risks, management requirements, input costs, perishability, etc.

6.   Conclusions

The terminology of the physical accounts presented by SEEAW is well defined, and allows a country to report annual flows of water in relation to economic sectors in a meaningful way. Such data can assist national planning and the formulation of approaches to scarcity and competition. Certainly, the availability of such analysis will improve inter-sectoral understanding of water issues.

In application, the SEEAW approach has proved difficult, even in a sophisticated and highly developed water economy such as Australia. Especially in the stock accounts, key data are not available – volume stored in ice-caps, volume in streams, and volume in soil moisture.

Since the SEEAW accounts are formulated on the basis of industrial sectors for which financial data are collected separately, it is relatively easy to link the accounts and provide first indications of the role of water in each sector and, by inference, the significance of water to the economy. Already at this stage, however, the interpretation can become problematic: the fact that an industry generates $x of value added and consumes $y units of water cannot be interpreted as indicating a value of $x/y per unit of water for a number of reasons:

- If water is plentiful for the industry in question, it may well be that usage could be curtailed significantly without additional investment or reduction in value added.
- Even where water is scarce, the relationship between the *marginal* value of water and the *average* value is uncertain.
- Financial prices, which are generally what we have available for this type of analysis, will often diverge from economic prices (which adjust financial prices for distortions caused by subsidies, quota restrictions and taxes), and even more from prices that reflect social issues and "externalities" such as damage to the environment.

Taken together, these issues suggest that we very rarely know the precise relationship between aggregate water availability and physical output; we know even less about the marginal relationship between water availability and economic output, and we typically know still less about the price that should properly be assigned to the non-financial impacts of water use and consumption.

Finally, it is clear that aggregating "water" over time and space will entirely mask the variability that so profoundly affects the value of water to a country.

While these points cast significant, perhaps insurmountable doubts on the possibility to construct a meaningful statement of a nation's water wealth, the first step of assembling data on the sources and uses of water within the economy can only help move important political debates forward as competition increases, and point to areas where interventions will be most appropriate.

To meet this need, and also to link water to the broader ecological and environmental status of a nation, SEEAW accounts should include the "unmanaged" natural landscape, including forests, rainfed rangelands, and wetlands, which are major features of the water economy and potential components of the financial economy; "managed" areas including rainfed agriculture feature in the financial economy as well as the water economy; and irrigated agriculture is a dominant feature of the water economy in many countries, as well as an important part of the financial economy.

REFERENCES

AUSTRALIAN BUREAU OF STATISTICS. (2006). Proposed methodology for producing regional water use estimates, 2004-05. Retrieved from http://www.abs.gov.au/ausstats/abs@.nsf/productsbytitle/7CD5E3C07FF9268FCA2571EC007C9CCD?OpenDocument

AUSTRALIAN BUREAU OF STATISTICS & NATIONAL WATER COMMISSION. (2006). *Water account Australia, 2004-05.* Retrieved from http://www.water.gov.au/publications/ABS_Water_Account_2004-05(complete_report).pdf

FALKENMARK, M. (1989). The massive water scarcity now threatening Africa - Why isn't it being addressed? *AMBIO, 18*, 112-118.

ISRAELSEN, O.W. (1950). *Irrigation principles and practices.* New York: John Wiley and Sons, Inc.

JENSEN, M.E. (1967). Evaluating irrigation efficiency. *Journal of Irrigation and Drainage Division, American Society of Civil Engineers, 93*, 83–98.

JENSEN, M.E. (1993). *Impacts of irrigation and drainage on the environment.* 5th N.D. Gulhati lecture. The Hague, Netherlands: ICID.

MOLDEN, D. (2007). *Water for food, water for life: A comprehensive assessment of water management in agriculture.* London: Earthscan.

NATIONAL WATER COMMISSION. (2007). *Water balance assessment method.* Retrieved from http://water.gov.au/WaterAvailability/Waterbalanceassessments/WaterBalanceAssessmentMethod/index.aspx?Menu=Level1_3_2_1

PERRY, C. (2007). Efficient irrigation; inefficient communication; flawed recommendations. *Irrigation and Drainage, 56*(4), 367–378.

SHIKLOMANOV, I. (1993). World fresh water resources. In P.H. Gleick (Ed.) *Water in crisis: A guide to the world's fresh water resources.* New York: Oxford University Press.

UNITED NATIONS (UN). (2007). *System for environmental-economic accounting for water (SEEAW).* Retrieved from http://unstats.un.org/unsd/statcom/doc07/SEEAW_SC2007.pdf

WILLARDSON, L.S., ALLEN, R.G. & FREDERIKSEN, H. (1994). *Eliminating irrigation efficiencies.* Retrieved from http://www.winrockwater.org/docs/Willardson.pdf

CHAPTER 11

Safeguarding the future of the wealth of nature

Sustainability, substitutability, measurement, thresholds, and aggregation issues in natural capital accounting for human well-being

Paul Ekins

KEY MESSAGES

Nature is very different from human, social, and manufactured capital stocks in that it predates humanity and it operates through its own complex laws and systems.

Most accounting for natural capital involves assigning monetary values to the flows of benefits from that capital. A monetary measure suggests that one capital stock can be substituted for another when trying to measure a country's total wealth in a multi-capital model. For natural capital, there is an emerging body of opinion that such substitutability is not complete, therefore accounting for it in this way could be seriously misleading.

The assumption of more or less complete substitutability between natural capital and other capital stocks is sometimes referred to as the "weak sustainability" assumption; while an assumption of limited substitutability is termed the "strong sustainability" assumption.

The assumption of strong sustainability in respect of certain important aspects of natural capital would seem more consistent with the scientific evidence. Starting with this assumption when trying to understand the interactions between different forms of capital allows substitutability to be considered to the extent appropriate. Starting with an assumption of complete substitutability (the weak sustainability perspective), and proceeding directly to monetary valuation, tends to obscure those situations where this assumption is not valid.

While consumption is important to well-being, it is also affected by a number of other important factors. The contribution of natural capital to well-being has not been widely recognized in the literature, but that has started to change in recent years as diverse contributions have been revealed through ecosystem assessments.

1. Introduction

This chapter reviews a number of actual or potentially problematic issues that have arisen in relation to wealth accounting, which can supplement or modify the overall picture of wealth accounting as described in this report, and that need to be taken into account in the practice of it.

All the issues explored here (as is true for wealth accounting as a whole) can be clearly related to, and in this chapter are based on, a four-capitals model of wealth creation. The model is described in Section 2, followed by definitions and discussions of human, social, and, in more length, natural capital – the three capitals usually given the least attention in wealth accounting because of the emphasis given to manufactured capital. As noted in earlier chapters, the concept of capital is well suited to framing a discussion of sustainability and sustainable development, and the four-capitals framework enables these subjects to be treated in an integrated way.

Most accounting for natural capital, including what is described in other chapters of this report, proceeds by assigning monetary values to the flows of benefits from that capital and thereby inferring the value of the natural capital stock. This assumes that, in a multi-capital model such as that presented here, there is complete substitutability between the capital stocks[1] that are being thus valued. For natural capital, there is now a considerable amount of literature giving reasons as to why such substitutability is incomplete, and therefore accounting for it by this method is also likely to be incomplete. Section 3 gives a brief overview of these reasons and discusses in the light of them the various methods by which natural capital

has been measured, and the advantages and disadvantages of these methods.

The concept of environmental sustainability has been developed largely to address issues involving what has been called "critical natural capital" (EKINS ET AL. 2003), when strong rather than weak sustainability seems a more appropriate starting assumption. This is the subject of Section 4, which starts by introducing the idea of environmental functions. Environmental sustainability is then defined as the maintenance of the minimum thresholds of natural capital that are required to sustain important environmental functions, and principles of environmental sustainability as well as sustainability standards, are articulated on this basis. This permits the definition of an indicator of environmental sustainability that shows the "gap" between current uses of the environment and the sustainability standard. The final part of this section describes the main, recently developed method of measuring the flows of resources through the economy with a view to identifying whether they are being used sustainably, and relates this to the concepts of resource efficiency and dematerialization, the achievement of which are important if sustainable resource use is to be achieved in a context of continuing economic growth.

If substitutability is one assumption at the heart of most natural capital accounting, another is that wealth is the stock that provides the flow of future consumption (the value of which then needs to be discounted to arrive at its present value). However, as shown in the four-capitals model, the purpose of wealth creation is not consumption *per se*, but the maintenance and increase of human welfare. There is now a considerable body of literature to show that there are many more influences on human welfare than material consumption. Section 5 briefly explores this literature, in which various terms for welfare (for example, well-being), tend to be used interchangeably. The literature surprisingly places very little emphasis on the influence of the environment on human well-being, despite the fact that it is intuitively obvious that environmental functions, or ecosystem

---

1   An assumption of substitutability between natural capital and other capital stocks is sometimes referred to as the "weak sustainability" assumption, while an assumption of limited substitutability is termed the "strong sustainability" assumption. This distinction is further explored below.

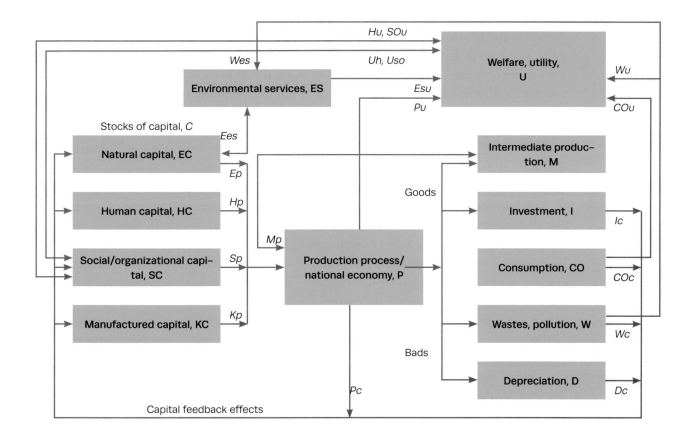

Stocks of capital, C

goods and services as they have also been called, are clearly crucial for both human survival and human welfare. This emerges clearly from the ecosystem assessments that have so far been carried out, and the section closes with estimates of some values delivered by ecosystem goods and services in the U.K. Section 6 concludes by briefly drawing together the various strands of the chapter.

2. The four–capitals model of wealth creation

In order to treat these issues adequately, it is necessary to be clear about the definition of wealth that is being employed and to locate the issues within a comprehensive theoretical framework that identifies the relationship between wealth and human welfare and shows how wealth can be created and destroyed. Such a framework was set out in Ekins (2000, P.53), and is illustrated here in Figure 1.

There is no space to elaborate the theory fully here, but Figure 1 suggests that wealth creation is the product of the joint application for productive purposes of different kinds of capital, where capital is a stock, or asset, that has the characteristic of producing a flow of income or some other benefit. The four-capitals model distinguishes between four different types of capital: manufactured (or physical) capital (e.g., buildings, built infrastructure); human capital (e.g., knowledge, skills, health); social capital (relationships and institutions); and natural (or environmental, ecological) capital.[2] The four capitals

FIGURE 1

A four–capitals model of wealth creation through a process of production

Note: In the flow descriptors, the upper case letters denote the source of the flow; lower case letters denote the destination. Those relating to the various capital stocks have the C omitted for simplicity.

Source: Ekins (2000), p.53.

---

2   It may be noted that in this formulation, financial capital is a form of social capital with the power to mobilize other forms of social capital and the other three capitals.

generally need to be combined in a production process in order to generate their benefits (this is least true of natural capital, which generates many benefits independently of humans).

Inclusive wealth accounting requires that the stocks of the four capitals, and changes in the stocks, be measured over time. This means that the forms of capital themselves need to be defined in terms of indicators that are subject to measurement. Indicators of manufactured capital, both monetary and non-monetary, are routinely used and need no further discussion here. Because most attention in the rest of this chapter will be paid to natural capital, human and social/organizational capital are discussed briefly first, and will then not be discussed further.

2.1 Human capital

Human capital is a well-established concept in economics, with a large literature (ZULA AND CHERMACK [2007] provide a brief overview), often associated with the name of Gary Becker (BECKER 1993). There has been considerable interest in the relationship between human capital and productivity (see, for example, STILES AND KULVISAECHANA [N.D., BUT AFTER 2003] for a literature review), and in how it might be measured.

In 2001, the OECD produced a publication specifically on human and social capital, in which it discusses measurement issues and the evidence that stocks of these types of capital are related to economic performance and personal well-being (as shown in Figure 1). Human capital was defined as "the knowledge, skills, competencies and attributes embodied in individuals that facilitate the creation of personal, social and economic well-being" (OECD 2001A, P.18).

The key function in the creation of human capital is learning. This may be learning within the family and early childcare settings, formal education and training, workplace training and informal learning at work, or in daily life. There is much evidence that learning is greatly influenced by "cultural capital" – "the collection of family-based resources such as parental education levels, social class, and family habits, norms and practices which influence academic success" (OECD 2001A, P.23). Major specific influences include work habits of the family; academic aspirations and expectations and the support and guidance to help achieve them; and a stimulating environment for thinking, imagination, and discussion of ideas and events.

Learning is negatively affected by social disadvantage, but can be positively affected by aspects of social capital to be discussed further in the next section: "The potential for school, community and family partnerships to support learning is especially relevant to families from disadvantaged areas and backgrounds where they can at a treble disadvantage of poor access to income and employment as well as social networks" (OECD 2001A, P.92). Putnam (2000) found that learning outcomes were strongly and significantly correlated with a composite measure of social capital comprised of the following indicators:

- Intensity of involvement in community and organizational life.
- Public engagement (e.g., voting).
- Community volunteering.
- Informal sociability (e.g., visiting friends).
- Reported levels of trust.

There is substantial evidence that human capital levels are positively related to wages, employment, and economic growth. Indeed, one would expect these to be the principal economic benefits to flow from human capital. There is also substantial evidence that human capital is positively related to non-economic social and personal well-being, which may in turn feed back into economic growth. In fact, "the indirect impact of education of economic growth via social benefits may be as large as the direct impacts" (OECD 2001A, P.33), where the social benefits include better health, lower crime, political and community participation, social cohesion, more volunteering and charitable giving, and better educated children.

There is a case for regarding health itself as an element of human capital, because it is clearly related positively to productivity. These other social benefits of education may be regarded as elements of social capital, to be discussed in the next section, so that human and social capital are obviously closely inter-related.

Human capital, the benefits flowing from it, or proxies for these may be measured in a number of different ways, all of them more or less problematic:

- Education spending, or other expenditures such as on research and development. These are input measures. There is no guarantee that they result in human capital and corresponding output benefits.
- Educational credentials (e.g., years of schooling or other education at various levels, or enrolment rates) and qualifications. These are output measures but there is no guarantee that these outputs are actually being put to productive use (i.e., they may be a stock of human capital in theory, but they may not be leading to a flow of benefits).
- Various measures of training and the higher skill levels to which they lead. It is likely that employment-based training, although an input measure, leads to its intended outputs and benefits because those qualified in this way often move into more advanced employment in a related field.
- Surveys of student achievements or adult skills, of which easily the most commonly investigated is various forms of literacy (e.g., prose, document, quantitative literacy).
- Health status.
- Indicators of motivation and productivity, such as absenteeism (for health or other reasons) from work.
- Employment, unemployment, and wages. All jobs presuppose a certain level of human capital, and the level of this should be related to wages.

- Indicators of disadvantage, leading to educational and learning disadvantages, or of the outcomes of measures and policies to reduce it.
- Levels of invention or entrepreneurship, as shown for example in numbers of patents or new business start-ups.

Some of these indicators are already measured in money terms, most obviously the first of the bullet points above, and it is therefore not surprising that this is the indicator most often used in accounts of human capital creation (e.g., WORLD BANK 2000). In chapter 2 of this report, human capital estimates are mainly driven by the years of total schooling of the population, which is subsequently weighted by its shadow price.[3] Efforts to improve the measurement of human capital have continued (see LE ET AL. [2005] for a review) and, because of the importance of human capital to business success, many business organizations have their own systems of indicators to measure their human capital, although there seems to be little standardization of these (ROBINSON ET AL. 2008). Further exploration of human capital measurement and related issues is beyond the scope of this chapter.

2.2 Social capital

In an early treatment of social capital Coleman (1988) defined it as aspects of social structure that facilitate action, in terms of the importance of obligations and expectations, information channels, and social norms to education and linked it explicitly to human capital, writing: "Social capital inheres in the structure of relations between actors and among actors." (COLEMAN 1988, P.S98). In essence, therefore, social capital derives from relationships. Distinctions in the literature include those between "bonding,"

---

3   In this study, the human capital shadow price is represented by the present value of the labor compensation received by workers over an entire working life.

"bridging," and "linking" relationships, where bonding relationships relate to the close ties mainly between kin and ethnic groups; bridging relationships to those that allow individuals to transcend those groups; while linking relationships connect individuals and groups to other groups and institutions. It should be noted that, unlike other forms of capital, the attitudes and activities generated by social capital may not necessarily be in the broad social interest: closely bonded groups may be exclusive; the activities of some closely bonded groups may be anti-social (e.g., criminal gangs); and other groups may pursue their own narrow interests at the expense of society at large (e.g., business associations or trade unions).

The definition of social capital in OECD (2001A, P.41) is "networks together with shared norms, values, and understandings that facilitate co-operation within or among groups." However, this seems to be an unnecessarily narrow definition, and social capital could also be taken to include various other social arrangements that are recognized by the OECD as being closely related to their preferred concept:

- Organizational capital, which "reflects the shared knowledge, teamwork and norms of behavior, and interaction within organisations" (OECD 2001A, P.19).
- Cultural capital, which are "the habits or cultural practices based on knowledge and demeanours learned through exposure to role models in the family and other environments" (OECD 2001A, P.23).
- Political, institutional, and legal arrangements, including the financial system.

Social capital is discussed in some detail in World Bank (1997, PP.77FF.). This publication notes that there are broadly three views on what forms social capital: informal and local horizontal associations; hierarchical organizations, such as firms and professional associations; and formalized national structures, such as government and its agencies and legal arrangements. These three descriptions of social capital share several common features:

- "All link the economic, social, and political spheres. They share the belief that social relationships affect economic outcomes and are affected by them.
- All focus on relationships among economic agents and how the formal or informal organization of those can improve the efficiency of economic activities.
- All imply that "desirable" social relationships and institutions have positive externalities. Because these cannot be appropriated by any one individual, each agent has a tendency to under-invest in social capital; hence, there is a role for public support of social capital building.
- All recognize the potential created by social relationships for improving development outcomes but also recognize the danger for negative effects. Which outcome prevails depends on the nature of the relationship (horizontal versus hierarchical) and the wider legal and political context" (WORLD BANK 1997, P.79).

Based on these definitions of social capital, the World Bank (1997, P.88) suggests a number of indicators of social capital. Table 1 compares the headings for social capital given in OECD (2001A) and World Bank (1997).

In the intervening years, publications have further explored the policy implications of the social capital concept (e.g., PRODUCTIVITY COMMISSION 2003); the health implications (e.g., LOCHNER ET AL. 2003); what kinds of social capital do most to increase productivity or other benefits (e.g., WELZEL ET AL. 2005); as well as taking forward the discussion about appropriate indicators (e.g., CAVAYE 2004). These issues are outside the scope of this paper, but are clearly relevant to any comprehensive articulation of the four-capitals framework.

As with human capital, inclusive wealth accounting should ideally seek to compute changes in quantities of social capital in monetary terms. For human capital, as already noted, education spending is often used. For social capital, the obvious difficulties of expressing relationships in monetary terms have so far ruled out this approach.

2.3 Environmental/natural capital

From Figure 1, a broad definition of natural capital might be everything in nature (biotic and abiotic) capable of contributing to human well-being, either through the production process or directly. As is discussed further below, because natural capital has featured regularly in various definitions of sustainability and sustainable development (see, for an early example, PEZZEY 1992, PP.55FF.), more attention has been paid to the concept as sustainable development has risen up the public policy agenda. In this context, considerable efforts have been invested in developing and making environmental indicators operational. For example, EUROSTAT produced a set of environmental indicators, based on a major expert consultation (EUROSTAT 2001A), while the European Environment Agency regularly publishes its "Environmental Signals" report (most recently EEA 2011).

The OECD's main source of environmentally relevant data is published as a compendium of indicators (OECD 2011).[4] It is structured according to a Pressure-State-Response (PSR) framework, where Pressures include both direct environmental pressures and the indirect pressure of the human activities producing the direct pressures; the States refer to various environmental conditions; and the Responses relate to societal intentions and actions in respect to the environmental conditions, and include general data. The compendium has been published roughly every two years since 1993 and is used as the indicator framework for the OECD's country environmental performance reviews. In 2001, 10 headline indicators were selected from this compendium (OECD 2001B), and the indicators were also selected or combined to form the environmental indicators of the OECD sustainable development indicator set (OECD 1998, 2001C).

TABLE 1

Headings for indicators of social capital

OECD (OECD, 2001a)	World Bank (World Bank, 1997)
Context indicators	Horizontal associations
Self-sufficiency	Civil and political society
Equity	Social integration
Health	Legal and governance aspects
Social cohesion	

The frameworks of environmental indicators produced by EUROSTAT and the OECD are listed in Table 2. There is substantial overlap, but also a few differences.

A relatively early attempt to define trends in the stock of capital through what were called *resource* indicators was made by the OECD (2001C, PP.69FF.). This was an early precursor for natural capital of the kind of inclusive wealth accounting approaches that have been developed since then and that are described in this report. The OECD indicators were:

- changes in air quality (changes in emissions of CO_2 or GHG, NO_x, and SO_x);
- changes in water resources (intensity of water use);
- changes in land and ecosystems (changes in land use);
- changes in biodiversity (protected areas);
- changes in use of energy resources (growth in consumption of energy resources);
- net changes in produced assets (change in value of the net [manufactured] capital stock);
- net changes in financial assets (current account balance to GDP ratio);
- technological change (multi-factor productivity growth rate);
- changes in the stock of human capital (changes in the proportion of the population with upper secondary/tertiary

---

4   In 2011, the compendium has different chapters in separate pdf files, with data in different chapters from different years, the latest being 2008.

TABLE 2

Structure of the environmental indicator sets of
EUROSTAT and OECD

EUROSTAT	OECD
Themes (pollution) Climate change Ozone depletion Air pollution Waste Water pollution Dispersion of toxic substances	**Pollution issues** Climate change Ozone layer depletion Air quality Waste Water quality
Themes and indicators (resource depletion) Water consumption Timber balance Urbanization of land Energy use Fishing pressure Loss of biodiversity	**Resource issues** Water resources Forest resources Land resources Energy resources Fish resources Biodiversity (and wildlife) Mineral resources
Mixed resource and pollution themes Marine environment and coastal zones Urban environmental problems	**Key sectors** Energy, transport, industry, agriculture **Other issues** Risks Environmental expenditure and taxes Multilateral environmental agreements

qualifications);

- investment in human capital (growth in expenditure on education); and
- depreciation of human capital (standardized unemployment rates).

OECD (2001C) also defines a number of *outcome* indicators, which are related more to the right hand side of Figure 1, from which they may contribute to human welfare (e.g., consumption) or feed back into the stocks of capital in a positive (e.g., health) or negative (e.g., waste generation) way. These indicators are:

- consumption (household final consumption expenditure per capita);
- sustainable consumption (waste generation intensities);
- income distribution (D9/D1 decile ratio/ Gini coefficient);
- health (life expectancy/disability-free life expectancy, environment-related health

expenditure);

- work status/employment (employment-to-population ratio); and
- education (enrolment rates).

3. Sustainability and sustainable development

Conceiving of wealth creation in terms of the interaction between different capital stocks allows the ideas of sustainability and sustainable development to be formulated in robust terms. Sustainability itself simply means that whatever is being considered has the capacity for continuance. As discussed in Ekins (2003), the literature on sustainable development has come to a broad consensus that sustainable development entails meeting human needs and increasing quality of life now and in the future, the multi-dimensional nature of which has led to sustainable development being regarded as having economic, social, and environmental "pillars," or dimensions.

With regard to the economic dimension (as is also true for the idea of manufactured capital), the sustainable development concept has contributed little that is new. Economists have long had guidelines as to whether economic growth and development should be regarded as sustainable. The rate of inflation, public sector net credit requirement, and balance of payments, among others, are all considered to be important indicators of economic sustainability.

The idea of social sustainability, in contrast, is both far less developed and seems much more intractable. It is true that social sustainability is affected by such conditions as poverty, inequality, unemployment, social exclusion, and the corruption or breakdown of social institutions. But the relationship between sustainability and these conditions is clearly very complex and quite different between different societies. It seems unlikely that a social sustainability threshold for unemployment or inequality, comparable for example to the target rate of inflation for economic sustainability, will be identified. What seems more important in this case, is to ensure that the direction of change is toward what is considered necessary for sustainability, rather than the attainment of some particular number.

Environmental sustainability is related to natural capital, which is the main concern of this chapter, and this concept is discussed and developed in some detail in Section 4. However, if sustainable development entails, at a minimum, sustaining the flows of benefits that give rise to human welfare and therefore the capital stock that produces the benefits, the issues that immediately arise are whether there is substitutability between capitals (in the literature, the difference between weak and strong sustainability); whether the flows from the capitals can be valued in monetary terms (especially problematic for natural capital) and, if so, how (valuation of the capital stocks depends on valuation of the flows from them); and the difference between the economic, social, and environmental dimensions of sustainability. These issues are explored briefly here (and in more detail in EKINS 2000), and lead naturally into a discussion as to how sustainable development and progress toward it, should be measured.

3.1 Weak and strong sustainability

It has been noted above that sustainable development is intended to deliver benefits across economic, social, and environmental dimensions of human life. The first point to be made about this combination of objectives is that their simultaneous achievement by an industrial economy across all major environmental dimensions would be unprecedented. In fact, if industrial production can be characterized as above as the judicious combination of four kinds of capital stock, then one of the main discernible aspects of this process in the history of industrialism is the systematic depletion of natural capital in favor of manufactured and human capital.

As illustrated in Figure 1, the purpose of production is to satisfy human needs and increase human welfare and quality of life. Sustainable production and, therefore, sustainable development require that the capital stocks from which the satisfaction of human needs and increased quality of life derive are maintained or increased over time.

This immediately raises the question as to whether it is the total stock of capital that must be maintained, with substitution allowed between various parts of it, or whether certain components of capital are non-substitutable, that is they contribute to welfare in a unique way that cannot be replicated by another capital component. With regard to natural capital, Turner (1993, PP.9–15) identifies four different kinds of sustainability, ranging from very weak (which assumes complete substitutability between this and other capital types) to very strong (which assumes no substitutability so that all natural capital must be conserved). Few would contend that all natural capital is substitutable, while very strong sustainability has been called "absurdly strong sustainability" (DALY 1995, P.49) in order to dismiss it from practical consideration. Turner's more interesting intermediate categories are:

- Weak environmental sustainability, which derives from a perception that welfare is not normally dependent on a specific form of capital and can be maintained by substituting manufactured for natural capital, though with exceptions.
- Strong environmental sustainability, which derives from a different perception that substitutability of manufactured for natural capital is seriously limited by such environmental characteristics as: irreversibility, uncertainty and the existence of "critical" components of natural capital, which make a unique contribution to welfare. An even greater importance is placed on natural capital by those who regard it in many instances as a complement to man-made capital (DALY 1992, PP.27FF.).

The point at issue is which perception most validly describes reality. Resolving this point should be an empirical rather than a theoretical or ideological matter. However, if weak sustainability is assumed *a priori*, it is impossible to show *ex post* whether the assumption was justified or not, for the following reason:

The assumption underlying weak sustainability is that there is no essential difference between different forms of capital, or between the kinds of welfare that they generate. This enables, theoretically at least, all types of capital and the services and welfare generated by them to be expressed in the same monetary unit. In practice, there may be insuperable difficulties in performing the necessary monetization and aggregation across the range of issues involved, but the theoretical position is clear and strenuous efforts are being made to make it operational. But the numbers that emerge from these efforts can only show if weak sustainability has been achieved, that is whether overall welfare has been maintained. They cannot shed any light on the question as to whether the assumption of commensurable and substitutable capitals was justified in the first place.

By keeping different kinds of capital distinct from each other, the strong sustainability assumption, in contrast, can examine each type's particular contribution to welfare. The examination may reveal that, in some cases, the welfare derived from one type of capital is fully commensurable with other welfare from production. It can be expressed in monetary form so that, in these cases, substitutability with other forms of capital exists, and the weak sustainability condition of a non-declining aggregate capital stock is sufficient to maintain welfare. In other cases, the outcome of the examination may be different. The important point is that starting from a strong sustainability assumption of non-substitutability in general, it is possible to shift to a weak sustainability position where that is shown to be appropriate. But starting from a weak sustainability assumption permits no such insights to enable exceptions to be identified. In terms of scientific methodology,

strong sustainability is therefore greatly preferred as the *a priori* position.

In respect to natural capital, there are other theoretical reasons for choosing the strong sustainability assumption, in addition to the practical reason of the sheer difficulty of carrying out the necessary weak sustainability calculations for complex environmental effects. Victor (1991, PP.210–211) notes that there is a recognition in economics going back to Marshall that manufactured capital is fundamentally different from environmental resources. The former is human-made and reproducible in the quantities desired, the latter is the "free gift of nature" and in many categories is in fixed or limited supply. The destruction of manufactured capital is very rarely irreversible (this would only occur if the human capital, or knowledge, that created the manufactured capital had also been lost), whereas irreversibility is common in the consumption of natural capital with such effects as species extinction, climate change, or even the combustion of fossil fuels. Moreover, to the extent that manufactured capital requires natural capital for its production, it can never be a complete substitute for resources.

Victor et al. (1998, P.206) identify the elements of natural capital that are essential for life as we know it as: water, air, minerals, energy, space, and genetic materials, to which might be added the stratospheric ozone layer and the relationships and interactions between these elements that sustain ecosystems and the biosphere. Some substitution of these essential elements by manufactured and human capital can be envisaged, but their wholesale substitutability as assumed by weak sustainability, appears improbable, certainly with present knowledge and technologies. In fact, if the process of industrialization is viewed as the application of human, social, and manufactured capital to natural capital to transform it into more human and manufactured capital, as suggested above, then it is possible to view current environmental problems as evidence that such substitutability is not complete. If our current development is unsustainable, it is because it is depleting some critical, non-substitutable components of the capital base on which it depends. This has important implications for how sustainable development, and progress toward it can and should be measured.

Summarizing this literature, Dietz and Neumayer (2007, p.619) list four reasons why the strong approach to sustainability may be preferred to the weak: risk and uncertainty; irreversibility; risk aversion; and the ethical non-substitutability of consumption for natural capital.

3.2 Measurement and indicators of sustainable development

Since the UN Conference on Environment and Development in 1992, which established the idea of sustainable development as an overarching policy objective, there has been an explosion of activity to develop sustainable development indicators (SDIs) in order to determine whether sustainable development is actually being achieved. Because the meaning of sustainable development was not particularly clear (and is still often the source of some confusion), this activity was characterized by much experimentation. Many indicator sets were put forward by different bodies at different levels (international, national, regional, local), and substantial efforts have since been invested in seeking to rationalize these into "core" sets that can be used for comparison and benchmarking, while the development of particular sets of indicators for specific purposes has continued to flourish.

There are two main approaches to constructing indicators of sustainable development: the framework approach which sets out a range of indicators intended the cover the main issues and concerns related to sustainable development; and the aggregation approach, which seeks to express development-related changes in a common unit (normally money), so that they can be aggregated. A limitation of the first approach is that unless all the indicators in the framework are moving in the same direction (i.e.,

all making development more or less sustainable), it is not possible to say whether, in total, sustainable development is being approached. In respect to the second approach, Kumar (2010) recently exposed the issues that arise with the economic valuation of the environment, while Foster (1997) explored many of the same issues more than 10 years earlier. While such valuation can be both meaningful and important, a major limitation is that it is often impossible, very difficult or very controversial to convert all changes of interest to money values, or any other common numeraire, and this limitation applies most strongly to precisely the largest environmental effects that are therefore of most policy interest. With the valuation approach, therefore, the change in respect of sustainable development may be expressed as a single number, but the number may lack credibility.

A third approach, confined to assessing environmental sustainability, involves establishing standards of environmental sustainability and calculating the "gap" between current environmental situations and the standards.

The first two of these approaches are now described briefly. The third is described in Section 4.

Frameworks of indicators for sustainable development

In 1996 the UNCSD published its first set of SDIs, comprising 134 economic, social, and environmental indicators (UN 1996). The indicators were structured in a matrix that related Driving Force, State, and Response indicators to the chapters in Agenda 21.[5] Because it felt that not all the indicators were relevant for the European Union, EUROSTAT carried out a study using a subset of 36 of these indicators, publishing the results of the study in 1997 (EUROSTAT 1997). UNCSD subsequently produced a "core" set of 59 SDIs based on its original set, and EUROSTAT (2001B) did another study involving 63 indicators,

---

5   Agenda 21 was the 'Plan of Action' that was agreed at the Rio Earth Summit in 1992

which related closely to the UNCSD core set and showed the very wide range of issues that sustainable development is considered to cover.

There are many other frameworks of SDIS. Internationally, one of the best known is that produced by the Organisation for Economic Co-operation and Development (OECD). The OECD was given a mandate to work on sustainable development in 1998. Pursuant to this its work has resulted in theoretical, methodological, and policy- and indicator-oriented publications (OECD 1998; 2000A,B; 2001C,D,E). The first publication in this field (OECD 1998) was largely environmentally focused, but this was followed by a conference on sustainable development indicators in 1999, the proceedings of which were published in 2000 (OECD 2000A). This contained a set of "possible core sustainable development indicators," a number of country case studies on different aspects of sustainable development indicators, and sectoral/environment indicators for the major environmentally significant sectors. It also contained a new set of social indicators, with context indicators and structured according to the themes: promoting autonomy (or self-sufficiency), equity, healthy living (or just health), and social cohesion. Within the themes the indicators were grouped according to social status and societal response (similar to the Pressure-State-Response framework it had used for environmental indicators).

Two other indicator frameworks should also be described:

- Those related to the EU Sustainable Development Strategy, adopted in 2006 and reviewed in 2009,[6] and Sixth Environmental Action Programme (6EAP), which was adopted to run for 10 years from 2002.[7] The priorities of the former were:
  — Combating poverty and social exclusion
  — Dealing with the economic and social implications of an ageing society
  — Climate change and the use of clean energy
  — Addressing threats to public health in relation to hazardous chemicals and food safety
  — Managing natural resources more responsibly
  — Improving the transport system and land-use management

  The main themes of the 6EAP are:
  — Climate change
  — Nature and biodiversity
  — Environment and human health
  — Waste and resources

  In December 2001 the EU Council of Ministers agreed a set of seven headline indicators to measure progress in relation to the 6EAP and the last four of the priorities of the EU Sustainable Development Strategy, and an "open list" of a further 33 indicators.

- The indicators related to the U.K. Sustainable Development Strategy, which were published as DETR (1999B). The framework contained 152 indicators, of which 15 were identified as Headline indicators. Regional and local versions of the indicators were produced (DETR 2000A,B) for use at the relevant levels.

Aggregations of indicators for sustainable development

An advantage of the framework approach to indicators of sustainable development is that each of the many aspects of sustainable development can be specifically reported on in its own terms, and trends for the separate aspects can be identified. However, a disadvantage is that without combining the indicators in some way, it is not possible to draw any overall conclusions about progress towards sustainable development unless all the indicators happen to be moving in the same direction in relation to that progress. This is most unlikely to be the case.

6   See http://ec.europa.eu/environment/eussd/

7   EC, 2001, also see http://ec.europa.eu/environment/newprg/

A number of methods have been developed for the aggregation of indicators so that overall impacts can be assessed:

Aggregation into environmental themes

This was the approach underlying the Netherlands National Environmental Policy Plan process. It is described in Adriaanse (1993).

Aggregation across environmental themes

One method of doing this is to weight the different themes according to perceptions of environmental performance. An example of this method is the Ecopoints system developed by BRE (BRE 2008). Another method depends on the setting of sustainability standards for the themes, and then aggregating them according to the distance from the standard. An example of this approach based on the concept of the "sustainability gap" is given in Section 4.

Aggregating across environmental and other themes

This can be implemented by using multi-criteria analysis, or relating the themes to some concept such as quality of life or human development. The annual United Nations Development Programme's Human Development Index is an example of this approach.

An innovative application of this method was implemented by the Consultative Group on Sustainable Development Indicators (CGSDI 2007), which was established in 1996 and is an Internet-based working group drawing members from many different institutions and countries. Their Dashboard of Sustainability is not a specific selection of indicators as such, but a way of presenting sustainability indicators in an aggregated form, with the aim of providing an informative and easily grasped and communicated overview of the complex relationships among the social, environmental, and economic dimensions of sustainable development issues. Indicators from the three sustainability dimensions form the basis for aggregated social, environmental, and economic indices, which are then further aggregated into one "policy

performance index" and presented as a pie chart organized in three concentric circles. The outer circle contains the actual indicators, the next level circle contains the three sub-indices, and the inner circle contains the overall policy performance index. Clearly, the Index is only as good as the indicators used for it and the proponents of this methodology stress the continued need for improved and broadened indicators. However, the methodology is being quite widely used at the local and regional as well as the national level.

Another use of indices to measures progress towards environmental sustainability is the calculation of the "sustainability gap," as described in the next section.

Expressing the different environmental impacts in monetary form

Starting from an assumption of weak sustainability, and using techniques of environmental valuation, environmental indicators can be expressed in monetary form and, once expressed in this form, they can be added them up according to some theoretical position. Some calculations are based on economic welfare theory (see NORDHAUS AND TOBIN [1972] for an early example), and these have been developed into proposals for the calculation of a Green GDP (see EKINS [2001] for a discussion of the theoretical problems associated with this). The Index of Sustainable Economic Welfare (ISEW) (first proposed by DALY AND COBB [1989]) starts from consumer expenditure and then adds various social or environmental impacts (which can be positive or negative) to arrive at a supposedly more realistic assessment of changes in human welfare than represented by changes in GDP. ISEW has been calculated for a number of countries (see POSNER AND COSTANZA [2011, P.1973] for a list of studies), while the Friends of the Earth website called Measuring Progress enables people to calculate their own ISEW.[8] ISEW was further developed into the Genuine Progress Indicator

---

8 See http://www.foe.co.uk/community/tools/isew/

(GPI),[9] which has been calculated for a number of countries, U.S. states, and other sub-national entities (again, see POSNER AND COSTANZA [2011] for a list). All the methods based on giving monetary values to different impacts essentially take the weak sustainability approach in the terms discussed earlier, assuming that the different aspects of sustainable development, and the different forms of welfare associated with them, are commensurable and can therefore be expressed in the same numeraire. As was noted earlier, the implementation of this assumption does not permit any subsequent attempt to assess whether it was justified, except in terms of the plausibility of the results and conclusions to which it leads.

The situation is well-illustrated by the World Bank's genuine savings indicator (WORLD BANK 2000), which is one of the best known methods to express different aspects of sustainable development in monetary terms. The indicator is explicitly based on a capitals methodology such as that described above. It is computed from the figure for net domestic savings (assumed to comprise net additions to, or investment in, physical capital), plus education expenditures (assumed to comprise net additions to, or investment in, human capital minus depletion of energy, mineral, and forest resources, and damages from CO_2 emissions (assumed to comprise net loss of natural capital). All the loss of natural capital has been computed in money terms, to enable the relevant calculation to be made. In addition to assuming weak sustainability, such an approach assumes that all education expenditures are converted into productive human capital, which may not be the case, and covers only a relatively small range of environmental issues compared to those assessed in frameworks of environmental indicators such as those presented above. Moreover, no attempt in this publication is made to incorporate changes in social capital in this indicator. More recent work by the World Bank (2006) incorporates a number

9 ee for some background to the GPI http://en.wikipedia.org/wiki/Genuine_progress_indicator

of changes to the genuine savings calculations, while preserving its essential methodology. For example, intangible (human and social capital) is now estimated through regression analysis of a residual once other aspects of wealth (natural, and produced ["manufactured" in Figure 1 above] capital) have been accounted for. A functioning justice system emerges as making a particularly important contribution to wealth creation (P.XVIII).

According to the calculations of genuine savings in World Bank (2000, TABLE A1, P.10), all OECD countries and the great majority of developing countries have positive genuine savings. This picture is broadly confirmed in the follow up genuine savings calculations by the World Bank (2006, P.41), with in addition the East Asian countries showing strongly positive genuine savings rates and Latin America and the Caribbean also showing positive rates (except for a brief period in the 1980s). Only North Africa and the Middle East emerges as a region with consistently negative genuine savings rates "reflecting high dependence on petroleum extraction," with the extent of this result being of course highly dependent on the oil price (the higher the price, the higher the calculated cost of oil depletion to be subtracted from other savings categories).

While a negative genuine savings rate is a clear sign of unsustainability, World Bank (2006) advocates caution in the interpretation of a positive genuine savings rate (P.38). This is because a number of important environmental issues are not included in the calculations of natural capital, because of a lack of data. Notwithstanding this, if the genuine savings rate truly is "a sustainability indicator," as both World Bank 2000 (P.2) and World Bank 2006 (P.36) appear to claim, this would seem to indicate that most countries, and all OECD countries, are sustainable. If this is true, then the issue of sustainability is much less important than often seems to be supposed in policy-making (it is not clear, for example, why the EU needs a "sustainable development strategy," if all EU countries are already sustainable, as the genuine savings indicator in this publication suggests). This appears to put in question either the weak sustainability assumption on which the indicator is based, or the methodology by which it has been computed.

As noted earlier, the indicator itself cannot help to address these questions, although World Bank (2006) does seek to address the issue at the heart of the weak/strong sustainability debate outlined earlier: the substitutability between natural and other kinds of capital. In Chapter 8 it uses a constant elasticity of substitution (CES) production to estimate the elasticities of substitutions between land, labor, and capital. It is encouraging to find that these appear to be quite high, suggesting that other capitals can indeed substitute for natural capital, at least in some cases. However, it also acknowledges that this is preliminary work which omits many important environmental functions so that the results are by no means definitive.

One other fairly strong conclusion from World Bank (2006) is also questionable from a strong sustainability perspective, namely: "The level of natural wealth per capita actually rises with income. This contradicts the common assumption, that development necessarily entails the depletion of the environment and natural resources" (P.32). But the level of natural wealth is the product of the quantity of natural wealth and its value. If its value increases at a faster rate than its quantity declines, then its level will increase even as the physical quantity declines (which is what is normally meant by the word "depletion"). Of course, if the natural wealth can be completely substituted by other wealth (as is assumed under weak sustainability and the very act of valuation), then depletion of it may not matter, but that is not the same as saying that depletion has not taken place.

Those who wish to start from a strong sustainability approach will therefore wish to go beyond the genuine savings indicator and assess sustainability separately across the different capitals to see whether the broad sustainability conclusions of the genuine saving indicator are justified. The next section describes

such an approach in respect of environmental sustainability.

There is also one other area in which World Bank (2006) seems to tell an incomplete story, in its treatment of wealth, welfare and consumption. Wealth is presented as "the present value of future consumption" (P.XIV), while under certain conditions "wealth per capita is the correct measure of social welfare" (P.17). This means that "current net saving should equal the change in future well-being, specifically the present value of future changes in consumption" (P.XVII). This is standard economic practice, with a detailed theoretical justification given in Box 1.1. (PP.15–17), but it is at variance with the increasing literature on well-being that identifies many factors apart from consumption that are important to this condition. Outlining a different perspective on human welfare and well-being is the purpose of Section 5.

Finally, it is clear that the methodology of World Bank (2006) is not the last word on comprehensive wealth accounting. Arrow et al. (2010), building on the theoretical foundations of Arrow et al. (2003), significantly changes several aspects of the methodology, in the calculation of comprehensive wealth and of several components of comprehensive investment (see P.14). They also extend the methodology to account for population growth, technological change, different aspects of human capital (including health) and environmental quality. However, the approach remains rooted in weak sustainability. In empirical analysis of the U.S., China, India, Brazil, and Venezuela, all the countries except the U.S. showed net natural capital depletion. But only with Venezuela was this not offset by investment in other kinds of capital (in China, in reproducible [manufactured] capital; in the other countries human capital). Only Venezuela therefore clearly emerges as "unsustainable" by this metric. Chapter 3, which relies methodologically on Arrow et al. (2010) reports a decrease of natural capital for 17 out of 20

FIGURE 2

The relationship between
environmental functions
and human benefits

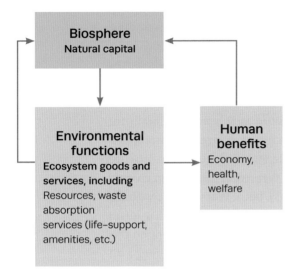

4. Environmental sustainability

4.1 Understanding environmental sustain–ability

As noted at the beginning of the previous section, sustainability itself simply means that whatever is being considered has the capacity for continuance. Its interpretation when applied to the environment must define what needs to be sustained for environmental sustainability to be achieved. In line with the overall capitals approach taken here, what needs to be sustained from the environment conceived as natural capital is the flow of benefits that humans derive from it.

The key contribution of the environment (in Figure 2 shown in total as the biosphere, or just natural capital) to the human economy, and to human life in general, can be envisaged to take place through the operation of a wide range of "environmental functions." This concept was first employed in economic analysis by Hueting, who defined environmental functions as "possible uses" of the environment (HUETING 1980, P.95). De Groot has subsequently defined them as "the capacity of natural processes and components to provide goods and services that satisfy human needs" (DE GROOT 1992, P.7). Linking with the discussion of capital above, these "natural processes and components" can in turn be identified as the flows from and stocks of natural capital. The flows may also be called ecosystem goods and services, some of which flow into the production process, and others of which contribute directly to human welfare, as shown in Figure 1.

As shown in Figure 2, the functions may be seen as being of three broad kinds: the provision of resources, the absorption and neutralization of wastes, and the generation of services ranging from life-support services (such as the maintenance of a stable climate) to amenity and recreation services (see PEARCE AND TURNER [1990, PP.35FF.] for more detail on this categorization). These three sets of functions collectively both maintain the biosphere itself (the positive

countries[10] studied (the three exceptions are Japan, France, and Kenya). Nonetheless, when looking at the different capital forms together, it is only Russia that has a decrease in inclusive wealth. It is also worth remarking that another five countries go into negative growth rates in wealth when changes are measured at a per capita level.

Those who feel that such a result fails to reflect the evidence from environmental science of great and increasingly threatening environmental dislocation will be inclined to turn to a stronger notion of sustainability for conceptual underpinning and associated indicators. This is the subject of the next section.

---

10 Australia, Brazil, Canada, Chile, China, Colombia, Ecuador, France, Germany, India, Japan, Kenya, Nigeria, Norway, Russian Federation, Saudi Arabia, South Africa, United Kingdom, United States of America, and Venezuela.

feedback on the left of the diagram), and contribute to the human economy, human health, and human welfare. However, the economy's use of the environment can impact negatively on the biosphere, which can in turn impair its ability to perform its environmental functions.

In terms of Figure 2, environmental sustainability requires the maintenance of important environmental functions and the natural capital which generates them, where important environmental functions may be considered to be those that are not substitutable, those whose loss is irreversible and is likely to lead to "immoderate" losses (i.e., those considerably greater than the costs of maintaining the functions), and those that are crucial for the maintenance of health, for the avoidance of substantial threats (such as climate stability), and for economic sustainability.

The interactions in Figure 2 also draw attention to a further distinction between environmental functions that needs to be emphasized, a distinction between "functions for" and "functions of" (EKINS ET AL. 2003). The "functions for" are those environmental functions that provide direct benefits for humans. These are the functions which are generally most easily perceived and appreciated, and towards the maintenance of which most environmental policy is directed.

The "functions of" the environment are those which maintain the basic integrity of natural systems in general and ecosystems in particular (shown in Figure 2 as the positive feedback to the biosphere). These functions are not easily perceived, and scientific knowledge about them is still uncertain and incomplete. What may be said with certainty, however, is that whether science understands these functions or not, and whether people value or are ignorant about them or not, the continued operation of the "functions of" the environment is a pre-requisite for the continued performance of many of the "functions for" humans. Looked at in isolation, these "functions of" the environment may appear useless in human terms, and therefore dispensable. Considered as part of a complex natural system, these functions may be essential for the continued operation of other functions of much more obvious importance to humans. The danger is that the isolated view, or scientific ignorance about the natural complexity, may result in "functions of" being sacrificed for economic or social benefits, without appreciation of the wider implications. It is these "functions of" the environment that present some of the greatest challenges for valuation, because there is no discrete flow of benefits to humans that can be identified from them.

The situation is made more complex still by the fact that there is clearly an impact from the performance of the "functions for," especially when they are enhanced by human intervention, on the "functions of" (shown in Figure 2 by the negative feedback to the biosphere). As an example, increases in agricultural productivity, perhaps through intensification, may have serious negative effects on the functions of ecosystems, as may the disposal of wastes above ecosystems' critical loads. Scientific uncertainty about these effects, and about thresholds of resilience for the "functions of," argues for caution over activities which may threaten them.

Thus, environmental sustainability in this characterization entails the maintenance of the environmental functions at such a level that they will be able both to sustain their contribution to human benefits (the economy, health. and welfare) and to maintain the biosphere from which they derive. The requisite level across different environmental functions may be estimated using both environmental science and social preferences for environmental quality. The environmental dimension of sustainability is therefore different from both the economic and social dimensions, in that it is possible to articulate principles of sustainability, and thence to derive thresholds and standards for environmental sustainability, as discussed below, according to which it is possible to distinguish between sustainable and unsustainable use of the environment and the functions which it performs for people.

4.2 Principles of environmental sustainability

Considerations of environmental sustainability must start from the recognition of the need for the sustainable use of resources and ecosystems, and be rooted in basic laws of physical science, which hold that indefinite physical expansion of the human economy (in terms of its use of materials and resources) on a finite planet is impossible; and that all use of non-solar forms of energy creates disorder, and potential disruption, in the natural world. The laws of thermodynamics mean that, at a certain physical scale, further physical growth becomes uneconomic (in the sense that the marginal environmental costs of this growth exceed the marginal benefits of the increased production), and there is now substantial evidence that, except from a very short-term perspective (involving high discount rates), there is little doubt that this scale has now been exceeded in respect of certain environmental effects. Rockström et al. (2009) characterize acceptable human impacts on the environment across different issues, taking risks into account, as "the safe operating space for humanity,"[11] and their work suggests, as shown in Figure 3, that human activities are already outside this space in respect of biodiversity loss, climate change, and the nitrogen cycle, with the phosphorus cycle also fast approaching the limit.

In the terms set out earlier, environmental sustainability requires that important environmental functions are sustained, which in turn requires that the capital stock which produces these functions, sometimes called "critical natural capital" (CNC) (EKINS ET AL. 2003), should also be maintained, although it may well not be possible to identify CNC as particular elements of natural capital. The complexity of natural systems is such that environmental functions

may be enabled or performed by processes resulting from the interactions between elements of natural capital as much as from the elements themselves. These interactions derive from certain characteristics of the natural capital stock, and it is these characteristics that need to be safeguarded if the functions are to be maintained. Thus it is important always to consider functions in relation to the interacting characteristics of natural capital as well as to the natural capital itself.

The major factor in the operationalization of this definition of environmental sustainability is the process for identifying environmental functions as "important." The conventional economic approach to such a process is to assign a monetary value to the benefit accruing from the function, which should then be maintained unless a larger monetary value would accrue from an activity which resulted in its necessary destruction. It may also be noted that the consistent application of even this conventional economic approach would result in far less environmental degradation than at present, because so much environmental damage is still given no value at all.

However, given the problems entailed in computing monetary valuations for complex environmental functions, as briefly mentioned above, it seems preferable instead to define the importance of environmental functions in more fundamental ways. De Groot et al. (2003) put forward the following criteria:

- *Maintenance of human health:* functions should be maintained at a level to avoid negative effects on human health. These effects may be physical or psychological, resulting from the loss of environmental quality or amenity.
- *Avoidance of threat:* functions should be maintained if there is any possibility that their loss would entail unpredictably large costs. This criterion is even stronger if there is any risk that the loss of the function would be irreversible. It is most obviously applicable to considerations of climate stability, biodiversity and the

---

11   The concept is very similar to the concept of 'safe minimum standards' related to resource conservation over 50 years ago by Ciriacy–Wantrup (1952), and significantly developed since. See Ekins (2000) for a discussion.

maintenance of ecosystem integrity.

- *Economic sustainability:* functions that provide resources for, or services to, economic activities should be used on a sustainable basis (i.e., one that can be projected to continue into the long-term future).

Brand (2009, P.608) identifies six "domains" that emerge from the literature as relevant to the categorization of critical natural capital: socio-cultural; ecological; sustainability; ethical; economic; and human survival. Clearly in the attribution of criticality to particular manifestations of natural capital, all the domains will need to be considered. Brand (2009, P.609) also develops a concept of ecological resilience to add to De Groot et al. (2003)'s three criteria above.

On the basis of these broad criteria, which establish in general terms whether an environmental function should be considered important, a number of principles of environmental sustainability may be derived, related to current environmental issues of concern. The principles spring from the perception that, in order for the environment to be able to continue to perform its functions, the impacts of human activities on it must be limited in some ways:

1. At the global level it would seem important not to disrupt the climate, or
2. deplete the ozone layer or
3. significantly reduce biodiversity.
4. For pollution generally, emissions should not exceed levels at which they cause damage to human health, or the critical loads of receiving ecosystems.
5. Renewable resources should be renewed,

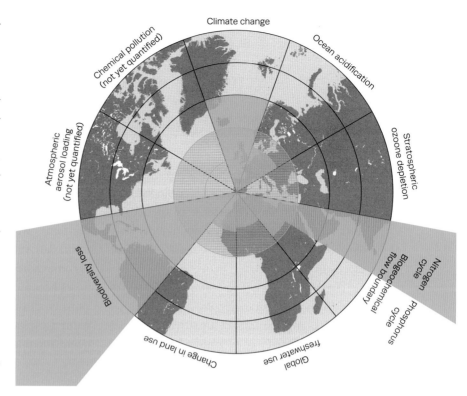

FIGURE 3

A safe operating space for humanity

Source: Rockström et al. 2009

and the development of renewable substitutes should accompany the depletion of non-renewable resources.

6. Given the great uncertainty attached to many environmental impacts, and the possibility that some of these may give rise to very large costs, the Precautionary Principle should also be used as a sustainability principle, to limit environmental risks.
7. Precious landscapes and elements of the human-made environment should be preserved.

The first five of the above principles are fairly straightforward conceptually. For one, two, and four, relating to pollution, quantitative standards describing the environmental states (e.g., concentrations of pollutants) and pressures (e.g., emissions of pollutants) that are consistent with them may be readily derived (though not without a broad range of uncertainty in some cases) from environmental science. For resources, it is depletion (or non-renewal) of renewable resources that is currently giving most cause for concern. For single, discrete resources, the idea of depletion may be unproblematic to apply, but this will not be the case in respect of biodiversity, especially related to more complex ecosystems, and there are many aspects of biodiversity which cannot readily be reduced to the idea of "resources" at all. Identifying sustainability standards for biodiversity is likely, therefore, to be especially challenging.

The sixth principle, a statement of adherence to the Precautionary Principle, acknowledges that an environmentally sustainable society will choose to forgo even quite large benefits rather than run even a very small risk of incurring potentially catastrophic costs in the future. Again, environmental science is the best source of insight into the existence of such risks, and the standards of environmental quality which are necessary to avoid them.

The seventh principle is rooted entirely in ethical, aesthetic and socio-cultural considerations, which are present to some extent too in the other principles, but which are outside the realm of environmental science. It is not therefore possible to specify in general terms which landscapes should, or should not, be conserved. On the other hand, it is also not possible to conceive, in the contemporary context, of an environmentally sustainable society that makes no attempt to identify outstandingly valuable landscapes (however value may be construed in these contexts), or to conserve the ones that had been identified. Most countries have now enacted landscape designations of various kinds, internationally, nationally, and at sub-national levels. Standards under this principle would assess the extent of these designations, and the rigor with which they were observed.

The ideas of critical natural capital and strong sustainability are intended to avoid the routine trade-offs associated with weak sustainability, yet even within this concept trade-offs need to be confronted and choices made. Pearson et al. (2012), building explicitly on Brand (2009) and Spash et al. (2009), distinguish between the utilitarian (based on consequentialist reasoning) and "protected" (based on deontological reasoning) motivations that may be differently reflected in the principles. They usefully differentiate between tragic decisions, which involve trade-offs between protected values; taboo decisions, which involves a trade-off between protected and utilitarian values; and routine decisions, where the trade-off only involves utilitarian values. As environmental damages become more serious, and environmental prognoses become more threatening, trade-off decisions of all three kinds, even related to critical natural capital, are likely to become more frequent and unavoidable. [12]

4.3   The sustainability gap

Once the standards according to these principles and criteria have been defined, then the difference between these standards and the environmental state or pressure indicator showing the current situation may be described as the "sustainability gap" (SGAP), in physical terms, between the current and a sustainable situation (EKINS AND SIMON 1999). SGAP indicates the degree of consumption of natural capital, either in the past or present, which is in excess of what is required for environmental sustainability. For the state indicators, the gap indicates the extent to which natural resource stocks are too low, or pollution stocks are too high. For pressure indicators, the gap indicates the extent to which the flows of energy and materials which contribute to environmental depletion and degradation are too high. SGAP indicates in physical terms the extent to which economic activity is resulting

---

12   A simple example related to energy is the dispute between those who advocate low-carbon energy sources – such as wind turbines or nuclear power – to protect climate stability, and those who reject these energy sources because of their landscape impacts or generation of radioactive wastes.

TABLE 3

Various sustainability measures for the Netherlands

	Environmental stress (ES)		Sustainability standard (SS)	Sustainability gap (SGAP) (ES–SS)		Normalized SGAP (100*SGAP/SS), EPeq		Years to sustainability
	1980	1991		1980	1991	1980	1991	
Climate change, Ceq	286	239	10	276	229	2760 1001	2290 83	54
Ozone depletion, Oeq	20000	8721	0	20000	8721	na	na	8.5
Acidification, Aeq	6700	4100	400	6300	3700	1575 100	925 59	16
Eutrophication, Eeq	302	273	86	216	187	251 100	217 86	71
Dispersion, Deq	251	222	12	239	210	1992 100	1750 88	80
Waste disposal, Weq	15.3	14.1	3	12.3	11.1	410 100	370 90	102
Disturbance, Neq	46	57	9	37	48	411 100	533 130	Never
TOTAL	na	na	na	na	na	7399 100	6085 82	51

Source: Ekins and Simon 2001, Table 4, p.14

1. The second entry in this column has converted the NSGAP to index numbers, with 1980=100.

in unsustainable impacts on important environmental functions.

The SGAP idea can be developed further to give an indication of the time that would be taken, on present trends, to reach the standards of environmental sustainability. Thus Ekins and Simon (2001, PP.11FF.) use calculations of various stresses across seven environmental themes in the Netherlands for two years, 1980 and 1991, measured in various "theme equivalent" units (taken from ADRIAANSE 1993), to derive both SGAPs and Years-to-Sustainability indicators for each theme.

Columns 1 and 2 of Table 3 show Adriaanse's environmental stresses, and Column 3 gives his sustainability standards. The next two columns calculate the SGAP for each theme for each year, where SGAP is the distance in theme equivalent units between current conditions and the sustainability standard. Thus in the SGAP columns the standard is subtracted from the stress for each year. The next two columns normalize

this SGAP (NSGAP) as shown. It can be seen that the NSGAP for climate change, for example, was reduced by 17 percent from 1980–91, while that for disturbance increased by 30 percent. The total NSGAP was reduced by 18 percent over this period. The final column gives the years required to reach the sustainability standard (to reduce SGAP and NSGAP to zero) given the trend established from 1980–91. It can be seen that the total NSGAP will be reduced to zero after 51 years, although individually climate change, eutrophication, dispersion and waste disposal will still not have reached their sustainability level by then.

It may also be noted from Table 3 that the various measures cannot all be derived for all the environmental themes. For ozone depletion, the sustainability standard of 0 means that no figure for normalized SGAP can be derived, although there is no problem computing the years to sustainability. For disturbance the increasing trend from 1980 to 1991 means that no figure for YS can be given. However, in this case there is no problem with normalizing the stress, and the increasing trend is factored into the total normalized figures, increasing the length of time before sustainability overall will be reached (removing disturbance from the total actually reduces the time before sustainability is reached to 43 years). Both the normalized SGAP (NSGAP) and Years-to-Sustainability (YS) indicators give useful information on the achievement of sustainable development. The SGAP indicator can also be expressed as a ratio of output to show the "unsustainability intensity" (similar to the energy intensity) of economic activity. Ekins and Simon (1999) also show how maintenance and restoration costs can be used to convert the SGAP into a monetary figure, which may be directly compared with GDP.

While all such aggregate indicators have limitations, the SGAP avoids the main ones identified by Pillarisetti and van den Bergh (2010) in their analysis of the Genuine Savings (GS) indicator, the Ecological Sustainability Index (ESI), and the Ecological Footprint (EF)[13]. SGAP takes explicit account of critical natural capital and does not make inappropriate assumptions of substitutability by setting sustainability standards for each environmental theme (unlike GS) and it is related to the carrying capacity of the Earth (unlike ESI), but without the methodological problems of EF. If the problem of environmental unsustainability is to increase its public profile and awareness, some way of simplifying and presenting the complexity of the issue is likely to be necessary.

4.4 Material flows, resource efficiency, and dematerialization

The sustainable use of resources in line with the fifth sustainability principle above will require,

firstly, that the flow of resources (materials with economic value) through the economy is measured and secondly, for those resources whose use is excessive and unsustainable, that use will need to be reduced.

New methods for measuring material flows have resulted in much information, organized through concepts such as Domestic or Total Material Consumption (DMC/TMC), Direct and Total Material Input (DMI/TMI) and Total Material Requirement (TMR), which includes Hidden Flows.[14] Through such studies as that for the U.K. by Bringezu and Schütz (2001), which utilize these concepts, it is increasingly possible to characterize material flows, making it possible for the first time to assess whether or not any reduction in resource use, or dematerialization, is taking or has taken place. For example, Bringezu et al. 2004 (P.120) found that for 26 countries, with the exception only of the Czech Republic, "no significant absolute decline of direct material input per capita has been observed so far in the course of economic growth." If incomes are to be simultaneously increased as resource use is reduced, the efficiency of resource use will have to increase. There are a number of related efficiency concepts, which need to be distinguished: *material efficiency* (which is some ratio of useful material output to material resource input and which may argue, for example, for increased recycling over the economy as a whole); and *economic efficiency* (which would argue for recycling to the extent that the marginal cost of recycling equaled its marginal benefit). The term *resource efficiency* may be applied to either of these concepts. Distinct is the more rigorous idea of *resource productivity*, which is some measure of economic output or value added per some unit of resources.

Resource efficiency is also important for reducing environmental impacts. The use of such indicators as TMR and TMO as sustainability indicators by themselves is obviously

13 The latter two are aggregate environmental/ecological indicators not discussed here for reasons of space. Further details can be found at YCELP (2005) (ESI) and WWF et al. 2006 (EF).

14 For definitions of these and other terms used in material flow analysis (MFA), see EC/EUROSTAT 2001

problematic, because different materials have such different environmental impacts per unit of weight (DIETZ AND NEUMAYER 2007, P.623). However, as Bringezu et al. (2009, P.30) point out, there is an intrinsic relationship between material flows and environmental impacts. It is in fact hard to think of an environmental impact that is not in some way or another linked to the flow of materials through the socio-industrial metabolism. Greater efficiency in the production and use of materials therefore helps to reduce environmental impacts. Environmental impacts may also be reduced by reducing most of those materials and resources with high negative impacts, or by replacing them with those with a lower environmental impact.

This is the thinking behind the European Commission's "Resource Efficiency Roadmap" (EC 2011), using a classification of resources and environmental impacts as set out in Table 4. Policy analysis must find ways of evaluating any trade off between the different resources and environmental impacts in Table 4 (e.g., recycling may entail greater energy use, transport emissions) throughout supply chains and product life-cycles.

Dematerialization is an absolute decrease in the quantity of resources, measured by mass, being used by an economy. It is clearly related to but is distinct from the concept of *decoupling*, which is a decline in the ratio of the amount used of a certain resource, or of the environmental impact, to the value generated or otherwise involved. The unit of decoupling is therefore a weight per unit of value. *Relative* decoupling

TABLE 4

A classification of resources and their indicators

| Resources | Unit | Indicator | |
		Home	Abroad
Materials: abiotic (inc. fossil fuels), biotic (land, freshwater, marine)	Tonnes	Components of DMC/DMI/TMI (inc. HF[2])	Components of TMC/TMR (inc. HF[2])
Water	Liters	Water exploitation index (WEI)	Embodied water in EU imports
Land: not built up[1]	Hectares	Protected areas	Protected areas
Land: built up	Hectares	Built-up area	Land use from EU imports
Marine area	Hectares	MPAs	MPAs
Energy	MJ/MWh	Energy productivity Absolute energy use Renewable energy use	Embodied energy in EU imports
Environment			
Greenhouse gases	Tonnes CO$_{2e}$	Emissions	Emissions
Air: non–GHG emissions, Water: emissions, Land: emissions	Tonnes various	Emissions	Emissions

1. This could be broken down by habitat (e.g., from the U.K. National Ecosystem Assessment, referred to below: Mountains, Moorlands and Heaths, Semi–natural Grasslands, Enclosed Farmland, Woodlands, Freshwaters [Openwaters, Wetlands and Floodplains], Coastal Margins; Urban included in Built up, Marine included separately)

2. Hidden flows

means that productivity/efficiency improvements have been realized, but total inputs, or pollution outputs, continue to increase as economic output increases. *Absolute* decoupling refers to the situation in which there is an overall reduction in required material inputs or pollution outputs, even while the economy grows, whether through productivity improvements or through a decrease in pollution, or a combination of the two.

If dematerialization occurs in a growing economy, then it is indicative of absolute decoupling. If it occurs in a shrinking economy, its relationship to decoupling is unclear. Decoupling may be defined in terms of emissions and other environmental impacts as well as resource use. Dematerialization is usually only defined in terms of resource use, although, especially in mass balance studies, there is no over-riding reason why this should be so. Obviously both resource use and emissions may lead to environmental impacts, although these impacts are normally considered as an extension to, rather than as part of, the dematerialization concept.

Three kinds of materials may be defined in an economy. There are virgin resources, those which enter the economy for the first time after their extraction from the natural environment; recycled resources, which circulate in the economy through multiple uses; and materials for disposal (not resources at this stage because they have no economic value). The dematerialization concept may be applied to any or all of these stages of resource and material use, depending on whether it is the use of virgin resources, the circulation of resources in the economy, or the disposal of materials, that has been reduced. The distinction between these stages of resource and material use is important, because the policies to affect the different stages may be very different.

Dematerialization, as opposed to decoupling, is not a concept that has received much explicit policy attention. In fact it is not easy to think of any policies that have been introduced with the explicit purpose of "dematerialization." It is therefore important, in thinking about policies that might achieve dematerialization, to be clear about the purpose of dematerialization. This may include one or more of the following objectives, associated with the different stages of resource and material use:

1. To reduce the depletion, and therefore extend the period of availability, of a scarce resource;
2. To reduce the environmental impacts associated with the extraction, transport, processing or use of the resource;
3. To reduce the environmental impacts of the disposal of the material at the end of its useful life.

Most economists would suggest that the main policy used to achieve dematerialization should be an economic instrument that explicitly increases the prices associated with resource use and environmental impacts.

Clearly different materials have very different environmental impacts (VAN DER VOET ET AL. 2003). In order to reduce environmental impacts, dematerialization needs to focus on the materials producing the greatest impacts, as well as reducing their quantity mobilized by the economy. However, the mobilization of any material by the economy is the source of some environmental impact, especially its mobilization in bulk, and if the related energy use and the whole life cycle of the material is taken into account. For example, bulk aggregates may be inert in environmental terms, but their mining and transport can be energy intensive and result in very great environmental disturbance in the location of the mine. This is the rationale for calling for the dematerialization of the economy in general, as well as seeking special control of substances with particularly harmful impacts.

Moll et al. (2003) provide a limited disaggregation of material flows into the four main materials by mass to flow through the economy (excluding water): biomass, construction minerals, industrial minerals and ores, and fossil fuels. The flow of these materials through the economies of the EU-15 countries since 1980 has been remarkably constant (MOLL ET AL. 2003, FIG.4-4, P.35). This confirms that, while technical progress tends continuously to improve the efficiency or productivity with which resources are employed, the decoupling has mainly been relative rather than absolute. The productivity or efficiency gains have overall been outweighed by growth in the scale of the economy, and there has been a small absolute increase in a number of both resource inputs and emission and waste outputs. It is clear that if absolute decoupling (dematerialization) is required to reduce the physical scale of the economy such that it becomes environmentally sustainable, then either current environmental policies will have to be applied much more stringently, or new, more effective, policies will have to be found.

5. The environment, the economy, and human well-being[15]

5.1 Influences on human well-being

Figure 1 shows that the purpose of economic activity is to contribute to human welfare or well-being, and that human welfare derives from a number of sources. It is obvious from any consideration of the issue that some level of output/income is clearly vital for well-being, and for prosperity, but the declining marginal utility of income is a well accepted notion in economics, and this means that, at some (high) level of income, economic growth may not be important for well-being and may, indeed, add a rather small increment to it. Notwithstanding, it is conventional to assume that the level of economic output is positively related to human well-being and that therefore the growth in that output, called economic growth and measured in money terms, will increase human well-being. Figures 1 and 2 already cast some doubt on the general validity of this assumption, because if economic growth results in the depletion of environmental resources and negative environmental impacts, as is the case in the absence of absolute decoupling, then any well-being increase from increased incomes may be offset by reductions in well-being from environmental damage. In economic parlance, if the generation of economic output has had a negative impact on some of the other arguments in the utility function (for example, work-life balance, or relationships, or income distribution, or the environment), which is entirely possible, then economic growth at high levels of income may actually reduce well-being.

Substantial recent empirical research on human happiness has in fact cast doubt on the presumed positive relationship between economic growth beyond a certain level of output and human well-being for reasons apart from environmental impacts. The issue has recently entered the mainstream, exemplified by the Stiglitz-Sen report (2009) commissioned by the French Government, the "Beyond GDP" conference (2007) and Communication[16] (2009) of the European Commission, and the ongoing initiative that also involves the OECD, Club of Rome, and WWF.[17] In the U.K., at the Prime Minister's request, the Office for National Statistics has produced a discussion paper on measuring well-being (BEAUMONT 2011). This section will very briefly review this research and its implications for accounting for natural capital.

The notion that human happiness is an important objective of human life goes back considerably further than the 1776 U.S. Declaration of Independence which famously identified its pursuit as one of "inalienable rights" given to human by their Creator. As Nettle (2005) notes, the ancient Greek philosopher Aristippus argued in the fourth century B.C. that the goal of life is to maximize the totality of one's pleasures. However it was not until the 1960s that psychologists began to investigate happiness in a scientific manner. Further, it was not until the 1970s that economists looked into the notion of happiness and its relationship with economic growth.

One of the first conclusions from this work is that the concept of well-being/happiness is not easy to define. Often different words are used to try to explain the concept. Indeed Easterlin (2003:11176) states that he takes the terms "happiness, utility, well-being, life satisfaction, and welfare to be interchangeable." However, despite different definitions of well-being, McAllister (2005) argues that there does appear to be common ground between the different descriptions and resulting measurements of well-being, although these may be

---

15 This section draws substantially on Ekins and Venn 2009

16 http://eur-lex.europa.eu/LexUriServ/LexUriServ. do?uri=COM:2009:0433:FIN:EN:PDF

17 http://www.beyond-gdp.eu/

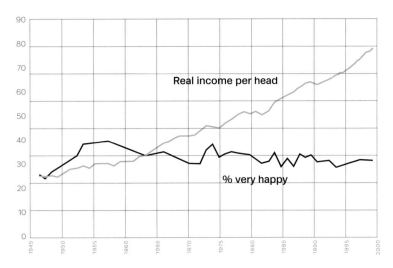

FIGURE 4

Income and happiness in
the United States

Source: Layard 2005, p.30

differentiated as to whether the measurements are subjective or objective. Most researchers agree about the elements that make up well-being: physical well-being; material well-being; social well-being; development and activity; and emotional well-being. The elements can be paraphrased as physical health, income and wealth, relationships, meaningful work and leisure, personal stability and (lack of) depression. Mental health is increasingly seen as fundamental to overall health and well-being. These elements are sometimes viewed as "drivers" of well-being. As is discussed further below, it is interesting and remarkable that the natural environment *per se* is absent from this list.

With regard to the influence on well-being of economic growth, one of the earliest and most influential papers was by Easterlin (1974), who found that, firstly, individual happiness appears to be the same across poor countries and rich countries, and secondly, economic growth does not appear to raise well-being. Rather Easterlin proposed that people compare themselves to their peers, and it is their relative income in respect of this group that delivers well-being, rather than its absolute level. Therefore, raising the income of all does not

increase the well-being of all (EASTERLIN 1995). Similar lines of investigation were taken up by Hirsch (1976), Scitvosky (1976), and Frank (1985), with similar conclusions, and although a later study (OSWALD 1997) criticized the approach taken, it also found that "it seems extra income is not contributing dramatically to the quality of people's lives" (OSWALD 1997:1818).

Income, relative or absolute, is however usually included in lists of factors which affect well-being. For example, Dolan et al. (2007, P.33) reviewed 150 peer reviewed papers and grouped their contributory factors to well-being under seven broad headings: 1) income; 2) personal characteristics: who we are, our genetic makeup; 3) socially developed characteristics: our health and education; 4) how we spend our time: the work we do, and activities we engage in; 5) attitudes and beliefs towards self/others/life: how we interpret the world; 6) relationships: the way we connect with others; and 7) the wider economic, social and political environment: the place we live. Again, the natural environment is at best implicit in this list.

Although measurements of well-being tend to be one of two types, subjective or objective, empirical work has shown that economic conditions, like unemployment, inflation and income, have a strong impact on people's subjective well-being. Clark and Oswald (1994) showed that unemployed people are significantly less happy than those with a job (see also WINKELMANN AND WINKELMANN 1998; DI TELLA ET AL. 2001; OUWENEEL 2002).

At best, the relationship between happiness and income seems to be nonlinear. Over time, happiness appears to be relatively unrelated to income. Research by Diener and Seligman (2012 FORTHCOMING) and Layard (2005) has found, as shown for the U.S. in Figure 4, that substantial real per capita income growth in developed countries over the last decades has led to no significant increases in subjective well-being – despite massive increases in purchasing power, people in developed nations seem no happier than they were fifty years ago. Figure 4 shows very much the same relationship between income and "mean life satisfaction" in the u.s.

Figure 5 shows that once average income in a country exceeds $20,000 per head, increases in income are no longer associated strongly, if at all, with increases in happiness.

Along with Easterlin, Layard (2005) argues that relative income is more important in explaining well-being than absolute wealth, explaining this through a process known as the "hedonic treadmill." As individuals and societies grow wealthier, they adapt to new and higher living standards and adjust expectations upwards. This means that aspirations are never satisfied, and that at higher income levels increases in income make less difference, as basic needs are satisfied but consumption desires remain. On the basis of his research, Layard also identifies seven main factors that influence the well-being of people: family relationships, financial situation, work, community and friends, health, personal freedom and personal values (LAYARD 2005, P.63). Again, the natural environment is conspicuous by its absence from this list.

5.2 Human well–being and the environment

Notwithstanding the near total absence of the environment from the well-being literature, as noted above, the landmark study of the natural environment, the Millennium Ecosystem Assessment (MA 2005) is in no doubt of the (intuitively fairly obvious) fact that human well-being is fundamentally dependent on the "ecosystem goods and services" (the same concept as the environmental "functions for" humans discussed above), the production of which depends on the continued functioning of basic environmental processes.

Carried out between 2001 and 2005, the MA sought to assess the consequences of ecosystem change for human well-being and to establish the scientific basis for actions needed to enhance the conservation and sustainable use of ecosystems. It resulted in one of the most comprehensive assessments to date, at the conceptual level, of the multiple inter-linkages between the environment and human well-being. Ecosystem services as defined by MA comprise *provisioning services* such as food, water, timber and genetic resources; *regulating services* that affect climate, floods, disease, wastes and water quality; *cultural services* that provide recreational, aesthetic, and spiritual benefits; and *supporting services* such as soil formation, pollination, and nutrient cycling. Supporting services are included as an overarching category as it is perceived that they are essential for sustaining each of the other three ecosystem services. The link between supporting services and human well-being is therefore crucial but indirect.

Human well-being is assumed to have multiple constituents (MA 2005, P.V), including the *basic material for a good life*, such as secure and adequate livelihoods, enough food at all times, shelter, clothing, and access to goods; *health*, including feeling well and having a

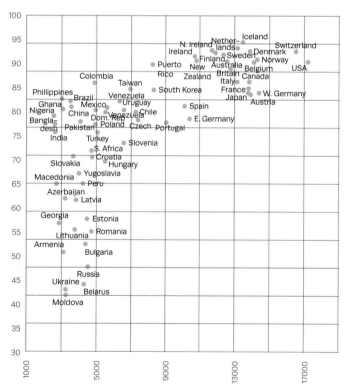

FIGURE 5

Income and happiness for different countries

Source: Layard 2005, p.32

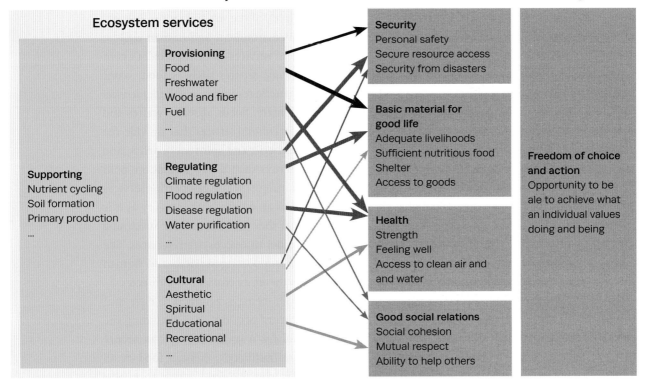

Life on Earth – biodiversity

Constituents of well-being

Ecosystem services

Supporting
Nutrient cycling
Soil formation
Primary production
...

Provisioning
Food
Freshwater
Wood and fiber
Fuel
...

Regulating
Climate regulation
Flood regulation
Disease regulation
Water purification
...

Cultural
Aesthetic
Spiritual
Educational
Recreational
...

Security
Personal safety
Secure resource access
Security from disasters

Basic material for good life
Adequate livelihoods
Sufficient nutritious food
Shelter
Access to goods

Health
Strength
Feeling well
Access to clean air and
and water

Good social relations
Social cohesion
Mutual respect
Ability to help others

Freedom of choice and action
Opportunity to be ale to achieve what an individual values doing and being

healthy physical environment, such as clean air and access to clean water; *good social relations*, including social cohesion, mutual respect, and the ability to help others and provide for children; *security*, including secure access to natural and other resources, personal safety, and security from natural and human-made disasters; and *freedom of choice and action*, including the opportunity to achieve what an individual values doing and being.

One of the rare studies to have investigated explicitly the relationship between natural capital (and manufactured, social and human capital) and human life satisfaction is Vemuri and Costanza (2006). They computed an "ecosystem services product (ESP)" from the land-cover dataset of the International Geosphere and Biosphere Programme (IGBP) and unit ecosystem service values from Costanza et al. (1997). To represent manufactured and human capital they used the Human Development Index (which combines measures of income, health, and education). Social capital was represented by a press freedom rating but was then excluded from the analysis because of its correlation with both HDI and ESP. Regressing life satisfaction against HDI and ESP for 56 countries found a significant relationship for both variables, with HDI having the stronger effect. Excluding six outlier countries (which, included both China and India) greatly improved the fit of the regression. They conclude that natural capital has a "significant impact" (VEMURI AND COSTANZA 2006, P.131) on life satisfaction, although the paper earlier said "we cannot conclude causal implications from this type of model" (IBID., P.128). However, it is at least intuitively plausible that natural capital and life satisfaction have a positive relationship.

It is clear that the MA approach to human well-being is close to those discussed above. Building on its classifications the MA (2005) maps ecosystem services onto human well-being as in Figure 6, with the arrows indicating the strength as well as the nature of the linkages, and their colors indicating of the extent to which it is possible for socioeconomic factors to mediate the linkage (for example, if it is possible to purchase a substitute for a degraded

FIGURE 6

Illustration of linkages
between ecosystem
services and human well–
being

Source MA (2005, p.50)

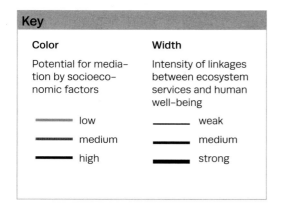

Key

Color	Width
Potential for mediation by socioeconomic factors	Intensity of linkages between ecosystem services and human well–being
——— low	——— weak
——— medium	——— medium
——— high	——— strong

ecosystem service, then there is a high potential for mediation).

The MA argues that both the strength of the linkages and the potential for mediation differ in different ecosystems and regions. The MA additionally identifies non-ecosystem factors which have the potential to influence human well-being (classified into economic, social, technological, and cultural factors), and notes that, as in Figure 2, these can feed back into the environment and affect ecosystem services, but these interactions are not shown in Figure 6.

All this suggests that well-being is the product of a range of different factors or conditions that include the environment. Two lists of these factors or conditions from the economics literature, to complement those above, but which in contrast do include environmental resources, are:

- Real income per capita; health and nutritional status; educational achievement; access to resources; income distribution; basic freedoms (PEARCE ET AL. 1990, PP.2–3)

- Income; income distribution; employment; working conditions; leisure ["work-life balance"]; environment; relationships; safety of the future/security (HUETING 1986, PP.243FF.)

While it is clear from the review of Dolan et al. (2007) that there are remarkably few studies that investigate environment-well-being relationships, or seek empirically to assess the strength of the linkages identified in Figure 6; and while both Dolan et al. (2007) and MA (2005:6) also note there is also a limited amount of information available to assess the consequences of changes in ecosystem services for human well-being; more recent research, including The Economics of Ecosystems and Biodiversity (TEEB 2010) and the U.K.'s recent National Ecosystem Assessment (UKNEA 2011) have produced clearer evidence that ecosystems, and the services they produce for humans, are valuable. Some of their value appears directly in marketed products. Some of it is not marketed, but can, with some difficulty and reservations, be expressed in monetary terms. The MA and UKNEA in particular have also shown that in past years pressure on many ecosystems has grown, a number of them have been lost or degraded, and the flow of ecosystem services has declined. In some cases this decline continues, with probable negative consequences for social well-being in the future. Figures from the economic analysis in UKNEA illustrate the possible scale of these consequences.

Natural capital in the UKNEA includes the eight kinds of ecosystems that are explored in detail in the UKNEA (Mountains, Moorlands and Heaths, Semi-natural Grasslands, Enclosed Farmland, Woodlands, Freshwaters [Openwaters, Wetlands and Floodplains], Urban, Coastal Margins, Marine). These ecosystems produce services which are involved in the production of both monetary and non-monetary output, and which contribute directly to human well-being. When ecosystems decline, so normally does their level of service production, thereby reducing their level of contribution to monetary and non-monetary output and their direct contribution to human well-being. Where their decline has been the result of other economic activity, then the value of the production attributed to this activity should be reduced by the value of the ecosystem service decline. In the extreme it may be that the value of the lost ecosystem services *exceeds* the value created by the so-called economic activity, so-called because such activity is not really economic activity at all, but wealth destroying activity. An example of such a wealth destroying activity might be a forestry business that clear fells a productive forest ecosystem for its timber, where the lost ecosystem services from the forest (many of which might have been non-monetary and therefore not taken properly into account) were more valuable than the timber that was produced.

The valuation work on the scenarios constructed for the UKNEA (see UKNEA 2011, P.14 FIGURE 8; the scenarios are called Green and Pleasant Land [GPL], Nature at Work [NW], Local Stewardship [LS], Go with the Flow [GF], National Security [NS] and World Markets [WM]) explored precisely such trade-offs as these, where developments in (High and Low) marketed agricultural output and in the value of three non-marketed ecosystem services (GHG emissions, recreation, and urban greenspace) were compared. Table 5 shows a summary of these values.

The three non-marketed ecosystem services are explicitly represented in the categories of Hueting's utility function above: GHG emissions (safety of the future); recreation (leisure), urban greenspace (environment), and of course it is their presence in people's utility functions that causes people to value them. At the same time, these values are highly dependent on context and circumstance, and it is not difficult to imagine situations in which they would change markedly, so that any estimated values should be taken as a snapshot from present perspectives, and are most unlikely to be the same in 2060, which is the year of the scenarios' projections.

In the scenarios with both high and low climate change, on the basis of the issues considered, the two scenarios (NS, WM) that give the most emphasis to marketed agricultural output have the highest increase over the Baseline in terms of marketed money values, but these two scenarios represent the worst social value in terms of total output. It might be surmised from this that NS would have the highest GDP of all the scenarios, followed by WM, but this would be wrong for two reasons.

First, agriculture is a relatively small sector of the monetized economy, and the scenarios could be expected to show very different outcomes for other sectors. For example, WM from its description would probably have the highest growth in other industries. Second, and more importantly here, there is no allowance made for the possible contribution of the increased natural capital in other scenarios to other sectors. For example, those scenarios with better protected ecosystems might have more developed U.K. tourism and leisure sectors, which have not been evaluated here. Third, there is no assessment of possible feedback between natural capital and other forms of capital. For example, the greater availability in some scenarios of urban greenspace may improve urban health and therefore increase human capital. All such considerations emphasize the desirability in any whole-economy assessment of such scenarios, even if only considering the scenarios' GDP outcomes, of carrying out an economy-wide assessment with a well specified national environment-economy model.

The work of TEEB, MA, and UKNEA, among others, seem now to have established indicators of the natural environment, or natural capital, as an important component of well-being measures. For example, the new framework being adopted by the U.K. Government (BEAUMONT 2011) to assess trends in human well-being, and social progress more widely, includes the natural environment as one of three "contextual domains" (along with governance and the economy) contributing to human well-being.

TABLE 5

Summary impacts for the change from the 2000 baseline to 2060 under each of the NEA scenarios: Great Britain. All values given in £Million per annum.

Source: UKNEA, 2011, Chapter 26, Table 26.23

	GF High	GF Low	GPL High	GPL Low	LS High	LS Low	NS High	NS Low	NW High	NW Low	WM High	WM Low
	£ millions pa (real values, £ 2010)											
Market agricultural output values[1]	590	220	−30	−290	430	350	1,200	680	−110	−510	880	420
Non−market GHG emissions[2]	−810	−800	2410	2410	570	−100	3400	3590	4570	4590	−1680	−2130
Non−market recreation[3]	4120	5710	5160	6100	1100	1540	3340	4490	23910	24170	−820	5040
Non−market urban greenspace[4]	−1960	−1960	2350	2350	2160	2160	−9940	−9940	4730	4730	−24000	−24000
Total monetized values[5]	1940	3170	9890	10570	4260	3950	−2000	−1180	33100	32980	−25620	−20670
Non−monetized impacts[6]												
Change in farmland bird species[7]	0	0	0	0	0	0	−1	−1	−1	−1	0	0
Bird diversity (all species)[8]	++	++	++	++	−	−	++	+++	++	++	− −	+
Rank: Market values only	4	8	9	11	5	7	1	3	10	12	2	6
Rank: All monetary values	8	7	4	3	5	6	10	9	1	2	12	11
Rank: +ve monetary values and no farmland bird losses	6	5	2	1	3	4						
Rank: +ve monetary values and biodiversity gains	4	3	2	1								

Notes: Scenarios are as follows: BAU = Business as Usual; GPL = Green and Pleasant Land; LS = Local Stewardship; NS = National Security; NW = Nature at Work; WM = World Markets.

1. Change in total GB farm gross margin.
2. Change from baseline year (2000) in annual costs of greenhouse gas (GHG) emissions from GB terrestrial ecosystems in 2060 under the NEA Scenarios (millions £/yr); negative values represent increases in annual costs of GHG emissions
3. Annual value change for all of Great Britain.
4. Annuity value; negative values indicate losses of urban greenspace amenity value.
5. There is some double counting between urban recreation and urban greenspace amenity values. Further data is needed to correct for this.
6. Note that some commentators prefer to use monetized values for biodiversity. See discussion in NEA Economics chapter.
7. Expected impact on the mean number of species in the seeds and invertebrates guild (including many farmland bird species) present in each 10km square in England and Wales from 1988 to 2060 (rounded to the nearest whole number). Note that the 2000 Baseline has 19 species in this guild.
8. Based on relative diversity scores for all species.

6. Conclusion

This chapter has reviewed a number of issues relating to wealth accounting with a view to extending and complementing the main approaches to the subject that have been discussed in this report, always in the context of a multi-capital framework for understanding wealth creation.

The most important of these issues are the distinction between weak and strong sustainability; and the identification of influences on human well-being beyond conventional measures of wealth as the discounted future flow of consumption.

The fact that some natural capital may be non-substitutable by other forms of capital shifts attention to ways of measuring such capital that take account of thresholds and minimum standards for its conservation to ensure the sustainability of the environmental functions which it generates. The main section of this chapter has identified principles of environmental sustainability that are particularly relevant to critical natural capital and shown how sustainability standards in relation to these standards may be formulated. This then permits an indicator to be derived that shows the "gap" between current use of the environment and its resources and the sustainability standard, showing in easily communicable form the extent to which current activities are sustainable, and the time that will be taken on current trends before the sustainability standards will be achieved. New methods of measuring the flows of resources through the economy have been developed, both to facilitate analysis of the sustainability of these flows, and to permit the construction of economic-environmental indicators of resource efficiency and dematerialization, which can provide further guidance to policymakers on the joint achievement of economic and environmental objectives.

The maintenance and increase of human well-being is the purpose of economic activity. There is little doubt of the importance of consumption to such well-being, but equally there is little doubt of the importance of a number of other factors and influences. The substantial literature on this subject has surprisingly underplayed the importance of natural capital as one of these factors and influences, but the balance here has started to be corrected through the various ecosystem assessments that have been produced in recent years, with their focus on the importance to human well-being of a whole range of ecosystem goods and services. Even the limited valuation of those that have been shown to be possible in these assessments suggests that it is beyond time that inclusive accounting for natural capital, both as suggested in other chapters of this report, and in the broader approaches outlined here, is long overdue.

REFERENCES

ADRIAANSE, A. (1993). *Environmental policy performance indicators.* The Hague: SDU.

ARROW, K.J., DASGUPTA, P. & MÄLER, K.G. (2003). Evaluating projects and assessing sustainable development in imperfect economies. *Environmental and Resource Economics, 26,* 647–685

ARROW, K.J., DASGUPTA, P., GOULDER, L.H., MUMFORD, K.J. & OLESON, K. (2010). Sustainability and the measurement of wealth. *NBER Working Paper No 16599.*

BEAUMONT, J. (2011). *Measuring national well-being: Discussion paper on domains and measures.* Retrieved from http://www.ons.gov.uk/ons/dcp171766_240726.pdf

BECKER, G.S. (1993). *Human capital: A theoretical and empirical analysis with special reference to education (3rd edition).* Chicago: University of Chicago Press.

BRAND, F. (2009). Critical natural capital revisited: Ecological resilience and sustainable development. *Ecological Economics, 68* (3), 605–612.

BRE. (2008). *Statement on the green guide from BRE Global and the Construction Products Association.* Retrieved from http://www.bre.co.uk/news/Statement-On-The-Green-Guide-From-BRE-Global-And-The-Construction-Products-Association-524.html

BRINGEZU, S. & SCHÜTZ, H. (2001). *Total resource flows of the United Kingdom.* Report for DEFRA. Wuppertal: Wuppertal Institute.

BRINGEZU, S., SCHÜTZ, H., STEGER, S. & BAUDISCH, J. (2004). International comparison of resource use and its relation to economic growth: The development of total material requirement, direct material inputs and hidden flows and the structure of TMR. Ecological Economics, 51, 97–124.

BRINGEZU, S., VAN DE SAND, I., SCHÜTZ, H., BLEISCHWITZ, R. & MOLL, S. (2009). Analysing global resource use of national and regional economies across various levels. In S. Bringezu & R. Bleischwitz (Eds.) Sustainable resource management. *Global trends, visions and policies* (pp. 10–51). Sheffield: Greenleaf Publishing.

CAVAYE, J. (2004). *Social capital: A commentary on issues, understanding and measurement.* Retrieved from http://www.communitydevelopment.com.au/Documents/Social%20Capital%20-%20A%20Commentry%20on%20Issues,%20Understanding%20and%20Measurement.pdf

CGSDI. (2007). *Consultative group on sustainable development indicators.* Retrieved from http://www.iisd.org/cgsdi/dashboard.asp

CIRIACY-WANTRUP, S.V. (1952). *Resource conservation: Economics and policies.* Berkeley: University of California Press.

CLARK, A.E. & OSWALD, A.J. (1994). Unhappiness and unemployment. *The Economic Journal, 104,* 648–659.

COLEMAN, J. (1988). Social capital in the creation of human capital. *The American Journal of Sociology, 94,* S95–S120.

COSTANZA, R., D'ARGE, R., DE GROOT, R., FARBER, S., GRASSO, M., HANNON, B.,...VAN DEN BELT, M. (1997). The value of the world's ecosystem services and natural capital. *Nature, 387,* 253–260.

DALY, H.E. (1992). From empty world to full world economics. In R. Goodland, H.E. Daly & S. Serafy (Eds.) *Population, technology and lifestyle: The transition to sustainability* (pp. 23-37). Washington, DC: Island Press.

DALY, H.E. (1995). On Wilfrid Beckerman's critique of sustainable development. *Environmental Values, 4,* 49–55.

DALY, H.E. & COBB, J. (1989). *For the common good: Redirecting the economy towards community, the environment and a sustainable future.* Boston: Beacon Press.

DE GROOT, R.S. (1992). *Functions of nature.* Groningen, Netherlands: Wolters-Noordhoff.

DE GROOT, R., VAN DER PERK, J., CHIESURA, A. & VAN VLIET, A. (2003). Importance and threat as determining factors for criticality of natural capital. *Ecological Economics, 44* (2–3), 187–204.

DETR (DEPARTMENT FOR THE ENVIRONMENT, TRANSPORT AND THE REGIONS). (1999). *Quality of life counts.* London: DETR.

DETR (DEPARTMENT FOR THE ENVIRONMENT, TRANSPORT AND THE REGIONS). (2000a). *Regional quality of life counts (December).* London: DETR.

DETR (DEPARTMENT FOR THE ENVIRONMENT, TRANSPORT AND THE REGIONS). (2000b). *Local quality of life counts (July).* London: DETR.

DI TELLA, R., MACCULLOCH, R.J. & OSWALD, A.J. (2001). Preferences over inflation and unemployment: evidence from surveys of happiness. *American Economic Review, 91* (1), 335–341.

DIENER, E. & SELIGMAN, M. (2012). Beyond money: Toward an economy of well-being. *Psychological Science in the Public Interest,* forthcoming.

DIETZ, S. & NEUMAYER, E. (2007). Weak and strong sustainability in the SEEA: Concepts and measurement. *Ecological Economics, 61,* 617–626.

DOLAN, P., PEASGOOD, T. & WHITE, M. (2006). *Review of research on the influences on personal well-being and application to policy making.* Retrieved from http://randd.defra.gov.uk/Document.aspx?Document=SD12005_4017_FRP.pdf

EASTERLIN, R. (1974). Does economic growth improve the human lot? Some empirical evidence. In P.A. David & M.W. Reder (Eds.) *Nations and households in economic growth: Essays in honour of Moses Abramowitz.* New York/London: Academic Press.

EASTERLIN, R.A. (1995). Will raising the incomes of all increase the happiness of all? *Journal of Economic Behavior and Organization, 27,* 35–47.

EASTERLIN, R.A. (2003). Explaining happiness. *Proceedings of the National Academy of Sciences, 100,* 11176–83.

EC (EUROPEAN COMMISSION). (2001). *A sustainable Europe for a better world: A European Union strategy for sustainable development.* Retrieved from http://www.eea.europa.eu/policy-documents/com-2001-264-final

EC (EUROPEAN COMMISSION). (2011). *Communication from the Commission to the Council, the European Parliament, the European Economic and Social Committee and the Committee of the Regions: Roadmap to a resource-efficient Europe.* Retrieved from http://ec.europa.eu/environment/resource_efficiency/pdf/com2011_571.pdf

EC (EUROPEAN COMMISSION)/EUROSTAT. (2001). *Economy-wide material flow accounts and derived indicators: A methodological guide.* Luxembourg: Office for Official Publications of the European Communities.

EEA (EUROPEAN ENVIRONMENT AGENCY). (2011). *EEA signals 2011: Globalisation, environment and you.* Retrieved from http://www.eea.europa.eu/publications/signals-2011-1

EKINS, P. (2000). *Economic growth and environmental sustainability: The prospects for green growth.* London/New York: Routledge.

EKINS, P. (2001). From green GNP to the sustainability gap: Recent developments in national environmental economic accounting. *Journal of Environmental Assessment, Policy and Management, 3,* 61–93

EKINS, P. (2003). Sustainable development. In J. Proops & E. Page (Eds.) *Environmental thought* (pp. 144-17).Cheltenham: Edward Elgar, Cheltenham.

EKINS, P., SIMON, S., DEUTSCH, L., FOLKE, C. & DE GROOT, R. (2003). A framework for the practical application of the concepts of critical natural capital and strong sustainability. *Ecological Economics, 44* (2–3), 165–185.

EKINS, P. & SIMON, S. (1999). The sustainability gap: A practical indicator of sustainability in the framework of the national accounts. *International Journal of Sustainable Development, 2* (1), 32–58.

EKINS, P. & SIMON, S. (2001). Estimating sustainability gaps: Methods and preliminary applications for the UK and the Netherlands. *Ecological Economics, 37* (1), 5–22.

EKINS, P. & VENN, A. (2009). *Economic growth, the environment and well-being.* PETRE Working Paper, University College London.

EUROSTAT. (1997). *Indicators of sustainable development.* Luxembourg: Office for Official Publications of the European Communities.

EUROSTAT. (2001A). *Environmental pressure indicators for the EU.* Luxembourg: Office for Official Publications of the European Communities.

EUROSTAT. (2001B). *Measuring progress towards a more sustainable Europe: Proposed indicators for sustainable development.* Luxembourg: Office for Official Publications of the European Communities.

FOSTER, J. (1997). *Valuing nature: Economics, ethics and environment.* London/New York: Routledge.

FRANK, R. (1985). *Choosing the right pond: Human behaviour and the quest for status.* Oxford: Oxford University Press.

HIRSCH, F. (1976). *Social limits to growth.* Cambridge, MA: Harvard University Press.

HUETING, R. (1980). *New scarcity and economic growth.* Amsterdam: North Holland.

HUETING, R. (1986). An economic scenario for a conserver economy. In P. Ekins (Ed.) *The living economy: A new economics in the making* (pp. 242-256). London: Routledge & Kegan Paul.

KUMAR, P. (2010). *The economics of ecosystems and biodiversity: Ecological and economic foundations.* London: Earthscan.

LAYARD, R. (2005). *Happiness.* London: Penguin Books.

LE, T., GIBSON, J. & OXLEY, L. (2005). Measures of human capital: A review of the literature. University of Canterbury, New Zealand Treasury Working Paper 05/10, November, Wellington.

LOCHNER, K., KAWACHI, I., BRENNAN, R. & BUKA, S. (2003). Social capital and neighborhood mortality rates in Chicago. *Social Science & Medicine, 56* (8), 1797–1805.

MCALLISTER, F. (2005). *Well-being concepts and challenges.* Retrieved from http://www.sd-research.org.uk/wp-content/uploads/finalwellbeingpolicybriefing.pdf

MA (MILLENNIUM ECOSYSTEM ASSESSMENT). (2005). *Ecosystems and human well-being: Synthesis.* Washington, DC: Island Press.

MOLL, S., BRINGEZU, S. & SCHÜTZ, H. (2003). *Resource use in European countries.* Copenhagen: European Topic Centre on Waste and Material Flows (ETC-WMF).

NETTLE, D. (2005). *Happiness: The science behind your smile.* Oxford: Oxford University Press.

NORDHAUS, W.D. & TOBIN, J. (1973). Is growth obsolete? In M. Moss (Ed.) *The measurement of economic and social performance* (pp. 509-532). New York: National Bureau of Economic Research/Columbia University.

OECD (ORGANISATION FOR ECONOMIC CO-OPERATION AND DEVELOPMENT). (1998). *Towards sustainable development: Environmental indicators.* Paris: OECD.

OECD (ORGANISATION FOR ECONOMIC CO-OPERATION AND DEVELOPMENT). (2000A). *Towards sustainable development: Indicators to measure progress: Proceedings of the OECD Rome conference.* Paris: OECD.

OECD (ORGANISATION FOR ECONOMIC CO-OPERATION AND DEVELOPMENT). (2000b). *Frameworks to measure sustainable development.* Paris: OECD.

OECD (ORGANISATION FOR ECONOMIC CO-OPERATION AND DEVELOPMENT). (2001a). *The well-being of nations: The role of human and social capital.* Paris: OECD.

OECD (ORGANISATION FOR ECONOMIC CO-OPERATION AND DEVELOPMENT). (2001b). *Key environment indicators.* Paris: OECD.

OECD (ORGANISATION FOR ECONOMIC CO-OPERATION AND DEVELOPMENT). (2001c). *Sustainable development: Critical issues.* Paris: OECD.

OECD (ORGANISATION FOR ECONOMIC CO-OPERATION AND DEVELOPMENT). (2001d). *OECD environmental indicators: Towards sustainable development.* Paris: OECD.

OECD (ORGANISATION FOR ECONOMIC CO-OPERATION AND DEVELOPMENT). (2001e). *Policies to enhance sustainable development.* Paris: OECD.

OECD (ORGANISATION FOR ECONOMIC CO-OPERATION AND DEVELOPMENT). (2011). *OECD environmental data: Compendium.* Paris: OECD. Retrieved from http://www.oecd.org/document/49/0,3746,en_2649_34283_39011377_1_1_1_1,00.html

OSWALD, A. J. (1997). Happiness and economic performance. *Economic Journal, 107,* 1815–1831.

OUWENEEL, P. (2002). Social security and well-being of the unemployed in 42 nations. *Journal of Happiness Studies, 3,* 167–192.

PEARCE, D., BARBIER, E. & MARKANDYA, A. (1990). *Sustainable development: Economics and environment in the third world.* Aldershot: Edward Elgar.

PEARCE, D. & TURNER, R.K. (1990). *Economics of Natural Resources and the Environment.* New York: Harvester Wheatsheaf.

PEARSON, L., KASHIMA, Y. & PEARSON, C. (2012). Clarifying protected and utilitarian values of critical capital. *Ecological Economics, 73,* 206–210.

PEZZEY, J. (1992). Sustainable development concepts: An economic analysis. *World Bank Environment Paper No.2.* Washington DC: World Bank.

POSNER, S. AND COSTANZA, R. (2011). A summary of ISEW and GPI studies at multiple scales and new estimates for Baltimore Coty, Baltimore County, and the State of Maryland. *Ecological Economics, 70*, 1972–1980.

PRODUCTIVITY COMMISSION. (2003). *Social capital: Reviewing the concept and its policy implications*. Retrieved from http://www.pc.gov.au/__data/assets/pdf_file/0018/8244/socialcapital.pdf

PUTNAM, R. (2000). *Bowling alone: The collapse and revival of American community*. New York: Simon Schuster.

ROBINSON, D., HOOKER, H. & MERCER, M. (2008). *Human capital measurement: Approaches, issues and case studies. Report 454*. London: Institute for Employment Studies.

ROCKSTRÖM, J., STEFFEN, W., NOONE, K., PERSSON, Å., CHAPIN III, F.S., LAMBIN, E.F.,...FOLEY, J.A. (2009). A safe operating space for humanity. *Nature, 461*, 472–475.

SCITOVSKY, T. (1976). *The joyless economy: The psychology of human satisfaction*. Oxford: Oxford University Press.

SPASH, C.L., URAMA, K., BURTON, R., KENYON, W., SHANNON, P. & HILL, G. (2009). Motives behind willingness to pay for improving biodiversity in a water ecosystem: economics, ethics and social psychology. *Ecological Economics, 68*, 955–964.

STIGLITZ, J., SEN, A. & FITOUSSI, J.P. (2009). *Report by the commission on the measurement of economic performance and social progress*. Retrieved from http://www.stiglitz-sen-fitoussi.fr/documents/rapport_anglais.pdf

STILES, P. & KULVISAECHANA, S. (N.D.). *Human capital and performance: A literature review*. Retrieved from http://webarchive.nationalarchives.gov.uk/+/http://www.bis.gov.uk/files/file38844.pdf

TEEB (THE ECONOMICS OF ECOSYSTEMS AND BIODIVERSITY). (2010). *Mainstreaming the economics of nature: A synthesis of the approach, conclusions and recommendations of TEEB*. Retrieved from http://www.teebweb.org/TEEBSynthesisReport/tabid/29410/Default.aspx

TURNER, R.K. (1993). Sustainability: Principles and practice. In R.K. Turner (Ed.) *Sustainable environmental economics and management: Principles and practice* (pp. 3-36). New York/London: Belhaven Press.

UKNEA (UK NATIONAL ECOSYSTEM ASSESSMENT). (2011). *Synthesis of key findings*. Retrieved from http://uknea.unep-wcmc.org/Resources/tabid/82/Default.aspx

UN (UNITED NATIONS). (1996). *Indicators of sustainable development: Framework and methodologies*. New York: UN.

UNDP (UNITED NATIONS DEVELOPMENT PROGRAMME). (Annual from 1990). *Human development report*. Oxford/New York: Oxford University Press.

VAN DER VOET, E., VAN OERS, L. & NIKOLIC, I. (2003). *Dematerialisation: not just a matter of weight*. Retrieved from http://www.leiden-univ.nl/cml/ssp/publications/demat.pdf

VEMURI, A. & COSTANZA, R. (2006). The role of human, social, built and natural capital in explaining life satisfaction at the country level: Toward a national well-being index (NWI). *Ecological Economics, 58*, 119–133.

VICTOR, P.A. (1991). Indicators of sustainable development: Some lessons from capital theory. *Ecological Economics, 4*, 191–213.

VICTOR, P., HANNA, E. & KUBURSI, A. (1998). How strong is weak sustainability? In S. Faucheux, M. O'Connor & J. van der Straaten (Eds.) *Sustainable development: Concepts, rationalities and strategies* (pp. 195-210). Dordrecht: Kluwer.

WELZEL, C., INGLEHART, R. & DEUTSCH, F. (2005). Social capital, voluntary associations and collective action: Which aspects of social capital have the greatest "civic" payoff? *Journal of Civil Society, 1* (2), 121–146.

WINKELMANN, L. & WINKELMANN, R. (1998). Why are the unemployed so unhappy? Evidence from panel data. *Economica, 65*, 1–15.

WORLD BANK. (1997). *Expanding the measure of wealth: Indicators of environmentally sustainable development*. Washington, DC: World Bank.

WORLD BANK. (2000). *Genuine saving as a sustainability indicator*. Washington, DC: World Bank.

WORLD BANK. (2006). *Where is the wealth of nations?* Washington, DC: World Bank. Retrieved from http://siteresources.worldbank.org/INTEEI/214578-1110886258964/20748034/All.pdf

WORLD BANK. (2011). *The changing wealth of nations: Measuring sustainable development in the new millennium*.Washington, DC: World Bank.

WWF (WORLD WILDLIFE FUND), ZOOLOGICAL SOCIETY OF LONDON & GLOBAL FOOTPRINT NETWORK. (2006). *Living planet report 2006*. Gland, Switzerland: WWF.

YCELP (YALE CENTRE FOR ENVIRONMENTAL LAW AND POLICY), CENTER FOR INTERNATIONAL EARTH SCIENCE INFORMATION NETWORK (CIESIN) & THE WORLD ECONOMIC FORUM. (2005). *2005 environmental sustainability index*. New Haven: YCELP.

ZULA, K. & CHERMACK, T. (2007). Human capital planning: A review of literature and implications for human resource development. *Human Resource Development Review, 6* (3), 245–262.

Lessons, findings, and recommendations

Anantha Duraiappah and Pablo Fuentenebro

For decades, economists and governments have used conventional production indicators such as per capita gross domestic product (GDP) or, more recently, the Human Development Index (HDI) to measure societies' overall "well-being."

The reliance on GDP per capita is understandable. It is easy to compute, and it is based on a rigorous and well-tested economic theory. Moreover, the data needed to compute GDP were relatively easy to compile and countries were quick to adopt this system of national accounts. However, as illustrated in this report, neither GDP per capita nor the HDI reflect the state of the natural environment and both focus on the short term, with no indication of whether current well-being can be sustained. Therefore, it is not surprising that we continue to see a degradation of the natural environment. It should also not come as a surprise if we continuously hear of the growth-versus-environment debate. We are basically using the wrong measurement approach to guide policy-making.

The Inclusive Wealth Report (IWR) provides a metric of measurement for sustainable development. While GDP and the HDI are based on a flow concept, inclusive wealth relies on the stocks of different assets: natural capital (natural resources, land, and ecosystem services, etc.); produced capital (machinery, buildings, etc.); and human capital (education, health, skills, etc.), which make up the productive base of a country. The Inclusive Wealth Index (IWI) is not intended to answer all of a decision-maker's questions, but it can lend insights about the use of assets over time.

In this report, the focus is on natural capital. Although it is true that many developing countries have been depleting their natural resources over the past several decades, we are not suggesting that countries should stop using their natural capital assets to achieve improvements in well-being; rather, we offer more sustainable solutions for achieving these improvements (e.g., making larger investments in other parts of the economy, such as human capital). In this sense, what the 2012 IWR puts on the table is the foundation for a more holistic approach to economic development than is currently practised.

To be clear, the IWI is an important step forward in understanding human well-being, the economy, wealth, and sustainability. Indeed, it's an enormously valuable input into decision-making. That said, as a nascent index, it should not be seen as the exclusive source of information and insight. For now, it is advised that the IWI be used in conjunction with GDP, the HDI and some of the specific environmental indicators such as the ecological footprint and the ecological sustainability index among others to gain the most comprehensive perspective possible.

Lessons learned

A number of key lessons emerge from this first report, including: 1. substitutions among the different capital assets; 2. the importance of not just one capital but the emphasis on a basket of interdependent capital assets; 3. population changes and their impact on the returns to a nation's productive base; 4. interconnected externalities that accrue, particularly from the degradation and decline of the natural capital base; and 5. estimation of shadow prices, which are so critical in computing the inclusive wealth of a country. These are elaborated in the following sections.

1. Substitution

The inclusive wealth framework allows substitution across the different forms of capital and refrains from asserting any specific interest of any particular constituency. Therefore, natural capital is not preserved for its own sake, but for its contribution to the overall productive base of a country. For example, a country with extensive commercially available forest stocks will, according to the inclusive wealth measure, be able to convert some of these forest stocks to other forms of capital assets that it might need to increase the well-being of its citizens and to maintain a sustainable path. The degree of substitutability is determined by the ratio of the shadow prices of the capitals in question. The shadow prices hold the key to the degree of substitution and/or transformation in the country.

2. Health and other forms of capital

One of the crucial features of the inclusive wealth framework is the emphasis on the importance of not just one form of capital, but all capitals, for ensuring sustainability and improvement of human well-being. Among the results is the importance of health and education in wealth accounts. However, the use of health through the value of a statistical life (VSL) does bring with it a number of issues related to morality and ethics. The fact that the report finds this dimension to be significantly larger than the rest of the other capitals is not surprising. Yet, if the authors were to extend the equation on health to include it as a function of the other capitals, specifically natural capital, this would likely have changed the results. This feedback loop between the different forms of capital can be captured to a certain extent by the shadow prices of the respective capital assets. We do understand that the report states that the shadow prices of an asset are a function of the stocks of all assets. That being the case, we would have expected higher shadow prices in natural capital, which might not be reflected in the proxy prices used in computing the values in this report. Examples of how the mental health of populations has changed with the state of natural capital can be used in computing the shadow price of nature. This shows again the importance of the shadow prices in making the inclusive wealth framework functional.

3. Population change

The other useful and important inclusion in the inclusive wealth framework is the explicit treatment of population. By including population, the framework acknowledges growing population as an important variable in determining a country's sustainable track. This is demonstrated strongly by comparing the results of changes in the IWI and the Natural Capital Index as illustrated clearly in Chapters 2 and 3. For instance, Saudi Arabia, which had a positive average growth rate in IWI of 1.57 percent over the period under study, showed a negative growth rate of 1.12 percent when population growth was factored in. Another example is the rapid decline in IWI per capita seen in Nigeria which was not compensated adequately by increases in the other capital assets and had a negative growth rate of 1.87 percent in its inclusive wealth per capita. This highlights the need for policy-makers to introduce strategies for increasing the marginal rate of transformation of natural capital to human and produced capital, to ensure the country is on a sustainable track. These are important investment guidelines that the inclusive wealth framework provides not only for national policy-makers, but also the international organizations responsible for development.

4. Interconnected externalities

The growing frequency of global environmental problems such as climate change, nitrogen deposition, and biodiversity loss, among others, has impacts on a country's wealth prospects and its ability to adopt a sustainable path. Therefore, even if a country adopts all the right measures to follow a sustainable path in order to maintain or increase its productive base, there are some external variables beyond its control that can either increase or reduce its inclusive wealth. This report takes climate change as one key externality and makes an important point about the impact of negative externalities on the inclusive wealth of a nation. Information on these transboundary externalities might also be useful in determining international compensations either in the form of financial or technology transfers, which has been a controversial issue in the international negotiations on climate change. The analysis on climate change can be extended to other externalities such as biodiversity loss, acidification of oceans, and the loss of fisheries. The report clearly highlights a need for a systematic research program on addressing these externalities.

5. Shadow prices

Shadow prices are both the strength and the Achilles heel of the inclusive wealth framework. On one hand, The shadow price captures the degree of substitution across the different forms of capital. It also reflects the contribution to inter-generational well-being at each time period by each capital asset. The shadow price also reflects expected future scarcities and captures the externalities produced in the use of the capital. For example, the shadow price of manufactured capital also reflects, in principle, the environmental externalities it caused in the transformation process.

On the other hand, just as the shadow price is the strength of the framework, it is also its Achilles heel. This is when we have to move from theory to practice. In many cases, the market prices we observe for many of the capitals are adequate for the exercise. However, in many other cases, as the report rightly highlights, it becomes a bit more problematic, especially for natural capital and, to a lesser extent, human and social capital. The fact that many of the prices are not observable suggests using different approaches to finding the shadow prices of these capitals.

Findings

A number of key findings are presented in this section. These are based on the material presented in the earlier chapters of the report.

70 percent of countries assessed in the 2012 Inclusive Wealth Report present a positive Inclusive Wealth Index (IWI) per capita growth, indicating sustainability.

14 countries of the 20 accessed in this report were found to have positive IWI growth rates. The 6 that experienced negative IWI growth rates were Colombia, Nigeria, Russia, Saudi Arabia, South Africa, and Venezuela. Of the 14 countries having positive growth rates, only China returned a growth rate above 2 percent over the past 19 years, while Chile, France, and Germany were in the second tier of countries having growth rates above 1 percent. The remaining 10 showed growth rates of between 0.1 and 1 percent. Therefore, although many of the countries in this first report had positive growth rates, many were at the margin and have a high probability of moving to an unsustainable trajectory. This was especially true for Kenya, with a growth rate of 0.06 percent.

High population growth with respect to IWI growth rates caused 25 percent of countries assessed to become unsustainable.

One of the primary reasons five of the six countries experienced negative growth rates were relatively high population growth rates with respect to their IWI growth rates. The five countries were Colombia, Nigeria, Saudi Arabia, South Africa, and Venezuela. Russia was the exception to the sample of 20 countries that were used in this report. It had a negative population growth rate, but was also the only country to have a negative IWI growth rate before population dynamics were included in the computations. This example illustrates how a negative population growth rate can counter a declining growth rate of IWI to return better growth rates of IWI on a per capita basis.

While 19 out of the 20 countries experienced a decline in natural capital, six of them also saw a decline in their inclusive wealth, thus following an unsustainable track.

Japan was the only country that experienced an increase in its natural capital. This was from an increase in forest cover. But for 12 countries, a decline in natural capital did not automatically translate to a decrease in the IWI growth rate. However, for six countries – Colombia, Nigeria, South Africa, Russia, Saudi Arabia, and Venezuela – decreases in their natural capital base did contribute to the negative IWI growth rate. Yet, for most of these countries, in particular South Africa, a major cause in the decrease of their natural capital came from the rapid drawdown of their fossil fuel asset base.

Human capital has increased in every country, being the prime capital form that offsets the decline in natural capital in most economies.

Brazil, in particular, has had success in increasing its human capital by over 1.2 percent as compared to its IWI growth rate of 0.4 percent. Much of that increase, however, has come from the drawdown of its natural capital base which has decreased at an average of 0.7 percent, with very little increase in its manufactured capital. The key inference to be derived from this finding is that the rate of changes of the three capital asset bases and the corresponding increase or decrease in the IWI growth rate, both at an absolute and a per capita basis, have to be analyzed in an integrated manner.

There are clear signs of trade-off effects among different forms of capital (manufactured, human, and natural capital) as witnessed by increases and declines of capital stocks for 20 countries over 19 years.

A clear picture of trade-offs across the different forms of capital emerges from the results presented in the report. In many countries, as highlighted in Key Finding 4, human capital has increased from the reduction in natural capital. The more important question to answer is if the transformation from one capital to another has been done in a manner as efficient as in the example of Brazil. However, there are examples such as Nigeria, where the massive drawdown of natural capital (primarily fossil fuels) has hardly been compensated by increases in human or manufactured capital.

Technological innovation and/or oil capital gains outweigh declines in natural capital and damages from climate change, moving a number of countries from an unsustainable to a sustainable trajectory.

Total factor productivity (TFP) and, for some countries, the capital gains from oil price fluctuations were found to play a key role in moving them from an unsustainable trajectory to a sustainable one. These countries included Russia, Nigeria, Saudi Arabia, and Venezuela. At the same time, Kenya, which had returned a positive IWI – albeit at a very low rate of 0.06 percent – returned negative IWI rates after adjustment for oil capital losses. This finding demonstrates the sensitivity of some countries to market price fluctuations of key commodities (such as oil) towards achieving sustainability in the long run.

25 percent of assessed countries, which showed a positive trend when measured by GDP per capita and the HDI, were found to have a negative IWI.

Colombia, Nigeria, Russia, Saudi Arabia, and Venezuela showed positive growth rates for the HDI and GDP per capita, but returned negative IWI growth rates. South Africa was the only country that had positive GDP per capita growth rates but returned negative growth rates for both the HDI and the IWI per capita. The biggest discrepancies were found in the cases of Nigeria, South Africa, and Venezuela. These results demonstrate how GDP per capita focuses purely on the present income and production flow while the IWI concentrates on the stocks of assets and their changes over time.

The primary driver of the difference in performance was the decline in natural capital.

The main factor for the differences between the GDP per capita and the HDI with the IWI per capita was the decline in natural capital. Prime examples of countries falling in this category include Australia, Brazil, China, India, and Canada where the differences between GDP per capita and the IWI per capita ranged between 75 percent in the case of Canada to 95 percent for Australia. Countries that performed better based on the IWI per capita were France and Germany. Main reasons for this were an increase in human capital and, in the case of France, some contribution of increase in natural capital.

KEY FINDING 9

Estimates of inclusive wealth can be improved significantly with better data on the stocks of natural, human, and social capital and their values for human well-being.

The results presented in this report are based on a partial set of data on the various categories of capital. For example, social capital was not included in the analysis and there is some the possibility that the results might change when this capital category is added. This, of course, has to be evaluated in more detail both on the theoretical foundations and the empirical estimates. The biggest gaps in data were found to be in the stocks of the different categories of natural capital and their corresponding values. Many of the challenges in addressing and filling these gaps were discussed in detail in Part II of this report. The task is not trivial, but it is not impossible either.

Recommendations

Inclusive wealth offers policy-makers a comprehensive accounting tool for measuring the assets available in the economy. The understanding of such asset portfolios and their changes over time has important implications for sustaining the consumption needs of present and future generations.

RECOMMENDATION 1

Countries witnessing diminishing returns in their natural capital should build up their investments in renewable natural capital to increase their inclusive wealth and the well-being of their citizens.

The majority of countries have been drawing down their natural capital base to increase their IWI per capita growth. However, the declining natural capital asset base cannot be continued indefinitely, and evidence from the IWI suggests that IWI can be increased substantially if more investment is directed at building up renewable natural capital assets in countries where IWI growth rates are low. Examples of investment in renewable natural capital include reforestation (REDD+ programs), agro-biodiversity landscapes, and seascapes.

Countries should mainstream the Inclusive Wealth Index within their planning and development ministries so that projects and activities are evaluated based on a balanced portfolio approach that includes natural, human, and manufactured capital.

Economic planning, poverty reduction, and conservation strategies are typically designed to meet their specific objectives and are evaluated on their project level targets. This is a necessary condition but not sufficient to ensure sustainability of the outcomes due to the high inter-dependency among the various social, economic, and environmental components. Trade-offs are inevitable, but not recognizing them can cause unintended consequences that might result in unwarranted overall decreases in well-being. In order to avert this outcome, governments might require all projects to be evaluated at the sectoral level of the impacts they have on the three capital asset bases and the changes that might occur as well as the overall change in the IWI. This might require some tweaking of the IWI if it is to be used at a sectoral level, but the benefits from getting a more inclusive view of the final consequences on some common denominator, such as the capital assets, might provide guidance in the transition toward sustainability.

Countries should support/speed up the process of moving from an income-based accounting framework to a wealth accounting framework.

GDP, as highlighted many times in this report, is a flow and is based on production and income. The present accounting systems used at the national level are based on economic production and geared towards computing GDP. There is limited information on the capital stocks and most of these are focused on manufactured capital. There is very little or no information on the human and natural capital assets within an integrated framework that can track the changes simultaneously to capture the inter-dependencies. There is work underway to revise the accounts to include environmental dimensions, but they are still conducted within an income-driven framework and the IWI suggests a move towards a wealth-based framework to give a fuller account of the changing productive base of a country and its change over time.

RECOMMENDATION 4

Governments should move away from GDP per capita and instead evaluate their macroeconomic policies – such as fiscal and monetary policies – based on their contribution to the IWI of the country.

Governments use a combination of fiscal and monetary policies to guide and steer an economy. The objective of these policies has traditionally been to increase economic growth as measured by GDP, keep inflation low, and, to some extent, generate employment. This would by conventional terms suggest a drawdown of the natural and human capital asset base, and sometimes even manufactured capital, if the outlook is myopic and seeking quick gains. The solution to the problem is to target increasing the IWI and therefore focus on the investment in the different capital asset bases to facilitate human development on a sustainable basis.

RECOMMENDATION 5

Governments and international organizations should establish research programs for valuing key components of natural capital, particularly ecosystem services.

The usefulness of the IWI will be fully realized once we have a set of functioning wealth accounts. The accounts developed in this report are only in their infancy with big data gaps in the natural and human capital categories. Although much progress has been made in developing a typology for the natural capital accounts, there is still much work to be done, both theoretically and empirically, to make them fully operational so that they become mainstream instruments in government policy-making. This can be achieved to a large extent if governments and international organizations form partnerships to design and fund research programs in order to get better estimates of natural capital stocks and their values.

The way forward

The IWR should not be a one-off report, but instead should be institutionalized as a periodic publication providing timely updates on the changes in the capital assets and the overall changes in the productive base of nations. The IWR 2012 should be seen as the beginning of a series of reports that will be produced every two years in order to monitor the well-being of countries. In the long term, we expect inclusive wealth to become an important criterion in assessments of societal progress. Each of the capital asset categories will be updated as described below. In addition, new theoretical insights and empirical data on total factor productivity, trade, and inequality with respect to the IWI will be further developed and presented in future reports.

Natural capital

Efforts will be made to link existing research networks investigating the valuation of ecosystem services to explore ways and means to get better estimates of the flows and stocks of ecosystem services. In parallel, valuation of these stocks will be undertaken using both monetary and non-monetary techniques. This meta-network will oversee the filling of the gaps identified in this report and also increase the number of countries in the data set from the existing 20 to a more representative sample of the global condition.

Human capital

Human capital presented in this report is limited to literacy rates and the wage rates prevalent in the various countries. Although there were estimates for health to be included in the human capital category, they were not included in the final computations because of their relative dominance in influencing the rate of change in the final levels of inclusive wealth. The use of the value of a statistical life (VSL) as an additional indicator within the human capital component caused the human capital contribution to dominate the overall Inclusive Wealth Index, making the other categories relatively small and insignificant. A number of revisions can be made to address this dominance. A significant modification that might address this issue will be making health dependent in part on the relative changes in natural capital. A well-documented example is the decline in water purification ecosystem services and the impacts on human health. Actual numerical estimates of this relationship are scarce, however, and need to be improved and presented in the next Inclusive Wealth Report.

Produced capital

The produced capital category is well documented due to the availability of data for many of the individual categories. These will be updated automatically.

Social capital

One of the most promising concepts that has emerged in recent times is without doubt that of social capital. Inspired by the work of Robert Putnam and other authors, the wealth accounting literature has picked up on this idea as one of the capital assets that could contribute to the well-being of any given nation.

Although first developed as a sociological term to address the value of human relationships for civil society and community-building, more recently the concept of social capital has taken a new dimension as it has become increasingly clear that social relationships and networks – and trust in individuals and institutions – play a decisive role for sustainable development and the well-being of nations.

The IWR 2014

The next publication of the Inclusive Wealth Report is expected in 2014. It is envisaged that the IWR 2014 will present updates on the various capital assets but with a specific emphasis on social capital. Participating organizations that focused on aspects of the natural capital for this IWR will continue collecting and improving the natural capital asset categories and expanding the list of ecosystem services covered by the wealth accounts. However, at the same time, efforts to improve the theoretical and empirical basis for including social capital will be pursued.

Annexes

Methodological annex

This annex aims to elaborate upon the methodological and data issues regarding the wealth accounts presented in Chapters 2 and 3. We focus here on the three capital forms (human, manufactured, natural capital); also health capital; and the three adjustments to them: carbon damages, total factor productivity, and oil capital gains.

1. Human capital

For human capital calculations, we followed Arrow et al. (2012) and Klenow and Rodríguez-Clare (1997). According to the method employed in these works, human capital per individual ("h") can be defined as a function of educational attainment ("A") and the additional compensation over time of this training, which is assumed to be equivalent to the interest rate, ("ρ"), which was fixed at 8.5 percent in this case. It is additionally assumed that the amount of human capital per person increases exponentially with the interest rate and the average educational attainment per person – consistent with an economy in steady state. Thus it is obtained that:

EQUATION 1

$$h=e^{(\rho \cdot A)}$$

"A" is represented here by the average years of total schooling per person and it is obtained from such sources as Barro and Lee (2011), where data are presented every five years for our time period of study (i.e., 1990, 1995, 2000, 2005 and 2010). This implied that we were forced to use linear interpolations for estimating the years of total schooling on an annual basis. There were, however, no estimates for Nigeria in the Barro and Lee (2010) dataset. In this case we modeled this country by combining educational attainment parameters from Nigeria, which were available in the Human Development Index database, and the progress made in this regard by other African countries, particularly Ghana, South Africa and Kenya using Barro and Lee (2010). Readers should particularly be cautious when interpreting the human capital trends for this country. Human capital per capita is further extended considering the population of the country who reach the year of total education, "P". For simplicity we have assumed that to be the age of 15. Therefore, the total amount of human capital is:

EQUATION 2

$$H=hP$$

As the interest rate ("ρ") is constant over time, changes in human capital are basically caused by either the change in the number of people educated, or an increase (decrease) in the years of education.

Regarding the shadow price per unit of human capital, $P_{k_{human}}$, it is obtained by computing the present value of the average labor compensation per unit of human capital, "r", received by workers over an entire life's working period, "T", i.e.:

EQUATION 3

$$P_{k_{human}}=\int_{t=0}^{T} r \cdot e^{-\delta t} dt$$

With regard to "T", this parameter is obtained by using various demographic inputs such as population and mortality rates by age and gender, as well as other parameters related to the labor market, particularly the participation of the population in the labor force by age and gender. In our case, for each nation we computed these shadow prices for every year within the time period 1990–2008. Concerning the discount rate, "δ", it was fixed in 8.5 percent. Subsequently we used the average of this rental price of one unit of human capital over time as the representative weight for entering human capital into the wealth accounting framework. For further details, see Arrow et al. (2012).

TABLE 1

Key variables and data sources used in the measurement of human capital

Variables	Data sources
Population by age and gender	United Nations Population Division (2011)
Mortality probability by age and gender	World Health Organization (2012)
Discount rate	Klenow and Rodríguez–Clare (1997)
Employment	Conference Board (2012)
Educational attainment	Barro and Lee (2010)
Employment compensation	Conference Board (2012); United Nations Statistics Division (2011a)
Labour force by age and gender	International Labour Organization (2011)

TABLE 2

Key variables and data sources used in the measurement of manufactured capital

Variables	Data sources
Investment	United Nations Statistics Division (2011b)
Depreciation rate	It is assumed a rate of 7%
Assets lifetime	It is assumed indefinite depreciation periods
Output growth	Conference Board (2012); United Nations Statistics Division (2011b)
Population	United Nations Population Division (2011)
Productivity	United Nations Statistics Division (2011b); Conference Board (2012); and United Nations Population Division (2011)

2. Manufactured capital

With regard to manufactured capital, we followed the method developed in King and Levine (1994), who based their calculations on the perpetual inventory method (PIM) by setting an initial capital estimate. Regarding the initial estimate, "K_o", it is assumed that the economy is in a steady-state, implying this that the capital-output ratio is constant in the long term, and can be derived as follows:

EQUATION 4

$$k = \frac{I/y}{(\delta + \gamma + n)}$$

where "k" is the capital-output ratio; "I" is investment; "y" is the output of the economy; "γ" is the steady-state growth rate of the economy, estimated as a weighted average growth rate of the economy under study, and that of the global economy (see King and Levine [1994]); "δ" is the depreciation rate of the capital (here is set at 7 percent, and it is additionally assumed to be constant across countries and time); and "n" is the population growth rate.

Once this ratio is measured, it is subsequently multiplied by the output of the economy under study, in order to obtain a first estimate of the manufactured capital stock in the initial period, K_o. Subsequently, the PIM allows capturing of the dynamics in the manufactured capital accumulation by looking at the annual changes in investment. The corresponding formula of the PIM combined with the initial estimate is:

EQUATION 5

$$K_t = \sum_{j=1}^{t} I_j (1-\gamma)^{t-j} + (1-\gamma)^t K_0$$

Finally, regarding the lifetimes of the assets, we have assumed indefinite depreciation periods. As mentioned in Chapter 2, we carried out our initial estimate in 1970 in order to minimize errors in the time period under study (1990–2008). As capital depreciates over time, the initial capital estimate retained in 1990 would be about 22 percent and only 5 percent in 2008. This means that any potential error in the departure point (year 1970) would be attenuated in the relevant period under analysis. For further details on this method, see King and Levine (1994).

3. Natural capital

3.1 Agricultural land

3.1.1 Cropland

Regarding the inclusion of this natural capital asset, we primarily obtained this by analyzing the physical amount of cropland area available every year, and its corresponding shadow price. We used cropland data from FAO for calculating the physical changes over the time span in study, 1990–2008. Concerning the valuing of this asset, we appealed conceptually to the net present value (NPV) of future rental flows. We applied this evaluation on an annual basis so as to obtain, subsequently, the average wealth value per hectare for the entire period of analysis. Once this later wealth value per hectare was obtained, we multiplied this by the total number of hectares available in the country for cropland. This method is also used in other studies, such as the World Bank (2011A). In our method, however, we introduce minor modifications by analyzing a vast number of crops (159) in order to arrive at a representative rental price per hectare for a specific year.

Concretely, we estimated the average rental price per hectare (*RPA*) for country "*i*" in the year "*j*" as follows:

EQUATION 6

$$RPA_{ij} = \frac{I}{A} \sum_{k=1}^{159} R_{ik} \cdot P_{ijk} \cdot Q_{ijk}$$

where "*Q*", "*P*" and "*R*" are the quantity of production of crop "*k*", (with *k*=1,2,..,159), price per amount of crop *k* and the rental rate of crop *k* respectively; "*j*" is the year of analysis, with "*j*" running from 1990 to 2008; and "*A*" is the total area harvested. To estimate the rent by crop we map FAO crop classification (HS) with those sectoral rental rates provided by Narayanan and Walmsley (2008) in order to get the rental rate by crop group.

To calculate the value of total wealth per hectare (*Wha*) we estimated the present value of future rental flows, as follows:

EQUATION 7

$$Wha_{ij} = \sum_{t=0}^{\infty} \frac{RPA_{ij}}{(1+r)^t}$$

where "*r*" is the discount rate, assumed to be equal to 5 percent and "*t*" is the planning horizon, here assumed up to infinity. Subsequently, we used the average wealth values per hectare ($\overline{Wha_i}$) over the study period as a proxy of the shadow price:

EQUATION 8

$$\overline{Wha_i} = \frac{I}{19} \sum_{t=1}^{19} Wha_{ij}$$

Finally, the total wealth in cropland land (WCL) for country "*i*" in year "*j*" is derived as follows:

EQUATION 9

$$WCL_{ij} = \overline{Wha_i} \cdot CLA_j$$

where "*CLA*" is the physical amount of total crop land area of country "*i*" and in the year "*j*", while "*WCL*" is the total wealth in cropland in the corresponding year.

3.1.2 Pastureland

For pastureland, we applied a similar methodology as with cropland in that we aimed at obtaining the total wealth per hectare of pastureland and the corresponding physical quantity available during the period of analysis. However, while it is possible to find data of production, prices, and rental rates of the products stemming from this kind of land, it is hard to link such rents to a particular amount of land involved in the production process (unlike cropland). Given this limitation, we assumed that the rents per hectare in pastureland are equal to that of the cropland. This also means that the total wealth per hectare in pastureland is identical to the estimates in the previous section for

TABLE 3.1

Key variables and data sources used in the measurement of agricultural land

Variables	Data sources
Quantity of crops produced	FAO (2011)
Price of crops produced	FAO (2011)
Rental Rate	Narayanan and Walmsley (2008)
Harvested area in crops	FAO (2011)
Discount rate	It is assumed a rate of 5%
Permant crops land area	FAO (2011)
Permanent pasture land area	FAO (2011)

TABLE 3.2

Key variables and data sources used in the measurement of forest wealth

Variables	Data sources
Forest stocks	FAO (2010); FAO (2006); FAO (2001); FAO (1995)
Forest stock com-mercially available	FAO (2006)
Wood production	FAO (2011)
Value of wood production	FAO (2011)
Rental rate	Bolt et al. (2002)
Forest area	FAO (2011)
Value of non–timber forest benefits (NTFB)	Lampietti and Dixon (1995)
Percentage of forest area used for the extraction of NTFB	World Bank (2006)
Discount rate	It is assumed a rate of 5%

cropland. Therefore the total wealth in pasture land (WPL) was estimated as follows:

EQUATION 10

$$WPL_{ij} = \overline{Wha_i} \cdot PLA_j$$

where "PLA" is the physical amount of pasture land area available in the period "j" and country "i".

3.2 Forest resources

3.2.1 Timber

In order to value forest timber stocks, we followed the methodology developed by Arrow et al. (2012), which differs to some extent from that of the World Bank (2006, 2011A). As a starting point, we estimated the volume of timber commercially available. This first measure basically stems from the multiplication of the forest area, timber density per area, and the percentage of such total volume that is commercially available – all these parameters are country-specific and were obtained from the Forest Resources Assessment (FAO, 2010; FAO, 2006; FAO, 2001; FAO, 1995). Unfortunately, parameters regarding the volume, area, and density of forest are only available for the following years: 1990, 2000, 2005, and 2010. We therefore carried out linear interpolations to derive estimates for those years where data is not available.

With regard to the stumpage price, we followed the World Bank's (2006) method by adopting a weighted average price of two different commodities: industrial roundwood and fuelwood, which are also country-specific parameters. The weight attached to the different prices is based on the quantity of the commodity manufactured, while industrial roundwood and fuelwood prices are obtained from the value and quantity exported and produced respectively. Three further steps were applied regarding the rental price estimates: (1) we converted the annual estimated values from current to constant prices by using each country-specific GDP deflator; (2) subsequently, we used information on the regional rental rates for timber estimated by Bolt et al. (2002). Such rates are assumed to be constant over time; and (3) lastly, we estimated the average price over the entire study period (1990–2008), thereby obtaining our proxy value for the shadow price of timber.

Concerning the estimates of total timber wealth, we multiplied the constant rental price over time obtained in the last step by the total volume of timber commercially available every year.

3.2.2 Non-timber forest resources

Consistent with the studies of Arrow et al. (2012) and the World Bank (2006, 2011B), we valued non-timber forest benefits (NTFB) following the work of Lampietti and Dixon (1995). These authors estimated the economic benefits of NTFR as US$190 per hectare for developed countries and as US$145 per hectare for developing countries. We then multiplied these coefficients by the forest area that is accessed by the population, which is assumed to be 10 percent of the total forest area. For the data on forest area, we used FAO (2012). Finally, the total wealth of NTFR was calculated as the present value of future benefits assuming an infinite time horizon and a discount rate of 5 percent.

3.3 Fisheries

We valued the wealth of fisheries for four countries: Australia, Canada, South Africa, and the United States. We restricted our analysis to only these countries due to lack of data in the other regions of interest. In this regard, we obtained the available stock of fisheries within these countries' fishing areas from the RAM Legacy Stock Assessment Database (RICHARD ET AL., IN PRESS). From this database, we were able to obtain the total biomass expressed in tonnes for several species which number vary according to the country. In the case of the above four countries, the RAM Legacy Stock Assessment Database reports 12 species for Australia; nine

species for Canada; 10 in South Africa; and 80 in the U.S. However, data on fisheries and prices were not found for the years 2007 and 2008. Therefore, we carried out our own estimates based on linear trends for these two years to be consistent with the rest of the wealth accounts.

Regarding the valuation of fisheries, our starting point was to derive prices per tonne from the total landing value and quantity of the Sea Around Us Project (SAUP 2011), which are available for the time period 1990–2006. It was however only possible to obtain such prices for 20 species in the case United states; 7 species for South Africa; 6 for Canada; and 20 for Australia. Given that the mapping between the stock assessed and the corresponding prices of such species was rather low, we opted for estimating a representative price per tonne of fisheries for each of the four countries. This was done by estimating a weighted (by extracted quantity) price of those species reported by the Sea Around Us Project, and using this as a proxy price for all the physical stocks. We subsequently averaged these weighted prices over time, and multiplied them by the fisheries rental rate from Narayanan and Walmsley (2008), thereby arriving at the average rental price for fisheries and country.

The last step for obtaining the wealth of fisheries consisted in multiplying the average rental price by the total stock of biomass available in each of the years under analysis.

TABLE 3.3

Key variables and data sources used in the measurement of fisheries

Variables	Data sources
Fishery stocks	Richard et al. (in press)
Value of capture fishery	SAUP (2011)
Quantity of capture fishery	SAUP (2011) and Sumaila et al. (2005)
Rental rate	Narayanan and Walmsley (2008)

TABLE 3.4

Key variables and data sources used in the measurement of fossil fuels

Variables	Data sources
Reserves	U.S. Energy Information Administration (2011)
Production	U.S. Energy Information Administration (2011)
Prices	U.S. Energy Information Administration (2011)
Rental rate	Narayanan and Walmsley (2008)

TABLE 3.5

Key variables and data sources used in the measurement of minerals

Variables	Data sources
Reserves	U.S. Geological Survey (2011)
Production	U.S. Geological Survey (2011)
Prices	U.S. Geological Survey (2011)) and World Bank (2011b)
Rental rate	Narayanan and Walmsley (2008)

3.4 Fossil fuels

In our analysis, we followed the approach used by Arrow et al. (2012). As noted in Chapter 2, fossil fuels consist of three main components: coal, natural gas, and oil. The methodology of valuing the wealth of these stated components largely follows the same procedure.

We referred to BP Statistical Review of World Energy (BP 2011) for prices of coal, natural gas, and oil. For coal, we averaged prices from four sources: the U.S., Northwest Europe, Japan Coking; and Japan Steam. For natural gas, we also averaged prices from five sources: the European Union (EU), United Kingdom, the U.S., Japan, and Canada. Lastly, we averaged the prices of four types of oil grades: Dubai, Brent, Nigerian Forcados, and West Texas Intermediate. We adjusted for inflation before averaging over time

by using the U.S. GDP deflator. We obtained the rental prices by multiplying the above estimated prices and the corresponding sectoral rental rates from Narayanan and Walmsley (2008).

We set the end of year reserves of coal, natural gas and oil to 2008 and obtained this dataset from the U.S. Energy Information Administration (2011).

The stocks of natural gas, oil, and coal for a previous year to 2008, were estimated as follows:

EQUATION 11

$$Stock_{t-1} = Stock_t + Production_t$$

where the corresponding stock under study in the year t-1 is derived from the production and stock in year "t". Finally, we computed the wealth coal, natural gas, and oil by multiplying the stocks and the unit rental price for each of our 20 countries for the period under study.

3.5 Metals and minerals

In order to value metals and minerals, we followed the method used by Arrow et al. (2012). We set the reserves base to 2008 and obtained reserves data from the United States Geological Survey published in their Mineral Commodity Summaries and/or Minerals Yearbooks (U.S. Geological Survey 2011). We focused on 10 mineral types: bauxite, copper, gold, iron, lead, nickel, phosphate, silver, tin, and zinc. As explained in Chapter 2 we only obtained reserves data for 12 countries: Australia, Brazil, Canada, Chile, China, Colombia, India, Japan, Russia, South Africa, the U.S., and Venezuela.

Production data are based on United States Geological Survey numbers published in their Mineral Commodity Summaries and/or Minerals Yearbook (U.S. Geological Survey 2011). We filled in the missing years by extrapolating linearly.

We calculated previous years' stocks by using the following equation:

EQUATION 12

$Stock_{t-1} = Stock_t + Production_t$

where the production and stock in year "t"are used to compute the amount of the mineral available in the year "t-1".

As far as prices are concerned, we obtained world annual market prices for the 10 mineral commodities from the World Bank (2011b) and u.s. Geological Survey (2011) for the period 1990–2008. We converted to year 2000 constant prices and computed average prices for each mineral. As with fossil fuels, we retrieved sectoral rental rates of different mineral industries from Narayanan and Walmsley (2008) and multiplied by the corresponding prices.

We finally valued minerals by multiplying mineral stocks by rental prices to obtain the total mineral wealth for each of the 12 countries for the period under study.

4. Health Capital

As discussed in chapter 2, our health capital estimates rely on the methodology developed in Arrow et al. (2012). In this work, the total value of health capital (V_{HeC}) stems from multiplying the value of the total expected discounted years of life remaining of a country's population (HeC) and the value of a statistical life year ($VSLY$), which is the constant shadow price of a unit of health capital. In other words:

As far as HeC is concerned, it is estimated as follows:

EQUATION 13

$V_{HeC} = HeC \; x \; VSLY$

where:

EQUATION 14

$$HeC = \sum_{a=0}^{100} P(a) \left[\sum_{t=a}^{100} f(t|t \geq a) \left(\sum_{u=0}^{t-a} (1-\delta)^u \right) \right]$$

"$P(a)$" is the population of age "a" available in the country. Years of life reaming are truncated at the age of 100.

"$f(t)=f(t|t \geq a)$" is the conditional density of age of death given survival to age "a" that results

from computing the density of age of death, "$f(t)$" – "t" being the year of death – and the cumulative distribution of age of death, "$F(a)$", in the following way:

EQUATION 15

$f(t|t \geq a) = [1-F(a)]^{-1} f(t)$

"δ" is the rate at which future years are discounted, assuming that the value of an additional year is independent of age.

"u" is time expressed in years.

Regarding the estimates of $VSLY$, these were obtained by dividing the value of the statistical life (vsl) and the average expected discounted years of life remaining per person.

Probability of dying, by age group, was obtained by the life tables of the World Health Organization (2012). The who life tables report the probability of death for five-year age groups. For our estimates, we additionally smoothed the data between age groups in order to get the parameter for every age. Moreover, as the who life tables are only available for the years 1990, 2000, and 2009, we used linear interpolations for obtaining all the years of interest, 1990–2008. Concerning the vsl, we used the value reported by epa of us$6.3 million in 2000 in the case of the u.s. For the remaining countries, we utilized an implied value of vsl estimated by multiplying the us$6.3 million value for the u.s. and the gdp (per capita) ratio of the country under analysis to the u.s. at the power of 0.6, as suggested by Viscusi and Aldy (2003) and applied in Arrow et al. (2012). Finally, we applied a discount rate of 5 percent.

5. Adjustments

5.1 Carbon damages

Carbon damage estimates are based on the method developed in Arrow et al. (2012). The key methodological steps can be described as follows: (1) obtain the total global carbon emissions for the period under analysis, 1990–2008; (2) derive the total global damages as a function

TABLE 4

Key variables and data sources used in the measurement of health capital

Variables	Data sources
Population by age	United Nations Population Division (2011)
Probability of dying by age	World Health Organization (2012)
Value of statistical life	U.S. Environmental Protection Agency (2000)
Discount rate	It is assumed a rate of 5%

TABLE 5.1

Key variables and data sources used in the measurement of carbon damages

Variables	Data sources
Carbon emission	Boden et al. (2011)
Forest area	FAO (2011)
carbon release per hectare of forest	Lampietti and Dixon 1995
Carbon cost	Tol (2009)
Climate change impacts	Nordhaus and Boyer (2000)
GDP	United Nations Statistics Division (2011b)

TABLE 5.2

Key variables and data sources used in the measurement of oil capital gains

Variables	Data sources
Carbon emission	Boden et al. (2011)
Reserves	U.S. Energy Information Administration (2011)
Oil production	U.S. Energy Information Administration (2011)
Oil consumption	U.S. Energy Information Administration (2011)
Prices	BP (2011)
Rental rate	Narayanan and Walmsley (2008)

of the emissions; and (3) allocate the global damages to the countries according to the potential effect of global warming in their economies.

Global carbon emissions: Two sources of carbon emissions were taken into account: (i) carbon emissions stemming from fuel consumption and cement, which were obtained from the Carbon Dioxide Information Analysis Center (BODEN ET AL. 2011); and (ii) emissions resulting from global deforestation. In this case, we used FAO (2011) data on the changes in annual global forest land. It is further estimated that the average carbon release per hectare is equal to 100 tonnes of carbon (LAMPIETTI AND DIXON 1995).

Global carbon damages: The damages per tonne of carbon released to the atmosphere are estimated at US$50 (see TOL ET AL., 2009). Multiplying the total global tonnes of carbon released to the atmosphere by the price per tonne, we obtain the total global carbon damages. Notice that this parameter is constant over time.

Assigning carbon damages to countries: to calculate the distribution of the damages that each region will suffer, we referred to the study of Nordhaus and Boyer (2000). This study presents the distribution of damages that different regions and the global economy as a whole will suffer as a percentage of the corresponding regional and global GDP. By using country and global GDP information, we were able to re-estimate regional percentage damages in terms of the total global GDP – and not related to the country GDP – as initially presented in Nordhaus and Boyer (2000). Finally, we apportioned the global damages estimated in step 2 according to this later percentage.

5.2 Oil capital gains

As noted in Chapter 2, gains in oil prices are separately accounted for in the wealth accounts. In order to include this adjustment, we assumed an annual increase of 5 percent in the rental price of oil, which corresponds to the annual average oil price increase during the years 1990–2008

TABLE 5.3

Total factor productivity estimates

	1990	1991	1992	1993	1994	1995	1996	1997	1998	1999	2000	2001	2002	2003	2004	2005	2006	2007	2008
Australia	0.15	-1.02	1.78	0.36	0.53	-0.12	2.14	1.19	1.78	0.64	-0.34	1.56	-0.28	-0.88	-0.23	-1.70	-1.82	0.11	-1.48
Brazil	-6.50	-0.27	-1.56	3.59	4.10	2.17	1.09	0.97	-2.58	-2.21	0.43	-0.71	-0.44	-0.89	1.63	-0.65	-0.40	1.13	-1.57
Canada	-1.68	-1.97	0.01	0.27	1.61	0.18	-1.21	1.23	0.33	1.05	1.33	-0.52	0.35	-0.67	-0.38	0.55	-0.41	-1.05	-1.82
Chile	-0.39	3.52	7.24	2.25	0.94	5.50	1.42	0.87	-2.20	-12.18	-0.07	-1.67	-1.96	-0.26	2.40	0.82	-3.76	0.61	-0.96
China	-0.73	2.14	4.33	3.07	2.97	7.52	-4.83	-1.36	-5.87	0.53	3.31	4.73	6.14	7.85	2.61	2.62	4.65	6.07	2.35
Colombia	-2.51	-3.11	2.24	-0.62	-2.14	3.57	-3.21	1.52	-2.49	-7.30	0.28	-1.58	1.41	-0.76	1.99	-0.24	4.33	1.43	-2.95
Ecuador	-0.02	2.42	-1.56	-2.58	1.27	-2.01	1.93	0.29	0.12	-5.30	2.33	0.46	-0.79	0.38	1.77	2.49	-0.15	-0.90	3.54
France	0.34	-0.27	-0.05	-0.86	0.92	0.90	-0.87	0.63	1.28	0.36	1.74	-0.46	0.74	-0.10	-0.54	-0.14	1.19	-0.51	-2.60
Germany	2.96	2.12	1.05	-0.34	1.97	1.76	1.36	1.66	-0.09	0.71	2.28	1.07	0.06	-0.25	0.35	1.45	2.90	1.31	-0.64
India	1.15	-2.37	1.57	1.83	2.60	2.81	3.58	0.45	2.61	2.20	-0.16	1.31	-0.60	3.69	2.33	3.65	3.38	2.79	0.72
Japan	2.32	0.30	-1.45	-0.16	-8.83	1.14	0.76	0.42	-2.15	0.01	1.00	0.14	0.73	0.98	1.47	0.74	0.58	1.57	-0.78
Kenya	0.60	-2.05	-4.13	-3.02	-0.07	1.56	1.09	-2.61	0.41	-0.50	-2.24	1.93	-2.47	0.02	1.60	2.36	1.96	2.22	-3.35
Nigeria	3.51	-2.22	-0.95	0.83	-0.45	-1.80	3.08	0.37	-0.39	-1.89	3.58	5.69	16.09	6.57	6.18	0.09	-0.43	0.32	-0.75
Norway	2.57	3.85	3.10	1.97	3.26	2.37	2.54	1.87	-1.17	-0.71	1.64	0.94	0.33	0.76	1.07	-0.34	-2.09	-2.56	-3.92
Russia*				-7.48	-10.59	-1.08	-1.66	3.92	-3.06	8.21	11.43	6.29	5.32	7.45	6.59	4.69	4.84	3.52	-0.37
Saudi Arabia	9.42	4.82	0.30	-4.64	-3.32	-2.80	0.99	0.54	0.59	-3.85	1.11	-3.92	-4.81	2.70	0.86	1.18	-1.38	-2.93	-1.39
South Africa	-3.72	-4.03	-5.08	-1.66	0.17	-0.44	0.27	-1.58	-4.02	-2.02	0.19	-0.92	0.35	-0.83	0.48	0.58	0.35	-0.17	-3.39
United Kingdom	-1.41	0.60	0.91	2.16	1.37	0.39	0.72	0.02	0.68	0.35	1.13	-0.01	0.49	1.15	1.08	-0.16	1.34	0.94	-0.85
United States	-0.06	-0.77	1.83	0.08	0.86	-0.11	1.29	0.66	0.44	1.47	1.26	-0.16	0.46	0.95	1.67	0.82	0.03	-0.09	-1.05
Venezuela	2.97	7.86	3.32	-2.34	-4.49	2.32	-1.97	4.40	-2.25	-8.34	1.49	0.90	-9.67	-8.14	16.57	8.30	2.62	2.12	0.62

*Note: The average TFP presented in Section 5 of Chapter 2 for the case of Russia is computed considering only the years 1993–2008.

Source: Conference Board (2012).

(BP 2011). These increments in the rental price of oil are multiplied by the stock of oil available in each period. Data on oil stock rely on the method presented above in Section 3.4.

Conversely, other countries that depend on oil imports may be negatively affected as their capacity to build other capital forms is frustrated by these higher prices. We therefore allocate those gains in oil prices to those nations that consume the commodity. To do so, we used data on oil consumption from our country sample as well as total world oil consumption. We were thus able to estimate the way in which the oil capital gains have to be distributed among each of the 20 countries in this study, as well as the rest of the world. Finally, we subtracted the oil capital gains from the losses due to oil consumption, thereby obtaining the net oil capital gains/losses.

5.3 Total factor productivity (TFP)

Country estimates on total factor productivity were obtained from the Total Economy Database (Conference Board, 2012). The corresponding values for all countries are listed in Table 5.3.

REFERENCES

ARROW, K., DASGUPTA, P., GOULDER, L., MUMFORD, K. & OLESON, K. (2012). Sustainability and the measurement of wealth. Forthcoming in *Environment and Development Economics*.

BARRO, R. & LEE, J. (2010). A new data set of educational attainment in the world, 1950-2010. *NBER Working Paper No. 15902*.

BODEN, T.A., MARLAND, G. & ANDRES, R. (2011). *Global, regional, and national fossil-fuel CO_2 emissions*. Carbon Dioxide Information Analysis Center. Retrieved from http://cdiac.ornl.gov/trends/emis/tre_usa.html

BOLT, K., MATETE, M. & CLEMENS, M. (2002). *Manual for calculating adjusted net savings*. Washington, DC: Environment Department, World Bank.

BP. (2011). *Statistical review of world energy 2011*. Retrieved May 2011, from http://www.bp.com/statisticalreview

CONFERENCE BOARD. (2012). *Total economy database*. Retrieved January 2012, from http://www.conference-board.org/data/economydatabase/

FAO. (1995). *Forest resources assessment 1990 - global synthesis*. Retrieved from http://www.fao.org/docrep/007/v5695e/v5695e00.htm

FAO. (2001). *Global forest resources assessment 2000 – main report*. Retrieved from http://www.fao.org/forestry/fra/2000/report/en/

FAO. (2006). *Global forest resources assessment 2005 – main report*. Retrieved from http://www.fao.org/docrep/008/a0400e/a0400e00.htm

FAO. (2010). *Global forest resources assessment 2010 – main report*. Retrieved from http://www.fao.org/forestry/fra/fra2010/en/

FAO. (2011). *FAOSTAT*. Retrieved May 2011, from http://faostat.fao.org/site/291/default.aspx

HERTEL, T., TSIGAS, M. & NARAYANAN, B. (2007). *Primary factor shares*. GTAP 7 Data Base Documentation. Center for Global Trade Analysis.

INTERNATIONAL LABOR ORGANIZATION. (2011). *LABORSTA*. Total economically active population. Available at http://laborsta.ilo.org/STP/guest, accessed in 2011.

KING, R.G. & LEVINE, R. (1994). Capital fundamentalism, economic development and economic growth. *Carnegie-Rochester Conference Series on Public Policy, 40*, 259-292.

KLENOW, P.J. & RODRÍGUEZ-CLARE, A. (2005). Externalities and growth. In P. Aghion & S. Durlauf (Eds.) *Handbook of economic growth*. Amsterdam: North Holland.

LAMPIETTI, J. & DIXON, J. (1995). *To see the forest for the trees: A guide to non-timber forest benefits*. Washington, DC: World Bank.

NARAYANAN, B.G. & WALMSLEY, T.L. (2008). *Global trade, assistance, and production: The GTAP 7 data base*. Retrieved from http://www.gtap.agecon.purdue.edu/databases/v7/v7_doco.asp

NORDHAUS, W.D. & BOYER, J. (2000). *Warming the world: Economic models of global warming*. Cambridge, MA: MIT Press.

RICARD, D., MINTO, C., JENSEN, O. & BAUM, J.K. (IN PRESS). Evaluating the knowledge base and status of commercially exploited marine species with the RAM legacy stock assessment database. *Fish and Fisheries*.

SAUP. (2011). *The Sea Around Us Project database*. Retrieved May 2011, from http://www.seaaroundus.org/data/

SUMAILA, U., MARSDEN, A., WATSON, R. & PAULY, D. (2005). *Global ex-vessel fish price database: Construction, spatial and temporal applications*. The University of British Columbia: Fisheries Center.

TOL, R.S.J. (2009). The economic effects of climate change. *Journal of Economic Perspectives, 23*, 29–51.

UNITED NATIONS. (2011). *UN data*. Retrieved May 2011, from http://data.un.org/Default.aspx

UNITED NATIONS DEVELOPMENT PROGRAMME. (2011). *Human development reports. HDI trends 1980-2010*. Retrieved May 2011, from http://hdr.undp.org/en/statistics/hdi/

UNITED NATIONS POPULATION DIVISION. (2011). *World population prospects: The 2010 Revision*. New York.

UNITED NATIONS STATISTICS DIVISION. (2011A). *National Accounts Estimates of Main Aggregates*. Available: http://data.un.org/Explorer.aspx?d=SNAAMA

UNITED NATIONS STATISTICS DIVISION. (2011B). *Nationals Accounts Main Aggregates Database*. Available: http://unstats.un.org/unsd/snaama/Introduction.asp

U.S. ENERGY INFORMATION ADMINISTRATION. (2011). *International energy statistics*. Retrieved May 2011, from http://www.eia.gov/countries/data.cfm

U.S. ENVIRONMENTAL PROTECTION AGENCY. (2000). *Guidelines for Preparing Economic Analyses*. EPA 240-R-00-003, Washington, DC, USA.

U.S. GEOLOGICAL SURVEY. (2011). *Mineral commodity summaries*. Retrieved May 2011, from http://minerals.usgs.gov/minerals/pubs/mcs/

U.S. GEOLOGICAL SURVEY. (2011). *Mineral yearbook: Volume I - Metals and minerals*. Retrieved May 2011, from http://minerals.usgs.gov/minerals/pubs/commodity/myb/

U.S. GEOLOGICAL SURVEY. (2011). *Mineral yearbook: Volume III - Area reports: International*. Retrieved May 2011, from http://minerals.usgs.gov/minerals/pubs/country/index.html#pubs

VISCUSI, W.K. & ALDY J.E. (2003). The value of a statistical life: A critical review of market estimates throughout the world. *Journal of Risk and Uncertainty, 27*(1), 5-76.

WORLD BANK. (2006). *Where is the wealth of nations?* Washington, DC: World Bank.

WORLD BANK. (2011A). *The changing wealth of nations*. Washington, DC: World Bank.

WORLD BANK. (2011B). *Gem commodity database*. Retrieved May 2011 from http://data.worldbank.org/data-catalog/commodity-price-data

WORLD HEALTH ORGANIZATION. (2012). *Life tables for WHO member states*. Retrieved January 2012 from http://www.who.int/healthinfo/statistics/mortality_life_tables/en/

Data annex: wealth by country

REFERENCES

CONFERENCE BOARD. (2012). *Total economy database*. Retrieved January 2012, from http://www.conference-board.org/data/economydatabase/

UNITED NATIONS POPULATION DIVISION. (2011). *World population prospects: The 2010 revision*. New York.

Australia

UNIT: millions of constant US$ of year 2000

		1990	1991	1992	1993	1994	1995	1996
1	Inclusive Wealth Index, rows 2 + 3 + 4	4,747,891	4,782,508	4,817,827	4,846,260	4,904,314	4,953,813	5,002,667
2	Produced capital	661,628	675,640	692,791	712,469	738,622	765,188	795,459
3	Human capital	2,100,350	2,127,023	2,146,937	2,166,146	2,194,588	2,228,303	2,250,604
4	Natural capital, rows 5 + 8 + 11 + 12 + 16	1,985,913	1,979,844	1,978,100	1,967,645	1,971,105	1,960,323	1,956,604
5	Agricultural land, rows 6 + 7	442,297	440,862	443,913	438,302	446,695	441,218	443,002
6	Cropland	45,785	43,683	45,115	44,266	45,231	38,375	34,757
7	Pastureland	396,512	397,179	398,798	394,037	401,464	402,843	408,245
8	Forest resources, rows 9 + 10	219,757	219,817	219,877	219,937	219,996	220,056	220,116
9	Timber	171,244	171,291	171,337	171,384	171,431	171,477	171,524
10	Non-timber forest resources	48,513	48,526	48,539	48,553	48,566	48,579	48,592
11	Fisheries	308	278	261	245	238	236	233
12	Fossil fuels, rows 13 + 14 + 15	1,222,824	1,218,953	1,214,907	1,210,834	1,206,702	1,202,237	1,197,664
13	Oil	11,639	11,634	11,629	11,625	11,620	11,615	11,610
14	Natural gas	50,848	50,096	49,293	48,431	47,501	46,470	45,408
15	Coal	1,160,337	1,157,222	1,153,984	1,150,778	1,147,581	1,144,152	1,140,647
16	Minerals, rows 17 + 18 +...+ 26	100,728	99,935	99,143	98,327	97,473	96,576	95,589
17	Bauxite	10,882	10,816	10,752	10,685	10,617	10,548	10,478
18	Appendix	7,131	7,069	6,997	6,927	6,851	6,769	6,667
19	Gold	8,951	8,744	8,530	8,312	8,086	7,863	7,607
20	Iron	44,159	43,892	43,637	43,361	43,069	42,743	42,408
21	Lead	1,917	1,886	1,855	1,827	1,798	1,773	1,745
22	Nickel	20,555	20,505	20,464	20,417	20,360	20,289	20,208
23	Phosphate	385	385	385	385	385	385	385
24	Silver	812	796	780	765	751	738	724
25	Tin	123	121	118	114	110	106	102
26	Zinc	5,812	5,720	5,627	5,535	5,445	5,361	5,264
27	Health capital	81,730,343	82,921,298	84,053,099	85,144,107	86,221,223	87,309,208	88,432,849
28	IWI adjustments excluding TFP, rows 29 + 30	-3,780	-3,819	-4,138	-4,650	-5,028	-5,401	-5,722
29	Carbon damages (annual change)	1,151	1,168	1,155	1,154	1,173	1,193	1,216
30	Oil capital gains (annual change)	-4,930	-4,987	-5,293	-5,804	-6,201	-6,594	-6,939

	Per Capita Values	1990	1991	1992	1993	1994	1995	1996
31	Per capita Inclusive Wealth Index	277,717	276,116	274,842	273,377	273,651	273,413	273,077
32	Per capita produced capital	38,700	39,008	39,521	40,190	41,214	42,233	43,421
33	Per capita human capital	122,855	122,803	122,476	122,192	122,453	122,986	122,852
34	Per capita natural capital	116,161	114,306	112,844	110,994	109,984	108,195	106,804
35	Per capita health capital	4,780,628	4,787,429	4,794,960	4,802,963	4,810,964	4,818,810	4,827,216
36	TFP (in percentage)	0.15	-1.02	1.78	0.36	0.53	-0.12	2.14
37	Population	17,096,153	17,320,633	17,529,469	17,727,413	17,921,818	18,118,416	18,319,637

Data for TFP and population was obtained from Conference Board (2012), and United Nations Population Division (2011) respectively.

	1997	1998	1999	2000	2001	2002	2003	2004	2005	2006	2007	2008
1	5,054,439	5,116,193	5,169,947	5,246,458	5,303,968	5,383,658	5,467,852	5,564,708	5,698,718	5,825,973	5,969,781	6,105,831
2	831,255	868,670	910,913	950,558	978,463	1,027,813	1,083,185	1,142,991	1,210,489	1,281,239	1,363,182	1,440,787
3	2,275,721	2,304,747	2,332,119	2,373,981	2,410,817	2,457,044	2,500,680	2,545,069	2,615,175	2,690,889	2,771,667	2,847,924
4	1,947,463	1,942,776	1,926,914	1,921,919	1,914,688	1,898,801	1,883,987	1,876,649	1,873,054	1,853,845	1,834,931	1,817,120
5	440,125	441,635	432,059	433,745	433,935	425,651	418,509	419,090	423,888	414,153	405,129	397,358
6	38,185	42,184	43,613	45,327	47,733	45,826	45,112	45,784	47,366	45,769	42,403	42,255
7	401,940	399,451	388,446	388,418	386,203	379,825	373,397	373,306	376,522	368,383	362,726	355,103
8	220,176	220,235	220,295	220,355	220,070	219,786	219,501	219,217	218,932	217,618	216,304	214,990
9	171,570	171,617	171,663	171,710	171,488	171,267	171,045	170,823	170,602	169,577	168,553	167,529
10	48,605	48,619	48,632	48,645	48,582	48,519	48,456	48,394	48,331	48,041	47,751	47,460
11	231	227	223	220	218	217	214	211	208	206	204	201
12	1,192,854	1,187,680	1,182,434	1,176,921	1,171,064	1,165,006	1,158,884	1,152,578	1,145,928	1,139,206	1,132,126	1,124,994
13	11,605	11,600	11,595	11,588	11,582	11,577	11,572	11,567	11,563	11,559	11,554	11,550
14	44,354	43,259	42,145	40,989	39,806	38,574	37,302	35,996	34,559	33,053	31,511	29,935
15	1,136,896	1,132,821	1,128,694	1,124,344	1,119,676	1,114,855	1,110,010	1,105,015	1,099,805	1,094,594	1,089,060	1,083,509
16	94,077	92,999	91,903	90,678	89,400	88,141	86,879	85,552	84,098	82,662	81,168	79,578
17	10,406	10,333	10,254	10,167	10,079	9,992	9,901	9,830	9,732	9,632	9,530	9,426
18	6,465	6,344	6,200	6,038	5,868	5,696	5,535	5,364	5,183	5,012	4,843	4,671
19	7,036	6,762	6,497	6,235	5,984	5,743	5,494	5,267	5,035	4,818	4,600	4,410
20	42,048	41,693	41,347	40,956	40,543	40,126	39,699	39,166	38,568	37,941	37,260	36,480
21	1,695	1,662	1,625	1,585	1,547	1,510	1,473	1,437	1,396	1,359	1,324	1,290
22	20,066	19,963	19,871	19,752	19,610	19,476	19,348	19,222	19,084	18,958	18,843	18,707
23	385	385	385	382	375	367	358	349	339	328	318	307
24	709	689	666	638	611	583	558	528	495	472	446	420
25	97	93	88	84	79	76	74	74	73	72	71	70
26	5,170	5,075	4,970	4,841	4,704	4,571	4,437	4,317	4,193	4,070	3,933	3,796
27	89,574,978	90,739,006	91,926,438	93,141,001	94,339,347	95,566,314	96,870,704	98,318,871	99,955,087	101,840,301	103,908,549	106,078,149
28	-6,018	-6,349	-6,765	-6,999	-7,336	-7,798	-8,049	-8,308	-8,836	-9,112	-9,672	-10,551
29	1,235	1,231	1,222	1,249	1,219	1,230	1,299	1,362	1,412	1,468	1,500	1,534
30	-7,253	-7,580	-7,987	-8,248	-8,555	-9,028	-9,348	-9,670	-10,248	-10,580	-11,172	-12,085

	1997	1998	1999	2000	2001	2002	2003	2004	2005	2006	2007	2008
31	272,842	273,084	272,851	273,761	273,652	274,620	275,596	276,799	279,301	280,847	282,660	283,810
32	44,872	46,366	48,075	49,600	50,483	52,429	54,596	56,854	59,327	61,763	64,545	66,970
33	122,845	123,019	123,081	123,875	124,383	125,333	126,042	126,596	128,173	129,717	131,234	132,376
34	105,125	103,698	101,695	100,286	98,786	96,858	94,958	93,348	91,801	89,367	86,881	84,463
35	4,835,316	4,843,320	4,851,539	4,860,118	4,867,322	4,874,825	4,882,566	4,890,556	4,898,914	4,909,316	4,919,915	4,930,699
36	1.19	1.78	0.64	-0.34	1.56	-0.28	-0.88	-0.23	-1.70	-1.82	0.11	-1.48
37	18,525,153	18,734,878	18,947,894	19,164,351	19,382,188	19,604,051	19,840,120	20,103,822	20,403,520	20,744,295	21,119,988	21,513,817

Brazil

UNIT: millions of constant US$ of year 2000

		1990	1991	1992	1993	1994	1995	1996
1	Inclusive Wealth Index, rows 2 + 3 + 4	4,922,507	5,034,400	5,141,044	5,252,759	5,380,368	5,523,537	5,668,095
2	Produced capital	1,059,810	1,069,536	1,073,024	1,081,225	1,100,729	1,125,808	1,150,665
3	Human capital	2,406,780	2,510,655	2,617,003	2,722,790	2,833,959	2,950,267	3,074,410
4	Natural capital, rows 5 + 8 + 11 + 12 + 16	1,455,917	1,454,210	1,451,016	1,448,744	1,445,680	1,447,463	1,443,019
5	Agricultural land, rows 6 + 7	231,816	235,014	236,710	239,353	241,228	247,997	248,521
6	Cropland	55,081	56,596	56,609	57,568	57,760	62,845	62,749
7	Pastureland	176,735	178,418	180,101	181,784	183,468	185,151	185,772
8	Forest resources, rows 9 + 10	1,019,148	1,014,845	1,010,542	1,006,238	1,001,935	997,631	993,328
9	Timber	878,888	875,289	871,691	868,093	864,494	860,896	857,297
10	Non-timber forest resources	140,261	139,556	138,851	138,146	137,440	136,735	136,030
11	Fisheries							
12	Fossil fuels, rows 13 + 14 + 15	151,293	151,128	150,959	150,779	150,587	150,389	150,178
13	Oil	81,482	81,476	81,471	81,465	81,459	81,452	81,445
14	Natural gas	13,564	13,468	13,362	13,243	13,120	12,990	12,846
15	Coal	56,246	56,184	56,126	56,071	56,009	55,946	55,888
16	Minerals, rows 17 + 18 +...+ 26	53,659	53,223	52,805	52,374	51,930	51,447	50,992
17	Bauxite	3,117	3,102	3,089	3,075	3,064	3,049	3,033
18	Appendix	2,688	2,681	2,675	2,667	2,660	2,652	2,644
19	Gold	2,345	2,276	2,209	2,154	2,099	2,050	2,003
20	Iron	40,220	39,914	39,620	39,300	38,967	38,597	38,246
21	Lead	44	43	43	43	43	42	42
22	Nickel	3,328	3,311	3,300	3,290	3,280	3,261	3,245
23	Phosphate	859	859	859	859	859	859	859
24	Silver	-	-	-	-	-	-	-
25	Tin	349	337	325	314	303	296	288
26	Zinc	710	700	686	671	656	641	632
27	Health capital	255,297,511	260,126,396	264,886,415	269,616,728	274,376,251	279,214,853	284,114,750
28	IWI adjustments excluding TFP, rows 29 + 30	-15,470	-15,963	-16,494	-17,346	-18,476	-19,884	-21,308
29	Carbon damages (annual change)	-8,590	-8,717	-8,624	-8,616	-8,754	-8,906	-9,081
30	Oil capital gains (annual change)	-6,880	-7,246	-7,870	-8,730	-9,722	-10,978	-12,226

	Per Capita Values	1990	1991	1992	1993	1994	1995	1996
31	Per capita Inclusive Wealth Index	32,893	33,089	33,258	33,460	33,754	34,128	34,490
32	Per capita produced capital	7,082	7,030	6,941	6,887	6,906	6,956	7,002
33	Per capita human capital	16,083	16,502	16,930	17,344	17,779	18,229	18,707
34	Per capita natural capital	9,729	9,558	9,387	9,229	9,070	8,943	8,781
35	Per capita health capital	1,705,962	1,709,706	1,713,565	1,717,459	1,721,322	1,725,165	1,728,796
36	TFP (in percentage)	-6.50	-0.27	-1.56	3.59	4.10	2.17	1.09
37	Population	149,650,206	152,146,887	154,582,103	156,985,824	159,398,558	161,848,162	164,342,524

Data for TFP and population was obtained from Conference Board (2012), and United Nations Population Division (2011) respectively.

	1997	1998	1999	2000	2001	2002	2003	2004	2005	2006	2007	2008
1	5,829,884	5,992,024	6,146,495	6,299,015	6,490,400	6,632,379	6,758,525	6,896,408	7,044,434	7,153,950	7,264,466	7,413,777
2	1,182,836	1,212,368	1,230,625	1,253,267	1,273,852	1,287,776	1,295,990	1,312,601	1,331,940	1,360,796	1,404,541	1,464,091
3	3,208,527	3,345,651	3,486,299	3,620,695	3,793,288	3,925,014	4,046,622	4,171,206	4,303,947	4,390,723	4,463,687	4,559,539
4	1,438,521	1,434,005	1,429,571	1,425,053	1,423,261	1,419,590	1,415,914	1,412,601	1,408,547	1,402,432	1,396,238	1,390,147
5	249,046	249,570	250,191	250,812	252,787	252,917	253,109	253,780	253,780	253,780	253,780	253,972
6	62,654	62,558	62,558	62,558	63,771	63,901	64,572	65,244	65,724	65,724	65,724	65,916
7	186,393	187,013	187,633	188,254	189,016	189,016	188,536	188,536	188,056	188,056	188,056	188,056
8	989,024	984,721	980,417	976,114	973,146	970,179	967,211	964,244	961,277	956,334	951,392	946,450
9	853,699	850,101	846,502	842,904	840,690	838,477	836,263	834,050	831,836	827,429	823,023	818,616
10	135,325	134,620	133,915	133,210	132,456	131,702	130,948	130,194	129,441	128,905	128,370	127,834
11												
12	149,944	149,702	149,448	149,147	148,879	148,572	148,250	147,895	147,526	147,157	146,788	146,330
13	81,437	81,428	81,419	81,408	81,398	81,386	81,374	81,362	81,348	81,334	81,318	81,302
14	12,687	12,521	12,344	12,135	11,945	11,712	11,459	11,182	10,901	10,618	10,336	9,974
15	55,820	55,753	55,685	55,604	55,536	55,474	55,417	55,352	55,277	55,206	55,134	55,054
16	50,507	50,012	49,515	48,980	48,448	47,922	47,343	46,681	45,964	45,160	44,277	43,395
17	3,016	2,999	2,979	2,960	2,940	2,921	2,896	2,866	2,834	2,801	2,764	2,724
18	2,637	2,631	2,626	2,620	2,615	2,610	2,605	2,588	2,565	2,539	2,504	2,466
19	1,958	1,919	1,878	1,839	1,798	1,769	1,738	1,701	1,671	1,637	1,598	1,556
20	37,871	37,474	37,083	36,656	36,233	35,807	35,335	34,809	34,243	33,604	32,890	32,183
21	41	41	40	40	40	39	39	38	37	36	34	33
22	3,225	3,201	3,175	3,146	3,118	3,089	3,060	3,027	2,980	2,928	2,891	2,856
23	859	859	859	859	859	859	859	859	859	859	859	859
24	-	-	-	-	-	-	-	-	-	-	-	-
25	280	275	269	263	258	252	247	242	237	233	228	223
26	620	613	605	597	588	577	565	552	538	524	508	494
27	289,110,033	294,156,897	299,191,599	304,164,825	309,009,448	313,756,570	318,372,370	322,807,862	327,020,940	330,966,728	334,654,704	338,164,850
28	-22,814	-23,930	-24,443	-25,521	-26,317	-26,196	-26,170	-27,392	-29,168	-31,194	-33,106	-35,036
29	-9,220	-9,189	-9,123	-9,327	-9,103	-9,183	-9,695	-10,168	-10,542	-10,958	-11,196	-11,449
30	-13,594	-14,740	-15,320	-16,194	-17,214	-17,013	-16,475	-17,223	-18,625	-20,236	-21,910	-23,587

	1997	1998	1999	2000	2001	2002	2003	2004	2005	2006	2007	2008
31	34,937	35,370	35,749	36,113	36,694	36,993	37,210	37,506	37,876	38,061	38,275	38,706
32	7,088	7,156	7,157	7,185	7,202	7,183	7,135	7,139	7,161	7,240	7,400	7,644
33	19,228	19,749	20,277	20,758	21,446	21,892	22,279	22,685	23,141	23,360	23,518	23,804
34	8,621	8,465	8,315	8,170	8,047	7,918	7,795	7,682	7,573	7,461	7,356	7,258
35	1,732,555	1,736,364	1,740,131	1,743,811	1,747,029	1,750,002	1,752,833	1,755,599	1,758,300	1,760,853	1,763,214	1,765,475
36	0.97	-2.58	-2.21	0.43	-0.71	-0.44	-0.89	1.63	-0.65	-0.40	1.13	-1.57
37	166,869,168	169,409,713	171,936,271	174,425,387	176,877,135	179,289,227	181,633,074	183,873,377	185,986,964	187,958,211	189,798,070	191,543,237

Canada

UNIT: millions of constant US$ of year 2000

		1990	1991	1992	1993	1994	1995	1996
1	Inclusive Wealth Index, rows 2 + 3 + 4	8,602,456	8,684,872	8,754,117	8,821,980	8,901,305	8,966,504	9,032,373
2	Produced capital	1,037,863	1,065,359	1,088,187	1,107,455	1,132,513	1,153,643	1,177,693
3	Human capital	3,984,467	4,045,095	4,097,546	4,152,545	4,213,547	4,264,748	4,313,830
4	Natural capital, rows 5 + 8 + 11 + 12 + 16	3,580,126	3,574,418	3,568,384	3,561,979	3,555,246	3,548,113	3,540,849
5	Agricultural land, rows 6 + 7	30,817	30,810	30,838	30,865	30,892	30,920	30,947
6	Cropland	23,585	23,551	23,611	23,670	23,729	23,788	23,848
7	Pastureland	7,232	7,259	7,227	7,195	7,164	7,131	7,099
8	Forest resources, rows 9 + 10	1,865,803	1,865,803	1,865,803	1,865,803	1,865,803	1,865,803	1,865,803
9	Timber	1,768,421	1,768,421	1,768,421	1,768,421	1,768,421	1,768,421	1,768,421
10	Non-timber forest resources	97,382	97,382	97,382	97,382	97,382	97,382	97,382
11	Fisheries	313	253	198	145	123	136	152
12	Fossil fuels, rows 13 + 14 + 15	1,661,199	1,656,219	1,650,857	1,645,063	1,638,865	1,632,305	1,625,626
13	Oil	1,393,134	1,393,118	1,393,102	1,393,084	1,393,066	1,393,047	1,393,027
14	Natural gas	162,323	158,319	153,858	149,012	143,815	138,285	132,649
15	Coal	105,742	104,782	103,898	102,967	101,984	100,973	99,950
16	Minerals, rows 17 + 18 +...+ 26	21,994	21,332	20,689	20,104	19,563	18,949	18,321
17	Bauxite	-	-	-	-	-	-	-
18	Appendix	4,149	3,994	3,847	3,707	3,587	3,448	3,317
19	Gold	3,996	3,843	3,703	3,571	3,444	3,312	3,168
20	Iron	5,159	5,078	5,004	4,936	4,854	4,767	4,690
21	Lead	172	157	139	130	121	109	96
22	Nickel	5,955	5,819	5,687	5,554	5,448	5,320	5,183
23	Phosphate	119	119	119	119	119	119	119
24	Silver	487	469	453	441	431	414	397
25	Tin	-	-	-	-	-	-	-
26	Zinc	1,956	1,853	1,736	1,647	1,559	1,460	1,351
27	Health capital	137,635,198	139,530,996	141,362,059	143,121,176	144,806,653	146,423,819	147,990,342
28	IWI adjustments excluding TFP, rows 29 + 30	58,780	62,250	64,895	67,866	71,304	74,683	78,232
29	Carbon damages (annual change)	1,986	2,015	1,993	1,992	2,023	2,058	2,099
30	Oil capital gains (annual change)	56,794	60,235	62,902	65,874	69,281	72,624	76,133

	Per Capita Values	1990	1991	1992	1993	1994	1995	1996
31	Per capita Inclusive Wealth Index	310,548	309,602	308,394	307,338	306,846	306,002	305,331
32	Per capita produced capital	37,467	37,978	38,335	38,581	39,040	39,371	39,811
33	Per capita human capital	143,839	144,201	144,350	144,665	145,249	145,544	145,825
34	Per capita natural capital	129,242	127,422	125,709	124,091	122,557	121,087	119,695
35	Per capita health capital	4,968,627	4,974,061	4,979,964	4,986,015	4,991,778	4,997,043	5,002,678
36	TFP (in percentage)	-1.68	-1.97	0.01	0.27	1.61	0.18	-1.21
37	Population	27,700,854	28,051,725	28,386,162	28,704,519	29,009,032	29,302,092	29,582,222

Data for TFP and population was obtained from Conference Board (2012), and United Nations Population Division (2011) respectively.

	1997	1998	1999	2000	2001	2002	2003	2004	2005	2006	2007	2008
1	9,140,269	9,241,793	9,355,364	9,475,508	9,663,691	9,900,493	10,149,382	10,374,359	10,605,677	10,744,377	10,909,131	11,062,192
2	1,216,007	1,254,582	1,299,425	1,352,879	1,397,071	1,445,944	1,500,496	1,563,323	1,637,394	1,719,229	1,802,291	1,883,697
3	4,390,833	4,461,389	4,537,908	4,612,564	4,764,641	4,960,580	5,162,654	5,332,617	5,497,739	5,562,490	5,651,995	5,731,080
4	3,533,428	3,525,822	3,518,031	3,510,065	3,501,979	3,493,970	3,486,232	3,478,420	3,470,544	3,462,658	3,454,846	3,447,416
5	30,897	30,847	30,796	30,746	30,696	30,703	30,711	30,719	30,726	30,735	30,740	30,740
6	23,817	23,787	23,757	23,727	23,697	23,700	23,703	23,706	23,710	23,713	23,715	23,715
7	7,079	7,059	7,039	7,019	6,999	7,003	7,008	7,012	7,017	7,022	7,026	7,026
8	1,865,803	1,865,803	1,865,803	1,865,803	1,865,803	1,865,803	1,865,803	1,865,803	1,865,803	1,865,803	1,865,803	1,865,803
9	1,768,421	1,768,421	1,768,421	1,768,421	1,768,421	1,768,421	1,768,421	1,768,421	1,768,421	1,768,421	1,768,421	1,768,421
10	97,382	97,382	97,382	97,382	97,382	97,382	97,382	97,382	97,382	97,382	97,382	97,382
11	165	172	171	179	193	187	187	194	200	207	213	219
12	1,618,858	1,611,926	1,604,744	1,597,405	1,589,924	1,582,459	1,575,228	1,567,915	1,560,535	1,553,156	1,545,862	1,538,956
13	1,393,007	1,392,986	1,392,965	1,392,944	1,392,922	1,392,899	1,392,874	1,392,850	1,392,826	1,392,800	1,392,773	1,392,747
14	126,962	121,064	114,881	108,496	101,986	95,441	89,072	82,674	76,199	69,737	63,405	57,438
15	98,889	97,876	96,898	95,965	95,016	94,119	93,281	92,391	91,510	90,620	89,684	88,770
16	17,706	17,075	16,516	15,931	15,363	14,818	14,303	13,790	13,280	12,758	12,227	11,697
17	-	-	-	-	-	-	-	-	-	-	-	-
18	3,191	3,056	2,945	2,824	2,702	2,588	2,481	2,373	2,259	2,144	2,030	1,914
19	3,019	2,876	2,739	2,603	2,466	2,336	2,214	2,101	1,996	1,906	1,817	1,735
20	4,607	4,522	4,446	4,367	4,306	4,237	4,162	4,098	4,030	3,955	3,881	3,811
21	86	76	67	59	51	46	42	38	34	29	25	21
22	5,049	4,901	4,776	4,641	4,511	4,385	4,269	4,137	3,996	3,831	3,650	3,467
23	119	119	119	117	115	111	107	103	100	98	96	92
24	380	364	349	333	316	298	280	263	248	234	223	213
25	-	-	-	-	-	-	-	-	-	-	-	-
26	1,255	1,161	1,075	986	896	817	747	677	617	561	505	444
27	149,470,088	150,915,058	152,396,756	153,962,880	155,530,462	157,198,315	158,945,088	160,738,032	162,558,738	164,417,500	166,306,372	168,210,367
28	81,676	85,906	89,682	94,385	98,833	103,634	107,831	113,065	118,800	125,873	131,604	139,034
29	2,131	2,124	2,109	2,156	2,104	2,123	2,241	2,350	2,437	2,533	2,588	2,646
30	79,544	83,782	87,573	92,229	96,729	101,511	105,590	110,714	116,363	123,340	129,016	136,388

	1997	1998	1999	2000	2001	2002	2003	2004	2005	2006	2007	2008
31	306,204	306,894	307,906	308,977	312,062	316,494	321,096	324,771	328,518	329,300	330,807	331,919
32	40,737	41,661	42,767	44,115	45,114	46,223	47,471	48,940	50,719	52,692	54,652	56,520
33	147,095	148,150	149,353	150,406	153,861	158,578	163,331	166,938	170,296	170,482	171,390	171,960
34	118,372	117,083	115,786	114,456	113,087	111,694	110,294	108,893	107,502	106,125	104,764	103,439
35	5,007,333	5,011,463	5,015,720	5,020,414	5,022,420	5,025,244	5,028,545	5,031,932	5,035,364	5,039,157	5,043,051	5,047,126
36	1.23	0.33	1.05	1.33	-0.52	0.35	-0.67	-0.38	0.55	-0.41	-1.05	-1.82
37	29,850,242	30,113,972	30,383,823	30,667,365	30,967,236	31,281,727	31,608,562	31,943,605	32,283,413	32,627,978	32,977,334	33,327,954

Chile

UNIT: millions of constant US$ of year 2000

		1990	1991	1992	1993	1994	1995	1996
1	Inclusive Wealth Index, rows 2 + 3 + 4	646,491	657,770	673,869	691,511	705,494	720,106	735,881
2	Produced capital	60,588	63,789	68,554	74,642	80,978	89,587	98,866
3	Human capital	360,831	369,882	382,991	395,363	403,536	410,714	418,377
4	Natural capital, rows 5 + 8 + 11 + 12 + 16	225,071	224,100	222,324	221,506	220,981	219,806	218,637
5	Agricultural land, rows 6 + 7	100,947	100,249	98,769	98,268	98,096	97,335	96,712
6	Cropland	19,359	18,661	17,181	16,362	16,191	15,238	14,603
7	Pastureland	81,588	81,588	81,588	81,906	81,906	82,096	82,109
8	Forest resources, rows 9 + 10	68,205	68,392	68,579	68,766	68,953	69,140	69,327
9	Timber	64,481	64,654	64,827	65,000	65,173	65,346	65,520
10	Non-timber forest resources	3,724	3,738	3,752	3,766	3,780	3,794	3,808
11	Fisheries							
12	Fossil fuels, rows 13 + 14 + 15	4,546	4,503	4,468	4,435	4,403	4,373	4,344
13	Oil	1,124	1,124	1,124	1,124	1,123	1,123	1,123
14	Natural gas	975	964	952	938	924	909	895
15	Coal	2,447	2,415	2,392	2,372	2,355	2,341	2,326
16	Minerals, rows 17 + 18 +...+ 26	51,373	50,956	50,509	50,038	49,529	48,958	48,253
17	Bauxite	-	-	-	-	-	-	-
18	Appendix	46,036	45,675	45,290	44,879	44,437	43,940	43,319
19	Gold	2,488	2,461	2,431	2,401	2,366	2,325	2,277
20	Iron	1,565	1,545	1,527	1,511	1,493	1,473	1,452
21	Lead	-	-	-	-	-	-	-
22	Nickel	-	-	-	-	-	-	-
23	Phosphate	-	-	-	-	-	-	-
24	Silver	1,284	1,275	1,261	1,247	1,233	1,219	1,204
25	Tin	-	-	-	-	-	-	-
26	Zinc	-	-	-	-	-	-	-
27	Health capital	27,245,613	27,833,091	28,440,705	29,056,234	29,661,663	30,243,946	30,796,048
28	IWI adjustments excluding TFP, rows 29 + 30	-2,235	-2,372	-2,458	-2,656	-2,815	-3,048	-3,308
29	Carbon damages (annual change)	-1,291	-1,310	-1,296	-1,295	-1,316	-1,338	-1,365
30	Oil capital gains (annual change)	-944	-1,062	-1,162	-1,361	-1,500	-1,710	-1,943

	Per Capita Values	1990	1991	1992	1993	1994	1995	1996
31	Per capita Inclusive Wealth Index	49,022	48,980	49,265	49,644	49,771	49,975	50,297
32	Per capita produced capital	4,594	4,750	5,012	5,359	5,713	6,217	6,757
33	Per capita human capital	27,361	27,543	28,000	28,383	28,468	28,503	28,596
34	Per capita natural capital	17,067	16,687	16,254	15,902	15,590	15,254	14,944
35	Per capita health capital	2,065,968	2,072,562	2,079,246	2,085,966	2,092,550	2,098,902	2,104,882
36	TFP (in percentage)	-0.39	3.52	7.24	2.25	0.94	5.50	1.42
37	Population	13,187,821	13,429,315	13,678,373	13,929,390	14,174,890	14,409,416	14,630,769

Data for TFP and population was obtained from Conference Board (2012), and United Nations Population Division (2011) respectively.

	1997	1998	1999	2000	2001	2002	2003	2004	2005	2006	2007	2008
1	757,556	779,700	794,206	807,011	827,664	847,814	869,697	901,137	924,828	953,410	983,475	1,018,637
2	109,137	119,010	124,999	132,510	138,822	145,617	152,876	161,374	173,859	186,027	200,076	218,389
3	430,446	443,394	453,707	459,514	474,533	486,143	502,619	523,379	535,952	553,969	571,489	589,384
4	217,973	217,296	215,500	214,986	214,309	216,054	214,202	216,384	215,017	213,414	211,910	210,864
5	96,649	96,630	95,620	95,938	96,192	98,827	97,938	101,176	100,858	100,319	99,912	99,919
6	14,584	14,565	13,524	13,397	13,651	13,111	12,222	12,286	11,968	11,429	10,940	10,933
7	82,064	82,064	82,096	82,541	82,541	85,715	85,715	88,890	88,890	88,890	88,973	88,985
8	69,514	69,701	69,889	70,076	70,185	70,293	70,402	70,511	70,620	70,732	70,843	70,954
9	65,693	65,866	66,039	66,212	66,311	66,410	66,508	66,607	66,706	66,808	66,910	67,012
10	3,822	3,836	3,850	3,863	3,874	3,884	3,894	3,904	3,914	3,924	3,933	3,942
11												
12	4,313	4,284	4,268	4,254	4,236	4,222	4,199	4,187	4,164	4,139	4,122	4,098
13	1,123	1,123	1,123	1,123	1,122	1,122	1,122	1,122	1,122	1,122	1,122	1,122
14	879	864	855	846	837	828	814	806	790	775	762	748
15	2,311	2,298	2,291	2,285	2,277	2,271	2,263	2,259	2,251	2,242	2,238	2,229
16	47,496	46,681	45,723	44,719	43,696	42,712	41,663	40,510	39,374	38,225	37,032	35,893
17	-	-	-	-	-	-	-	-	-	-	-	-
18	42,643	41,908	41,032	40,115	39,170	38,257	37,279	36,200	35,139	34,070	32,962	31,900
19	2,232	2,192	2,148	2,099	2,061	2,026	1,991	1,955	1,918	1,880	1,843	1,807
20	1,432	1,410	1,391	1,370	1,350	1,333	1,314	1,295	1,277	1,257	1,236	1,215
21	-	-	-	-	-	-	-	-	-	-	-	-
22	-	-	-	-	-	-	-	-	-	-	-	-
23	-	-	-	-	-	-	-	-	-	-	-	-
24	1,189	1,171	1,152	1,134	1,116	1,097	1,079	1,060	1,040	1,018	991	972
25	-	-	-	-	-	-	-	-	-	-	-	-
26	-	-	-	-	-	-	-	-	-	-	-	-
27	31,322,020	31,826,576	32,319,014	32,806,209	33,191,814	33,570,962	33,943,159	34,307,277	34,663,583	35,020,770	35,371,110	35,715,824
28	-3,478	-3,667	-3,765	-3,796	-3,820	-3,949	-4,121	-4,330	-4,657	-5,015	-5,293	-5,752
29	-1,386	-1,381	-1,371	-1,402	-1,368	-1,380	-1,457	-1,528	-1,584	-1,647	-1,683	-1,721
30	-2,092	-2,286	-2,394	-2,394	-2,452	-2,569	-2,664	-2,802	-3,073	-3,368	-3,611	-4,032

	1997	1998	1999	2000	2001	2002	2003	2004	2005	2006	2007	2008
31	51,048	51,845	52,142	52,336	53,041	53,714	54,493	55,859	56,732	57,892	59,127	60,649
32	7,354	7,913	8,207	8,594	8,896	9,226	9,579	10,003	10,665	11,296	12,029	13,003
33	29,006	29,483	29,787	29,800	30,411	30,800	31,493	32,443	32,877	33,638	34,358	35,092
34	14,688	14,449	14,148	13,942	13,734	13,688	13,421	13,413	13,190	12,959	12,740	12,555
35	2,110,643	2,116,247	2,121,846	2,127,535	2,127,108	2,126,899	2,126,792	2,126,632	2,126,375	2,126,508	2,126,530	2,126,500
36	0.87	-2.20	-12.18	-0.07	-1.67	-1.96	-0.26	2.40	0.82	-3.76	0.61	-0.96
37	14,840,038	15,039,162	15,231,557	15,419,820	15,604,200	15,783,991	15,959,793	16,132,209	16,301,726	16,468,677	16,633,254	16,795,593

China

		1990	1991	1992	1993	1994	1995	1996
1	Inclusive Wealth Index, rows 2 + 3 + 4	11,903,258	12,117,426	12,358,580	12,633,483	12,938,297	13,263,921	13,614,788
2	Produced capital	962,551	1,019,570	1,103,917	1,233,621	1,385,242	1,552,091	1,734,193
3	Human capital	5,647,423	5,807,404	5,967,512	6,126,514	6,285,442	6,446,801	6,627,185
4	Natural capital, rows 5 + 8 + 11 + 12 + 16	5,293,284	5,290,452	5,287,152	5,273,349	5,267,612	5,265,029	5,253,409
5	Agricultural land, rows 6 + 7	2,463,917	2,466,208	2,468,489	2,461,321	2,463,347	2,470,029	2,467,822
6	Cropland	609,245	611,535	613,816	606,648	608,674	615,356	613,149
7	Pastureland	1,854,673	1,854,673	1,854,673	1,854,673	1,854,673	1,854,673	1,854,673
8	Forest resources, rows 9 + 10	778,586	787,996	797,406	806,816	816,225	825,635	835,045
9	Timber	740,244	749,169	758,094	767,019	775,945	784,870	793,795
10	Non–timber forest resources	38,342	38,827	39,311	39,796	40,281	40,765	41,250
11	Fisheries							
12	Fossil fuels, rows 13 + 14 + 15	1,953,591	1,939,754	1,925,533	1,910,368	1,894,090	1,876,385	1,858,563
13	Oil	119,345	119,324	119,302	119,281	119,259	119,236	119,212
14	Natural gas	28,126	27,979	27,831	27,675	27,511	27,343	27,144
15	Coal	1,806,120	1,792,451	1,778,400	1,763,412	1,747,320	1,729,806	1,712,207
16	Minerals, rows 17 + 18 +...+ 26	97,190	96,494	95,723	94,844	93,950	92,980	91,980
17	Bauxite	1,487	1,483	1,479	1,473	1,467	1,459	1,449
18	Appendix	7,015	6,957	6,892	6,826	6,758	6,672	6,587
19	Gold	4,025	3,920	3,797	3,657	3,517	3,395	3,268
20	Iron	60,883	60,484	60,036	59,505	58,962	58,397	57,833
21	Lead	1,319	1,300	1,282	1,264	1,246	1,218	1,184
22	Nickel	1,459	1,437	1,414	1,392	1,369	1,339	1,307
23	Phosphate	15,237	15,237	15,237	15,237	15,237	15,237	15,237
24	Silver	735	733	731	728	725	713	697
25	Tin	1,493	1,474	1,453	1,430	1,407	1,379	1,346
26	Zinc	3,537	3,469	3,401	3,332	3,262	3,171	3,071
27	Health capital	1,221,152,645	1,240,178,816	1,257,491,628	1,273,548,469	1,289,016,309	1,304,308,252	1,318,367,691
28	IWI adjustments excluding TFP, rows 29 + 30	-13,116	-15,094	-16,998	-20,222	-22,423	-24,811	-27,575
29	Carbon damages (annual change)	-1,930	-1,959	-1,938	-1,936	-1,967	-2,001	-2,041
30	Oil capital gains (annual change)	-11,186	-13,136	-15,060	-18,286	-20,456	-22,810	-25,535

	Per Capita Values	1990	1991	1992	1993	1994	1995	1996
31	Per capita Inclusive Wealth Index	10,394	10,439	10,516	10,628	10,768	10,926	11,104
32	Per capita produced capital	841	878	939	1,038	1,153	1,279	1,414
33	Per capita human capital	4,931	5,003	5,078	5,154	5,231	5,310	5,405
34	Per capita natural capital	4,622	4,558	4,499	4,436	4,384	4,337	4,285
35	Per capita health capital	1,066,327	1,068,383	1,069,996	1,071,390	1,072,819	1,074,401	1,075,223
36	TFP (in percentage)	-0.73	2.14	4.33	3.07	2.97	7.52	-4.83
37	Population	1,145,195,229	1,160,799,514	1,175,230,312	1,188,687,527	1,201,522,570	1,213,986,610	1,226,134,423

Data for TFP and population was obtained from Conference Board (2012), and United Nations Population Division (2011) respectively.

	1997	1998	1999	2000	2001	2002	2003	2004	2005	2006	2007	2008
1	13,970,089	14,358,243	14,758,174	15,233,596	15,615,719	16,094,833	16,632,529	17,244,067	17,845,470	18,525,829	19,206,254	19,960,009
2	1,926,842	2,140,688	2,363,037	2,642,738	2,866,569	3,168,772	3,532,122	3,940,841	4,399,104	4,919,505	5,514,849	6,159,399
3	6,797,566	6,967,572	7,149,236	7,346,155	7,510,958	7,693,865	7,882,376	8,068,536	8,241,502	8,416,403	8,577,371	8,727,850
4	5,245,681	5,249,984	5,245,902	5,244,704	5,238,192	5,232,196	5,218,031	5,234,690	5,204,864	5,189,921	5,114,035	5,072,761
5	2,463,713	2,470,515	2,467,947	2,467,650	2,463,305	2,459,123	2,450,485	2,477,916	2,461,512	2,461,493	2,422,971	2,422,864
6	609,041	615,843	613,274	612,977	608,633	604,450	595,812	623,244	606,839	606,821	568,298	568,192
7	1,854,673	1,854,673	1,854,673	1,854,673	1,854,673	1,854,673	1,854,673	1,854,673	1,854,673	1,854,673	1,854,673	1,854,673
8	849,909	864,773	879,637	894,501	909,663	926,898	944,133	961,368	978,602	995,729	992,779	989,830
9	808,175	822,554	836,933	851,313	865,692	882,144	898,596	915,048	931,500	947,952	944,328	940,705
10	41,734	42,219	42,704	43,188	43,971	44,754	45,537	46,320	47,103	47,777	48,451	49,125
11												
12	1,841,176	1,824,750	1,809,295	1,794,460	1,778,062	1,759,973	1,738,295	1,711,565	1,682,444	1,652,403	1,620,284	1,584,641
13	119,188	119,163	119,139	119,114	119,088	119,062	119,035	119,008	118,980	118,951	118,922	118,893
14	26,921	26,692	26,444	26,175	25,877	25,555	25,217	24,816	24,324	23,747	23,065	22,316
15	1,695,067	1,678,895	1,663,713	1,649,171	1,633,097	1,615,356	1,594,042	1,567,741	1,539,140	1,509,704	1,478,297	1,443,433
16	90,883	89,945	89,023	88,093	87,161	86,202	85,119	83,841	82,306	80,296	78,001	75,426
17	1,436	1,423	1,409	1,395	1,379	1,361	1,340	1,313	1,277	1,234	1,185	1,129
18	6,492	6,397	6,297	6,183	6,069	5,959	5,842	5,698	5,551	5,383	5,203	5,022
19	3,114	2,959	2,807	2,650	2,488	2,320	2,140	1,952	1,755	1,541	1,300	1,050
20	57,226	56,667	56,131	55,627	55,129	54,606	54,015	53,291	52,341	50,981	49,381	47,517
21	1,146	1,115	1,086	1,051	1,015	980	930	876	816	745	669	587
22	1,274	1,239	1,204	1,168	1,131	1,093	1,049	995	943	885	837	785
23	15,237	15,237	15,237	15,237	15,237	15,237	15,237	15,237	15,237	15,237	15,237	15,237
24	680	663	644	623	597	557	525	492	459	424	387	350
25	1,315	1,282	1,245	1,199	1,155	1,126	1,079	1,024	966	907	840	789
26	2,962	2,962	2,962	2,962	2,962	2,961	2,961	2,961	2,961	2,961	2,960	2,960
27	1,332,617,688	1,346,598,128	1,359,666,865	1,371,523,323	1,382,958,035	1,393,156,143	1,402,473,188	1,411,505,672	1,420,612,032	1,429,087,741	1,437,692,473	1,446,348,252
28	-30,953	-33,921	-37,125	-42,923	-45,754	-50,254	-56,480	-67,159	-72,187	-81,938	-88,792	-99,404
29	-2,072	-2,065	-2,050	-2,096	-2,046	-2,064	-2,179	-2,285	-2,369	-2,462	-2,516	-2,573
30	-28,881	-31,856	-35,075	-40,827	-43,708	-48,190	-54,302	-64,874	-69,818	-79,476	-86,276	-96,831

	1997	1998	1999	2000	2001	2002	2003	2004	2005	2006	2007	2008
31	11,286	11,496	11,718	12,003	12,220	12,516	12,860	13,259	13,648	14,093	14,534	15,027
32	1,557	1,714	1,876	2,082	2,243	2,464	2,731	3,030	3,364	3,742	4,173	4,637
33	5,491	5,578	5,676	5,788	5,878	5,983	6,094	6,204	6,303	6,402	6,491	6,571
34	4,238	4,203	4,165	4,133	4,099	4,069	4,034	4,025	3,980	3,948	3,870	3,819
35	1,076,558	1,078,124	1,079,549	1,080,691	1,082,208	1,083,381	1,084,333	1,085,313	1,086,432	1,087,105	1,087,940	1,088,892
36	-1.36	-5.87	0.53	3.31	4.73	6.14	7.85	2.61	2.62	4.65	6.07	2.35
37	1,237,849,861	1,249,020,152	1,259,476,966	1,269,116,737	1,277,903,627	1,285,933,789	1,293,396,654	1,300,552,134	1,307,593,489	1,314,581,402	1,321,481,935	1,328,275,524

Colombia

UNIT: millions of constant US$ of year 2000

		1990	1991	1992	1993	1994	1995	1996
1	Inclusive Wealth Index, rows 2 + 3 + 4	903,171	914,042	928,157	946,140	967,300	986,640	1,008,714
2	Produced capital	168,089	171,135	175,807	184,987	196,129	206,709	216,208
3	Human capital	283,546	293,004	302,567	312,409	323,278	334,553	345,796
4	Natural capital, rows 5 + 8 + 11 + 12 + 16	451,536	449,903	449,783	448,743	447,893	445,378	446,710
5	Agricultural land, rows 6 + 7	232,755	231,727	232,238	231,825	231,629	229,812	231,913
6	Cropland	25,814	24,787	25,298	24,885	24,689	22,871	21,147
7	Pastureland	206,941	206,941	206,941	206,941	206,941	206,941	210,766
8	Forest resources, rows 9 + 10	89,454	89,310	89,165	89,021	88,876	88,731	88,587
9	Timber	74,200	74,080	73,960	73,840	73,720	73,600	73,480
10	Non–timber forest resources	15,255	15,230	15,205	15,181	15,156	15,131	15,107
11	Fisheries							
12	Fossil fuels, rows 13 + 14 + 15	127,176	126,732	126,264	125,800	125,310	124,776	124,173
13	Oil	11,666	11,663	11,660	11,656	11,653	11,648	11,643
14	Natural gas	7,984	7,830	7,681	7,525	7,364	7,205	7,039
15	Coal	107,526	107,239	106,924	106,619	106,293	105,923	105,491
16	Minerals, rows 17 + 18 +...+ 26	2,150	2,134	2,116	2,097	2,079	2,059	2,037
17	Bauxite	-	-	-	-	-	-	-
18	Appendix	-	-	-	-	-	-	-
19	Gold	-	-	-	-	-	-	-
20	Iron	-	-	-	-	-	-	-
21	Lead	-	-	-	-	-	-	-
22	Nickel	2,150	2,134	2,116	2,097	2,079	2,059	2,037
23	Phosphate	-	-	-	-	-	-	-
24	Silver	-	-	-	-	-	-	-
25	Tin	-	-	-	-	-	-	-
26	Zinc	-	-	-	-	-	-	-
27	Health capital	46,460,586	47,397,148	48,336,059	49,277,776	50,223,541	51,173,868	52,125,802
28	IWI adjustments excluding TFP, rows 29 + 30	-2,266	-2,377	-2,607	-2,753	-2,839	-2,953	-3,260
29	Carbon damages (annual change)	-1,379	-1,399	-1,384	-1,383	-1,405	-1,429	-1,457
30	Oil capital gains (annual change)	-887	-978	-1,223	-1,370	-1,434	-1,524	-1,803

	Per Capita Values	1990	1991	1992	1993	1994	1995	1996
31	Per capita Inclusive Wealth Index	27,201	27,003	26,905	26,920	27,021	27,066	27,180
32	Per capita produced capital	5,062	5,056	5,096	5,263	5,479	5,670	5,826
33	Per capita human capital	8,540	8,656	8,771	8,889	9,031	9,178	9,317
34	Per capita natural capital	13,599	13,291	13,038	12,768	12,512	12,218	12,037
35	Per capita health capital	1,399,275	1,400,212	1,401,154	1,402,079	1,402,972	1,403,818	1,404,530
36	TFP (in percentage)	-2.51	-3.11	2.24	-0.62	-2.14	3.57	-3.21
37	Population	33,203,321	33,849,971	34,497,319	35,146,220	35,797,965	36,453,337	37,112,621

Data for TFP and population was obtained from Conference Board (2012), and United Nations Population Division (2011) respectively.

	1997	1998	1999	2000	2001	2002	2003	2004	2005	2006	2007	2008
1	1,028,526	1,048,333	1,058,760	1,065,335	1,057,391	1,068,058	1,083,506	1,100,426	1,118,978	1,142,433	1,172,824	1,205,200
2	224,561	230,849	229,093	228,540	226,654	227,993	231,215	236,346	243,934	255,351	270,082	286,995
3	357,270	369,287	381,683	393,953	405,032	416,085	427,195	438,464	449,914	465,389	481,217	497,366
4	446,695	448,197	447,985	442,842	425,706	423,979	425,096	425,616	425,130	421,693	421,525	420,839
5	232,750	235,130	235,775	231,598	215,521	214,809	217,101	218,856	219,713	217,736	219,089	220,008
6	21,978	22,598	22,530	23,465	21,348	19,288	19,355	19,144	18,653	17,395	18,431	17,868
7	210,771	212,532	213,244	208,133	194,173	195,521	197,746	199,713	201,060	200,341	200,658	202,139
8	88,442	88,298	88,153	88,009	87,864	87,720	87,575	87,430	87,286	87,141	86,997	86,852
9	73,360	73,240	73,120	73,000	72,881	72,761	72,641	72,521	72,401	72,281	72,161	72,041
10	15,082	15,057	15,033	15,008	14,984	14,959	14,934	14,910	14,885	14,860	14,836	14,811
11												
12	123,490	122,780	122,121	121,368	120,526	119,737	118,801	117,808	116,722	115,522	114,245	112,869
13	11,638	11,632	11,626	11,620	11,615	11,611	11,607	11,603	11,598	11,594	11,590	11,585
14	6,830	6,611	6,429	6,230	6,017	5,801	5,588	5,372	5,138	4,886	4,618	4,303
15	105,022	104,537	104,066	103,518	102,893	102,325	101,606	100,834	99,985	99,042	98,037	96,980
16	2,013	1,989	1,936	1,867	1,794	1,713	1,619	1,521	1,409	1,294	1,194	1,110
17	-	-	-	-	-	-	-	-	-	-	-	-
18	-	-	-	-	-	-	-	-	-	-	-	-
19	-	-	-	-	-	-	-	-	-	-	-	-
20	-	-	-	-	-	-	-	-	-	-	-	-
21	-	-	-	-	-	-	-	-	-	-	-	-
22	2,013	1,989	1,936	1,867	1,794	1,713	1,619	1,521	1,409	1,294	1,194	1,110
23	-	-	-	-	-	-	-	-	-	-	-	-
24	-	-	-	-	-	-	-	-	-	-	-	-
25	-	-	-	-	-	-	-	-	-	-	-	-
26	-	-	-	-	-	-	-	-	-	-	-	-
27	53,078,951	54,032,565	54,985,580	55,936,715	57,032,036	58,131,789	59,236,536	60,347,508	61,466,017	62,591,840	63,723,927	64,859,114
28	-3,387	-3,478	-3,379	-3,474	-3,439	-3,411	-3,579	-3,669	-3,809	-3,983	-4,180	-4,260
29	-1,480	-1,475	-1,464	-1,497	-1,461	-1,474	-1,556	-1,632	-1,692	-1,759	-1,797	-1,837
30	-1,908	-2,003	-1,915	-1,977	-1,978	-1,938	-2,023	-2,037	-2,117	-2,225	-2,383	-2,423

	1997	1998	1999	2000	2001	2002	2003	2004	2005	2006	2007	2008
31	27,228	27,273	27,076	26,791	26,158	26,001	25,963	25,962	25,998	26,145	26,443	26,779
32	5,945	6,006	5,859	5,747	5,607	5,550	5,540	5,576	5,668	5,844	6,089	6,377
33	9,458	9,607	9,761	9,907	10,020	10,129	10,237	10,345	10,453	10,650	10,850	11,051
34	11,825	11,660	11,457	11,137	10,531	10,321	10,186	10,042	9,877	9,650	9,504	9,351
35	1,405,132	1,405,667	1,406,185	1,406,712	1,410,895	1,415,152	1,419,454	1,423,770	1,428,095	1,432,421	1,436,766	1,441,128
36	1.52	-2.49	-7.30	0.28	-1.58	1.41	-0.76	1.99	-0.24	4.33	1.43	-2.95
37	37,775,054	38,439,099	39,102,653	39,764,166	40,422,597	41,078,136	41,731,914	42,385,712	43,040,558	43,696,540	44,352,327	45,005,782

Ecuador

UNIT: millions of constant US$ of year 2000

		1990	1991	1992	1993	1994	1995	1996
1	Inclusive Wealth Index, rows 2 + 3 + 4	245,770	251,957	258,419	264,907	271,747	278,107	283,372
2	Produced capital	40,293	40,965	41,831	42,677	43,713	44,595	45,247
3	Human capital	133,539	139,272	145,128	151,052	156,958	162,778	167,871
4	Natural capital, rows 5 + 8 + 11 + 12 + 16	71,938	71,720	71,460	71,178	71,076	70,734	70,254
5	Agricultural land, rows 6 + 7	10,750	10,843	10,896	10,926	11,137	11,108	10,943
6	Cropland	4,007	4,103	4,138	4,075	4,160	4,112	4,098
7	Pastureland	6,742	6,739	6,759	6,852	6,978	6,997	6,845
8	Forest resources, rows 9 + 10	21,396	21,090	20,784	20,478	20,172	19,866	19,560
9	Timber	18,025	17,767	17,509	17,252	16,994	16,736	16,478
10	Non–timber forest resources	3,371	3,323	3,275	3,227	3,178	3,130	3,082
11	Fisheries							
12	Fossil fuels, rows 13 + 14 + 15	39,792	39,786	39,780	39,773	39,766	39,759	39,751
13	Oil	38,991	38,989	38,986	38,983	38,980	38,976	38,973
14	Natural gas	438	434	431	427	423	419	414
15	Coal	364	364	364	364	364	364	364
16	Minerals, rows 17 + 18 +...+ 26	-	-	-	-	-	-	-
17	Bauxite	-	-	-	-	-	-	-
18	Appendix	-	-	-	-	-	-	-
19	Gold	-	-	-	-	-	-	-
20	Iron	-	-	-	-	-	-	-
21	Lead	-	-	-	-	-	-	-
22	Nickel	-	-	-	-	-	-	-
23	Phosphate	-	-	-	-	-	-	-
24	Silver	-	-	-	-	-	-	-
25	Tin	-	-	-	-	-	-	-
26	Zinc	-	-	-	-	-	-	-
27	Health capital	9,817,970	10,065,068	10,311,540	10,554,806	10,791,625	11,020,030	11,236,968
28	IWI adjustments excluding TFP, rows 29 + 30	993	1,006	950	1,074	1,085	1,133	1,169
29	Carbon damages (annual change)	-230	-233	-231	-231	-234	-238	-243
30	Oil capital gains (annual change)	1,223	1,239	1,181	1,304	1,319	1,371	1,412

	Per Capita Values	1990	1991	1992	1993	1994	1995	1996
31	Per capita Inclusive Wealth Index	23,953	24,011	24,094	24,185	24,320	24,429	24,462
32	Per capita produced capital	3,927	3,904	3,900	3,896	3,912	3,917	3,906
33	Per capita human capital	13,015	13,272	13,531	13,791	14,047	14,298	14,492
34	Per capita natural capital	7,011	6,835	6,663	6,498	6,361	6,213	6,065
35	Per capita health capital	956,862	959,172	961,424	963,629	965,810	967,985	970,036
36	TFP (in percentage)	-0.02	2.42	-1.56	-2.58	1.27	-2.01	1.93
37	Population	10,260,587	10,493,498	10,725,281	10,953,182	11,173,647	11,384,506	11,584,074

Data for TFP and population was obtained from Conference Board (2012), and United Nations Population Division (2011) respectively.

	1997	1998	1999	2000	2001	2002	2003	2004	2005	2006	2007	2008
1	287,461	292,988	296,813	301,890	307,366	311,820	319,020	327,184	335,370	344,192	351,206	360,032
2	45,955	46,766	46,406	47,189	47,150	48,644	50,025	51,546	53,506	55,540	57,574	60,420
3	171,531	176,539	180,972	185,592	191,807	195,484	201,947	208,528	215,111	222,296	227,640	233,896
4	69,975	69,683	69,436	69,109	68,408	67,691	67,047	67,110	66,753	66,355	65,991	65,716
5	10,977	10,997	11,063	11,051	10,666	10,262	9,933	10,312	10,275	10,199	10,155	10,200
6	4,116	4,116	4,083	4,081	3,836	3,562	3,407	3,457	3,439	3,351	3,309	3,425
7	6,861	6,882	6,980	6,970	6,830	6,700	6,526	6,856	6,837	6,848	6,846	6,775
8	19,254	18,948	18,642	18,336	18,030	17,724	17,418	17,112	16,806	16,500	16,194	15,888
9	16,221	15,963	15,705	15,447	15,189	14,932	14,674	14,416	14,158	13,901	13,643	13,385
10	3,034	2,986	2,937	2,889	2,841	2,793	2,745	2,696	2,648	2,600	2,552	2,503
11												
12	39,744	39,737	39,730	39,721	39,712	39,705	39,696	39,685	39,671	39,656	39,642	39,628
13	38,969	38,966	38,963	38,959	38,956	38,953	38,949	38,944	38,940	38,935	38,931	38,926
14	411	407	403	398	392	389	383	377	367	357	347	338
15	364	364	364	364	364	364	364	364	364	364	364	364
16	-	-	-	-	-	-	-	-	-	-	-	-
17	-	-	-	-	-	-	-	-	-	-	-	-
18	-	-	-	-	-	-	-	-	-	-	-	-
19	-	-	-	-	-	-	-	-	-	-	-	-
20	-	-	-	-	-	-	-	-	-	-	-	-
21	-	-	-	-	-	-	-	-	-	-	-	-
22	-	-	-	-	-	-	-	-	-	-	-	-
23	-	-	-	-	-	-	-	-	-	-	-	-
24	-	-	-	-	-	-	-	-	-	-	-	-
25	-	-	-	-	-	-	-	-	-	-	-	-
26	-	-	-	-	-	-	-	-	-	-	-	-
27	11,445,958	11,651,848	11,861,388	12,079,502	12,301,842	12,532,058	12,767,501	13,003,969	13,238,154	13,468,576	13,696,772	13,922,913
28	1,211	1,273	1,474	1,548	1,554	1,635	1,697	1,774	1,809	1,747	1,759	1,282
29	-247	-246	-244	-250	-244	-246	-260	-272	-282	-293	-300	-307
30	1,458	1,520	1,718	1,798	1,798	1,881	1,957	2,047	2,091	2,040	2,059	1,588

	1997	1998	1999	2000	2001	2002	2003	2004	2005	2006	2007	2008
31	24,415	24,498	24,433	24,454	24,487	24,423	24,563	24,770	24,978	25,235	25,358	25,613
32	3,903	3,910	3,820	3,822	3,756	3,810	3,852	3,902	3,985	4,072	4,157	4,298
33	14,569	14,761	14,897	15,034	15,281	15,311	15,549	15,787	16,022	16,298	16,436	16,639
34	5,943	5,827	5,716	5,598	5,450	5,302	5,162	5,081	4,972	4,865	4,765	4,675
35	972,138	974,269	976,392	978,492	980,067	981,566	983,023	984,488	985,979	987,453	988,957	990,480
36	0.29	0.12	-5.30	2.33	0.46	-0.79	0.38	1.77	2.49	-0.15	-0.90	3.54
37	11,774,005	11,959,586	12,148,188	12,345,023	12,552,036	12,767,415	12,987,992	13,208,869	13,426,402	13,639,708	13,849,721	14,056,740

France

UNIT: millions of constant US$ of year 2000

		1990	1991	1992	1993	1994	1995	1996
1	Inclusive Wealth Index, rows 2 + 3 + 4	9,153,530	9,380,150	9,593,125	9,786,530	9,982,546	10,183,155	10,405,136
2	Produced capital	2,120,057	2,180,924	2,233,377	2,269,909	2,307,108	2,345,287	2,382,088
3	Human capital	6,882,044	7,047,584	7,207,779	7,364,404	7,522,874	7,684,895	7,869,655
4	Natural capital, rows 5 + 8 + 11 + 12 + 16	151,429	151,641	151,969	152,217	152,564	152,973	153,394
5	Agricultural land, rows 6 + 7	68,416	68,093	67,881	67,594	67,406	67,272	67,135
6	Cropland	42,947	43,005	43,048	43,504	43,614	43,625	43,554
7	Pastureland	25,468	25,088	24,833	24,090	23,792	23,647	23,582
8	Forest resources, rows 9 + 10	80,806	81,481	82,156	82,832	83,507	84,182	84,858
9	Timber	76,241	76,891	77,541	78,190	78,840	79,490	80,139
10	Non–timber forest resources	4,565	4,590	4,616	4,641	4,667	4,693	4,718
11	Fisheries							
12	Fossil fuels, rows 13 + 14 + 15	2,207	2,067	1,932	1,791	1,651	1,519	1,401
13	Oil	473	473	472	472	471	471	471
14	Natural gas	1,445	1,345	1,248	1,142	1,033	930	840
15	Coal	289	249	211	177	146	118	90
16	Minerals, rows 17 + 18 +...+ 26	-	-	-	-	-	-	-
17	Bauxite	-	-	-	-	-	-	-
18	Appendix	-	-	-	-	-	-	-
19	Gold	-	-	-	-	-	-	-
20	Iron	-	-	-	-	-	-	-
21	Lead	-	-	-	-	-	-	-
22	Nickel	-	-	-	-	-	-	-
23	Phosphate	-	-	-	-	-	-	-
24	Silver	-	-	-	-	-	-	-
25	Tin	-	-	-	-	-	-	-
26	Zinc	-	-	-	-	-	-	-
27	Health capital	269,378,375	270,773,126	272,137,184	273,481,644	274,817,762	276,168,209	277,447,481
28	IWI adjustments excluding TFP, rows 29 + 30	-40,671	-42,507	-42,856	-43,095	-43,890	-45,384	-46,668
29	Carbon damages (annual change)	-27,056	-27,454	-27,160	-27,137	-27,571	-28,048	-28,602
30	Oil capital gains (annual change)	-13,616	-15,052	-15,696	-15,957	-16,319	-17,336	-18,067

	Per Capita Values	1990	1991	1992	1993	1994	1995	1996
31	Per capita Inclusive Wealth Index	161,414	164,691	167,742	170,461	173,221	176,044	179,221
32	Per capita produced capital	37,385	38,291	39,052	39,537	40,034	40,545	41,030
33	Per capita human capital	121,359	123,737	126,033	128,272	130,540	132,854	135,549
34	Per capita natural capital	2,670	2,662	2,657	2,651	2,647	2,645	2,642
35	Per capita health capital	4,750,249	4,754,071	4,758,507	4,763,473	4,768,749	4,774,321	4,778,834
36	TFP (in percentage)	0.34	-0.27	-0.05	-0.86	0.92	0.90	-0.87
37	Population	56,708,260	56,956,057	57,189,616	57,412,239	57,628,904	57,844,501	58,057,570

Data for TFP and population was obtained from Conference Board (2012), and United Nations Population Division (2011) respectively.

	1997	1998	1999	2000	2001	2002	2003	2004	2005	2006	2007	2008
1	10,572,275	10,769,237	10,995,980	11,243,897	11,380,112	11,575,374	11,836,216	12,023,558	12,198,377	12,425,226	12,690,734	12,955,131
2	2,417,481	2,465,405	2,528,515	2,608,251	2,677,189	2,741,261	2,806,191	2,875,263	2,951,230	3,032,756	3,126,767	3,215,068
3	8,000,912	8,149,438	8,312,538	8,480,548	8,546,143	8,675,649	8,869,402	8,985,972	9,083,079	9,228,001	9,399,180	9,574,982
4	153,881	154,394	154,927	155,099	156,781	158,464	160,623	162,323	164,068	164,468	164,788	165,081
5	67,050	66,977	66,916	66,482	66,314	66,144	66,442	66,269	66,133	66,028	65,837	65,616
6	43,603	43,641	43,675	43,824	43,831	43,827	43,829	43,829	43,961	43,858	43,683	43,435
7	23,448	23,336	23,242	22,658	22,483	22,317	22,613	22,440	22,172	22,170	22,154	22,181
8	85,533	86,209	86,884	87,559	89,476	91,393	93,310	95,226	97,143	97,687	98,230	98,774
9	80,789	81,439	82,089	82,738	84,632	86,527	88,421	90,315	92,209	92,737	93,266	93,795
10	4,744	4,770	4,795	4,821	4,844	4,866	4,889	4,912	4,934	4,949	4,964	4,979
11												
12	1,298	1,209	1,127	1,057	990	927	872	827	792	753	720	691
13	470	470	470	469	469	468	468	468	467	467	467	466
14	760	690	627	569	510	453	403	360	324	286	253	225
15	67	49	31	20	12	6	1	-	-	-	-	-
16	-	-	-	-	-	-	-	-	-	-	-	-
17	-	-	-	-	-	-	-	-	-	-	-	-
18	-	-	-	-	-	-	-	-	-	-	-	-
19	-	-	-	-	-	-	-	-	-	-	-	-
20	-	-	-	-	-	-	-	-	-	-	-	-
21	-	-	-	-	-	-	-	-	-	-	-	-
22	-	-	-	-	-	-	-	-	-	-	-	-
23	-	-	-	-	-	-	-	-	-	-	-	-
24	-	-	-	-	-	-	-	-	-	-	-	-
25	-	-	-	-	-	-	-	-	-	-	-	-
26	-	-	-	-	-	-	-	-	-	-	-	-
27	278,757,355	280,152,845	281,710,499	283,485,355	285,664,955	288,042,974	290,548,401	293,092,341	295,612,510	298,007,774	300,324,825	302,615,437
28	-47,743	-49,139	-49,323	-50,406	-51,140	-51,524	-53,999	-55,906	-57,593	-59,809	-61,452	-63,205
29	-29,039	-28,943	-28,733	-29,376	-28,670	-28,922	-30,534	-32,026	-33,203	-34,513	-35,261	-36,059
30	-18,704	-20,197	-20,590	-21,030	-22,469	-22,601	-23,465	-23,880	-24,389	-25,295	-26,192	-27,146

	1997	1998	1999	2000	2001	2002	2003	2004	2005	2006	2007	2008
31	181,435	184,102	187,161	190,420	191,614	193,651	196,668	198,419	199,985	202,438	205,536	208,623
32	41,487	42,146	43,037	44,172	45,078	45,860	46,627	47,449	48,384	49,411	50,640	51,774
33	137,307	139,316	141,486	143,622	143,897	145,140	147,372	148,291	148,911	150,347	152,227	154,190
34	2,641	2,639	2,637	2,627	2,640	2,651	2,669	2,679	2,690	2,680	2,669	2,658
35	4,783,857	4,789,254	4,794,944	4,800,947	4,809,926	4,818,824	4,827,678	4,836,771	4,846,384	4,855,281	4,863,986	4,873,159
36	0.63	1.28	0.36	1.74	-0.46	0.74	-0.10	-0.54	-0.14	1.19	-0.51	-2.60
37	58,270,419	58,496,138	58,751,572	59,047,795	59,390,720	59,774,531	60,183,884	60,596,691	60,996,506	61,378,065	61,744,596	62,098,413

Germany

UNIT: millions of constant US$ of year 2000

		1990	1991	1992	1993	1994	1995	1996
1	Inclusive Wealth Index, rows 2 + 3 + 4	13,494,774	14,083,223	14,372,673	14,673,642	14,977,692	15,315,106	15,615,130
2	Produced capital	3,429,436	3,537,002	3,653,438	3,746,853	3,848,136	3,941,350	4,026,148
3	Human capital	8,745,701	9,236,828	9,417,687	9,631,571	9,840,253	10,090,276	10,311,159
4	Natural capital, rows 5 + 8 + 11 + 12 + 16	1,319,637	1,309,393	1,301,548	1,295,218	1,289,303	1,283,481	1,277,823
5	Agricultural land, rows 6 + 7	35,266	33,514	33,152	33,565	33,850	33,919	33,907
6	Cropland	24,279	23,092	22,898	23,295	23,542	23,589	23,594
7	Pastureland	10,988	10,422	10,254	10,270	10,309	10,330	10,313
8	Forest resources, rows 9 + 10	74,024	75,455	76,886	78,317	79,748	81,179	82,610
9	Timber	70,651	72,071	73,492	74,913	76,333	77,754	79,174
10	Non-timber forest resources	3,373	3,383	3,394	3,404	3,415	3,425	3,436
11	Fisheries							
12	Fossil fuels, rows 13 + 14 + 15	1,210,347	1,200,424	1,191,510	1,183,336	1,175,704	1,168,383	1,161,306
13	Oil	1,373	1,373	1,372	1,372	1,371	1,371	1,370
14	Natural gas	19,496	18,908	18,311	17,715	17,096	16,441	15,733
15	Coal	1,189,478	1,180,144	1,171,826	1,164,250	1,157,237	1,150,571	1,144,203
16	Minerals, rows 17 + 18 +...+ 26	-	-	-	-	-	-	-
17	Bauxite	-	-	-	-	-	-	-
18	Appendix	-	-	-	-	-	-	-
19	Gold	-	-	-	-	-	-	-
20	Iron	-	-	-	-	-	-	-
21	Lead	-	-	-	-	-	-	-
22	Nickel	-	-	-	-	-	-	-
23	Phosphate	-	-	-	-	-	-	-
24	Silver	-	-	-	-	-	-	-
25	Tin	-	-	-	-	-	-	-
26	Zinc	-	-	-	-	-	-	-
27	Health capital	380,997,967	384,853,746	389,092,265	393,437,706	397,520,567	401,044,675	403,078,784
28	IWI adjustments excluding TFP, rows 29 + 30	-247,407	-61,240	-61,947	-63,567	-64,703	-66,180	-68,035
29	Carbon damages (annual change)	-38,778	-39,349	-38,928	-38,894	-39,516	-40,200	-40,993
30	Oil capital gains (annual change)	-208,630	-21,892	-23,019	-24,672	-25,187	-25,980	-27,041

	Per Capita Values	1990	1991	1992	1993	1994	1995	1996
31	Per capita Inclusive Wealth Index	170,608	176,810	179,025	181,321	183,786	186,930	189,964
32	Per capita produced capital	43,357	44,406	45,507	46,300	47,219	48,107	48,980
33	Per capita human capital	110,568	115,965	117,306	119,017	120,746	123,158	125,439
34	Per capita natural capital	16,684	16,439	16,212	16,005	15,821	15,666	15,545
35	Per capita health capital	4,816,778	4,831,696	4,846,510	4,861,690	4,877,841	4,895,001	4,903,615
36	TFP (in percentage)	2.96	2.12	1.05	-0.34	1.97	1.76	1.36
37	Population	79,098,094	79,651,903	80,282,985	80,926,118	81,495,194	81,929,441	82,200,333

Data for TFP and population was obtained from Conference Board (2012), and United Nations Population Division (2011) respectively.

	1997	1998	1999	2000	2001	2002	2003	2004	2005	2006	2007	2008
1	15,887,971	16,164,650	16,394,381	16,643,601	17,134,904	17,597,384	18,059,692	18,618,523	19,187,437	19,300,630	19,415,161	19,473,621
2	4,108,484	4,199,334	4,300,666	4,391,920	4,490,123	4,544,070	4,589,704	4,631,312	4,672,874	4,741,768	4,824,522	4,908,363
3	10,507,000	10,697,589	10,831,148	10,993,968	11,392,897	11,807,459	12,229,877	12,752,922	13,285,925	13,336,130	13,373,728	13,353,882
4	1,272,486	1,267,727	1,262,566	1,257,714	1,251,884	1,245,856	1,240,112	1,234,290	1,228,639	1,222,732	1,216,911	1,211,377
5	33,888	33,978	33,545	33,381	33,315	33,184	33,250	33,273	33,309	33,142	33,150	33,096
6	23,587	23,678	23,544	23,508	23,510	23,463	23,534	23,665	23,669	23,594	23,616	23,729
7	10,301	10,299	10,002	9,873	9,804	9,720	9,716	9,609	9,640	9,548	9,534	9,366
8	84,041	85,472	86,903	88,334	88,721	89,107	89,494	89,880	90,267	90,437	90,608	90,779
9	80,595	82,015	83,436	84,856	85,243	85,629	86,016	86,402	86,789	86,960	87,130	87,301
10	3,446	3,457	3,467	3,478	3,478	3,478	3,478	3,478	3,478	3,478	3,478	3,478
11												
12	1,154,558	1,148,277	1,142,118	1,135,999	1,129,849	1,123,565	1,117,368	1,111,136	1,105,063	1,099,152	1,093,153	1,087,502
13	1,370	1,369	1,369	1,368	1,368	1,367	1,367	1,366	1,366	1,366	1,365	1,365
14	15,035	14,355	13,630	12,945	12,253	11,560	10,869	10,230	9,613	9,003	8,424	7,924
15	1,138,153	1,132,553	1,127,118	1,121,686	1,116,227	1,110,638	1,105,132	1,099,540	1,094,084	1,088,784	1,083,364	1,078,214
16	-	-	-	-	-	-	-	-	-	-	-	-
17	-	-	-	-	-	-	-	-	-	-	-	-
18	-	-	-	-	-	-	-	-	-	-	-	-
19	-	-	-	-	-	-	-	-	-	-	-	-
20	-	-	-	-	-	-	-	-	-	-	-	-
21	-	-	-	-	-	-	-	-	-	-	-	-
22	-	-	-	-	-	-	-	-	-	-	-	-
23	-	-	-	-	-	-	-	-	-	-	-	-
24	-	-	-	-	-	-	-	-	-	-	-	-
25	-	-	-	-	-	-	-	-	-	-	-	-
26	-	-	-	-	-	-	-	-	-	-	-	-
27	404,625,745	405,791,197	406,783,838	407,810,922	408,497,310	409,124,395	409,709,013	410,285,656	410,858,766	411,078,165	411,293,753	411,500,848
28	-69,282	-70,327	-69,878	-71,143	-71,740	-72,254	-74,908	-77,314	-79,615	-83,583	-82,496	-87,106
29	-41,621	-41,482	-41,182	-42,104	-41,092	-41,453	-43,763	-45,901	-47,589	-49,466	-50,538	-51,681
30	-27,661	-28,845	-28,696	-29,039	-30,648	-30,801	-31,145	-31,413	-32,026	-34,116	-31,959	-35,425

	1997	1998	1999	2000	2001	2002	2003	2004	2005	2006	2007	2008
31	192,988	196,291	199,102	202,110	207,988	213,478	218,948	225,612	232,460	233,845	235,289	236,115
32	49,905	50,993	52,230	53,333	54,502	55,125	55,643	56,121	56,613	57,451	58,467	59,513
33	127,627	129,903	131,539	133,505	138,290	143,239	148,269	154,535	160,962	161,579	162,074	161,914
34	15,457	15,394	15,333	15,273	15,196	15,114	15,035	14,957	14,885	14,815	14,748	14,688
35	4,914,919	4,927,613	4,940,202	4,952,225	4,958,439	4,963,173	4,967,126	4,971,692	4,977,648	4,980,584	4,984,394	4,989,385
36	1.66	-0.09	0.71	2.28	1.07	0.06	-0.25	0.35	1.45	2.90	1.31	-0.64
37	82,326,019	82,350,467	82,341,545	82,349,027	82,384,256	82,432,026	82,484,111	82,524,343	82,540,739	82,536,138	82,516,297	82,475,271

India

UNIT: millions of constant US$ of year 2000

		1990	1991	1992	1993	1994	1995	1996
1	Inclusive Wealth Index, rows 2 + 3 + 4	3,841,876	3,915,155	3,985,438	4,055,314	4,154,840	4,245,038	4,344,540
2	Produced capital	474,905	499,132	525,665	553,714	587,458	632,813	676,302
3	Human capital	1,682,622	1,735,084	1,783,266	1,828,822	1,898,877	1,949,002	2,009,276
4	Natural capital, rows 5 + 8 + 11 + 12 + 16	1,684,349	1,680,939	1,676,508	1,672,777	1,668,505	1,663,223	1,658,962
5	Agricultural land, rows 6 + 7	529,078	529,370	528,786	529,072	529,049	528,318	528,614
6	Cropland	495,172	494,886	494,681	496,046	496,201	496,084	496,817
7	Pastureland	33,906	34,485	34,105	33,026	32,848	32,234	31,796
8	Forest resources, rows 9 + 10	63,280	63,642	64,004	64,366	64,728	65,090	65,453
9	Timber	47,679	48,005	48,332	48,659	48,986	49,312	49,639
10	Non–timber forest resources	15,601	15,637	15,672	15,707	15,743	15,778	15,814
11	Fisheries							
12	Fossil fuels, rows 13 + 14 + 15	1,039,306	1,035,400	1,031,344	1,027,122	1,022,672	1,017,936	1,013,200
13	Oil	47,143	47,138	47,132	47,128	47,122	47,116	47,109
14	Natural gas	54,576	54,109	53,613	53,060	52,443	51,790	51,066
15	Coal	937,587	934,154	930,598	926,934	923,107	919,030	915,024
16	Minerals, rows 17 + 18 +...+ 26	52,685	52,527	52,374	52,217	52,055	51,878	51,696
17	Bauxite	1,582	1,574	1,566	1,557	1,548	1,539	1,529
18	Appendix	27,515	27,504	27,493	27,481	27,471	27,461	27,452
19	Gold	109	108	106	104	102	100	98
20	Iron	19,909	19,774	19,643	19,511	19,371	19,216	19,058
21	Lead	3,569	3,568	3,566	3,564	3,563	3,561	3,559
22	Nickel	-	-	-	-	-	-	-
23	Phosphate	-	-	-	-	-	-	-
24	Silver	-	-	-	-	-	-	-
25	Tin	-	-	-	-	-	-	-
26	Zinc	-	-	-	-	-	-	-
27	Health capital	479,444,845	491,428,918	503,451,427	515,506,557	527,592,037	539,698,924	551,765,844
28	IWI adjustments excluding TFP, rows 29 + 30	-23,275	-23,921	-24,737	-25,388	-26,752	-28,762	-30,324
29	Carbon damages (annual change)	-16,906	-17,155	-16,971	-16,957	-17,228	-17,526	-17,872
30	Oil capital gains (annual change)	-6,370	-6,767	-7,766	-8,432	-9,524	-11,236	-12,452

	Per Capita Values	1990	1991	1992	1993	1994	1995	1996
31	Per capita Inclusive Wealth Index	4,397	4,390	4,379	4,369	4,390	4,401	4,422
32	Per capita produced capital	544	560	578	597	621	656	688
33	Per capita human capital	1,926	1,945	1,959	1,970	2,006	2,021	2,045
34	Per capita natural capital	1,928	1,885	1,842	1,802	1,763	1,724	1,688
35	Per capita health capital	548,699	550,985	553,204	555,367	557,488	559,571	561,563
36	TFP (in percentage)	1.15	-2.37	1.57	1.83	2.60	2.81	3.58
37	Population	873,785,449	891,910,180	910,064,576	928,226,051	946,373,316	964,486,155	982,553,253

Data for TFP and population was obtained from Conference Board (2012), and United Nations Population Division (2011) respectively.

	1997	1998	1999	2000	2001	2002	2003	2004	2005	2006	2007	2008
1	4,444,223	4,547,857	4,660,523	4,783,274	4,887,274	5,015,770	5,153,632	5,317,030	5,504,897	5,709,605	5,938,610	6,163,964
2	718,617	765,762	822,034	881,774	929,645	989,505	1,063,654	1,161,489	1,279,094	1,415,941	1,578,775	1,736,341
3	2,071,594	2,132,517	2,194,344	2,257,997	2,325,478	2,400,173	2,468,580	2,540,713	2,618,017	2,692,677	2,767,258	2,843,220
4	1,654,012	1,649,578	1,644,144	1,643,503	1,632,150	1,626,092	1,621,398	1,614,829	1,607,786	1,600,988	1,592,577	1,584,404
5	528,540	529,102	528,815	533,558	527,120	526,147	526,942	526,281	525,624	525,960	525,188	525,185
6	496,867	497,265	497,259	502,417	496,195	495,453	496,420	495,821	495,187	495,412	494,722	494,827
7	31,673	31,837	31,556	31,141	30,925	30,694	30,522	30,461	30,437	30,548	30,466	30,358
8	65,815	66,177	66,539	66,901	68,035	69,169	70,303	71,437	72,570	73,393	74,215	75,037
9	49,966	50,293	50,619	50,946	51,967	52,987	54,008	55,029	56,049	56,836	57,623	58,410
10	15,849	15,884	15,920	15,955	16,068	16,181	16,295	16,408	16,521	16,556	16,592	16,627
11												
12	1,008,148	1,002,987	997,666	992,127	986,291	980,289	973,931	967,206	960,081	952,580	944,659	936,238
13	47,103	47,097	47,090	47,084	47,077	47,070	47,064	47,057	47,050	47,042	47,035	47,028
14	50,321	49,530	48,748	47,921	47,036	46,074	45,072	44,036	42,938	41,807	40,655	39,472
15	910,724	906,360	901,828	897,121	892,177	887,145	881,795	876,113	870,093	863,730	856,969	849,738
16	51,508	51,313	51,124	50,917	50,704	50,487	50,223	49,905	49,511	49,056	48,515	47,943
17	1,519	1,509	1,497	1,484	1,471	1,455	1,438	1,419	1,398	1,374	1,340	1,304
18	27,444	27,436	27,429	27,422	27,416	27,409	27,403	27,397	27,392	27,386	27,379	27,373
19	95	93	91	85	82	78	75	72	69	67	64	62
20	18,893	18,721	18,554	18,374	18,185	17,995	17,760	17,473	17,112	16,692	16,200	15,678
21	3,557	3,555	3,553	3,552	3,550	3,549	3,547	3,544	3,541	3,537	3,532	3,527
22	-	-	-	-	-	-	-	-	-	-	-	-
23	-	-	-	-	-	-	-	-	-	-	-	-
24	-	-	-	-	-	-	-	-	-	-	-	-
25	-	-	-	-	-	-	-	-	-	-	-	-
26	-	-	-	-	-	-	-	-	-	-	-	-
27	563,822,972	575,855,439	587,844,529	599,778,823	612,478,869	625,147,836	637,802,472	650,470,761	663,176,750	675,852,825	688,566,885	701,324,474
28	-31,631	-32,870	-34,930	-36,936	-37,819	-39,670	-42,204	-44,284	-46,696	-50,685	-53,782	-57,529
29	-18,145	-18,085	-17,954	-18,356	-17,915	-18,072	-19,079	-20,011	-20,747	-21,566	-22,033	-22,531
30	-13,486	-14,785	-16,976	-18,580	-19,904	-21,598	-23,124	-24,273	-25,949	-29,119	-31,749	-34,998

	1997	1998	1999	2000	2001	2002	2003	2004	2005	2006	2007	2008
31	4,442	4,465	4,497	4,539	4,562	4,607	4,660	4,735	4,829	4,935	5,059	5,176
32	718	752	793	837	868	909	962	1,034	1,122	1,224	1,345	1,458
33	2,070	2,094	2,118	2,143	2,171	2,205	2,232	2,262	2,296	2,327	2,357	2,388
34	1,653	1,620	1,587	1,559	1,523	1,494	1,466	1,438	1,410	1,384	1,357	1,330
35	563,508	565,412	567,276	569,105	571,676	574,218	576,735	579,231	581,712	584,123	586,528	588,921
36	0.45	2.61	2.20	-0.16	1.31	-0.60	3.69	2.33	3.65	3.38	2.79	0.72
37	1,000,558,144	1,018,471,141	1,036,258,683	1,053,898,107	1,071,374,264	1,088,694,080	1,105,885,689	1,122,991,192	1,140,042,863	1,157,038,539	1,173,971,629	1,190,863,679

Japan

UNIT: millions of constant US$ of year 2000

		1990	1991	1992	1993	1994	1995	1996
1	Inclusive Wealth Index, rows 2 + 3 + 4	45,239,588	46,482,041	47,572,051	48,484,836	49,282,111	50,076,142	50,769,414
2	Produced capital	10,477,873	11,023,621	11,502,652	11,914,529	12,279,380	12,629,497	13,010,380
3	Human capital	34,210,115	34,902,509	35,509,166	36,005,829	36,433,990	36,875,690	37,183,925
4	Natural capital, rows 5 + 8 + 11 + 12 + 16	551,600	555,911	560,233	564,478	568,741	570,955	575,108
5	Agricultural land, rows 6 + 7	238,273	236,641	235,008	233,292	231,576	227,810	225,968
6	Cropland	219,439	217,807	216,174	214,458	212,742	210,859	209,017
7	Pastureland	18,834	18,834	18,834	18,834	18,834	16,951	16,951
8	Forest resources, rows 9 + 10	272,350	278,657	284,964	291,270	297,577	303,883	310,190
9	Timber	264,516	270,825	277,134	283,443	289,752	296,061	302,370
10	Non–timber forest resources	7,834	7,832	7,830	7,827	7,825	7,823	7,820
11	Fisheries							
12	Fossil fuels, rows 13 + 14 + 15	10,695	10,356	10,029	9,706	9,398	9,090	8,794
13	Oil	344	343	342	342	341	341	340
14	Natural gas	4,124	3,917	3,709	3,496	3,291	3,080	2,878
15	Coal	6,228	6,096	5,977	5,868	5,765	5,670	5,576
16	Minerals, rows 17 + 18 +...+ 26	30,281	30,257	30,233	30,210	30,190	30,172	30,156
17	Bauxite	-	-	-	-	-	-	-
18	Appendix	15	12	10	8	7	6	6
19	Gold	243	236	229	221	213	205	198
20	Iron	-	-	-	-	-	-	-
21	Lead	22	21	20	19	19	18	18
22	Nickel	-	-	-	-	-	-	-
23	Phosphate	-	-	-	-	-	-	-
24	Silver	29,797	29,794	29,792	29,790	29,789	29,787	29,786
25	Tin	-	-	-	-	-	-	-
26	Zinc	205	193	182	171	163	154	148
27	Health capital	804,473,747	806,782,226	809,339,559	812,004,560	814,522,375	816,723,323	818,419,057
28	IWI adjustments excluding TFP, rows 29 + 30	-57,150	-59,545	-62,047	-63,420	-67,346	-69,578	-71,733
29	Carbon damages (annual change)	-17,467	-17,724	-17,534	-17,519	-17,800	-18,108	-18,465
30	Oil capital gains (annual change)	-39,683	-41,821	-44,512	-45,900	-49,547	-51,470	-53,269

	Per Capita Values	1990	1991	1992	1993	1994	1995	1996
31	Per capita Inclusive Wealth Index	370,054	378,817	386,207	392,103	397,124	402,261	406,757
32	Per capita produced capital	85,708	89,840	93,383	96,354	98,949	101,453	104,237
33	Per capita human capital	279,835	284,447	288,276	291,183	293,591	296,222	297,912
34	Per capita natural capital	4,512	4,531	4,548	4,565	4,583	4,586	4,608
35	Per capita health capital	6,580,499	6,575,081	6,570,512	6,566,779	6,563,560	6,560,725	6,557,058
36	TFP (in percentage)	2.32	0.30	-1.45	-0.16	-8.83	1.14	0.76
37	Population	122,251,184	122,703,017	123,177,552	123,653,405	124,097,649	124,486,744	124,814,986

Data for TFP and population was obtained from Conference Board (2012), and United Nations Population Division (2011) respectively.

	1997	1998	1999	2000	2001	2002	2003	2004	2005	2006	2007	2008
1	51,455,643	51,890,580	52,249,233	52,625,167	53,089,312	53,541,390	53,716,452	53,898,780	54,181,705	54,496,153	54,902,443	55,105,917
2	13,361,418	13,596,956	13,806,766	14,004,745	14,199,502	14,312,635	14,411,869	14,520,082	14,655,788	14,787,389	14,896,443	14,956,648
3	37,514,964	37,710,158	37,854,589	38,027,036	38,292,340	38,625,921	38,696,227	38,764,627	38,906,104	39,089,726	39,387,731	39,531,806
4	579,261	583,467	587,878	593,386	597,470	602,834	608,355	614,071	619,814	619,037	618,268	617,463
5	224,085	222,243	220,611	220,067	217,555	216,300	215,170	214,249	213,328	212,449	211,570	210,650
6	207,134	205,292	203,660	202,153	200,605	199,349	198,219	197,298	196,378	195,499	194,620	193,699
7	16,951	16,951	16,951	17,913	16,951	16,951	16,951	16,951	16,951	16,951	16,951	16,951
8	316,497	322,803	329,110	335,416	342,256	349,096	355,936	362,776	369,615	369,897	370,179	370,461
9	308,679	314,987	321,296	327,605	334,441	341,277	348,114	354,950	361,786	362,065	362,344	362,623
10	7,818	7,816	7,813	7,811	7,815	7,818	7,822	7,826	7,830	7,832	7,835	7,838
11												
12	8,539	8,294	8,047	7,807	7,574	7,366	7,190	6,999	6,834	6,663	6,499	6,339
13	339	338	337	337	336	335	334	333	332	331	330	329
14	2,684	2,496	2,306	2,111	1,928	1,721	1,546	1,355	1,192	1,022	858	699
15	5,516	5,460	5,404	5,359	5,310	5,310	5,310	5,310	5,310	5,310	5,310	5,310
16	30,141	30,126	30,111	30,096	30,084	30,072	30,060	30,048	30,036	30,028	30,020	30,014
17	-	-	-	-	-	-	-	-	-	-	-	-
18	6	6	6	5	5	5	5	5	5	5	5	5
19	191	184	176	169	162	155	148	141	134	126	119	113
20	-	-	-	-	-	-	-	-	-	-	-	-
21	17	17	17	16	16	16	16	15	15	15	15	15
22	-	-	-	-	-	-	-	-	-	-	-	-
23	-	-	-	-	-	-	-	-	-	-	-	-
24	29,785	29,784	29,783	29,781	29,780	29,779	29,778	29,777	29,776	29,776	29,776	29,776
25	-	-	-	-	-	-	-	-	-	-	-	-
26	141	136	130	125	121	117	113	109	105	105	105	105
27	819,853,210	821,081,383	822,196,152	823,267,869	824,263,392	825,174,647	826,012,559	826,799,277	827,555,249	828,344,866	829,085,774	829,794,623
28	-72,983	-73,194	-75,822	-77,049	-77,787	-79,326	-83,447	-83,977	-86,801	-88,408	-89,519	-90,194
29	-18,747	-18,685	-18,550	-18,965	-18,509	-18,672	-19,712	-20,675	-21,436	-22,281	-22,764	-23,279
30	-54,235	-54,509	-57,273	-58,084	-59,278	-60,654	-63,735	-63,301	-65,365	-66,127	-66,755	-66,915

	1997	1998	1999	2000	2001	2002	2003	2004	2005	2006	2007	2008
31	411,344	414,046	416,224	418,589	421,700	424,769	425,699	426,754	428,677	430,920	433,958	435,466
32	106,813	108,493	109,986	111,396	112,790	113,549	114,213	114,966	115,954	116,929	117,744	118,193
33	299,900	300,897	301,554	302,473	304,164	306,437	306,665	306,926	307,819	309,096	311,327	312,394
34	4,631	4,656	4,683	4,720	4,746	4,783	4,821	4,862	4,904	4,895	4,887	4,879
35	6,554,024	6,551,585	6,549,714	6,548,408	6,547,301	6,546,492	6,546,088	6,546,343	6,547,480	6,550,004	6,553,236	6,557,327
36	0.42	-2.15	0.01	1.00	0.14	0.73	0.98	1.47	0.74	0.58	1.57	-0.78
37	125,091,571	125,325,617	125,531,619	125,720,310	125,893,623	126,048,366	126,184,149	126,299,414	126,392,944	126,464,789	126,515,486	126,544,640

Kenya

UNIT: millions of constant US$ of year 2000

		1990	1991	1992	1993	1994	1995	1996
1	Inclusive Wealth Index, rows 2 + 3 + 4	74,061	75,976	78,006	79,677	82,141	84,475	85,973
2	Produced capital	16,194	16,505	16,732	16,893	17,228	17,772	18,300
3	Human capital	31,422	32,937	34,572	36,300	38,082	39,893	41,567
4	Natural capital, rows 5 + 8 + 11 + 12 + 16	26,445	26,534	26,703	26,484	26,831	26,810	26,105
5	Agricultural land, rows 6 + 7	24,300	24,398	24,575	24,364	24,720	24,707	24,011
6	Cropland	4,965	5,063	5,240	5,029	5,385	5,372	4,676
7	Pastureland	19,335	19,335	19,335	19,335	19,335	19,335	19,335
8	Forest resources, rows 9 + 10	2,145	2,136	2,128	2,120	2,111	2,103	2,094
9	Timber	1,240	1,235	1,229	1,224	1,219	1,213	1,208
10	Non-timber forest resources	905	902	899	896	892	889	886
11	Fisheries							
12	Fossil fuels, rows 13 + 14 + 15	-	-	-	-	-	-	-
13	Oil							
14	Natural gas	-	-	-	-	-	-	-
15	Coal	-	-	-	-	-	-	-
16	Minerals, rows 17 + 18 +...+ 26	-	-	-	-	-	-	-
17	Bauxite	-	-	-	-	-	-	-
18	Appendix	-	-	-	-	-	-	-
19	Gold	-	-	-	-	-	-	-
20	Iron	-	-	-	-	-	-	-
21	Lead	-	-	-	-	-	-	-
22	Nickel	-	-	-	-	-	-	-
23	Phosphate	-	-	-	-	-	-	-
24	Silver	-	-	-	-	-	-	-
25	Tin	-	-	-	-	-	-	-
26	Zinc	-	-	-	-	-	-	-
27	Health capital	11,515,272	11,795,499	12,068,500	12,331,103	12,579,972	12,813,141	13,030,845
28	IWI adjustments excluding TFP, rows 29 + 30	-689	-666	-706	-732	-766	-807	-844
29	Carbon damages (annual change)	-375	-380	-376	-376	-382	-389	-396
30	Oil capital gains (annual change)	-314	-285	-330	-356	-384	-418	-448

	Per Capita Values	1990	1991	1992	1993	1994	1995	1996
31	Per capita Inclusive Wealth Index	3,159	3,134	3,115	3,083	3,083	3,080	3,050
32	Per capita produced capital	691	681	668	654	647	648	649
33	Per capita human capital	1,340	1,359	1,381	1,404	1,429	1,455	1,474
34	Per capita natural capital	1,128	1,095	1,066	1,025	1,007	978	926
35	Per capita health capital	491,116	486,611	481,924	477,091	472,170	467,194	462,224
36	TFP (in percentage)	0.60	-2.05	-4.13	-3.02	-0.07	1.56	1.09
37	Population	23,447,177	24,240,108	25,042,330	25,846,436	26,642,887	27,425,720	28,191,597

Data for TFP and population was obtained from Conference Board (2012), and United Nations Population Division (2011) respectively.

	1997	1998	1999	2000	2001	2002	2003	2004	2005	2006	2007	2008
1	88,293	90,488	93,194	95,806	98,657	101,533	104,343	107,371	110,893	114,503	118,496	122,812
2	18,847	19,504	20,099	21,078	21,726	22,446	22,936	23,544	24,724	26,345	28,309	30,498
3	43,220	44,890	46,629	48,457	50,517	52,701	54,979	57,302	59,646	61,595	63,591	65,636
4	26,227	26,095	26,466	26,271	26,414	26,386	26,427	26,525	26,524	26,563	26,596	26,678
5	24,141	24,017	24,397	24,211	24,363	24,344	24,395	24,502	24,511	24,558	24,600	24,691
6	4,806	4,682	5,062	4,876	5,028	5,009	5,060	5,167	5,176	5,223	5,265	5,356
7	19,335	19,335	19,335	19,335	19,335	19,335	19,335	19,335	19,335	19,335	19,335	19,335
8	2,086	2,078	2,069	2,061	2,051	2,042	2,032	2,023	2,013	2,004	1,996	1,987
9	1,203	1,197	1,192	1,187	1,180	1,173	1,167	1,160	1,154	1,148	1,142	1,136
10	883	880	877	874	871	868	865	862	859	857	854	851
11												
12	-	-	-	-	-	-	-	-	-	-	-	-
13												
14	-	-	-	-	-	-	-	-	-	-	-	-
15	-	-	-	-	-	-	-	-	-	-	-	-
16	-	-	-	-	-	-	-	-	-	-	-	-
17	-	-	-	-	-	-	-	-	-	-	-	-
18	-	-	-	-	-	-	-	-	-	-	-	-
19	-	-	-	-	-	-	-	-	-	-	-	-
20	-	-	-	-	-	-	-	-	-	-	-	-
21	-	-	-	-	-	-	-	-	-	-	-	-
22	-	-	-	-	-	-	-	-	-	-	-	-
23	-	-	-	-	-	-	-	-	-	-	-	-
24	-	-	-	-	-	-	-	-	-	-	-	-
25	-	-	-	-	-	-	-	-	-	-	-	-
26	-	-	-	-	-	-	-	-	-	-	-	-
27	13,237,214	13,436,135	13,632,749	13,831,408	14,325,900	14,839,376	15,371,173	15,919,376	16,482,552	17,061,690	17,654,765	18,267,227
28	-821	-909	-929	-1,006	-966	-985	-1,060	-1,148	-1,268	-1,410	-1,457	-1,448
29	-402	-401	-398	-407	-397	-401	-423	-444	-460	-478	-489	-500
30	-419	-508	-531	-598	-569	-584	-637	-705	-808	-931	-969	-948

	1997	1998	1999	2000	2001	2002	2003	2004	2005	2006	2007	2008
31	3,050	3,047	3,059	3,065	3,076	3,083	3,087	3,094	3,114	3,134	3,161	3,194
32	651	657	660	674	677	682	678	678	694	721	755	793
33	1,493	1,512	1,531	1,550	1,575	1,600	1,626	1,651	1,675	1,686	1,696	1,707
34	906	879	869	841	823	801	782	764	745	727	710	694
35	457,326	452,450	447,531	442,553	446,621	450,663	454,697	458,743	462,804	466,920	470,979	475,024
36	-2.61	0.41	-0.50	-2.24	1.93	-2.47	0.02	1.60	2.36	1.96	2.22	-3.35
37	28,944,780	29,696,410	30,462,154	31,253,701	32,076,186	32,927,864	33,805,301	34,702,176	35,614,576	36,540,948	37,485,246	38,455,418

Nigeria

UNIT: millions of constant US$ of year 2000

		1990	1991	1992	1993	1994	1995	1996
1	Inclusive Wealth Index, rows 2 + 3 + 4	811,870	814,540	817,352	821,034	824,682	827,780	827,903
2	Produced capital	64,805	63,416	62,030	61,229	60,124	58,263	56,958
3	Human capital	127,568	131,746	136,237	141,017	146,048	151,300	155,188
4	Natural capital, rows 5 + 8 + 11 + 12 + 16	619,497	619,378	619,086	618,788	618,510	618,216	615,757
5	Agricultural land, rows 6 + 7	86,285	86,597	86,743	86,889	87,034	87,190	85,189
6	Cropland	38,398	38,710	38,857	39,003	39,147	39,398	37,397
7	Pastureland	47,887	47,887	47,887	47,887	47,887	47,792	47,792
8	Forest resources, rows 9 + 10	10,261	10,029	9,796	9,564	9,332	9,100	8,868
9	Timber	6,056	5,923	5,791	5,659	5,527	5,395	5,262
10	Non-timber forest resources	4,205	4,105	4,005	3,905	3,805	3,705	3,605
11	Fisheries							
12	Fossil fuels, rows 13 + 14 + 15	522,952	522,752	522,546	522,335	522,143	521,927	521,700
13	Oil	311,466	311,449	311,432	311,416	311,399	311,382	311,365
14	Natural gas	209,543	209,360	209,172	208,978	208,804	208,604	208,395
15	Coal	1,943	1,942	1,941	1,941	1,941	1,940	1,940
16	Minerals, rows 17 + 18 +...+ 26	-	-	-	-	-	-	-
17	Bauxite	-	-	-	-	-	-	-
18	Appendix	-	-	-	-	-	-	-
19	Gold	-	-	-	-	-	-	-
20	Iron	-	-	-	-	-	-	-
21	Lead	-	-	-	-	-	-	-
22	Nickel	-	-	-	-	-	-	-
23	Phosphate	-	-	-	-	-	-	-
24	Silver	-	-	-	-	-	-	-
25	Tin	-	-	-	-	-	-	-
26	Zinc	-	-	-	-	-	-	-
27	Health capital	50,334,009	51,609,921	52,888,276	54,172,647	55,468,850	56,782,764	58,139,943
28	IWI adjustments excluding TFP, rows 29 + 30	12,187	12,809	13,499	14,204	15,177	15,735	16,609
29	Carbon damages (annual change)	-1,511	-1,534	-1,517	-1,516	-1,540	-1,567	-1,598
30	Oil capital gains (annual change)	13,698	14,343	15,016	15,720	16,717	17,302	18,207

	Per Capita Values	1990	1991	1992	1993	1994	1995	1996
31	Per capita Inclusive Wealth Index	8,322	8,147	7,978	7,824	7,675	7,524	7,351
32	Per capita produced capital	664	634	605	584	560	530	506
33	Per capita human capital	1,308	1,318	1,330	1,344	1,359	1,375	1,378
34	Per capita natural capital	6,350	6,195	6,043	5,897	5,756	5,619	5,468
35	Per capita health capital	515,971	516,171	516,261	516,266	516,217	516,138	516,257
36	TFP (in percentage)	3.51	-2.22	-0.95	0.83	-0.45	-1.80	3.08
37	Population	97,552,057	99,986,136	102,444,773	104,931,559	107,452,627	110,014,688	112,618,306

Data for TFP and population was obtained from Conference Board (2012), and United Nations Population Division (2011) respectively.

	1997	1998	1999	2000	2001	2002	2003	2004	2005	2006	2007	2008
1	829,093	834,028	837,054	839,902	844,121	847,825	856,984	862,814	870,189	878,882	886,129	892,512
2	55,989	54,935	53,871	52,649	52,219	51,630	52,621	52,437	51,900	54,177	56,604	58,437
3	159,284	163,596	168,129	172,868	178,281	181,094	190,175	196,559	203,192	209,160	215,480	222,139
4	613,820	615,497	615,054	614,385	613,621	615,100	614,188	613,817	615,097	615,545	614,045	611,936
5	83,728	85,883	85,957	86,017	86,077	88,351	88,471	89,189	91,584	93,379	93,379	92,781
6	36,799	38,954	39,028	39,088	39,147	41,662	41,781	43,098	45,492	47,887	48,485	47,887
7	46,929	46,929	46,929	46,929	46,929	46,690	46,690	46,091	46,091	45,492	44,894	44,894
8	8,635	8,403	8,171	7,939	7,707	7,475	7,242	7,010	6,778	6,546	6,314	6,082
9	5,130	4,998	4,866	4,734	4,601	4,469	4,337	4,205	4,072	3,940	3,808	3,676
10	3,505	3,405	3,305	3,205	3,105	3,006	2,906	2,806	2,706	2,606	2,506	2,406
11												
12	521,457	521,212	520,926	520,429	519,838	519,274	518,475	517,618	516,735	515,620	514,352	513,073
13	311,346	311,328	311,309	311,291	311,271	311,253	311,233	311,213	311,191	311,170	311,150	311,131
14	208,170	207,944	207,677	207,199	206,627	206,082	205,302	204,465	203,605	202,511	201,264	200,004
15	1,940	1,940	1,940	1,940	1,940	1,940	1,939	1,939	1,939	1,939	1,939	1,939
16	-	-	-	-	-	-	-	-	-	-	-	-
17	-	-	-	-	-	-	-	-	-	-	-	-
18	-	-	-	-	-	-	-	-	-	-	-	-
19	-	-	-	-	-	-	-	-	-	-	-	-
20	-	-	-	-	-	-	-	-	-	-	-	-
21	-	-	-	-	-	-	-	-	-	-	-	-
22	-	-	-	-	-	-	-	-	-	-	-	-
23	-	-	-	-	-	-	-	-	-	-	-	-
24	-	-	-	-	-	-	-	-	-	-	-	-
25	-	-	-	-	-	-	-	-	-	-	-	-
26	-	-	-	-	-	-	-	-	-	-	-	-
27	59,515,600	60,919,166	62,362,819	63,857,618	66,234,181	68,697,758	71,251,916	73,896,825	76,632,906	79,480,595	82,415,435	85,446,251
28	17,644	18,806	19,983	21,125	21,668	22,865	24,250	25,721	26,667	28,413	30,122	31,661
29	-1,622	-1,617	-1,605	-1,641	-1,602	-1,616	-1,706	-1,789	-1,855	-1,928	-1,970	-2,014
30	19,266	20,423	21,588	22,766	23,269	24,480	25,955	27,510	28,522	30,341	32,092	33,676

	1997	1998	1999	2000	2001	2002	2003	2004	2005	2006	2007	2008
31	7,193	7,069	6,930	6,790	6,662	6,530	6,440	6,326	6,223	6,131	6,030	5,924
32	486	466	446	426	412	398	395	384	371	378	385	388
33	1,382	1,387	1,392	1,398	1,407	1,395	1,429	1,441	1,453	1,459	1,466	1,474
34	5,325	5,217	5,092	4,967	4,843	4,738	4,616	4,500	4,399	4,294	4,179	4,062
35	516,320	516,337	516,315	516,278	522,744	529,126	535,459	541,768	548,069	554,494	560,834	567,125
36	0.37	-0.39	-1.89	3.58	5.69	16.09	6.57	6.18	0.09	-0.43	0.32	-0.75
37	115,268,715	117,983,368	120,784,408	123,688,536	126,704,722	129,832,447	133,067,097	136,399,438	139,823,340	143,338,939	146,951,477	150,665,730

Norway

		1990	1991	1992	1993	1994	1995	1996
1	Inclusive Wealth Index, rows 2 + 3 + 4	1,234,748	1,237,315	1,241,297	1,247,372	1,256,971	1,269,777	1,282,556
2	Produced capital	285,082	285,719	285,846	287,239	289,670	292,817	298,124
3	Human capital	745,122	747,655	752,401	757,810	765,750	775,809	784,547
4	Natural capital, rows 5 + 8 + 11 + 12 + 16	204,545	203,941	203,050	202,323	201,551	201,152	199,886
5	Agricultural land, rows 6 + 7	5,031	5,206	5,170	5,222	5,310	5,810	5,835
6	Cropland	4,454	4,598	4,552	4,588	4,645	5,114	5,155
7	Pastureland	577	608	619	634	665	696	680
8	Forest resources, rows 9 + 10	19,885	20,152	20,420	20,688	20,955	21,223	21,490
9	Timber	17,018	17,280	17,542	17,805	18,067	18,329	18,591
10	Non-timber forest resources	2,867	2,872	2,878	2,883	2,888	2,894	2,899
11	Fisheries							
12	Fossil fuels, rows 13 + 14 + 15	179,629	178,583	177,460	176,413	175,286	174,119	172,560
13	Oil	57,108	57,092	57,074	57,054	57,032	57,008	56,981
14	Natural gas	122,128	121,103	120,003	118,980	117,879	116,740	115,211
15	Coal	392	387	383	379	375	371	368
16	Minerals, rows 17 + 18 +...+ 26	-	-	-	-	-	-	-
17	Bauxite	-	-	-	-	-	-	-
18	Appendix	-	-	-	-	-	-	-
19	Gold	-	-	-	-	-	-	-
20	Iron	-	-	-	-	-	-	-
21	Lead	-	-	-	-	-	-	-
22	Nickel	-	-	-	-	-	-	-
23	Phosphate	-	-	-	-	-	-	-
24	Silver	-	-	-	-	-	-	-
25	Tin	-	-	-	-	-	-	-
26	Zinc	-	-	-	-	-	-	-
27	Health capital	27,441,713	27,647,776	27,865,291	28,094,258	28,333,341	28,580,953	28,821,708
28	IWI adjustments excluding TFP, rows 29 + 30	-1,981	-1,869	-1,753	-1,717	-1,700	-1,716	-1,766
29	Carbon damages (annual change)	-3,350	-3,399	-3,363	-3,360	-3,414	-3,473	-3,541
30	Oil capital gains (annual change)	1,369	1,530	1,610	1,643	1,713	1,757	1,775

	Per Capita Values	1990	1991	1992	1993	1994	1995	1996
31	Per capita Inclusive Wealth Index	291,112	290,250	289,642	289,456	290,030	291,294	292,478
32	Per capita produced capital	67,213	67,024	66,699	66,655	66,838	67,174	67,985
33	Per capita human capital	175,675	175,385	175,564	175,852	176,687	177,975	178,910
34	Per capita natural capital	48,225	47,841	47,379	46,950	46,505	46,145	45,583
35	Per capita health capital	6,469,836	6,485,625	6,502,044	6,519,344	6,537,562	6,556,624	6,572,587
36	TFP (in percentage)	2.57	3.85	3.10	1.97	3.26	2.37	2.54
37	Population	4,241,485	4,262,932	4,285,620	4,309,369	4,333,931	4,359,096	4,385,139

Data for TFP and population was obtained from Conference Board (2012), and United Nations Population Division (2011) respectively.

	1997	1998	1999	2000	2001	2002	2003	2004	2005	2006	2007	2008
1	1,298,103	1,316,951	1,330,194	1,343,194	1,368,686	1,391,764	1,414,575	1,441,934	1,475,161	1,496,853	1,530,436	1,565,688
2	307,134	319,590	329,345	336,940	344,354	350,550	356,364	364,862	377,202	393,111	411,441	431,416
3	793,050	800,885	806,048	813,177	832,884	851,923	871,422	893,013	916,759	925,420	943,660	962,294
4	197,919	196,476	194,802	193,078	191,448	189,290	186,789	184,060	181,199	178,322	175,335	171,978
5	5,351	5,397	5,351	5,371	5,397	5,392	5,361	5,361	5,340	5,335	5,320	5,280
6	4,650	4,655	4,572	4,557	4,567	4,552	4,516	4,505	4,469	4,449	4,420	4,378
7	701	742	778	814	830	840	845	856	871	887	900	902
8	21,758	22,025	22,293	22,560	23,017	23,473	23,929	24,385	24,841	25,297	25,753	26,209
9	18,853	19,116	19,378	19,640	20,072	20,504	20,936	21,368	21,801	22,233	22,665	23,097
10	2,904	2,910	2,915	2,921	2,945	2,968	2,992	3,016	3,040	3,064	3,088	3,112
11												
12	170,811	169,054	167,158	165,146	163,035	160,426	157,499	154,314	151,018	147,689	144,262	140,488
13	56,954	56,928	56,902	56,874	56,846	56,819	56,791	56,765	56,741	56,718	56,696	56,676
14	113,494	111,767	109,903	107,926	105,867	103,314	100,453	97,332	94,081	90,807	87,454	83,746
15	363	359	354	345	322	293	255	216	197	165	111	66
16	-	-	-	-	-	-	-	-	-	-	-	-
17	-	-	-	-	-	-	-	-	-	-	-	-
18	-	-	-	-	-	-	-	-	-	-	-	-
19	-	-	-	-	-	-	-	-	-	-	-	-
20	-	-	-	-	-	-	-	-	-	-	-	-
21	-	-	-	-	-	-	-	-	-	-	-	-
22	-	-	-	-	-	-	-	-	-	-	-	-
23	-	-	-	-	-	-	-	-	-	-	-	-
24	-	-	-	-	-	-	-	-	-	-	-	-
25	-	-	-	-	-	-	-	-	-	-	-	-
26	-	-	-	-	-	-	-	-	-	-	-	-
27	29,070,870	29,324,031	29,575,192	29,821,168	30,054,703	30,280,821	30,518,786	30,795,961	31,130,935	31,529,132	31,983,651	32,467,125
28	-1,682	-1,566	-1,398	-1,232	-1,095	-973	-1,119	-912	-873	-1,096	-941	-852
29	-3,595	-3,583	-3,557	-3,637	-3,550	-3,581	-3,780	-3,965	-4,111	-4,273	-4,366	-4,464
30	1,914	2,017	2,159	2,405	2,455	2,608	2,661	3,053	3,238	3,177	3,425	3,612

	1997	1998	1999	2000	2001	2002	2003	2004	2005	2006	2007	2008
31	294,215	296,661	297,872	299,095	303,212	306,853	310,305	314,349	319,071	320,607	324,106	327,621
32	69,612	71,992	73,750	75,028	76,287	77,289	78,173	79,542	81,587	84,200	87,133	90,274
33	179,745	180,410	180,499	181,074	184,513	187,830	191,158	194,682	198,291	198,214	199,843	201,361
34	44,858	44,259	43,622	42,993	42,413	41,734	40,974	40,126	39,193	38,194	37,131	35,986
35	6,588,908	6,605,630	6,622,798	6,640,415	6,658,178	6,676,256	6,694,683	6,713,680	6,733,491	6,753,152	6,773,304	6,793,765
36	1.87	-1.17	-0.71	1.64	0.94	0.33	0.76	1.07	-0.34	-2.09	-2.56	-3.92
37	4,412,092	4,439,248	4,465,664	4,490,859	4,513,953	4,535,599	4,558,660	4,587,046	4,623,298	4,668,802	4,722,016	4,778,959

Russia

UNIT: millions of constant US$ of year 2000

		1990	1991	1992	1993	1994	1995	1996
1	Inclusive Wealth Index, rows 2 + 3 + 4	11,309,075	11,351,800	11,306,998	11,201,869	11,073,422	10,978,441	10,885,180
2	Produced capital	2,202,470	2,234,585	2,187,143	2,114,905	2,026,699	1,939,838	1,847,614
3	Human capital	1,811,819	1,822,524	1,853,463	1,849,791	1,836,557	1,855,028	1,879,906
4	Natural capital, rows 5 + 8 + 11 + 12 + 16	7,294,786	7,294,690	7,266,393	7,237,173	7,210,166	7,183,574	7,157,660
5	Agricultural land, rows 6 + 7	175,215	175,215	175,215	172,973	172,116	171,079	170,851
6	Cropland	105,705	105,705	105,705	103,798	103,093	102,300	101,171
7	Pastureland	69,509	69,509	69,509	69,175	69,022	68,779	69,679
8	Forest resources, rows 9 + 10	2,241,902	2,242,485	2,243,068	2,243,651	2,244,234	2,244,818	2,245,401
9	Timber	1,987,892	1,988,465	1,989,038	1,989,611	1,990,184	1,990,757	1,991,330
10	Non–timber forest resources	254,010	254,020	254,030	254,040	254,050	254,060	254,070
11	Fisheries							
12	Fossil fuels, rows 13 + 14 + 15	4,794,458	4,794,458	4,766,279	4,739,354	4,713,237	4,687,710	4,662,013
13	Oil	496,396	496,396	496,332	496,275	496,223	496,172	496,122
14	Natural gas	2,166,073	2,166,073	2,142,138	2,119,051	2,096,350	2,074,119	2,051,645
15	Coal	2,131,988	2,131,988	2,127,809	2,124,028	2,120,665	2,117,420	2,114,245
16	Minerals, rows 17 + 18 +...+ 26	83,212	82,533	81,831	81,196	80,579	79,968	79,396
17	Bauxite	459	450	443	436	431	426	421
18	Appendix	6,045	5,911	5,776	5,663	5,552	5,451	5,350
19	Gold	6,705	6,580	6,452	6,321	6,192	6,076	5,968
20	Iron	60,100	59,919	59,733	59,561	59,395	59,223	59,065
21	Lead	-	-	-	-	-	-	-
22	Nickel	8,283	8,096	7,896	7,722	7,550	7,371	7,206
23	Phosphate	1,440	1,399	1,356	1,321	1,291	1,258	1,226
24	Silver	-	-	-	-	-	-	-
25	Tin	180	177	175	172	167	163	160
26	Zinc	-	-	-	-	-	-	-
27	Health capital	224,248,712	223,050,376	221,414,260	219,436,772	217,271,210	215,018,298	212,398,067
28	IWI adjustments excluding TFP, rows 29 + 30	-6,024	-6,375	-7,136	-1,738	3,776	6,253	10,457
29	Carbon damages (annual change)	1,455	1,476	1,461	1,459	1,483	1,508	1,538
30	Oil capital gains (annual change)	-7,479	-7,851	-8,596	-3,197	2,293	4,744	8,919

	Per Capita Values	1990	1991	1992	1993	1994	1995	1996
31	Per capita Inclusive Wealth Index	76,287	76,354	75,938	75,208	74,385	73,830	73,322
32	Per capita produced capital	14,857	15,030	14,689	14,199	13,614	13,045	12,445
33	Per capita human capital	12,222	12,259	12,448	12,419	12,337	12,475	12,663
34	Per capita natural capital	49,208	49,065	48,801	48,589	48,434	48,310	48,214
35	Per capita health capital	1,512,705	1,500,267	1,487,022	1,473,268	1,459,506	1,446,001	1,430,705
36	TFP (in percentage)				-7.48	-10.59	-1.08	-1.66
37	Population	148,243,501	148,673,813	148,897,737	148,945,559	148,866,314	148,698,582	148,456,965

Data for TFP and population was obtained from Conference Board (2012), and United Nations Population Division (2011) respectively.

	1997	1998	1999	2000	2001	2002	2003	2004	2005	2006	2007	2008
1	10,790,061	10,698,680	10,694,557	10,653,287	10,561,905	10,504,167	10,439,861	10,402,659	10,367,033	10,341,726	10,337,446	10,327,366
2	1,758,121	1,669,937	1,590,359	1,527,453	1,464,410	1,411,687	1,369,602	1,337,632	1,314,714	1,306,155	1,315,707	1,335,387
3	1,897,227	1,919,639	2,020,765	2,067,294	2,063,814	2,084,155	2,088,485	2,110,408	2,125,437	2,132,756	2,142,820	2,135,477
4	7,134,713	7,109,104	7,083,434	7,058,540	7,033,681	7,008,324	6,981,773	6,954,619	6,926,882	6,902,815	6,878,918	6,856,502
5	172,335	171,780	171,387	171,682	171,444	171,278	170,982	170,747	170,510	170,358	170,338	170,363
6	102,287	101,160	100,260	99,800	99,389	99,058	98,325	97,996	97,699	97,533	97,531	97,589
7	70,048	70,620	71,127	71,882	72,055	72,219	72,656	72,751	72,811	72,825	72,807	72,773
8	2,245,984	2,246,567	2,247,150	2,247,733	2,248,739	2,249,746	2,250,752	2,251,759	2,252,765	2,257,969	2,263,172	2,268,376
9	1,991,903	1,992,477	1,993,050	1,993,623	1,994,659	1,995,696	1,996,732	1,997,769	1,998,805	2,003,990	2,009,175	2,014,360
10	254,080	254,090	254,100	254,110	254,080	254,050	254,020	253,990	253,960	253,979	253,998	254,017
11												
12	4,637,588	4,612,565	4,587,367	4,562,303	4,537,392	4,511,938	4,485,436	4,458,247	4,430,490	4,402,134	4,373,825	4,346,947
13	496,072	496,021	495,969	495,914	495,855	495,791	495,721	495,644	495,566	495,486	495,404	495,324
14	2,030,300	2,008,215	1,986,175	1,964,340	1,942,633	1,920,380	1,897,342	1,873,649	1,849,707	1,825,189	1,800,779	1,778,009
15	2,111,216	2,108,328	2,105,222	2,102,048	2,098,905	2,095,767	2,092,373	2,088,953	2,085,217	2,081,459	2,077,642	2,073,614
16	78,806	78,192	77,530	76,822	76,106	75,363	74,603	73,866	73,117	72,355	71,582	70,816
17	415	410	404	397	390	383	374	365	354	344	333	323
18	5,252	5,156	5,053	4,943	4,827	4,693	4,562	4,432	4,296	4,156	4,013	3,868
19	5,868	5,767	5,657	5,531	5,398	5,250	5,101	4,958	4,814	4,674	4,537	4,382
20	58,905	58,741	58,557	58,360	58,173	57,983	57,775	57,555	57,336	57,105	56,867	56,640
21	-	-	-	-	-	-	-	-	-	-	-	-
22	7,021	6,813	6,599	6,373	6,141	5,919	5,698	5,506	5,308	5,110	4,910	4,719
23	1,189	1,152	1,109	1,068	1,029	989	948	907	866	825	783	744
24	-	-	-	-	-	-	-	-	-	-	-	-
25	156	154	152	150	147	146	145	144	143	141	140	139
26	-	-	-	-	-	-	-	-	-	-	-	-
27	209,844,768	207,288,365	204,622,041	201,820,230	201,686,715	201,456,825	201,232,379	201,168,744	201,353,170	201,492,543	201,828,067	202,342,203
28	12,079	13,555	14,244	14,802	15,561	15,994	16,877	18,033	19,111	20,248	22,902	21,608
29	1,562	1,556	1,545	1,580	1,542	1,555	1,642	1,722	1,786	1,856	1,896	1,939
30	10,517	11,998	12,699	13,222	14,019	14,438	15,235	16,311	17,325	18,392	21,006	19,668

	1997	1998	1999	2000	2001	2002	2003	2004	2005	2006	2007	2008
31	72,837	72,411	72,610	72,591	72,262	72,184	72,058	72,087	72,072	72,063	72,141	72,137
32	11,868	11,303	10,798	10,408	10,019	9,701	9,453	9,269	9,140	9,101	9,182	9,328
33	12,807	12,993	13,720	14,086	14,120	14,322	14,415	14,624	14,776	14,861	14,954	14,916
34	48,162	48,116	48,093	48,097	48,123	48,161	48,190	48,193	48,156	48,100	48,005	47,893
35	1,416,537	1,402,974	1,389,277	1,375,195	1,379,887	1,384,396	1,388,954	1,394,033	1,399,811	1,404,031	1,408,484	1,413,368
36	3.92	-3.06	8.21	11.43	6.29	5.32	7.45	6.59	4.69	4.84	3.52	-0.37
37	148,139,274	147,749,214	147,286,725	146,757,517	146,161,742	145,519,641	144,880,469	144,306,982	143,843,159	143,510,059	143,294,533	143,163,100

Saudi Arabia

UNIT: millions of constant US$ of year 2000

		1990	1991	1992	1993	1994	1995	1996
1	Inclusive Wealth Index, rows 2 + 3 + 4	3,737,877	3,774,763	3,812,699	3,854,090	3,892,059	3,931,841	3,978,736
2	Produced capital	251,105	259,288	267,701	277,482	281,622	286,148	290,429
3	Human capital	749,332	779,068	809,853	842,842	878,168	914,935	959,551
4	Natural capital, rows 5 + 8 + 11 + 12 + 16	2,737,441	2,736,406	2,735,144	2,733,767	2,732,270	2,730,758	2,728,756
5	Agricultural land, rows 6 + 7	222,981	223,227	223,322	223,372	223,372	223,372	223,006
6	Cropland	4,474	4,720	4,815	4,865	4,865	4,865	4,499
7	Pastureland	218,507	218,507	218,507	218,507	218,507	218,507	218,507
8	Forest resources, rows 9 + 10	307	307	307	307	307	307	307
9	Timber	-	-	-	-	-	-	-
10	Non-timber forest resources	307	307	307	307	307	307	307
11	Fisheries							
12	Fossil fuels, rows 13 + 14 + 15	2,514,153	2,512,873	2,511,516	2,510,088	2,508,591	2,507,080	2,505,444
13	Oil	2,208,253	2,208,180	2,208,105	2,208,032	2,207,956	2,207,880	2,207,804
14	Natural gas	305,900	304,693	303,410	302,056	300,634	299,200	297,640
15	Coal	-	-	-	-	-	-	-
16	Minerals, rows 17 + 18 +...+ 26	-	-	-	-	-	-	-
17	Bauxite	-	-	-	-	-	-	-
18	Appendix	-	-	-	-	-	-	-
19	Gold	-	-	-	-	-	-	-
20	Iron	-	-	-	-	-	-	-
21	Lead	-	-	-	-	-	-	-
22	Nickel	-	-	-	-	-	-	-
23	Phosphate	-	-	-	-	-	-	-
24	Silver	-	-	-	-	-	-	-
25	Tin	-	-	-	-	-	-	-
26	Zinc	-	-	-	-	-	-	-
27	Health capital	43,005,876	44,546,954	46,065,521	47,506,994	48,802,269	49,923,521	50,867,503
28	IWI adjustments excluding TFP, rows 29 + 30	99,401	104,148	109,058	114,326	120,119	126,703	132,668
29	Carbon damages (annual change)	-2,743	-2,783	-2,754	-2,751	-2,795	-2,844	-2,900
30	Oil capital gains (annual change)	102,144	106,932	111,811	117,077	122,915	129,547	135,568

	Per Capita Values	1990	1991	1992	1993	1994	1995	1996
31	Per capita Inclusive Wealth Index	231,604	226,444	221,809	217,995	214,818	212,626	211,787
32	Per capita produced capital	15,559	15,554	15,574	15,695	15,544	15,474	15,459
33	Per capita human capital	46,430	46,735	47,114	47,673	48,469	49,478	51,077
34	Per capita natural capital	169,616	164,154	159,121	154,627	150,804	147,674	145,251
35	Per capita health capital	2,664,709	2,672,321	2,679,930	2,687,090	2,693,584	2,699,759	2,707,667
36	TFP (in percentage)	9.42	4.82	0.30	-4.64	-3.32	-2.80	0.99
37	Population	16,139,053	16,669,764	17,189,075	17,679,720	18,117,969	18,491,845	18,786,467

Data for TFP and population was obtained from Conference Board (2012), and United Nations Population Division (2011) respectively.

	1997	1998	1999	2000	2001	2002	2003	2004	2005	2006	2007	2008
1	4,027,123	4,074,370	4,123,822	4,178,275	4,246,410	4,324,887	4,414,396	4,505,246	4,599,901	4,712,636	4,829,904	4,946,619
2	297,222	305,305	315,320	326,649	336,670	347,554	362,693	377,769	399,295	427,445	465,583	509,424
3	1,002,567	1,043,575	1,084,828	1,129,909	1,190,117	1,259,918	1,336,631	1,415,084	1,490,981	1,578,481	1,660,501	1,736,685
4	2,727,335	2,725,490	2,723,674	2,721,717	2,719,624	2,717,415	2,715,072	2,712,394	2,709,625	2,706,711	2,703,820	2,700,510
5	223,372	223,372	223,372	223,372	223,380	223,382	223,389	223,274	223,285	223,229	223,231	223,044
6	4,865	4,865	4,865	4,865	4,873	4,875	4,882	4,767	4,778	4,722	4,724	4,537
7	218,507	218,507	218,507	218,507	218,507	218,507	218,507	218,507	218,507	218,507	218,507	218,507
8	307	307	307	307	307	307	307	307	307	307	307	307
9	-	-	-	-	-	-	-	-	-	-	-	-
10	307	307	307	307	307	307	307	307	307	307	307	307
11												
12	2,503,656	2,501,811	2,499,995	2,498,038	2,495,937	2,493,726	2,491,377	2,488,813	2,486,034	2,483,175	2,480,283	2,477,159
13	2,207,726	2,207,647	2,207,574	2,207,495	2,207,420	2,207,347	2,207,263	2,207,177	2,207,085	2,206,996	2,206,912	2,206,822
14	295,930	294,164	292,421	290,543	288,518	286,379	284,113	281,636	278,949	276,178	273,371	270,337
15	-	-	-	-	-	-	-	-	-	-	-	-
16	-	-	-	-	-	-	-	-	-	-	-	-
17	-	-	-	-	-	-	-	-	-	-	-	-
18	-	-	-	-	-	-	-	-	-	-	-	-
19	-	-	-	-	-	-	-	-	-	-	-	-
20	-	-	-	-	-	-	-	-	-	-	-	-
21	-	-	-	-	-	-	-	-	-	-	-	-
22	-	-	-	-	-	-	-	-	-	-	-	-
23	-	-	-	-	-	-	-	-	-	-	-	-
24	-	-	-	-	-	-	-	-	-	-	-	-
25	-	-	-	-	-	-	-	-	-	-	-	-
26	-	-	-	-	-	-	-	-	-	-	-	-
27	51,653,325	52,451,038	53,491,637	54,931,509	56,599,668	58,633,721	60,885,016	63,138,334	65,242,255	67,192,578	69,013,598	70,732,235
28	139,214	145,897	153,298	160,616	168,263	176,146	184,165	192,817	201,949	211,667	220,903	230,153
29	-2,944	-2,934	-2,913	-2,978	-2,907	-2,932	-3,096	-3,247	-3,366	-3,499	-3,575	-3,656
30	142,159	148,831	156,211	163,594	171,169	179,079	187,261	196,064	205,315	215,166	224,478	233,809

	1997	1998	1999	2000	2001	2002	2003	2004	2005	2006	2007	2008
31	211,724	211,583	210,626	208,442	205,323	201,504	197,650	194,076	191,335	190,030	189,377	189,043
32	15,626	15,855	16,105	16,296	16,279	16,193	16,239	16,273	16,609	17,236	18,255	19,468
33	52,709	54,193	55,408	56,368	57,545	58,702	59,846	60,959	62,018	63,650	65,107	66,370
34	143,388	141,535	139,113	135,778	131,500	126,609	121,565	116,844	112,708	109,144	106,015	103,204
35	2,715,646	2,723,788	2,732,103	2,740,372	2,736,719	2,731,842	2,726,068	2,719,866	2,713,778	2,709,440	2,705,972	2,703,146
36	0.54	0.59	-3.85	1.11	-3.92	-4.81	2.70	0.86	1.18	-1.38	-2.93	-1.39
37	19,020,639	19,256,649	19,578,923	20,045,276	20,681,576	21,463,072	22,334,371	23,213,767	24,041,116	24,799,436	25,504,176	26,166,639

South Africa

UNIT: millions of constant US$ of year 2000

		1990	1991	1992	1993	1994	1995	1996
1	Inclusive Wealth Index, rows 2 + 3 + 4	1,395,238	1,428,824	1,464,157	1,501,291	1,540,528	1,580,925	1,589,202
2	Produced capital	210,303	210,742	210,353	209,911	210,679	213,045	216,788
3	Human capital	647,995	682,885	720,559	760,164	800,745	841,487	849,058
4	Natural capital, rows 5 + 8 + 11 + 12 + 16	536,941	535,197	533,246	531,215	529,105	526,393	523,356
5	Agricultural land, rows 6 + 7	77,509	77,989	78,390	78,790	79,271	79,691	79,831
6	Cropland	11,450	11,690	11,931	12,171	12,411	12,671	12,651
7	Pastureland	66,059	66,299	66,459	66,619	66,860	67,020	67,180
8	Forest resources, rows 9 + 10	9,156	9,156	9,156	9,156	9,156	9,156	9,156
9	Timber	6,901	6,901	6,901	6,901	6,901	6,901	6,901
10	Non–timber forest resources	2,255	2,255	2,255	2,255	2,255	2,255	2,255
11	Fisheries	344	425	432	432	429	510	521
12	Fossil fuels, rows 13 + 14 + 15	422,948	420,745	418,487	416,159	413,683	411,077	408,473
13	Oil	131	131	131	131	129	128	126
14	Natural gas	907	907	906	856	802	748	696
15	Coal	421,910	419,707	417,450	415,173	412,752	410,202	407,650
16	Minerals, rows 17 + 18 +...+ 26	26,984	26,881	26,781	26,677	26,567	25,958	25,375
17	Bauxite	-	-	-	-	-	-	-
18	Appendix	2,879	2,879	2,879	2,879	2,878	2,846	2,817
19	Gold	10,012	10,012	10,011	10,011	10,010	9,550	9,114
20	Iron	3,705	3,639	3,575	3,508	3,435	3,363	3,293
21	Lead	86	82	78	72	67	62	58
22	Nickel	3,107	3,087	3,067	3,045	3,023	3,001	2,977
23	Phosphate	5,778	5,766	5,754	5,745	5,736	5,725	5,714
24	Silver	-	-	-	-	-	-	-
25	Tin	-	-	-	-	-	-	-
26	Zinc	1,417	1,417	1,417	1,417	1,417	1,411	1,404
27	Health capital	65,694,193	66,518,470	67,381,812	68,216,264	68,931,906	69,468,059	69,855,871
28	IWI adjustments excluding TFP, rows 29 + 30	-6,693	-7,074	-7,252	-7,325	-7,555	-7,842	-8,084
29	Carbon damages (annual change)	-3,898	-3,956	-3,913	-3,910	-3,972	-4,041	-4,121
30	Oil capital gains (annual change)	-2,794	-3,118	-3,339	-3,415	-3,582	-3,800	-3,963

	Per Capita Values	1990	1991	1992	1993	1994	1995	1996
31	Per capita Inclusive Wealth Index	37,920	37,909	37,890	37,902	37,998	38,184	37,680
32	Per capita produced capital	5,716	5,591	5,444	5,300	5,197	5,146	5,140
33	Per capita human capital	17,611	18,118	18,647	19,191	19,751	20,325	20,131
34	Per capita natural capital	14,593	14,200	13,800	13,411	13,051	12,714	12,409
35	Per capita health capital	1,785,464	1,764,841	1,743,753	1,722,220	1,700,258	1,677,875	1,656,305
36	TFP (in percentage)	-3.72	-4.03	-5.08	-1.66	0.17	-0.44	0.27
37	Population	36,793,907	37,690,924	38,641,823	39,609,488	40,542,036	41,402,400	42,175,740

Data for TFP and population was obtained from Conference Board (2012), and United Nations Population Division (2011) respectively.

	1997	1998	1999	2000	2001	2002	2003	2004	2005	2006	2007	2008
1	1,596,272	1,602,714	1,606,490	1,611,499	1,632,188	1,655,592	1,677,745	1,708,515	1,741,738	1,770,990	1,804,168	1,846,068
2	221,340	226,513	229,755	234,073	237,523	242,010	248,344	257,232	268,383	282,294	299,798	321,335
3	854,820	859,425	863,252	867,165	887,510	909,670	928,775	954,703	980,525	999,666	1,019,044	1,042,978
4	520,112	516,776	513,484	510,261	507,155	503,912	500,626	496,580	492,831	489,030	485,326	481,755
5	79,791	79,813	79,783	79,783	79,783	79,783	79,783	79,733	79,733	79,573	79,573	79,573
6	12,611	12,611	12,581	12,581	12,581	12,581	12,581	12,531	12,531	12,371	12,371	12,371
7	67,180	67,202	67,202	67,202	67,202	67,202	67,202	67,202	67,202	67,202	67,202	67,202
8	9,156	9,156	9,156	9,156	9,156	9,156	9,156	9,156	9,156	9,156	9,156	9,156
9	6,901	6,901	6,901	6,901	6,901	6,901	6,901	6,901	6,901	6,901	6,901	6,901
10	2,255	2,255	2,255	2,255	2,255	2,255	2,255	2,255	2,255	2,255	2,255	2,255
11	690	706	749	893	1,157	1,241	1,461	979	736	603	428	382
12	405,683	402,871	400,106	397,266	394,393	391,571	388,548	385,482	382,390	379,282	376,135	372,965
13	125	123	122	120	119	117	116	114	113	111	110	108
14	648	608	569	523	465	401	338	276	215	134	51	1
15	404,910	402,140	399,415	396,623	393,810	391,053	388,094	385,092	382,063	379,036	375,974	372,856
16	24,792	24,229	23,690	23,163	22,666	22,161	21,678	21,229	20,815	20,416	20,034	19,678
17	-	-	-	-	-	-	-	-	-	-	-	-
18	2,787	2,755	2,727	2,701	2,673	2,648	2,625	2,605	2,585	2,564	2,541	2,520
19	8,682	8,273	7,877	7,498	7,151	6,801	6,474	6,177	5,918	5,679	5,458	5,271
20	3,217	3,142	3,075	2,999	2,920	2,837	2,750	2,661	2,571	2,478	2,382	2,271
21	53	49	45	40	38	35	33	31	29	26	24	21
22	2,952	2,925	2,899	2,873	2,847	2,819	2,790	2,762	2,731	2,701	2,674	2,651
23	5,703	5,693	5,682	5,672	5,662	5,652	5,642	5,632	5,622	5,612	5,603	5,594
24	-	-	-	-	-	-	-	-	-	-	-	-
25	-	-	-	-	-	-	-	-	-	-	-	-
26	1,398	1,391	1,385	1,380	1,374	1,368	1,364	1,362	1,359	1,356	1,353	1,350
27	70,083,468	70,186,497	70,218,336	70,217,206	70,721,432	71,206,093	71,659,780	72,062,790	72,399,448	72,701,292	72,935,830	73,098,253
28	-8,350	-8,625	-8,860	-9,048	-9,142	-9,581	-10,147	-10,603	-11,359	-11,970	-12,505	-12,550
29	-4,184	-4,170	-4,140	-4,233	-4,131	-4,167	-4,399	-4,614	-4,784	-4,973	-5,080	-5,195
30	-4,166	-4,455	-4,720	-4,815	-5,011	-5,414	-5,747	-5,989	-6,575	-6,997	-7,424	-7,355

	1997	1998	1999	2000	2001	2002	2003	2004	2005	2006	2007	2008
31	37,232	36,830	36,398	36,003	35,960	35,979	35,979	36,177	36,444	36,643	36,939	37,431
32	5,163	5,205	5,205	5,229	5,233	5,259	5,326	5,447	5,616	5,841	6,138	6,515
33	19,938	19,750	19,558	19,373	19,553	19,769	19,917	20,215	20,516	20,684	20,864	21,147
34	12,131	11,875	11,634	11,400	11,173	10,951	10,736	10,515	10,312	10,118	9,937	9,768
35	1,634,663	1,612,881	1,590,905	1,568,736	1,558,099	1,547,440	1,536,729	1,525,892	1,514,861	1,504,240	1,493,287	1,482,141
36	-1.58	-4.02	-2.02	0.19	-0.92	0.35	-0.83	0.48	0.58	0.35	-0.17	-3.39
37	42,873,355	43,516,225	44,137,342	44,760,380	45,389,577	46,015,405	46,631,364	47,226,670	47,792,787	48,330,914	48,842,462	49,319,363

United Kingdom

UNIT: millions of constant US$ of year 2000

		1990	1991	1992	1993	1994	1995	1996
1	Inclusive Wealth Index, rows 2 + 3 + 4	10,718,589	10,759,091	10,791,161	10,814,707	10,876,817	10,925,053	11,014,382
2	Produced capital	858,527	858,756	863,088	870,846	885,913	902,168	922,850
3	Human capital	9,690,694	9,734,250	9,765,131	9,785,201	9,835,566	9,870,866	9,943,081
4	Natural capital, rows 5 + 8 + 11 + 12 + 16	169,368	166,085	162,941	158,661	155,338	152,019	148,451
5	Agricultural land, rows 6 + 7	38,260	38,134	37,981	36,854	36,591	36,528	36,770
6	Cropland	14,053	13,942	13,910	12,931	12,552	12,596	12,935
7	Pastureland	24,207	24,192	24,071	23,923	24,039	23,932	23,835
8	Forest resources, rows 9 + 10	17,155	17,317	17,479	17,641	17,803	17,965	18,128
9	Timber	16,335	16,491	16,648	16,804	16,961	17,117	17,273
10	Non-timber forest resources	820	826	831	837	843	848	854
11	Fisheries							
12	Fossil fuels, rows 13 + 14 + 15	113,953	110,634	107,481	104,165	100,943	97,525	93,554
13	Oil	29,953	29,936	29,919	29,901	29,900	29,899	29,897
14	Natural gas	72,095	69,969	67,886	65,433	62,819	59,992	56,624
15	Coal	11,905	10,728	9,676	8,831	8,224	7,634	7,033
16	Minerals, rows 17 + 18 +...+ 26	-	-	-	-	-	-	-
17	Bauxite	-	-	-	-	-	-	-
18	Appendix	-	-	-	-	-	-	-
19	Gold	-	-	-	-	-	-	-
20	Iron	-	-	-	-	-	-	-
21	Lead	-	-	-	-	-	-	-
22	Nickel	-	-	-	-	-	-	-
23	Phosphate	-	-	-	-	-	-	-
24	Silver	-	-	-	-	-	-	-
25	Tin	-	-	-	-	-	-	-
26	Zinc	-	-	-	-	-	-	-
27	Health capital	299,858,301	301,328,111	302,861,135	304,446,186	306,066,282	307,718,160	309,247,775
28	IWI adjustments excluding TFP, rows 29 + 30	-41,741	-42,841	-43,194	-43,901	-44,794	-45,590	-46,880
29	Carbon damages (annual change)	-29,973	-30,415	-30,089	-30,064	-30,544	-31,073	-31,686
30	Oil capital gains (annual change)	-11,768	-12,426	-13,105	-13,837	-14,250	-14,517	-15,194

	Per Capita Values	1990	1991	1992	1993	1994	1995	1996
31	Per capita Inclusive Wealth Index	187,341	187,540	187,589	187,490	188,055	188,372	189,391
32	Per capita produced capital	15,005	14,969	15,004	15,097	15,317	15,555	15,868
33	Per capita human capital	169,375	169,676	169,753	169,642	170,052	170,196	170,970
34	Per capita natural capital	2,960	2,895	2,833	2,751	2,686	2,621	2,553
35	Per capita health capital	5,240,952	5,252,398	5,264,819	5,278,043	5,291,731	5,305,741	5,317,476
36	TFP (in percentage)	-1.41	0.60	0.91	2.16	1.37	0.39	0.72
37	Population	57,214,474	57,369,629	57,525,459	57,681,639	57,838,596	57,997,210	58,156,871

Data for TFP and population was obtained from Conference Board (2012), and United Nations Population Division (2011) respectively.

	1997	1998	1999	2000	2001	2002	2003	2004	2005	2006	2007	2008
1	11,135,097	11,234,807	11,411,886	11,559,921	11,712,256	11,936,976	12,189,626	12,405,182	12,639,749	12,926,705	13,151,028	13,423,672
2	949,730	978,851	1,013,382	1,045,854	1,067,088	1,110,234	1,159,837	1,214,277	1,276,785	1,342,894	1,420,522	1,494,113
3	10,040,361	10,114,759	10,261,920	10,382,294	10,517,359	10,702,768	10,909,691	11,074,183	11,249,633	11,471,386	11,620,942	11,822,300
4	145,006	141,196	136,584	131,774	127,809	123,974	120,098	116,723	113,331	112,425	109,564	107,260
5	36,961	36,820	36,192	35,656	35,633	35,681	35,639	35,839	35,639	37,493	37,092	37,169
6	13,504	13,254	12,544	12,460	11,985	12,266	11,997	12,334	12,140	12,903	12,887	12,718
7	23,457	23,566	23,648	23,196	23,648	23,415	23,642	23,505	23,499	24,590	24,205	24,451
8	18,290	18,452	18,614	18,776	19,138	19,501	19,863	20,226	20,588	21,042	21,496	21,950
9	17,430	17,586	17,743	17,899	18,258	18,617	18,976	19,336	19,695	20,147	20,598	21,050
10	860	866	871	877	880	884	887	890	893	896	898	900
11												
12	89,756	85,924	81,779	77,342	73,038	68,792	64,596	60,658	57,103	53,890	50,977	48,140
13	29,896	29,895	29,893	29,892	29,891	29,890	29,890	29,889	29,888	29,887	29,887	29,886
14	53,409	50,076	46,380	42,323	38,411	34,532	30,680	27,048	23,742	20,753	18,046	15,428
15	6,450	5,954	5,506	5,126	4,736	4,370	4,025	3,721	3,473	3,249	3,044	2,826
16	-	-	-	-	-	-	-	-	-	-	-	-
17	-	-	-	-	-	-	-	-	-	-	-	-
18	-	-	-	-	-	-	-	-	-	-	-	-
19	-	-	-	-	-	-	-	-	-	-	-	-
20	-	-	-	-	-	-	-	-	-	-	-	-
21	-	-	-	-	-	-	-	-	-	-	-	-
22	-	-	-	-	-	-	-	-	-	-	-	-
23	-	-	-	-	-	-	-	-	-	-	-	-
24	-	-	-	-	-	-	-	-	-	-	-	-
25	-	-	-	-	-	-	-	-	-	-	-	-
26	-	-	-	-	-	-	-	-	-	-	-	-
27	310,802,832	312,411,630	314,120,704	315,967,570	317,959,110	320,082,456	322,350,792	324,786,151	327,406,927	330,007,489	332,781,801	335,698,193
28	-47,291	-47,601	-47,905	-48,711	-48,350	-49,194	-51,668	-53,780	-56,049	-57,931	-58,687	-60,474
29	-32,171	-32,064	-31,832	-32,544	-31,762	-32,041	-33,827	-35,479	-36,784	-38,235	-39,063	-39,947
30	-15,120	-15,537	-16,073	-16,166	-16,588	-17,153	-17,842	-18,301	-19,265	-19,696	-19,624	-20,527

	1997	1998	1999	2000	2001	2002	2003	2004	2005	2006	2007	2008
31	190,935	192,087	194,505	196,350	198,187	201,162	204,509	207,127	209,953	213,530	215,958	219,089
32	16,285	16,736	17,272	17,764	18,057	18,710	19,459	20,275	21,208	22,183	23,327	24,386
33	172,163	172,937	174,905	176,347	177,967	180,364	183,035	184,903	186,863	189,490	190,832	192,953
34	2,486	2,414	2,328	2,238	2,163	2,089	2,015	1,949	1,882	1,857	1,799	1,751
35	5,329,379	5,341,463	5,353,897	5,366,833	5,380,280	5,394,045	5,408,176	5,422,883	5,438,407	5,451,232	5,464,747	5,478,969
36	0.02	0.68	0.35	1.13	-0.01	0.49	1.15	1.08	-0.16	1.34	0.94	-0.85
37	58,318,771	58,488,026	58,671,413	58,874,117	59,097,129	59,339,971	59,604,347	59,891,788	60,202,727	60,538,143	60,896,101	61,270,318

United States

UNIT: millions of constant US$ of year 2000

		1990	1991	1992	1993	1994	1995	1996
1	Inclusive Wealth Index, rows 2 + 3 + 4	86,441,991	87,502,754	88,869,537	90,148,995	91,772,804	93,471,285	95,000,514
2	Produced capital	11,049,849	11,288,591	11,565,418	11,897,811	12,298,176	12,747,787	13,276,863
3	Human capital	68,515,458	69,356,545	70,467,276	71,436,979	72,685,177	73,955,459	74,986,345
4	Natural capital, rows 5 + 8 + 11 + 12 + 16	6,876,684	6,857,618	6,836,843	6,814,205	6,789,452	6,768,039	6,737,306
5	Agricultural land, rows 6 + 7	1,058,225	1,058,225	1,054,460	1,048,311	1,043,827	1,041,349	1,031,848
6	Cropland	465,418	465,418	461,462	458,409	456,404	456,404	449,382
7	Pastureland	592,807	592,807	592,998	589,902	587,424	584,945	582,467
8	Forest resources, rows 9 + 10	2,065,797	2,076,896	2,087,996	2,099,095	2,110,195	2,121,294	2,132,394
9	Timber	1,972,748	1,983,726	1,994,704	2,005,683	2,016,661	2,027,639	2,038,618
10	Non-timber forest resources	93,049	93,170	93,292	93,413	93,534	93,655	93,776
11	Fisheries	19,566	18,287	19,265	20,417	19,639	19,820	18,306
12	Fossil fuels, rows 13 + 14 + 15	3,685,096	3,657,176	3,629,102	3,601,334	3,571,923	3,542,734	3,512,969
13	Oil	148,197	148,122	148,047	147,975	147,902	147,830	147,757
14	Natural gas	569,377	552,088	534,660	516,983	498,597	480,428	462,009
15	Coal	2,967,522	2,956,967	2,946,395	2,936,376	2,925,424	2,914,477	2,903,203
16	Minerals, rows 17 + 18 +...+ 26	48,001	47,033	46,019	45,048	43,867	42,842	41,788
17	Bauxite	32	32	32	32	32	32	32
18	Appendix	11,876	11,565	11,228	10,884	10,537	10,184	9,817
19	Gold	7,349	7,094	6,809	6,522	6,240	5,966	5,684
20	Iron	17,697	17,570	17,445	17,321	17,190	17,050	16,911
21	Lead	824	799	777	758	739	718	695
22	Nickel	-	-	-	-	-	-	-
23	Phosphate	6,961	6,784	6,611	6,481	6,330	6,170	6,003
24	Silver	890	866	842	820	623	602	581
25	Tin	-	-	-	-	-	-	-
26	Zinc	2,373	2,324	2,275	2,230	2,177	2,119	2,064
27	Health capital	1,575,703,370	1,593,219,496	1,610,863,123	1,628,934,347	1,647,854,829	1,667,943,485	1,689,419,253
28	IWI adjustments excluding TFP, rows 29 + 30	-150,531	-153,489	-161,467	-169,287	-177,953	-183,066	-192,933
29	Carbon damages (annual change)	-31,046	-31,504	-31,166	-31,140	-31,638	-32,185	-32,820
30	Oil capital gains (annual change)	-119,484	-121,986	-130,301	-138,147	-146,316	-150,881	-160,113

	Per Capita Values	1990	1991	1992	1993	1994	1995	1996
31	Per capita Inclusive Wealth Index	341,211	342,065	344,088	345,659	348,325	350,969	352,646
32	Per capita produced capital	43,617	44,129	44,779	45,620	46,678	47,866	49,284
33	Per capita human capital	270,450	271,128	272,837	273,911	275,878	277,690	278,352
34	Per capita natural capital	27,144	26,808	26,471	26,128	25,769	25,413	25,009
35	Per capita health capital	6,219,740	6,228,201	6,236,985	6,245,836	6,254,455	6,262,842	6,271,192
36	TFP (in percentage)	-0.06	-0.77	1.83	0.08	0.86	-0.11	1.29
37	Population	253,339,097	255,807,342	258,275,919	260,803,255	263,468,980	266,323,717	269,393,632

Data for TFP and population was obtained from Conference Board (2012), and United Nations Population Division (2011) respectively.

	1997	1998	1999	2000	2001	2002	2003	2004	2005	2006	2007	2008
1	96,860,029	98,635,343	100,559,984	102,540,187	104,697,019	106,716,286	108,575,657	110,319,477	112,347,445	114,286,433	116,089,191	117,832,867
2	13,894,079	14,621,021	15,452,515	16,331,550	17,170,541	17,870,398	18,581,882	19,365,782	20,206,106	21,039,001	21,778,585	22,338,447
3	76,252,680	77,322,887	78,436,760	79,557,553	80,875,168	82,198,111	83,348,548	84,319,434	85,513,573	86,631,596	87,691,545	88,872,818
4	6,713,270	6,691,435	6,670,709	6,651,084	6,651,309	6,647,777	6,645,227	6,634,260	6,627,767	6,615,835	6,619,061	6,621,602
5	1,028,326	1,027,590	1,025,853	1,027,122	1,028,473	1,023,813	1,020,838	1,009,987	1,005,176	993,517	997,579	1,002,242
6	446,373	444,365	441,356	441,356	441,435	435,504	432,175	420,828	416,018	404,110	407,677	412,339
7	581,954	583,225	584,497	585,766	587,037	588,309	588,663	589,159	589,159	589,407	589,902	589,902
8	2,143,493	2,154,593	2,165,693	2,176,792	2,207,871	2,238,950	2,270,029	2,301,108	2,332,187	2,363,276	2,394,365	2,425,454
9	2,049,596	2,060,574	2,071,553	2,082,531	2,113,490	2,144,448	2,175,407	2,206,366	2,237,325	2,268,294	2,299,263	2,330,232
10	93,898	94,019	94,140	94,261	94,381	94,502	94,622	94,742	94,862	94,982	95,102	95,223
11	17,885	17,280	18,327	17,510	17,376	18,416	18,644	18,268	15,994	15,873	15,753	15,632
12	3,482,881	3,452,382	3,422,254	3,392,068	3,360,886	3,330,729	3,300,646	3,270,632	3,240,943	3,210,480	3,179,443	3,147,142
13	147,685	147,613	147,544	147,475	147,406	147,337	147,269	147,202	147,138	147,074	147,009	146,944
14	443,544	424,960	406,563	387,824	368,661	350,170	331,513	313,351	295,717	277,641	258,820	239,003
15	2,891,652	2,879,809	2,868,147	2,856,769	2,844,819	2,833,222	2,821,864	2,810,079	2,798,087	2,785,765	2,773,614	2,761,195
16	40,685	39,590	38,582	37,593	36,704	35,869	35,069	34,265	33,466	32,688	31,921	31,131
17	32	32	32	32	32	32	32	32	32	32	32	32
18	9,447	9,092	8,786	8,511	8,255	8,038	7,824	7,602	7,385	7,156	6,932	6,682
19	5,371	5,054	4,759	4,454	4,164	3,906	3,666	3,443	3,221	3,003	2,797	2,596
20	16,770	16,630	16,501	16,359	16,256	16,141	16,032	15,910	15,788	15,670	15,553	15,433
21	671	645	617	593	568	544	520	497	474	451	428	406
22	-	-	-	-	-	-	-	-	-	-	-	-
23	5,835	5,672	5,523	5,381	5,264	5,132	5,003	4,872	4,739	4,628	4,519	4,408
24	552	525	499	473	450	431	414	398	381	366	349	332
25	-	-	-	-	-	-	-	-	-	-	-	-
26	2,008	1,941	1,865	1,790	1,715	1,646	1,578	1,512	1,446	1,382	1,310	1,241
27	1,711,797,760	1,734,673,570	1,757,474,908	1,779,726,753	1,800,392,264	1,820,588,825	1,840,361,793	1,859,838,765	1,879,204,928	1,898,185,434	1,916,894,686	1,935,521,474
28	-200,119	-209,639	-219,761	-229,270	-235,612	-245,425	-256,481	-269,037	-278,151	-286,892	-297,843	-296,327
29	-33,323	-33,211	-32,971	-33,709	-32,899	-33,188	-35,038	-36,749	-38,101	-39,604	-40,462	-41,377
30	-166,797	-176,427	-186,789	-195,561	-202,713	-212,236	-221,444	-232,288	-240,050	-247,288	-257,382	-254,950

	1997	1998	1999	2000	2001	2002	2003	2004	2005	2006	2007	2008
31	355,263	357,392	360,043	362,979	366,657	369,942	372,740	375,156	378,503	381,509	384,039	386,351
32	50,961	52,977	55,326	57,812	60,133	61,949	63,792	65,856	68,075	70,232	72,047	73,243
33	279,679	280,170	280,833	281,623	283,231	284,948	286,135	286,739	288,099	289,192	290,096	291,397
34	24,623	24,246	23,884	23,544	23,293	23,045	22,813	22,561	22,329	22,085	21,897	21,711
35	6,278,524	6,285,366	6,292,426	6,300,000	6,305,114	6,311,248	6,317,953	6,324,624	6,331,120	6,336,484	6,341,358	6,346,200
36	0.66	0.44	1.47	1.26	-0.16	0.46	0.95	1.67	0.82	0.03	-0.09	-1.05
37	272,643,340	275,986,072	279,300,030	282,496,310	285,544,778	288,467,308	291,290,823	294,063,120	296,820,296	299,564,470	302,284,564	304,989,064

Venezuela

UNIT: millions of constant US$ of year 2000

		1990	1991	1992	1993	1994	1995	1996
1	Inclusive Wealth Index, rows 2 + 3 + 4	2,285,995	2,314,030	2,346,965	2,381,450	2,411,767	2,444,462	2,473,349
2	Produced capital	314,531	315,583	323,326	328,782	328,775	328,951	327,659
3	Human capital	811,085	839,333	867,927	898,270	929,890	963,691	995,198
4	Natural capital, rows 5 + 8 + 11 + 12 + 16	1,160,380	1,159,113	1,155,712	1,154,397	1,153,103	1,151,820	1,150,492
5	Agricultural land, rows 6 + 7	191,961	191,934	189,739	189,704	189,765	189,853	189,958
6	Cropland	31,701	31,718	29,523	29,523	29,593	29,681	29,786
7	Pastureland	160,260	160,216	160,216	160,181	160,172	160,172	160,172
8	Forest resources, rows 9 + 10	61,686	61,345	61,004	60,664	60,323	59,982	59,641
9	Timber	48,992	48,721	48,450	48,180	47,909	47,638	47,367
10	Non-timber forest resources	12,694	12,624	12,554	12,484	12,414	12,344	12,273
11	Fisheries							
12	Fossil fuels, rows 13 + 14 + 15	895,522	894,678	893,859	892,966	892,003	891,029	889,989
13	Oil	704,519	704,499	704,478	704,457	704,435	704,411	704,385
14	Natural gas	181,824	181,033	180,273	179,461	178,588	177,701	176,745
15	Coal	9,180	9,146	9,107	9,047	8,980	8,917	8,860
16	Minerals, rows 17 + 18 +...+ 26	11,210	11,156	11,110	11,064	11,011	10,957	10,904
17	Bauxite	696	692	690	685	677	668	660
18	Appendix	-	-	-	-	-	-	-
19	Gold	-	-	-	-	-	-	-
20	Iron	10,515	10,463	10,419	10,379	10,334	10,288	10,244
21	Lead	-	-	-	-	-	-	-
22	Nickel	-	-	-	-	-	-	-
23	Phosphate	-	-	-	-	-	-	-
24	Silver	-	-	-	-	-	-	-
25	Tin	-	-	-	-	-	-	-
26	Zinc	-	-	-	-	-	-	-
27	Health capital	40,519,332	41,511,144	42,485,864	43,447,231	44,402,602	45,356,546	46,303,369
28	IWI adjustments excluding TFP, rows 29 + 30	30,086	31,625	33,277	34,949	36,727	38,630	40,766
29	Carbon damages (annual change)	-2,185	-2,217	-2,193	-2,191	-2,226	-2,265	-2,310
30	Oil capital gains (annual change)	32,271	33,842	35,470	37,141	38,953	40,895	43,076

	Per Capita Values	1990	1991	1992	1993	1994	1995	1996
31	Per capita Inclusive Wealth Index	116,128	114,768	113,736	112,846	111,813	110,936	109,930
32	Per capita produced capital	15,978	15,652	15,669	15,579	15,242	14,929	14,563
33	Per capita human capital	41,203	41,628	42,060	42,565	43,111	43,735	44,233
34	Per capita natural capital	58,947	57,488	56,007	54,701	53,459	52,273	51,135
35	Per capita health capital	2,058,368	2,058,804	2,058,899	2,058,760	2,058,566	2,058,395	2,057,996
36	TFP (in percentage)	2.97	7.86	3.32	-2.34	-4.49	2.32	-1.97
37	Population	19,685,177	20,162,745	20,635,233	21,103,592	21,569,680	22,034,909	22,499,248

Data for TFP and population was obtained from Conference Board (2012), and United Nations Population Division (2011) respectively.

	1997	1998	1999	2000	2001	2002	2003	2004	2005	2006	2007	2008
1	2,507,152	2,542,069	2,572,990	2,606,770	2,641,291	2,699,686	2,751,639	2,812,216	2,881,059	2,960,935	3,026,548	3,093,738
2	331,648	336,840	337,252	341,656	342,361	341,265	331,778	330,120	336,861	351,871	375,717	396,201
3	1,026,470	1,057,782	1,089,829	1,122,793	1,158,235	1,220,119	1,282,936	1,346,215	1,409,677	1,476,011	1,519,055	1,567,039
4	1,149,034	1,147,447	1,145,909	1,142,320	1,140,695	1,138,302	1,136,926	1,135,881	1,134,521	1,133,053	1,131,776	1,130,499
5	189,994	190,046	189,967	187,877	187,904	187,043	187,043	187,482	187,482	187,482	187,482	187,482
6	29,822	29,874	29,795	29,813	29,839	28,978	28,978	29,418	29,418	29,418	29,418	29,418
7	160,172	160,172	160,172	158,065	158,065	158,065	158,065	158,065	158,065	158,065	158,065	158,065
8	59,300	58,959	58,618	58,277	57,936	57,595	57,254	56,913	56,572	56,231	55,890	55,549
9	47,097	46,826	46,555	46,285	46,014	45,743	45,472	45,201	44,930	44,660	44,389	44,118
10	12,203	12,133	12,063	11,993	11,923	11,852	11,782	11,712	11,642	11,572	11,502	11,431
11												
12	888,890	887,639	886,563	885,454	884,193	883,054	882,071	880,986	880,025	878,964	878,093	877,222
13	704,356	704,329	704,304	704,276	704,249	704,225	704,204	704,181	704,158	704,135	704,114	704,092
14	175,755	174,649	173,706	172,750	171,634	170,635	169,776	168,819	167,995	167,080	166,351	165,621
15	8,779	8,662	8,553	8,429	8,310	8,195	8,091	7,985	7,872	7,749	7,629	7,509
16	10,850	10,802	10,761	10,711	10,662	10,610	10,557	10,500	10,442	10,376	10,310	10,245
17	652	643	636	629	621	612	602	592	582	572	562	553
18	-	-	-	-	-	-	-	-	-	-	-	-
19	-	-	-	-	-	-	-	-	-	-	-	-
20	10,199	10,159	10,125	10,083	10,042	9,998	9,955	9,908	9,860	9,804	9,748	9,692
21	-	-	-	-	-	-	-	-	-	-	-	-
22	-	-	-	-	-	-	-	-	-	-	-	-
23	-	-	-	-	-	-	-	-	-	-	-	-
24	-	-	-	-	-	-	-	-	-	-	-	-
25	-	-	-	-	-	-	-	-	-	-	-	-
26	-	-	-	-	-	-	-	-	-	-	-	-
27	47,249,928	48,195,525	49,138,680	50,079,442	51,001,632	51,920,979	52,838,203	53,754,606	54,670,550	55,587,690	56,502,565	57,414,082
28	42,885	45,170	47,626	49,722	51,944	54,388	57,578	60,542	63,355	66,033	68,680	71,646
29	-2,345	-2,337	-2,320	-2,372	-2,315	-2,335	-2,466	-2,586	-2,681	-2,787	-2,847	-2,912
30	45,229	47,508	49,946	52,095	54,259	56,723	60,043	63,128	66,037	68,820	71,528	74,557

	1997	1998	1999	2000	2001	2002	2003	2004	2005	2006	2007	2008
31	109,186	108,523	107,719	107,062	106,458	106,820	106,916	107,337	108,050	109,144	109,684	110,264
32	14,443	14,380	14,119	14,032	13,799	13,503	12,891	12,600	12,633	12,970	13,616	14,121
33	44,703	45,157	45,626	46,114	46,683	48,277	49,849	51,382	52,868	54,408	55,051	55,851
34	50,040	48,985	47,974	46,916	45,976	45,040	44,176	43,354	42,549	41,766	41,016	40,292
35	2,057,725	2,057,498	2,057,198	2,056,794	2,055,631	2,054,378	2,053,054	2,051,703	2,050,341	2,049,035	2,047,682	2,046,302
36	4.40	-2.25	-8.34	1.49	0.90	-9.67	-8.14	16.57	8.30	2.62	2.12	0.62
37	22,962,221	23,424,338	23,886,213	24,348,304	24,810,691	25,273,336	25,736,393	26,199,994	26,664,122	27,128,721	27,593,427	28,057,485

Glossary of terms

Absolute decoupling: refers to a situation in which there is an overall reduction in required material inputs or pollution outputs, even while the economy grows, whether through productivity improvements or through a decrease in pollution, or a combination of the two.

Adjusted net savings: a measure of net change in the value of a country's capital stocks, including produced, human, and at least some stocks of natural capital.

Adjusted Inclusive Wealth Index (IWIadj): an index that reflects when a country's capital assets are corrected for specific factors that affect the size of its productive base. In this report we take into account the following three components: carbon damages; oil capital gains and; total factor productivity.

Biodiversity: the variability among living organisms from all sources and the ecological complexes of which they are part, including diversity within species, between species, and of ecosystems.

Biosphere: a limited space made up of air, earth, and water and in which life is possible.

Carbon emissions: the release of carbon dioxide gas into the atmosphere.

Comprehensive wealth: the shadow value of all the capital assets in a country. See inclusive wealth.

Decoupling: a decline in the ratio of the amount used of a certain resource, or of the environmental impact, to the value generated or otherwise involved in the resource use or environmental impact.

Dematerialization: an absolute decrease in the quantity of resources, measured by mass, being used by an economy.

Ecosystem: a mesh of human and natural resources interacting with one another at a multitude of speeds and across often overlapping spatial scales.

Ecosystem services: provisioning services such as food, water, timber, and genetic resources; regulating services that affect climate, floods, disease, wastes, and water quality; cultural services that provide recreational, aesthetic, and spiritual benefits; and supporting services such as soil formation, pollination, and nutrient cycling.

Environmental sustainability: the maintenance of the minimum thresholds of natural capital that are required to sustain important environmental functions.

Externalities: the effects of activities on the well-being of people who have not been parties to the negotiations that led to those activities.

Fossil fuels: fuels such as natural gas, coal, and petroleum that are formed in the earth from plant or animal remains.

Global genuine saving rate: the world's gross savings plus educational expenditures minus produced capital depreciation and the values of natural resource depletion and carbon emissions.

Gross domestic product: the market value of all final goods and services produced within an economy.

Health capital: measured here essentially by the extensions (reductions) in the individual's life expectancy. Such changes are basically analyzed by calculating the expected discounted years of life remaining of a given population.

Human capital: the knowledge, skills, competencies, and attributes embodied in individuals that facilitate the creation of personal, social, and economic well-being.

Human Development Index: a measure of development designed by the United Nations that combines indicators of life expectancy, educational attainment, and income.

Inclusive investment: the measurement of the physical changes in the assets of the economy, while holding shadow prices constant.

Inclusive wealth: the shadow value of all the capital assets in a country. In this report comprehensive wealth and inclusive wealth are used interchangeably.

Manufactured capital: includes roads, buildings, ports, machinery, and equipment. In common parlance, including national accounts, this category pretty much exhausts the list of capital assets. When national income accountants and international organizations speak of investment, they usually mean the accumulation of manufactured capital, also known as produced capital.

Millennium Ecosystem Assessment: a pioneering study from 2005 of the services humanity enjoys from ecosystems.

Natural capital: everything in nature (biotic and abiotic) capable of providing human beings with well-being, either directly or through the production process.

Non-renewable resources: Natural resources that cannot be regenerated or grown at a sustainable rate to meet demand, including fossil fuels, metals, and minerals.

Oil capital gains: measure of a change in wealth due to changes in price given a fixed quantity of oil.

Produced capital: see manufactured capital.

Relative decoupling: refers to a situation where productivity/efficiency improvements have been realized but total inputs, or pollution outputs, continue to increase as economic output increases.

Renewable resources: natural resources whose supply can essentially never be exhausted, usually because they are continuously produced.

Rental prices: market prices minus production costs of resources.

Shadow price: the shadow price of a capital asset is the contribution a marginal unit of the asset is forecast to make to human well-being.

Social capital: aspects of social structure that facilitate action, in terms of the importance of obligations and expectations, information channels, and social norms to education.

Strong sustainability: perception that substitutability of manufactured for natural capital is seriously limited by such environmental characteristics as irreversibility, uncertainty, and the existence of "critical" components of natural capital, which make a unique contribution to welfare.

Sustainable development: development that meets the needs of the present without compromising the ability of future generations to meet their own needs.

Sustainability gap: indicates the degree of consumption of natural capital, either in the past or present, that is in excess of what is required for environmental sustainability.

Total factor productivity: the proportion of output not explained by the amount of inputs used in production, and captures the effect of technical progress, the efficiency with which inputs are used, institutional conditions, and the impact of environmental factors such as climate.

Value of statistical life: an approach measuring a society's willingness to pay to avoid additional occurrences of death.

Weak sustainability: the perception that welfare is not normally dependent on a specific form of capital and can be maintained by substituting manufactured for natural capital, though with exceptions.

Contributing organizations

The IWR is a joint initiative of the United Nations University International Human Dimensions Programme on Global Environmental Change (UNU-IHDP) and the United Nations Environment Programme (UNEP), in collaboration with the UN-Water Decade Programme on Capacity Development (UNW-DPC) and the Natural Capital Project.

UNU–IHDP

The International Human Dimensions Programme on Global Environmental Change (IHDP) is an interdisciplinary science program, working towards a better understanding of the interactions of humans with and within their natural environment. IHDP advances interdisciplinary research and collaborates with the natural and social sciences. It enhances the capacities of science and policy communities through a large network and furthers a shared understanding of the social causes and implications of global change. The program facilitates dialogue between science and policy to ensure that research results feed into policy-planning and law-making processes, and offers education and training to future leaders in the field.

IHDP was founded by the International Council for Science (ICSU) and the International Social Science Council (ISSC) of UNESCO in 1996. The IHDP Secretariat is hosted by the United Nations University (UNU) in Bonn who joined as third sponsor in 2007. IHDP's research is guided by an international Scientific Committee comprised of renowned scientists from various disciplinary and regional backgrounds. Visit www.ihdp.unu.edu for more information.

UNEP

The United Nations Environment Programme (UNEP) is the voice for the environment in the UN system. Established in 1972, UNEP's mission is to provide leadership and encourage partnership in caring for the environment by inspiring, informing, and enabling nations and peoples to improve their quality of life without compromising that of future generations. UNEP is an advocate, educator, catalyst and facilitator promoting the wise use of the planet's natural assets for sustainable development. It works with many partners, UN entities, international organizations, national governments, non-governmental organizations, business, industry, the media and civil society. UNEP's work involves providing support for: environmental assessment and reporting; legal and institutional strengthening and environmental policy development; sustainable use and management of natural resources; integration of economic development and environmental protection; and promoting public participation in environmental management. For more information, please visit: www.unep.org

UNW–DPC

The UN-Water Decade Programme on Capacity Development (UNW-DPC), established in 2007, is a joint program of UN-Water, the interagency mechanism formed by the United Nations High Level Committee on Programmes in 2003. UNW-DPC's mission is to enhance the coherence and effectiveness of the capacity development activities of UN-Water and seeks to strengthen the ability of the UN-Water members and partners to support Member States to achieve the Millennium Development Goals (MDGS) related to freshwater and sanitation. UNW-DPC is funded by the German Federal Government, located in Bonn, Germany, and hosted by the United Nations University.

Natural Capital Project

People all over the world rely on functioning ecosystems to live healthy and productive lives. One effective strategy to protect our environment and human well-being is to focus conservation on the protection of ecosystem services. The Natural Capital Project works to develop and provide practical ecosystem services concepts and tools, apply these tools in select areas around the world in order to demonstrate the impact of ecosystem service approaches in policy and decision outcomes, and engage and educate influential leaders and practitioners to advance change in policy and practice. The Natural Capital Project is an innovative partnership among Stanford University, The Nature Conservancy, University of Minnesota, and World Wildlife Fund aimed at aligning economic forces with conservation. Its vision is a world in which people and institutions recognize natural systems as capital assets, appreciate the vital roles they play in supporting human well-being and incorporate the intrinsic and economic values of natural capital into decision making.